10648061

MHCC WITH

D1013701

PR 1262 .C68 1972
Creeth, Edmund.
Tudor plays

DATE DUE			

MT. HOOD COMMUNITY COLLEGE
LIBRARY RESOURCE CENTER

MHCC WITHDRAWN

Mt. Hood Community
College Library
Gresham, Oregon

Presented by

Winifred Casterline

TUDOR PLAYS

An Anthology of
Early English Drama

EDITED WITH AN INTRODUCTION
NOTES AND VARIANTS BY
EDMUND CREETH

The Norton Library
W · W · NORTON & COMPANY · INC ·
NEW YORK

COPYRIGHT © 1966 BY DOUBLEDAY & COMPANY, INC.

First published in the Norton Library 1972
by arrangement with Doubleday & Company, Inc.

ALL RIGHTS RESERVED
Published simultaneously in Canada by
George J. McLeod Limited, Toronto

W. W. Norton & Company, Inc. also publishes *The Norton
Anthology of English Literature,* edited by M. H. Abrams et al;
The Norton Anthology of Poetry, edited by Arthur M. Eastman
et al; *World Masterpieces,* edited by Maynard Mack et al; *The
Norton Reader,* edited by Arthur M. Eastman et al; *The Norton
Facsimile of the First Folio of Shakespeare,* prepared by Charlton
Hinman; and the Norton Critical Editions.

Library of Congress Cataloging in Publication Data

Creeth, Edmund.
  Tudor plays.

  (The Norton library)
  Original ed. issued as AO-1 of Anchor octavo.
  Bibliography: p.
  1. English drama—Early modern and Elizabethan.
I. Title.
[PR1262.C68   1972]   822'.2'08   72-2931
ISBN 0-393-00614-X

PRINTED IN THE UNITED STATES OF AMERICA

1 2 3 4 5 6 7 8 9 0

To Willard Farnham

ACKNOWLEDGMENTS

I owe thanks to Miss Harriet C. Jameson, Head of the
Department of Rare Books and Special Collections at the
University of Michigan Library, and to my co-laborer
in preparation of the manuscript, Mrs. Dorothy Foster.
Three texts and a number of sets of variants are from
facsimiles of holdings of the Henry E. Huntington Library, San Marino, California, and I thank the directors
of that noble foundation for allowing me to use these
facsimiles, particularly the Huntington Facsimile Reprint
of *Fulgens and Lucres*, and to reproduce title pages
from them. Nor have the Bodleian Library, Oxford, the
Master and Fellows of Magdalene College, Cambridge,
the Provost and Fellows of Eton College, and the British
Museum refused permission to make similar use of materials in their possession. Eton has kindly allowed the
unique copy of Udall's play to be microfilmed at my
request.

E. C.

CONTENTS

INTRODUCTION

*The best in this kind are but
shadowes, and the worst are no worse,
if imagination amend them.*

The seven plays collected in this volume will introduce the reader to the chief varieties of Tudor drama from its emergence as a secular art under Henry VII until the first manifestations of English tragedy early in the reign of Elizabeth I. The anthology represents the various auspices under which plays might be produced and the places where makeshift stages were most frequently set up before the building of the Theatre (the first playhouse) in 1576—the Tudor banquet hall, the innyard, the hall or chapel of school and university, and, especially after Elizabeth's accession in 1558, the law colleges of London, the Inns of Court. It opens with an interlude by the first English playwright whom we can identify by name, the first English play that we have, apart from folk drama, not written in the service of religion. It includes two masterpieces of an art in which Tudor dramatists excelled, the art of farce, and makes available the oldest specimen of English drama based on chronicle history. It represents the best in native comedy as well as tragedy before the appearance of the University Wits and Shakespeare. Students of Shakespeare will perceive in these plays how well he knew the earlier Tudor drama when he looked back upon it with sympathetic mockery and how much he learned from it.

The two surviving plays by Henry Medwall, chaplain to Cardinal and Archbishop John Morton, establish an important dichotomy in early Tudor drama. His *Interlude of Nature* is the original of many humanistic adaptations of the English theological plays of the fifteenth century which dealt with the struggle between forces of good and evil for the allegiance of Mankind. The protagonist of *Nature* is Man, and the design of his experience—innocence or virtue, temptation, sin, awakening and regeneration—resembles that of Mankynde in *The Castell of Perseverance* (ca. 1405), even though God no longer presides, Nature is Aristotelian and

Ovidian, Death has made his exit, and Reson vs. a Sensualyte by no means wholly improper to Man replace the Bonus and Malus Angelus of the religious play. Moral interludes after *Nature* apply the inherent didacticism of the temptation plot to a variety of secular themes: the upbringing of youth, the right conduct of kings and magistrates, religious polemics. The plot survives, with its tendency to favor personified abstractions, by informing story materials from romance, from the Bible, or from history, thus yielding hybrid drama, as in Bale's *Kyng Johan* and Preston's *Cambises* in the present collection.

But in his other interlude, *Fulgens and Lucres*, "a play based on an English translation of a French version of an Italian work of fiction,"[1] Medwall makes a clean break with the tradition of the morality play. And in this respect, though not in the high comic romance of his main plot, he is followed by John Heywood. Medwall works with but seven characters, either types or concrete individuals, as against the twenty-one of *Nature*, and retains no trace of personification or allegory. *Fulgens and Lucres* probably did not spring full-panoplied from the brow of the chaplain into Cardinal Morton's banquet hall. There surely existed slightly earlier secular plays now lost, and Medwall uses much traditional material.[2] Although English drama at this point did not show any influence from Roman comedy, *Fulgens* draws upon the courts of love, upon Christmas festivals and folk drama generally, and in particular upon the tradition of the wooing contest as seen, for instance, in *The Parlement of Foules*.

Medwall's two extant plays thus represent two originally separate strands in early Tudor drama which later began to intertwine: secularized versions of the morality play and romantic comedy, new, as such, to England. In the pre-Elizabethan period this distinction is perhaps clearer and more useful than another which it is fashionable to stress, that between the popular tradition and the theatre of a coterie.

A. W. Reed has shown that in composing *Fulgens and Lucres* Medwall worked directly from a version printed by Caxton (1481) of *De Vera Nobilitate* by Bonaccorso of Pistoja.[3] This Italian humanist, who died in 1429, had dedicated

[1] A. W. Reed, *Early Tudor Drama* (London, 1926), p. 100.

[2] C. R. Baskervill, "Conventional Features of Medwall's *Fulgens and Lucres, MP*, XXIV (1927), 419–42.

[3] *Early Tudor Drama*, pp. 97–99.

the work to his patron, Carlo Malatesta, Lord of Rimini. A *novella* of life in Republican Rome, it reveals in its Ciceronian Latin Bonaccorso's discipleship to Petrarch. In 1449 Jean Mielot made a French translation of the tale that was published in Bruges by Caxton's collaborator Colard Mansion. The English version was the work of John Tiptoft (d. 1470), Earl of Worcester under Edward IV. This Caxton published in a single volume with English renderings of the *De Amicitia* (also translated by Tiptoft) and the *De Senectute* of Cicero.

In Bonaccorso, Mielot, and Tiptoft, the plot runs as follows: Lucres, poised and beautiful daughter to Fulgens, a Senator of Rome, has two suitors, the nobly born Publius Cornelius, skilled in hunting, hawking, singing, and disport, and the plebian Gayus Flamyneus, moderately well-to-do but virtuous and patriotic to the full and in time of peace, as Tiptoft phrases it, "right busye and laboryous in his bokes." Fulgens refers the problem of the choice to the Senate, before whom the lovers plead their cases. But in a kind of 'lady-and-the-tiger denouement, the narrator pretends not to know "the sentence dyffynytyf" of the Senate and leaves it to the reader to decide which of the twain was more noble, "and to him juge ye this noble & vertuous lady Lucresse to be maryed." Medwall's treatment for the Tudor stage differs in two most important respects. He puts the decision up to Lucres, who herself presides in what thereby becomes a wooing contest and who chooses Gayus, and he adds the parallel low-comic plot in which A and B having become servants to Gayus and Publius woo Jone, the heroine's maid.

The problem *de vera nobilitate* was not merely academic in early Tudor England. Humanists held the Platonic ideal of the philosopher-ruler but were ruled by an aristocracy based on heredity rather than on learning, the avenue to virtuous discipline.[4] The talents of the aristocracy in fact were likely to be those of a Publius Cornelius. Various practical methods of bringing the New Learning to bear on government presented themselves. The philosopher might tutor king or nobleman, playing Seneca to his Nero. In the long run the nobility itself might be educated, or rather the nobility of the future through children. Bale's character Nobilyte, it is worth

[4] The Tudor resolution of this problem is studied by Fritz Caspari, *Humanism and the Social Order in Tudor England* (Chicago, 1954).

noting, resisted the process: "From the new lernyng, mary, God of hevyn save me! / I never lovyd yt of a chyld, so mote I the."[5] But as Erasmus explained to young Charles, the future emperor, since rulership now goes by blood rather than by merit "the chief hope for a good prince is from his education."[6] The remaining means of improving the ruling class was to grant favor and place to the Tudor equivalent of Gayus Flamyneus. By leaving the choice of suitors up to the lady, Medwall was able to do what Bonaccorso, perhaps because of Malatesta, had not dared: to imply the superiority of mere virtuous accomplishment over mere ancestors. Still, Medwall's Lucres is careful to say that she is but a woman, that her decision offers no sort of general precedent, and that moreover the nobility which a member of the hereditary aristocracy can achieve if he will is beyond that accessible to any commoner.

If its definitive resolution makes *Fulgens and Lucres* a major document in English humanism, Medwall's original stroke—of giving the heroine the power of choice—raises the main plot to the level of high comedy. Medwall's Rome, like settings of Shakespeare's romantic comedies, is a woman's world; Lucres, the Senator's daughter, who eschews the material advantages of marrying a sneering descendant of the Scipios and prefers the earnest commoner, is the quaint prototype of Portia. Medwall's freedom with his source may be due, as Reed suggests, to the difficulty of presenting the Senate in session with a small troupe of professional players, but it transforms what might have been only a dramatized *débat* into a play, and on the whole the sympathetic reader will find the chaplain's characterization of Lucres worthy of the responsibility that he has given her.

Medwall's use of the low-comic subplot is also strikingly in harmony with more mature romantic drama of a century hence. Much of the uncouth material comes from folk drama such as the *Revesby Sword Play*[7] and from the Christmas tradition of misrule, and Medwall several times asserts through speeches of A and B the idea that these "tryfyllis

---

[5] See *Kyng Johan,* II, 37–38. Bale of course regards the New Learning as the foe of Catholicism.

[6] *The Education of a Christian Prince,* trans. L. K. Born (New York, 1936), p. 140.

[7] Ed. J. M. Manly, *Specimens of the Pre-Shaksperean Drama* (Boston and London, 1900), I, 296–311.

be impertinent / To the matter principall." But in fact he uses low comedy exactly as it is used in *Endymion, Twelfth Night,* and *I Henry IV.* The wooing of Jone is, in the phrase of Boas and Reed, a farcical fantasia on the theme *de vera nobilitate.* The uncouth vying of A and B in singing, wrestling, and tilting, like the plays extempore between Falstaff and Prince Hal, is a kind of proleptic parody of the climactic scene of the high plot. It gives artistic balance and integrity to the whole, preventing us (along with the lords who watched the performance) from taking the serious theme too seriously and the play too largely as a didactic demonstration.

The lively lads designated (in speech-headings only) as A and B are also responsible in large measure for the peculiar relationship of stage illusion and banquet-hall reality in *Fulgens and Lucres.*[8] In early Tudor drama generally, and in all the plays here collected except *Gorboduc,* dramatic objectivity is little heeded. The actors are quite aware of the audience, who in fact may become part of the cast as when Johan Johan in Heywood's play asks one of them to hold his gown and, since he isn't doing anything else, to scrape off the dirt from it while Johan goes to fetch Syr Johan the priest. The boy A lists the audience among those to be present during the Second Part of *Fulgens:*

> Mary, here shall be Fulgens,
> And Publius Cornelius hymselfe also,
> With dyverse other many moo
> Besyde this honorable audyence.
>
> (I, ll. 1312–15)

It is the presence of the audience which makes B's obscene garbling of the message from Cornelius so embarrassing to Lucres. The members of the audience are asked to open a door so that a character can enter, and to look for a missing letter. They are regularly the confidants of any character who needs someone to talk to. But Medwall complicates this relationship uniquely when he has A and B, who during the induction pretend to be servants in the hall awaiting the performance of a troupe of traveling players like those who later

[8] See Anne Righter, *Shakespeare and the Idea of the Play* (London, 1962), pp. 36–38. The book studies the changing relationship of illusion and reality from the religious drama to Shakespeare.

come to Elsinore, step across into the play world. A and B woo the heroine's maid and attach themselves as servants to the rival suitors for Lucres in ancient Rome. Medwall is aware that he risks shattering illusion altogether, for when B is about to enter the play within the play, A cries out (ll. 362–63) "Pece, let be! / Be God, thou wyll distroy all the play." But A rightly replies:

> Distroy the play, quod a? nay, nay,
> The play began never till now.

No other such fascinating study in illusion and reality in English drama offers itself until the time of *The Spanish Tragedy, A Looking Glass for London and England,* and *The Taming of the Shrew.*

Among what audience and in what banquet hall *Fulgens and Lucres* was given its first production is not known with certainty, but Boas and Reed speculate plausibly that Morton entertained the ambassadors of Flanders and Spain with this play at his house at Lambeth during the Christmas festivities in their honor in 1497. The Spanish dance, the line of Flemish, the reference to "the season," and the blazing fire in the hall accord with this hypothesis. Trade relations had just been re-established with Flanders. Spain, through Pedro de Ayala, had helped to negotiate a truce between Henry VII and James IV of Scotland, and Ferdinand and Isabella were seeking an alliance with England through marriage of their daughter Catherine of Aragon to Arthur, Henry's eldest son.[9] Of the chaplain who rose to the occasion we know very little that can be said to illuminate his work. Evidently he did not proceed in holy orders beyond the degree of acolyte, which according to Morton's register at Lambeth he achieved in April 1490. John Bale, his earliest biographer, says that he flourished ca. 1500 and was *consuetudine domestica*—from which Reed surmises that like other early English playwrights he may have been a tutor. Pitseus (1619) describes him as *"nobilissimus in Anglia parentibus ortus"* and asserts that he was beloved by Morton and left behind many literary works lost through carelessness but mentions only *Nature.*

---

[9] F. S. Boas and A. W. Reed, eds., *Fulgens & Lucres* (Oxford, 1926), pp. xix–xx. A glimpse into Morton's household about the time of these festivities may be had in the opening pages of More's *Utopia.*

He was still alive in July 1501 when his benefice at Calais
was assigned to someone else. An interesting lawsuit brought
against him after Morton's death in 1500 perhaps reveals
some of the steadiness of nerve which it must have required
to present *Fulgens and Lucres* between courses of a banquet
attended by many a hereditary lord.[10]

John Heywood, alone among the early Tudor playwrights,
was a professional entertainer, and if the six plays usually
ascribed to him are indeed his, Heywood is the major figure
among them. Evidently born in 1497 (about the time that
Medwall produced *Fulgens and Lucres*), he enjoyed favor
in the court of Henry VIII as a protégé of Sir Thomas More
during the period 1519 to 1528. An annual wage of £20
was paid by the Crown to "John Haywode the synger" during these years. He is also called "player of the virginals."
He received as well an annuity of ten marks *"in considera-
cione boni et fidelis servicie."* The six extant plays belong to
this early period in Heywood's career. By marriage, about
1523, Heywood became More's kinsman, for he married
Joan, the daughter of John Rastell, the printer of *Fulgens*,
whose wife was Elizabeth More, Sir Thomas' sister. Heywood's son Jasper became an important translator of Seneca's
tragedies. In due course Heywood's daughter Elizabeth gave
him the distinction of being John Donne's grandfather.

All of his long life Heywood shared his patron More's devotion to the old faith, and it was inevitable that during the
last dark twenty years of Henry VIII and much of the reign
of Edward VI he should lose his prominence at court. In
1532 More, doomed to the block by his own integrity, re-
signed as Lord Chancellor, and soon Henry's marriage to
Catherine of Aragon was voided, their daughter Mary declared illegitimate, and Anne Boleyn crowned queen. When
in 1533 the younger Rastell, John's son William, began printing the plays associated with Heywood it was, as Reed remarks, as if to commemorate the close of a chapter in history.
In that year William published *A Play of Love, The Play of
the Wether, The Pardoner and the Frere,* and *Johan Johan
the Husbande*—the last two however with no statement as to
authorship. *The Foure P. P.,* "Made by John Heewood," was
not printed until about 1544 but was probably written be-

10 Reed, *Early Tudor Drama*, pp. 102–3.

tween 1520 and 1522. Reed speculates that it may have been brought forth to show Heywood's willingness to satirize the parasites of the old order now that his life was in danger for conspiring against Cranmer. The remaining play of the canon, *Wytty and Wyttles,* is a mere debate and certainly very early work. It remained in manuscript.

As a maker of plays, Heywood did not begin where Medwall left off, despite their mutual fondness for debate and some resemblances between Heywood's best plays and the subplot of *Fulgens.* Heywood never in his extant interludes adapted a story from nondramatic literature. Nor, despite a curious critical tradition that it was Heywood who modified moral drama by substituting type characters for its abstractions, has he any appreciable indebtedness to that drama. He is not, that is, in the tradition of Medwall's *Nature* and John Skelton's *Magnyfycence.* This can be seen by contrasting *Wytty and Wyttles* with another manuscript play, *Wyt and Science,* by Heywood's fellow playwright, musician and teacher of boys, John Redford.[11] In Redford's allegory for Tudor schoolboys the linear temptation plot informs a comic romance of knight errantry. If Wyt marries Science, they may have about them Fame, Favor, Ryches, and Worshyp —gifts of a World which is no longer vanity, as it was in the *Castell* play. Wyt, like Medwall's protagonist Man, is Nature's child. Against the advice of Instruccion, his Good Angel, he goes toward Tediousnes, who knocks him dead. Reson revives him and leaves him with Honest Recreacion. As in the old full-scope plays, the pattern is repeated with variations. In a second scene of moral struggle Wyt stands between Honest Recreacion and Idlenes. He receives the smudged face and coxcomb of Ignorance while asleep quite literally in the lap of Idlenes. Chancing to hold up the glass of Reson which he carries with him, Wyt is astonished: "Gogs sowle a foole!" he cries. The scene with the mirror is Redford's adaptation of the old scene of realization from the theological moralities. Confession and absolution are also humanistically refashioned. Reson brings Shame, who beats the repentant sinner while Reson reads off a list of his offenses: that he has set his love upon Idlenes, let her make a fool of him, sworn oaths as great as a man can, and so forth. Wyt

[11] Ed. Manly, *Specimens,* I, 421–56. Poems by Heywood occur in the same MS. with *Wyt and Science.*

departs with Instruccion, Study, and Dylygence to get his
face washed and costume restored to that proper to him. In
what is hardly more than epilogue, Wyt slays Tediousnes
and marries Science. The discursive plot has shown how
Wyt, the typical schoolboy, falls prey successively to Tediousnes and Idlenes, sins of all academic endeavor, and how
Reson is at hand each time to shame and regenerate him. Instruction in the curriculum of Colet and Lyly, with study
and diligence, promotes virtue and brings the gifts of the
World. The moral resembles that of *Fulgens* but is pleasantly
embodied in a fable that parallels that of *Nature*. A whole
series of early Tudor plays, including *Kyng Johan*, consists
of such secular incarnations of the temptation plot.

Wytty and Wyttles in contrast argues for the life of reason
by staging an intellectual disputation. John and James take
opposite positions on the question whether it is better to be
a wise man or a sot, and the argument is settled by Jerome,
whose logic and scriptural learning convince John that wit—
that is, the ability to perceive and reason—brings finer pleasure in this life and joy in the next, and it is better after all
to be Solomon than Will Somers, the King's Fool, for a man
without reason is the same as a beast.

Heywood the dramatist thus began from scratch, or more
precisely from *débat*, and gradually worked out his own
unique kind of interlude. *A Play of Love* is a more complex
debate among The Lover Loved, The Lover Not Beloved,
The Woman Beloved Not Loving, and No Lover Nor Loved,
the first character in English drama designated as the Vice.
The static debating is abruptly but insufficiently enlivened
by a song and by a Chaucerian anecdote told by No Lover
Nor Loved, but then (after 1293 lines) occurs an actual bit
of stage business:

> *Here the vyse cometh in ronnynge sodenly aboute
> the place among the audiens with a hye copyn tank on
> his hed full of squybs fyred, cryeng watere water, fyre,
> fyre, fyre, water, water, fyre, tyll the fyre in the squybs
> be spent.*

Lover Loved is made to think that his house is on fire, and
his distraction goes to prove the Vice's point.

Wether edges yet further from mere preciosity and debate toward farce and a truly dramatic technique. The Gentylman, the Marchaunt, the Watermyller and Wyndmyller

who debate the merits of water vs. wind, and the Gentylwoman who tangles with the Launder (laundress) provide
at least a series of entertaining and varied episodes as they
bring their suits to Jupiter. Most charming of these episodes
is the last, of the little boy, "the lest that can play," who
wants plenty of snow for his snowballs. The Chaucerian note
is stronger, the Vice, here called Mery-report, by far more
active than in *Love*.

Johan Johan the Husbande is the high point of what Reed
has distinguished as a second trilogy in the Heywood plays.
The others comprising it are *The Pardoner and the Frere* and
The Foure P. P. These three are intimately related. Unlike
Wytty and Wyttles, Love, and *Wether,* each "makes notable
work with the then Clergy,"[12] recalling Chaucer's portrait of
the Pardoner. They also draw upon the conventions of French
farce and even upon particular farces.[13] In *The Pardoner
and the Frere* Heywood adapts from *La Farce d'un Pardonneur* the idea of a contest between two rascals, substituting Frere for Triacleur and replacing the French ending with
his own. For a confidence trick played upon La Tavernière
he substitutes assault and battery. The knaves beat up the
Parson and neighbor Prat, sober men who tried to end their
strife. This ending finds its parallel in *Johan Johan* when the
three characters *"fyght by the erys a whyle, and than the
preest and the wyfe go out of the place"* to continue trium-
phant in their iniquity. The amorality of the denouement in
The Pardoner and the Frere and *Johan Johan* is alien to the
rest of Tudor drama. In *The Foure P. P.* Heywood develops
the crude *estrif* between Pardoner and Frere into a formal
lying contest among a Pothecary who tells of a remarkable
cure, a Pardoner who rescued a woman from hell, and a
Palmer who solemnly states that in all his wide experience
with women he never saw or knew one out of patience. The
Pedlar, designated arbiter, cannot but judge him the winner.
Here Heywood adapts his own "relic" passage from *The
Pardoner and the Frere,* which in turn owes something to
Chaucer's prologue as well as to *Pardonneur.* The influence
of the French farce reaches through *The Foure P. P.* into

[12] Francis Kirkman in his play list of 1671, quoted by Reed,
Early Tudor Drama, pp. 118–20.

[13] Karl Young, "The Influence of French Farce upon the Plays
of John Heywood," *MP,* II (1904), 97–104. Ian Maxwell, *French
Farce and John Heywood* (Melbourne and London, 1946).

Johan Johan, betraying itself in the miracles claimed by Syr Johan the Preest. These also may stand in debt to the "marvelous case" in the subplot of *Fulgens* (I, ll. 947 ff.).

But *Johan Johan,* masterpiece of the Heywood canon and of the misogyny of farce, is primarily an improved version of the French *Pernet qui va au vin.* Heywood modifies the triangle of *Pernet* by making the lover a priest, not merely "cousin" and "Amoureux," so that to cry out against him is to hinder God's word. He transforms Nicolle into that study in untamed shrewishness, Tyb, and he conceives of the exasperated husband as a mixture of luckless defiance and cringing servility that is surely one of the funniest things in English drama. The English playwright makes his comic effects more broad and obvious, but also tightens the plot and increases its ironies—for example, Johan Johan actually beseeches his wife's lover to come to dinner in the dim-witted belief that the priest's admonitions will stint the strife between the couple.

That *Johan Johan,* best of the Heywood plays, is least certainly attributable to Heywood scarcely diminishes our enjoyment of it. But of the plays of the second trilogy, only *The Foure P. P.* is assigned to Heywood by its printer. *Johan Johan* was first attributed to him in Francis Kirkman's play list of 1671. It lacks stylistic traits considered to be Heywoodian—his recapitulations, reiterations, and logic-chopping, for example—and Reed has raised the interesting possibility that the play shows the hand of Sir Thomas More himself. More had written in his youth *A Mery Jest of How a Sergeant Would Play the Frere,* which is a playlet in the spirit of the Heywood trilogy—fourteen pages of verse printed by William Rastell in the English *Works* (1557). More had lived as a child in the household where *Fulgens and Lucres* was performed. He was known as an actor extempore and a writer of *Comoediae.* His participation might explain the absence of an author's name in the edition of 1533.

Heywood's writing for the stage did not end with the period of his extant plays. Princess Mary's Book of Expenses for March 1538 records a payment "to Heywood playing an interlude with his children before my lady grace," and in the next year he put on an elaborate *Maske of King Arturs Knights* for the fallen Cromwell. Stowe provides a charming image of Heywood celebrating the coronation of Mary. When she was on her way to Westminster, he writes, "one Master

Haywood sate in a pageant under a vine and made to her an oration in Latin and in English." He had probably written and directed the pageant himself. Mary's death in 1558 eventually sent him into exile on the Continent, whence it had prompted the immediate return of his opposite number among Tudor playwrights, John Bale. His last jest was at the expense of the priest who as Heywood neared death spoke only of the frailty of flesh and whom Heywood accused of seeming to reproach God for not having made him a fish.

Heywood's reputation in the sixteenth century was based upon his personal mirth and wit and his collections of proverbs and epigrams. His major work was not a play but *A Parable of the Spider and the Flie,* begun about the time of More's death in 1535 and published in 1556, with remarkable woodcuts, as a compliment to Queen Mary, who is the Maid who brushes from her lattice the cobwebs of controversy. Heywood included no plays in his *Woorkes* of 1562 and would seem not to have greatly valued the function he attributed to himself in his best-known epigram: "Art thou Heywood that hath made many mad plaies?"

As Heywood celebrated Mary's coronation in a pageant, John Bale (1495–1563) defied her proclamation as queen in Ireland by putting on three of his plays "at the Market Crosse" in Kilkenny "to the small contentacion of the Prestes and other Papistes there."[14] He was at the time Bishop of Ossory, and the plays were *The Chefe Promyses of God, Johan Baptystes Preachynge in the Wyldernesse,* and *The Temptacyon of Our Lorde,* the latter an early and touching Protestant treatment of the subject of *Paradise Regained.* These plays survive along with two others, which, however, align themselves with the morality play rather than with the mysteries: *Thre Lawes, or Nature, Moses, and Christ* and Bale's most powerful and original play, *Kyng Johan.* In his *Scriptores* of 1548 Bale lists seventeen additional plays *"in idiomate materno"* now lost, including a translation of *Pammachius* by the Lutheran Thomas Kirchmayer. The Latin play tells of a fictitious pope, Pammachius, who became Antichrist and ruled till the return of Veritas, whose agent is the

[14] E. K. Chambers, *The Mediaeval Stage* (Oxford, 1903), II, 374.

German Theophilis. *Pammachius* doubtless influenced *Kyng Johan*,[15] which also bears some evidence of kinship with the contemporary *Ane Satyre of the Thrie Estaitis* by the Scotsman Sir David Lyndsay.

Though he took orders as a priest, Bale was an early and passionate convert to Protestantism, in whose cause all of his dramatic work seems to have been written. Evidently he organized a troupe of traveling players to spread the New Gospel and sought for it the patronage of the Protestant great. A deposition included with a letter from Thomas Cranmer to Thomas Cromwell in January 1539 mentions "an enterlude concernynge king John" enacted "aboute viij or ix of the clocke at nyght on thursdaye the seconde Daye of Januarye" which demonstrated that "king John was as noble a prince as ever was in England" and "the begynnyng of the puttyng down of the bisshop of Rome." This description of an interlude played "in Christmas tyme at my lorde of Canterbury's" fits Bale's play well, and the presumption that it was indeed Bale's *Kyng Johan* is brought near certainty by an entry in Cromwell's account books concerning thirty shillings paid to "Bale & his ffelowes" on the last day of January 1539, "gyven to him & his ffelowes for playing before my lorde."[16]

Upon the fall of his patron, Cromwell, in 1540 Bale perforce shifted his base of operations against Rome to Germany. When he returned to England after Henry's death early in 1547 he became rector of Bishopstoke in Hampshire and, in 1551, of Swaffham in Norfolk. His tenure in Ireland occupied most of 1553. Under Mary he again went into exile, at Basle, and he returned with the accession of Elizabeth, for whose pleasure he revised the play about John's struggle with the pope which he had written under her father.

The lost play by Bale whose lack is most regrettable is perhaps the one *"de imposturis Thomae Becketi."* But in *Kyng Johan* we can see what it was like. In his effort to find means to dramatize his view that Crown must have supremacy over Church, Bale turned instinctively to the struggle between John of England and Innocent III over the institution of

[15] C. H. Herford, *Studies in the Literary Relations of England and Germany in the Sixteenth Century* (Cambridge, 1886), pp. 134–38.

[16] The quotations are taken from the Malone Society Reprint of *Kyng Johan,* ed. J. H. P. Pafford (Oxford, 1931), pp. xvii–xviii.

Stephen Langton as Archbishop of Canterbury. This, as readily as the conflict between John's father, Henry II, and Thomas Becket, could be made to illustrate the corrupting subversion of government, and the breath-taking hypocrisy, of the Catholic Church. "There is no malyce," declares the dying king in one of Bale's few memorable lines (II, l. 1040), "to the malyce of the clergye." Permitting England's worst king to assume the qualities of sainthood, Bale achieves an almost Websterian satiric vision of helpless virtue pitted against Italianate villainy. England wallowed in sin for three hundred years, Bale asserts, until Henry VIII succeeded where John had failed. The major chronicles available to Bale were those of Fabyan and Polydore Vergil—who, since he vilified John, gets special attention in the play. Bale lists a dozen other historians, even finding a few who had something good to say of John. He does not seem to have drawn extensively upon any of these as Shakespeare drew upon Holinshed. Nonetheless by making drama out of the reigns of Henry II and John he invented the English chronicle play, and he made it from the start a mirror of Tudor policy.[17]

Though all literary works may be called transitional, some are more transitional than others, and *Kyng Johan* is one of them. Bale's mind hovers ambivalently between the personified abstraction of the old allegorical drama and the literal concreteness of history. Private Welth and Cardinal Pandulphus are the same character, sedition personified is also Stevyn Langton, and Usurpyd Power by a change of costume becomes the Pope. These shifts are distinct from the doubling of parts, frequently specified in the stage directions, which enabled Bale and his fellows to impersonate fourteen characters, and they help to make *Kyng Johan* the most challenging play in this collection.

The play's ambivalence is also structural. As a morality play it bears striking resemblances to *A Morality of Wisdom who is Christ* (ca. 1460),[18] and from this point of view Nobilyte, Clergye, and Civyle Order are central, a composite protagonist like Mind, Will, and Understanding who play Mankind's role in *Wisdom*. Johan, not at all "a sort of Eng-

[17] Lily B. Campbell, *Shakespeare's Histories, Mirrors of Eliza-bethan Policy* (San Marino, 1947), pp. 129–32.

[18] Ed. F. J. Furnivall and A. W. Pollard, *The Macro Plays*, E. E. T. S. Extra Series 91 (London, 1904), pp. 35–74. The other Macro plays are *The Castell of Perseverance* and *Mankind*.

lish Everyman" as he has been called, takes rather the role
of Wisdom; he is a Christ figure. Lucifer's part goes fittingly
to the Pope and his agents. The passive soul, Anima, resembles poor Widow England. At the outset each multiple
protagonist exhibits susceptible allegiance to Christ or king.
After an introduction of the boisterous and sinister power
of evil there is a temptation scene. Sedicyon alias Stevyn
Langton deceives Nobilyte, Clergye, and Civyle Order as
Lucifer had deceived the Mind, Will, and Understanding
of man. The long phase of error concludes with what the
author of *Wisdom* calls "þe recogyncion ye have clere."
Veryte, truth itself, in Bale's play forces this recognition
upon the central figures, and the conventional plot ends
with contrition, absolution, and instruction—here in the Gospel according to Bale that virtue lies in direct allegiance to
the king. As the Interpretour promised, Henry has restored
his country (like Anima in *Wisdom*) "To hir first bewtye."

But of course from the point of view of later chronicle
drama Johan himself is the protagonist and the play's parallels in older moral drama fade from prominence. Since Johan
is dead (and presumably died in the original version as well)
the play is also chronicle tragedy such as compels qualifica-
tion of the common opinion that *Gorboduc* is the first English tragedy. The revised ending is pervaded by Elizabethan tragic feeling akin to that of *A Mirrour for Magistrates*,
Gorboduc, and *Cambises*. Sedicyon is condemned to death,
and Nobilyte, despite his childhood distaste for the New
Learning, shows education enough to think fleetingly of
"Brute," "Catilyne," "Cassius," and "fayer Absolon"—men to
whom God dealt terrible punishment for their sedition.

Kyng Johan, historical-comical-tragical though it is, remains a moral interlude. For practical purposes, what distinguishes Tudor comedy and tragedy from Tudor interludes is
the formal imitation of Roman comedy and tragedy, and in
the extant vernacular drama of England this begins with
Royster Doyster and *Gammer Gurtons Nedle*. Toward the
end of the fifteenth century, plays of Plautus, Terence, and
Seneca had begun to be performed in Latin in various cities
in Italy. Pupils of Pomponius Laetus put on Plautus' *Asinaria*
and Seneca's *Hippolytus* about 1485 at the University of
Rome, and the *Menaechmi* of Plautus was played in Ferrara
in 1486 under the patronage of Ercole I. The practice spread

very rapidly to the north and to England, and Greek
dramatists joined the Roman, especially Aristophanes and
Euripides, usually but not always in Latin translations. Such
revivals were soon joined by neo-Latin and neo-Greek drama
in almost every possible combination of humanism and
medievalism. Sacred subjects were dramatized in the meter
and style of Plautus or of Euripides. In *Thersites,* one of the
Dialogi of J. Ravisius Textor, Professor of Rhetoric at the
College of Navarre, the Plautine Miles Gloriosus figures in
a medieval fable. (The English adaptation, apparently an
Oxford play, was acted in 1537.) The so-called Christian-
Terence plays chiefly by Dutch, Rhenish, and Swiss school-
masters, staged the career of a Prodigal Son in terms of Roman comedy. But the great step in the advance of modern
European drama was to adapt conventions of Roman drama
to the depiction of Renaissance life in plays written in the
vernacular. In the resultant *commedia erudita* the pioneer
is Lodovico Ariosto, the author of *Orlando Furioso,* who during the first two decades of the *cinquecento* wrote for performance at the ducal court of Ferrara a series of five
scintillating comedies. Of these the best known to English
readers is *I Suppositi* (1509 in prose, revised into verse
1529) which was translated (1566) into the witty prose of
George Gascoigne as *Supposes* and thence supplied the subplot for *The Taming of the Shrew. Supposes,* the first play
in English prose and the first comedy produced in England
with a modern Italian setting, is on a different level of sophistication from that of the contemporary native comedy. It
points up what every English reader of Ariosto must acknowledge: that he is of the stature of Jonson rather than of Udall.
Indeed, *Il Negromante* (1520, in verse) anticipates *Vol-
pone* and *The Alchemist.* In tragedy Ferrara could boast,
though somewhat less proudly, the work of Giraldi Cinthio,
who during the middle part of the century wrote two Senecan
tragedies on classical subjects, *Cleopatra* and *Didone,* and
seven using stories from his own collection of *novelle,* the
Ecatomithi, later to supply the source for *Othello.* It was
the example of Cinthio, according to J. W. Cunliffe,[19] which
turned Renaissance tragedy toward the Senecan model and
away from the Greek.

[19] *Early English Classical Tragedies* (Oxford, 1912), pp. xxxii–
xxxiii.

Inevitably Plautus and Terence were first assimilated to English drama and made to mirror English life upon the academic stage. Nicholas Udall most probably wrote *Royster Doyster* for his boys at Eton school, where he was headmaster from 1534 to 1541 and numbered among his responsibilities the superintending of the Christmas play. *Gammer Gurtons Nedle*, made by the elusive "Mr. S. Mr. of Art" most likely during the reign of Edward VI, was "Played on Stage . . . in Christes Colledge in Cambridge." It is the only play extant in English that we can be sure was offered at one of the universities during the Tudor period. *The Tragidie of Ferrex and Porrex*, better known as *Gorboduc*, in which Thomas Sackville and Thomas Norton first bled Seneca through English veins, was acted at the Inner Temple for the Christmas Revels early in January 1560/61 and again, before Elizabeth at Whitehall, on January 18, 1561/62.[20] Thus the progress of Roman drama into the vernacular may be said to have run parallel for the Italians and the English, erudite comedy being joined after a few years by tragedy. Plautus could not prove too light for them, nor Seneca too heavy. Seneca was transmitted to the Inns of Court through Italian tragedy, but in *Royster Doyster* and *Gammer Gurton* the influence of Roman comedy would appear to be direct.

[20] Old system beginning the year on the Annunciation (March 25); modern system beginning the year with the Circumcision (January 1). But the authorities do not agree on the year of the performance at the Inner Temple. F. A. Inderwick, *A Calendar of the Inner Temple Records* (London, 1896), I, lxx, dates it "Twelfth Night of 1560 or 1561." Chambers, *Mediaeval Stage*, I, 415–16, dates the festivities of which *Gorboduc* was part 1561. Then the performance at the Temple and that at Whitehall were separated by about a year and two weeks. Yet the undated authorized edition states on the title page that the tragedy "was shewed on stage before the Queenes Majestie, about nine years past, viz., the xviij day of Januarie 1561" and in its letter to the reader that the tragedy was "furniture of part of the grand Christmasse in the Inner Temple first written about nine yeares ago" by Sackville and Norton, suggesting that both early performances were in the same January, 1561/62. Chambers, *Elizabethan Stage*, III, 457, cites a reference from the diary of Henry Machyn to the performance on January 18: "a play in the quen hall at Westmynster by the gentyll-men of the Tempull, and after a grett maske, for ther was a grett skaffold in the hall, with grett tryhumpe as has bene sene; and the morow after the skaffold was taken done."

Udall adapts it to bourgeois English life, not wholly unlike the Greek middle-class life reflected in New Comedy of Menander, Plautus, and Terence. Mr. S. in contrast frankly lets it inform a farce of rustic English low life and, unexpectedly, achieves the more perfect fusion. Both perpetuate the jigging veins of rhyming mother wits from native drama as against the prose or unrhymed verse of the Italians.

Royster Doyster draws primarily upon the *Miles Gloriosus* of Plautus and the *Eunuchus* of Terence. The action of the *Miles* involves the rescue of the girl Philocomasium from the braggart warrior Pyrgopolinices, who abducted her from Athens to Ephesus, and her restoration to her Athenian lover, Pleusicles. The feat is accomplished by two intrigues practiced by the witty slave Palaestrio. He convinces the warrior's less witty servant that the girl seen next door making love with Pleusicles is not Philocomasium but her twin sister, and he causes Pyrgopolinices to reject Philocomasium by persuading him that a supposed lady, in reality a courtesan, wishes to marry him. Royster Doyster, Custance, her espoused Goodlucke, and the witty Merygreeke play roles roughly similar to those of the chief characters in the *Miles*. Close resemblance occurs not in plot but in certain exchanges, particularly between Rafe and Merygreeke, and in specific lines echoed from Plautus, lending the play a somewhat inkhorn quality. Goodlucke's marriage with Custance is impeded by nothing but his momentary misunderstanding of the relationship between her and Rafe. Custance herself and the testimony of Tristram Trusty remove the obstacle. The chief subject is original: Rafe's absurd suit, encouraged for the sake of mirth by Merygreeke, to gain the hand of Custance. From the *Eunuchus* Udall took the hint for the mock battle in his fourth act and for his closing scene. Pyrgopolinices was finally beaten for his lechery. But Thraso, the Miles Gloriosus of *Eunuchus*, is allowed to join the others who share the favors of Thais—a somewhat different kind of cheer, to be sure, from that in which Rafe is invited to partake. Merygreeke resembles the parasite Gnatho in *Eunuchus*, though he may also be regarded as a combination of Palaestrio ("the slippery one") and of the parasite Artotrogus ("bread chewer") who plumes up Pyrgopolinices in the first scene of the *Miles*. At the outset (I, i, ii) Merygreeke exhibits the parasite's perennial concern with his belly. He seeks also, like Iago, to make his fool his purse. But after a

scene or two the English playwright turns to English convention for the motivation of Merygreeke. The intriguer's
true motive is mirth, and his closest affinity is to Heywood's
Vice.

Finding his way into the writing of the first English comedy, Udall shows other signs of uncertainty. His Prologue
calls the play "thys Enterlude" then, after mentioning Plautus and Terence, "Our Comedie or Enterlude." Udall never
quite domesticates the Miles Gloriosus, as does Jonson in
Bobadill and Shakespeare in Falstaff. Rafe remains too much
a Greco-Roman boastful warrior in England. In its conventional New Comedy setting of a public street before a
house and in many aspects of technique *Royster Doyster*
takes Tudor England back to Roman comedy rather than
incorporates that comedy with the art that conceals art. It
is pedantic, not alone in its echoes of ancient comedy and
its jest based on punctuation. Yet Udall freely adds true English social types to the Greek or Roman, notably in Custance's maids and the old nurse Mage Mumble-crust; mod-
ernizes his heroine and the whole New Comic system of
sexual mores; and casually adapts to English the principle
of the name revelatory of type. In these respects like Ariosto
he domesticates New Comedy more thoroughly than had
the Roman *fabula palliata* itself, with its Greek plots, social
setting, costumes, and names.

What chiefly distinguishes *Royster Doyster* from *fabula
palliata* and *commedia erudita* alike is its moral tone and
propriety, unusual in pre-Elizabethan drama, as the reader
of this volume will quickly discover. The Prologue promises
a play "Wherin all scurilitie we utterly refuse, / Avoiding
such mirth wherin is abuse." Thinking presumably of his
schoolboys, Udall eschews the scurrility of Heywood and
of Plautus both and moralistically inveighs with the author
of *Thersites* "against the vayne glorious." Merygreeke will
not help Rafe's cause without assurance that his love for
Custance is in the way of Marriage rather than of Merchan-
dise, and Rafe has never the remotest prospect of the
physical possession which is a matter of course in Plautine
comedy. The contrast is sharpest in the women. Thais and
Philocomasium ("lover of revelry") are courtesans, the widow
Custance the embodiment of feminine dignity and constancy. Capable of sternness toward her foolish maidservant
but also of joining in the fun against Rafe, capable also of

pathos, she combines the virtues of Desdemona with worldly experience and practical wit. She is Udall's most charming achievement, too charming for the smug Goodlucke, who, as Flügel aptly remarks, is no Romeo. He is no Pleusicles either, eager to receive back his beloved from the arms of Pyrgopolinices. But Udall's play is not satiric of the priggish London merchant.

Nicholas Udall's recorded career as a dramatist begins with undistinguished verses which he wrote in collaboration with the king's antiquary John Leland for pageants celebrating the coronation of Anne Boleyn in 1533. He gained reputation and credentials for his appointment to Eton with his *Floures for Latine Spekynge, selected and gathered oute of Terence* (1534), which enjoyed several sixteenth-century editions. In 1538 "Woodall, the schoolmaster of Eton," received £5 for playing before Lord Cromwell. After his dismissal in 1541, he engaged chiefly in theological work. He shared in the great project of translating into English Erasmus' paraphrase of the New Testament and dedicated his rendering of Luke to Catherine Parr in 1545. Princess Mary did part of the Gospel of St. John, and perhaps it was due to this association that Udall, of Lutheran persuasion since his Oxford days, nonetheless remained in England when she became queen. For a time he was a tutor in the household of Bishop Gardiner, and about 1553 he returned finally to his old profession of schoolmastering, this time at Westminster. He wrote dialogues, interludes, and devises for Mary, and Bale in his *Scriptores* of 1557, the year after Udall's death, credits him with a tragedy on the papacy and *"Comoedias plures."* Among the extant anonymous Tudor plays none but *Royster Doyster* has been identified as one of these.

Royster Doyster is preserved in a single copy of a sixteenth-century edition, presented in 1818 to Eton College Library, where it fittingly resides. It lacks title page and colophon. The Stationers' *Registers* for 1566/67 list 4d. "Recevyd of Thomas hackett for hys lycense for pryntinge of a play intituled Rauf Ruyster Duster." The extant copy, with its reference to a queen who is presumably Elizabeth, may represent Hackett's edition. However, Thomas Wilson in the 1553 edition of *The Rule of Reason, conteinyng the Arte of Logique* quotes the two versions of Rafe's letter as "An example of soche doutbfull writing, whiche by reason of poincting maie have double sense, and contrarie meaning, taken out of an entrelude made by Nicolas Udal."[21] Wilson, whose allusion establishes the play's authorship, must have had a manuscript or a copy of an edition earlier than Hackett's. Internal evidence points toward the period of Udall's headmastership at Eton as the most likely time of the composition of this landmark of English drama.[22] Wilson was in fact a pupil at Eton during Udall's tenure and might have recalled the example of the power of punctuation from his own experience there, necessarily waiting until 1553 before he could obtain the text. Flügel suggests plausibly that *Royster Doyster* was "unpretentiously offered by Udall to his boys" in place of the usual Latin school comedy, "modestly put aside after the performance and printed long afterwards."[23] Redford's *Wyt and Science,* written under similar auspices, was never printed. Later (ca. 1560), perhaps through the precedent established by Udall, the *ludi magister* at Eton was explicitly permitted to exhibit English plays instead of Latin provided they had *"acumen et leporem,"* wit and grace.[24]

In *Gammer Gurtons Nedle* it is as though Heywood had written farce in the shape of Roman comedy. The types, the idiom, the manners are indigenous, and five-act structure, the unities, and the necessary intriguer shape the play unself-consciously. Neoclassicism obtrudes itself nowhere but in the formal divisions of the printed play into act and scene according to Renaissance principles for printing Roman comedy.

The language and behavior of yokels, Diccon remarks during the comedy, are entertaining enough for a man to make a play of "Being but halfe a Clarke" (II, ii, l. 12). Although the dialect is not quite authentic from a philological point of view, very likely the Master of Art drew the society of his play from life. Brett-Smith describes it well:

[21] Fol. 66ᵛ. Wilson's text of the letters is reprinted in full in the Malone Society edition of the play and in Scheurweghs' edition.

[22] For discussion of the date, see E. Flügel's introduction in C. M. Gayley, ed., *Representative English Comedies* (New York, 1903), pp. 95–97.

[23] Ibid., p. 90.

[24] Warton, *History of English Poetry* (London, 1871), III, 308. Quoted in Flügel, loc. cit., note.

. . . a society unlike anything to be found in the greater dramatists who followed him, for they were interested, like Shakespeare, either in the towns or in a more remote and pastoral life. The bustling folly of Dogberry or Bottom, the tinge of a rural philosophy in Corin or the old Bohemian shepherd, are alike unknown to Gammer Gurton's village, where everything is realistically sordid, and the author has achieved a singular absence of even a suggestion of abstract thought in his characters. . . . The miry winter weather, the impassable roads, the sluttishly kept houses, the state of society in which a needle is a coveted possession, and therewithall the rude comfort which does not lack a slip of bacon, a draught of ale, and a game of trump by the fire—all these are real enough, and not so long out of date.[25]

The play is worth the reading simply for the farmyard life it re-creates in sharp detail and for portraits like that of the indispensable Hodge, superstitious, uncouth, long-suffering, and honest, who remarks with unwitting truth (III, iv, ll. 7–8) that Gyb, the plaguiest cat between Thames and Tyne, has "as much wyt in her head almost as chave in mine." The sole character drawn from dramatic convention is Diccon. Boas points out rightly that despite his nominal designation, Diccon does not much resemble the Bedlam beggars who, as Shakespeare describes them,

with roaring voices,
Strike in their num'd and mortified Armes,
Pins, Wodden-prickes, Nayles, Sprigs of Rosemarie:
And with this horrible object, from low Farmes,
Poore pelting Villages, Sheeps-Coates, and Milles,
Sometimes with Lunaticke bans, sometime with Praiers
Inforce their charitie.[26]

Like Merygreeke, Diccon is the Vice in the role of Plautine intriguer.

Beneath an artless surface, *Gammer Gurtons Nedle* reveals true unity of action. To be sure, the progress of the

[25] H. F. B. Brett-Smith, ed., *Gammer Gurtons Nedle* (Oxford, 1920), pp. vii–viii.

[26] *King Lear*, II, iii, ll. 14–20. F. S. Boas, *University Drama in the Tudor Age* (Oxford, 1914), p. 74.

plot toward the seat of Hodge's britch, where the needle
has all along resided, is most elliptical. Sweepings must be
winnowed, Hodge terrified, Gyb the cat "groped," Chat
and Gammer tricked into a Heywoodian battle, and Doctor
Rat's head broken before the needle can be found. But "al
this great ado," as the Gammer calls it, is not really about
nothing. The course of the mirth leads efficiently toward in-
creased charity within the little community. Diccon's prac-
ticing upon Hodge, Gammer, Chat, and Rat serves to bring
everyone before the sanguine Baylye in the right state of
mind to benefit from his comic wisdom. Forerunner of Jonson's Justice Clement, Baylye probes to the truth and
negotiates reconciliation. "You must both learne, and teach
us to forgeve" (V, ii, l. 256) he tells the hitherto grudging
and vindictive Curate. And when Dame Chat cries out that
she is as glad at Gammer's fortune as if "mine owne selfe as
good a turne had," Baylye thinks such an access of good feeling worth three needles as a reason for rejoicing. Even Rat
concurs. They have Diccon to thank not so much for enabling
Hodge to locate the needle by a last prank as for the "perfect
securytie" of heart that ensues as the Prologue promised and
for the renewing of social bonds.

The date of *Gammer Gurtons Nedle* and the identity of
Mr. S. have yet to be specified definitively, but it may be that
like *Royster Doyster* it is pre-Elizabethan comedy. The king
referred to in Act V (ii, l. 236) might be Edward VI. The
religious attitude is consistently pre-Reformation. Thus Dame
Chat, the Prologue says, knows no more the whereabouts of
the needle than knows Tom, the clerk, what the priest says
at Mass. But these things may be mere artifice. Thomas Colwell's edition is dated 1575 and says on the title page that
the play was acted "not longe ago." But there are reasons
for thinking that it was printed earlier, among them that
Colwell was licensed to print a *Dyccon of Bedlam* in 1562/63.
Two Martin Marprelate tracts of 1588 state in so many
words that the playwright of *Gammer Gurton* was John
Bridges.[27] Bridges, a literate opponent of Papist as well
as of Puritan, would therefore be accepted as the author

[27] Boas, in the work just cited, pp. 81–87, makes the case for
Bridges. He supplies, and discounts, the case for John Still and
counters the persuasive argument for William Stevenson put forth
by Henry Bradley in Gayley's *Representative English Comedies*,
pp. 198–202.

except that he was a fellow of Pembroke's, not of Christ's, and that his name does not begin with S. A William Stevenson, fellow of Christ's College from 1551 to 1554, who produced, but did not necessarily write, a play performed there in 1553/54 is another likely candidate. Isaac Reed in 1782 nominated John Still, who was a Master of Art with the right initial at Christ's in 1567, when, at Christmas, 20d. was paid "for the Carpenters setting upp the scaffold at the Plaie," the latest recorded performance before 1575, when *Gammer Gurton* was printed. John Still, at least in later life, was a man of awesome gravity unmodified by wit, and in 1592 as Vice Chancellor of Cambridge he was capable of writing to Lord Burghley, "Englishe Comedies, for that wee never used any, wee presently have none."

Gorboduc and *A Lamentable Tragedy Mixed Full of Pleasant Mirth of Cambises, King of Persia* offer an interesting study in the academic vs. the popular in nascent Elizabethan tragedy. The former, written "for furniture of part of the grand Christmasse in the Inner Temple," in 1560/61, and afterward "shewed on stage before the Queenes Majestie" at Whitehall, was composed by Thomas Sackville and Thomas Norton, gentlemen of the Temple and members of Elizabeth's first Parliament. Norton, according to the Stationers' *Registers* and to the first (unauthorized) edition wrote Acts I–III and Sackville the rest. *Cambises*, intended for performance at hall and innyard by a traveling troupe of six men and two boys, may well have been produced at as early a date, though it was not licensed for printing until 1569/70. There is reason to believe that *Cambises* belonged to the repertory of the Earl of Leicester's men, which featured James Burbage and which in 1576 moved into his Theatre. If so, the tyrant-tragedy may well have been played at Stratford, on the occasion of the company's visits there in 1572 and 1576, and have impressed the future author of *Macbeth*. It is the work of one Thomas Preston, whom recent opinion tends to identify with the fellow of King's College, Cambridge, of that name, who in 1564 won favor and a pension from the Queen for disputing before her and acting in *Dido*.[28] If the identification is correct Preston

[28] W. A. Armstrong, "The Authorship and Political Meaning of *Cambises*," *English Studies*, XXXVI (1955), 289–99. Chambers,

anticipates the University Wits of the late 1580s and 1590s who mediated between Learning and the commercial theatre.

As vehicles of moral and political comment, *Gorboduc* and *Cambises* are not utterly dissimilar, but they differ radically in style and dramaturgy. *Gorboduc* is the first play in what was to become the medium for great English tragedy, blank verse, the suggestion for which Norton and Sackville perhaps owe jointly to Surrey's translation of Books II and IV of the *Aeneid* and to the unrhymed, eleven-syllable line of Italian tragedy. In quality of dramatic blank verse there is no advance until Marlowe beyond the best passages in *Gorboduc*. Sidney thought it "full of stately speeches and well sounding Phrases, clyming to the height of *Seneca* his stile," and, he added, "as full of notable moralitie, which it doth most delightfully teach, and so obtayne the very end of Poesie."[29] In contrast the verse of the serious parts of *Cambises* is an artistic disaster. Holding to the native tradition, Preston remains in troublesome bondage to rhyme and commits himself to the impossible fourteener. Though he was an erudite man, his experiments in tragic heightening are nonetheless laughable, and we have Shakespeare's laughter at "King Cambyses' vaine."[30]

The contrast is equally sharp between the off-stage, reported quality of events in *Gorboduc* and Preston's effort to bring all the important deeds, however violent and bloody, before the eyes of the spectator. Here, following the practice of English drama from its very origin in the mystery plays, Preston intuits the future course of Elizabethan tragedy. The Senecan model leads Sackville and Norton to convey everything exciting indirectly in the speech of a Nuntius or other character, sometimes perfunctorily and sometimes, as with Marcella's description of the murder of Porrex, movingly, but in a manner unsatisfying to the Elizabethan longing for immediacy. The messenger's report is often the

---

Elizabethan Stage, III, 469, is not alone in thinking it incredible that such a scholar wrote such a play.

[29] *An Apologie for Poetrie* (ca. 1583), in *Elizabethan Critical Essays*, ed. Gregory Smith (Oxford, 1904), I, 196–97.

[30] *I Henry IV*, II, iv, ll. 426 ff. What follows is not a close parody of Preston's style. Compare however the rhetoric of the "very tragicall mirth" involving Pyramus and Thisbe, *A Midsummer Night's Dream*, V, i, ll. 56 ff.

price paid by the neoclassic dramatist for unity of time and place and a late point of attack. Norton and Sackville begin at the beginning of the story and violate these unities, as Sidney could not forbear complaining, and still depend heavily upon narration. Preston stops at nothing to gain immediacy. Sisamnes' body is flayed on stage according to instructions in the most famous stage direction in Tudor drama, and the heart of Praxaspes' son is cut out and held up before the crowd to show that even when Cambises has drunk his fill his arrow hits the mark. The doubling of parts, more frequent than in *Kyng Johan*, permits Preston's little company to represent thirty-six characters as if Persian life at court and among the people were being glimpsed in all its remarkable heterogeneity. Its vitality often topples *Cambises* into absurdity, and no doubt Preston by his chronic incompetence deserves the epithet which one unkind scholar has given him of University half-wit. As often in Tudor drama (for example when Kyng Johan declares to the audience that he finds it convenient to tell them who he is) one has the sense in Preston's serious scenes of reading one of Shakespeare's parodies of his predecessors and not the thing itself. Shame comes on before Cambises does anything wrong, and the king's death, wherein he has to explain to the audience how the sword became accidentally stuck into his side, reads indeed like the work of Peter Quince. Yet *Cambises* helps prepare the way for *Tamburlaine*, for *Henry IV*, and for *Macbeth*. What the dramatist is attempting is profoundly important in the evolution of English drama even though he lacks the skill, and the tradition behind him, to enable him to carry it off. This would remain true even if Preston himself had played Cambises and hanged himself in the "cosin-jarmins" garter. Whereas after a series of similar Inn of Court tragedies the spiritual descendants of *Gorboduc*, in its neoclassic dignity and sententiousness, are *Sejanus* and *Catiline*.

Rarely, the pre-Elizabethan moral interludes involve death, as in the death of Kyng Johan, but no vernacular play that can be called, or that calls itself, a tragedy seems to have appeared before 1558. It is therefore tempting to connect the birth of tragedy in England with Elizabeth's accession, and to an extent this can be done on political and religious grounds. The earliest tragedies are all political object lessons, mirrors for magistrates, and as a rule those in the popular tradition are darkly Protestant.

The great collection of stories of political misjudgment, *A Mirrour for Magistrates*, prepared in its original form under Mary, was hindered from publication by her chancellor Stephen Gardiner, but the first edition followed Elizabeth's coronation within the year. *Gorboduc* is a Senecan mirror for the queen and her advisors, and in *Cambises* Preston tries to adapt the instructive fall of magistrates to the form of the native morality play. Sackville is directly linked to the *Mirrour* by his contribution of the famed *Induction* and *The Complaynt of Henrye Duke of Buckingham* to its second edition (1563), and he must have had these in hand as he worked on *Gorboduc*. But William Baldwin's view in the preface to the *Mirrour* of the magistrate as God's vicegerent whom God, out of justice, may plague with shameful death if he turns corrupt or presumptuous is patently exemplified by Preston's Sisamnes and Cambises. Here, Baldwin says to Elizabethan magistrates, "as in a loking glas, you shall see (if any vice be in you) howe the like hath bene punished in other heretofore, whereby admonished, I trust it will be a good occasion to move you to the soner amendment."[31] The ideas were not new, but the *Mirrour* gave them new prominence and systematic illustration out of British history.

The orthodox Tudor theory of the magistrate, Lily Bess Campbell reminds us, was the same as that which ecclesiastical necessity forced upon the mind of Calvin.[32] One wonders if the abrupt emergence of English tragedy is not part of the sudden release of Protestant thought after five years of suppression under Mary. Tragedies like *Inough Is as Good as a Feast, The Longer Thou Livest the More Fool Thou Art*, and *The Conflict of Conscience*, all probably written in the 1560s, merge catastrophe with predestination and reprobation. Preston's bias, judging from his reference (l. 1146) to ex-Bishop Bonner, is frankly Protestant. And during 1559–61, when he presumably wrote his share of *Gorboduc*, Thomas Norton was more heavily engaged in making the Tudor translation of *The Institution of Christian Religion*.

In his *Historia Regum Britanniae* Geoffrey of Monmouth accords only a summary account to the events dramatized by the gentlemen of the Temple: King Gorbodugo, he writes,

---

[31] *The Mirror for Magistrates*, ed. Lily B. Campbell (Cambridge, 1938), pp. 65–66.

[32] *Mirror for Magistrates*, p. 52.

had two sons, the one Ferreux, the other Porrex, and as their
father approached senility contention broke out between
them about the succession. Porrex planned to kill Ferreux,
who learned of the plot, went to the king of France for aid,
and returned to fight his brother. Ferreux and all his host
however were killed in the fighting. Their mother, Iuden,
who favored Ferreux, came with her maids to Porrex while
he slept, killed him, and cut him into pieces by way of revenge. For a long time civil discord afflicted the people, and
five kings clashed one with another.

Later chroniclers like Fabyan and Grafton vary Geoffrey's
account but slightly except for some confusion of the roles
of the two sons. Norton and Sackville, as Tucker Brooke remarks, "did not scruple to distort Geoffrey's narrative in order to bring into bold relief the favorite Latin themes of an-
cestral impiety and avenging fate."[33] They play up the role
of Videna and cause Gorboduc, "In kinde a father, not in
kindlinesse" (I, i, l. 18), to sin in her eyes against primogeni-
ture. His well-intended folly, for which the dramatists may
have taken their hint from the preceding history of Leir,
sets going revenge and counter-revenge. In a chain of un-
natural deeds, brother slays brother, mother kills son, subject
kills prince until the house of Gorboduc has been obliterated
as by a curse. The adaptation matches Seneca's treatment
in the fragmentary *Thebaïs* of the strife between the two
sons of Oedipus.

Unlike the tragedies of Seneca and their Italian counter-
parts as well, however, *Gorboduc* is an object lesson rich in
contemporary political applications. Even as playwrights,
Norton and Sackville seek to guide the new government of
which both were members. Gorboduc's fall, like the complaints in the *Mirrour*, remains a tragedy in the medieval
sense, one of the stories *de casibus virorum illustrium*, but
adapted to teach a point in government. Gorboduc, the first
chorus tells us:

> From blisfull state of joye and great renowne,
> A myrrour shall become to Princes all,
> To learne to shunne the cause of suche a fall.
>
> (I, ii, ll. 391–93)

[33] *The Tudor Drama* (Boston, 1911), p. 192.

The cause, of course, was dividing the land. The second dumb show and chorus do not let us fail to draw the moral from the three parallel scenes in which Gorboduc, Ferrex, and Porrex each listens to wise and unwise counsel. A prince should accept sound counsel however retrograde to his desires and see flattery for what it is. (The humanistic preoccupation of Norton and Sackville with the role of counselors to the prince and with their treatment is shared by the author of *Cambises*, though expressed there in his more flamboyant way.) We learn something of the consequences of "lust of kingdom" or ambition, of the giddiness of the people, and, especially in a didactic passage omitted from the authorized edition, of the necessity for ordinary subjects to remain subject to their sovereign in deed and even in secret thought during extremity and not to judge his acts. But the great lesson was that the succession of the crown of England must be at once established. In the printed play the theme that civil war otherwise follows the death of the monarch is introduced in the argument and stressed in the description of the fifth dumb show. The fifth act, which is really postlude since all the principals are dead, is an apocalyptic vision of what might happen in England should the childless and seemingly frail queen die. Such horrors follow, Eubulus-Sackville tells the audience toward the close:

> when, loe, unto the prince,
> Whom death or sodeine happe of life bereaves,
> No certaine heire remaines, such certaine heire
> As not all onely is the rightfull heire
> But to the realme is so made knowen to be,
> And trouth therby vested in subjectes hartes,
> To owe fayth there where right is knowen to rest.
> (V, ii, ll. 246–52)

Parliament, Eubulus goes on, should have been convened to establish the succession while the prince still lived. Now it is too late. Elizabeth could hardly have failed to understand the lesson that she should marry or limit the succession, although she took it not to heart.

The result of Thomas Preston's struggle to fashion a mirror out of Persian history and the English morality play is a tragical interlude, lamentable in more senses than one. But it offers a rewarding study in hybridization and in what might have been. Preston's chief fault is unwillingness or inability fully to adapt the source material to the tried and true dramatic pattern.

In *The Second Booke of the Garden of Wysedome* (1539) Richard Taverner concludes a very short section on the merits of English and Egyptian judges by remarking that any unjust judge ought to be "served as a certayn juge of whome I shall nowe make relation." He then begins a new section "Of Cambyses." "Cambyses kynge of Persia," writes Taverner, "was otherwyse a verye wycked and cruell tyraunte. Yet there is no prynce of so disperat an hope of so naughtye a lyfe, but that at the lest waye otherwhyles doth some honest acte. For Gods propertye is, to garnyshe and exonerate the office of the magistrat and rulers, and he causeth, that for the conservation of civil governaunce in the common weale, sometyme excellente and profytable workes be of necessitie done of them that beare rule." Cambises' honest act was to execute the unjust judge Sisamnes. Having entered, however awkwardly, upon the career of Cambises, in which such an act was the exception, Taverner decides to recount the whole reign. "And albeit at the begynnynge he subdued and conquered Egypte, yet anone he forgatte all goodnes. . . ."[34] The three crimes that form the life-in-sin of the play follow in Preston's order.

At first, it seems that Preston's Cambises will re-enact in terms of his own exciting life the pattern of Mankind's experience in the traditional temptation play: Virtue, Temptation, Sin. Preston, it will be noted, magnifies the praiseworthy Egyptian campaign. Moreover, he combines it with the Sisamnes episode as reinforcement by making Sisamnes the deputy who rules Persia while Cambises is away. He conceives of all of this as occurring at the very outset of Cambises' reign, whereas Taverner, though circumstances led him to recount the Sisamnes episode first, made it one of the necessary exceptions to a generally vicious rule. Preston's protagonist, newly crowned after the death of his worthy father, Cyrus, wishes to perpetuate his father's golden praises and rejoices Councell, who urges him "to proceed in vertuous life."

---

[34] The quotations are from Fol. 17ʳ–18ᵛ. Willard Farnham, who discovered that Taverner was Preston's source, discusses the relationship of the *Garden of Wysedome* to the tragedy in *The Medieval Heritage of Elizabethan Tragedy* (Berkeley, 1936), pp. 263–69.

Preston now introduces the Vice as if, guided by the fable of the moral play, he were preparing for Temptation. But he is not. The second scene is the first of two major installments of the "pleasant mirth." Ambidexter, as a fantastic soldier, fights disgracefully with three ruffian soldiers, Huf, Ruf, and Snuf. The trull Meretrix, apparently an old acquaintance, kisses him and thrashes Ruf and Snuf. This is comic balance for the serious martial talk of the scene before, much in the manner of *Henry IV*. But to undercut the virtues of Cambises' Egyptian campaign is no part of making his career into a concrete re-enactment of the temptation plot. It is true that we learn the duplicity of Ambidexter, who turns to Sisamnes and encourages that judge's natural dishonesty.

The traditional design breaks down rapidly. (It does so in other Elizabethan interludes of a tragical cast—John Phillip's *Patient Grissill*, for instance, the interlude prototype of *Othello*.) To our surprise Shame enters to announce that the king has given over virtue for lechery and drunkenness and "nought esteemes his Councel grave ne vertuous bringing-up." The news is premature, since Cambises, entering at once, reveals as yet no sign of this defection, and in fact proceeds to the celebrated "one good deed of execution," to order the corrupt judge beheaded and flayed.

His handling of the king's transition to crime offers another measure of Preston's inadequacy to his task. He places the temptation scene *after* the first of the three crimes, the killing of Praxaspes' child, which is left entirely gratuitous. He puts the Vice to work persuading Cambises to the second crime, the murder of Smirdis. By comparing play and source we may infer the reason for this otherwise inexplicable placement of the Temptation. Taverner tells the Praxaspes episode in such detail that Preston can translate it intact to the stage without straining his inventive powers. It is here that Farnham can adduce verbal parallels. But Taverner recounts the second offense most perfunctorily, in a single sentence: "He murdered also hys owne brother Smerdis, whom he prively caused to be put to deth, lest he might at any tyme be king."[35] Here was little for Preston to work upon. How, he perhaps asked himself, does Cambises get the impression that Smirdis has such dangerous ambition? Preston

[35] Fol. 20.

turns to moral drama for the technique with which to elaborate this episode for the stage. For Smirdis, whose virtues
plead like angels, he causes Cambises to have what appears
to be genuine fraternal affection. Thus the Vice has oppor-
tunity to break up a close human relationship. Ambidexter,
Iago-like, pretends to have heard Smirdis admit to praying
day and night for the king's death and hoping by his own
merits to eclipse the king's praises. Cambises' faith in Smirdis
causes him at first to react, Othello-like, in a manner dangerous to the calumniator, and the Vice cleverly retreats
while leaving the seed of suspicion:

> CAMBISES. Did he speake thus of my Grace in such dis-
>   pightful wise?
>   Or els doost thou presume to fil my princely eares with
>   lyes?
> LORD. I cannot think it in my hart that he would report
>   so.
> CAMBISES. How sayst thou? Speake the trueth, was it so or
>   no?
> AMBIDEXTER. I think so, if it please your Grace, but I can-
>   not tel.
> CAMBISES. Thou plaist with bothe hands, now I perceive
>   well!   (ll. 682–87)

Cambises, no man to take chances, departs to arrange the
murder, and the Vice exults in the style of other tempters in
the Tudor morals: "Dooth not this geer cotten? . . . I tolde
him a notable lye." Crueltie and Murder dispose of Smirdis
bloodily. His innocence never comes to light.

For the third crime and the catastrophe Taverner again
supplies materials which Preston may simply translate to
the stage. The queen, Cambises' cousin-german whom he
married after Cupid shot him with an arrow, injudiciously
remarks that the loyalty of two dogs was greater than that
of Cambises toward his brother. Cambises' wrath is tickle
o' the sere, and he sends again for Crueltie and Murder.
The "odious death by Gods justice appointed" follows as
in Taverner, and it is worth noting that it lacks the protagonist's recognition of his folly and the consequent regeneration
of his spirit which regularly conclude the temptation plays
written between 1400 and 1558. Recognition had always
prepared for a merciful denouement by returning the central figure to grace. To retain it and its salutary effect upon

his spirit in face of a just reward for his misdeeds, to make
it tragic recognition, was beyond the conception of any early
Elizabethan playwright. That is one reason why Gorboduc's
experience is after all so little like King Lear's. It is too much
to expect a miniature *Macbeth* in the 1560s, yet in theory
the potential for it was present. The Egyptian victory and
just treatment of Sisamnes are the kind of good deeds that
imply a propensity for cruel misdeeds. If Preston had let the
Vice play upon this underlying cruelty and so turn the king
from virtue, Cambises would have committed his three
crimes as Macbeth commits his—the murder of Duncan, the
murder of Banquo, and the slaughter of Macduff's family—
under the same delusion under which he commits the second, namely that such cruelty is required to secure his king-
ship and peace of mind.

A unifying theme of some sophistication runs through
Cambises nonetheless, and its emblem is Ambidexter. He
represents the equivocal nature of a magistrate, Sisamnes or
Cambises, in whom good so easily changes to evil. But, as
he says, he reaches to all estates, and his presence among
soldiers and country fellows as well as at court suggests
moral uncertainty throughout the realm. He may in part be
a projection of Taverner's idea that no prince is so naughty
"but that at the lest waye otherwhyles doth some honest acte,"
but he is also a product of dramatic tradition. The Vice is
the most conspicuous character in Tudor drama taken as a
whole. From Heywood's No Lover Nor Loved to Preston's
Ambidexter his essence, as the names imply, is to be uncom-
mitted, *dégagé.* He is likely to be evasive about his local
habitation and his name. He cannot "abide." He may work
for good or evil or for both in the same play. Fansy in John
Skelton's *Magnyfycence* (ca. 1523), a morality warning
Henry against the extravagant new faction at court, both
leads the king into error and awakens him from it. Ambidexter laughs and weeps about the same events. Cushman and,
more recently, Spivack have argued that the Vice condenses
or stands for the numerous moral vices personified in the
theological moralities, but as Chambers long ago demonstrated, the facts will not support this neat hypothesis.[36] It

[36] L. W. Cushman, *The Devil and the Vice in the English Dramatic Literature before Shakespeare* (Halle, 1900), p. 63. Bernard
Spivack, *Shakespeare and the Allegory of Evil* (New York, 1958),

may be that his designation refers rather to Latin *vicis*, a change or turn, and so matches the "vice" in vice versa rather than that which opposes virtue. He is not yet really understood. The reader of the present collection may begin a study of the Vice and of his near relatives not only with Ambidexter but with Sedicyon, Merygreeke, Diccon, and, first in Tudor drama to exhibit his traits, the boy A in *Fulgens and Lucres*.

All of the texts in this edition are taken from photographic facsimiles either of original editions or, in the case of *Kyng Johan*, of the unique MS. I retain the old spelling, for it is time that modern editors should cease their dull labor of erasing the distinctive character and subtle associations of the language of our older literature. Readers unfamiliar with Tudor English might well begin with one of the academic plays—*Royster Doyster*, *Gammer Gurton*, or *Gorboduc*—or with Heywood's easy interlude, and thus prepare themselves for the more archaic *Fulgens* and the vagaries of *Kyng Johan*. The language of the plays is simple, much simpler than that of Shakespeare, and will soon yield itself. I do however regularize the names of characters, adopting consistently the form favored by playwright or printer, so that the reader will not be distracted by shifts like that from "Hodge" to "hogge." In *Kyng Johan* I adopt insofar as possible the forms that Bale himself uses in the parts of the MS. written in his own hand. I also expand most abbreviations and divide or join certain words according to modern practice: thus "ado" for "a do" and "shal be" for "shalbe." The letters *i, j, u,* and *v* I treat in the modern fashion. I retain original punctuation where it might conceivably control meaning or rhythm but lightly supplement the old pointing, if any (*Fulgens* is virtually without any), to bring out the sense. I have inserted the few apostrophes in the texts, always denoting contractions, as "th'empire" for "thempire." I have also added some initial capitalization without notice, chiefly of proper names. All the original stage directions I of course retain, supplementing them in brackets. *Royster Doyster, Gammer Gurton,* and *Gorboduc,* however, in their original

pp. 135–40. Chambers, *Mediaeval Stage*, II, 203–5. Cf. F. H. Mares, "The Origin of the Figure called 'the Vice' in Tudor Drama," *HLQ*, XXII (1958), 289–302.

editions follow the neoclassic practice of listing at the head
of each scene all the characters who will participate in it. I
retain only the names of those on stage at the outset and
indicate in brackets the later entrances of the others. From
the nature of the directions in these academic plays and in
Fulgens, and often from the absence of directions, it is clear
that the old editions were intended for the sixteenth-century
reader. It seems equally apparent that the MS. of *Kyng
Johan* and the editions of *Johan Johan* and *Cambises* (with
its instructions for the doubling of parts) were prepared for
the use of players.

Ann Arbor, Michigan   E. C.
1965

A Note on Footnotes

There are three sets of footnotes for the text in this edition.

(a) Footnotes, or glosses, to difficult or obscure words, indicated in the text by a superscript number, as, for example, [1], [2], [3], are to be found at the bottom of the page.

(b) Variants, or alternative readings from old copies and occasionally from modern editions, designated in the text by a superscript number in brackets, as, for example, [1], [2], [3], are to be found in the back of the book.

(c) Explanatory notes, or extended commentary, designated by a superscript number in parentheses in the text, as, for example, (1), (2), (3), are to be found also in the back of the book.

FULGENS AND LUCRES

by

HENRY MEDWALL

¶Here is côteyned a godely interlude of Fulgens
Senatoure of Rome. Lucres his doughter. Gayus
flaminius. ⁊ Publi9. Corneli9. of the disputacyon of
noblenes. ⁊ is deuyded in two ptyes/to be played at
ii.tymes. Côppyled by mayster Henry medwall. late
chapelayne to þ ryght reuerent fader in god Johan
Morton cardynall ⁊ Archebysshop of Cauterbury.

PD

[DRAMATIS PERSONAE.

FULGENS, *a Senator of Rome.*
PUBLIUS CORNELIUS, *a young Patrician.*
GAYUS FLAMYNEUS, *a young Plebian.*
A, *a Tudor youth.*
B, *another.*[1]
LUCRES, *daughter to* FULGENS.
JONE, *her handmaiden* (ANCILLA).

SCENE.

A cleared space in an actual Tudor banqueting hall during dinner and again about supper time. For part of the play this space represents ancient Rome.]

[PARS PRIMA]

Intrat A, *dicens.*[1]

A. For Goddis will,
What meane ye, syrs, to stond so still?
Have not ye etyn and your fill,[1]
And payd nothinge therfore?
Iwys,[2] syrs, thus dare I say,   5
He that shall for the shott[3] pay
Vouchsaveth that ye largely assay
Suche mete[4] as he hath in store.
I trowe your disshes be not bare,
Nor yet ye do the wyne spare;   10
Therfore be mery as ye fare.
Ye ar welcom eche oon
Unto this house withoute faynynge.
But I mervayle moche of one thinge,
That after this mery drynkynge   15
And good recreacyon
There is no wordes amonge this presse.

PARS PRIMA
  1 *Intrat . . . dicens:* Let A
    enter, saying.

2 *Iwys :* certainly.
3 *shott :* reckoning.
4 *mete :* food, provisions.

Non sunt loquele neque sermones.[5,(1)]
But as it were men in sadnes
Here ye stonde musynge,   20
Whereaboute[6] I can not tell.
Or some els praty[7] damesell[(2)]
For to daunce and sprynge.
                    [*He catches sight of* B.]
Tell me, what cal't,[8] is it not so?
I am sure here shal be somewhat ado,   25
And Iwis I will know it or[9] I go
Withoute I be dryvyn hens.[10]
                    Intrat B.
[B.] Nay, nay, hardely[11] man I undertake
No man wyll suche mastryes[12] make,
And it were but for the maner sake.[13]   30
Thou maist tary by licence[[2]]
Among other men and see the pley,
I warand no man wyll say the[e] nay.
A. I thinke it well evyn as ye say,
That no man wyll me greve.   35
But I pray you, tell me that agayn,
Shall here be a play?
B.   Ye, for certeyn.
A. By my trouth, therof am I glad and fayn,
And[14] ye will me beleve.
Of all the worlde I love suche sport,   40
It dothe me so myche plesure and comfort,
And that causith me ever to resort
Wher suche thing is to do.
I trowe your owyn selfe be oon
Of them that shall play.
B.   Nay, I am none.   45
I trowe thou spekyst in derision
To lyke[15] me therto.

---

5 *Non . . . sermones:* There
    is no speech nor lan-
    guage. (Psalms 19)
6 *Whereaboute:* about what.
7 *praty:* pretty, perhaps
    with something of the
    old sense of clever.
8 *what cal't:* whatever you
    call yourself.

9 *or:* ere, before.
10 *hens:* hence.
11 *hardely:* assuredly.
12 *mastryes:* difficulties.
13 *And . . . sake:* Merely for
    the sake of fashion.
14 *And:* If.
15 *lyke:* liken, compare.

A. Nay, I mok not, wot ye well,
   For I thought verely by your apparell
   That ye had bene a player.
B.   Nay, never a dell.[3]   50
A. Than I cry you mercy,
   I was to blame, lo, therfor I say.
   Ther is so myche nyce aray[16]
   Amonges these galandis[17] nowaday
   That a man shall not lightly   55
   Know a player from another man.
   But now to the purpose wher I began,
   I see well here shal be a play than.
B. Ye, that ther shall doutles,
   And I trow ye shall like it well.   60
A. It semeth than that ye can tell
   Sumwhat of the mater.[18]
B.   Ye, I am of counsell,[19]
   One tolde me all the processe.
·A. And I pray you, what shall it be?
B. By my fayth, as it was tolde me   65
   More than ones or twyse,
   As fare as I can bere it awaye,
   All the substaunce of theyr play
   Shall procede this wyse :

   When th'empire of Rome was in such floure[4]   70
   That all the worlde was subgett to the same
   Than was there an nobill senatour,
   And as I remember Fulgens was his name,
   Whiche had a doughter of nobill fame.
   And yet as th'auctor sayth in veray dede,   75
   Her nobill vertu dide her fame excede.
   Allbeit there was not one allmost
   Thoroughoute all the cyte yong ne olde
   That of her beaute did not boste.
   And over that her verteuse manyfolde   80
   In suche maner wyse were praysid and tolde
   That it was thought she lakkede no thing

16 *nyce aray :* fancy attire.   18 *the mater :* the subject
17 *galandis :* gallants, elegant   matter.
     young men.   19 *of counsell :* informed, in
                                             the know.

To a nobill woman that was accordyng.[20, (5)]

Grete labour was made her favour to attayne
In the way of mariage, and among all   85
That made suche labour were specially twayn
Whiche more than other dyd besily on her call,
On the whiche twayn she sett her mynde especiall
So that she utterly determyned in her hert
The one of them to have, all other sett aparte.   90

One of them was called Publius[3] Cornelius,
Borne of noble blode, it is no nay.
That other was one Gayus Flamyneus,
Borne of a pore stocke as men doth say.
But for all that many a fayre day   95
Thorough his grete wisedome and vertueous be-
            havyour
He rulyd the comenwele to his grete honoure.

And how so be it that the vulgare opynion
Hade both these men in lyke favour and rever-
            ence,
Supposing they had bene of lyke condycion,   100
Yet this seyd woman of inestimable prudence
Sawe that there was some maner of difference,
For the whiche her answere she differred and
            spared[21]
Tyll both theyre condycions were openly declared.

And yet to them both this comfort she gave,   105
He that coude be founde more noble of them
            twayne
In all godely maner her harte sholde he have.
Of the which answere they both were glade and
            fayne,
For ether of them trustede therby to attayne
Th'effecte of his desyre; yet when they had do   110
One of them must nedis his appetit forgoo.

Hereuppon was areysyd a grete doute and ques-
            tion :
Every man all after as he was affeccionate

20 *accordynge :* fitting.   21 *differred and spared :* de-
                                      ferred and withheld.

Unto the parties seyd his opynion,
But at the laste in eschewyng of debate   115
This matter was brought before the cenate[6]
They to gyve therin an utter sentence
Whiche of these two men sholde have the pre-
        eminence.[4]

And finally they gave sentence and awarde
That Gayus Flamyneus was to be commende   120
For the more nobill man, havynge no regarde
To his lowe byrthe of the whiche he dyde dys-
        cende.
But onely to his vertue thay dyde therin attende,
Whiche was so grete that of convenience[22, 5]
All the cyte of Rome dyd hym honour and rever- 125
        ence.

A. And shall this be the process[6] of the play?
B. Ye, so I understonde be credible informacyon.[23]
A. By my fayth, but yf it be evyn as ye say,
    I wyll advyse them to change that conclusion.
    What, wyll they afferme that a chorles[24] son   130
    Sholde be more noble than a gentilman born?
    Nay, beware, for men wyll have therof grete
            scorn,
    It may not be spoken in no maner of case.
B. Yes, suche consyderacions may be layde
    That every resonable man in this place   135
    Wyll holde hym therin right well apayde,[25]
    The matter may be so well convayde.
A. Let them convay and cary clene than,
    Or els he wyll repent that this play began.
    How be it the matter touchith me never a dell,   140
    For I am nether of vertue excellent
    Nor yet of gentyl blode, this I know well,
    But I speke it onely for this entent:
    I wolde not that any man sholde be shent.[26]
    And yet there can no man blame us two,   145
    For why[27] in this matter we have nought to do.

22 of convenience: accord-   24 chorles: churl's, lowborn
        ingly.   fellow's.
23 be . . . informacyon: from   25 apayde: satisfied.
        reliable sources.   26 shent: blamed.
                                      27 For why: Because.

B. Wel no, God wott, nothing at all,
 Save that we come to see this play
 As farre as we may by the leve of the marshall.[7]
 I love to beholde suche myrthes alway   150
 For I[7] have sene byfore this day
 Of suche maner thingis in many a gode place
 Both gode examples and right honest solace.
 This play in like wyse I am sure
 Is made for the same entent and[8] purpose,   155
 To do every man both myrth and pleasure.[9]
 Wherfor I cannot think or suppose
 That they wyll ony worde therin disclose
 But suche as shall stond with treuth and reason
 In godely maner according to the season.[8]   160
A. Ye, but trouth may not be sayde alway,
 For somtyme it causith gruge and despite.
B. Ye, goth the worlde so nowaday
 That a man must say the crow is white.
A. Ye, that he must, be God Allmyght,   165
 He must both lye and flater now and then[10]
 That castith hym to dwell amonge worldly men.
 In some courtis such men shall most wyn.
B. Ye, but as for the parish[11] where I abide
 Suche flaterye is abhorride as dedly syn,   170
 And specially lyars be sett asyde
 As sone as they may with the faute[28] be spied.
 For every man that favoreth and loveth vertue
 Wyll suche maner of folke utterly esscheue.
 Wherfor I can think these folke wyll not spare 175
 After playne trouth this matter to procede,
 As the story seyth; why shulde they care?
 I trow here [*Indicating the audience.*] is no man
    of the kyn or sede
 Of either partie, for why they were bore
 In the cytie of Rome, as I sayd before.   180
 Therfor leve all this doutfull question
 And prayse at the parting evyn as ye fynde.
A.[12] Yes, be ye sure whan thei have all done
 I wyll not spare to shew you my mynd,
 Praise who wyll or dispraise, I will not be behynd. 185
 I wyll gest[29] theron whatsoever shal befall,
 If I can fynd any man to gest withall.

28 *faute*: fault.   29 *gest*: jest, make merry.

B. Pees, no moo wordes, for now they come,
   The plears[30] bene evyn here at hand.
A. So thei be, so help[13] me God and halydome,   190
   I pray you, tell me where I shall stand.
B. Mary, stand evyn here by me, I warand.
   Geve rome there, syrs, for God avowe
   Thei wold cum in if thei myght for you.(9)
A. Ye, but I pray the[e,] what cal't, tell me this,   195
   Who is he that now comyth yn?
B. Mary, it is Fulgens the senatour.
A. Ye, is? What, the father of the forseide virgyn?
B. Ye, forseth. He shall this matere begyn.
A. And wher is feyr doughter Lucres?   200
B. She comyth Anon, I say hold thy pece.
          Intrat FULGENS, *dicens.*
[FULGENS.] Everlastyng joy with honoure and praise
   Be unto our most drad Lord and Savyour(10)
   Whiche doth us help and comfort many ways,
   Not lefyng us destitute of his ayde and socour,   205
   But lettith his son shyne on[14] the riche and
          poore
   And of his grace is ever indifferent,[31]
   Allbeyt he diversely commytteth his talent.[32]

   To some he lendith the sprete[33] of prophecy,
   To some the plenty of tonges eloquence,   210
   To some grete wisdome and worldly policy,
   To some litterature and speculatyf science,[34]
   To some he geveth the grace of pre-emynence
   In honour and degre, and to some abundance
   Of tresoure, riches, and grete inheritaunce.   215

   Every man oweth[35] to take gode hede
   Of this distribution, for whoso doth take
   The larger benefite, he hath the more nede
   The larger recompense and thank therfor to make.
   I spede[36] these wordes onely for myne owne sake   220
   And for non other person, for I know well
   That I am therin chargid as I shall you tell.

---

30 *plears:* players.
31 *indifferent:* impartial.
32 *talent:* human potentiali-
      ties (from figurative use
      in Matthew 25:14–30).
33 *sprete:* spirit.
34 *litterature . . . science:*
      learning and philosophy.
35 *oweth:* ought.
36 *spede:* utter, send forth.

When I consider and call to my remembraunce
Ϝhe prosperous lyfe that I have allwey
Hyderto endured withoute any grevaunce   225
Of worldly adversitie, well may I sey
And thynke that I am bound to yeld and pay
Grete prayse and thankes to the hye Kynge
Of whom procedith and growith every gode thing.

And certes if I wold not praise or[15] boste   230
The benefyts that he hath done unto me,
Yet is it well know of lest and most
Thrughoute all Rome th'emperiall[16] cyte
What place in the cenate and honorable degre
I occupye and how I demean me[37] in the same.   235
All this can they tell that knowith but my name.

To speke of plenty and grete abundaunce
Of worldly[17] riches therunto belongyng,
Houses of pleasure and grete inheritaunce
With riche apparell and every other thing   240
That to a worthy man shold be according,
I am and ever have be in metely[38] gode case,
For the whiche I thank Allmighty God of his grace.

Than have I a wyfe of gode condicyon
And right conformable to myn entent   245
In every thing that is to be done,
And how be it that God hath me not sent
An hayr[39] male[18] whiche were convenient
My name to continew and it to repeyre,
Yet am I not utterly destitute of an heyre.   250

For I have a doughter in whom I delight
As for the chefe comfort of myn olde age,
And surely my seyd doughter Lucres doth hight.[40]
Men seyth she is as lyke me in visage
As though she were evyn myn owne ymage,   255
For the whiche cause nature doth me force and
            bynde
The more to favour and love here[41] in my
            mynde.[19]

37 *demean me :* deport my-   39 *hayr :* heir.
    self.   40 *doth hight :* is named.
38 *metely :* satisfactorily.   41 *here :* her.

But yet to the principall and grettist occasion
That makyth me to love her as I do
Is this whiche I speke not of affection   260
But evyn as the treuth movith me therto,
Nature hath wrought in my Lucres so
That to speke of beaute and clere understanding
I can not thinke in here what shold be lakking.

And besides all that yet a gretter thing   265
Whiche is not oft sene in so yong a damesell,
She is so discrete and sad[42] in all demeanyng
And therto[43] full of honest and verteous counsell
Of here owne mynd that wonder is to tell
The giftes of nature and of especiall grace.   270

Am not I gretly bound in this case
To God, as I rehersid you bifore?
I were to[o] voyd of all reson[20] and grace
If I wold not serve and prayse hym therfore
With due love and drede; he askyth no more.   275
As far as he will me grace therto send
The rest of my lif therin will I spend,

Albeyt that I must partely intend[21]
To the promocyon[22] of my doughter Lucres
To some metely mariage, ellis God defend!   280
She is my chief jewell and riches,
My comfort agayn[44] all care and hevynes,
And also she is now of gode and ripe age
To be a mannes fere[45] by wey of mariage.

Wherfor if I might see or I dye   285
That she were bestowid sumwhat accordyng,
Then were my mynd dischargid utterly
Of every grete cure[46] to me belongyng.
It was the chief cause of my hider cummyng
To have a communication in this same matere   290
With on Cornelius; cam ther non suche here?
         Intrat PUBLIUS CORNELIUS, *dicens.*
CORNELIUS. Yes, now am I come here at the last,
    I have taried long, I cry you mercy.

42 *sad :* serious.   45 *fere :* companion, mate.
43 *therto :* in addition.   46 *cure :* care.
44 *agayn :* against, in the
       event of.

FULGENS. Nay, no offence, ther is no waste
    Nor losse of tyme yet hardely,   295
    For this is the oure that ye and I
    Apoyntid here to mete this other day.
    Now shew me your mynd, lete me here what ye
        say.
CORNELIUS. Than wyll I leve superfluite awey,
    For why ye know alredy my minde in sub-   300
        stance.[23]
FULGENS. I what[47] not whether I do, ye or nay.
CORNELIUS. Why, is it now oute of your remem-
        braunce
    That my desire is to honour and advaunce
    Your doughter Lucres, if she will agree
    That I so pore a man her husbonde shuld be?   305
FULGENS. Ye nede not, syr, to use these wordis to me,
    For non in this cyte knowith better than I
    Of what grete birth or substaunce ye be.
    My doughter Lucres is full unworthy
    Of birth and goodis to loke so hye,   310
    Savyng that happily her gode condicyon
    May her enable to suche a promocyon.
    But if this be youre mynde and suche intent
    Why do ye not laboure to her therfore?
    For me semyth it were ryght expedient   315
    That we know therin her mynde before
    Or ever we shold commune therof any more,
    For if she wold to your mynde apply[48]
    No man shal be so glad therof as I.
CORNELIUS. Suppose ye that I dyde not so begyn   320
    To gete fyrste her favoure? Yes, truste me well.
FULGENS. And what comfort wolde she gyve you
        therin?
CORNELIUS. By my feyth, no grete comfort to tell,
    Save that she abideth to have youre counsell,
    For as she seyth she will nothing   325
    In suche mater to do withoute your counsel-
        lyng,[24]
    Nor other wyse than ye shal be contente.
    And theruppon it was my mynde and desire
    To speke with you of her for the same intent

47 *what* : wot, know.   48 *to your mynde apply* :
                             agree to your intention.

Your gode will in this behalfe to requyre,[49]   330
For I am so brent[50] in loves fyre
That nothing may my payne aslake[51]
Withoute that ye wyll my cure undertake.

FULGENS. Syr, I shall do you the comfort that I can,
As far as she wil be advised by me.   335
How be it certeynly I am not the man
That wyll take from her the liberte
Of her owne choice, that may not be.
But when I speke with her I shall her advyse
To love you before other in all godely wyse.   340

CORNELIUS. I thanke you, syr, with all myn harte,
And I pray you do it withoute delay.

FULGENS. As sone as I shall fro you departe
I wyll her mynde therin assay.

CORNELIUS.[25] For I shall think that every howre is   345
                         twayne
Till I may speke with you agayne.
                                   [*Exeat* FULGENS.]
Now a wise felow that had sumwhat a brayne
And of suche thingis had experience,
Such one wolde I with me retayne
To gyve me counseile and assistence,   350
For I will spare no cost or expence
Nor yet refuse ony laboure or payne
The love of fayre Lucres therby to attayne.
So many gode felowes as byn in this hall,
And is ther non, syrs, among you all   355
That wyll enterprise this gere?
Some of you can do it if ye lust.
But if ye wyl not than I must
Go seche a man ellis where.   *Et exeat.*
          Deinde loquitur B.[52]

B. Now have I spied a mete office for me,   360
For I wyl be of counsell and I may
With yonder man—

A.   Pece, let be!
Be God, thou wyll distroy all the play.[(11)]

B. Distroy the play, quod a?[53] nay, nay,
The play began never till now.   365

49 *requyre :* request.   52 *Deinde . . .* B : Then B
50 *brent :* burnt.   speaks.
51 *aslake :* diminish.   53 *quod a :* quoth he.

I wyll be doyng, I make God avow,
For there is not in this hondred myle
A feter bawde[54] than I am one.

A. And what shall I do in the meanewhile?

B. Mary, thou shalt com in anone   370
With another pageant.[55]

A.   Who? I?

B.   Ye, by saynt Johan.

A. What, I never uside suche thing before.

B. But folow my counsell and do no more.
Loke that thou abide here still,
And I shall undertake for to fulfyll   375
All his mynde withouten delay.
And whether I do so, ye or nay,
At the lest well dare I undertake
The mariage utterly to mare or to make.
If he and I make any bargeyn   380
So that I must gyve hym attendaunce,
When thou seest me com in ageyn,
Stond evyn still and kepe thy contenaunce,
For when Gayus Flamyneus comyth in,
Than must thou thy pageaunt begyn.   385

A. Shall ony profyt grow therby?

B. Hold thy pece, speke not so hye!
Leste any man of this company
Know oure purpose openly
And breke all oure daunce,   390
For I assure the[e] feithfully
If thou quyte the[e][56] as well as I
This gere[57] shall us both avaunce.

Exeat [into the audience.]

A.[26] Nay then let me alone, hardely!
Yf ony advauntage honge therby,   395
I can myselfe thereto apply
By helpe of gode counsell.
This felowe and I be maysterles[58]
And lyve moste parte in ydelnes;

54 *feter bawde :* more adroit   57 *gere :* device.
   go-between.   58 *maysterles :* without mas-
55 *pageant :* ruse, stratagem,   ters (in a statutory
   blind.   sense).
56 *quyte thee :* acquit, do jus-
   tice to, yourself.

Therefore some maner of besenes   400
Wolde become us both well.
At the leste wyse it is mery beynge
With men in tyme of woynge,[59]
For all that whyle they do nothynge
But daunce and make revell,   405
Synge and laugh with greate shoutynge,
Fyll in wyne with revell routynge.[60]
I trowe it be a joyfull thinge
Amonge suche folke to dwell.

    Intrat FULGENS,[27] LUCRES,
     et ANCILLA *et dicat.*

[FULGENS.] Doughter Lucres, ye knowe well ynough   410
 What study and care I have for youre promocyon
 And what fatherly love I bere to you,
 So that I thynke in myne opynyon
 It were tyme loste and wastfull occupacyon
 This matter to reherse or tell you ony more   415
 Syth ye it best knowe, as I sayde before.

 But the specyall cause that I speke fore
 Is touchynge youre mariage; as ye knowe well
 Many folke there be that desyreth sore
 And laboureth in that behalve with you to mell.[61]   420
 Ye knowe what is for you, ye nede no counsell.
 Howe so be it, yf ye lyste my counseyle to
   requyre,
 I shall be glad to satysfye therein youre desyre.

LUCRES. Trought[62] it is, fader, that I am bounde
 As moche unto you as ony chylde may be   425
 Unto the fader lyvynge on the grounde.
 And where it pleaseth you to gyve unto me
 Myne owne fre choyse and my lyberte,
 It is the thynge that pleaseth me well,
 Sith I shall have therein youre counsell.   430

 And nowe accordynge to this same purpose,
 What thynke ye best for me to do?
 Ye knowe ryghte well, as I suppose,
 That many folke doth me greatly woo,

---

59 *woynge :* wooing.   61 *mell :* wed.
60 *Fyll . . . routynge :* Drink   62 *Trought :* troth, truth.
  wine with uproarious
  merriment.

Amonge the whiche there be specyally twoo   435
In whome, as I trowe and so do ye,
The choyce of this matter must fynally be.
In that poynt your mynde and myne dothe agre.
But yet ryght now er I came here
For Publius Cornelius ye advysed me,   440
As touchinge ye wolde have me only reste there.
Yf that be youre mynde, I shall gladly forbere
All other and only to hym assente
To have me in wedlocke at his commaundemente.

FULGENS. Naye, doughter Lucres, not so I mente,   445
For though I dyde somwhat to hym enclyne,
Yet for all that it is not myne entente
That ye shulde so thereupon utterly diffyne,[63]
But loke whom ye wyll, on Godys blessing and
       myne.
For truste ye me verely, it is all one to me,   450
Whether Gayus Flamyneus wedde you or els he.

LUCRES. Than syth I have so greate lyberte
And so gode choyce, I were unfortunable
And also to[o] unwyse yf I wolde not see
That I had hym whiche is moste honorable.   455
Wherfore, may it lyke you to be agreable
That I may have respyte to make inquisycyon
Whiche of this two men is better of condicyon?

FULGENS. I holde me content, that shall be well done,
It may be respyted for a day or twayne.   460
But in the meanetyme use this provysyon,
Se that ye indyfferently them both entertayne
Tyll that youre mynde be sett at a certayne
Where ye shall rest : now, can ye do so?
LUCRES. At the leste my gode wyll shall I put thereto.   465
FULGENS. Than syth I have bysynes at whome[64] for
      to do,
I wyll go thetherwarde as fast as I may.
LUCRES. Is it youre pleasure that I shall with you go?
FULGENS. Nay, I had lever that ye went your way
Aboute this matter.

                            Et exeat.

63 *diffyne :* decide.   64 *whome :* home.

LUCRES.   Well, God be with you than!   470
  I shall do therein the best that I can.
          Et facta[28] *aliqua pausatione dicat* LUCRES.[65]
  I[29] wyll not dysclaunder[66] nor blame no man,
  But neverthelesse by that I here saye
  Pore maydens be dissayved[67] now and than,
  So greate dyssemblynge nowadaye   475
  There is convayed under wordes gaye
  That if—
ANCILLA.[30]   Peace, lady! ye must forbere
  Se ye not who cometh here?
LUCRES. Who is it, wot ye ere?
ANCILLA. It is Gayus Flamyneus, parde,   480
  He that wolde your husbonde be.
                              [*Exeat* ANCILLA.]
LUCRES. Ey, gode Lorde, how wyste he
  For to fynde me here?
                Intrat GAYUS FLAMYNEUS.
GAYUS.[31] Yes, gode lady, wheresoever ye go
  He that lysteth to do his dylygence   485
  In suche manere wyse as I have do
  At the laste he may come to youre presence.
  For whosoever oweth obedyence
  Unto love, he hath greate nede
  To attendaunce if he wyll spede.   490
LUCRES. Syr, ye be welcome; what is your mynde?
GAYUS. Why, fayre Lucres, is that your gyse,[68]
  To be so straunge[69] and so unkynde
  To hym that owith you lovyng servyce?
  I trow I have tolde you twyse or thrise   495
  That myn desyre is to mary with you.
  Have ye not herde this matter or now?
LUCRES. Yes, in veray trouth I have herde you say
  Att dyverse tymes that ye bare me affeccyon.
  To suche an intent I say not nay.   500
GAYUS. What nede ye than to aske the question,
  What I wolde with you at this season?
  Me semyth ye sholde therin doubt no more
  Sith ye know well myn erande before.

65 *Et . . .* LUCRES: After a   67 *dissayved :* deceived.
        slight pause let LUCRES   68 *gyse :* fashion.
        say.   69 *straunge :* distant.
66 *dysclaunder :* speak evil of.

Iwys your strangnes greveth me sore.   505
But notwithstonding now wyll I sece,[70]
And at this tyme I wyll chide no more
Lest I geve you cause of hevynes.
I cam hyder onely for youre sake, doubtles,
To glade you and please you in all that I can   510
And not for to chyde with you, as I began.
For thynke it in your mynde I am the man
That wolde you please in all that I may,
And to that purpose I wyll do what I can,
Though ye forbyde it and say therin nay.   515
In that poynt onely I wyll you disobay.
My hart shall ye have in all godely wise,
Whether ye me take or utterly dispise.
And to say that I will folow the gise
Of wanton lovers nowaday   520
Whiche doth many flatering wordis devise,
With gyftis of ringis and broches gay
Theyr lemmans[71] hartis for to betray,
Ye must have me therin excusid,
For it is the thing that I never usid.   525
Therfore I will be short and playne,
And I pray you hartely, feyre Lucres,
That ye wyll be so to me agayne.
Ye know well I have made labour and besynes
And also desyrid you by wordis expresse   530
That ye wold vouchesave in your harte
To be my wife till deth us departe.[(12)]
Lo, this is the mater that I come fore,
To know therin your mynde and plesoure,
Whether ye sett by me ony store   535
To th'effect of my seyd desire.
And nothing ellis I wyll require
But that I may have a playne ye or nay,
Whereto I may trust withoute delay.

LUCRES. Me thinketh that by that that ye[[32]] say   540
  Ye force not[72] what myne answere be.
GAYUS. A, wyll ye take it that way?
  My lady, I ment not so, parde.
  Th'affirmatyfe were most lefe[73] to me,

70 *sece:* cease.   72 *force not:* don't care.
71 *lemmans:* beloveds'.   73 *lefe:* pleasing.

For as ye yourself knowith best,   545
That was and is my principall request.
But ye may say I am a homely gest[74]
On a gentilwoman[33] so hastely to call.
LUCRES. Nay, nay, syr, that guyse is best,
Ye cannot displeyse me withall.   550
And accordyng to your desire I shall
Evyn as sone as I godely may
Answere you therin withoute delay.
Howbeit, it can not be done strait way
If I myght gett a realme therby.   555
Fyrst wyll I my faders mynde assay,
Whether he wyll ther unto applye,[75]
For if he like you as well as I
Your mynde in this behalf shal be sone easid,
If my seyd fader can be content and pleysid.   560
GAYUS.[34] Gramercy, myne owne swete Lucres,
Of you desire can I no more at all,
Save onely that ye do your besynes
Upon[35] youre fader besily to call,
So that whatsoever shal befall   565
Within few days I may verily know
To what effect this mater shal grow.
LUCRES. Ye shall know by tomorow nyght
What my fader wyll sey therto.
GAYUS. Than shall ye make myne harte full light   570
If it pleyse you so to do.
LUCRES. Yes, doubt ye not it shal be so,
And for that cause I wyll even now departe.
GAYUS. Now farewell than, myne owne sweteharte!
Et exeat LUCRES. *Deinde* A, *accedens ad* GAYUM
            FLAMYNEUM, *dicat ei*[36] *sic.*[76]
A. Syr, ye seme a man of grete honoure,   575
And that moveth me to be so bolde.
I rede[77] you adventure not over moche laboure
Upon[37] this woman, leste ye take colde.
I tell you, the mater is bought and solde.[78]

---

74 *homely gest*: rude fellow.   77 *rede*: advise.
75 *applye*: agree.   78 *bought and solde*: already
76 *Deinde . . . sic*: Then let   settled behind your
    A, approaching GAYUS   back.
    FLAMYNEUS, speak to
    him as follows.

Withoute ye take the better hede,   580
For all these feyre wordes ye shall not spede.
GAYUS. Thynkest thou so in very dede?
A. Ye, so helpe me God! and I shall tell you why. [13]
Syr, ryght now this way as I yede[79]
This gentylwoman cam even by   585
And a fresshe galant in her company.
As God wolde, nere them I stalked
And herde every worde that they talked.
GAYUS. But [38] spake they ony worde of me?
A. Nay, nay, ye were nothinge in her thoughte.   590
They were as besy as they myghte be
Aboute suche a matter as ye have wroughte,
And by God that me dere boughte
Loke what answer that ye now have :
Even the same wordes to hym she gave.   595
Iwys, syr, I am but a pore knave,
But yet I wolde take on me a greate payne
Youre honeste in this matter to save,
Though it be unto me no profyte nor gayne.
But therefore I speke and have dysdayne   600
To se in a woman of suche dyssemblaunce
Towarde a gentylman of youre substaunce. [39]
GAYUS. Why, hast thou of me ony acquentaunce?
A. Ye, syr, and some tyme ye knewe me,
Though it be now oute of youre remembraunce.   605
GAYUS. By my fayth, it may well be,
But neverthelesse I thank the[e.]
Me semeth thou woldest that all were well
Betwyxte me and yonder fayre damesell.
A. Ye, by God, I wolde fyghte in the quarell   610
Rather than ye sholde lese youre entente. [40]
GAYUS. I praye the[e] felowe, where doste thou
                dwell?
A. By my fayth, I am now at myn owne commaunde-
                ment.
I lacke a mayster, and that I me repente.
To serve you and please I wolde be fayne   615
Yf it myghte lyke you me to retayne,
And of one thynge I wyll acertayne :
I doubte not I shall do you better stede

79 *yede* : went, walked.

Towarde this maryage than some other twayne,
And yf I do not, let me be dede.   620
GAYUS. Well than wyll I do by thy rede,
   And in my servyce thou shalt be,
   Yf thou canst fynde me any surete.
A. Yes, I can have sureties plente
   For my trouth, within this place :   625
   Here is a gentilman that wolde truste me
   For as moche gode as he hase.
      [*Indicating* B, *who steps forward from*
                        the audience.]
GAYUS. Ye, and that is but litle, percase.[80]
A. By my fayth go where he shall,
   It is as honest a man as ony in the reall.[81]   630
   I have no more acqueyntaunce within this hall.
   If I wolde ony frendis assay,
   By God, here is one best of all.
   I trow he wyll not say me nay,
   For he hath knowen me many a day.   635
   Syr, wyll not ye for my trouth undertake?[41]
B. Yes,[42] for God, els I wolde I were bake!
   Syr, my maister, wyll ye beleve me?
   I dare trust hym for all that I can make,
   Yf ye fynde me sufficient surete.   640
   As for his trouth, doubt not ye.
   I never coude by hym anything espie
   But that he was as true a man as I.
   He and I dwelled many a feyre day
   In one scole, and yet I wot well   645
   From thens he bare never away
   The worth of an halfe peny that I can tell.[14]
   Therefore he is able with you to dwell.
   As for his trought, that dare I well saye
   Hardely truste hym therein ye maye.   650
GAYUS.[43] Upon youre worde I shall assaye.
   And syr, after thi gode deservynge,
   So shall I thy wagys pay.
   But now to remembre one thinge :
   Me thought thou saydist at the begynnynge   655
   That Lucres favoreth better than me
   Another lover; what man is he?

80 *percase :* perhaps.   81 *reall :* realm.

A. Cornelius I wene his name sholde be.

GAYUS. A, then I knowe him well, by the rode.

Ther is not within all this cyte   660
A man borne of a better blode.
But yet Lucres hath a wytt so gode
That, as I thynke, she wyll before see
Whether his condicyons therto agree.
And if they do not, farewell he.   665
But therin I have nought ado,
He shall not be dispraysid for me
Withoute that I be compellid therto.
I can not let[82] hym for to woo
A woman beyng at her owne liberte,   670
For why it is as fre for hym as for me.
I wyll forbere never the more
Tyll I knowe what shall be the ende.
Go thy waye unto Lucres, therfore,
And hertly me unto her recommende,   675
Praying her that she wyll me sende
A redy answere of that thing
That she promised me at her departing.

A. Mary, I shall without any tarying,
I knowe myne erand well Inow.   680
Ye shall se me apoynte a metynge
Where she agayne shall speke wyth you.

GAYUS. Than shall I thy wyt alowe,
Yf thou can brynge that aboute.

A. Yes, that I shall do, have ye no doubte.   685

Et exeat GAYUS FLAMYNEUS *et dicat* B.

B. Now, by my trought, I wolde not have thoughte
That thou haddest bene halfe so wyse,
For thou hast this matter featly[83] wrought
And convayed it poynt devyse,[84]
To brynge thyselfe to suche a servyce.   690
I se well thou hast some wytt in thy hede.

A. Ye, a lytell, but hast thou spede?[85]

B. Even lykewyse, have thou no drede.
I have goten a maister for my prowe.[86]
I never thryvede as I shall do now.   695

---

82 *let :* stop.   85 *spede :* succeeded.
83 *featly :* adroitly.   86 *prowe :* advantage.
84 *poynt devyse :* to
     perfection.

A. No, whiche way?

B.   I shall tell the[e] how.
　It is no maystry[87] to thryve at all
　Under a man that is so liberall.
　Ther is now late unto hym fall
　So grete goodis by inheritaunce   700
　That he wote never what to do withall
　But lassheth it forth daily, escaunce[88]
　That he had no dayly remembraunce
　Of tyme to come, nor makyth no store,
　For he carith not whiche ende goth before.   705
　And, by Oure Lady, I commende hym the more.
　Why sholde he those goodis spare
　Sith he laborede never therfore?
　Nay, and every man sholde care
　For goodis, and specially suche as are   710
　Of gentil blode, it were grete syn,
　For all liberalite in them sholde begyn.
　Many a pore man therby doth wyn
　The chef substauns of his lyving.
　My maister were worthy to be a kyng   715
　For liberall expensis in all his deling.
　I trow thou shalt se hym com yn
　Lyke a rutter[89] somwhat according,
　In all apparell to hym belongyng.
　How moche payeth he, as ye suppose,   720
　For the makyng of a peyre of his hose?

A. Mary, .xii. d.[90] were a feyre thing.

B. Ye, by the rode, .xx. tymes tolde,
　That is evyn .xx. shelynges for the makyng.

A. It cannot be so, withoute a man wolde   725
　Make them all with sylke and golde.

B. Nay, by yes,[91] non erthly thing
　But evyn the bare cloth and the lynynge,
　Save onely that ther is in cuttinge
　A new maner of fascyon nowaday.[(15)]   730
　Because they sholde be somwhat straunge

87 *maystry*: problem.
88 *escaunce*: as if.
89 *rutter*: gaily dressed member of the German cavalry.
90 *.xii. d.*: twelvepence, a shilling. Roughly, two dollars in modern purchasing power.
91 *yes*: Jesus.

They moste be strypide all this way,
With small slypes of coloures gay,
A codpece[92] before allmost thus large,
And therin restith the gretist charge.[93]   735
To speke of gowns, and that gode chaunge,[94]
Of them he hath store and plenty,
And that the fascyons be new and straunge,
For non of them passith the mydde thy,[95]
And yet he puttyth in a gown communely   740
How many brode yardis,[96] as ye gesse?

A. Mary, .ii. or .iii.

B.   Nay, .vii. and no lesse.

A. By my trouth, that is lyke a lye.

B. But it is as true as ye stond there,
And I shall tell you a reson why.   745
All that doth that fascyon were
They have whingis behynd redy to flye,
And a sleve that wolde cover all the body.
Than .xl. playtis,[97] as I think in my mynde,
They have before and as many behynde.   750

A. Well, as for gentilmen it is full kynde
To have theyr plesyrs that may well paye.

B. Ye, but than this grugeth my mynde:
A gentylman shall not were it a daye
But every man wyll hymself araye   755
Of the same fascyon even by and by[98]
On the morow after.

A.   Nay, that I defy.
But then I marvell gretly why
You are not garnysshyd after that gyse.

B. There is never a knave in the house save I   760
But his gowne is made in the same wyse,
And for bycause I am new come to servyce,
I must for a whyle be content
To were stylle myn olde garment.

[A.][4¹] Ye, but abyde, to what intent   765
Doth thy mayster take in honde

92 *codpece:* the bag cover-   95 *thy:* thigh.
   ing the opening in the   96 *brode yardis:* yards of
   front of tight breeches.   broadcloth.
93 *charge:* expense.   97 *.xl. playtis:* forty pleats.
94 *gode chaunge:* in ample   98 *by and by:* immediately.
   variety.

To make hym so moche costely rayment?
B. Mary, that is esy to understonde :
   All is done for Lucres sake.
   To wedde her he doth his rekenynge make.   770
A. I put case that she do hym forsake,
   So that she be my maysters wyf.
B. By my fayth, then I say it wyll make
   Many a man to lose his lyf,
   For therof wyll ryse a gret stryf.   775
A. Mary, I pray God send us pes.
B. Be my fayth, it wyll be no lesse,
   Yf my master have not Lucres.
A. I can no more, God sped the ryght!
   Lo, thes folke wyll stryve and fyght   780
   For this womans sake,
   And whan they have done ther uttyrmest,
   I wene veryly he shall sped best
   That must her forsake.
   He is well at ease that hath a wyf,   785
   Yet he is better that hath none, be my lyf.
   But he that hath a good wyf and wyll forsake her,
   I pray God the devyll take her.
B. Now, in Gode fayth, thou art a made knave.
   I se well thou hast wedyd a shrew.   790
A. The devyll I have!
   Nay, I have marryed .ii. or .iii.
   Syth the tyme that I her lost.
B. And kepist thou them all stylle with the[e?]
A. Nay, that wolde not quyte[99] the cost.   795
   To say the trouth thay fond[100] me most.
B. Than they have some maner gettynge
   By some occupacione, have thay?
A. Syr, thay have a prety waye.
   The chef meane of ther levynge   800
   Is lechery—lech crafte I wolde say—
   Wherein thay labore nyght and day,
   And ease many a man in some case.
B. And where do thay dwell?
A. Att the commen place.   805
   There thou mayst them all fynde.
   Goddis mercy, where is my mynde?

99 *quyte* : requite, repay.   100 *fond* : support.

By God, I shall be shent,
I shold have gone to Lucres
Abowte my maysters besynes.   810
Thetherwarde I was bent.

B. By my fayth, my mayster is there
All the whyle that thou arte here,
As I veryly suppose.

A. I shrow thy face, by Saynt Mary.   815
With thy chaterynge thou doyst me tary
Evyn for the same purpose.

B. I say, whan thou hast with Lucres spoken,
I pray the[e,] wyll thou delyver me a token
In myne name to her mayde?   820

A. Nay, ye muste beware of that gere,
For I have bene afore you there.

B. Why, hast thou hyr assayed?

[A.][45] Ye, ye, that matyr ys sped full.
I may have her and she wull,[101]   825
That comfort she me gave.

B. And hast thou no noder[102] comfort att all?
I truste to God than yet I shall
All this matyr save,
How be it I wyll not the matter begyn   830
Withoute I were sure she were a virgyn.

A. By my trought, this comfort shall I putt the[e] in :
I cam never on her backe in the way of synne.
                    Avoyde the place A.[(16)]

B. Than all is well and fyne.
Yf the matter be in that case,   835
I trust that within a lytyll space
That wenche shall be myne.
I tell you it is a trull of trust
All to quenche a mannes thrust[103]
Bettyr then ony wyne   840
It is a lytyll praty moucet,
And her voyce is as doucett[104]
And as swete as resty[105] porke.
Her face is somewhat browne and yelow,
But for all that she hath no felow   845

---

101 *and she wull :* if she will.   104 *doucett :* sweet.
102 *no noder :* none other.   105 *resty :* rancid.
103 *thrust :* thirst.

In syngynge hens to Yorke.⁽¹⁷⁾
But the worst that grevyth me,
She hath no layser nor lybarte
For an howre or twayne
To be owte of her maystres syght.   850
I wachyde for her this odyr nyght,
But all was in vayne.
How be it I thinke that at the laste
    Come in the maydyn.
I shall come within two stonys caste
Of her. I aske no more.   855
And yf I do so, then my mate
Shall have no lust therin to prate
As he dyde before.
Cockis body,¹⁰⁶ here she is.
Now wellcome, by hevyn blys,   860
The last that was in my thought! [*Embraces her.*]
ANCILLA. Tusshe, I pray you, let me go.
I have somewhat els to do.
For this howre I have soughte
A man that I sholde speke withall   865
Fro my maystres.
B.   What do you hym call?
ANCILLA. Mayster Gayus or his man.
B. Am not I he that ye wolde have?
ANCILLA. No, no, I wolde have another knave.
B. Why, am I a knave than?   870
ANCILLA. Nay, I sayd not so, perde,
But where trow ye these folkis be?
B. I can not veryly say.
His man went evyn now frome me,
And I marvell gretly that ye   875
Met hym not by the way,
For he is gone to speke with Lucres
From his maystyr.
ANCILLA. What, with my maystres? Nay.
B. Ye, so I harde hym say.   880
ANCILLA. Goddis mercy, and I was sent
Evyn hedyr for the same intent
To brynge an answere

106 *Cockis body :* by God's
  body.

Of the erande that he is gone fore.
Wherefore now ther is no more   885
But I must go seche hym there.
B. Nay, tary here a whyle, gentyll Jone,
For he wyll come hedyr anone.
ANCILLA. Tary? Why shold I so?
B. Mary, to laugh and[46] talke with me.   890
ANCILLA. Nay, loke where suche gyglottis[107] be,
For I am none of them, I warne the[e,]
That use so to do.
B. I mene nothinge but good and honest
And for your wele, and you lyst   895
To assent therunto.
ANCILLA. For my wele, quod a! How may that be?
That is a thinge that I can not se.
B. Mary, this, lo, is myne entent:
I mene yf ye wolde be content
Or ony wyse agree   900
For to be my sacrament of penaunce
Ey, God gyve it a very, very vengeaunce![47]
Of wedlocke, I wolde have sayde.[18]
ANCILLA. Tush, by seynt Jame, ye do but mocke,   905
To speke to me of ony wedlocke,
And I so yonge a mayde.
B. Why, are ye a mayde?
ANCILLA.   Ye, ellis I were to blame.
B. Whereby wote ye?
ANCILLA.   Mary, for I ame.
B. A, that is a thinge. [*Turns to the audience.*]   910
Here ye not, syrs, what she sayth?
So resonable a cause thereto she layth.
ANCILLA. A straw for your mockynge,
Have ye none to mocke but me?
B. Mocke? Nay, so mote I the,[108]   915
I mene evyne gode ernest.
Geve me your honde and you shall se
What I wyll promes you.
ANCILLA. That way were not best for my prow.
Wold ye hondefast[109] me forth withall?   920

107 *gyglottis*: wantons.   109 *hondefast*: contract mar-
108 *so mote I the*: as I may   riage with.
        prosper.

Nay, be the roode, fyrst ye shall
Chepe or ever you by.[110]
We must fyrst of the price agre,
For whosomeever shall have me,
I promes you faythfully,[48]   925
He shall me fyrst assure
Of .xx. pound londe in joyncture.[19]
B. Why, are ye so costely?
Nay, nay, then ye be not for me.
As prety a woman as ye be   930
I can sometyme by
For moche les wagis and hyre
As for the season that I desyre
To have hyr in company.
Therefore, yf ye can fynde in youre harte   935
To leve all sucche joynter aparte
And take me as I am,
I shall do you as greate a pleasure,
And therto I wyll love you oute of mesure,
Els I were to blame.   940
ANCILLA. Ye, but oure housholde shall be full small
But yf we have somewhat els withall
Oure charges for to bere.
B. Ye, God sende us mery wether!
I may not wed and thryve all together,   945
I loke not for that gere.
I shall tell you a marvelous case:
I knewe twayne marryed in a place
Dwellyng together in one house,
And I am sure they were not worth a louse   950
At the begynnynge,
And or ever the yere were do,
They were worth an hondred or two.
ANCILLA. That was a marvelous thynge,
But yet I can tell the[e] a gretter marvayle,   955
And I knewe the persons ryght well.
Syr, I knewe two certayne
That when they were wedded they had in store
Scarce halfe a bed and no more
That was worth an hawe,[111]   960

110 *Chepe . . . by:* Bargain   111 *worth an hawe:* of any
      before you buy.   value at all.

And within a yere or twayne
They had so greate encrease and gayne
That at the last they were fayne
To shove theyre hedes in the strawe.[20]

B. Tusshe, ye do but mocke and rayle,   965
And I promesse you withouten fayle
Yf ye lyste to have me,
I woot where is an .c. pound in store,[112]
And I ow never a grot[113] therfore.

ANCILLA. All that may be,   970
I beleve hyt evyn as ye say,
But ye tary me here all day.
I pray you, let me goo.
And for my mariage that is a thing
In the whyche I purpose to geve a sparyng   975
For a yere or two.

B. A yere or .ii., quod a, nay, God forbede!
I wis hyt had be tyme fore you to wedde
Vii. or .viii. yere agoo.
And ye wyst how mery a lyfe   980
Hyt is to be a wedded wyf,
Ye wold chaunge that mynde.

ANCILLA. Ye, so hyt is as I understonde,
If a woman have a gode husbonde,
But that ys herd to fynde.   985
Many a man blamyth his wyf, parde,
And she is more to blame than he.

B. As true as the Gospell now say ye.
But now tell me one thing,
Shall I have none other answere but this   990
Of my desyre?

ANCILLA.   No syr, Iwys,
Not at this metyng.

B. Wyll ye now nede be agoo? Than
[49]Take your leve honestly.

                Et conabitur eam osculari.[114]

ANCILLA.   Se the man!
Let me alone, with Sorowe![115]   995

112 *an . . . store:* £ 100 in re-   114 *Et . . . osculari:* He shall
    serve.   try to kiss her.
113 *grot:* groat, a silver coin   115 *with Sorowe:* sorrow be-
    worth only fourpence.   tide you.

B. Mary, so be hyt; but one worde,
   I wyll kys the[e] or thou goo.
ANCILLA. The devyllis torde,
   The man is madde, I trowe.
[B.][50] So madde I am that nedis I must   1000
   As in this poynt have my lust,
   Howsoever I doo.
[ANCILLA.][51] Parde, ye may do me that request,
   For why it is but good and honest.
        Et osculabitur.[116] *Intrat* A.
A. Now a felychip,[117] I thee beseche,   1005
   Set even suche a patche one my breche.
B. A wyld feyre therone![21]
ANCILLA. Goddis mercy, this is he
   That I have sought so.
A.   Have ye sought me?
ANCILLA. Ye, that have I do.   1010
   This gentylman can wytnes bere
   That all this owre I have stonde here
   Sechyng even for you.
A. Have ye two be togeder so longe?
ANCILLA. Ye, why not?
A.   Mary, then all is wrong,   1015
   I fere me so now.
B. Nay, nay, here be to[o] many wytnes
       [*Indicating the audience.*]
   For to make ony syche besynes
   As thou wenest, hardely.
ANCILLA. Why, what is the mannes thought?   1020
   Suppose ye that I wolde be nowght
   Yf no man were by?
B.[52] Nay, for God, I[53] ment not so,
   But I wolde no man sholde have to do
   With you but onely I.   1025
ANCILLA. Have to do, quod a, what call ye that?
   Hyt sowndyth to a thing I wote ner what.
[A.] Ey, Godes mercy,[54]
   I se well a man must bewarre
   How he spekyth theras ye ar,   1030
   Ye take it so straungely.

116 *Et osculabitur:* He shall   117 *felychip:* for the sake of
   kiss (her).   fellowship.

Nay, I mene nothyng but well,
For by my wyll no man shall dele
With you in way of maryage
But onely I—this wyse I ment.   1035
ANCILLA. Ye, but though it were youre entent,
Yet ye do but rage
To use suche wordes unto me,
For I am yet at my lyberte.
A. Ye, that I know well,   1040
But neverthelesse, sythen I beganne
To love you longe before this man,
I have veray greate mervell
That ever ye wolde his mynde fulfyll
To stonde and talke with hym styll   1045
So long as ye have do.
[B.][55] Before me, quod a? Nay, I make avowe
I mevyde this matter long byfore you,
How sey ye therto?
ANCILLA. I wyll nothinge in the matter say   1050
Lest I cause you to make a fray,
For therof I wolde be lothe.
A. By Cokkes body, butt whosoever it be
That weddythe her bysydes me
I shall make hym wrothe.   1055
B. Ye, but he that is so hasty at every worde
For a medsyn[118] must ete his wyves torde.
ANCILLA. Holde your tongis there, I say!
For and ye make this warke[119] for me
Ye shall bothe dyspoyntyd be,   1060
As fare as I may.
A. By my trouthe, but marke me well,
Yf ever thou with this man dwell
As a woman with here make,[120]
Thou shalt fynde hym the most froward man   1065
That ever thou sawiste sythe the worlde bygan,
For I dare undertake
That .xl. tymes on a day
Withoute ony cause he wyll thee afray
And bete the[e] bake and syde.   1070
ANCILLA. He shall not nede so to do

118 *medsyn*: medicine, cure.   120 *here make*: her mate.
119 *and . . . warke*: if you go
     to this trouble.

For he shall have .xl. causes and .xl. too[121]
Yf I with hym abyde.

A. Mary, that ys a remedy accordynge.[122]
But I can tell the[e] another thynge,   1075
And it is no lye:
Thow maist well be hys weddyd wyf,
But he wyll never love the[e] in his lyf.

ANCILLA. Yet I know a remedy.

A. How so?

ANCILLA. Mary, I wyll love hym as lytyll agayne.   1080
For every shrewed turne he shall have twayne,
And he were my brother.

B. Iwys, Jone, he spekythe but of males.[123]
There ys no man hens to Cales,[124]
Whosoever be the tother,[125]   1085
That can hymselfe better applye
To please a woman better then I.

ANCILLA. Ye, so I harde you say,
But yet, be ye never so wrothe,
There ys never one of you bothe   1090
For all youre wordes gay
That shal be assured of me
Tyll I may fyrst here and se
What ye bothe can do.

And he that can do most maystry,[126]   1095
Be it in cokery or in pastry,
In fettis of warre or dedys of chevalry,[127]
With hym wyll I go.

A. By my trowthe that lykythe me well.
There is no maystry that a man can tell   1100
But I am mete thereto,
Wherefor that wagere I dare well undertake.
Lett me se, wylt thou go coyt[128] for thy ladis sake,
Or what thyng shall we do?

---

121 *and . . . too:* and another forty in addition.
122 *accordynge:* appropriate.
123 *males:* malice.
124 *hens to Cales:* from here to Calais.
125 *Whosoever . . . tother:* Whoever the other fellow may be.
126 *do . . . maystry:* perform with the greatest mastery.
127 *fettis . . . chevalry:* feats of war or deeds of chivalry.
128 *go coyt:* go play quoits.

B. Nay, yf thou wylt her with maystry wynne,   1105
   With boyes game thou mayst not begyn.
   That is not her intent.
A. What is best that we do than?
B. Mary, canst thou syng?
A.   Ye, that I can,
   As well as ony man in Kent.   1110
B. What maner of song shall it be?
A. Whatsoever thou wylt chose thee,
   I holde me well content.
   And yf I mete thee not at the close,
   Hardely let me the wager lose   1115
   By her owne jugement.
   Go to now, wyll ye set in?
B. Nay, be the rode, ye shall begyn.
A. By seynt Jame, I assent.
   Abyde, Jone, ye can gode skyll,[129]   1120
   And if ye wolde the song fulfyll
   With a thyrd parte,
   It wolde do ryght well in my mynde.
ANCILLA. Synge on hardely, and I wyll not be
         behynde,
   I pray the[e] with all my hert.   1125
       Et tunc cantabunt.[130]
B. I am so whorse it wyll not be.
A. Horse, quod a? nay, so mot I the,
   That was not the thynge,
   And a man sholde the trowth saye
   Ye lost a crochet[131] or .ii. by the waye,   1130
   To myne understondynge.
B. Why, was I a mynyme[132] before?
A. Ye, be the rode, that ye were and more.
B. Then were ye a mynyme behynde.
   Let me se, yet syng agayne   1135
   And marke whyche of us twayne
   Plesyth best your mynde.
ANCILLA. Nay, nay, ye shall this matter try
   By some other maner of mastry
   Than by your syngynge.   1140

129 *can . . . skyll:* have tal-   131 *crochet:* crotchet, a quar-
    ent.   ter note.
130 *Et . . . cantabunt:* Then   132 *mynyme:* minim, a half
    they shall sing.   note.

B. Let hym assay what mastry he wull.

A. Mary, and my bely were not so full
   I wolde wrestell with hym a fayre pull.
   That were a game accordynge
   For suche valyaunt men as we be.   1145

B. I shrew thyn hert and thou spare me.
              Et deinde luctabuntur.[133]

ANCILLA. Nay, by my fayth, that was no fall.

B. A, than I se well ye be parcyall,
   Whan ye juge so.
   Well, I shall do more for your love: 1150
   Evyn here I cast to hym my glove
   Or ever I hens goo,
   On the condycion that in the playne fylde
   I shall mete hym with spere and shelde
   My lyf theron to jeoparde.   1155
   Let me se and he dare take hyt.
              Tunc proiiciet cirothecam.[134]

A. Yes, hardely, I wyll not forsake hyt.
   I am not suche a coward
   But I dare mete thee at all assays.
              [*Picks up the glove.*]
   Whan shall hyt be do?

B.   Evyn streyghtways,   1160
   Withoute furthere delay.
   And I shrewe his hert that feris
   Eyther with cronall[135] or sharpe speris
   This bargyn to assay.

A. And I beshrewe hym for me.   1165
   But abyde now, let me se,
   Where shall I have a hors?

B. Nay, we shall nede no horse ne mule
   But let us just[136] at farte pryke in cule.[(22)]

A. Be seynt Jame, no forse.[137]   1170

---

133 *Et . . . luctabuntur:* Then
     they shall wrestle.
134 *Tunc . . . cirothecam:*
     Then let him throw
     down his glove.
135 *cronall:* tilting lance de-
     signed for unhorsing the
opponent but not (like
the "sharpe speris") for
wounding him.
136 *just:* joust.
137 *no forse:* I have no objec-
     tion.

Evyn so be it, but where is oure gere?

B. By my fayth, all thing is redy
That belongethe therto.
Com forthe, ye flowre of the frying pane,
Helpe ye to aray us as well as ye can,   1175
And howsoever ye do
Se that ye juge indifferently
Whiche of us twayne hathe the mastry.

ANCILLA. Yes, hardely, that I shall.
I shall juge after my mynde.   1180
But see ye hold fast behynd
Lest ye troble us in all.

B. Tushe, that is the lest[138] care of .xv.
And yf I do not, on my game be yt sene!
Go to, bynd me fyrst hardely :   1185
                [*She binds his hands.*]
So—lo, now geve me my spere
And put me a staffe thorow here,
Than am I all redy.

A. Abyde, who shall helpe to harnys me?[139]

ANCILLA. That shall I do, so mott I the,   1190
With a ryght gode wyll.

A. Soft and fayre, myne arme is sore,
Ye may not bynd me strayt[140] therfore.

ANCILLA. Nay, no more I wyll,
I wyll not hurte the[e] for .xx. pounde.   1195
Come of now, syt downe on the grounde,
Evyn upon thy tayle.
          [A *sits while she binds his hands.*]

A. Ey, gode Lorde, whan wyll ye have do?

ANCILLA. Now all is redy hardely, go to,
Bydde hym bayle, bayle![141]   1200
                [A *gets up.*]

A. [*To the audience.*] Fall to prayer, syrs, it is nede,
As many of you as wolde me Gode spede,
For this gere stondyth me uppon.[142]

B. Ye, and that shall thou fynde or we departe,
And yf thou spare me I shrow thy harte :   1205

138 *lest:* least.   141 *bayle:* go to it, engage.
139 *harnys me:* get me into   142 *this gere . . . uppon:* this
      my armor.   encounter will prove de-
140 *strayt:* tightly.   manding upon me.

Let[56] me se, com on!
> *Et proiectus dicat* A.[143]

[A.][57] Out, out, alas, for payne!
Let me have a pryst or I be slayne,
My syn to dysclose.[144]

B. And bycause he sayth so, it is nede,   1210
For he is not in clene lyfe indede,
I fele it at my nose .for fo. &c.(23)
Now ye are myne lady.

ANCILLA.   Nay, never the more!

B. No, why so?

ANCILLA.   For I am taken up before.[145]

B. Mary, I beshrew your hart therefore.   1215
It shold better content me
That ye had be taken up behynde.(24)

ANCILLA. Nay, nay, ye understond not my mynde
In that poynt.

B.   It may well be.
But tell me, how ment ye then?[58]   1220

ANCILLA. Mary, I am sure to another man,
Whose wyfe I intende to be.

B. Nay, I trow by Cockis passyon
Ye wyll not mocke us of that fascyon,
Ye may not for very shame.   1225

ANCILLA. Shame or not, so shall it be,
And bycause that fore the love of me
Ye .ii. have made this game,
It shall not be done all in vayne,
For I wyll rewarde you bothe twayne,   1230
And ellis I were to blame.
Somewhat thereby ye must nedis wyn,
And therfore to everyche of you wyll I spyn
A new peyre of breches.
Take the[e] that fore thy dole, [*Strikes* B.]   1235
And bycause he is blacke in the hole,
He shall have as moche. [*Strikes* A.]
> *Et utroque flagellato recedit* ANCILLA.[146]

143 *Et . . . dicat* A: Let A,
    having been thrown
    down, say.
144 *dysclose:* confess.
145 *taken up before:* already
    engaged.
146 *Et . . .* ANCILLA: Hav-
    ing beaten both of
    them, let the maid de-
    part.

A. Oute, alas, what woman was this?

B. It is Lucres mayde.

A.   The devyll it is!
   I pray God a vengeance take her!   1240
   How saist thou, shall she be thy wyfe?

B. Nay, I had lever she had etyn my knyfe.[147]
   I utterly forsake her.

                    Intrat GAYUS.

GAYUS. How, syrs, who hath arayde you thys?[148]

A. Fals thevys, maister, Iwys,   1245
   And all for your quarell.[(25)]

GAYUS. What, and this other man too?

A. Ye, and ye wolde oure hondes undo,
   The matter whe shall tell.

GAYUS. Yes, mary wyll I. [*Unties their hands.*] Now   1250
                    tell on,
   Who hathe you these wrongis done?

A. Mary, that I shall.
   Cornelyus Servantis,[(26)] whiche is your enmy,
   Espyed me goyng toward Lucres place
   That[149] I coude brynge the matter to passe   1255
   Of that gentylwoman,[[59]] as your desyre was.
   They leyd awayte for me in the way
   And so they lefte me in this araye.

GAYUS. Ye, but haste thou ony dedely wounde?
   That is the thinge that feryth my mynde.   1260

A. I'faythe, I was lefte for dede on the grounde,
   And I have a grete garce[150] here byhynde
   Out of the whiche ther commythe suche a wynde
   That yf ye holde a candyll therto
   Hyt wyll blowe it oute, that wyll hyt do.   1265

GAYUS. Se to hyt betyme, by myne advyse,
   Lest the wounde fewster[151] within.

A. Then have I nede of a gode surgyn,
   For hyt is so depe within the skyn
   That ye may put youre nose therin   1270
   Evyn up to the harde eyes.[152]
   Here is a man that quyt hym as well

147 *she . . . knyfe:* I had   150 *garce:* gash.
    stabbed her.   151 *fewster:* fester.
148 *thys:* thus.   152 *the harde eyes:* the very
149 *That:* So that.   eyes.

For my defence as ever I see.
He toke suche parte that in the quarell
His arme was strykyne of by the harde kne[153]   1275
And yet he slew of them .ii. or .iii.

GAYUS. Be they slayne? nay, God forbyde!

A. Yes, so helpe me God, I warande them dede.
How be it I stonde in grete drede
That yf ever he[60] come in theyr way   1280
They wyll kyt of[154] his arme or his hede,
For so I herde them all .iii. say.

GAYUS. Whiche? thay that were slayne?

A.   Ye, by this day.
What nedyth me therfore to lye?
He herd it hymselfe as well as I.   1285

GAYUS. Well then, ye lye both two.   [*Exeat* B.]
But now tell me, what hast thou do
As touchynge my commaundement
That I badde the[e] do to Lucres?
Spakyst thou with her?

A.   Ye, syr, dowtles,   1290
And this is her intent :
Sche commaundyth[155] hyr to you by the same
            tokyn
That with hyr father she hath spokyn
Accordynge to your requeste,
And so she wyllythe you to be of gode chere,   1295
Desyrynge you this nyght to appere,
Or tomorow at the furthest,
And she wyll mete you here in this place
To gyve you a fynall answare in this case,
Whereto ye shall trust.   1300

GAYUS. That is the thing that I desyre,
But sayd she so?

A.   Ye, be thys fyre,[(27)]
I tell you verey juste,
In so moche that she bad me say
And warne you that ye shulde purvay[156]   1305
For your owne besenes,

153 *strykyne . . . kne:* struck   155 *commaundyth:* com-
       off at the very elbow.   mends, sends her re-
154 *kyt of:* cut off.   gards.
                                        156 *purvay:* arrange.

For than it shall determyde be
Whether Publius Cornelius or ye
Shall have the preemynence.

GAYUS. All that purpose lykythe me well,   1310
But who shall be here more, canst thou tell?

A. Mary, here shall be Fulgens,
And Publius Cornelius hymselfe also,
With dyverse other many moo
Besyde this honorable audyence.   1315
Wherfore yf ye wyll youre honour save,
And your intent in this matter have,
It is best that ye go hens
For to study and call to mynde
Suche argumentis as ye can best fynde   1320
And make yourselfe all prest.[157]

GAYUS. Thy counsell is gode, be it so,
And evyn thereafter wyll I do,
For I holde it best.   *Et exeat* GAYUS.[61]

                    Intrat B.

B. Goddes body, syr, this was a ffytt!   1325
I beshrew the horys[158] hart yett
When I thinke theron.
And yet the strokys be not so sore
But the shame grevyth me more,
Sith that it was done   1330
Before so many as here be present.
But and I myght take her
By my trowth I shall make her
This dede to repent.

A. Yet thou were as gode holde thy pease,   1335
For ther is no remedy, doutles,
Therfore lett itt go.
It is to us bothe grete foly and shame
This matter ony more to reherse or name.

B.[62] Well than, be it so,   1340
And yet because she hathe made me smart,
I trust onys to ryde in her carte,[159]
Be it shame or no.
I can not suffre it paciently
To be rebuked openly   1345

157 *prest :* ready.   159 *onys . . . carte :* once to
158 *horys :* whore's.   seduce her.

And to be mockyd also.
Another thing grevythe me werst of all:
I shall be shent,[160] that I shall,
Of my mayster too,
Because I have ben so long away   1350
Oute of his presence.
A.   Nay, nay,
I have harde so much syth I went hens
That he had lityll mynd to thyn offens.
B. I pray you tell me why.
A. For as I brought my mayster on hys way   1355
I harde one of Lucres men say
That thy mayster hathe ben
All this houre at her place
And that he his answere hase,
This wyse as I mene: 1360
Shè hathe appoynted hym to be here
Sone in the evynyng aboute Suppere,
And[63] than he shall have a fynall answere
What she entendith to do.
And so than we shal know here intent,   1365
For as I understond she wyll be content
To have one of them too.
But furst she wyll nedis know the certayn[161]
Whether is the most noble of them twayne,
This she sayeth alway.   1370
B. Why, that is easy to understonde,
Yf she be so wyse as men bere in honde.[162]
A. Ye, so I hard you say.
Let me se now, what is your oppynion
Whether of them is most noble of condycion?   1375
B. That can I tell, hardely:
He that hathe moste nobles[163] in store,
Hym call I the most noble evermore,
For he is most sett by.
And I am sure Cornelius is able   1380
With his owne goodis to bye a rable[164]
Of suche as Gayus is.
And over that, yf noblenes of kynn

160 *shent*: blamed.
161 *the certayn*: for a cer-
        tainty.
162 *bere in honde*: claim.

163 *nobles*: gold coins worth
        6s. 8d.
164 *bye a rable*: buy a whole
        crowd.

May this womans favour wynn,
I am sure he can not mys.   1385
A. Ye, but come hether sone to the ynde[165] of this
            playe,
And thou shalt se wherto all that wyll wey.[166]
It shall be for thy lernynge.
B. Ye, cum agayne[164] who wyll for me,
For I wyll not be here, so mot I thel   1390
It is a gentylmanly thinge
That I shulde awayt and com agayne
For other mennys causes and take suche payne.
I wyll not do it, I make God avowe.
Why myght not this matter be endyd nowe?   1395
A. Mary, I shall tell the[e] why:
Lucres and her father may not attende
At this seson to make an ende,
So I hard them say.
And also it is a curteyse gyse[167]   1400
For to respyte the matter this wyse
That the partyes may
In the meanetyme advyse them well,
For eyther of them bothe must tell
And shew the best he can   1405
To force[168] the goodnes of his owne condycion,
Bothe by example and gode reason.
I wold not for a swan
That thou sholdest be hens at that season,
For thou shalt here a reyal[169] disputacyon   1410
Bitwext them or thay have do.
Another thing must be considred withall:
These folke that sitt here in the halle
May not attende theretoo.
Whe may not with oure long play   1415
Lett[170] them fro theyre dyner all day.
Thay have not fully dyned.
For and this play where ones overe past
Some of them wolde falle to fedyng as fast
As thay had bene almost pyned.[171]   1420

165 *ynde*: end.   168 *force*: urge, press home.
166 *wey*: tend.   169 *reyal*: royal.
167 *curteyse gyse*: courteous   170 *Lett*: Keep.
        procedure.   171 *pyned*: starved.

But no forse, hardely, and they do,[172]
Ussher, gete them goode wyne therto,
Fyll them of the best.
Let it be do or ye wyll be shent,
For it is the wyll and commaundement   1425
Of the master of the fest.
And[65] therefore we shall the matter forbere
And make a poynt[173] evyn here,
Lest we excede a mesure.
And we shall do oure labour and trewe entent   1430
For to play the remenant
At my lordis pleasure.   [*Exeant.*]

    Finis prime partis.

PARS SECUNDA

    Intrat A, *dicens.*
[A.] Muche gode do it you everyche one,
Ye wyll not beleve how fast I have gone,
For fere that I sholde come to[o] late.
No forse, I have lost but a lytyll swete[1]
That I have taken upon this hete,   5
My colde corage to abate.
But now to the matter that I cam fore:
Ye know the cause therof before,
Your wittis be not so short.
Perde, my felowys and I were here   10
Today whan ye where at dyner
And shewed you a lytyll disport
Of one Fulgens and his doughter Lucres
And of two men that made grett besynes
Her husbonde for to be.   15
She answered to them bothe than,
Loke whiche was the more noble man,
To hym she wolde agre.
This was the substance of the play
That[1] was shewed here today,   20
Allbeit that there was

---

172 *But . . . do:* But it cer- PARS SECUNDA
  tainly doesn't matter if   1 *a lytyll swete:* a little
  they do.   sweat.
173 *poynt:* pause.

Dyvers toyes mengled[2] yn the same
To styre folke to myrthe and game
And to do them solace—
The whiche tryfyllis be impertinent[3]   25
To the matter principall,
But neverthelesse they be expedient
For to satisfye and content
Many a man withall.
For some there be that lokis and gapys[(1)]
Only for suche tryfles and japys,[4]   30
And some there be amonge[5]
That forceth[6] lytyll of suche madnes
But delytyth them in matter of sadnes,
Be it never so longe.   35
And every man must have hys mynde,
Ellis thay will many fautys[7] fynde
And say the play was nought.
But no force, I car not,
Let them say and spare not,   40
For God knoweth my thought :
It is the mynde and intent
Of me and my company to content
The leste that stondyth here,
And so I trust ye wyll it alowe.[(2)]   45
By Godis mercy, where am I now?
It were almys[8] to wrynge me by the eare
Bycause I make suche degression
From the matter that I began
Whan I entred the halle.   50
For had I made a gode contynuaunce
I sholde have put you in remembraunce
And to your myndis call
How Lucres wyll come hyder agayne
And her sayde lovers bothe twayne   55
To dyffyne thys question,
Whether of them ys the more noble man.
For theron all this matter began.

2 *Dyvers toyes mengled :*   5 *amonge :* as well, at the
    Various trifling matters   same time.
    intermixed.   6 *forceth :* care.
3 *impertinent :* irrelevant.   7 *fautys :* faults.
4 *japys :* jokes.   8 *almys :* alms, charity, i.e.
                                          fitting.

It is the chefe foundacyon
Of all thys proces, both all and some.   60
And yf thes players where ons come
Of this matter will they speke.
I mervell gretely in my mynde
That thay tary so long behynde
Theyre howre for to breke.   65
But what, syrs, I pray you everychone,
Have pacyens, for thay come anone.
I am sure they wyll not fayle
But thay wyll mete in this place
As theyre promys and apoyntment wase,   70
And ellis I have merveyle.
Let me se, what is now a cloke?[9]
               [B *knocks offstage.*]
A, there commyth one, I here hym knoke.
He knokythe as he were wood.[10]
One of you go loke who it is.   75
     [*One of the audience opens the door for*
       B, *who enters.*]
B. Nay, nay, all the meyny[11] of them, Iwis,
Can not so moche gode :
A man may rappe tyll his naylis ake
Or[12] ony of them wyll the labour take
To gyve hym an answere.   80
A. I have grete marvell on the[e]
That ever thou wylt take upon the[e]
To chyde ony man here.
No man is so moche to blame as thow
For longe taryinge.
B.   Ye, God avow!   85
Wyll ye play me that?
Mary, that shall be amended anone.
I am late comen, and I wyll sone be gone,
Ellis I shrew my catt.
Kockis body, syr, it is a fayre resone,   90
I am com hedyr att this season
Only at thy byddynge,
And now thou makyst to me a quarell
As though all the matter were in parell[13]

9 *a cloke :* o'clock.   12 *Or :* Before.
10 *wood :* mad.   13 *parell :* peril.
11 *meyny :* crowd.

By my longe taryynge.   95
Now God be with you, so mote I the,
Ye shall play the knave alone for me.
                    [*Starts to leave.*]
A. What? I am afrayde,
Iwis, ye are but lewyde :[14]
Turne agayne, all be shrewyde!   100
Now are you fayre prayde.
B. Why, than is your angyr all do?
A. Ye, mary is it, lo.[2]
B. So is myne too,
I have done clene.   105
But now, how goyth this matter forth
Of this mariage?
A. By saynt Jame, ryght nought[3] worth.
I wot nere[15] what thay meane,
For I can none other wise thinke   110
But that some of them begyn to shrinke
Bycause of ther longe tariage.
B. Shrynke now, quod a! mary, that were mervele.
But one thinge of surete I can the[e] tell
As touchynge this mariage :   115
Cornelius my mayster apoyntyth hym therupone,[16]
And dowtles he wyll be here anone
In payne of forty pens,[17]
In so muche that he hath devysyde
Certayne straungers fresshly disgisyd   120
Att his owne exspens
For to be here this nyght also.
A. Straungers, quod a! what to do?
B. Mary, for to glade withall
This gentylwoman at her hedyr comynge.   125
A. A, then I se well we shall have a mummynge.
B. Ye, surely that we shall,
And therfor never thinke it in thy mynde
That my mayster wyll be behynde
Nor slacke at this bargyn.   130
Mary, here he commyth, I have hym aspyde.

14 *lewyde :* ignorant, foolish.   *one :* has determined
15 *I wot nere :* I wot never, I   upon it.
        haven't the least idea.   17 *In payne . . . pens :*
16 *apoyntyth   hym   therup-*   Under penalty of forty
                                            pence.

No more wordis; stonde thou asyde,
For it is he playne.
                [*Intrat* CORNELIUS.]
CORNELIUS. My frynde, whereabowt goist thou all
                day?
B. Mary, syr, I came heder to asay   135
    Whedyr these folke had ben here,
    And yet thay be not come,
    So helpe me God and holydome!
    Of that I have moche marvaile that thay tary so.
CORNELIUS. Mary, go thi way, and wit where[18] thay   140
                wyll or no.
B. Ye, God avow, shall I so?
CORNELIUS. Ye, mary, so I say.
B. Yet in that poynt, as semyth me,
    Ye do not accordynge to your degre.
CORNELIUS. I pray the[e,] tell me why.   145
B. Mary, it wolde becom them well Inow
    To be here afore and to wayte upon you,
    And not you to tary
    For theyr laysyr[19] and abyde them here,
    As it were one that were ledde by the eare,   150
    For that I defy.
    By this mene you sholde be theyr druge,[20]
    I tell you trought, I.
    And yet the worst that greveth me
    Is that your adversary sholde in you se   155
    So notable a foly.
    Therfore witdraw you for a seasone.
CORNELIUS. By seynt Johan, thou sayst but reasone.
B. Ye, do so hardely,
    And whan the tyme drawith upon   160
    That thay be com everychone
    And all thinge redy,
    Than shall I come streyghtaway[4]
    For to seche you withoute delay.
CORNELIUS. Be it so, hardely.   165
    But one thinge whyle I thinke[5] therone,
    Remember this when I am gone:
    Yef hit happon so
    That Lucres come in fyrst alone,

18 *wit where*: learn whether.   20 *druge*: drudge.
19 *laysyr*: leisure.

Go in hand with her anone,[21]   170
Howsoever thou do,
For to fele her mynde toward me,
And by all meanis possyble to be,
Induce her therunto.

B. Than some token you must gyve me,   175
For ellis she wyll not beleve me
That I cam from you.

CORNELIUS. Mary, that is evyn wysely spoken.
Commaunde me to her by the same token,
She knowyth it well Inow,   180
That as she and I walkyde onis togedyr
In her garden hedyr and thedyr
There happonde a straunge case,
For at the last we dyd se
A byrd sittynge on a holow tre,   185
An ashe I trow it was.
Anone she prayde me for to assay
Yf I coude start the byrde away.

B. And dyde ye so? Alas, alas!

CORNELIUS. Why the devyll sayst thou so?   190

B. By Cokkis[6] bonis, for it was a kocko,[22]
And men say amonge,
He that throwyth stone or[7] stycke
At suche a byrde he is lycke[23]
To synge that byrdes songe.   195

CORNELIUS. What the devyll recke I therfore?
Here what I say to thee evermore,
And marke thine erand well.
Syr, I had no stone to throw withall,
And therfore she toke me her musc[8] ball,   200
And thus it befell :
I kyst[24] it as strayght as ony pole
So that it lyghtyde evyn in the hole
Of the holow ashe.
Now canst thou remember all this?   205

B. By God, I wolde be loth to do amys,
For some tyme I am full rashe.
Ye say that ye kyst it evyn in the hole

21 *Go . . . anone :* Sound her
     out at once.
22 *kocko :* cuckoo.
23 *lycke :* likely.
24 *kyst :* cast, threw. But the
humor of the following
scene between B and
LUCRES depends on his
takyng "kyst" to mean
"kissed."

Of the holow ashe as strayte as a pole?
Sayde ye not so?   210
CORNELIUS. Yes.
B.   Well then, let me alone.
  As for this erande it shall be done
  As sone as ye be go.
CORNELIUS. Farewell then. I leve the[e] here.
  And remembyr well all this gere,   215
  Howsoever thou do.   *Et exeat* CORNELIUS.
B. Yes, hardely this erande shall be spoken.
          [B *turns to the audience.*]
  But how say you, syrs, by this tokene?
  Is it not a quaynt thinge?
  I went[25] he hade bene a sad[26, [9]] man   220
  But I se well he is a made[27] man
  In this message doynge.
  But what, chose he for me![28]
  I am but a messanger, perde.
  The blame shall not be myne but his,   225
  For I wyll his token reporte.
  Whether she take it in ernest[10] or sporte,
  I wyll not therof mys.
  Be she wroth or well apayde,[29]
  I wyll tell her evyn as he sayde.   230
          Intrat LUCRES.
  God avow, here she is.
  It is tyme for me to be wyse.
  Now welcome, lady, floure of prise,
  I have sought you twyse or thryse
  Wythin this houre, Iwys.   235
LUCRES. Me syr? Have ye sought me?
B. Ye, that I have, by God that bowght me.
LUCRES. To what intent?
B. Mary, for I have thingis a few
  The which I must to you shew   240
  By my maysters commaundement.
  Publius Cornelius is hys name,
  Your veray lover in payne of shame,[30]

25 *went*: weened, thought.   29 *well apayde*: pleased.
26 *sad*: serious.   30 *in payne of shame*: shame
27 *made*: mad.   on him (or on me) if he
28 *But . . . me*: Oh well, let   isn't.
   him take the responsibil-
   ity.

And yf ye love hym not ye be to blame.
For this dare I say,   245
And on a boke make it gode,
He lovyd you better than his one hart blode.[31]
LUCRES. Hys harde[32] bloode? Nay, nay,
Half that love wolde serve for me.
B. Yet sithe he dyde you fyrst se   250
In the place where he dwellis,
He had lovyd you so in hys hart
That he settyth not by hymself a fart,
Nor by noo man ellis.
And bycause ye shulde gyve credence   255
Unto my sayng in hys absence
And trust to that I say,
He tolde me tokyns .ii. or .iii.
Whiche I know well as he tolde me.
LUCRES. Tokyns? What be thay?   260
B. Let me se, now I had nede to be wyse,
For one of his tokyns is very nyse[33]
As ever I harde tell:
He prayd you for to beleve me
By the same tokyn that ye and he   265
Walkyd togeder by a holow tre.
LUCRES. All that I know well.
B. A, than I am yet in the ryght way,
But I have som other thyng to say
Towchyng my credence   270
Whiche as I thynke were best to be spared,
For happely ye wold not have it declared
Byfore all this audience.
LUCRES. Nay, nay, hardely, spare not.
As for my dedis I care not   275
Yf all the worlde it harde.
B. Mary, than shall I procede.
He shewde me also in very dede
How ther satt a byrde,
And than ye delyveryd hym your muskball   280
For to throw at the byrd withall,
And than, as he sayd, ye dyd no wors

31 *one . . . blode:* own
   heart's blood.
32 *harde:* heart's, perhaps
   with a play on the meaning "very."
33 *very nyse:* very much to
   be handled with deli-
   cacy.

But evyn fayr kyst hym on the noke[34] of the ars.

LUCRES. Nay, ther thow lyest falsely, by my fay.[35]

B. Trouth, it was on the hole of th'ars I shulde say.   285
   I wyst well it was one of the too,
   The noke or the hole.

LUCRES.   Nay, nor yet so.

B. By my fayth, ye kyst hym or he kyst you
   On the hole of th'ars, chose you now,
   This he tolde me sure.   290
   Howbeit I speke it not in reprove,[36]
   For it was done but for gode love
   And for no synfull pleasure.

LUCRES. Nay, nay, man, thow art farr amys.
   I know what thyn erande is,   295
   Though thow be neclygent.
   Of thy foly thou mayst well abasshe,[37]
   For thou shuldis have sayde the holow asshe,
   That hole thy mayster ment.

B. By God avow, I trow it was.   300
   I crye you mercy, I have done you trespas.
   But I pray you take it in pacyence,
   For I mystoke it by necligence.
   A myscheef com theron!
   He myght have sent you this gere in a letter,   305
   But I shall go lerne myn erande better
   And cum ayen anon.   *Et exeat.*

LUCRES. Ye, so do hardely.
   Now, forsoth, this was a lewed message
   As ever I harde sith I was bore,   310
   And yf his mayster have therof knowlege
   He wyll be angry with hym therfore.
   Howbeit I will speke therof no more,
   For hyt hath ben my condiscyon alwey
   No man to hender but to helpe where I may.   315

                 Intrat A.

A. Feyr maysters,[38] lyketh it you to know
   That my mayster comaunde[39] me to you?

LUCRES. Commaundeth you to me?

A. Nay, commaundeth you to hym.

LUCRES. Wele amendyd, by saynt Sym.   320

---

34 *noke :* nook, corner.
35 *fay :* faith.
36 *reprove :* reproof.
37 *abasshe :* be ashamed.

38 *Feyr maysters :* Fair mistress.
39 *comaunde :* commends.

A. Commaundeth he to you, I wolde say,
   Or ellis you to he; now chose ye may,
   Whether lyketh you better.
   And here he sendyth you a letter—
   Godis mercy, I had it ryght now.   325
   Syrs [*Addressing the audience.*], is there none
                       there among you
   That toke up suche a wrytyng?
   I pray you, syrs, let me have it agayne.
LUCRES. Ye ar a gode messanger, for certeyne.
   But I pray you, syr, of one thyng,   330
   Who is your mayster? Tell me that.
A. Maister what call ye hym. Perde, ye wott
   Whome I mene well and fyne.
LUCRES. Yet I know not, so mot I go.
A. What? Yes, perde, he that wolde have you so.   335
LUCRES. I suppose there be many of tho
   Yf I wolde enclyne.
   But yet know I not who ye mene.
   I holde best that ye go ageyene
   To lerne your maysters name.   340
A. By my fayth and I holde it best,
   Ye may say I am a homely gest[40]
   In ernest and in game.
LUCRES. Abyde, I shall go to you nere honde.[41]
   What ys your owne name, I wolde understonde?   345
   Tell me that or I go.
   I trow thou canst not well tell.
A. By my fayth, not verely well
   Bycause ye say so.
      Et scalpens caput post modicum intervallum
                        dicat.[42]
   By this lyght, I have forgoten.[(3)]   350
   Howbeit by that tyme I have spoken
   With som of my company
   I shall be acerteyned of this gere.[43]
   But shall I fynde you agayne here?
LUCRES. Ye, that thow shalt, happely.   *Et exeat* A.   355

40 *homely gest*: uncouth fel-   scratching his head after
   low.   a little while let him say.
41 *go . . . honde*: come near   43 *acerteyned of this gere*:
   you, get more personal.   made certain about this
42 *Et . . . dicat*: And   matter.

[*Intrant* CORNELIUS *et* B.]

CORNELIUS. Now, fayr Lucres, accordyng to th'ap-
           poyntement
   That ye made with me here this day
   Bycause ye shall not fynde me there neclygent,
   Here I am come your wyll to obey,
   And redy am I for myselfe to sey   360
   That as towchyng the degre of noble condycion,
   Betwyxt me and Gayus there may be no com-
        parison,
   And that shall I shew you by apparent reason
   Yf it shall lyke you that I now begynne.
LUCRES. Nay, ye shall spare it for a lytyll season   365
   Tyl[11] suche tyme that Gayus, your adversary,
        come in,
   For I wyll gyve you therin none audience
   Tyll ye be both togeder[12] in presence.
   And in ony wyse kepe well your patience,
   Lyke as I have bound you both to the peace.   370
   I forbyde you utterly all maner of violence
   Durynge this matter, and also that ye seace
   Of all suche wordis as may gyve occasion
   Of brallynge or other ongodely condycion.
CORNELIUS. There shal be in me no suche abusyon   375
   In worde nor dede, I you promyse.
   But now, let me se, what occupation
   Or what maner of passetyme wyll ye devyse
   Whyle that these folke dothe tary this wyse?
   Wyll ye see a bace daunce after the gyse   380
   Of Spayne,[4] whyle ye have nothynge to do?
   All thynge have I purvaide that belongyth therto.
LUCRES. Syr, I shall gyve you the lokynge on.
CORNELIUS. Wyll ye do so? I aske no more.
   [*To* B.] Go sone and bidde them come thens anone,   385
   And cause the mynstrelles to come in beffore.
                 [*Exeat* B.]

    [*Intrant Musicians, Mummers, et* B.]
B. Mary, as for one of them his lippe is sore,
   I trow he may not pype, he is so syke.[5]
   Spele up tamboryne, ik bide owe frelike.[6]
       Et deinde corisabunt.[44]

  44 *Et . . . corisabunt:* Then
    they shall dance.

LUCRES. Forsothe, this was a godely recreacyon.   390
    But I pray you, of what maner nation
    Be these godely creatours?
    Were they of Englonde or of Wales?
B. Nay, they be wylde Irissh Portyngales[7]
    That dyde all these pleasures.   395
    Howbeit it was for my maysters sake,
    And he wyll deserve it,[45] I undertake,
    On the largest wyse.
CORNELIUS. Go thyselfe, why stondis thou so?
    And make them chere; let it be do,   400
    The best thou canst devyse.
B. Yes, they shall have chere hevyn hye,
    [Aside.] But one thing I promyse you faithfully,
    They get no drynke therto.   Exeat.
        [Intrat GAYUS.] Dicat LUCRES.
LUCRES. Lo, here thys man ys come now.   405
    Now may ye in your matter procede.
    Ye remembre both what I sayde to you
    Touchynge myne answere. I trow it is no nede
    Ony more to reherse it.
CORNELIUS.   No, in veray dede,
    For moche rehersall wolde let the spede[46]   410
    Of all this matter; it nedyth no more.
    Let us roundely to the matter we come for.
LUCRES. Ye, that I pray you as hartly as I can.
    But fyrst me semyth it were expedient
    That ye both name some indifferent man   415
    For to gyve betwyxt you the forseyde jugement.
CORNELIUS. Nay, as for that, by myne assent
    No man shall have that office but ye.
GAYUS. And I holde me well content that it so be.
LUCRES. Ye, but notwythstondyng that ye therto agre   420
    That I sholde this question of nobles diffine,
    It is a grete matter whiche, as semyth me,
    Pertayneth to a philosopher or ellis a devyne.
    Howbeit sith the choyse of this matter is myne
    I can be content under certayne protestacyon,   425
    Whan that I have harde you, to say myne opinion.
    Lo, this wyse I mene and thus I do intende,

---

45 *deserve it :* requite it.   46 *let the spede :* hinder the
                                    progress.

That whatsoever sentence I gyve betwyxt you two
After myne owne fantasie, it shall not extende
To ony other person. I wyll that it be so,   430
For why, no man ellis hath theryn ado :
It may not be notyde for a generall precedent,
Allbeit that for your partis ye do therto assent.

GAYUS. As touchyng that poynt we holde us well
             content,
Your sentence shall touche no man but us twayne,   435
And sith ye shall gyve it by our owne agrement,
None other man ought to have thereat disdayne.
Wherfor all thys dout ye may well refrayne,
And in the matter principall this tyme wolde be
             spent.

CORNELIUS. Than wyll I begynne.
GAYUS.   I holde me well content.   440
CORNELIUS. Syth ye have promysed, fayre Lucres,
             heretofore,
That to the more noble man ye wyll enclyne,
Vary not fro that worde, and I aske no more,
For than shall the victory of this cause be myne,
As it shal be easy to jugge and diffyne   445
For every creature that ony reason hase.
Me semyth I durst make hymself jugge in this case,
          [*Indicating* GAYUS.]
Save that I fere me the beaute of your face
Sholde therin blynde hym so that he ne myght
Egally disserne the wronge fro the right.   450
And if he were half so wyse a man indede
As he reputeth hymself for to be,
Upon your saide answere he sholde not nede
To gaynesay in this matter or travers[47] with me.
My noblenes is knowen thorow all the cyte.   455
He knoweth hymselfe the noblenes of my kyn,
And at that one poynt my proces I wyll begyne.

Amonge all th'istoryes of Romaynes that ye rede,
Where fynde ye ony blode of so grete noblenes
As hath ben the Cornelys wherof I am brede?   460
And if so be that I wolde therin holde my pease,
Yet all your cornecles[48] beryth gode witnes

---

47 *travers*: oppose.   48 *cornecles*: chronical his-
                                  tories.

That my progenytours and auncetours have be
The chefe ayde and diffence of this noble cyte.

How ofte have myne auncetours in tymes of   465
          necessite
Delyverd this cyte from dedely parell
As well by theyr manhode as by theyr police,
What jeopardi and paine they have suffred in the
          quarell
Th'empire to encrece and for the comune wele,
It nedith not the specialties[49] to reherse or name,   470
Sith every trew Romaine knoweth the same.

In every manys howse that histories be rife[50]
And wrytten in bookes, as in some placis be
The gestis[13] of Arthur, or of Alexandyrs life,[8]
In the whiche stories ye may evidently se   475
And rede how Cartage that royall cyte
By Cipion of Affrick my grete graunte sire
Subduede was and also ascribede to his empire.

And many other cyties that dyde conspire,
Ageynst the noble senatoure makynge resistence,   480
As often as necessite did it require
They were reducyd unto due obedience
Eyther by the policy or by the violence
Of my sayde aunceters; th'istories be playne
And witnesse that I speke not these wordis in   485
          vayne.

My blode hath ever takyn suche payne
To salvegarde the comune wele fro ruyn and decay
That by one advyse[51] the Cenat dyde ordeyne
Them to be namyd the faders of the contray,[14]
And so were myne auctours reputed alway,   490
For in every nede they dyde upon them call
For helpe as the chylde doth on the fader naturall.

Howbeit, to praye them it was no nede at all,
For of their owne myndis they were redy alway.
In tokyn of the same, for a memoriall   495
Of theyr desertis, the cytie dyde edifye[52]
Triumphall arches wheruppon ye may

49 *specialties* : particulars.   51 *advyse* : decision.
50 *that . . . rife* : those stories   52 *edifye* : build.
      are current.

To my grete honour se at this day
Th'ymages of myn auncetours evyn by and by[53]
Bycause that theyr noblenes sholde never dye.   500

In token also that they were worthy
Grete honour and prayse of all the contray,
It is commaunded and used generally
That every cytezen that passith that way
By the sayde Images he must obey,[54]   505
And to those fygures[15] make a due reverence,
And ellis to the lawes he dothe grete offence.

Sith it is so, than, that of convenience
Such honoure and homage must nedis be do
To these dede ymagis, than muche more reverence   510
To me sholde be gevyn, I trow ye thinke so,
For I am theyr very ymage and relyque to[o]
Of theyr flesch and blode, and veray Inherytoure
As well of theyr godes as of theyr sayde honoure.

To me they have left many a castell and toure   515
Whiche in theyr triumphes thay rightfully wan,
To me they have also left all theyr tresoure
In suche abundaunce that I trow no man
Within all Rome sith it fyrst began
Had half the store as I understonde   520
That I have evyn now at ons in my honde.

Lo, in these thynges my noblenes doth stonde,
Whiche in myne oppynyon suffiseth for this intent,
And I trow there is no man throwgh all this londe
Of Italy but if he were here present   525
He wolde to my sayng in this matter assent,
And gyve unto me the honoure and preeminence
Rather than make agayne me resistence.

[*To* GAYUS.] I marvayle gretly what shulde thy
           mynde insence
To thinke that thy tytle therin sholde be gode :   530
Parde, thow canst not say for thy deffence
That ever there was gentilman of thy kyn or blode,
And if there were oone it wolde be under-
           stoode,[16]

53 *by and by :* here at hand.   54 *obey :* bow, do obeisance
                                         to.

Without it be thyself, whiche now of late
Among noble gentylmen playest checkmate.[55]   535
LUCRES. No more therof, I pray you! such wordis I
          hate,
    And I dyde forbid you them at the begynnyng,
    To eschue th'occasyon of stryfe and debate.
GAYUS. Nay, let hym alone, he speketh after his
          lernyng,
    For I shall answer hym to everythyng   540
    Whan he hath all said, if ye woll here me,
    As I thinke ye wyll of your equyte.
CORNELIUS. Abide, I must make an ende fyrst, perde.
    To you, swete Lucres, I wolde have said beffore[(9)]
    That yf ye wyll to my desyre in this matter agre, 545
    Doubtles ye shall blesse the tyme that ever ye
          were bore,
    For riches shall ye have at your will evermore
    Without care or study of laboriouse besynes
    And spend all your dayes in ease and plesaunt
          idelnesse.

    About your owne apparell ye can do non excesse   550
    In my company that sholde displese my mynd.
    With me shall ye do non other maner of besynes
    But hunt for your solace at the hart and hynde,
    And sometyme where we convenient game fynde
    Oure hawkis shal be redy to shew you a flight   555
    Whiche shal be right plesaunt and chereful to
          your sight.

    And yf so be that in huntyng ye have no delyght,
    Than may ye daunce a whyle for your disport.
    Ye shall have at your pleasure both day and night
    All maner of mynstralsy to do you comfort.   560
    Do what thyng ye wyll, I have to support
    Our chargis,[56] and over that I may susteyne
    At myne owne fyndyng an .L.[57] or twayne.

    And as for hym, I am certayn [Indicating GAYUS.]
    Hys auncetours were of full poore degre,   565

55 *playest checkmate:* pre-   have the wherewithal to
    sumes to offer opposi-   pay our expenses.
    tion.   57 *an .L.:* a poand, £1.
56 *I . . . chargis:* I shall

Allbeit that now withyn a yere or twayne,
By cause that he wold a gentilman be,
He hath hym goten both office and fee,
Whiche after the rate of hys wrechyd sparyng
Suffiseth scarsely for hys bare lyvynge.   570

Wherfore, swete Lucres, it were not accordyng[58]
For your grete beaute with hym to dwell,
For there sholde ye have a thredebare lyvynge
With wrechyd scarcenes, and I have herde tell
That maydens of your age love not ryght well   575
Suche maner of husbondis, without it be thay
That forceth lytyll to cast[59] themself away.

I mene specyally for suche of them as may
Spede better if they wyll, as ye be yn the case,
And therfore, Lucres, whatsoever he wyll say   580
Hys title agaynst you to force and embrace,
Ye shall do your owen selfe to[o] grete a trespas
Yf ye folow hys part and enclyne therto.
Now say what ye wyll, syr, for I have all doo.

[GAYUS.][17] With ryght gode will I shall go to,   585
So that ye will here me with as grete pacience
As I have harde you; reason wolde soo.
And whatsoever I shall speke in this audience
Eyther of myn owne merites or of hys insolence,
Yet fyrst unto you all, syrs, I make this request,   590
That it wolde lyke you to construe it to the best.

For lothe wolde I be as ony creature
To boste of myne owne dedis; it was never my
        gyse.
On that other syde, loth I am to make ony re-
        portur[60]
Of this mans foly or hym to dispice,   595
But neverthelesse this matter towchith me in suche
        wise
That whatsoever ye thinke in me I must procede
Unto the veray trouth therof, as the matter is
        indede.

58 *accordyng*: fitting.   60 *reportur*: mention.
59 *without . . . cast*: except
        those who don't care
        about casting.

To make a grete rehersall of that ye have saide
The tyme will not suffre, but neverthelesse   600
Two thinges for yourself in substaunce ye have
        layd
Whiche as ye suppose maketh for your nobles,
Upon the whiche thingis dependith all your
        processe.[61]
Fyrst, of your auncetours ye allege the noble
        gestis,[62]
Secondly, the substaunce that ye have of theyr
        bequestes.   605

In the whiche thingis onely by your owne con-
        fession
Standeth all your noblenes, this sayd ye beffore,
Whereunto this I say, under the correction
Of Lucres, oure jugge here, that ye ar never the
        more
Worthy in myne oppynion to be callyd noble   610
        therfore,
And withoute ye have better causes to shew than
        these
Of reson ye must the victory of this matter lese.[63]

To the fyrst parte, as touching your auncetours
        dedes,
Some of them were noble lyke as ye declare.
Th'estoris bereth witnes, I must graunt them   615
        nedes.[64]
But yet for all that some of them ware
Of contrary disposycion, like as ye are,
For they dyde no proffite, no more do ye,
To the comon wele of this noble cytie.

Yf ye wyll the title of noblenes wynne,   620
Shew what have ye done yourself therfore.
Some of your owne meritis let se bryng in,[65]
Yf ever ye dyde ony syth ye were bore.
But surely ye have no suche thyng in store
Of your owne merites, wherby of right   625
Ye shulde appere noble to ony mannys sight.

61 *processe*: argument.
62 *gestis*: deeds.
63 *lese*: lose.

64 *I . . . nedes*: I must needs
    grant that they were.
65 *let . . . in*: let me see you
    bring in.

But neverthelesse I wyll you not blame
Thowgh ye speke not of your owne dedes at all,
And to say the trowght, ye may not for shame.
Your lyfe is so voluptuouse and so bestiall   630
In folowynge of every lust sensuall
That I marvaille nothynge in my mynde
Yf ye leve your owne dedis behynde.

He wenyth that by hys proude contenaunce
Of worde and dede with nyse aray,[66]   635
Hys grete othys and open mayntenaunce
Of theftis and murdres every day,
Also hys ryotouse disportis and play,
Hys sloth, his cowardy and other excesse,
Hys mynde disposed to all unclennesse,   640
By these thyngis oonly he shall have noblenesse.

Nay, the title of noblenes wyll not ensue[67]
A man that is all gevyn to suche insolence,
But it groweth of longe continued vertu,
As I trust, lady, that youre indifference[68]   645
Can well diffyne by your sentence.[69]
Hys auncetours were not of suche condicion,
But all contrary to hys disposicyon.

And therfore they were noble, withouten faile,
And dyde grete honoure to all the contrey.   650
But what can theyr sayde noblenes advayle[70]
To hym that takyth a contrary way,
Of whome men spekith every day
So grete dishonoure that it is marvel
The contrey suffereth hym therin to dwelle?   655

And where he to wyteth me of pore kyn[71]
He doth me therin a wrongfull offence,
For no man shall thankis or praysyng wyn
By the gyftis that he hath of natures influence.
Lykewyse, I thinke by a contrary sense   660
That if a man be borne blynde or lame
Not he hymselfe but nature therin is to blame.

66 *nyse aray*: elegant dress.
67 *ensue*: attach itself to.
68 *indifference*: impartiality.
69 *diffyne . . . sentence*: de-
    cide when you make
    your judgment.
70 *advayle*: avail.
71 *to wyteth . . . kyn*: re-
    proaches me for being of
    humble ancestry.

Therfor he doth not me therin repreve,
And as for that poynt this I wott welle,
That both he and I cam of Adam and Eve.   665
There is no difference that I can tell
Whiche makith oon man another to excell
So moche as doth vertue and godely maner,
And therin I may well with hym compare.

Howbeit I speke it not for myne one prayse,   670
But certeynly this hath ever be my condicion :
I have[18] borne unto God all my daies
His laude and prayse with my[19] due devocion,
And next that I bere allwayes
To all my neyghbours charitable affeccyon.   675
Incontynency and onclennes I have had in abhomi-
                  nacion,
Lovyng to my frende and faythfull withall,
And ever I have withstonde my lustis sensuall.

One tyme with study my tyme I spende
To eschew Idelnes, the causer of syn.   680
Another tyme my contrey manly I deffend,
And for the victoryes that I have done therin
Ye have sene yourself, syr, that I have come in
To this noble cytee twyse or thryse[20]
Crownyd with lawryel, as it is the gyse.   685

By these wayes, lo, I do aryse
Unto grete honoure fro low degre,
And yf myn heires will do likewyse,
Thay shal be brought to nobles by me.
But Cornely, it semyth by the[e,]   690
That the nobles of thyn auncetours everycheon
Shall utterly starve[72, 21] and die in the[e] alone.

And where he to witeth me on that other syde
Of small possession and grete scarecenes,[22]
For all that, lady, if ye will with me abidde,   695
I shall assure you of moderate richesse,
And that sufficient for us both, doutles.
Ye shall have also a man accordyng
To youre owne condicions in every thing.

72 *starve :* perish.

Now, Lucres, I have shewyd unto you a parte 700
Of my title that I clayme you by,
Besechynge you therfore with all my hart
To considre us both twayne indifferently,
Whiche of us twayne ye will rather alow
More worthy for nobles to marry with you. 705
LUCRES. Syrs, I have hard you both at large—
CORNELIUS. Nay, abide Lucres, I pray you hertly,
Sithe he leyeth many thynges to my charge,
Suffre that I may therunto repply.
LUCRES. Iwis replication shall not be necessary 710
Withoute that ye have some other thing in store
To shew for yourself than ye dyde beffore.
CORNELIUS. Why lady, what thing will ye desyre more
Than I have shewyd to make for noblenes?
LUCRES. Yes, somthyng ther ys that makyth therfore 715
Better than ye have shewid in your processe.
But now let me se what man of witnes
Or what other proves will ye forth bryng
By the whiche eyther of you may justifie his
      sayng.
GAYUS. As for my parte, I wyll stonde gladly 720
To the commune voyce of all the contrey.
LUCRES. And ye lykewyse, syr?
CORNELIUS.   Ye, certaynly,
I shall in no wyse your worde dissobey.
LUCRES. Than wyll I betwyxt you both take this way :
I shall go enquyre as faste as I may 725
What the commune fame wyll theryn reporte,
And whan I have therof a due evidence,
Than shall I agayne to you resorte
To shew you th'opynyon of my sentence,[73]
Whome I wyll jugge to have the preemynence. 730
CORNELIUS. Nay, fayre Lucres, I you requyre,
Let me not now depart in vayne,
Not knowyng th'effect of my desyre.
LUCRES. Syr, allthough it be to you a payne
Yet must ye do so evyn both twayne. 735
Eche of you depart hens to hys owne place
And take no more labour or payne in this case,

73 *th'opynyon of my sen-*   bodied in my judgment.
    tence : the opinion em-

For as towchyng th'effect of my sentence
I shall go write it by gode advysement
Sone after that I am departed fro hens.   740
And than to eyther of you both shal be sent
A copy of the same to this intent
That of none other person it shall be sayn[74]
Sith it concerneth but onely unto you twayne.[(10)]

GAYUS. This is a gode waye, as in my mynde.   745
    Ar not ye, syr, content in lyke wyse?

CORNELIUS. I wot nere yet. I wyll prayse as I fynde
    And as I have cause; that is evyr my gyse.

GAYUS. Well, Lucres, will ye commaunde me ony
        servyce?

LUCRES. No servyce at all, syr. Why say ye so?   750
    Our Lorde spede you both wheresoever ye goo.

        Et exeant PUBLIUS CORNELIUS[23] *et*
                GAYUS FLAMYNEUS.
                [*Intrat* B.][(11)]

[*To the audience.*] Now som mayde happely, and
        she were in my case,
Wolde not take that way that I do intend,
For I am fully determyned with Godis grace
So that to Gayus I wyll condyscend,[75]   755
For in this case I do hym commend
As the more noble man, sith he thys wyse
By meane of hys vertue to honoure doth aryse.
And for all that, I wyll not dispise
The blode of Cornelius; I pray you, thinke not so.   760
God forbede that ye sholde note me that wyse,
For truely I shall honoure them[76] wheresoever I go
And all other that be of lyke blode also,
But unto the blode I wyll have lytyl respect
Where tho condicyons be synfull and abject.   765
I pray you all, syrs, as meny as be here,
Take not my wordis by a sinistre way.[77]

B. Yes, by my trouth, I shall witnes bere,
    Wheresoever I becom another day,
    How suche a gentylwoman did opynly say   770

74 *sayn* : seen.   77 *by a sinistre way* : other-
75 *condyscend* : consent.   wise than I intend.
76 *them* : i.e. the Scipios, COR-
    NELIUS' family.

That by a chorles son she wolde set more
Than she wolde do by a gentylman bore.
LUCRES. Nay, syr, than ye report me amys.
B. I pray you, tell me how sayd ye than?
LUCRES. For God, syr, the substaunce of my wordis   775
           was this—
I say evyn as I saide whan I began,
That for vertue excellent I will honoure a man
Rather than for hys blode, if it so fall
That gentil condicyons agre not withall.
B. Than I put case that a gentilman bore   780
Have godely maners to his birth accordyng.
LUCRES. I say of hym is to be set gret store.
Suche one is worthy more lawde and praysyng
Than many of them that hath their begynnyng
Of low kynred, ellis God forbede!   785
I wyll not afferme the contrary for my hede,
For in that case ther may be no comparyson.
But neverthelesse I said this before,
That a man of excellent vertuouse condicions,
Allthough he be of a pore stoke bore,   790
Yet I wyll honour and commende hym more
Than one that is descendide of ryght noble kyn
Whose lyffe is all dissolute and rotyde in syn.
And therfore I have determyned utterly
That Gayus Flamyneus shall have his intent.   795
To hym onely I shall myself apply,
To use me in wedloke at his commaundement,
So that to Cornelius I wyll never assent,
Allthough he had as grete possession
As ony one man in Cristen region.   800
I shall in no wyse favour or love hys condicyon,
Howbeit that his blode requyreth due reverence,
And that shall I gyve hym with all submyssion,
But yet shall he never have the preemynence,
To speke of very nobles, by my sentence.   805
Ye be hys servaunt, syr, go your way
And report to your mayster evyn as I say.
                         [*Exeat* LUCRES.]
B. Shall I do that erand? Nay, let be,
By the rode, ye shall do it yourselfe for me!
            [B *turns to the audience.*]
I promyse you faythfully,   810

    I wolde my mayster had be in Scotland[12]
    Whan he dyd put this matter in her hand
    To stond to her jugement.
    But forasmoche as it is so
    That this wrong to hym is doo   815
    By a woman, he must let it goo
    And holde hym content.
    But he is of suche disposycion
    That whan he hereth of this conclusion
    He wyl be starke madd,   820
    Ye, by my trowth, as made as an hare.
    It shall make hym so full of care
    That he wyll with hymself fare
    Evyn as it were a lade.[78]
    And so wold not I, so mote I thee,   825
    For this matter and I were as he,
    It shulde never anger me.
    But this wold I do,
    I wolde let her go, in the mare name.[79]
             [*Intrat* A.]
A. [*To the audience.*] What now, syrs? How goth   830
        the game?
    [*To* B.] What, is this woman go?
B. Ye, ye man.
A.   And what way hathe she takyn?
B. By my fayth, my mayster is forsakyn,
    And nedis[80] she wyll agre
    Unto thy mayster; thus she saieth,   835
    And many causes therfore she leyeth
    Why it shulde so be.
A. I marvayle gretely wherof that grue.[81]
B. By my fayth, she saide, I tell the[e] true,
    That she wolde nedis have hym for his vertue   840
    And for none other thynge.
A. Vertue, what the devyll is that?
    And I can tell, I shrew my catt,
    To myne understondynge.
B. By my fayth, no more can I,   845
    But this she said here opynly,

78 *lade* : lad.   80 *nedis* : necessarily.
79 *in the mare name* : to the   81 *grue* : grew.
    devil with her.

All these folke can tell. [*Indicates the audience.*]

A. How say ye, gode women,[24] is it your gyse
To chose all your husbondis that wyse?
By my trought, than I marvaile.   850

B. Nay, this is the fere, so mot I goo,
That men chise not theyr wyffes so
In placis where I have be,
For wiffes may well complayne and grone,
Albeit that cause have they none   855
That I can here or se.
But of weddyd men there be ryght fewe
That welle not say the best is a shrew.
Therin they all agree.
I warne you, weddyd men everichone,   860
That other remede have ye none
So moche for your ease,
And ye wold study tyll tomorow,
But let them evyn alone with sorow[82]
Whan they do you displease.   865

A. Tusshe, here is no man that settyth a blank[83]
By thy consell or konneth the[e] thank.[84]
Speke therof no more.
They know that remedy better than thow.
But what shall we twayne do now?   870
I care most therfore;
Methinketh that matter wolde be wist.

B. Mary, we may goo hens whan we lyst,
No man saith us nay.

A. Why, than, is the play all do?   875

B. Ye, by my feyth, and we were ons go
It were do streghtwey.

A. And I wolde have thought in vere dede
That this matter sholde have procede
To som other conclusion.   880

B. Ye, thou art a maister mery man,[85]
Thou shall be wyse I wot nere whan.
Is not the question
Of noblenes now fully defynde,

---

82 *let . . . sorow:* let evil betide them, let them go
   to the devil.
83 *settyth a blank:* cares a
   farthing.

84 *konneth thee thank:* gives
   you thanks.
85 *maister mery man:* a great
   fool.

As it may be so by a womans mynde? 885
What woldyst thow have more?
Thow toldest me that other day[13]
That all the substaunce of this play
Was done specially therfor,
Not onely to make folke myrth and game, 890
But that suche as be gentilmen of name
May be somwhat movyd
By this example for to eschew
The wey of vyce and favour vertue,
For syn is to be reprovyd 895
More in them, for the degre,
Than in other parsons such as be
Of pour kyn and birth.
This was the cause principall,
And also for to do withall 900
This company some myrth.
And though the matter that we have playde
Be not, percase, so wele conveyde
And with so great reason
As th'istory itself requyreth, 905
Yet the auctour therof desyrith
That for this season
At the lest ye will take it in pacience.
And yf ther be ony offence—
Show us wherein or we go hence— 910
Done in the same,
It is onely for[25] lacke of connynge,
And not he but his wit runnynge
Is thereof to blame.
And glade wolde he be and ryght fayne 915
That some man of stabyll brayne
Wolde take on hym the labour and payne
This mater to amende.
And so he wyllyd me for to say,
And that done, of all this play 920
Shortely here we make an end.

Emprynted at London by Johan Rastell
dwellynge on the south syde of Paulys
chyrche bysyde Paulys cheyne.[14]

JOHAN JOHAN THE HUSBANDE

attributed to

JOHN HEYWOOD

¶ A mery play
betwene Johan Johan the
husbande / Tyb his
wyfe / & syr Jhan
the preest.

[Dramatis Personae.

JOHAN JOHAN, *the husbande.* (1)
TYB, *his wyfe.*
SYR JOHAN, *the preest.*

THE SCENE
LONDON.]

[*Enter*] JOHAN JOHAN, *the husbande.*
JOHAN JOHAN. God spede you,[1] maysters, everychone.
  Wote[2] ye not whyther my wyfe is gone?
  I pray God the dyvell take her.
  For all that I do I can not make her
  But she wyll go a gaddynge very myche   5
  Lyke an Anthony pyg[(1)] with an olde wyche[3]
  Whiche ledeth her about hyther and thyther,
  But by Our Lady I wote not whyther.
  But by Gogges[4] blod, were she come home
  Unto this my house, by our lady of Crome,[(2)]   10
  I wolde bete her or that[5] I drynke.
  Bete her, quod a?[6] yea, that she shall stynke,
  And at every stroke lay her on the grounde
  And trayne her by the here[7] about the house
             round.
  I am evyn mad that I bete her not nowe,   15
  But I shall rewarde her hardly[8] well ynowe.
  There is never a wyfe betwene heven and hell
  Whiche was ever beten halfe so well.
    Beten, quod a? yea, but what and she therof
           dye?
  Than I may chaunce to be hanged shortly.   20
  And whan I have beten her tyll she smoke
  And gyven her many a C.[9] stroke
  Thynke ye that she wyll amende yet?

---

1 *spede you:* cause you to prosper.
2 *Wote:* Know.
3 *wyche:* witch.
4 *Gogges:* God's.
5 *or that:* before (ere that).
6 *quod a?:* did I say?
7 *trayne . . . here:* drag her by the hair.
8 *hardly:* severely.
9 *C.:* hundred.

Nay, by Our Lady, the devyll spede whyt![10]
Therfore I wyll not bete her at all.   25
    And shall I not bete her? no shall?[11]
Whan she offendeth[1] and doth amys,
And kepeth not her house, as her duetie is?
Shall I not bete her, if she do so?
Yes, by Cokkes[12] blood, that shall I do.   30
I shall bete her and thwak her, I trow,
That she shall beshyte the house for very wo.
    But yet I thynk what my neybour wyll say than,
He wyll say thus : "Whom chydest thou, Johan
            Johan?"
"Mary," will I say, "I chyde my curst wyfe,   35
The veryest drab that ever bare lyfe,
Whiche doth nothying but go and come,
And I can not make her kepe her at home."
Than I thynke he will say by and by,
"Walke her cote,[13] Johan Johan, and bete her   40
            hardely."
But than unto hym myn answer shal be,
"The more I bete her the worse is she.
And wors and wors make her I shall."
    He wyll say than, "Bete her not at all."
"And why?" shall I say, "this wolde be wyst,[14]   45
Is she not myne to chastice as I lyst?"
    But this is another poynt worst of all,
The folkes wyll mocke me whan they here me
            brall.[15]
But for all that, shall I let[16] therfore
To chastyce my wyfe ever the more,   50
And to make her at home for to tary?
Is not that well done? Yes, by Saynt Mary,
That is a poynt[17] of an honest man
For to bete his wyfe well nowe and than.
    Therfore I shall bete her, have ye no drede!   55
And I ought to bete her, tyll she be starke dede.

---

10 *devyll . . . whyt:* the   14 *wolde be wyst:* would be
   devil she will (whyt =   known.
   whit).   15 *brall:* scold, revile.
11 *no shall?:* shall I not?   16 *let:* cease.
12 *Cokkes:* God's.   17 *poynt:* mark.
13 *Walke her cote:* Drub or
   beat her.

And why? By God, bicause it is my pleasure,
And if I shulde suffre her, I make you sure,
Nought shulde prevayle[18] me, nother staffe nor
   waster,[19]
Within a whyle she wolde be my mayster. 60
 Therfore I shall bete her, by Cokkes mother,
Both on the tone syde and on the tother,
Before and behynde; nought shall be her bote,[20]
From the top of the heed to the sole of the fote.
 But, masters, for Goddes sake, do not entrete 65
For her, whan that she shal be bete.
But, for Goddes passion, let me alone,
And I shall thwak her that she shall grone.
Wherfore I beseche you, and hartely you pray,
And I beseche you say me not nay, 70
But that I may beate her for this ones.
And I shall beate her, by Cokkes bones,
That she shall stynke lyke a polekat.
But yet, by Gogges body, that nede nat,
For she wyll stynke without any betyng, 75
For every nyght ones she gyveth me an hetyng,[21]
From her issueth suche a stynkyng smoke,
That the savour therof almost doth me choke.
But I shall bete her nowe, without fayle,
I shall bete her toppe and tayle, 80
Heed, shulders, armes, legges, and all,
I shall bete her, I trowe that I shall.
And, by Gogges boddy, I tell you trewe,
I shall bete her tyll she be blacke and blewe.
 But where the dyvell trowe ye she is gon? 85
I holde a noble[22] she is with Syr Johan.
I fere I am begyled alway,
But yet in faith I hope well nay.
Yet I almost enrage[23] that I ne can
Se the behavour of our gentylwoman. 90
And yet, I thynke, thyther as she doth go
Many an honest wyfe goth thyther also,
For to make some pastyme and sporte.

18 *prevayle* : avail.
19 *waster* : cudgel.
20 *bote* : salvation.
21 *hetyng* : heating, bawling
 out.

22 *holde a noble* : bet a noble
 (6s. 8d.).
23 *enrage* : become enraged.

But than my wyfe so ofte doth thyther resorte
That I fere she wyll make me weare a fether.[24]   95
But yet I nede not for to fere nether,
For he is her gossyp,[25] that is he.

    But abyde a whyle, yet let me se,
Where the dyvell hath our gyssypry begon?
My wyfe had never chylde, doughter nor son.   100

    Nowe if I forbede her that she go no more,
Yet wyll she go as she dyd before,
Or els wyll she chuse some other place,
And then the matter is in as yll case.

    But in fayth all these wordes be in wast,   105
For I thynke the matter is done and past.
And whan she cometh home she wyll begyn to
    chyde.

            [*Enter* TYB.]

But she shall have her payment styk[(3)] by her
    syde,
For I shall order her, for all her brawlyng,
That she shall repent to go a catterwawlyng.[26]   110

TYB. Why, whom wylt thou beate, I say, thou knave?
JOHAN JOHAN. Who, I, Tyb? None, so God me save.
TYB. Yes, I harde thee say thou woldest one bete.
JOHAN JOHAN.[2] Mary, wyfe, it was stokfysshe[(4)]
    in Temmes Strete,

Whiche wyll be good meate agaynst Lent.   115
Why, Tyb, what haddest thou thought that I had
    ment?
TYB. Mary, me thought I harde thee bawlyng.
Wilt thou never leve this wawlyng?
Howe the dyvell dost thou thy selfe behave?
Shall we ever have this worke, thou knave?   120
JOHAN JOHAN. What, wyfe, how sayst thou? Was it
    well gest of me[27]

That thou woldest be come home in safete,
As sone as I had kendled a fyre?
Come warme thee, swete Tyb, I thee requyre.

---

24 *weare a fether:* become a
    cuckold. (From "wear
    the bull's feather," i.e.
    horn, the sign of cuck-
    oldry.)

25 *gossyp:* sponsor of her
    child at its baptism.
26 *catterwawlyng:* catcalling,
    i.e. lovemaking.
27 *Was it well gest of me:*
    Could I guess.

TYB. O, Johan Johan, I am afrayd, by this lyght, 125
    That I shal be sore syk this nyght.

JOHAN JOHAN. [*Aside.*] By Cokkes soule, nowe, I dare
        lay a swan
    That she comes nowe streyght fro Syr Johan.
    For ever whan she hath fatched of hym a lyk,[28]
    Than she comes home, and sayth she is syk. 130

TYB. What sayst thou?

JOHAN JOHAN.   Mary, I say,
    It is mete for a woman to go play
    Abrode in the towne for an houre or two.

TYB. Well, gentylman, go to, go to.

JOHAN JOHAN. Well, let us have no more debate. 135

TYB. [*Aside.*] If he do not fyght, chyde, and rate,
    Braule and fare as one that were frantyke,
    There is nothyng that may hym lyke.[29]

JOHAN JOHAN. [*Aside.*] If that the parysshe preest,
        Syr Johan,
    Dyd not se her nowe and than, 140
    And gyve her absolution upon a bed,
    For wo and payne she wolde sone be deed.

TYB. For Goddes sake, Johan Johan, do thee not
        displease,
    Many a tyme I am yll at ease.
    What thynkest nowe, am not I somwhat syk? 145

JOHAN JOHAN. [*Aside.*] Nowe wolde to God, and
        swete Saynt Dyryk,[30]
    That thou warte in the water up to the throte,
    Or in a burnyng oven red hote,
    To se an I wolde pull thee out.

TYB. Nowe, Johan Johan, to put thee out of dout, 150
    Imagyn thou where that I was
    Before I came home.

JOHAN JOHAN.   My percase,[31]
    Thou wast prayenge in the Churche of Poules
    Upon thy knees for all Chrysten soules.

TYB. Nay.

JOHAN JOHAN. Than if thou wast not so holy, 155
    Shewe me where thou wast, and make no lye.

---

28 *fatched . . . a lyk :* fetched   30 *Saynt Dyryk :* St. Theo-
    of him a lick.   doric.
29 *lyke :* please.   31 *percase :* supposition.

TYB. Truely, Johan Johan, we made a pye,
  I and my gossyp Margery,
  And our gossyp the preest, Syr Johan,
  And my neybours yongest doughter An.   160
  The preest payde for the stuffe and the makyng,
  And Margery she payde for the bakyng.
JOHAN JOHAN. [*Aside.*] By Kokkes lylly woundes,[32]
        that same is she
  That is the most bawde hens to Coventre.[33]
TYB. What say you?
JOHAN JOHAN.   Mary, answere me to this: 165
  Is not Syr Johan a good man?
TYB.   Yes, that he is.
JOHAN JOHAN. Ha, Tyb, if I shulde not greve thee,
  I have somewhat wherof I wolde meve thee.[34]
TYB. Well, husbande, nowe I do conject
  That thou hast me somewhat in suspect.   170
  But, by my soule, I never go to Syr Johan
  But I fynde hym lyke an holy man,
  For eyther he is sayenge his devotion,
  Or els he is goynge in processyon.
JOHAN JOHAN. [*Aside.*] Yea, rounde about the bed   175
        doth he go,
  You two together, and no mo,
  And for to fynysshe the processyon,
  He lepeth up and thou lyest downe.
TYB. What sayst thou?
JOHAN JOHAN.   Mary, I say he doth well,
  For so ought a shepherde to do, as I harde tell,   180
  For the salvation of all his folde.
TYB. Johan Johan!
[JOHAN JOHAN.]   What is it that thou wolde?
TYB. By my soule I love thee too too,[35]
  And I shall tell thee, or I further go,
  The pye that was made, I have it nowe here,   185
  And therwith I trust we shall make good chere.
JOHAN JOHAN. By Kokkes body, that is very happy.
TYB. But wotest who gave it?

32 *Kokkes . . . woundes:*   34 *meve thee:* broach to thee.
    God's lovely wounds.   35 *too too:* overmuch.
33 *most . . . Coventre:* worst
    bawd between here and
    Coventry.

JOHAN JOHAN.   What the dyvel rek I?
TYB. By my fayth, and I shall say trewe, than
    The dyvell take me, and it were not Syr Johan.   190
JOHAN JOHAN. O holde the peas, wyfe, and swere no
        more,
    But I beshrewe both your hartes therfore.
TYB. Yet peradventure, thou hast suspection
    Of that that was never thought nor done.
[JOHAN JOHAN.] Tusshe, wife, let all suche matters   195
        be,
    I love thee well, though thou love not me.
    But this pye doth nowe catche harme,
    Let us set it upon the harth to warme.
TYB. Than let us eate it as fast as we can.
    But bycause Syr Johan is so honest a man,   200
    I wolde that he shulde therof eate his part.
[JOHAN JOHAN.][3] That were reason, I thee ensure.
[TYB.][4] Than, syns that it is thy pleasure,
    I pray thee than go to hym ryght,
    And pray hym come sup with us tonyght.   205
JOHAN JOHAN. [*Aside.*] Shall he cum hyther? By
        Kokkes soule I was acurst
    Whan that I graunted to that worde furst.
    But syns I have sayd it, I dare not say nay,
    For than my wyfe and I shulde make a fray.
    But whan he is come, I swere by Goddes mother,   210
    I wold gyve the dyvell the tone to cary away the
        tother.
TYB. What sayst?
JOHAN JOHAN.   Mary, he is my curate, I say,
    My confessour and my frende alway,
    Therfore go thou and seke hym by and by,[36]
    And tyll thou come agayne, I wyll kepe the pye.   215
TYB. Shall I go for him? Nay, I shrewe me than!
    Go thou, and seke, as fast as thou can,
    And tell hym it.
JOHAN JOHAN.   Shall I do so?
    In fayth, it is not mete for me to go.
TYB. But thou shalte go tell hym, for all that.   220
JOHAN JOHAN. Than shall I tell hym, wotest what?[5]
    That thou desyrest hym to come make some chere.

36 *by and by* : immediately.

TYB. Nay, that thou desyrest hym to come sup
        here.
JOHAN JOHAN. Nay, by the rode, wyfe, thou shalt
        have the worshyp
And the thankes of thy gest, that is thy gossyp.   225
TYB. [Aside.] Full ofte I se my husbande wyll me
        rate,
For this hether commyng of our gentyll curate.
JOHAN JOHAN. What sayst, Tyb? let me here that
        agayne.
TYB. Mary, I perceyve very playne
That thou hast Syr Johan somwhat in suspect.   230
But by my soule, as far as I conject,
He is vertuouse and full of charyte.
JOHAN JOHAN. [Aside.] In fayth, all the towne
        knoweth better, that he
Is a horemonger, a haunter of the stewes,
An ypocrite, a knave that all men refuse,   235
A lyer, a wretche, a maker of stryfe,
Better than they knowe that thou art my good
        wyfe.
TYB. What is that, that thou hast sayde?
JOHAN JOHAN. Mary, I wolde have the table set and
        layde,
In this place or that, I care not whether.   240
TYB. Than go to, brynge the trestels hyther.
JOHAN JOHAN.[6] Abyde a whyle, let me put of[37]
        my gown.
But yet I am afrayde to lay it down,
For I fere it shal be sone stolen.
And yet it may lye safe ynough unstolen.   245
It may lye well here, and I lyst.
But, by Cokkes soule, here hath a dogge pyst,
And if I shulde lay it on the harth bare,
It myght hap to be burned, or I were ware.
Therfore [To one in the audience.] I pray you,   250
        take ye the payne
To kepe my gowne tyll I come agayne.
    But yet he shall not have it, by my fay.
He is so nere the dore he myght ron away.

37 *put of:* take off.

But bycause that ye [*To another spectator.*] be
    trusty and sure,
Ye shall kepe it, and[38] it be your pleasure.   255
    [*Gives him the gown.*]
And bycause it is arrayde[39] at the skyrt,
Whyle ye do nothyng, skrape of the dyrt.
    Lo, nowe am I redy to go to Syr Johan,
And byd hym come as fast as he can.
[TYB.] Ye, do so without ony taryeng.   260
    But I say, harke! thou hast forgot one thyng:
Set up the table, and that by and by.
    [*Johan puts the board on the trestles.*]
Nowe go thy ways.
JOHAN JOHAN.   I go shortly.
But se your candelstykkes be not out of the way.
TYB. Come agayn, and lay the table, I say.   265
    What! methynkes ye have sone don.
JOHAN JOHAN. [*Aside, laying the table.*] Nowe I pray
    God that his malediction
Lyght on my wyfe, and on the baulde[40] preest.
TYB. Nowe go thy ways and hye thee, seest?
JOHAN JOHAN. [*Aside.*] I pray to Christ, if my wyshe   270
    be no synne,
That the preest may breke his neck whan he comes
    in.
TYB. Now[7] cum agayn.
JOHAN JOHAN. [*Aside.*] What a myschefe wylt thou,
    fole?
TYB. Mary, I say, brynge hether yender stole.
JOHAN JOHAN. [*Aside.*] Nowe go to, a lyttell wolde
    make me
For to say thus: a vengaunce take thee!   275
TYB. Nowe go to hym, and tell hym playn,
    That tyll thou brynge hym, thou wylt not come
    agayn.
JOHAN JOHAN. This pye doth borne here as it doth
    stande.
TYB. Go, washe me these two cuppes in my hande.
JOHAN JOHAN. I go, [*Aside.*] with a myschyefe lyght   280
    on thy face! [*Washes the cups.*]

38 *and*: if.
39 *arrayde*: soiled. Cf. *ray,*
    l. 510.
40 *baulde*: bald, with shaven
    head.

TYB. Go, and byd hym hye hym apace,
    And the whyle I shall all thynges amende.
JOHAN JOHAN. This pye burneth here at this ende.
    Understandest thou?
TYB.   Go thy ways, I say.
JOHAN JOHAN. I wyll go nowe, as fast as I may.   285
TYB. Now,[8] come ones agayne. I had forgot.
    Loke and there be ony ale in the pot.
JOHAN JOHAN. [*Aside, filling the ale pot.*] Nowe a
                        vengaunce and a very myschyefe
    Lyght on the pylde[41] preest and on my wyfe,
    On the pot, the ale, and on the table,   290
    The candyll, the pye, and all the rable,
    On the trystels, and on the stole;
    It is moche ado to please a curst fole.
TYB. Go thy ways nowe, and tary no more,
    For I am a hungred very sore.   295
JOHAN JOHAN. Mary, I go.
TYB.   But come ones agayne yet.
    Brynge hyther that breade, lest I forget it.
                [JOHAN *brings it.*]
JOHAN JOHAN. Iwys it were tyme for to torne
    The pye, for ywys it doth borne.
TYB. Lorde! how my husbande nowe doth patter,   300
    And of the pye styl doth clatter.
    Go nowe, and byd hym come away.
    I have byd thee an hundred tymes today.
JOHAN JOHAN. [*Aside.*] I wyll not gyve a strawe, I
                        tell you playne,
    If that the pye waxe cold agayne.   305
TYB. What! art thou not gone yet out of this place?
    I had went,[42] thou haddest ben come agayn in
                        the space.
    But, by Cokkes soule, and I shulde do thee ryght,
    I shulde breke thy knaves heed tonyght.
JOHAN JOHAN. [*Aside.*] Nay, than if my wyfe be set a   310
                        chydyng,
    It is tyme for me to go at her byddyng.
    There is a proverbe, whiche trewe nowe preveth,
    He must nedes go that the dyvell dryveth.
                [*He crosses the stage.*]

41 *pylde*: shorn.   42 *went*: thought.

How, mayster curate, may I come in
At your chamber dore, without ony syn?   315
    [*Enter*] SYR JOHAN, *the Preest.*
SYR JOHAN. Who is there nowe that wolde have me?
  What! Johan Johan! what newes with thee?
JOHAN JOHAN. Mary, syr, to tell you shortly,
  My wyfe and I pray you hartely,
  And eke[43] desyre you wyth all our myght,   320
  That ye wolde come and sup with us tonyght.
SYR JOHAN. Ye must pardon me, in fayth I ne can.
JOHAN JOHAN. Yes, I desyre you, good Syr Johan,
  Take payne this ones, and, yet at the lest,
  If ye wyll do nought at my request,   325
  Yet do somewhat for the love of my wyfe.
SYR JOHAN. I wyll not go, for makyng of stryfe.
  But I shall tell thee what thou shalte do,
  Thou shalt tary and sup with me, or thou go.
JOHAN JOHAN. Wyll ye not go than? why so?   330
  I pray you tell me, is there ony dysdayne,
  Or ony enmyte betwene you twayne?
SYR JOHAN. In fayth, to tell thee, betwene thee and
      me,
  She is as wyse a woman as any may be.
  I know it well, for I have had the charge   335
  Of her soule, and serchyd her conscyens at large.
  I never knew her but honest and wyse,
  Without any yvyll, or any vyce,
  Save one faut, I know in her no more,
  And because I rebuke her, now and then, therfore,   340
  She is angre with me and hath me in hate.
  And yet that that I do, I do it for your welth.
JOHAN JOHAN. Now God yeld it yow,[44] god master
      curate,
  And as ye do, so send you your helth,
  Ywys I am bound to you a plesure.   345
SYR JOHAN. Yet thou thynkyst amys, peradventure,
  That of her body she shuld not be a good woman,
  But I shall tell thee what I have done, Johan,
  For that matter; she and I be somtyme aloft,
  And I do lye uppon her, many a tyme and oft,   350

---

43 *eke*: also.   44 *yeld it yow*: repay you for
                                it.

> To prove her, yet could I never espy
> That ever any dyd worse with her than I.

JOHAN JOHAN. Syr, that is the lest care I have of nyne,
Thankyd be God, and your good doctryne.
But yf it please you, tell me the matter,   355
And the debate betwene you and her.

SYR JOHAN. I shall tell thee, but thou must kepe
secret.

JOHAN JOHAN. As for that, syr, I shall not let.[45]

SYR JOHAN. I shall tell thee now the matter playn.
She is angry with me and hath me in dysdayn   360
Because that I do her oft intyce
To do some penaunce, after myne advyse,
Because she wyll never leve her wrawlyng,[46]
But alway with thee she is chydyng and brawlyng.
And therfore, I knowe, she hatyth me[9] presens.   365

JOHAN JOHAN. Nay, in good feyth, savyng your
reverens.

SYR JOHAN. I know very well she hath me in hate.

JOHAN JOHAN. Nay, I dare swere for her, master
curate.

[Aside.] But was I not a very knave?
I thought surely, so God me save,   370
That he had lovyd my wyfe, for to deseyve me,
And now he quytyth[47] hymself, and here I se
He doth as much as he may, for his lyfe,
To stynte[10] the debate betwene me and my
wyfe.

SYR JOHAN. If ever she dyd or thought[11] me any   375
yll,
Now I forgyve her with me fre wyll.
Therfore, Johan Johan, now get thee home,
And thank thy wyfe, and say I wyll not come.

JOHAN JOHAN. Yet, let me know, now, good Syr
Johan,
Where ye wyll go to supper than.   380

SYR JOHAN. I care nat greatly and I tell thee.
On Saterday last, I and two or thre
Of my frendes made an appoyntement,
And agaynst this nyght we dyd assent

---

45 *let*: hesitate.   47 *quytyth*: acquits.
46 *wrawlyng*: squalling,
   bawling.

That in a place we wolde sup together. 385
And one of them sayd, he[12] wolde brynge
    thether
Ale and bread, and for my parte, I
Sayd that I wolde gyve them a pye,
And there I gave them money for the makynge.
And another sayd she wolde pay for the bakyng. 390
And so we purpose to make good chere
For to dryve away care and thought.

JOHAN JOHAN. Than I pray you, syr, tell me here,
Whyther shulde all this geare be brought?

SYR JOHAN. By my fayth, and I shulde not lye, 395
It shulde be delyvered to thy wyfe, the pye.

JOHAN JOHAN. By God, it is at my house, standyng by
    the fyre.

SYR JOHAN. Who bespake that pye, I thee requyre?

JOHAN JOHAN. By my feyth, and I shall not lye,
It was my wyfe, and her gossyp Margerye, 400
And your good masshyp, callyd Syr Johan,
And my neybours yongest doughter An.
Your masshyp payde for the stuffe and makyng,
And Margery she payde for the bakyng.

SYR JOHAN. If thou wylte have me nowe, in faithe I 405
    wyll go.

JOHAN JOHAN. Ye, mary, I beseche your masshyp do
    so,
My wyfe taryeth for none but us twayne.
She thynketh longe or I come agayne.

SYR JOHAN. Well nowe, if she chyde me in thy
    presens,
I wyl be content and take[13] in pacyens. 410

JOHAN JOHAN. By Cokkes soule, and she ones chyde,
Or frowne, or loure,[48] or loke asyde,
I shall brynge you a staffe as myche as I may heve,
Than bete her and spare not, I gyve you good leve,
To chastyce her for her shreude varyeng.[49] 415

    [*They return to* TYB.]

TYB. The devyll take thee for thy long taryeng!
Here is not a whyt of water, by my gowne,
To washe our handes that we myght syt downe.

---

48 *loure*: scowl.   49 *shreude varyeng*: shrew-
                                ish changeableness.

Go and hye thee, as fast as a snayle,
And with fayre water fyll me this payle.   420
JOHAN JOHAN. I thanke our Lorde of his good grace
  That I cannot rest longe in a place.
TYB. Go fetche water, I say, at a worde,
  For it is tyme the pye were on the borde.
  And go with a vengeance, and say thou art prayde.   425
SYR JOHAN. A! good gossyp! is that well sayde?
TYB. Welcome, myn owne swete harte,
  We shall make some chere or we departe.
JOHAN JOHAN. [Aside.] Cokkes soule, loke howe he
            approcheth nere
  Unto my wyfe; this abateth my chere.   430
                          [Exit with the pail.]
SYR JOHAN. By God, I wolde ye had harde the tryfyls,
  The toys, the mokkes, the fables, and the nyfyls;[50]
  That I made thy husbande to beleve and thynke!
  Thou myghtest as well into the erthe synke,
  As thou coudest forbeare laughyng any whyle.   435
TYB. I pray thee let me here part of that wyle.
SYR JOHAN. Mary, I shall tell thee as fast as I can.
  But peas, no more; yonder cometh thy good man.
                  [Re-enter JOHAN.]
JOHAN JOHAN. [Aside.] Cokkes soule, what have we
            here?
  As far as I sawe, he drewe very nere   440
  Unto my wyfe.
TYB.   What, art come so sone?
  Gyve us water to wasshe nowe; have done.
    Than he bryngeth the payle empty.
JOHAN JOHAN. By Kockes soule, it was even nowe full
            to the brynk,
  But it was out agayne or I coude thynke,
  Wherof I marveled, by God Almyght,   445
  And than I loked betwene me and the lyght,
  And I spyed a clyfte,[51] bothe large and wyde.
  Lo, wyfe! here it is, on the tone syde.
TYB. Why dost not stop it?
JOHAN JOHAN.   Why, howe shall I do it?
TYB. Take a lytle wax.
JOHAN JOHAN.   Howe shal I come to it?   450

----

50 *nyfyls*: fictions.   51 *clyfte*: cleft, split.

SYR JOHAN. Mary, here be two wax candyls, I say,
 Whiche my gossyp Margery gave me yesterday.
TYB. Tusshe, let hym alone, for, by the rode,
 It is pyte to helpe hym or do hym good.
SYR JOHAN. What! Johan Johan, canst thou make no 455
   shyfte?
Take this waxe, and stop therwith the clyfte.
JOHAN JOHAN. This waxe is as harde as any wyre.
TYB. Thou must chafe[5] it a lytle at the fyre.
    [JOHAN *does so*.]
JOHAN JOHAN. She that boughte thee these waxe
   candelles twayne,
 She is a good companyon, certayn.   460
TYB. What, was it not my gossyp Margery?
SYR JOHAN. Yes, she is a blessed woman surely.
TYB. Nowe wolde God I were as good as she,
 For she is vertuous, and full of charyte.
JOHAN JOHAN. [*Aside*.] Nowe, so God helpe me, and 465
   by my holydome,
 She is the erranst baud betwene this and Rome.
TYB. What sayst?
JOHAN JOHAN. Mary, I chafe the wax,
 And I chafe it so hard that my fingers krakkes.
 But take up this py that I here torne.
 And it stand long, ywys it wyll borne.   470
TYB. Ye,[14] but thou must chafe[15] the wax, I say.
JOHAN JOHAN. Byd hym syt down, I thee pray—
 Syt down, good Syr Johan, I you requyre.
TYB. Go, I say, and chafe the wax by the fyre,
 Whyle that we sup, Syr Johan and I.   475
JOHAN JOHAN. And how now, what wyll ye do with
   the py?
 Shall I not ete therof a morsell?
TYB. Go and chafe the wax whyle thou art well,
 And let us have no more pratyng thus.
SYR JOHAN. [*Starting to say grace*.] Benedicite . . .
JOHAN JOHAN.   *Dominus*. 480
TYB. Now go chafe the wax, with a myschyfe.
JOHAN JOHAN. What! I come to blysse the bord,[6]
   swete wyfe!
 It is my custome now and than.
 Mych good do it you, Master Syr Johan.
TYB. Go chafe the wax, and here no lenger tary. 485

[JOHAN *retreats to the fire.*]

JOHAN JOHAN. [*Aside.*] And is not this a very purga-
    tory
    To se folkes ete, and may not ete a byt?
    By Kokkes soule, I am a very wodcok.[52]
    This payle here, now a vengaunce take it!
    Now my wyfe gyveth me a proud mok!   490
TYB. What dost?

JOHAN JOHAN.   Mary, I chafe the wax here,
    And I ymagyn to make you good chere,
    [*Aside.*] That a vengaunce take you both as ye syt,
    For I know well I shall not ete a byt.
    But yet, in feyth, yf I myght ete one morsell,   495
    I wold thynk the matter went very well.

SYR JOHAN. Gossyp Johan Johan, now mych good do
    it you.
    What chere make you, there by the fyre?

JOHAN JOHAN. Master parson, I thank yow now.
    I fare well inow after myne own desyre.   500

SYR JOHAN. What dost, Johan Johan, I thee requyre?

JOHAN JOHAN. I chafe the wax here by the fyre.

TYB. Here is good drynk, and here is a good py.

SYR JOHAN. We fare very well, thankyd be Our Lady.

TYB. Loke how the kokold chafyth the wax that is   505
    hard,
    And for his lyfe, daryth not loke hetherward.

SYR JOHAN. What doth my gossyp?

JOHAN JOHAN.   I chafe the wax—
    [*Aside.*] And I chafe it so hard that my fyngers
        krakkes,
    And eke the smoke puttyth out my eyes two.
    I burne my face and ray my clothys also,   510
    And yet I dare nat say one word,
    And they syt laughyng yender at the bord.

TYB.[16] Now, by my trouth, it is a pretty jape,[53]
    For a wyfe to make her husband her ape.[54]
    Loke of Johan Johan, which maketh hard shyft   515
    To chafe the wax, to stop therwith the clyft.

JOHAN JOHAN. [*Aside.*] Ye, that a vengeance take ye
    both two,

---

52 *wodcok :* woodcock (noted   53 *jape :* jest.
    for stupidity).   54 *ape :* fool.

Both hym and thee, and thee and hym also,
And that ye may choke with the same mete
At the furst mursell that ye do ete. 520
TYB. Of what thyng now dost thou clatter,
Johan Johan? Or whereof dost thou patter?
JOHAN JOHAN. I chafe the wax, and make hard shyft
To stopt herwith of the payll the ryft.[17]
SYR JOHAN. So must he do, Johan Johan, by my father 525
kyn,
That is bound of wedlok in the yoke.
JOHAN JOHAN. [Aside.] Loke how the pyld preest
crammyth in,
That wold to God he myght therwith choke.
TYB. Now, Master Parson, pleasyth your goodnes
To tell us some tale of myrth or sadnes, 530
For our pastyme, in way of communycacyon.
SYR JOHAN. I am content to do it for our recreacyon,
And of three myracles I shall to you say.[7]
JOHAN JOHAN. What, must I chafe the wax all day,
And stond here, rostyng by the fyre? 535
SYR JOHAN. Thou must do somwhat at thy wyves
desyre!
I know a man whych weddyd had a wyfe,
As fayre a woman as ever bare lyfe,
And within a senyght after, ryght sone
He went beyond[18] se, and left her alone, 540
And taryed there about a seven yere.
And as he cam homeward he had a hevy chere,
For it was told hym that she was in heven.
But when that he comen home agayn was,
He found his wyfe, and with her chyldren seven, 545
Whiche she had had in the mene space.
Yet had she not had so many by thre
Yf she had not had the help of me.
Is not this a myracle, yf ever were any,
That this good wyfe shuld have chyldren so many 550
Here in this town, whyle her husband shuld be
Beyond[19] the se, in a farre contre?
JOHAN JOHAN. Now, in good soth, this is a wonderous
myracle,
But for your labour, I wolde that your tacle[55]

55 *tacle*: genitals.

Were in a skaldyng water well sod.[56]   555
TYB. Peace, I say, thou lettest[57] the worde of God.
SYR JOHAN. Another myracle eke I shall you say,
    Of a woman whiche that many a day
    Had ben wedded, and in all that season
    She had no chylde, nother doughter nor son.   560
    Wherfore to Saynt Modwin[(8)] she went on pil-
                grimage,
    And offered there a lyve pyg, as is the usage
    Of the wyves that in London dwell.
    And through the vertue therof, truly to tell,
    Within a moneth after, ryght shortly,   565
    She was delyvered of a chylde as moche as I.
    How say you, is not this myracle wonderous?[20]
JOHAN JOHAN. Yes, in good soth, syr, it is marvelous.
    But surely, after myn opynyon,
    That chylde was nother doughter nor son.   570
    For certaynly, and I be not begylde,
    She was delyvered of a knave chylde.
TYB. Peas, I say, for Goddes passyon,
    Thou lettest Syr Johans communication.
SYR JOHAN. The thyrde myracle also is this: 575
    I knewe another woman eke, ywys,
    Whiche was wedded, and within five monthis after
    She was delyvered of a fayre doughter,
    As well formed in every membre and joynt,
    And as perfyte in every poynt   580
    As though she had gone five monthis full to th'
                ende.
    Lo! here is five monthis of advantage.
JOHAN JOHAN. A wonderous myracle, so God me
                mende!
    I wolde eche wyfe that is bounde in maryage,
    And that is wedded here within this place,   585
    Myght have as quicke spede in every suche case.
TYB. Forsoth, Syr Johan, yet for all that
    I have sene the day that Pus, my cat,
    Hath had in a yere kytlyns eyghtene.
JOHAN JOHAN. Ye, Tyb, my wyfe, and that have I sene.   590
    But howe say you, Syr Johan, was it good, your
                pye?[(9)]

56 *sod* : boiled.   57 *lettest* : hinderest.

The dyvell the morsell that therof eate I.
By the good Lorde this is a pyteous warke.[58]
But nowe I se well the olde proverbe is treu:
The parysshe preest forgetteth that ever he was   595
    clarke!
But, Syr Johan, doth not remembre you
How I was your clerke, and holpe you Masse to
    syng,
And hylde the basyn alway at the offryng?
Ye never had halfe so good a clarke as I!
But, notwithstandyng[21] all this, nowe our pye   600
Is eaten up, there is not lefte a byt,
And you two together there do syt,
Eatynge and drynkynge at your owne desyre,
And I am Johan Johan, whiche must stande by the
    fyre,
Chafyng the wax, and dare none other wyse do.   605
SYR JOHAN. And shall we alway syt here styll, we two?
That were to[o] mych.
TYB.   Then ryse we out of this place.
SYR JOHAN. And kys me than in the stede of grace,
And farewell leman[59] and my love so dere.
JOHAN JOHAN. Cokkes body, this waxe it waxte colde   610
    agayn here.
But what! shall I anone go to bed,
And eate nothyng, nother meate nor brede?
I have not be wont to have suche fare.
TYB. Why! were ye not served there as ye are,
Chafyng the waxe, standying by the fyre?   615
JOHAN JOHAN. Why, what mete gave ye me, I you re-
    quyre?
SYR JOHAN. Wast thou not served, I pray thee
    hartely,
Both with the brede, the ale, and the pye?
JOHAN JOHAN. No, syr, I had none of that fare.
TYB. Why! were ye not served there as ye are,   620
    Standyng by the fyre, chafyng the waxe?
JOHAN JOHAN. Lo, here be many tryfyls and knakkes[60]
    By Kokkes soule, they wene I am other dronke or
    mad.

58 *warke*: chore, or perhaps
    in the sense of pain,
    ache.
59 *leman*: sweetheart.
60 *tryfyls and knakkes*: lies
    and tricks.

TYB. And had ye no meate, Johan Johan? no had?

JOHAN JOHAN. No, Tyb my wyfe, I had not a whyt.   625

TYB. What, not a morsel?

JOHAN JOHAN.   No, not one byt.

   For honger, I trowe, I shall fall in a sowne.

SYR JOHAN. O, that were pyte, I swere by my crowne.

TYB. But is it trewe?

JOHAN JOHAN.   Ye, for a surete.

TYB. Dost thou ly?

JOHAN JOHAN.   No, so mote I the![61]   630

TYB. Hast thou had nothyng?

JOHAN JOHAN.   No, not a byt.

TYB. Hast thou not dronke?

No, not a whyt.   JOHAN JOHAN.

TYB. Where wast thou?

JOHAN JOHAN.   By the fyre I dyd stande.

TYB. What dydyst?

JOHAN JOHAN.   I chafed this waxe in my hande,

   Whereas I knewe of wedded men the payne   635

   That they have, and yet dare not complayne.

   For the smoke put out my eyes two,

   I burned my face, and rayde my clothes also,

   Mendyng the payle, whiche is so rotten and olde,

   That it will not skant together holde.   640

   And syth it is so, and syns that ye twayn

   Wold gyve me no meate for my suffysaunce

   By Kokes soule I wyll take no lenger payn,

   Ye shall do all yourself, with a very vengaunce,

   For me, and take thou there thy payle now,   645

           [*Throws it down.*]

   And yf thou canst mend it, let me se how.

TYB. A! horson knave! hast thou brok my payll?

   Thou shalt repent, by Kokes lylly nayll.

   Rech me my dystaf, or my clyppyng sherys :

   I shall make the blood ronne about his erys.   650

JOHAN JOHAN. Nay, stand styll, drab, I say, and come no nere,

   For by Kokkes blood, yf thou come here,

   Or yf thou onys styr toward this place,

        [*Takes a shovel full of coals from the fire.*]

  61 *so mote I the:* as I may
     prosper.

I shall throw this shovyll full of colys in thy face.

TYB. Ye horson dryvyll! Get thee out of my dore. 655

JOHAN JOHAN. Nay! get thee[22] out of my house,
    thou prestes hore.

SYR JOHAN. Thou lyest, horson kokold, evyn to thy
    face.

JOHAN JOHAN. And thou lyest, pyld preest, with an
    evyll grace.

TYB. And thou lyest.

JOHAN JOHAN.   And thou lyest, syr.

SYR JOHAN.   And thou lyest agayn.

JOHAN JOHAN. By Kokkes soule, horson preest, thou 660
    shalt be slayn.

Thou hast eate our pye, and gyve me nought.

By Kokkes blod, it shal be full derely bought.

TYB. At hym, Syr Johan, or els God gyve thee sorow.

JOHAN JOHAN. And have at you,[23] hore and thefe,.
    Saynt George to borow.[62]

Here they fyght by the erys a whyle, and
than the preest and the wyfe go out
of the place.

JOHAN JOHAN. A! syrs! I have payd some of them 665
    even as I lyst,

They have borne many a blow with my fyst.

I thank God, I have walkyd them well,

And dryven them hens. But yet, can ye tell

Whether[63] they be go? for, by God, I fere me,

That they be gon together, he and she, 670

Unto his chamber, and perhappys she wyll,

Spyte of my hart, tary there styll,

And peradventure there he and she

Wyll make me cokold evyn to anger me,

And then had I a pyg in the woyrs panyer.[64] 675

Therfore, by God, I wyll hye me thyder

To se yf they do me any vylany.

And thus fare well this noble company.   [*Exit.*]

FINIS.

62 *to borow:* to protect me.
63 *Whether:* Whither

64 *woyrs panyer:* worse bas-
ket (proverbial).

Imprynted by Wyllyam Rastell
the xii day of February
the yere of our Lord
MCCCCC and xxxiii
Cum privilegio.

KYNG JOHAN

by

JOHN BALE

take vecte with ye, for every acte ye doo ⌐
So shall ye be sure, not out of the waye to goo

Sedicyon in that

here I see ye, I am glad I have spyed ye.

Hab be

there is Sedicyon, stande you asyde a whyle
ye shall see how we. shall catche hym by a wyle ⌐

Sedicyon No noyse amonge ye, where is the mery chere
that was wont to be, with quaffyng of dowble bere ⌐
the worlde is not yet, as some men wolde it have
I have bene abroade, and I thynke I have playde ye knave ⌐

Dyssyle Thou canst do none other, except thou change thy mude

Sedicyon what myschiefe ayle ye, that ye are to me so blunte
I have sene this daye, ye have fancyed me perfectyon

Dyssyle thy selfe is not so, this art of any other complexyon
for thys is thy fee. that fyrst subdued kynge John
very yonge other persons. that sens have ruled thys regyon
And now he doth saye, he hath so played the knave
that the worlde is not yet, as some men wolde it have
It wolde be knowne syr, what he hath done of late ⌐

Sedicyon what is thy name fryde, to us here intymate ⌐

[DRAMATIS PERSONAE.

KYNG JOHAN *of Englande.*
ENGLANDE, *a widow.*
NOBILYTE.
CLERGYE.
CIVYLE ORDER.[1]
SEDICYON, *also called* STEVYN LANGTON.
DISSYMULACYON, *once referred to as Raymundus and finally
  identified with Simon of Swynsett.*
USURPYD POWER, *also called the* POPE (*Innocent III*).
PRIVATE WELTH, *also called* CARDYNALL (*Pandulphus*).
COMMYNALTE.
TREASON, *a monk.*
VERYTE.
IMPERYALL MAJESTYE.
THE INTERPRETOUR.

THE SCENE
ENGLANDE–ROME.]

[ACTUS PRIMUS

ENGLANDE.]

KYNG JOHAN. To declare the powres[1] and their
            force[1] to enlarge
The Scriptur of God doth[2] flow in most abown-
            daunce.
And of sophysteres the cauteles[1], [3] to dyscharge
Bothe Peter and Pawle makyth plenteosse utter-
            auns.
How that all pepell shuld shew there trew ale-   5
            gyauns
To ther lawfull kyng, Christ Jesu dothe consent,
Whych to the hygh powres was ever obedyent.
    To shew what I am, I thynke yt convenyent.
Johan, Kyng of Englande, the cronyclys[2] doth
            me call.

ACTUS PRIMUS
  1 *of . . . cauteles:* the de-
    ceptions of sophists.

My granfather was an empowre[2] excelent,   10
My father a Kyng, by successyon lyneall.
A Kyng my brother, lyke as to hym ded fall.
Rychard Curdelyon, they callyd hym in Fraunce,
Whych had over[4] enymyes most fortynable
          chaunce.

By the wyll of God, and his hygh ordynaunce,   15
In Yerlond and Walys, in Angoye and Normandye,
In Englande also,[3] I have had the governaunce.
I have worne the crown and wrowght vycto-
          ryouslye[4]
And now do purpose, by practyse and by stodye,
To reforme the lawes and sett men in good order,   20
That trew Justyce may be had in every border.
          [*Here enter Widow* ENGLANDE.]
ENGLANDE. Than I trust yowr grace wyll waye[3] a
          poore wedowes cause,
Ungodly usyd, as ye shall know in short clause.
KYNG JOHAN. Yea, that I wyll swer, yf yt be trew and
          just.
ENGLANDE. Lyke as yt beryth trewth, so lett yt be   25
          dyscust.
KYNG JOHAN. Than, gentyll wydowe, tell me what
          the mater ys.
ENGLANDE. Alas, yowr clargy hath done very sore
          amys
In mysusyng me, ageynst all ryght and justice,
And for my more greffe,[4] therto they others intyce.
KYNG JOHAN. Whom do they intyce for to do thee in-   30
          jurye?
ENGLANDE. Soch as hath enterd by false hypocrysye,
Moch worse frutes havyng than hathe the thornes
          unplesaunt,
For they are the trees that God dyd never plant
And as Christ dothe saye, blynd leaders of the
          blynd.[5]
KYNG JOHAN. Tell me whom thow menyst, to satysfy   35
          my mynd.
ENGLANDE. Such lubbers[5] as hath dysgysed heades
          in their hoodes

2 *empowre :* emperor (Geof-   4 *greffe :* grief.
     frey of Anjou).   5 *lubbers :* louts (commonly
3 *waye :* weigh, consider.   applied to priests).

Whych in ydelnes do lyve by other mens goodes :
Monkes, chanons, and nones,[6] in dyvers coloure
    and shappe,
Bothe whyght, blacke, and pyed, God send ther
    increase yll happe.

KYNG JOHAN. Lette me know thy name, or[7] I go fer-   40
    ther with thee.

ENGLANDE. Englande, syr, Englande my name ys, ye
    may trust me.

KYNG JOHAN. I mervell ryght sore, how thow commyst
    chaungyd thus.

      [*Here enter* SEDICYON.]

SEDICYON. What, yow two alone? I wyll tell tales, by
    Jesus,

And saye that I se yow fall here to lycherye.[5]

KYNG JOHAN. Avoyd,[8] lewde person, for thy wordes   45
    are ungodlye.

SEDICYON. I crye yow mercy, sur. I pray yow be not
    angrye.

Be me fayth and trowth, I cam hyther to be
    merye.

KYNG JOHAN. Thow canst with thy myrth in no
    wysse[9] dyscontent me,

So that thow powder yt with wysdom and honeste.

SEDICYON. I am no spycer, by the Messe, ye may be-   50
    leve me.

KYNG JOHAN. I speke of no spyce, but of cyvyle
    honeste.

SEDICYON. Ye spake of powder, by the Holy Trynyte.

KYNG JOHAN. Not as thow takyst yt, of a grosse
    capasyte,

But as Saynt Pawle meanyth, unto the Collessyans
    playne,[(6)]

So seasyne yowr speche that yt be withowt dys-   55
    dayne.

Now, Englande, to thee : Go thow forth with thy
    tale,

And showe the cause why thow lokyst so wan and
    pale.

6 *chanons, and nones :* can-   8 *Avoyd :* Clear out, leave
    ons, and nuns.   us.

7 *or :* ere, before.   9 *in no wysse :* in no wise,
                                 not at all.

ENGLANDE. I told yow before the faulte was in the
            clergye

That I a wedow apere to yow so barelye.

SEDICYON. Ye are a wylly wat[10] and wander here   60
            full warelye.

KYNG JOHAN. Why in the clargye, do me to under-
            stande?

ENGLANDE. For they take from me my cattell,[11]
            howse, and land,

My wodes and pasturs, with other commodyteys,

Lyke as Christ ded saye, to the wyckyd Phary-
            seys,[(7)]

Pore wydowys howsys, ye grosse up by long   65
            prayers,

In syde cotys[12] wandryng, lyke most dysgysed
            players.

SEDICYON. [*Aside.*] They are well at ese, that hath
            soch sothsayers.

KYNG JOHAN. They are thy chylderne, thou owghtest
            to say them good.

ENGLANDE. Nay, bastardes they are, unnaturall, by
            the rood.

Sens ther begynnyng they ware never good to me.   70

The wyld bore of Rome, God let hym never to
            thee,[13]

Lyke pygges they folow in fantysyes, dreames,
            and lyes,

And ever are fed with hys vyle cerymonyes.

SEDICYON. [*Aside.*] Nay, sumtyme they eate bothe
            flawnes[14] and pygyn pyes.

KYNG JOHAN. By the bore of Rome, I trow, thou   75
            menyst the pope.

ENGLANDE. I mene non other but hym, God geve
            hym a rope.

KYNG JOHAN. And why dost thow thus compare hym
            to a swyne?

ENGLANDE. For that he and hys to such bestlynes
            inclyne.

10 *wylly wat :* wily person.   13 *thee :* prosper.
11 *cattell :* possessions.   14 *flawnes :* custards.
12 *syde cotys :* long coats.

They forsake Godes word, whych is most puer
    and cleane,

And unto the lawys of synfull men they leane.   80

Lyke as the vyle swyne the most vyle metes
    dessyer,

And hath gret plesure to walowe themselvys in
    myre,

So hath this wyld bore with his church unyversall,

His sowe with hyr pygys, and monstros bestyall,

Dylyght in mennys draffe[15] and covytus lucre all,   85

Yea, *aper de sylva*[16] the prophet dyd hym call.

SEDICYON. Hold yowr peace, ye whore, or ellys by
    Masse, I trowe,

I shall cawse the pope to curse thee as blacke as
    a crowe.

KYNG JOHAN. What art thow, felow, that seme so
    braggyng bolde?

SEDICYON. I am Sedicyon, that with the pope wyll   90
    hold

So long as I have a hole within my breche.

ENGLANDE. Commaund this felow to avoyd, I you
    beseche,

For dowghtles he hath done me great injury.

KYNG JOHAN. Avoyd, lewd felow, or thou shalt rewe
    yt truly.

SEDICYON. I wyll not away for that same wedred[17]   95
    wytche.

She shall rather kysse where as it doth[6] not
    ytche.

Quodcunque ligaveris,[18] I trow, wyll playe soch a
    parte,

That I shall abyde in Englande magry[19] yowr
    harte.

Tushe, the pope ableth me to subdewe bothe kyng
    and keyser.

---

15 *mennys draffe:* men's
    swill.

16 *aper de sylva:* boar of the
    forest. (Vulgate Psalms
    79:14, A. V. Psalms
    80:13)

17 *wedred:* weathered.

18 *Quodcunque ligaveris:*
    Whatever you may have
    bound (on earth shall
    be bound in heaven).
    Matthew 16:19.

19 *magry:* despite.

KYNG JOHAN. Off that thow and I wyll common more   100
        at leyser.[20]

ENGLANDE. Truly[7] of the devyll they are that do
        ony thyng

To the subdewyng of any Christen kyng,

For be he good or bade, he is of Godes apoyntyng,

The good for the good, the badde ys for yll doyng.

KYNG JOHAN. Of that we shall talke hereafter. Say   105
        forth thy mynd now,

And show me how thou art thus becum a wedowe.

ENGLANDE. Thes vyle popych swyne hath clene
        exyled my hosband.

KYNG JOHAN. Who ys thy husbond, tel me, good gen-
        tyll Englande?

ENGLANDE. For soth, God hymselfe, the spowse of
        every sort

That seke hym in fayth to the sowlys helth and   110
        comfort.

SEDICYON. He is scant honest that so many wyfes wyll
        have.

KYNG JOHAN. I saye hold yowr peace, and stond
        asyde lyke a knave.

Ys God exylyd owt of this regyon, tell me?

ENGLANDE. Yea, that he is, ser, yt is the much more
        pete.[21]

KYNG JOHAN. How commyth yt to passe that he is thus   115
        abusyd?

ENGLANDE. Ye know he abydyth not where his word
        ys refusyd,

For God is his word, lyke as seynt John dothe tell

In the begynnyng of his moste blyssyd Gospell.

The popys pyggys may not abyd this word to be
        hard,[22]

Nor knowyn of pepyll, or had in anye regard :   120

Ther eyes are so sore they may not abyd the lyght,

And ther[8] bred so hard ther gald gummes may
        yt not byght.

I, knowyng yowr grace to have here the gover-
        nance

By the gyft of God, do knowlege my allegeance,

20 *common . . . leyser:* talk   21 *pete :* pity.
        further at leisure.   22 *hard :* heard.

Desyeryng yowr grace to waye suche injuryes   125
As I daylye suffer by thes same subtyll spyes,
And lett me have ryght, as ye are a ryghtfull kyng
Apoyntyd of God to have such mater in doyng.
For God wyllyth yow to helpe the pore wydowes
     cause,
As he by Esaye protesteth in this same clause,   130
Querite judicium, subvenite oppresso,
Judicate pupillo, defendite viduam :[8]
Seke ryght to poore, to the weake and fater-
     lesse,[9]
Defende the wydowe whan she is in dystresse.
SEDICYON. [*Aside.*] I tell ye, the woman ys in great   135
     hevynes!
KYNG JOHAN. I may not in no wyse leve thi ryght
     undyscuste,
For God hath sett me by his apoyntment just
To further thy cause, to mayntayne thi ryght,
And therfor I wyll supporte thee daye and nyght :
So long as my symple lyffe shall here indewer   140
I wyll se thee have no wrong, be fast and swer.[23]
I wyll fyrst of all call my Nobilyte,
Dwkis, erlyes and lords, yche one in ther degre,
Next them the Clergye or fathers spirituall,
Archebysshopes, bysshoppes, abbottes, and pryers   145
     all,
Than the great juges and lawers everych one,
So opynyng to them thi cause and petyfull mone,
By the meanys wherof I shall their myndes under-
     stande.
Yf they helpe thee not, myselfe wyll take yt in
     hande,
And sett such a waye as shall be to thi comforte.   150
ENGLANDE. Than for an answere I wyll shortly
     ageyne resort.
KYNG JOHAN. Do, Englande, hardly,[24] and thow shalt
     have remedy.
ENGLANDE. God reward yowr grace, I beseche hym
     hartely,
And send yow longe dayes to governe this realme
     in peace.

23 *swer :* sure.   24 *hardly :* certainly, by all
                      means.

KYNG JOHAN. Gramercy, Englande, and send thee   155
    plentyus increse.

Go owt ENGLANDE *and drese for* CLERGYE. (9)

SEDICYON. Of bablyng matters, I trow, yt is tyme to
    cease.

KYNG JOHAN. Why dost thow call them bablyng mat-
    ers, tell me?

SEDICYON. For they are not worth the shakyng of a
    pertre²⁵

    Whan the peres are gone, they are but dyble
    dable.

    I marvell ye can abyd suche byble bable.   160

KYNG JOHAN. Thow semyst to be a man of symple
    dyscrescyon.

SEDICYON. Alas, that ye are not a pryst to here con-
    fessyon.

KYNG JOHAN. Why for confessyon? Lett me know thi
    fantasye.

SEDICYON. Becawse that ye are a man so full of
    mercye,

    Namely²⁶ to women that wepe with a hevy harte   165
    Whan they in the churche hath lett but a lytyl
    farte.

KYNG JOHAN. I perseyve well now thow speakyst all
    this in mockage,

    Becawse I take parte with Englandes ryghtfull
    herytage.

    Say thu[¹⁰] what thow wylt, her mater shall not
    peryshe.

SEDICYON. Yt is joye of hym that women so can cher-   170
    yshe.[¹¹]

KYNG JOHAN. God hathe me ordeynned in this same
    princely estate

    For that I shuld helpe such as be desolate.

SEDICYON. Yt is as great pyte to se a woman wepe

    As yt is to se a sely dodman²⁷ crepe,

    Or, as ye wold say, a sely goose go barefote.   175

KYNG JOHAN. Thou semyste by thy wordes to have no
    more wytt than a coote.

    I mervell thou arte to Englande so unnaturall,

---

25 *pertre* : pear tree.   27 *sely dodman* : harmless
26 *Namely* : Especially.   snail.

 Beyng her owne chyld. Thou art worse than a[12]
  best brutall.

SEDICYON. I am not her chyld, I defye hyr, by the
  Messe.

 I her sone, quoth he! I had rather she were hed- 180
  lesse.

 Thowgh I sumtyme be in Englande for my past-
  aunce,

 Yet was I neyther borne here, in Spayne, nor in
  Fraunce,

 But under the pope in the holy cyte of Rome,

 And there wyll I dwell unto the daye of dome.

KYNG JOHAN. But what is thy name, tell me yett onys 185
  agayne?

SEDICYON. As I sayd afore, I am Sedicyon playne :

 In every relygyon and munkysh secte I rayne,

 Havyng yow prynces in scorne, hate and dysdayne.

KYNG JOHAN. I pray thee, good frynd, tell me, what
  ys thy facyon?

SEDICYON. Serche and ye shall fynd in every congre- 190
  gacyon

 That long to the pope, for they are to me full swer,

 And wyll be so long as they last and endwer.

KYNG JOHAN. Yff thow be a cloysterer, tell of what
  order thow art.

SEDICYON. In every estate of the clargye I playe a
  part.

 Sumtyme I can be a monke in a long syd cowle, 195

 Sumtyme I can be a none and loke lyke an owle,

 Sumtyme a chanon in a syrples[28] fayer and
  whyght,

 A chapter howse monke sumtyme I apere in syght.

 I am ower syre John sumtyme with a new shaven
  crowne,

 Sumtyme the person[29] and swepe the stretes with 200
  a syd gowne,

 Sumtyme the bysshoppe with a myter and a cope,

 A graye fryer sumtyme with cutt[30] shoes and a
  rope.

---

28 *syrples* : surplice.   30 *cutt* : ornamentally
29 *person* : parson.   slashed.

Sumtyme I can playe the whyght monke, sumtyme
      the fryer,
The purgatory prist and every mans wyffe desyer.
This cumpany hath provyded for me mortt-   205
      mayne,[31]
For that I myght ever among ther sort remayne.
Yea, to go farder, sumtyme I am a cardynall;
Yea, sumtyme a pope and than am I lord over[13]
      all,
Bothe in hevyn and erthe and also in purgatory,
And do weare three crownes whan I am in my   210
      glorye.
KYNG JOHAN. But what doeste thow here in[14] Eng-
      lande, tell me shortlye?
SEDICYON. I hold upp the pope, as in other places
      many,
For his ambassador I am contynwally,
In Sycell, in Naples, in Venys and Ytalye,
In Pole, Spruse,[32] and Berne, in Denmarke and   215
      Lumbardye,
In Aragon, in Spayne, in Fraunce and in Ger-
      manye,
In Englande, in Scotland,[15] and in other re-
      gyons elles.
For his holy cawse I mayntayne traytors and
      rebelles,
That no prince can have his peples obedyence,
Except yt doth stond with the popes prehemy-   220
      nence.
KYNG JOHAN. Gett thee hence, thow knave, and
      moste presumptuows wreche,
Or as I am trew kyng thow shalt an halter streche.
We wyll thow know yt, owr power ys of God,
And therfore we wyll so execute the rod
That no lewde pryst shall be able to mayneteyne   225
      thee.
I se now they be at to[o] mych lyberte.
We wyll short ther hornys, yf God send tyme and
      space.
SEDICYON. Than I in Englande am lyke to have no
      place.

31 *morttmayne :* mortmain,   32 *Spruse :* Prussia.
    inalienable possession.

KYNG JOHAN. No, that thow arte not, and therfor
           avoyd apace.

SEDICYON. By the holy Masse, I must lawgh to here   230
           yowr grace.

Ye suppose and thynke that ye cowd me sub-
           dewe :

Ye shall never fynd yowr supposycyon trewe,

Thowgh ye wer as strong as Hector and Diomedes,

Or as valyant as ever was Achylles.

Ye are well content that bysshoppes contynew   235
           styll?

KYNG JOHAN. We are so indede, yf they ther dewte
           fullfyll.

SEDICYON. Nay than, good inowgh, yowr awtoryte
           and power

Shall passe as they wyll, they have sawce bothe
           swet and sower.

KYNG JOHAN. What menyst thow by that? Shew me
           thy intente this hower.

SEDICYON. They are Godes vycars, they can both save   240
           and lose.

KYNG JOHAN. Ah, thy meenyng ys that they maye a
           prynce depose.

SEDICYON. By the rood they may, and that wyll ap-
           pere by yow.

KYNG JOHAN. Be the helpe of God we shall se to that
           well inow.

SEDICYON. Nay, that ye can not, thowgh ye had Argus
           eyes,

In abbeyes they have so many suttyll spyes,   245

For ones in the yere they have secret vysytacyons,

And yf ony prynce reforme ther ungodly facyons,

Than two of the monkes must forthe to Rome by
           and by[33]

With secrett letters to avenge ther injury.

For a thowsand pownd they shrynke not in soch   250
           matter,

And yet for the tyme the prynce to his face they
           flater.

I am ever more[16] ther gyde and ther advocate.

KYNG JOHAN. Than with the bysshoppes and monkes
           thu art checke mate.[34]

33 *by and by* : at once.   34 *checke mate* : coequal.

SEDICYON. I dwell among them and am one of ther
    sorte.

KYNG JOHAN. For thy sake they shall of me have but   255
    small comforte.
  Loke wher I fynd thee, that place wyll I put
    downe.

SEDICYON. What yf ye do chance to fynd me in every
    towne
  Where as is fownded any sect monastycall?

KYNG JOHAN. I pray God I synke yf I dystroye them
    not all.

SEDICYON. Well, yf ye so do, yett know I where to   260
    dwell.

KYNG JOHAN. Thow art not skoymose[35] thy fantasy
    for to tell.

SEDICYON. Gesse, at a venture ye may chance the
    marke to hytt.

KYNG JOHAN. Thy falssed[36] to shew no man than
    thyselfe more fytt.

SEDICYON. Mary, in confessyon undernethe *bene-
    dicite.*

KYNG JOHAN. Nay, tell yt agayne, that I may under-   265
    stond thee.

SEDICYON. I say I can dwell, whan all other placys
    fayle me,
  In ere confessyon undernethe *benedicite,*
  And whan I am there, the pryst may not bewray
    me.

KYNG JOHAN. Why wyll ere confesshon soch a secret
    traytor be?

SEDICYON. Whan all other fayle he is so sure as stele.   270
  Offend Holy Churche and I warant ye shall yt fele,
  For by confessyon the holy father knoweth
  Throwowt all Christendom what to his holynes
    growyth.

KYNG JOHAN. Oh, where ys Nobilyte, that he myght
    knowe[17] thys falshed?

SEDICYON. Nay, he is becum a mayntener of owr god-   275
    hed.
  I know that he wyll do Holy Chyrche no wronge,
  For I am his gostly father and techear amonge.[37]

---

35 *skoymose :* squeamish.   37 *amonge :* as well, at the
36 *falssed :* falsehood.   same time.

He belevyth nothyng but as Holy Chyrch doth tell.

KYNG JOHAN. Why, geveth he no credence to Cristes
       holy Gospell?

SEDICYON. No, ser, by the Messe, but he callyth them   280
       heretyckes

That preche the Gospell, and sedycyows scys-
       matyckes,

He tache[38] them, vex them, from prison to prison
       he turne them,

He indygth them, juge them, and in conclusyon
       he burne them.

KYNG JOHAN. We rewe to here this of owr Nobilyte.

But in this behalfe what seyst of the spretuallte?[39]   285

SEDICYON. Of this I am swer, to them to be no
       stranger,

And spesyally, whan ther honor ys in dawnger.

KYNG JOHAN. We trust owr lawers have no such
       wyckyd myndes.

SEDICYON. Yes, they many tymys are my most secrett
       fryndes.

With faythfull prechers they can play legerde-   290
       mayne,

And with falce colores procure them to be slayne.

KYNG JOHAN. I perseyve this worlde[18] is full of iniq-
       uite.

As God wold have yt here cummyth Nobilyte.

SEDICYON. Doth he so in dede, by owr Lord than wyll
       I hence.

KYNG JOHAN. Thow saydest thou woldyst dwell where   295
       he kepyth resydence.

SEDICYON. Yea, but fyrst of all I must chaunge myn
       apparell

Unto a bysshoppe, to maynetayene with my
       quarell,

To a monke or pryst, or to sum holy fryer.

I shuld never elles accomplych my dysyre.

KYNG JOHAN. Why, art thow goyng? Naye, brother,   300
       thow shalte not hence.

SEDICYON. I wold not be sene as I am for fortye
       pence.

---

38 *tache*: arrests, or perhaps   39 *spretuallte*: spirituality,
    merely stigmatizes.   the clergy.

Whan I am relygyouse I wyll returne agayne.

KYNG JOHAN. Thow shalt tary here, or I must put
thee to payne.

SEDICYON. I have a great mynd to be a lecherous
man—

A wengonce take yt, I wold saye a relygyous man.   305
I wyll go and cum so fast as evyr I can.

KYNG JOHAN. Tush, dally not with me. I saye thou
shalt abyde.

[*Tries to hold* SEDICYON.]

SEDICYON. Wene yow to hold me that I shall not
slyppe asyde?

KYNG JOHAN. Make no more prattyng, for I saye
thou shalt abyde.

SEDICYON. Stoppe not my passage, I must over see at   310
the next tyde.

KYNG JOHAN. I wyll ordeyne so, I trowe, thou shalt
not over.

SEDICYON. Tush, tush, I am sewer of redy passage at
Dover.

Her go out SEDICYON *and drese for* CIVYLE ORDER.

KYNG JOHAN. The devyll go with hym, the unthriftye
knave is gon.

[*Enter* NOBILYTE.]

NOBILYTE. Troble not yowrsylfe with no soch dys-
solate persone,

For ye knowe full well very lyttell honeste   315
Ys gote at ther handes in every commynnalte.

KYNG JOHAN. This is but dallyaunce, ye do not speke
as ye thynke.

NOBILYTE. By my trowthe I do, or elles I wold I shuld
synke.

KYNG JOHAN. Than must I marvell at yow of all men
lyvynge.

NOBILYTE. Why mervell at me? Tell me yowr very   320
menyng.

KYNG JOHAN. For no man levynge is in more famyl-
yerite

With that wycked wrech, yf it be trew that he told
me.

NOBILYTE. What wrech speke ye of, for Jesus love
intymate?

KYNG JOHAN. Of that presumtous wrech that was with
      me here[19] of late,

Whom yow wyllyd not to vexe myselfe withall.   325

NOBILYTE. I know hym not I, by the waye that my
      sowll to shall.

KYNG JOHAN. Make yt not so strange, for ye know
      hym wyll inow.

NOBILYTE. Beleve me yff ye wyll, I know hym not, I
      assuer yow.

KYNG JOHAN. Ware ye never yett aquantyd with
      Sedicyon?

NOBILYTE. Syns I was a chyld both[20] hym and his   330
      condycyon

I ever hated for his iniquite.

KYNG JOHAN. A clere tokyn that is of trew nobilyte,

But I pray to God we fynde yt not otherwyse.

Yt was never well syns the clergye wrowght by
      practyse

And left the Scripture for mens ymagynacyons,   335

Dyvydyng themselvys in so many congrygacyons

Of monkes, chanons, and fryers of dyvers colors
      and facyons.

                [*Enter* CLERGYE.]

CLERGYE. I do trust yowr grace wyll be as lovyng
      now

As yowr predysessowrs have[21] bene to us before
      yow.

KYNG JOHAN. I wyll suer wey my love with yowr   340
      behavers,

Lyke as ye deserve, so wyll I bere yow favers.

Clergye, marke yt well, I have more to yow to say

Than, as the sayeng is,[22] the prist dyd speke a
      Sonday.

CLERGYE. Ye wyll do us no wrong, I hope, nor in-
      jurye.

KYNG JOHAN. No, I wyll do yow ryght in seyng yow   345
      do yowr dewtye.

We know the cawtelles of yowr sotyll companye.

CLERGYE. Yf ye do us wrong we shall seke remedy.

KYNG JOHAN. Yea, that is the cast of all yowr com-
      pany.

When kynges correcte yow for yowr actes most
      ungodly,

To the pope, syttyng in the chayer of pestoolens,   350
Ye ronne to remayne in yowr concupysens.
Thus sett ye at nowght all princely prehemynens,
Subdewyng the order of dew obedyens.
But within a whyle I shall so abate yowr pryde
That to yowr pope ye shall noyther runne nor   355
    ryde,
But ye shall be glad to seke to me yowr prynce
For all such maters as shall be within this
    provynce,
Lyke as God wyllyth yow by his Scripture
    evydente.
NOBILYTE. To the Church, I trust, ye wyll be
    obedyent.
KYNG JOHAN. No mater to yow whether I be so or no.   360
NOBILYTE. Yes, mary is yt, for I am sworne ther-
    unto.
I toke a great othe whan I was dubbyd a knyght
Ever to defend the Holy Churches ryght.
CLERGYE. Yea, and in her quarell ye owght onto
    deth to fyght.
KYNG JOHAN. Lyke backes in the darke ye always   365
    take yowr flyght,
Flytteryng in fanseys and ever abhorre[23] the
    lyght.
I rew yt in hart that yow, Nobilyte,
Shuld thus bynd yowrselfe to the grett captyvyte
Of blody Babulon, the grownd and mother of
    whordom,
The Romych churche I meane, more vyle than   370
    ever was Sodom,
And to say the trewth a mete spowse for the
    fynd.[40]
CLERGYE. Yowr grace is fare gonne. God send yow a
    better mynd.
KYNG JOHAN. Hold yowr peace, I say, ye are a lytyll
    to[o] fatte.
In a whyle, I hope, ye shall be lener sumwhatte.
We shall loke to yow and to Civyle Order also.   375
Ye walke not so secrett but we know wher abowght
    ye goo.
        [*Enter* CIVYLE ORDER.]

40 *fynd:* fiend.

CIVYLE ORDER. Why, yowr grace hath no cawse with
            me to be dysplesyd.

KYNG JOHAN. All thynges consyderyd, we have small
            cause to be plesyd.

CIVYLE ORDER. I besech yowr grace to graunt me a
            word or too.

KYNG JOHAN. Speke on yowr pleasure, and yowr hole   380
            mynd also.

CIVYLE ORDER. Ye know very well to set all thynges
            in order

I have moche ado, and many thynges passe fro me
For yowr commonwelth, and that in every border
For offyces, for londes, for lawe and for lyberte,
And for transgressors I appoynt the penalte,   385
That cytes and townes maye stand in quiotose
            peace,
That all theft and murder with other vyce maye
            seace.
Yff I have chaunsed for want of cyrcumspeccyon
To passe the lymytes of ryght and equite,
I submyte myselfe unto yowr graces correccyon,   390
Desyryng pardon of yowr benygnyte.
I wot I maye fall throwgh my fragylyte,
Therfore I praye yow tell me what the mater ys,
And amendes shall be where as I have done amyse.

KYNG JOHAN. Aganste amendement no resonnable   395
            man can be.

NOBILYTE. That sentence rysyth owt of an hygh
            charyte.

KYNG JOHAN. Now that ye are here assembled all
            together,

Amongeste other thynges ye shall fyrst of all
            consyder
That my dysplesure rebounyth on to yow all.

CLERGYE. To yow non of us ys prejudycyall.   400

KYNG JOHAN. I shall prove yt, yes, how have ye usyd
            Englande?

NOBILYTE. But as yt becommyth us, so fare as I
            understond.

KYNG JOHAN. Yes, the pore woman complayneth her
            grevosly,

And not withowt a cawse, for she hath great in-
            jurye.

I must se to yt, ther ys no remedy,   405
For it ys a charge gevyn me from God All-
          myghtye.
How saye ye, Clergye, apperyth it[24] not so to
          yow?
CLERGYE. Yf it lykyth yowr Grace, all we know that
          well ynow.
KYNG JOHAN. Than yow, Nobilyte, wyll affyrme yt, I
          am suer.
NOBILYTE. Ye, that I wyll, sur, so long as my lyfe   410
          indure.
KYNG JOHAN. And yow, Civyle Order, I thynke wyll
          graunte the same?
CIVYLE ORDER. Ondowghted, sir, yea, elles ware yt
          to me gret shame.
KYNG JOHAN. Than for Englandes cause I wyll be
          sumewhat playne.
Yt is yow, Clergye, that hathe her in dysdayne,
With yowr Latyne howrs, serymonyes, and popetly   415
          playes.[41]
In her more and more[25] Godes holy worde
          decayes,
And them to maynteyn unresonable ys the spoyle
Of her londes, her goodes, and of her pore
          chylderes toyle.
Rekyn fyrst yowr tythis, yowr devocyons, and
          yowr offrynges,
Mortuaryes,[42] pardons, bequestes, and other   420
          thynges,
Besydes that ye cache for halowed belles and
          purgatorye,
For jwelles, for relyckes, confessyon, and cowrtes
          of baudrye,
For legacyes, trentalles, with scalacely messys,[43]
Wherby ye have made the people very assys.
And over all this ye have browght in a rabyll   425
Of Latyne mummers and sects desseyvabyll,

41 *popetly playes*: popish   43 *trentalles . . . messys*: sets
      tricks.   of thirty requiem masses,
42 *Mortuaryes*: gifts to priests   and Scala Celi (ladder
      upon the death of pa-   of heaven) masses.
      rishioners

Evyn to dewore her and eat her upp attonnys.[44]

CLERGYE. Yow wold have no Churche, I wene, by
     thes sacred bones.

KYNG JOHAN. Yes, I wold have a churche not of
     dysgysyd shavelynges,

But of faythfull hartes and charytable doynges, 430
For whan Christes Chyrch was in her hyeste glory
She knew neyther thes sectes nor their ipocrysy.

CLERGYE. Yes, I wyll prove yt by David sub-
     stancyally.

Astitit Regina a dextris tuis in vestitu
Deaurato, circumdata varietate.[10]   435

A quene, sayth Davyd, on thy ryght hand, Lord,
     I se

Apparrellyd with golde and compassyd with
     dyversyte.

KYNG JOHAN. What ys yowr meanyng by that same
     Scriptur, tell me?

CLERGYE. This quene ys the Chyrch, which thorow
     all Cristen regions

Ys beawtyfull deckyd with many holy relygyons, 440
Munks, chanons and fryers, most excellent dyvynis,
As Grandy Montensers and other Benedictyns,[11]
Primonstratensers, Bernards, and Gylbertynys,
Jacobytes, Mynors, Whyght Carmes, and Augus-
     tynis,

Sanbenets, Cluniackes, with holy Carthusyans, 445
Heremytes and Ancors, with most myghty
     Rodyans,

Crucifers, Lucifers, Brigettis, Ambrosyanes,[26]
Stellifers, Ensifers, with Purgatoryanes,
Sophyanes, Indianes and Camaldulensers,
Jesuytes, Joannytes, with Clarimontensers, 450
Clarynes and Columbynes, Templers, newe
     Ninivytes,

Rufyanes, Tercyanes, Lorytes and Lazarytes,
Hungaryes, Tuetonykes, Hospitelers, Honofrynes,
Basyles and Bonhams, Solanons and Celestynes,
Paulynes, Hieronymytes, and Monkes of Josaph- 455
     athes Valleye,

44 *attonnys* : at once.

Fulygynes, Flamynes, with bretherne of the black
      alleye,

Donates and Dimysynes, with Canons of S. Marke,

Vestals and Monyals, a worlde to heare them
      barke,

Abbottes and doctors, with bysshoppes and
      cardynales,

Archedecons and pristes, as to ther fortune falles.   460

CIVYLE ORDER. Methynkyth yowr fyrst text stondeth
      nothyng with yowr reson,

For in Davydes tyme wer no such sectes of re-
      lygyon.

KYNG JOHAN. Davyd meanyth vertuys by the same
      diversyte,

As in the sayd psalme yt is evydent to se,

And not munkysh sects, but it is ever yowr cast   465

For yowr advauncement the Scripturs for to wrast.

CLERGYE. Of owr holy father in this I take my
      grownd,

Which hathe awtoryte the Scripturs to expond.

KYNG JOHAN. Nay, he presumyth the Scripturs to
      confownd.

Nowther thow nor the pope shall do pore Eng-   470
      lande wronge,

I beyng governor and kyng her peple amonge.

Whyle yow for lucre sett forth yowr popysh lawys

Yowrselvys to advaunce, ye wold make us pycke
      strawes.

Nay, ipocrytes, nay, we wyll not be scornyd soo

Of a sort of knavys, we shall loke yow otherwyse   475
      too.

NOBILYTE. Sur, yowr sprytes are movyd, I persayve
      by yowr langage.

KYNG JOHAN. I wonder that yow for such veyne
      popych baggage

Can suffyr Englande to be impoveryshyd

And mad a begger. Yow are very yll advysyd.

NOBILYTE. I marvell grettly that ye say thus to me.   480

KYNG JOHAN. For dowghtles ye do not as becummyth
      Nobilyte.

Ye spare nouther landes nor goodes, but all ye
      geve

To thes cormerants. Yt wold any good man
    greve
To see yowr madnes, as I wold God shuld save me.

NOBILYTE. Sur, I suppose yt good to bylde a   485
    perpetuite
For me and my frendes to be prayed for evermore.

KYNG JOHAN. Tush, yt is madnes all to dyspayre in
    God so sore,
And to thynke Christes deth to be unsufficient.[27]

NOBILYTE. Sur, that I have don was of a good intent.

KYNG JOHAN. The intente ys nowght whych hath no   490
    sewer grounde.

CLERGYE. Yff yow continue, ye wyll Holy Chyrch
    confunde.

KYNG JOHAN. Nay, no Holy Chyrch, nor feythfull
    congregacyon,
But an hepe of adders of Antecristes[12] gen-
    eracyon.

CIVYLE ORDER. Yt pyttyth me moche that ye are to
    them so harde.

KYNG JOHAN. Yt petyeth me more that ye them so   495
    mych regarde.
They dystroye mennys sowlles with damnable su-
    persticyon,
And decaye all realmys by meyntenaunce of
    Sedicyon.
Ye wold wonder to know what profe I have of
    this.

NOBILYTE. Well, amenment shal be wher anythyng
    is amysse,
For undowtted God doth open soche thyngs to   500
    prynces
As to none other men in the Crystyen provynces,
And therfor we wyll not in this with yowr Grace
    contend.

CIVYLE ORDER. No, but with Godes grace we shall
    owr mysededes amend.

CLERGYE. For all such forfets as yowr pryncely
    mageste
For yowr owne person or realme can prove by me   505
I submytte myselfe to yow bothe body and goodes.
             Knele.

KYNG JOHAN. We pety yow now consyderyng yowr
    repentante modes,

 And owr gracyous pardone we grawnte yow upon
    amendment.

CLERGYE. God preserve yowr grace and mageste
    excelent.

KYNG JOHAN. Aryse, Clergye, aryse, and ever be 510
    obedyent,

 And as God commandeth yow take us for yowr
    governer.

CLERGYE. By the grace of God the pope shall be my
    ruler.

KYNG JOHAN. What saye ye, Clergye, who is yowr
    governer?

CLERGYE. Ha! ded I stomble? I sayd my prynce ys my
    ruler.

KYNG JOHAN. I pray to owr Lord this obedyence 515
    maye indewre.

CLERGYE. I wyll not breke yt, ye may be fast and
    suer.

KYNG JOHAN. Than cum hether all thre : ye shall
    know more of my mynde.

CLERGYE. Owr kyng to obeye the Scriptur doth us
    bynde.

KYNG JOHAN. Ye shall fyrst be sworne to God and to
    the crowne

 To be trew and juste in every cetye and towne, 520
 And this to performe set hand and kysse the
    bocke.

CIVYLE ORDER. With the wyffe of Loth[45] we wyll
    not backeward locke,

 Nor turne from owr oth, but ever obeye yowr
    Grace.

KYNG JOHAN. Than wyll I gyve yow yowr chargys
    her in place

 And accepte yow all to be of owr hyghe councell. 525

CLERGYE.
NOBILYTE. } To be faythfull than, ye us more
CIVYLE ORDER. streytly compell.

KYNG JOHAN. For the love of Gode, loke to the state
    of Englande.

 45 *Loth* : Lot.

Leate non enemy holde her in myserable bond.
[*To* NOBILYTE.] Se yow defend her as yt becum-
            myth Nobilyte.
[*To* CLERGYE.] Se yow instrutte her acordynge to   530
            yowr degre.
[*To* CIVYLE ORDER.] Fournysh her yow with
            cyvyle honeste.
Thus shall she florysh in honor and grett plente.
With godly wysdom yowr matters so conveye
That the commynnalte the powers maye obey,
And ever beware of that false thefe Sedicyon,   535
Whych poysenneth all realmes and bryng them to
            perdycyon.
NOBILYTE. Sur, for soche wrecches we wyll be so
            circumspectte
That neyther ther falsed nor gylle shall us infecte.
CLERGYE. I warrant yow sur no, and that shall well
            apere.
CIVYLE ORDER. We wyll so provyde, yffe anye of   540
            them cum here
To dysturbe the realme, they shall be full glad to
            fle.
KYNG JOHAN. Well, yowr promyse includeth no small
            dyffyculte.
But I put the[28] case that this false thefe
            Sedicyon
Shuld cum to yow thre, and call hymselfe
            Relygyon,
Myght he not under the pretence of holynes   545
Cawse yow to consent to myche ungodlynes?
NOBILYTE. He shall never be able to do yt, veryly.
KYNG JOHAN. God graunt ye be not deceyvyd by
            hypocresye.
I say no more, I. In shepes aparell sum walke,
And seme relygeyose that deceyvably can   550
            calke.46, [29]
Beware of soche hypocrites as the kyngdom of
            hevyn fro man
Do hyde for awantage, for they deceyve now and
            than.

46 *calke :* calculate.

Well, I leve yow here : yche man consyder his
　　　　dewtye.

NOBILYTE. With Godes leve no faute[47] shall be in
　　　　this companye.

KYNG JOHAN. Cum, Civyle Order, ye shall go hence　　555
　　　　with me.

CIVYLE ORDER. At your commandmente. I wyll
　　　　gladlye wayte upon ye.

　　Here KYNG JOHAN *and* CIVYLE ORDER *go owt,*
　　and CIVYLE ORDER *drese hym for* SEDICYON.

NOBILYTE. Methynke the kyng is a man of a wonder-
　　　　full wytt.

CLERGYE. Naye, saye that he is of a vengeable,
　　　　craftye wytt,

　　Than shall ye be sure the trewth of the thyng to
　　　　hytt.

　　Hard ye not how he of the Holy Church dyd　　560
　　　　rayle?

　　His extreme thretynyngs shall lytyll hym avayle.

　　I wyll worke soch wayes that he shall of his pur-
　　　　pose fayle.

NOBILYTE. Yt is meet a prince to saye sumwhat for
　　　　his plesure.

CLERGYE. Yea, but yt is to[o] moch to rayle so with-
　　　　owt mesure.

NOBILYTE. Well, lett every man speke lyke as he　　565
　　　　hathe a cawse.

CLERGYE. Why, do ye say so? Yt is tyme for me than
　　　　to pawse.

NOBILYTE. This wyll I saye, sur, that he ys so noble
　　　　a prynce

　　As this day raygneth in ony Cristyen provynce.

CLERGYE. Mary, yt apereth well by that he wonne in
　　　　Fraunce.

NOBILYTE. Well, he lost not there so moche by mar-　　570
　　　　tyall chaunce,

　　But he gate moche more in Scotland, Ireland, and
　　　　Wales.

CLERGYE. Yea, God sped us well, Crystmes songes
　　　　are mery tales.

　　47 *faute :* fault.

NOBILYTE. Ye dysdayne soche mater as ye know
        full evydent.
    Are[30] not both Ireland and Wales to hym
        obedyent?
    Yes, he holdyth them bothe in pessable possessyon,   575
    And bycause I wyll not from yowr tale make de-
        gressyon,
    For his lond in Fraunce he gyveth[31] but
        lytell forsse,[48]
    Havyng to Englande all his love and remorse,[49]
    And Angoye he gave to Artur his nevy in
        chaunge. (13)
CLERGYE. Our changes are soch that an abbeye   580
        turneth to a graunge.
    We are so handled we have scarce eyther[32]
        horse or male.[50]
NOBILYTE. He that dothe hate me the worse wyll tell
        my tale.
    Yt is yowr fassyon soche kynges to dyscommend
    As yowr abuses reforme or reprehend.
    You pristes are the cawse that chronycles doth   585
        defame
    So many prynces, and men of notable name,
    For yow take upon yow to wryght them evermore,
    And therfore Kyng Johan ys lyke to rewe yt sore,
    Whan ye wryte his tyme, for vexcyng of the
        Clergye.
CLERGYE. I mervell ye take his parte so ernestlye.   590
NOBILYTE. Yt becomyth Nobilyte his prynces fame
        to preserve.
CLERGYE. Yf he contynew, we are lyke in a whyle to
        starve.[51]
    He demaundeth of us the tenth parte of owr
        lyvyng.
NOBILYTE. I thynke yt is then for sum nessessary
        thyng.
CLERGYE. Mary, to recover that he hath lost in   595
        Fraunce,
    As Normandy dewkedom, and his land beyond
        Orleaunce.

48 *gyveth . . . forsse:* cares   50 *male:* pack, trunk.
    little about.   51 *starve:* perish.
49 *remorse:* compassion.

NOBILYTE. And thynke ye not that a mater
    nessesary?

CLERGYE. No, sur, by my trowth, he takyng yt of the
    Clergye.

NOBILYTE. Ye cowde be content that he shuld take yt
    of us.

CLERGYE. Yea, so that he wold spare the Clergye, by   600
    swet Jesus.

This takyng of us myght sone growe to a custom,

And than Holy Churche myght so be browght to
    thraldom,

Whych hath ben ever from temporall prynces free,

As towchyng trybute or other captyvyte.

NOBILYTE. He that defendeth yow owght to have   605
    parte of yowr goodes.

CLERGYE. He hath the prayers of all them that hathe
    hoodes.

NOBILYTE. Why, ys that inowgh to helpe hym in his
    warre?

CLERGYE. The Churche he may not of lyberte debarre.

NOBILYTE. Ded[33] not Crist hymselfe pay tryb-
    ute[34] unto Ceser?

Yf he payd trybute, so owght his holy vycar.   610

CLERGYE. To here ye reson so ondyscretlye I wonder.

Ye must consyder that Crist that tyme was under,

But his vycar now ys above the prynces all.

Therfor beware ye do not to herysy fall.

Ye owght to beleve as Holy Churche doth teche   615
    yow,

And not to reason in soche hygh materes now.

NOBILYTE. I am unlernyd, my wyttes are sone
    confowndyd.

CLERGYE. Than leve soch materes to men more
    depely growndyd.

NOBILYTE. But how wyll ye do for the othe that ye
    have take?

CLERGYE. The keyes of the Church can all soche   620
    materes off shake.

NOBILYTE. What call ye those kyes, I pray yow hartly
    tell me?

CLERGYE. Owr holy fathers power, and hys hygh
    autoryte.

NOBILYTE. Well, I can no more say, ye are to[o] well
    lernyd for me.
My bysynes ys soche that here now I must leve ye.
CLERGYE. I must hence also so fast as ever maye be   625
To sewe unto Rome for the Churches lyberte.
            Go owt NOBILYTE *and* CLERGYE.
    [*The scene changes to Rome.*]
      Here SEDICYON *cummyth in.*
SEDICYON. Have in[35] onys ageyne[52] in spyght of all
    my enymyes,
For they cannot dryve me from all mennys
    companyes,
And thowgh yt were so that all men wold forsake
    me,
Yet dowght I[36] yt not but sume good women   630
    wold take me.
I loke for felowys that here shuld make sum
    sporte.
I mervell yt is so longe ere they hether[37] re-
    sorte.
By the Messe, I wene the knaves are in the bryers,
Or ells they are[38] fallen into sum order of
    fryers.
Naye, shall I gesse ryght? They are gon into the   635
    stwes.[53]
I holde ye my necke, anon we shall here newes.
    [*Hears* DISSYMULACYON] *seying the leteny.*
Lyst, for Godes passyon! I trow her cummeth sum
    hoggherd
Callyng for hys pygges. Such a noyse I never herd.
    Here cum DISSYMULACYON *syngyng*
      of the letany.[39]
DISSYMULACYON. (*syng*). *Sancte Dominice, ora pro*
    nobis.[54]
SEDICYON. (*syng*). *Sancte pyld monache, I beshrow*   640
    vobis.[55]
DISSYMULACYON. (*syng*). *Sancte Francisse, ora pro*
    nobis.

52 *Have . . . ageyne:* Back to   54 *Sancte . . . nobis:* Holy
    work once again.   Dominic, pray for us.
53 *stwes:* whorehouses.   55 *Sancte . . . vobis:* Holy
                           shorn monk, I curse you.

SEDICYON. Here ye not? Cockes sowle, what meaneth
      this ypocrite knave?

DISSYMULACYON. *Pater noster*, I pray God bryng hym
      sone to his grave,
  Qui es in celis, with an vengeable[40] *sancti-*
    ficetur,(14)

Or elles Holy Chyrche shall never thryve, by saynt   645
      Peter.

SEDICYON. Tell me, good felowe, makyste thou this
      prayer for me?

DISSYMULACYON. Ye are as ferce as thowgh ye had
      broke yowr nose[41] at the buttre.[56]

I medyll not with thee, but here to good sayntes I
    praye

Agenst soch enmyes as wyll Holy Chyrche decaye.
       Here syng this:

A *Johanne Rege iniquo, libera nos, domine*.[57]   650

SEDICYON. Leve, I saye, or by Messe I wyll make yow
      grone.

DISSYMULACYON. Yff thow be jentyll, I pray thee leate
      me alone,

For within a whyle my devocyon wyll be gone.

SEDICYON. And wherfor[42] dost thou praye here so
      bytterly,

Momblyng thy pater noster and chauntyng the   655
      letany?

DISSYMULACYON. For that Holy Chyrch myght save
      hyr patrymonye,

And to have of Kyng Johan a tryumphant vyctorye.

SEDICYON. And why of Kyng Johan? Doth he vexe
      yow so sore?

DISSYMULACYON. Bothe chyrchys and abbeys he op-
      pressyth more and more,

And take[s] of the clergye yt is onresonable to   660
      tell.

SEDICYON. Owte with the popys bulles than, and
      cursse hym downe to hell.

DISSYMULACYON. Tushe, man, we have done so, but
      all wyll not helpe.

56 *buttre :* buttery.

57 *A . . . domine :* From Jo-   han the bad king free us,
                             Lord.

He regardyth no more the pope than he dothe a
     whelpe.

SEDICYON. Well, lett hym alone, for that wyll I geve
     hym a scelpe.[58]

But what arte thou callyd of thyn owne munkych   665
     nacyon?

DISSYMULACYON. Kepe yt in counsell, dane[59] Davy
     Dissymulacyon.

SEDICYON. What, Dissymulacyon! Cokes sowle, myn
     old aquentence.

Par me faye, mon amye, je tote ad voutre
     plesaunce. [15]

DISSYMULACYON. Gramercyes, good frend, with all
     my very hert.

I trust we shall talke more frely or we deperte.[60]   670

SEDICYON. Why, vylyn horson, knowyst not thi cosyn
     Sedicyon?

DISSYMULACYON. I have ever loved both thee and
     thy condycyon.

SEDICYON. Thow must nedes, I trowe, for we cum of
     two bretherne.

Yf thou remember, owr fatheres were on mans
     chylderne.

Thow comyst of Falsed and I of Prevy Treason.   675

DISSYMULACYON. Than Infydelyte owr granfather ys
     by reason.

SEDICYON. Mary, that ys trewe, and his begynner
     Antycrist,

The great pope of Rome, or fyrst veyne popysh
     prist.

DISSYMULACYON. Now welcum, cosyn, by the waye
     that my sowle shall to.

SEDICYON. Gramercy, cosyn, by the holy bysshope   680
     Benno. [16]

Thow kepyst thi old wont, thow art styll an abbe
     man.

DISSYMULACYON. To hold all thynges up I play my
     part now and than.

---

58 *scelpe*: smack, blow.   60 *or we deperte*: before we
59 *dane*: dan, i.e. master **or**   part.
     sir.

SEDICYON. Why, what maner of offyce hast thou
    within the abbey?

DISSYMULACYON. Of all relygyons I kepe the chyrch-
    dore keye.

SEDICYON. Than of a lykelyhod thow art ther generall   685
    porter?

DISSYMULACYON. Nay, of munkes and chanons I am
    the suttyll sorter.

Whyle sum talke with Besse, the resydewe kepe
    sylence.

Thowgh we playe the knavys we must shew a good
    pretence.

Wheresoever sum eate, a serten kepe the froyter.[61]

Wheresoever sum slepe, sum must nedes kepe the   690
    dorter.[62]

Dedyst thou never know the maner of owr
    senyes?[63]

SEDICYON. I was never with them aqueynted, by
    Seynt Denyes.

DISSYMULACYON. Than never knewyst thou the
    knavery of owr menyes.[64]

Yf I shuld tell all, I cowd saye more than that.

SEDICYON. Now, of good felowshyppe, I beseche   695
    thee, shew me what.

DISSYMULACYON. The profytable lucre cummyth ever
    in by me.

SEDICYON. But by what meane? Tell me, I hartely
    pray thee.

DISSYMULACYON. To wynne the peple I appoynt yche
    man his place,

Sum to syng Latyn, and sum to ducke at grace,

Sum to go mummyng, and sum to beare[43] the   700
    crosse,

Sum to stowpe downeward as the heades ware
    stopt with mosse,

Sum rede the Epystle and Gospell at hygh Masse,

Sum syng at the lectorne with long eares lyke an
    asse.

    The pawment of the Chyrche the aunchent
        faders tredes,

---

61 *froyter*: refectory.   63 *senyes*: synods.
62 *dorter*: dormitory.   64 *menyes*: means.

Sum tyme with a portas,[65] sumtyme with a payre   705
    of bedes,
And this exedyngly drawt peple to devoycyone,
Specyally whan they do se so good relygeone.
Than have we imagys of Seynt Spryte and Seynt
    Savyer.[17]
Moche is the sekynge of them to gett ther faver.
Yong whomen berfote, and olde men seke them   710
    brecheles.
The myracles wrought there I can in no wyse ex-
    presse.
We[44] lacke noyther golde nor sylwer, gyrdles
    nor rynges,
Candelles nor taperes, nor other customyd offer-
    ynges.
Thowgh I seme a shepe I can play the suttle foxe.
I can make Latten to bryng this gere to the   715
    boxe.[66]
Tushe, Latten is alone to bryng soche mater to
    passe.
Ther ys no Englyche that can soche prof-
    yghtes[45] compasse,
And therfor we wyll no servyce to be songe,
Gospell nor Pystell, but all in Latten tonge.
Of owr suttell dryftes many more poyntes are   720
    behynde.
  If I tolde yow all we shuld never have an ende.
SEDICYON. *In nomine patris,* of all that ever I hard
    Thow art alone yet of soche a dremyng bussard.[67]
DISSYMULACYON. Nay, dowst thou not se how I in my
    colours jette?[68]
To blynd the peple I have yet[46] a farther   725
    fette.[69]
This is for Bernard, and this is for Benet,
This is for Gylbard, and this is for Jhenet,
For Frauncys this is, and this is for Domynyke,
For Awsten and Elen, and this is for seynt
    Partryk.

65 *portas:* portable breviary.   67 *Thow . . . bussard:* You
66 *bryng . . . boxe:* make   are uniquely stupid.
    this device succeed.   68 *jette:* strut.
                                       69 *fette:* fetch, device.

We have many rewlles, but never one we kepe.   730
Whan we syng full lowde our hartes be fast[47]
    aslepe.
We resemble sayntes in gray, whyte, blacke, and
    blewe,
Yet unto prynces not one of owr nomber trewe,
And that shall Kyng Johan prove shortly, by the
    rode.
SEDICYON. But in the meanetyme yowrselves gett   735
    lytyll good.
Yowr abbeys go downe, I here saye, everywhere.
DISSYMULACYON. Yea, frynd Sedicyon, but thow must
    se to that gere.
SEDICYON. Than must I have helpe, by swete
    saynt[48] Benettes cuppe.
DISSYMULACYON. Thow shalt have a chylde of myn
    owne bryngyng uppe.
SEDICYON. Of thy bryngyng uppe! Cokes sowle, what   740
    knave is that?
DISSYMULACYON. Mary, Private Welth, now hayve I
    tolde thee what.[49]
I made hym a monke and a perfytt cloysterer,
And in the abbeye he becam[50] fyrst celerer,[70]
Than pryor, than abbote, of a thowsand pownd
    land, no wors.
Now he is a bysshoppe and rydeth with an hon-   745
    dryd hors,
And, as I here say, he is lyke to be a Cardynall.
SEDICYON. Ys he so indede? By the Masse, than have
    att all.
DISSYMULACYON. Nay, fyrst Private Welth shall bryng
    in Usurpyd Power
With hys autoryte, and than the gam ys ower.
SEDICYON. Tush, Usurpyd Power dothe faver me of   750
    all men,
For in his trobles I ease his hart now and then.
Whan prynces rebell agenste hys autoryte,
I make ther commons agenst them for[51] to be.
Twenty M^d men[71] are but a mornyng breckefast

70 *celerer:* cellarer, in charge   71 *M^d men:* thousand men.
    of cellar and provisions.

To be slayne for hym, he takyng his repast.   755

DISSYMULACYON. Thow hast I persayve a very
    suttyll cast.

SEDICYON. I am for the pope, as for the shyppe the
    mast.

DISSYMULACYON. Than helpe, Sedicyon, I may styll
    in Englande be.

Kyng Johan hath thretned[52] that I shall over
    see.

SEDICYON. Well, yf thow wylte of me have remedy   760
    this ower,

Go feche[53] Private Welth and also Usurpyd
    Power.

DISSYMULACYON. I can bryng but one, be Mary,
    Jesus mother.

SEDICYON. Bryng thow in the one, and let hym bryng
    in the other.

Here cum in USURPYD POWER *and* PRIVATE
    WELTH, *syngyng on after another.*

USURPYD POWER *syng this. Super flumina Babilonis
    suspendimus organa nostra.*[72]

PRIVATE WELTH *syng this. Quomodo cantabimus*   765
    canticum bonum in terra aliena?[73]

SEDICYON. By the Mas, methynke they are syngyng
    of *placebo.*[74]

DISSYMULACYON. Peace, for with my spectakles *vadam
    et videbo.*[75]

Cokes sowll, yt is they, at the last I have smellyd
    them[54] owt.

Her go and bryng them [*to the rear of the stage.*]

SEDICYON. Thow mayst be a sowe, yf thow hast so
    good a snowt.

[*Aside, to audience.*] Sures, marke well this gere,   770
    for now yt begynnyth to worke.

---

72 *Super . . . nostra:* Over
   the river of Babylon we
   hang our instruments.
   (Cf. Psalms 137:1–2.)

73 *Quomodo . . . aliena:*
   How shall we sing the
   good song in an alien
   land? (Psalms 137:4)

74 *placebo:* I shall assuage.
   First word, and hence
   designation, of the office
   for the dead, from Vulgate Psalms 114:9.

75 *vadam et videbo:* I'll go
   and see.

False Dissymulacyon doth bryng in Private Welth,
And Usurpyd Power, which is more ferce than a
    Turcke,
Commeth in by hym to decaye all spyrytuall helth,
Than I by them bothe, as clere experyence telth.
We four by owr crafts Kyng Johan wyll so   775
    subdwe
That for[55] three C[18] yers all Englande shall
    yt rewe.
DISSYMULACYON. [*Aside, leading* PRIVATE WELTH *for-*
    ward.] Of the clergy, frynds, report
    lyke as ye se,
That ther Private Welth cummyth ever in by me.
SEDICYON. But by whom cummyst thou? By the
    Messe, evyn by the devyll,
For the grownd thow art of the Cristen peplys   780
    evyll.
DISSYMULACYON. And what are yow, ser? I pray yow,
    say good by me.
SEDICYON. By my trowth, I cum by thee and thy
    affynyte.
DISSYMULACYON. [*To* PRIVATE WELTH.] Feche thow
    in thy felow so fast as ever thow can.
PRIVATE WELTH. I trow, thow shalt se me now playe
    the praty man.
Of me, Private Welth, cam fyrst Usurpyd Power.   785
Ye may perseyve yt in pagent here this hower.
      [PRIVATE WELTH *brings* USURPYD
        POWER *forward.*]
SEDICYON. Now welcum, felowys, by all thes bonys
    and naylys.
USURPYD POWER. Among companyons good felyshyp
    never faylys.
SEDICYON. Nay, Usurpyd Power, thou must go backe
    ageyne,
For I must also put thee to a lytyll payne.   790
USURPYD POWER. Why, fellaue Sedicyon, what wylt
    thou have me do?
SEDICYON. To bare me on thi backe and bryng me in
    also,
That yt may be sayde that fyrst Dissymulacyon

Browght in Private Welth to every Cristen nacion,
And that Private Welth browght in Usurpyd   795
    Power,
And he Sedicyon in cytye, towne, and tower,
That sum man may know the feche of all owr
    sorte.

USURPYD POWER. Cum on thy wayes than, that thow
    mayst make thee fort.[76]

DISSYMULACYON. Nay, Usurpyd Power, we shall bare
    hym all thre,
Thyselfe, he, and I, yf ye wyll be rewlyd by me,   800
For ther is non of us but in hym hath a stroke.

PRIVATE WELTH. The horson knave wayeth and yt
    were a croked[56] oke.

Here they shall bare hym in, and
    SEDICYON *saythe.*

SEDICYON. Yea, thus it shuld be, mary, now I am
    alofte.[57]
I wyll beshyte yow all yf ye sett me not downe
    softe.
In my opynyon, by swete saynt Antony,   805
Here is now gatheryd a full honest company.
Here is nowther Awsten, Ambrose, Hierom nor
    Gregory,
But here is a sorte of companyons moch more
    mery.
  They of the Chirch than were fower holy
    doctors,
We of the Chirch now are the fower generall   810
    proctors.
Here ys fyrst of all good father Dissymulacyon,
The fyrst begynner of this same congregac[y]on.
Here is Private Welth, which hath the Chyrch in-
    fecte
With all abusyons, and brought yt to a synfull
    secte.
  Here ys Usurpyd Power that all kynges doth   815
    subdwe
With such autoryte as is neyther good ner trewe,
And I last of all am evyn sance pere[77] Sedicyon.

---

76 *fort*: strong.   77 *sance pere*: peerless.

USURPYD POWER. Under hevyn ys not a more knave
    in condycyon.
  Wher as thou dost cum that commonwelth cannot
    thryve.
  By owr Lord, I marvell that thow art yet alyve.   820
PRIVATE WELTH. Wher herbes are pluckte upp the
    wedes many tymes remayne.
DISSYMULACYON. No man can utter an evydence more
    playn.
SEDICYON. Yea, ye thynke so, yow, now Godes
    blyssyng breke yowr heade,
  I can do but lawgh to her yow, by thys breade.
  I am so mery that we are mett, by saynt John,   825
  I fele not the ground that I do go uppon.
  For the love of God lett us have sum mery songe.
USURPYD POWER. Begyne thyself than, and we shall
    lepe in amonge.
          Here syng.
SEDICYON. I wold ever dwell here to have such mery
    sporte.
PRIVATE WELTH. Thow mayst have yt, man, yf thow   830
    wylt hether resorte,
  For the holy father ys as good a felowe as we.
DISSYMULACYON. The holy father? Why, I pray thee,
    whych is he?
PRIVATE WELTH. Usurpyd Power here, which, thowgh
    he apparaunt be
  In this apparell, yet hathe he autoryte
  Bothe in Hevyn and Erth, in Purgatory and in   835
    Hell.
USURPYD POWER. Marke well his saynges, for a trew
    tale he doth tell.
SEDICYON. What, Usurpyd Power? Cockes sowle, ye
    are owr pope.
  Where is yowr thre crounnys, yowr crosse keys,
    and yowr cope?
  What meanyth this mater? Methynke ye walke
    astraye.
USURPYD POWER. Thow knowest I must have sum   840
    dalyaunce and playe,
  For I am a man lyke as another ys.
  Sumtyme I must hunt, sumtyme I must Alysen kys.

I am bold of yow, I take ye for no straungers,

We are as spirituall, I dowght in yow no daungers.

DISSYMULACYON. I owght to conseder yowr holy fa-   845
    therhode,

From my fyrst infancy ye have ben to me so good.

For Godes sake, wytsave[78] to geve me yowr
    blyssing here

A pena et culpa,[79] that I may stand this day clere.
             Knele.

SEDICYON. From makyng cuckoldes? Mary, that were
    no mery chere.

DISSYMULACYON. A pena et culpa. I trow thow canst   850
    not here.

SEDICYON. Yea, with a cuckoldes wyff ye have dronke
    dobyll bere.

DISSYMULACYON. I pray thee, Sedicyon, my pacyens
    no more stere.[80]

A pena et culpa I desyre[581] to be clere,

And than all the devylles of hell I wold not fere.

USURPYD POWER. But tell me one thyng : dost thou   855
    not preche the Gospell?

DISSYMULACYON. No, I promyse yow, I defye yt to the
    devyll of Hell.

USURPYD POWER. Yf I knewe thow dydest, thou
    shuldest have non absolucyon.

DISSYMULACYON. Yf I do, abjure me, or put me to
    execucyon.

PRIVATE WELTH. I dare say he brekyth no popyshe
    constytucyon.

USURPYD POWER. Soche men are worthy to have owr   860
    contrybucyon.

I assoyle thee here, behynde and also beforne.

Now art thou as clere as that daye thow wert
    borne.

Ryse, Dissymulacyon, and stond uppe lyke a bold
    knyght.

Dowght not of my power, thowgh my aparell be
    lyght.

78 wytsave : vouchsafe.   80 stere : disturb.
79 A . . . culpa : From pun-
    ishment and guilt.

SEDICYON. A man, be the Masse, can not know yow   865
     from a knave,

Ye loke so lyke hym, as I wold God shuld me save.

PRIVATE WELTH. Thow art very lewde owr father so
     to deprave.

Thowgh he for his plesure soche lyght apparell
     have,[59]

Yt is now sommer and the heate ys withowt
     mesure,

And among us he may go lyght at his owne   870
     plesure.

Felow Sedicyon, thowgh thou dost mocke and
     scoffe,

We have other materes than this to be commyned
     of.[81]

Frynd Dissymulacyon, why dost thou not thy
     massage

And show owt of Englande the causse of thi
     farre[60] passage.

Tush, blemysh not, whoreson, for I shall ever as-   875
     syst thee.

SEDICYON. The knave ys whyght leveryd, by the Holy
     Trynyte.

USURPYD POWER. Why so, Private Welth, what ys the
     mater, tell me?

PRIVATE WELTH. Dissymulacyon ys a massanger for
     the Clergye.

I must speke for hym, there ys no remedy.

The Clergye of Englande, which ys yowr specyall   880
     frynde

And of a long tyme hath borne yow very good
     mynde,

Fyllyng yowr coffars with many a thowsande
     pownde,

Yf ye sett not to hand, he ys lyke to fall to the
     grownde.

I do promyse yow truly[61] his hart ys in his
     hose.[62]

Kyng Johan so usyth hym that he reconnyth all to   885
     lose.[63]

81 *commyned of*: discussed.

USURPYD POWER. Tell, Dissymulacyon, why art thow
    so asshamed
  To shewe thy massage? Thow art moche to be
    blamed.
  Late me se those wrytynges. Tush, man, I pray
    thee cum nere.

DISSYMULACYON. Yowr horryble[64] holynes putth
  me in wonderfull fere.

USURPYD POWER. Tush, lett me se them, I pray thee   890
  hartely.

Here DISSYMULACYON *shall delever the*
wrytynges to USURPYD POWER.

I perseyve yt well, thow wylt lose no ceremony.[65]

SEDICYON. Yet is he no lesse than a false knave,
  veryly.
  I wold thow haddyst kyst hys ars, for that is holy.

PRIVATE WELTH. How dost thow prove me that his
  arse ys holy, now?

SEDICYON. For yt hath an hole evyn fytt for the nose   895
  of yow.

PRIVATE WELTH. Yowr parte ys not elles but for to
  playe the knave,[66]
  And so ye must styll contynew to yowr grave.

USURPYD POWER. I saye leve yowr gawdes, and attend
  to me this hower.
  The bysshoppes writeth here to me, Usurpyd
    Power,
  Desyryng assystence of myne auctoryte   900
  To save and support the Chyrches lyberte.
  They report Kyng Johan to them to be very harde,
  And to have the Church in no pryce nor regarde.
  In his parliament he demaundeth of the Clergye
  For his warres the tent[82] of the Chyrches pat-   905
    rymony.

PRIVATE WELTH. Ye wyll not consent to that, I trow,
  by saynt Mary.

SEDICYON. No, drawe to yow styll, but lett none from
  yow cary.

USURPYD POWER. Ye know yt is cleane agenst owr
  holy decrees

82 *tent :* tenth.

That princes shuld thus contempne owr lybertees.

He taketh uppon hym to reforme the tythes and   910
    offrynges,

And intermedleth with other spyrytuall thynges.

PRIVATE WELTH. Ye must sequester hym, or elles that
    wyll mare all.

USURPYD POWER. Naye, besydes all this, before juges
    temporall

He conventeth clarkes of cawses crymynall.

PRIVATE WELTH. Yf ye se not to that, the Churche   915
    wyll have a fall.

SEDICYON. By the Masse, than pristes are lyke to have
    a pange.

For treson, murder, and thefte they are lyke to
    hange.

By Cockes sowle, than I am lyke to walke for
    treasone,

Yf I be taken, loke to yt therfore in seasone.

PRIVATE WELTH. Mary, God forbyd that ever yowr   920
    holy anoynted

For tresone or thefte shuld be hanged, racked, or
    joynted,

Lyke the rascall sorte of the prophane layete.

USURPYD POWER. Naye, I shall otherwyse loke to yt,
    ye may trust me.

Before hymselfe also the bysshoppes he doth con-
    vent,

To the derogacyon of ther dygnyte excelent,   925

And wyll suffer non to the court of Rome to appele.

DISSYMULACYON. No, he contemnyth yowr autoryte
    and seale,

And sayth in his lond he wyll be lord and kyng,

No prist so hardy to enterpryse anythyng.

For the whych of late with hym ware at veryaunce   930

Fower of the bysshoppes, and in maner at
    defyaunce,

Wyllyam of London, and Eustace, bysshope of
    Hely,

Water of Wynchester, and Gylys of Hartford
    trewly.

Be yowr autoryte they have hym excom-
    munycate.[19]

USURPYD POWER. Than have they done well, for he is   935
    a reprobate.
To that I admytt, he ys alwayes[67] contrary.
I made this fellow here the Archebysshope of
    Canterbery,
And he wyll agree therto in no condyc[y]on.
PRIVATE WELTH. Than hath he knowlege that his
    name ys Sedicyon.
DISSYMULACYON. Dowtles he hath so, and that drown-   940
    nyth his opynyon.
USURPYD POWER. Why do ye not saye his name ys
    Stevyn Langton?
DISSYMULACYON. Tush, we have done so, but that
    helpyth not the mater.
The bysshope of Norwych for that cawse doth
    hym flater.
USURPYD POWER. Styke thow to yt fast, we have onys
    admytted thee.
SEDICYON. I wyll not one jote from my admyssyon   945
    fle :
The best of them all shall know that I am he.
Naye, in suche maters lett men beware of me.
USURPYD POWER. The monkes of Canterbery ded more
    at my request
Than they wold at his concernyng that eleccyon.
They chase Sedicyon, as yt is now manyfest,   950
In spytt of his harte. Than he for ther rebellyon
Exyled them all, and toke ther hole possessyon
Into his owne handes, them sendyng over see
Ther lyvynges to seke in extreme poverte.
    This custum also he hath, as it is tolde me :   955
Whan prelates depart, yea bysshope, abbott, or
    curate,
He entreth theyr londes withowt my lyberte,
Takyng the profyghtes tyll the nexte be con-
    secrate,
Instytute, stallyd, inducte, or intronyzate,[83]
And of the pyed monkes he entendeth to take a   960
    dyme.[84]

---

83 *stallyd . . . intronyzate :*   84 *dyme :* tithe amounting to
    installed, inducted, or   a tenth of their posses-
    enthroned.   sions.

All wyll be marryd yf I loke not to yt in tyme.

DISSYMULACYON. Yt is takyn, ser. The some ys un-
             resonnable,

A nynne thowsand marke, to lyve they are not
       able.

His suggesteon was to subdew the Yryshmen.

PRIVATE WELTH. Yea, that same peple doth ease the   965
             Church, now and then.

For that enterpryse they wold be lokyd uppon.

USURPYD POWER. They gett no mony, but they shall
             have clene remyssion,

For those Yryshmen are ever good to the Church.

Whan kynges dysobeye yt, than they begynne to
       worch.

PRIVATE WELTH. And all that they do ys for indul-   970
             gence and pardon.

SEDICYON. By the Messe, and that is not worth a rot-
             tyn wardon.[85]

USURPYD POWER. What care we for that? To them yt
             is venyson.

PRIVATE WELTH. Than lett them have yt, a Godes
             dere benyson.

USURPYD POWER. Now, how shall we do for this
             same wycked kyng?

SEDICYON. Suspend hym and curse hym, both with   975
             yowr word and wrytyng.

Yf that wyll not holpe, than interdyght his land

With extreme cruellnes, and yf that wyll not stand,

Cawse other prynces to revenge the Churchys
       wronge,

Yt wyll profytte yow to sett them aworke amonge.

For clene remyssyon one kyng wyll subdew an-   980
       other,

Yea, the chyld sumtyme wyll sle both father and
       mother.

USURPYD POWER. This cownsell ys good, I wyll now
             folow yt playne.

Tary thow styll here tyll we returne agayne.

       Her go owt USURPYD POWER *and* PRIVATE
             WELTH *and* SEDICYON. USURPYD POWER
             shall drese for the POPE, PRIVATE

85 *wardon:* pear.

WELTH *for a* CARDYNALL [*Pan-*
dulphus], *and* SEDICYON *for*
[STEVYN LANGTON,] *a*
Monke. The CARDY-
NALL *shall bryng*
in the crose and
STEVYN LANGTON
the bocke,
bell, and
candell.

DISSYMULACYON. This Usurpyd Power, whych now is
        gone from hence,

For the Holy Church wyll make such ordynance   985
That all men shall be under his obedyens.

Yea, kynges wyll be glad to geve hym their[68]
        alegyance,

And than shall we pristes lyve here withowt
        dysturbans.

As Godes owne vyker anon ye shall se hym sytt,
His flocke to avaunse by his most polytyke wytt.   990
He shall make prelates, both byshopp and car-
        dynall,[69], (20)

Doctours and prebendes with furde whodes and
        syde[86] gownes.

He wyll also create the orders monastycall,
Monkes, chanons, and fryers with graye coates
        and shaven crownes,

And buylde them places to corrupt cyties and   995
        townes.

The dead sayntes shall shewe both visyons and
        myracles

With ymages and rellyckes he shall wurke ster-
        racles.[87]

He wyll make mattens, houres, Masse and even-
        songe

To drowne the Scriptures for doubte of heresye,
He wyll sende pardons to save mennys sowles   1000
        amonge,

Latyne devocyons with the holye rosarye.

---

86 *syde :* long.
87 *sterracles :* spectacles, per-   haps with play on "miracles."

He wyll apoynt fastynges, and plucke downe
    matrimonye.
Holy water and breade shall dryve awaye the
    devyll.
Blessynges with blacke bedes wyll helpe in every
    evyll.
  Kyng Johan of Englande, bycause he hath re-   1005
    belled
Agaynst Holy Churche, usynge it wurse than a
    stable,
To gyve up his crowne shall shortly be compelled,
And the Albygeanes, lyke heretykes detestable,
Shall be brent bycause agaynst our father they
    babble.[21]
Through Domynyckes preachynge an xviij thou-   1010
    sande are slayne,
To teache them how they shall Holye Churche
    disdayne.
All this to performe he wyll cawse a generall
    cowncell
Of all Cristendom to the church of Laternense.[88]
His intent shall be for to supprese the Gospell,
Yet wyll he glose yt with a very good pretens   1015
To subdwe the Turkes by a Cristen vyolens.
Under this coloure he shall grownd ther many
    thynges,
Whych wyll at the last be Cristen mennys un-
    doynges.
The popys power shall be abowe the powers all,
And eare confessyon a matere nessessary.   1020
Ceremonys wyll be the ryghtes ecclesyastycall.
He shall sett up there both pardowns and pur-
    gatory.
The Gospell prechyng wyll be an heresy.
Be this provyssyon, and be soch other kyndes,
We shall be full suere allwaye to have owr   1025
    myndes.
[*Re-enter* USURPYD POWER *as* THE POPE, PRIVATE
    WELTH *as a* CARDYNALL, *and* SEDICYON
        as STEVYN LANGTON.]

88 *church of Laternense:* the
    church of St. John Lat-
    eran in Rome.

THE POPE. Ah, ye are a blabbe, I perseyve ye wyll
  tell all.

I lefte ye not here to be so lyberall.

DISSYMULACYON. *Mea culpa, mea culpa, gravissima*
  mea culpa.

Geve me yowr blyssyng *pro Deo et sancta*
  Maria.[89]

  Knele and knoke on thi bryst.

THE POPE. Thow hast my blyssyng, aryse now and 1030
  stond asyde.

DISSYMULACYON. My skyn ys so thyke, yt wyll not
  throw glyde.

THE POPE. Late us goo abowght owr other materes
  now.

Say this all thre. We wayte her upon the great holynes of yow.

THE POPE. Forasmoch as Kyng Johan doth Holy
  Church so handle,

Here I do[70] curse[90] hym wyth crosse, boke, 1035
  bell and candle.

Lyke as this same roode[91] turneth now from me
  his face,

So God I requyre to sequester hym of his grace.

As this boke doth speare[92] by my worke man-
  nuall,

I wyll God to close uppe from hym his benyfyttes
  all.

As this burnyng flame goth from this candle in 1040
  syght,

I wyll God to put hym from his eternall lyght.

I take hym from Crist, and after the sownd of this
  bell,

Both body and sowle I geve hym to the devyll of
  hell.

I take from hym baptym, with the other sacra-
  mentes

And suffrages of the churche, bothe ember dayes 1045
  and lentes.

Here I take from hym bothe penonce and confessyon,

89 *pro . . . Maria:* for God
  and Saint Mary.
90 *curse:* excommunicate.
91 *roode:* cross.
92 *speare:* shut, close up.

Masse of the five wondes, with sensyng[93] and
    processyon.
Here I take from hym holy water and holy brede,
And never wyll them to stande hym in any sted.
This thyng to publyshe I constytute yow thre,   1050
Gevyng yow my power and my full autoryte.
Say this all thre. With the grace of God we shall per-
    forme yt than.
THE POPE. Than gett yow foreward so fast as ever ye
    can
Uppon a bone vyage. Yet late us syng meryly.
SEDICYON. Than begyne the song, and we shall folow   1055
    gladly.
        Here they shall syng.
THE POPE. To colour this thyng thow shalte be callyd
    Pandulphus,
Thow Stevyn Langton, thy name shall be Ray-
    mundus.(22)
Fyrst thow Pandulphus shall opynly hym suspend
With boke, bell, and candle. Yff he wyll not so[71]
    amend,
Interdycte his lande, and the churches all up   1060
    speare.
PRIVATE WELTH. I have my massage, to do yt I wyll
    not feare.
      Here go owt and drese for NOBILYTE.
THE POPE. And thow, Stevyn Langton, cummand the
    bysshoppes all
So many to curse as are to hym benefycyall,
Dwkes, erles and lords, wherby they may forsake
    hym.
SEDICYON. Sur, I wyll do yt, and that I trow shall   1065
    shake hym.
THE POPE. Raymundus, go thow forth to the Crysten
    princes all.
Byd them in my name that they uppon hym fall
Bothe with fyre and sword, that the Churche may
    hym conquarre.
DISSYMULACYON. Yowr plesur I wyll no lengar tyme
    defarre.

93 *wondes,   with   sensyng:*
    wounds, with incensing.

THE POPE. Saye this to them also : Pope Innocent the   1070
    Thred
  Remyssyon of synnes to so many men hath
    graunted,
As wyll do ther best to slee hym yf they may.
DISSYMULACYON. Sur, yt shall be don withowt ony
    lenger delay.
THE POPE. In the meane season I shall soch gere
    avaunce
  As wyll be to us a perpetuall furderaunce.   1075
  Fyrst eare confessyon, than pardons, than pur-
    gatory,
  Sayntes worchyppyng than, than sekyng of
    ymagery,
  Than Laten servyce, with the cerymonyes many,
  Wherby owr bysshoppes and abbottes shall get
    mony.
    I wyll make a law to burne all herytykes,   1080
And kynges to depose whan they are sysmatykes.
I wyll allso reyse up the fower beggyng or-
    deres,[23]
That they may preche lyes in all the Cristen
    borderes.
For this and other I wyll call a generall cownsell
To ratyfye them in lyke strength with the Gospell. · 1085
           Here THE POPE, [DISSYMULACYON,
             and SEDICYON] *go owt.*[72]
      [*Enter*] THE INTERPRETOUR.
[THE INTERPRETOUR.] In thys present acte we have to
    yow declared,[73]
As in a myrrour, the begynnynge of Kyng Johan,
How he was of God a magistrate appoynted
To the governaunce of thys same noble regyon,
To see mayntayned the true faythe and relygyon.   1090
But Satan the Devyll, whych that tyme was at
    large,
Had so great a swaye that he coulde it not dis-
    charge.

  Upon a good zele he attempted very farre
For welthe of thys realme to provyde reformacyon
In the Churche therof, but they ded hym debarre   1095
Of that good purpose, for by excommunycacyon

The space of seven yeares they interdyct thy
    nacyon.
These bloudsuppers thus of crueltie and spyght
Subdued thys good kynge for executynge ryght.

In the second acte thys wyll apeare more playne,   1100
Wherin Pandulphus shall hym excommunycate
Within thys hys lande, and depose hym from hys
    reigne.
All other princes they shall move hym to hate,
And to persecute after most cruell rate.
They wyll hym poyson in their malygnyte,   1105
And cause yll report of hym always to be.

This noble Kyng Johan, as a faythfull Moyses,
Withstode proude Pharao for hys poore Israel,
Myndynge to brynge yt owt of the lande of darke-
    nesse,
But the Egyptyanes did agaynst hym so rebell,   1110
That hys poore people ded styll in the desart dwell,
Tyll that duke Josue, whych was our late Kynge
    Henrye,[24]
Clerely brought us in to the lande of mylke and
    honye.

As a stronge David, at the voyce of verytie,
Great Golye, the pope, he strake downe with hys   1115
    slynge,
Restorynge agayne to a Christen lybertie
Hys lande and people, lyke a most vyctoryouse
    kynge,
To hir first bewtye intendynge the Churche to
    brynge
From ceremonyes dead, to the lyvynge wurde of
    the Lorde.
Thys the seconde acte wyll plenteously recorde.   1120

Finit Actus Primus.

[ACTUS SECUNDUS
ENGLANDE.]

SEDICYON *and* NOBILYTE *cum in and say*

NOBILYTE. It petyeth my hart to se the controvercye
 That nowadayes reygnethe betwyn the Kyng and
  the Clergye.
 All Cantorbery monks are now the realme exyled,
 The prystes and bysshoppes contyneally[1] re-
  vyled,
 The Cystean monkes are in soche perplexyte   5
 That owt of Englande they reken all to flee.
 I lament the chaunce, as I wold God shuld me
  save.

SEDICYON. Yt is gracyously sayd. Godes blyssyng
  myght ye have.
 Blyssyd is that man that wyll graunte or con-
  dyssend
 To helpe relygyon or Holy Churche defend.   10

NOBILYTE. For ther mayntenance I have gevyn
  londes full fayer.
 I have dysheryted many a laufull ayer.

SEDICYON. Well, yt is yowr owne good, God shall reward yow for ytt,
 And in hevyn full hyghe for soch good workes shall
  ye sytt.

NOBILYTE. Yowr habyte showyth ye to be a man of 15
  relygeon.

SEDICYON. I am no worse, sur : my name is Good Per-
  feccyon.

NOBILYTE. I am the more glad to be aquented with
  ye.

SEDICYON. Ye show yowrselfe here lyke a noble man,
  as ye be.
 I perseyve ryght well yowr name ys Nobilyte.

NOBILYTE. Yowr servont and umfrey,[1] of trewthe, 20
  father, I am he.

SEDICYON. From Innocent the pope, I am cum from
  Rome evyn now.

ACTUS SECUNDUS
 1 *umfrey :* underling (?)

A thowsand tymes, I wene, he commendyth hym
    unto yow,
And sent yow clene remyssyon to take the
    Chyrches parte.

NOBILYTE. I thanke his holynes, I shall do yt with
    all my harte.

Yf ye wold take paynes for heryng my confessyon,   25
I wold owt of hand resayve this cleane[2] re-
    myssyon.

SEDICYON. Mary, with all my hart. I wyll be full glad
    to do ytt.

NOBILYTE. Put on yowr stolle then, and I pray yow
    in Godes name sytt.

    Here sett downe, and NOBILYTE *shall say*
        benedycyte.

NOBILYTE. *Benedicite.*

SEDICYON.   *Dominus. In nomine Domini*
    Pape,[1] *amen.* Say forth yowr mynd,
    in Godes name.

NOBILYTE. I have synnyd agaynst God, I knowledge   30
    myselfe to blame.
In the vij dedly synnys I have offendyd sore.
Godes ten commaundymentes I have brokyn ever
    more.
My .v. boddyly wytes I have ongodly kepte.
The workes of charyte in maner I have owt slepte.

SEDICYON. I trust ye beleve as Holy Chyrch doth   35
    teache ye,
And from the new lernyng[2] ye are wyllyng for
    to fle.

NOBILYTE. From the new lernyng, mary, God of
    hevyn save me!
I never lovyd yt of a chyld, so mote I the.[2]

SEDICYON. Ye can say yowr crede and yowr Laten
    Ave Mary?

NOBILYTE. Yea, and dyrge also, with sevyn psalmes   40
    and letteny.

SEDICYON. Do ye not beleve in purgatory and holy
    bred?

NOBILYTE. Yes, and that good prayers shall stand my
    soule in stede.

    2 *so mote I the :* so help me.

SEDICYON. Well than, good enowgh, I warant my
           soulle for yowr.

NOBILYTE. Than execute on me the holy fatheres
           power.

SEDICYON. Naye! whyll I have yow here underneth   45
           benedicite,

  In the popes behalfe I must move[3] other
           thynges to ye.

NOBILYTE. In the name of God, saye here what ye
           wyll to me.

SEDICYON. Ye know that Kyng Johan ys a very wycked
           man,

  And to Holy Chyrch a contynuall adversary.

  The pope wyllyth yow to do the best ye canne   50

  To his subduyng for his cruell tyranny,

  And for that purpose this privylege gracyously

  Of clene remyssyon he hath sent yow this tyme,

  Clene to relesse yow of all yowr synne and cryme.

NOBILYTE. Yt is clene agenst the nature of Nobilyte   55

  To subdew his kyng withowt Godes autoryte,

  For his princely estate and power ys of God.

  I wold gladly do ytt, but I fere his ryghtfull[4]
           rode.

SEDICYON. Godes holy vycare gave me his whole[5]
           autoryte.

  Loo, yt is here, man, beleve yt, I beseche thee,   60

  Or elles thow wylte faulle in danger of damnacyon.

NOBILYTE. Than I submyt me to the Chyrches ref-
           ormacyon.

SEDICYON. I assoyle thee here from the kynges
           obedyence

  By the auctoryte of the popys magnifycence.[6]

  Auctoritate Romani pontyficis ego absolvo te.[3]   65

  From all possessyons gevyn to the spiritualte,

  In nomine Domini Pape, amen.

  Kepe all thynges secrett, I pray yow hartely.

NOBILYTE. Yes, that I wyll, sur, and cum agayne
        hether shortly.   *Go owt* NOBILYTE.

      Here enter CLERGYE *and* CIVYLE ORDER
      together, and SEDICYON *shall go up and
      down a praty whyle.*

---

3 *Auctoritate . . . te:* By   pontiff I absolve you.
  authority of the Roman

CLERGYE. Ys not yowr fatherhod Archbysshope of   70
      Canterbery?

SEDICYON. I am Stevyn Langton. Why make ye here
      inquyry?

[CLERGYE *and* CIVYLE ORDER] *knele and say both.*
      Ye are ryght welcum to this same re-
      gyon, trewly.

SEDICYON. Stond up, I pray yow. I trow thou art the
      Clergye.

CLERGYE. I am the same, sur, and this is Civyle Or-
      der.

SEDICYON. Yf a man myght axe yow, what make yow   75
      in this border?

CLERGYE. I herd tell yesterdaye ye were cum into
      the land.

I thowght for to se yow sum newes to understand.

SEDICYON. In[7] fayth, thow art welcum. Ys Civyle
      Order thy frynd?

CLERGYE. He is a good man and beryth the Chyrch
      good mynd.

CIVYLE ORDER. Ryght sory I am of the great con-   80
      trovarsy

Betwyn hym and the kyng, yf I myght yt remedy.

SEDICYON. Well, Civyle Order, for thy good wyll
      gramercy.

That mater wyll be of an other facyon shortly.

Fyrst to begyne with, we shall interdyte the land.

CIVYLE ORDER. Mary, God forbyde we shuld be in   85
      soche band.[4]

But who shall do yt, I pray yow hartyly?

SEDICYON. Pandulphus and I: we have yt in owr
      legacy.

He went to the kyng for that cawse yesterdaye,

And I wyll folow so fast as ever I maye.

Lo, here ys the bull of myn auctoryte.   90

CLERGYE. I pray God to[8] save the popes holy
      majeste.

SEDICYON. Sytt downe on yowr kneys, and ye shall
      have absolucion

A pena et culpa, with a thowsand dayes of pardon.

Here ys fyrst a bone of the blyssyd trynyte.[(3)]

_____

4 *band :* restraint.

A dram of the tord of swete seynt Barnabe.   95
Here ys a fedder of good seynt Myhelles wyng,
A toth of seynt Twyde, a pece of Davyds harpe
    stryng,
The good blood of Haylys, and Owr Blyssyd Ladys
    mylke,
A lowse of seynt Fraunces in this same[9]
    crymsen sylke,
A scabbe of seynt Job, a nayle of Adams too,   100
A maggot of Moyses, with a fart of saynt Fandigo.
Here is a fygge leafe and a grape of Noes vyne-
    yearde,
A bede of saynt Blythe, with the bracelet of a
    berewarde,[5]
The devyll that was hatcht in maistre Johan
    Shornes bote,
That the tree of Jesse did plucke up by the   105
    roote.[(4)]
Here ys the lachett of swett seynt Thomas shewe,
A rybbe of seynt Rabart, with the[10] huckyll
    bone of a Jewe.
Here ys a joynt of Darvell Gathyron,[(5)]
Besydes other bonys and relyckes many one.
In nomine Domini Pape, amen.
Aryse now lyke men, and stande uppon yowr   110
    fete,
For here ye have caught an holy and[11] a
    blyssyd hete.
Ye are now as clene as that day ye were borne,
And lyke to have increase of chylderne, catell,[6]
    and corne.
CIVYLE ORDER. Chyldryn he can have non, for he ys
    not of that loade.[7, [12]]
SEDICYON. Tushe, thowgh he hath non at home, he   115
    may have sume abroade.
Now, Clergye, my frynd, this must thow do for
    the pope,
And for Holy Chyrch: thow must mennys con-
    scyence grope,[8]

5 *berewarde* : bear keeper.   7 *loade* : way of life.
6 *catell* : possessions.   8 *grope* : search into.

And as thow felyst them so cause them for to
    wurcke :

Leat them show Kyng Johan no more faver than
    a Turcke.

Everywher sture them to make an insurreccyon.   120

CLERGYE. All that shall I do, and to provoke them
    more

This interdyccyon I wyll lament very sore

In all my[13] prechynges, and saye throwgh his
    occacyon

All we are under the danger of dampnacyon.

And this wyll move peple to helpe to put hym   125
    downe,

Or elles compell hym to geve up septur and
    crowne.

Yea! and that wyll make those kynges that shall
    succede

Of the Holy Chyrche to stond evermore in drede.

And bysydes all this, the chyrch dores I wyll up-
    seale

And closse up the belles that they ryng never a   130
    pele.

I wyll spere up the chalyce, crysmatory, crosse
    and all,

That Masse they shall have non, baptym nor
    beryall,

And thys I know well wyll make the peple
    madde.

SEDICYON. Mary, that yt wyll, soche sauce he never
    had.

And what wylte thow do for Holy Chyrche, Civyle   135
    Order?

CIVYLE ORDER. For the clargyes sake I wyll in every
    border

Provoke the gret men to take the commonys parte.

With cautyllys[9] of the lawe I wyll so tyckle[14]
    ther hart

They shall thynke all good that they shall passe
    upon,

9 *cautyllys* : deceptions.

And so shall we cum to ower full intent anon,   140
For yf the Church thryve than do we lawers
        thryve,
And yf they decay ower welth ys not alyve.
Therfore we must helpe yowr state masters to up-
        hold,
Or elles owr profyttes wyll cache a wynter colde.
I never knew lawer whych had ony crafty   145
        lernyng
That ever escapte yow withowt a plentyows
        levyng.
Therfore we may not leve Holy Chyrchys quarell,
But ever helpe yt, for ther fall ys owr parell.

SEDICYON. Gods blyssyng have ye, this ger[10] than
        wyll worke I trust.

CIVYLE ORDER. Or elles sum of us are lyke to lye in   150
        the dust.

SEDICYON. Let us all avoyde[11]—be the Messe, the
        Kyng cummyth her.

CLERGYE. I wold hyde myselfe for a tyme yf I wyst
        where.

CIVYLE ORDER. Gow we hence apace, for I have spyed
        a corner.

Here go owt all and KYNG JOHAN *cummyth in.*

KYNG JOHAN. For non other cawse God hathe kynges
        constytute
And gevyn them the sword, but forto correct all   155
        vyce.
I have attempted this thyng to execute
Uppon transgressers accordyng unto justyce,—
And becawse I wyll not be parcyall in myn offyce
For theft and murder to persones spyrytuall,
I have ageynst me the pristes and the bysshoppes   160
        all.
A lyke dysplesure in my fatheres tyme ded fall,
Forty yeres ago, for ponyshment of a clarke.[(6)]
No cunsell myght them to reformacyon call,
In ther openyon they wer so stordy and starke,
But ageynst ther prynce to the pope they dyd so   165
        barke

10 *ger :* device.   11 *avoyde :* depart.

That here in Englande in every cyte and towne
Excommunycacyons as thonder bolts cam downe.
    For this ther captayn had after a pared[15]
        crowne,
And dyed upon yt with owt the kynges consent.
Than interdiccyons were sent from the popes re-   170
        nowne,
Whych never left hym tyll he was penytent,
And fully agreed unto the popes apoyntment
In Englande to stand with the Chyrches lyberte
And suffer the pristes to Rome for appeles to flee.
    They bownd hym also to helpe Jerusalem cyte   175
With ij hundrid men the space of a yere and more,
And thre yere after to maynteyne battell free
Ageynst the Sarazens, whych vext the Spanyardes
        sore.
Synce my fathers tyme I have borne them groge
        therfore,
Consyderyng the pryde and the capcyose[12] dys-   180
        dayne
That they have to kyngs whych oughte over them
        to rayne.
    PRIVATE WELTH *cum in lyke a* CARDYNALL.
God save you, sur Kyng, in yowr pryncly mageste.
KYNG JOHAN. Frynd, ye be welcum, what is yowr
        plesur with me?
PRIVATE WELTH. From the holy father, Pope Innocent
        the thred,
As a massanger I am to yow dyrectyd,   185
To reforme the peace betwyn Holy Chyrch and
        yow,
And in his behalfe I avertyce[13] yow here now
Of the Chyrchys goods to make full restytucyon,
And to accepte also the popes hely constytucyon
    For Stevyn Langton, archebysshop of Cantur-   190
        bery,
And so admytt hym to his state and primacy.
The monkes exilyd ye shall restore agayne
To ther placys and londes, and nothyng of theres
        retayne.

---

12 *capcyose*: captious.   13 *avertyce*: notify.

Owr holy fatheres mynde ys that ye shall agayne
    restore
All that ye have ravyshyd from Holy Chyrche with   200
    the more.
KYNG JOHAN. I reken yowr father wyll never be so
    harde
But he wyll my cawse as well as theres regarde.
I have done nothyng but that I may do well,
And as for ther taxe I have for me the Gospell.
PRIVATE WELTH. Tushe, Gospell or no, ye must make   205
    a recompens.
KYNG JOHAN. Yowr father is sharpe and very quycke
    in sentence,
Yf he wayeth the word of God no mor than so.
But I shall tell yow in this what I[16] shall do.
I am well content to receyve the monkes agayne
Upon amendement, but as for Stevyn Langton   210
    playne
He shall not cum here, for I know his dysposycyon :
He is moche inclyned to sturdynesse[14, 17] and
    sedycyon.
There shall no man rewle in the lond wher I am
    kyng
Withowt my consent, for no mannys plesur lyvyng.
Neverthelesse, yet upon a newe behaver   215
At the popys request hereafter I may hym faver
And graunt hym to have sum other benyfyce.
PRIVATE WELTH. By thys I perseyve ye bare hym
    groge[15] and malyce.
Well, thys wyll I say bycause ye are so blunte,
A prelate to dyscharge Holy Chyrche was never   220
    wont,
But her custome ys to mynyster ponyshment
To kynges and princes beyng dyssobedyent.
KYNG JOHAN. Avant, pevysh prist, what, dost thow
    thretten me?
I defye the worst both of thi pope and thee.
The power of princys ys gevyn from God above,   225
And, as sayth Salomon, ther hartes the Lord doth
    move.

14 *sturdynesse*:   contumacy,   15 *groge*: grudge.
    rebelliousness.

God spekyth in ther lyppes whan they geve juge-
　　　ment :
The lawys that they make are by the Lordes ap-
　　　poyntment.
　　Christ wylled not his the princes to correcte
But to ther precepptes rether to be subjecte.　　　230
The offyce of yow ys not to bere the sword
But to geve cownsell acordyng to Godes word.
He never tawght his to weare nowther sword nor
　　　sallett[16]
But to preche abrode withowt staffe, scrypp, or
　　　walett.[17]
　　Yet are ye becum soche myghty lordes this　　　235
　　　hower
That ye are able to subdewe all princes power.
I can not perseyve but ye are becum Belles
　　　prystes,[18]
Lyvyng by ydolls, yea, the very antychrystes.
PRIVATE WELTH. Ye have sayd yowr mynd, now wyll
　　　I say myn also.
Here I cursse yow for the wrongs that ye have do　　　240
Unto Holy Churche, with crosse, bocke, bell and
　　　candell,
And bysydes all thys I must yow otherwyse han-
　　　dell.
Of contumacy the pope hath yow convyt :
From this day forward yowr lond stond interdytt.
　　The bysshope of Norwyche and the bysshope　　　245
　　　of Wynchester
Hath full autoryte to spred it[18] in Englande here.
The bysshope of Salysbery and the bysshope of
　　　Rochester
Shall execute yt in Scotland everywhere.
The bysshope of Landaffe, seynt Assys, and seynt
　　　Davy
In Walles and in Erlond shall puplyshe yt openly.　　　250
　　Throwghowt all crystyndom the bysshoppes
　　　shall suspend
All soche as to yow any mayntnenance pretend,
And I cursse all them that geve to yow ther harte,

16 *sallett :* headpiece.
17 *scrypp, or walett :* satchel,
　　or knapsack.
18 *Belles prystes :* priests who
　　attach undue importance
　　to bell ringing.

Dewkes, erlles, and lordes so many as take yowr
      parte.
And I assoyle yowr peple from yowr obedyence,   255
That they shall owe yow noyther sewte[19] nor
      reverence.
  By the popys awctoryte I charge them yow to
      fyght
As with a tyrant agenst Holy Chyrchys ryght,
And by the popes auctoryte I geve them abso-
      lucyon
A *pena et culpa,* and also clene remyssyon.   260
SEDICYON *extra locum.* Alarum! Alarum! tro ro ro ro
      ro, tro ro ro ro ro, tro ro ro ro ro![19]
Thomp, thomp, thomp, downe, downe, downe, to
      go, to go, to go!
KYNG JOHAN. What a noyse is thys that without the
      dore is made.
PRIVATE WELTH. Suche enmyes are up as wyll your
      realme invade.
KYNG JOHAN. Ye cowde do no more and ye cam from   265
      the devyll of hell
Than ye go abowt here to worke by yowr wyckyd
      cownsell.
Ys this the charyte of that ye call the Churche?
God graunt Cristen men not after yowr wayes to
      worche.
I sett not by yowr curssys the shakyng of a rod,
For I know they are of the devyll and not of God.   270
Yowr curssys we have that we never yet de-
      maundyd,
But we can not have that God hath yow com-
      maundyd.
PRIVATE WELTH. What ye mene by that I wold ye
      shuld opynlye tell.
KYNG JOHAN. Why, know ye it[20] not? The prechyng
      of the Gospell.
Take to ye yowr traysh, yowr ryngyng, syngyng,   275
      and pypyng,
So that we may have the Scryptures openyng.
But that we can not have, yt stondyth not with
      yowr avantage.

19 *sewte* : suit.

PRIVATE WELTH. Ahe, now I fell yow for this herety-
        call langage.

I thynke noyther yow nor ony of yowres, iwys,[21]
We wyll so provyd, shall ware the crowne after   280
        this.
                Go owt and dresse for NOBILYTE.
KYNG JOHAN. Yt becum not the Godes secret workes to
        deme.[20]

Gett thee hence, or elles we shall teche thee to
        blaspheme.
Oh Lord, how wycked ys that same generacyon
That never wyll cum to a godly reformacyon.
The prystes report me to be a wyckyd tyrant   285
Because I correct ther actes and lyfe unplesaunt.
    Of thy prince, sayth God, thow shalt report non
        yll,
But thyselfe applye his plesur to fulfyll.
The byrdes of the ayer shall speke to ther gret
        shame,
As sayth Ecclesyastes, that wyll a prynce dyf-   290
        fame.[7]
The powrs are of God, I wot Powle hath soch sen-
        tence,
He that resyst them agenst God maketh resys-
        tence.
    Mary and Joseph at Cyryus appoyntment
In the descripcyon to Cesar were obedyent.
Crist ded paye trybute for hymselfe and Peter   295
        to[o,]
For a lawe prescrybyng the same unto pristes also.
To prophane princes he obeyed unto dethe.
So ded John Baptyst so longe as he had brethe.
    Peter, John, and Powle, with the other apostles
        all,
Ded never withstand the powers imperyall.   300
Prystes are so wycked they wyll obeye no power,
But seke[22] to subdewe ther prynces day and
        hower,
As they wold do me, but I shall make them smart,
Yf that Nobilyte and Law wyll take my parte.
        [*Enter* NOBILYTE, CLERGYE, *and*
                CIVYLE ORDER.]

20 *deme* : judge.

CIVYLE ORDER. Dowghtles we can not tyll ye be rec-   305
    onsylyd
  Unto Holy Chyrche, for ye are a man defylyd.

KYNG JOHAN. How am I defylyd, tel me, good gentyll
    mate?

CIVYLE ORDER. By the popes hye power ye are ex-
    comynycate.

KYNG JOHAN. By the word of God, I pray thee, what
    power hath he?

CIVYLE ORDER. I spake not with hym, and therfore I   310
    cannot tell ye.

KYNG JOHAN. With whom spake ye not? Late me know
    yowr intent.

CIVYLE ORDER. Mary, not with God sens the latter
    wecke of Lent.

KYNG JOHAN. Oh mercyfull God, what an unwyse
    clawse ys this,
  Of hym that shuld se that nothyng ware amys!
  That sentence or curse that Scriptur doth not   315
    dyrect
  In my opynyon shall be of non effecte.

CLERGYE. Ys that yowr beleve? Mary, God save me
    from yow.

KYNG JOHAN. Prove yt by Scriptur, and than wyll I yt
    alowe.
  But this know I well, whan Baalam gave the curse
  Uppon Godes peple they war never a whyt the   320
    worse.

CLERGYE. I passe not on the Scriptur, that is inow for
    me
  Whyche the holy father approvyth by his auc-
    toryte.

KYNG JOHAN. Now, alas, alas, what wreched peple ye
    are!
  And how ygnorant yowr owne wordes doth de-
    clare.
  Woo ys that peple whych hath so wycked   325
    techeres.

CLERGYE. Naye, wo ys that peple that hathe so[23]
    cruell rewlars.
  Owr holy father, I trow, cowd do no lesse,
  Consyderyng the factes of yowr owtragyosnes.

NOBILYTE. Com awaye for shame, and make no more
                  ado.

   Ye are in gret danger for commynyng with hym so.   330

   He is accursyd, I mervell ye do not waye yt.

CLERGYE. I here by his wordes that he wyll not
                  obeye yt.

NOBILYTE. Whether he wyll or no, I wyll not with
                  hym talke

   Tell he be assoyllyd. Com on, my frynds, wyll ye
                  walke?

KYNG JOHAN. Oh, this is no tokyn of trew Nobilyte   335

   To flee from yowr kyng in his extremyte.

NOBILYTE. I shall dyssyer yow as now to pardone me.

   I had moche rather do agaynst God veryly

   Than to Holy Chyrche to do any injurye.

KYNG JOHAN. What blyndnes is this? On this peple   340
                  Lord have mercy!

   Ye speke of defylyng, but ye are corrupted all

   With pestylent doctryne or leven pharesayycall.[21]

   Good to[24] faythfull Susan sayd that yt was
                  moche better

   To fall in daunger of men than do the gretter,[22]

   As to leve Godes lawe, whych ys his word most   345
                  pure.

CLERGYE. Ye have nothyng yow to allege to us but
                  Scripture.

   Ye shall[25] fare the worse for that, ye may be
                  sure.

KYNG JOHAN. What shuld I allege elles, thu[26]
                  wycked pharyse?

   To yowr false lernyng no faythfull man wyll agree.

   Dothe not the Lord say, *nunc reges intellege*,[23]   350

   The kyngs of the erthe that worldly cawses juge,

   Seke to the Scriptur, late that be yowr refuge?

CIVYLE ORDER. Have ye nothyng elles but this? than
                  God be with ye.

KYNG JOHAN. One questyon more yet ere ye departe
                  from me.

---

21 *leven pharesayycall:*   23 *nunc reges intellege:* now,
    hypocritical influence   kings, be instructed.
    (leaven Pharisaical).   (Psalms 2 :10).

22 *the gretter:* the greater
    (sin).

I wyll fyrst demaund of yow, Nobilyte,   355
Why leve ye yowr prince and cleave to the pope
      so sore?

NOBILYTE. For I toke an othe to defend the Chyrche
      ever more.

KYNG JOHAN. Clergye, I am sure than yowr quarell
      ys not small?

CLERGYE. I am professyd to the ryghtes ecclesyas-
      tycall.

KYNG JOHAN. And yow, Civyle Order, oweth her sum   360
      offyce of dewtye?

CIVYLE ORDER. I am hyr feed[24, 27] man, who shuld
      defend her[28] but I?

KYNG JOHAN. Of all thre partyes yt is spoken reson-
      ably.

   [*To* NOBILYTE.] Ye may not obeye becawse of the
      othe ye mad.

   [*To* CLERGYE.] Yowr strong professyon maketh
      yow of that same trad.

   [*To* CIVYLE ORDER.] Yowr fee provokyth yow to   365
      do as thes men do,

Grett thyngs to cawse men from God to the devyll
      to go!

Yowr othe is growndyd fyrst uppon folyshenes,
And yowr professyon uppon moche pevyshenes;
Yowr fee last of all ryseth owt of covetusnes,
And thes are the cawses of yowr rebellyosnes.   370

CLERGYE. Cum, Civyle Order, lett us departe from
      hence.

KYNG JOHAN. Than are ye at a poynt[25] for yowr
      obedyence?

CIVYLE ORDER. We wyll in no wysse be partakers of
      yowr yll.

   Here go owt CLERGYE *and dresse for* ENGLANDE
     and CIVYLE ORDER *for* COMMYNALTE.

KYNG JOHAN. As ye have bene ever, so ye wyll con-
      tynew styll.

Thowgh they be gone, tarye yow with me a   375
      whyle:

The presence of a prynce to yow shuld never be
      vyle.

24 *feed:* in fee, obliged, in   25 *at a poynt:* decided.
  feudal sense.

NOBILYTE. Sir, nothyng grevyth me but yowr excom-
　　　　　ynyca[i]on.
KYNG JOHAN. That ys but a fantasy in yowr ymagy-
　　　　　nacyon.

The Lord refuse not soch as hath his great cursse,
But call them to grace, and faver them never the　　　380
　　　worsse.
Saynt Pawle wyllyth you whan ye are among soch
　　　sort,
Not to abhore them but geve them words of[29]
　　　comfort.
Why shuld ye than flee from me yowr lawfull
　　　kyng,
For plesure of soch as owght to do no suche
　　　thyng?
The Chyrches abusyons, as holy seynt Powle do　　　385
　　　saye,
By the princes power owght for to be takyn awaye.
He baryth not the sword withowt a cawse (sayth
　　　he).
In this neyther bysshope nor spirituall man is free,
Offendyng the lawe they are under the poweres
　　　all.

NOBILYTE. How wyll ye prove me that the fathers　　　390
　　　sprytuall
Were under the princes ever contynewally?
KYNG JOHAN. By the actes of kynges I wyll prove yt
　　　by and by.[26]

David and Salomon the pristes ded constitute,
Commandyng the offyces that they shuld execute.
Josaphat the kyng the mynysters ded appoynt,　　　395
So ded kyng Ezechias whom God hymselfe ded
　　　anoynt.
Dyverse of the princes for the pristes ded make
　　　decrees,
Lyke as yt is[30] pleyn in the fyrst of Machabees.
Owr prists are rysyn throwgh lyberte of kyngs
By ryches to pryd and other unlawfull doynges,　　　400
And that is the cawse that they so oft dysobeye.
NOBILYTE. Good Lord, what a craft have you thes
　　　thynges to convaye!

26 *by and by :* at once.

KYNG JOHAN. Now, alas, that the false pretence of
        superstycyon
  Shuld cawse yow to be a mayntener of Sedicyon!
  Sum thynkyth Nobilyte in natur to consyst   405
  Or in parentage, ther thowght is but amyst.
  Wher habundance is of vertu, faith, and grace,
  With knowlage of the Lord, Nobilyte is ther in
        place,
  And not wher as in the wylfull contempte of
        thyngs
  Pertaynyng to God in the obedyence of kynges.   410
  Beware ye synke not with Dathan and Abiron[8]
  For dysobeyng the power and domynyon.
NOBILYTE. Nay, byd me beware I do not synke with
        yow here.
  Beyng acurssyd, of trewth ye put me in fere.
KYNG JOHAN. Why, are ye gone hence and wyll ye no   415
        longar tarrye?
NOBILYTE. No, wher as[31] yow are in place, by
        swete[32] seynt Marye.
    Here NOBILYTE *go owt and dresse for the*
        CARDYNALL.
KYNG JOHAN. Blessed Lord of Heaven, what is the
        wretchednesse[33]
  Of thys wycked worlde? An evyll of all evyls,
        doubtlesse.
  [*To the audience.*] Perceyve ye not here how the
        Clergye hath rejecte
  Their true allegeaunce to maynteyne the popysh   420
        secte?
  See ye not how lyghte the lawyers sett the poure,
  Whanne God commaundeth them to obeye yche
        daye and howre?
  Nobilyte also, whych ought hys prynce to assyste,
  Is vanyshed awaye as it we[re] a wynter myste.
  All they are from me, I am now left alone,   425
  And God wote knowe not to whome to make my
        mone.
  Oh, yet wolde I fayne knowe the mynde of my
        Commynalte,
  Whether he wyll go with them or abyde with me.
    Here enter ENGLANDE *and* COMMYNALTE.[34]

ENGLANDE. He is here at hond, a symple creatur as
    may be.

KYNG JOHAN. Cum hether, my[35] frynde, stand nere,   430
    ys thyselfe he?

COMMYNALTE. Yf it lyke yowr grace, I am yowr pore
    Commynalte.

KYNG JOHAN. Thou art poore inowgh, yf that be good,
    God helpe thee.

    Methynke thow art blynd. Tell me, frynde, canst
      thou not see?

ENGLANDE. He is blynd in dede, yt is the more rewth
    and pytte.

KYNG JOHAN. How cummyst thow so blynd, I pray   435
    thee, good fellow, tell me?

COMMYNALTE. For want of knowlage in Christes
    lyvely[36] veryte.

ENGLANDE. This spirituall blyndnes bryngeth men
    owt of the waye

    And cause them ofttymes ther kynges to dysso-
      baye.

KYNG JOHAN. How sayst thow, Commynalte, wylt
    not thou take my parte?

COMMYNALTE. To that I cowd be contented, with all   440
    my hart,

    But, alas, in me are two[37] great impedymentes.

KYNG JOHAN. I pray thee shew me, what are those im-
    pedymentes?

COMMYNALTE. The fyrst is blyndnes, wherby I myght
    take with the pope

    Soner than with yow, for alas I can but grope,

    And ye know full well ther are many nowghty   445
      gydes.

    The nexte is poverte, whych cleve so hard to my
      sydes

    And ponych me so sore that my power ys lytyll or
      non.

KYNG JOHAN. In Godes name tell me how cummyth
    thi substance gone?

COMMYNALTE. By pristes, channons, and monkes,
    which do but fyll ther bely

    With my swett and labour for ther popych purga-   450
      tory.

ENGLANDE. Yowr grace promysed me that I shuld
    have remedy

In that same mater, whan I was last here trewly.

KYNG JOHAN. Dowghtles I ded so, but alas yt wyll not
be.

In hart I lament this great infelycyte.

ENGLANDE. Late me have my spowse and my londes   455
at lyberte,

And I promyse you my sonne here, your Commynalte,

I wyll make able to do ye dewtyfull servyce.

KYNG JOHAN. I wold I ware able to do to[38] thee that
offyce,

But alas I am not, for why my Nobilyte,

My Lawers and Clergye hath cowardly forsake   460
me,

And now last of all, to my most anguysh of mynd,

My Commynalte here I fynd both poore and
blynde.

ENGLANDE. Rest upon this, ser, for my governor ye
shall be

So long as ye lyve. God hath so apoynted me.[39]

His owtward blyndnes ys but a sygnyficacion   465

Of blyndnes in sowle for lacke of informacyon

In the word of God, which is the orygynall grownd

Of dyssobedyence, which all realmies doth con-
fund.

Yf yowr Grace wold cawse Godes word to be
tawght syncerly

And subdew those pristes that wyll not preche yt   470
trewly,

The peple shuld know to ther prynce ther lawfull
dewty.

But yf ye permytt contynuance of ypocresye

In monke[s,] chanons, and pristes, and mynysters
of the clargy,

Yowr realme shall never be withowt moch traytery.

KYNG JOHAN. All that I perseyve, and therfore I kepe   475
owt fryers,

Lest they shuld bryng thee moch farder into the
bryers.

They have mad labur to inhabytt this same
regyon.

They shall for my tym not enter my domynyon.

We have to[o] many of soch vayne lowghtes[27] all-
    redy.

I beshrew ther hartes, they have[40] made you ij   480
    full nedy.

Here enter Pandulphus the CARDYNALL *and*
sayth

CARDYNALL. What, Commynalte, ys this the cove-
    naunt[41] kepyng?

Thow toldyst me thou woldest take hym no more
    for thy kyng.

COMMYNALTE. *Peccavi, mea culpa.*[28] I submit me to
    yowr holynes.

CARDYNALL. Gett thee hence than shortly, and go
    abowt thi besynes.

Wayet on thy capttaynes, Nobilyte and the   485
    Clergye,

With Civyle Order, and the other company.

Blow owt yowr tromppettes and set forth manfully.

The Frenche kyng Phelype by sea doth hether
    apply

With the powr of Fraunce, to subdew this hery-
    tyke.

KYNG JOHAN. I defye both hym and thee, lewde scys-   490
    matyke.

Why wylt thou forsake thi prince, or[29] thi prince
    leve thee?

COMMYNALTE. I must nedes obbay, whan Holy
    Chirch commandyth me.

ENGLANDE. Yf thow leve thy kyng, take me never for
    thy mother.

CARDYNALL. Tush, care not thou for that, I shall
    provyd thee another.

                        Go out COMMYNALTE.[42]

Yt ware fytter for yow to be in another place.   495

ENGLANDE. Yt shall becum me to wayte upon his
    Grace

And do hym servyce where as he ys resydente,

For I was gevyn hym of the Lord omnypotente.

---

27 *lowghtes :* louts.   29 *or :* before.
28 *Peccavi . . . culpa :* I have
    sinned, the blame is
    mine.

CARDYNALL. Thow mayst not abyde here, for
    whye,[43] we have hym curssyd.

ENGLANDE. I beshrow yowr hartes, so have ye[44]   500
    me onpursed.

Yf he be acurssed, than are we a mete cuppell,

For I am interdyct,[45] no salve that sore can sup-
    pell.

CARDYNALL. I say gett thee hence, and make me no
    more pratyng.

ENGLANDE. I wyll not awaye from myn owne lawfull
    kyng,

Appoynted of God, tyll deth shall us departe.   505

CARDYNALL. Wyll ye not indede! Well, than ye are
    lyke to smarte.

ENGLANDE. I smarte allready throw yowr most suttell
    practyse

And am clene ondone by yowr false merchan-
    dyce—

Yowr pardons, yowr bulles, yowr purgatory pycke-
    purse,

Yowr Lent fastes, yowr schryftes— that I pray   510
    God geve yow his cursse.

CARDYNALL. Thou shalt smart better, or we have
    done with thee,

For we have this howr great navyes upon the see

In every quarter, with this Loller[9] here to fyght

And to conquarre hym, for the[46] Holy Chyrchis
    ryght.

We have on the northe, Alexander the kyng of   515
    Scottes,

With an armye of men that for their[47] townnes
    cast lottes.

On the sowthe syde we have the French kyng with
    his powr,

Which wyll sle and burne, tyll he cum to Londen
    towr.

In the west partes we have[48] kyng Alphonse
    with the Spanyardes

With sheppes full of gonepowder, now cummyng 520
    hether towardes,

And on the est syde we have Esterlynges,[30] Danes,
    and Norwayes

30 *Esterlynges*: men of east-
    ern Germany.

With soch powr landynge[49] as can be resystyd
    nowayes.

KYNG JOHAN. All that is not true that yow have here
    expressed.[50]

CARDYNALL. By the Messe, so true as I have now con-
    fessed.

KYNG JOHAN. And what do ye meane by such an   525
    hurly burlye?

CARDYNALL. For the Churches ryght, to subdue ye
    manfully.

        [*Enter* SEDICYON.]

SEDICYON. To all that wyll fyght, I proclame a
    jubyle[31]

Of cleane remyssyon, thys tyraunt here to slee,

Destroye hys people, burne up both cytie and
    towne,

That the Pope of Rome maye have hys scepture   530
    and crowne.

In the Churches cause, to dye thys daye be bolde.

Your sowles shall to heaven, ere your fleshe and
    bones be colde.

KYNG JOHAN. Most mercyfull God, as my trust is in
    thee,

So comforte me now, in this extremyte.

As thow holpyst David in his most hevynes,   535

So hele me this hour, of thy grace, mercye,[51] and
    goodnes.

CARDYNALL. This owtward remorse that ye show here
    evydent

Ys a grett lykelyhod and token of amendment.

How say ye, Kyng Johan, can ye fynd now in yowr
    hart

To obaye Holy Chyrch and geve ower yowr fro-   540
    ward part?

KYNG JOHAN. Were yt so possyble to hold thes enmyes
    backe,

That my swete Englande perysh not in this shepp-
    wracke.

CARDYNALL. Possyble, quoth he! Yea, they shuld go
    bake indede,

---

31 *jubyle :* period when speci-   remission of punishment
fied religious acts secure   for sin.

And ther gret armyes to some other quarteres
    leede,[52]

Or elles they have not so many good blyssynges   545
    now

But as many cursynges they shall have, I make
    God avowe.

I promyse yow sur, ye shall have specyall faver

If ye wyll submyt yowrsylfe to Holye Chyrch here.

KYNG JOHAN. I trust than ye wyll graunt some delyb-
    eracyon[53]

To have an answere of thys your protestacyon.   550

SEDICYON. Tush, gyve upp the crowne, and make no
    mor ado.

KYNG JOHAN. Your spirytuall charyte wyll be better to
    me than so.

The crowne of a realme is a matter of great
    wayght.

In gyvynge it upp, we maye not be too slayght.

SEDICYON. I say, gyve it up, lete us have no more ado.   555

CARDYNALL. Yea, and in our warres we wyll no farder
    go.

KYNG JOHAN. Ye wyll gyve me leave to talke first
    with my clergye?

SEDICYON. With them ye nede not, they are at a
    poynt alreadye.

KYNG JOHAN. Than with my lawers, to heare what
    they wyll tell.

SEDICYON. Ye shall ever have them as the clergye   560
    gyve them counsell.

KYNG JOHAN. Then wyll I commen with my Nobilyte.

SEDICYON. We have hym so jugled he wyll not to
    yow agree.

KYNG JOHAN. Yet shall I be content to do as he coun-
    sell me.

CARDYNALL. Than be not too longe from hence, I wyll
    advyse ye.   [*Here go out the Kyng.*]

SEDICYON. Is not thys a sport? By the Messe it is, I   565
    trowe.

What welthe and pleasure wyll now to our kynge-
    dom growe!

Englande is our owne, whych is the most ples-
    aunt grounde

In all the rounde worlde; now maye we realmes
    confounde.
Our holye Father maye now lyve at hys pleasure
And have habundaunce of wenches, wynes, and   570
    treasure.
  He is now able to kepe downe Christe and hys
    Gospell,
True fayth to exyle, and all vertues to expell.
Now shall we ruffle it in velvattes, golde, and
    sylke,
With shaven crownes, syde[32] gownes, and roch-
    ettes[33] whyte as mylke.
By the Messe, Pandulphus, now maye we synge   575
    Cantate
And crowe *Confitebor* with a joyfull *Jubilate*.
Holde me, or els for laughynge I must burste.
CARDYNALL.. Hold thy peace, whorson, I wene thu
    art accurst.
Kepe a sadde countenaunce, a very vengeaunce
    take thee.
SEDICYON. I can not do it, by the Messe, and thu   580
    shuldest hange me.
If Solon were here, I recken that he woulde laugh
Whych never laught yet, yea, lyke a whelpe he
    woulde waugh.
Ha, ha, ha, laugh, quoth he, yea, laugh and laugh
    agayne.
We had never cause to laugh more free, I am
    playne.
    [*Re-enter* KYNG JOHAN.]
CARDYNALL. I praye thee, no more, for here come the   585
    kynge agayne.
Ye are at a poynt wherto ye intende to stande?
SEDICYON. Yea, hardely sir, gyve up the crowne of
    Englande.
KYNG JOHAN. I have caste in mynde the great dis-
    pleasures of warre,
  The daungers, the losses, the decayes both nere
    and farre,
  The burnynge of townes, the throwynge downe of   590
    buyldynges,

32 *syde*: long.   33 *rochettes*: linen vestments
                                                resembling surplices.

Destructyon of corne and cattell with other
     thynges,
Defylynge of maydes, and shedynge of Christen
     blood,
With suche lyke outrages, neyther honest, true,
     nor good.
These thynges consydered, I am compelled thys
     houre
To resigne up here both crowne and regall poure.   595

ENGLANDE. For the love of God, yet take some better
     advysement.

SEDICYON. Holde your tunge, ye whore, or by the
     Messe, ye shall repent.
Downe on your mary bones,[34] and make no more
     ado.

ENGLANDE. If ye love me, sir, for Gods sake do never
     so.

KYNG JOHAN. O Englande, Englande, shewe now thy-   600
     self a mother.
Thy people wyll els be slayne here without nom-
     ber.
As God shall judge me, I do not thys of coward-
     nesse
But of compassyon in thys extreme heavynesse.
Shall my people shedde their bloude in suche
     habundaunce?
Naye, I shall rather gyve upp my whole gover-   605
     naunce.

SEDICYON. Come of[f] apace than, and make an ende
     of it shortly.

ENGLANDE. The most pytiefull chaunce yt hath bene
     hytherto, surely.

KYNG JOHAN. Here I submyt me to pope Innocent[54]
     the Thred,
Dyssyering mercy of hys holy fatherhed.

CARDYNALL. Geve up the crowne than,[55] yt shal   610
     be the better for ye.
He wyll unto yow the more favorable be.
     Here the KYNG *delevyr the crowne to the*
                    CARDYNALL.

34 *mary bones:* marrow
     bones, i.e. knees.

KYNG JOHAN. To hym I resygne here[56] the septer
    and the crowne
Of Englande and Yrelond, with the powr and re-
    nowne,
And put me wholly to his mercyfull ordynance.
CARDYNALL. I may say this day the Chyrch hath a   615
    full gret chaunce.
Thes five dayes I wyll kepe this crowne in myn
    owne hande
In the popes behalfe, upseasyng[35] Englande and
    Yerlond.
In the meane season, ye shall make an oblygacyon
For yow and yowr ayers in this synyficacyon :
To resayve yowr crowne of the pope for ever more   620
In maner of fefarme,(10) and for a tokyn therfor,
Ye shall every yere paye hym a thowsand marke
With[57] the Peter pens,[36] and not agenst yt
    barke.
Ye shall also geve to the bysshoppe of Cantorbery
A thre thowsand marke, for his gret injury.   625
To the Chyrch besydes, for the great[58] scathe
    ye have done,
Forty thowsand marke ye shall delyver sone.
KYNG JOHAN. Ser, the[59] taxe that I had of the hole
    realme of Englande
Amownted to no more but unto thirty thowsand.
Why shuld I than paye so moche unto the   630
    Clergye?
CARDYNALL. Ye shall geve yt them, ther is no remedy.
KYNG JOHAN. Shall they paye no tribute, yf the
    realme stond in rerage?
CARDYNALL. Sir, they shall paye none, we wyll have
    no soch bondage.
KYNG JOHAN. The pope had at once thre hundred
    thowsand marke.
CARDYNALL. What is that to yow? Ah, styll ye wyll be   635
    starke.
Ye shall paye yt, sir, ther is no remedy.
KYNG JOHAN. Yt shall be performed as ye wyll have yt,
    trewly.

---

35 *upseasyng* : seizing (?)   from householders to be
36 *Peter pens* : pence levied   paid to the papal see.

ENGLANDE. So noble a realme to stande tributarye,
alas,[60]

To the Devyls vycar, suche fortune never was.

SEDICYON. Out with thys harlot, Cockes sowle, she   640
hath lete a fart.

ENGLANDE. Lyke a wretche thu lyest, thy report is
lyke as thu art.   [Exit SEDICYON.]

CARDYNALL. [To JOHAN.] Ye shall suffer the monkes
and channons to make reentry

Into ther abbayes, and to dwell ther peacebly.

Ye shall se also to my great labur and charge.

For other thynges elles, we shall commen[61]   645
more at large.

KYNG JOHAN. Ser, in every poynt I shall fulfyll yowr
plesur.

CARDYNALL. Than plye yt apace and lett us have the
tresur.

ENGLANDE. Alacke for pyte, that ever ye grantyd this.

For me, pore Englande, ye have done sore amys.

Of a fre woman ye have now mad a bonde[62]   650
mayd.

Yowrselfe and heyres ye have for ever decayd.

Alas, I had rether be underneth the Turke

Than under the wynges of soch a[63] thefe to
lurke.

KYNG JOHAN. Content thee, Englande, for ther ys no
remedy.

ENGLANDE. Yf yow be plesyd, than I must consent   655
gladly.

KYNG JOHAN. If I shoulde not graunt, here woulde be
a wondrefull spoyle.[64]

Everywhere the enemyes woulde ruffle and tur-
moyle.

The losse of people stycketh most unto my harte.

ENGLANDE. Do as ye thynke best, yche waye is to my
smarte.

CARDYNALL. Are ye at a poynt with the same obly-   660
gacyon?

KYNG JOHAN. Yt is here redye, at yowr interrogacyon.

Here KYNG JOHAN *shall delevyr*
the oblygacyon.

CARDYNALL. Wher is[65] the mony for yowr full
    restytucyon?

KYNG JOHAN. Here, ser, accordyng to yowr last con-
    stytucyon.

CARDYNALL. [*To* SEDICYON, *alias* STEVYN LANGTON.]
    Cum hether, my lorde. By the popys
    autoryte

Assoyll this man here of irregularyte.   665

    Here the bysshop STEVYN LANGTON *cum in.*

KYNG JOHAN. Methynke this bysshope resembleth
    moch Sedicyon.

CARDYNALL. I cownsell yow yet to be ware of wrong
    suspycyon.

This is Stevyn Langton, yowr meteropolytan.[37]

KYNG JOHAN. Than do the offyce of the Good Sa-
    marytan

And pore oyle and wyne in my old festerd wownd.   670

Releace me of synne, that yt doth not me con-
    fownd.

Confiteor domino pape et omnibus cardinalibus
eius et vobis quia peccavi nimis exigendo ab ec-
clesia tributum. Mea culpa. Ideo precor sanctis-
simum dominum papam et omnes prelatos eius
et[66] vos orare pro me.[38]   675

STEVYN LANGTON. *Misereatur tui omnipotens papa et*
dimittat tibi omnes erratus tuos, liberetque te a
suspencione, excominicac[i]one, et interdicto, et
restituat te in regnum tuum.[39]

KYNG JOHAN. Amen.

STEVYN LANGTON. *Dominus papa noster te absoluat,*   680
et ego absolvo te, auctoritate eius et apostolorum
Petri et Pauli, in hac[67] parte mihi[68] comissa,

---

37 *meteropolytan*: metropoli-
    tan, archbishop.

38 *Confiteor . . . me*: I con-
    fess to the lord pope and
    all his cardinals and to
    you that I have sinned
    overmuch in exacting
    tribute from the church.
    I am guilty. For that
    reason I ask the most
    holy lord pope and all

his prelates and you to
    pray for me.

39 *Misereatur . . . tuum*:
    The almighty pope takes
    pity on you and dis-
    charges you of your sins
    and frees you from sus-
    pension, excommunica-
    tion, and interdiction,
    and restores you to your
    kingdom.

ab omnibus impietibus tuis, et restituo te corone
et regno, in nomine pape, amen.[40, (11)]

CARDYNALL. Ye are well content to take thys man
         for yowr primate?

KYNG JOHAN. Yea, and to use hym accordyng to his   685
         estate.

    [*To* LANGTON.] I am ryght sory that ever I yow of-
         fendyd.

SEDICYON. [(12)] And I am full gladde that ye are so
         welle amended.[69]

    Unto Holy Churche ye are now an obedyent
         chylde,

    Where ye were afore with heresye muche de-
         fyelde.

ENGLANDE. Sir, yonder is a clarke which is con-   690
         dempned for treason.

    The shryves[41] woulde fayne knowe what to do
         with hym thys season.

KYNG JOHAN. Come hyther, fellawe.

        [*Here* TREASON *come in, chained.*]

              What? Methynke thu art a pryste.

TREASON. He hath ofter gessed, that of the truthe
         have myste.

KYNG JOHAN. A pryste and a traytour, how maye
         that wele agree?

TREASON. Yes, yes, wele ynough, underneth Bene-   695
         dicite.

    Myself hath played it, and therfor I knowe it the
         better.

    Amonge craftye cloyners[42] there hath not bene a
         gretter.

KYNG JOHAN. Tell some of thy feates, thu mayest the
         better escape.

SEDICYON. [*Aside to* TREASON.] Hem, not too bolde
         yet, for a mowse the catte wyll gape.

---

40 *Dominus . . . amen:* Our
    lord pope absolves you,
    and I absolve you, by
    his authority and that of
    the apostles Peter and
    Paul, in the office com-
    missioned to me, from
all your sins, and I re-
store you in crown and
rule, in the name of the
pope, amen.

41 *shryves:* examiners.

42 *cloyners:* deceivers.

TREASON. Twenty thousande traytour I have made in   700
    my tyme.

  Undre Benedicite, betwyn hygh Masse and
    pryme,[43]

  I made Nobilyte to be obedyent

  To the churche of Rome, whych most kynges
    maye repent.

  I have so convayed that neyther priest nor lawer

  Wyll obeye Gods wurde, nor yet the Gospell faver.   705

    In the place of Christe I have sett up super-
    sticyons,

  For preachynges, ceremonyes, for Gods wurde,
    mennys tradicyons.

  Come to the temple and there Christe hath no
    place,

  Moyses and the paganes doth utterly hym deface.

ENGLANDE. Marke wele, sir. Tell what we have of   710
    Moyses.

TREASON. All your ceremonyes, your copes and your
    sensers doubtlesse,

  Your fyers, your waters, your oyles, your aulters,
    your ashes,

  Your candlestyckes, your cruettes, your salte, with
    suche lyke trashes.

  Ye lacke but the bloude of a goate or els a calfe.

ENGLANDE. Lete us heare sumwhat also in the   715
    paganes behalfe.

TREASON. Of the paganes ye have your gylded
    ymages all,

  In your necessytees upon them for to call,

  With crowchynges, with kyssynges and settynge
    up of lyghtes,

  Bearynge them in processyon and fastynges upon
    their nyghtes.

  Some for the tothe ake, some for the pestylence   720
    and poxe,

  With ymages of waxe to brynge moneye to the
    boxe.

ENGLANDE. What have they of Christe in the
    churche, I praye the[e] tell?

43 *betwyn . . . pryme:* from
  night to morn.

TREASON. Marry, nothynge at all, but the epystle and
          the Gospell,

  And that is in Latyne, that no man shoulde it
    knowe.

SEDICYON. Peace, noughty whoreson, peace, thu   725
          playest the knave I trowe.

KYNG JOHAN. Hast thu knowne suche wayes, and
          sought no reformacyon?

[TREASON.] It is the lyvynge of our whole congre-
          gacyon.

  If supersticyons and ceremonyes from us fall,

  Farwele monke and chanon, priest, fryer, bysh-
    opp, and all.

  Our conveyaunce is suche that we haue both   730
    moneye and ware.

SEDICYON. Our occupacyon thu wylt marre, God gyve
          the[e] care.

ENGLANDE. Very fewe of ye wyll Peters offyce take!

TREASON. Yes, the more part of us our maistre hath
          forsake.

ENGLANDE. I meane for preachynge, I pray God thu
          be curste.

TREASON. No, no, with Judas we love wele to be   735
          purste.

  We selle owr maker so sone as we have hym
    made,

  And as for preachynge, we meddle not with that
    trade,

  Least Annas, Cayphas, and the lawers shulde us
    blame,[13]

  Callyng us to reckenynge for preachynge in that
    name.

KYNG JOHAN. But tell to me, person, whie wert thu   740
          cast in preson?

[TREASON.] For no great matter, but a lyttle petye
    treason,

  For conjurynge, calkynge,[44] and coynynge of newe
    grotes,

  For clippynge of nobles, with suche lyke pratye
    motes.

44 *calkynge :* calculating.

ENGLANDE. Thys is hygh treason, and hath bene
            evermor.

KYNG JOHAN. It is suche treason as he shall sure hange   745
            for.

TREASON. I have holy orders, by the Messe, I defye
            your wurst.

Ye can not towche me but ye must be accurst.

KYNG JOHAN. We wyll not towche thee, the halter
            shall do yt alone.

Curse the rope therfor whan thu begynnest to
            grone.

TREASON. And sett ye no more by the holy ordre of   750
            prestehode?

Ye wyll prove yourselfe an heretyke, by the rode.

KYNG JOHAN. Come hyther, Englande, and here what
            I say to the[e.]

ENGLANDE. I am all readye to do as ye commaunde
            me.

KYNG JOHAN. For so much as he hath falsefyed our
            coyne,

As he is worthie, lete hym with an halter joyne.   755

Thu shalt hange no priest, nor yet none honest
            man,

But a traytour, a thefe, and one that lyttle good
            can.

CARDYNALL. What, yet agaynst the Churche? Gett me
            boke, belle, and candle.

As I am true priest, I shall ye yett better handle.

Ye neyther regarde hys crowne nor anoynted   760
            fyngers,

The offyce of a priest, nor the grace that therin
            lyngers.

SEDICYON. Sir, pacyent yourselfe, and all thynge shall
            be well.

Fygh, man, to the Churche that ye shulde be styll
            a rebell!

ENGLANDE. I accompt hym no priest that worke such
            haynouse treason.

SEDICYON. It is a worlde to heare a folysh woman   765
            reason.

CARDYNALL. After thys maner ye used Peter Pom-
            frete, [14]

A good symple man, and as they saye a profete.

KYNG JOHAN. Sir, I did prove hym a very supersti-
cyouse wretche

And blasphemouse lyar, therfor did the lawe hym
upstretche.

He prophecyed first I shulde reigne but xiiij years,   770
Makynge the people to beleve he coulde bynde
bears,

And I have reigned a seventene yeares and more.
And anon after he grudged at me very sore
And sayde I shulde be exyled out of my realme
Before the ascencyon, whych was turned to a fan-   775
tastycall dreame,

Saynge he woulde hange if hys prophecye were not
true.

Thus hys owne decaye hys folyshnesse did brue.

CARDYNALL. Ye shuld not hange hym whych is a
frynde to the Churche.

KYNG JOHAN. Alas, that ye shoulde counte them
fryndes of the Churche

That agaynst all truthe so hypocritycally lurche.   780
An yll Churche is it that hath such fryndes, indede.

ENGLANDE. Of maister Morres suche an other fable
we reade,[15]

That in Morgans fyelde the sowle of a knyght
made verses,

Apearynge unto hym, and thys one he rehearses,
Destruat hoc regnum Rex regum duplici plaga,[45]   785
Whych is true as God spake with the Ape at
Praga.

The sowles departed from thys heavye mortall
payne

To the handes of God returneth never agayne.

A marvelouse thynge that ye thus delyght in
lyes.

SEDICYON. Thys queane doth not els but mocke the   790
blessed storyes.

That Peter angred ye whan he called ye a devyll
incarnate.

KYNG JOHAN. He is now full sure no more so uncomely
to prate.

45 *Destruat . . . plaga:* The
King of kings shall de-
stroy this realm with
double plague.

Well, as for thys man, because that he is a priste
I gyve hym to ye : do with hym what ye lyste.
CARDYNALL. In the Popes behalfe I wyll sumwhat   795
    take upon me.
Here I delyver hym by the Churches lyberte
In spyght of your hart, make of it what ye lyste.
KYNG JOHAN. I am pleased, I saye, because he ys
    pryste.
CARDYNALL. Whether ye be or no, it shall not greatly
    force.
Lete me see those cheanes.
           [*Unchains* TREASON.]
           Go thy waye and have remorce.   800
TREASON. God save your Lordeshypps, I trust I shall
    amende
And do no more so, or els, sir, God defende.[46]
SEDICYON. I shall make thee, I trowe, to kepe thy
    benefyce.   [*Exit* TREASON.]
By the Marye Messe, the knave wyll never be wyse.
ENGLANDE. Lyke lorde, like chaplayne, neither barrell   805
    better herynge.[(16)]
SEDICYON. Styll she must trattle, that tunge is alwayes
    sterynge.
A wurde or two, sir, I must tell yow in your eare.
CARDYNALL. Of some advauntage I woulde very
    gladly heare.
SEDICYON. Releace not Englande of the generall in-
    terdictyon
Tyll the kynge hath graunted the dowrye and the   810
    pencyon
Of Julyane, the wyfe of kynge Richarde Cour de
    Lyon.
Ye knowe very well she beareth the Churche good
    mynde.
Tush, we must have all, manne, that she shall leave
    behynde.
As the saynge is, he fyndeth that surely bynde.[(17)]
    It were but folye suche louce endes for to lose.   815
The lande and the monye wyll make well for our
    purpose.

46 *defende :* forbid.

Tush, laye yokes upon hym, more then he is able
    to beare,
Of Holy Churche so he wyll stande ever in feare.
Suche a shrewe as he it is good to kepe undre awe.

ENGLANDE. Woo is that persone whych is undreneth   820
    your lawe.

[*To the audience.*] Ye may see, good people, what
    these same merchantes are.

Their secrete knaveryes their open factes[47] declare.

SEDICYON. Holde thy peace, callet.[48] God gyve the[e]
    sorowe and care.

CARDYNALL. Ere I releace yow of the interdyctyon
    heare,

In the whych yowr realme contynued hath thys   825
    seven yeare,

Ye shall make Julyane, your syster in lawe, thys
    bande,[49]

To gyve her the thirde part of Englande and of Ire-
    lande.

KYNG JOHAN. All the worlde knoweth, sir, I owe her
    no suche dewtye.

CARDYNALL. Ye shall gyve it to hir, there is no
    remedye.

Wyll ye styll withstande our holy fathers pre-   830
    cepte?

SEDICYON. In peyne of dampnacyon hys commaunde-
    ment must be kepte.

KYNG JOHAN. Oh, ye undo me, consyderynge my
    great paymentes.

ENGLANDE. Sir, disconfort not, for God hath sent de-
    batementes.[50]

Yowr mercyfull maker hath shewed upon ye hys
    powere,

From thys heavye yoke delyverynge yow thys   835
    howre.

The woman is dead, suche newes are hyther
    brought.

KYNG JOHAN. For me a synnar thys myracle hath God
    wrought.

---

47 *factes*: deeds.
48 *callet*: trull, strumpet.
49 *bande*: bond, contract.

50 *debatementes*: relief,
    abatement.

In most hygh paryls he ever me preserved,
And in thys daunger he hath not from me swerved.
In genua procumbens Deum adorat, dicens,[51]
As David sayth, Lorde, thu dost not leave thy ser-   840
    vaunt
That wyll trust in the[e] and in thy blessyd cove-
    naunt.

SEDICYON. A vengeaunce take it! by the Messe, it is
    unhappye
She is dead so sone. Now is it past remedye.
So must we lose all now that she is clerely gone.
If that praye had bene ours, oh, it had bene alone!   845
The chaunce beynge suche, by my trouth, even
    lete it go:
No grote, no pater noster, no penye, no placebo.[52]
The devyll go with it, seynge it wyll be no better.

ENGLANDE. Their myndes are all sett upon the fylthie
    luker.

CARDYNALL. Than here I releace yow of yowr inter-   850
    dictyons all
And strayghtly commaunde yow upon daungers
    that may fall
No more to meddle with the Churches refor-
    macyon
Nor holde men from Rome whan they make ap-
    pellacyon,[53]
By God and by all the contentes of thys boke.

KYNG JOHAN. Agaynst Holy Churche I wyll no more   855
    speake nor loke.

SEDICYON. Go, open the churche dores and lete the
    belles be ronge,
And throughout the realme see that *Te Deum* be
    songe.
Pryck upp your candels before saynt Loe and
    saynt Legearde.
Lete saynt Antonyes hogge be had in some re-
    garde.[18]
If yowr ale be sowre, and yowr breade moulde   860
    certayne,

51 *In . . . dicens:* Falling to
    his knees let him wor-
    ship God, saying.

52 *placebo:* I shall assuage.
    (Beginning of vespers
    for the dead)

53 *appellacyon:* appeal.

Now wyll they waxe swete, for the pope hath blest
　　ye agayne.

ENGLANDE. Than within a whyle I trust ye wyll
　　preache the Gospell.

SEDICYON. That shall I tell the[e], kepe thu it in
　　secrete counsell :

It shall neyther come in churche nor yet in
　　chauncell.

CARDYNALL. Goo your wayes apace, and see my   865
　　pleasure be done.

KYNG JOHAN. As ye have commaunded all shall be
　　perfourmed sone.

　　[*Exeunt* KYNG JOHAN *and* ENGLANDE.]

CARDYNALL. By the Messe, I laugh to see thys
　　cleane conveyaunce.

He is now full glad as our pype goeth to daunce.

By Cockes sowle, he is now become a good parrysh
　　clarke.

SEDICYON. Ha, ha, wylye whoreson, dost that so   870
　　busyly marke?

I hope in a whyle we wyll make hym so to rave,

That he shall become unto us a commen slave

And shall do nothynge but as we byd hym do.

If we byd hym slea, I trowe he wyll do so.

If we byd hym burne suche as beleve in Christe,   875

He shall not say naye to the byddynge of a priste.

But yet it is harde to trust what he wyll be,

He is so crabbed : by the holye Trinyte,

To save all thynges up I holde best we make hym
　　more sure,

And gyve hym a sawce that he no longar endure.   880

Now that I remembre, we shall not leave hym
　　thus.

CARDYNALL. Whye, what shall we do to hym els, in
　　the name of Jesus?

SEDICYON. Marry, fatche in Lewes, Kynge Phylyppes
　　sonne of Fraunce,

To falle upon hym with his menne and ordy-
　　naunce,

With wyldefyer, gunpouder, and suche lyke myrye   885
　　trickes,

To dryve hym to holde and searche hym in the
    quyckes.[54]
I wyll not leave hym tyll I brynge hym to hys
    yende.

CARDYNALL. Well, farwele, Sedicyon, do as shall lye
    in thy myende.   [*Exit* CARDYNALL.]

SEDICYON. I mervele greatly where Dissymulacyon is.
    [*Enter* DISSYMULACYON.]

DISSYMULACYON. I wyll come anon, if thu tarry tyll I   890
    pysse.

SEDICYON. I beshrewe your hart, where have ye bene
    so longe?

DISSYMULACYON. In the gardene, man, the herbes and
    wedes amonge,
And there have I gote the poyson of toade.
I hope in a whyle to wurke some feate abroade.

SEDICYON. I was wonte sumtyme of thy prevye coun-   895
    sell to be.
Am I nowadayes become a straunger to the[e]?

DISSYMULACYON. I wyll tell the[e] all, undreneth
    Benedicite,
What I mynde to do, in case thu wylte assoyle me.

SEDICYON. Thu shalt be assoyled by the most holy
    fathers auctoryte.

DISSYMULACYON. Shall I so indede? By the Masse,   900
    than now have at thee.
    Benedicite.

SEDICYON.   *In nomine pape, amen.*

DISSYMULACYON. Sir, thys is my mynde. I wyll gyve
    Kyng Johan this poyson,
So makynge hym sure that he shall never have
    foyson.[55]
And thys must thu saye to colour with the thynge,
That a penye lofe he wolde have brought to a   905
    shyllynge.

SEDICYON. Naye, that is suche a lye as easely wyll be
    felte.

DISSYMULACYON. Tush, man, amonge fooles it never
    wyll be out smelte.

---

54 *quyckes :* quick grass,   55 *foyson :* plenty, prosperity.
    fields.

Though it be a foule great lye : Set upon it a good
    face,

And that wyll cause men beleve it in every place.

SEDICYON. I am sure than thu wylt geve it hym in a   910
    drynke.

DISSYMULACYON. Marry, that I wyll, and the one half
    with hym swynke,[56]

To encourage hym to drynke the botome off.

SEDICYON. If thu drynke the halfe, thu shalt fynde it
    no scoff.

Of terryble deathe thu wyllt stacker in the
    plashes.[57]

DISSYMULACYON. Tush, though I dye, man, there   915
    wyll ryse more of my ashes.

    I am sure the monkes wyll praye for me so
        bytterlye

That I shall not come in helle, nor in purgatorye.

In the popes kychyne the scullyons shall not
    brawle

Nor fyght for my grese : If the priestes woulde for
    me yewle[58]

And grunt a good *pace placebo*[59] with Requiem   920
    Masse,

Without muche tarryaunce I shulde to paradyse
    passe,

    Where I myght be sure to make good cheare and
        be myrye,

For I can not away with that whoreson pur-
    gatorye.

SEDICYON. To kepe the[e] from thens thu shalt have
    five monkes syngynge

In Swynsett abbeye, so longe as the worlde is   925
    durynge.

They wyll daylye praye for the sowle of father
    Symon,[(19)]

A Cisteane monke whych poysened Kyng Johan.

---

56 *swynke :* drink deeply.
57 *stacker in the plashes :* stagger in the marshes.
58 *yewle :* pray.
59 *pace placebo :* in peace I shall assuage. (By con-fusion with *requiescat in pace.* The office prop-erly begins : *Placebo Domino in regione viv-orum.*)

DISSYMULACYON. Whan the worlde is done, what
        helpe shall I have than?

SEDICYON. Than shyft for thyself so wele as ever thu
        can.

DISSYMULACYON. Cockes sowle, he cometh here. As-   930
        soyle me that I were gone then.

SEDICYON. *Ego absolvo te in nomine pape, amen.*[60]
        [*Exeunt* SEDICYON *and* DISSYMULACYON.]
        [*Come in the* KYNG *with* ENGLANDE.]

KYNG JOHAN. No prince in the worlde in such
        captivyte

As I am thys houre, and all for ryghteousnesse.

Agaynst me I have both the lordes and com-
        mynalte,

Byshoppes and lawers, whych in their cruell mad-   935
        nesse

Hath brought in hyther the French kynges eldest
        sonne Lewes.

The chaunce unto me is not so dolourrouse

But my lyfe thys daye is muche more tedyouse.

  More of compassyon for shedynge of Christen
        blood

Than anythynge else, my sceptre I gave up latelye   940

To the pope of Rome, whych hath no tytle good

Of jurisdycton, but of usurpacyon onlye,

And now to the Lorde I woulde resygne up gladlye
        Flectit genua.[61]

Both my crowne and lyfe, for thyne owne ryght it
        is,

If it would please the[e] to take my sowle to thy   945
        blys.

ENGLANDE. Sir, discomfort ye not, in the honour of
        Christe Jesu

God wyll never fayle yow, intendynge not els but
        vertu.

KYNG JOHAN. The anguysh of sprete so pangeth me
        everywhere

That incessauntly I thyrst tyll I be there.

60 *Ego . . . amen:* I absolve   61 *Flectit genua:* Bends his
    you in the name of the   knees.
    pope, amen.

ENGLANDE. Sir, be of good chere, for the pope hath   950
    sent a legate,
  Whose name is Gualo, your foes to excommuny-
      cate,[20]
  Not only Lewes, whych hath wonne Rochestre,
  Wynsore and London, Readynge and Wynchestre,
  But so many els as agaynst ye have rebelled
  He hath suspended and openly accursed.   955
KYNG JOHAN. They are all false knaves, all men of
    them beware.
  They never left me tyll they had me in their snare.
  Now have they Otto, the emproure, so wele as
    me,[21]
  And the French kynge, Phylypp, undre their
    captivyte.
  All Christen princes they wyll have in their   960
    bandes.
  The pope and his priestes are poyseners of all
    landes.
  All Christen people be ware of trayterouse pristes,
  For of truthe they are the pernicyouse Antichristes.
ENGLANDE. Thys same Gualo, sir, in your cause doth
    stoughtly barke.
KYNG JOHAN. They are all nought, Englande, so many   965
    as weare that marke.
  From thys habytacyon, swete Lorde, delyver me,
  And preserve thys realme of thy benygnyte.
DISSYMULACYON. [Offstage.] Wassayle, wassayle out
    of the mylke payle,
  Wassayle, wassayle, as whyte as my nayle,
  Wassayle, wassayle in snowe, froste, and hayle,   970
  Wassayle, wassayle with partriche and rayle,[62]
  Wassayle, wassayle that muche doth avayle,
  Wassayle, wassayle that never wyll fayle.
KYNG JOHAN. Who is that, Englande? I praye the[e]
    stepp fourth and see.
ENGLANDE. He doth seme afarre some relygyous man   975
    to be.
      [Enter DISSYMULACYON with a cup.]
DISSYMULACYON. Now Jesus preserve your worthye
    and excellent grace,

  62 rayle: rail, a game bird.

For doubtlesse there is a very angelyck face.
Now forsoth and God, I woulde thynke myself in
    heaven,
If I myght remayne with yow but yeares alevyn.
I woulde covete here none other felicyte.   980

KYNG JOHAN. A lovynge persone thu mayest seme for
    to be.

DISSYMULACYON. I am as gentle a worme as ever ye
    see.

KYNG JOHAN. But what is thy name, good frynde, I
    praye the[e] tell me?

DISSYMULACYON. Simon of Swynsett my very name is,
    per dee.
I am taken of men for Monastycall Devocyon,   985
And here have I brought yow a marvelouse good
    pocyon,
For I hearde ye saye that ye were very drye.

KYNG JOHAN. Indede I wolde gladlye drynke. I praye
    the[e] come nye.

DISSYMULACYON. The dayes of your lyfe never felt
    ye suche a cuppe,
So good and so holsome, if ye woulde drynke it   990
    upp.
It passeth malmesaye, capryck, tyre, or ypocras.[63]
By my faythe, I thynke a better drynke never was.

KYNG JOHAN. Begynne, gentle monke, I pray the[e]
    drynke half to me.

DISSYMULACYON. If ye dronke all up, it were the bet-
    ter for ye.
It woulde slake your thirst and also quycken your   995
    brayne.
A better drynke is not, in Portyngale nor Spayne.
Therfore suppe it of, and make ·an ende of it
    quycklye.

KYNG JOHAN. Naye, thu shalte drynke half, there is
    no remedye.

DISSYMULACYON. Good lucke to ye than! Have at it
    by and bye.
Halfe wyll I consume, if there be no remedye.   1000
    [Drinks.]

63 *passeth . . . ypocras*: sur-   —kinds of sweet or
   passes malmsey, cap-   spiced wine.
   ryck, tyre, and hippocras

KYNG JOHAN. God saynt the[e,] good monke, with all
  my very harte!

DISSYMULACYON. I have brought ye half, conveye me
  that for your parte.
    [KYNG JOHAN *drinks.*]

 [*Aside.*] Where art thu, Sedicyon? By the Masse I
  dye, I dye.

 Helpe now at a pynche! Alas, man, cum awaye
  shortlye.
    [*Enter* SEDICYON.]

SEDICYON. Come hyther apace, and gett thee to the 1005
  farmerye.[64]

 I have provyded for the[e], by swete saynt Powle,

 Fyve monkes that shall synge contynually for thy
  sowle,

 That, I warande the[e,] thu shalt not come in
  helle.

DISSYMULACYON. To sende me to heaven goo rynge
  the holye belle,

 And synge for my sowle a Masse of Scala Celi, 1010

 That I maye clyme up aloft with Enoch and
  Heli,[(22)]

 I do not doubte it but I shall be a saynt.

 Provyde a gyldar myne image for to paynt.

 I dye for the Churche with Thomas of Canter-
  berye.

 Ye shall fast my vigyll and upon my daye be 1015
  merye.

 No doubt but I shall do myracles in a whyle,

And therfore lete me be shryned in the north yle.

SEDICYON. To the[e] than wyll offer both crypple,
  halte, and blynde,

 Mad men and mesels,[65] with such as are woo
  behynde.
    Exeunt [SEDICYON *and* DISSYMULACYON.]

KYNG JOHAN. My bodye me vexeth, I doubt much of 1020
  a tympanye.[66]

ENGLANDE. Now, alas, alas! your Grace is betrayed
  cowardlye.

---

64 *farmerye* : farm.   66 *tympanye* : swelling of the
65 *mesels* : lepers.   abdomen.

KYNG JOHAN. Where became the monke that was
    here with me latelye?

ENGLANDE. He is poysened, sir, and lyeth a-dyenge
    surelye.

KYNG JOHAN. It can not be so, for he was here even
    now.

ENGLANDE. Doubtlesse, sir, it is so true as I have tolde   1025
    yow.

A false Judas kysse he hath gyven yow and is gone.

The halte, sore, and lame thys pitiefull case wyll
    mone.

Never prynce was there that made to poore peoples
    uses

So many masendewes,[67] hospytals and spyttle
    howses,[68]

As your Grace hath done yet sens the worlde   1030
    began.

KYNG JOHAN. Of priestes and of monkes I am counted
    a wycked man,

For that I never buylte churche nor monasterye,

But my pleasure was to helpe suche as were nedye.

ENGLANDE. The more grace was yours, for at the daye
    of judgement

Christe wyll rewarde them whych hath done hys   1035
    commaundement.

There is no promyse for voluntarye wurkes,

No more than there is for sacrifyce of the Turkes.

KYNG JOHAN. Doubtlesse I do fele muche grevaunce
    in my bodye.

ENGLANDE. As the Lorde wele knoweth, for that I
    am full sorye.

KYNG JOHAN. There is no malyce, to the malyce of the   1040
    clergye.

Well, the Lorde God of heaven on me and them
    have mercye.

For doynge justyce they have ever hated me.

They caused my lande to be excommunycate

And me to resygne both crowne and princely
    dygnyte,

From my obedyence assoylynge every estate.   1045

67 *masendewes*: poorhouses.   for the indigent or foully
68 *spyttle houses*: hospitals   diseased.

And now last of all they have me intoxycate.[69]
I perceyve ryght wele their malyce hath none
    ende.
I desyre not els but that they maye sone amende.
  I have sore hungred and thirsted ryghteousnesse
For the offyce sake that God hath me appoynted,   1050
But now I perceyve that synne and wyckednesse
In thys wretched worlde, lyke as Christe
    prophecyed,
Have the overhande, in me it is verefyed.
Praye for me, good people, I besych yow hartely,
That the Lorde above on my poore sowle have   1055
    mercy.
  Farwell, noble men, with the clergye spirytuall,
Farwell men of lawe, with the whole commynalte.
Your disobedyence I do forgyve yow all
And desyre God to perdon your iniquyte.
Farwell, swete Englande, now last of all to the[e].   1060
I am ryght sorye I coulde do for the[e] no more.
Farwele ones agayne, yea, farwell for evermore.
ENGLANDE. With the leave of God I wyll not leave
    ye thus,
But styll be with ye tyll he do take yow from us,
And than wyll I kepe your bodye for a memoryall.   1065
KYNG JOHAN. Than plye it, Englande, and provyde
    for my buryall.
A wydowes offyce, it is, to burye the deade.
      [KYNG JOHAN *dies.*]
ENGLANDE. Alas, swete maistre, ye waye so heavy as
    leade.
Oh horryble case, that ever so noble a kynge
Shoulde thus be destroyed and lost for rythteouse   1070
    doynge,
By a cruell sort of disguysed bloud-souppers,
Unmercyfull murtherers, all dronke in the bloude
    of marters!
Report what they wyll in their most furyouse
    madnesse,
Of thys noble kynge muche was the godlynesse.
    Exeunt [, ENGLANDE *bearing out the King.*]
      [*Enter* VERYTE.]

69 *intoxycate:* poisoned.

[VERYTE. *To the audience.*] I assure ye, fryndes, lete   1075
    men wryte what they wyll,
Kyng Johan was a man both valeaunt and godlye.
What though Polydorus reporteth hym very yll[23]
At the suggestyons of the malicyouse clergye.
Thynke yow a Romane with the Romans can not
    lye?
Yes, therfore, Leylande, out of thy s[l]umbre   1080
    awake,[24]
And wytnesse a trewthe for thyne owne contrayes
    sake.
  For hys valeauntnesse many excellent writers
    make,
As Sigebertus, Vincentius, and also Nauclerus,
Giraldus and Mathu Parys with hys noble vertues
    take,
Yea, Paulus Phrigio, Johan Major, and Hector   1085
    Boethius.[25]
Nothynge is allowed in hys lyfe of Polydorus
Whych discommendeth hys ponyshmentes for tray-
    terye,
Advauncynge very sore hygh treason in the
    clergye.
  Of hys godlynesse thus muche report wyll I :
Gracyouse provysyon for sore, sycke, halte, and   1090
    lame
He made in hys tyme, he made both in towne and
    cytie,
Grauntynge great lyberties for mayntenaunce of
    the same,
By markettes and fayers in places of notable name.
Great monymentes are in Yppeswych, Donwych
    and Berye,
Whych noteth hym to be a man of notable mercye.   1095
  The cytie of London, through his mere graunt
    and premye,
Was first privyleged to have both mayer and
    shryve,
Where before hys tyme it had but baylyves onlye.
In hys dayes the brydge the cytiezens ded con-
    tryve.
Though he now be dead, hys noble actes are alyve,   1100

Hys zele is declared, as towchynge Christes re-
        ligyon,
In that he exyled the Jewes out of thys regyon.[26]
[*Enter* NOBILYTE, CLERGYE, *and* CIVYLE ORDER.]
NOBILYTE. Whome speake ye of, sir, I besyche ye
        hartelye?
VERYTE. I talke of Kyng Johan, of late your prynce
        most worthye.
NOBILYTE. Sir, he was a man of a very wycked sorte.   1105
VERYTE. Ye are muche to blame your prynce so to re-
        porte.
    How can ye presume to be called Nobilyte,
    Diffamynge a prynce in your malygnyte?
    Ecclesiastes sayth, If thu with an hatefull harte
    Misnamest a kynge, thu playest suche a wycked   1110
        parte
    As byrdes of ayer to God wyll represent,
    To thy great parell and excedynge ponnyshment.
        Saynt Hierome sayth also that he is of no re-
            nowne,
    But a vyle traytour, that rebelleth agaynst the
        crowne.
CLERGYE. He speaketh not agaynst the crowne but   1115
        the man, per dee.
VERYTE. Oh, where is the sprete whych ought to
        reigne in the[e]?
    The crowne of itselfe without the man is nothynge.
    Learne of the Scriptures to have better undre-
        standynge.
    The harte of a kynge is in the handes of the Lorde,
    And he directeth it, wyse Salomon to recorde,   1120
    They are abhomynable that use hym wyckedlye.
CLERGYE. He was never good to us, the sanctifyed
        Clergye.
VERYTE. Wyll ye know the cause, before thys wor-
        shypfull companye?
    Your conversacyon and lyves are very ungodlye.
        Kynge Salomon sayth, Who hath a pure mynde   1125
    Therin delyghtynge, shall have a kynge to frynde.
    On thys wurde Cleros, whych signyfieth a lott,
    Or a sortynge out into a most godly knott,
    Ye do take your name, for that ye are the Lordes
    Select, of hys wurde to be the specyall recordes.   1130

As of saynt Mathias we have a syngular
    mencyon,
That they chose hym owt anon after Christes
    ascencyon.
Thus do ye recken, but I feare ye come of Clerus,
A very noyfull worme, as Aristotle sheweth us,
By whome are destroyed the honycombes of bees,   1135
For poore wydowes ye robbe, as ded the
    Pharysees.

CIVYLE ORDER. I promyse yow it is uncharytably
    spoken.

VERYTE. Trouthe ingendereth hate, ye shewe therof a
    token.

Ye are suche a man as ought everywhere to see
A godly order, but ye loose yche mare com-   1140
    mynalte.[70]
Plato thowght always that no hyghar love coulde
    be
Than a man to peyne hymself for hys own coun-
    treye.
David for their sake the proude Phelistian slewe,
Aioth mad Eglon hys wyckednesse to rewe.

Esdras from Persye for hys owne countreys sake   1145
Came to Hierusalem their strongeholdes up to
    make.
But yow lyke wretches cast over both contreye
    and kynge.
All manhode shameth to see your unnaturall
    doynge.
Ye wycked rulers, God doth abhorre ye all.
As Mantuan reporteth in hys Egloges pastorall,   1150
  Ye fede not the shepe, but ever ye pylle[71] the
    flocke,
And clyppe them so nygh that scarsely ye leve one
    locke.
Your jugementes are suche that ye call to God in
    vayne,
So longe as ye have your prynces in disdayne.
Chrysostome reporteth that nobilyte of fryndes   1155
Avalyeth nothynge, except ye have godly myndes.

70 *ye . . . commynalte :* each   71 *pylle :* pillage, or pull the
    (day) ye lose more of   wool from.
    the commons (?)

What profiteth it yow to be called spirytuall,
Whyls yow for lucre from all good vertues fall?
What prayse is it to yow to be called cyvylyte,
If yow from obedyence and godly order flee?   1160
Anneus Seneca hath thys most provable sentence,
The gentyll free hart goeth never from obedy-
          ence. [27]

CIVYLE ORDER. Sir, my bretherne and I woulde
          gladly knowe your name.

VERYTE. I am Veritas, that come hyther yow to blame
For castynge awaye of our most lawfull kynge.   1165
Both God and the worlde detesteth your damp-
          nable doynge.

     How have ye used Kyng Johan here now of
          late?

I shame to rehearce the corruptyons of your state.
Ye were never wele tyll ye had hym cruelly slayne,
And now beynge dead, ye have hym styll in dis-   1170
          dayne.

Ye have raysed up of hym most shamelesse lyes,
Both by your reportes and by your wrytten storyes.

     He that slewe Saul throwgh fearcenesse vyolent
Was slayne sone after at Davids just commaunde-
          ment

For bycause that Saul was anoynted of the Lorde.   1175
The seconde of Kynges of thys beareth plenteouse
          recorde.

He was in those dayes estemed wurthie to dye
On a noynted kynge that layed handes violentlye.

     Ye are not ashamed to fynde fyve priestes to
          synge

For that same traytour that slewe your naturall   1180
          kynge.

A trayterouse knave ye can set upp for a saynte,
And a ryghtheouse kynge lyke an odyouse tyraunt
          paynte.

I coulde shewe the place where yow most spyght-
          fullye

Put out your torches upon hys physnomye.

     In your glasse wyndowes ye whyppe your natu-   1185
          rall kynges. [28]

As I sayde afore, I abhorre to shewe your doynges.

The Turkes, I dare say, are a thowsande tymes bet-
    ter than yow.

NOBILYTE. For Gods love no more. Alas, ye have
    sayde ynough.

CLERGYE. All the worlde doth knowe that we have
    done sore amys.

CIVYLE ORDER. Forgyve it us, so that we never   1190
    heare more of thys.

VERYTE. But are ye sorye for thys ungodly wurke?

NOBILYTE. I praye to God else I be dampned lyke a
    Turke.

VERYTE. And make true promyse ye wyll never more
    do so?

CLERGYE. Sir, never more shall I from true obedyence
    goo.

VERYTE. What say you, brother? I must have also   1195
    your sentence.

CIVYLE ORDER. I wyll ever gyve to my prynce due rev-
    erence.

VERYTE. Well than, I doubt not but the Lorde wyll
    condescende

To forgyve yow all, so that ye mynde to amende.

Adewe to ye all, for now I must be gone.

        [*Enter* IMPERYALL MAJESTYE.]

IMPERYALL MAJESTYE. Abyde, Veryte, ye shall not   1200
    depart so sone.

Have ye done all thynges as we commanded yow?

VERYTE. Yea, most gracyouse prynce, I concluded the
    whole even now.

IMPERYALL MAJESTYE. And how do they lyke the cus-
    toms they have used

With our predecessours whome they have so
    abused,

Specyally Kyng Johan? Thynke they they have   1205
    done well?

VERYTE. They repent that ever they folowed sedi-
    cyouse counsell,

And have made promes they wyll amende all
    faultes.

IMPERYALL MAJESTYE. And forsake the pope with
    all hys cruell assaultes?

VERYTE. Whie do ye not bowe to Imperyall Majestye?

Knele and axe pardon for yowr great enormyte.   1210

NOBILYTE. Most godly governour, we axe your gracyouse pardon.

Promysynge nevermore to maynteyne false Sedicyon.

CLERGYE. Neyther Private Welth, nor yet Usurpyd
Power

Shall cause me disobeye my prynce from thys
same houre.

False Dissymulacyon shall never me begyle.   1215

Where I shall mete hym I wyll ever hym revyle.

IMPERYALL MAJESTYE. I perceyve, Veryte, ye have
done wele your part,

Refowrmynge these men. Gramercyes with all my
hart.

I praye yow take paynes to call our Commynalte

To true obedyence, as ye are Gods Veryte.   1220

VERYTE. I wyll do it, sir, yet shall I have muche
adoo

With your popish prelates, they wyll hunte me to
and fro.

IMPERYALL MAJESTYE. So longe as I lyve they shall
do yow no wronge.

VERYTE. Than wyll I go preache Gods wurde your
commens amonge.

But first I desyre yow their stubberne factes to   1225
remytt.

IMPERYALL MAJESTYE. I forgyve yow all, and perdon your frowarde wytt.

OMNES UNA. The heavenly Governour rewarde your
goodnesse for it.

VERYTE. For Gods sake obeye, lyke as doth yow befall,

For in hys owne realme a kynge is judge over all,

By Gods appoyntment, and none maye hym judge   1230
agayne

But the Lorde hymself: in thys the Scripture is
playne.

He that condempneth a kynge condempneth God
without dought,

He that harmeth a kynge to harme God goeth
abought,

He that a prynce resisteth doth dampne Gods
ordynaunce

And resisteth God in withdrawynge hys affyaunce.   1235
All subjectes offendynge are undre the kynges
      judgement.
A kynge is reserved to the Lorde omnypotent.
He is a mynyster immedyate undre God,
Of hys ryghteousnesse to execute the rod.
    I charge yow, therfore, as God hath charge   1240
      me,
To gyve to your kynge hys due supremyte,
And exyle the pope thys realme for evermore.
OMNES UNA. We shall gladly doo accordynge to your
      loore.
VERYTE. Your Grace is content I shewe your people
      the same?
IMPERYALL MAJESTYE. Yea, gentle Veryte, shewe   1245
      them their dewtye in Gods name.
                  [*Exit* VERYTE.]
To confyrme the tale that Veryte had now
The seconde of Kynges is evydent to yow.
    The yonge man that brought the crowne and
      bracelett
Of Saul to David, saynge that he had hym slayne,
David commaunded, as though he had done the   1250
      forfett,
Strayghtwaye to be slayne. Gods sprete ded hym
      constrayne
To shewe what it is a kynges bloude to distayne.
So ded he those two that in the fyelde hym mett,
And unto hym brought the heade of Isboset.[72]
    Consydre that Christe was undre the obedyence   1255
Of worldly prynces so longe as he was here,
And alwayes used them with a lowly reverence,
Payinge them tribute, all his true servauntes to
      stere
To obeye them, love them, and have them in rev-
      erent feare.
Dampnacyon it is to hym that an ordre breake   1260
Appoynted of God, lyke as the Apostle speake.
    No man is exempt from thys, Gods ordynaunce,
Bishopp, monke, chanon, priest, cardynall nor
      pope.

72 *Isboset :* Ishbosheth (II
    Samuel).

All they by Gods lawe to kynges owe their alle-
       geaunce.
Thys wyll be wele knowne in thys same realme I   1265
       hope.
Of Verytes wurdes the syncere meanynge I grope :
He sayth that a Kynge is of God immedyatlye.
Than shall never pope rule more in thys monarchie.
CLERGYE. If it be your pleasure we wyll exyle hym
       cleane,
That he in thys realme shall nevermore be seane.   1270
And your Grace shall be the supreme head of the
       churche.
To brynge thys to passe, ye shall see how we wyll
       wurche.
IMPERYALL MAJESTYE. Here is a nyce tale! He sayth,
       if it be my pleasure
He wyll do thys acte to the popes most hygh dis-
       pleasure,
As who sayth I woulde for pleasure of my persone   1275
And not for Gods truthe have suche an enterpryse
       done.
Full wysely convayed : the crowe wyll not chaunge
       her hewe.
It is marvele to me and ever ye be trewe.
  I wyll the auctoryte of Gods holy wurde to do
       it,
And it not to aryse of your vayne, slypper[73] wytt.   1280
That Scripture doth not is but a lyght fantasye.
CLERGYE. Both Daniel and Paule calleth hym Gods
       adversarye,
And therfore ye ought as a devyll hym to expell.
IMPERYALL MAJESTYE. Knewe ye thys afore, and
       woulde it never tell?
Ye shoulde repent it, had we not now forgyven ye.   1285
Nobilyte, what say yow? Wyll ye to thys agree?
NOBILYTE. I can no lesse, sir, for he is wurse than the
       Turke,
Whych none other wayes but by tyrannye doth
       wurke.
Thys bloudy bocher with hys pernycyouse bayte
Oppresse Christen princes by frawde, crafte, and   1290
       dissayte,

73 *slypper* : slippery.

Tyll he compell them to kysse hys pestylent fete,
Lyke a levyathan syttynge in Moyses sete.

I thynke we can do unto God no sacrifyce
That is more accept, nor more agreynge to justyce,
Than to slea that beaste and slauterman of the   1295
    devyll,
That Babylon boore, whych hath done so muche
    evyll.

IMPERYALL MAJESTYE. It is a clere sygne of a true
    Nobilyte
To the wurde of God whan your conscyence doth
    agree,
For as Christe ded saye to Peter, *Caro et sanguis*
Non revelavit tibi, sed Pater meus celestis:[29]   1300
Ye have not thys gyfte of carnall generacion,
Nor of noble bloude, but by Gods owne demon-
    stracyon.
    Of yow, Civyle Order, one sentence woulde I
    heare.

CIVYLE ORDER. I rewe it that ever any harte I ded
    hym beare.
    I thynke he hath spronge out of the bottomlesse   1305
    pytt
And in mennys conscyence in the stede of God
    doth sytt,
Blowynge fourth a swarme of grassopers and flyes,
Monkes, fryers and priestes, that all truthe pu-
    trifyes.
Of the Christen faythe playe now the true de-
    fendar,
Exyle thys monster and ravenouse devourar,   1310
With hys venym wormes, hys adders, whelpes and
    snakes,
Hys cuculled[74] vermyne that unto all myschiefe
    wakes.

IMPERYALL MAJESTYE. Than in thys purpose ye are
    all of one mynde?

CLERGYE. We detest the pope, and abhorre hym to
    the fynde.[75]

IMPERYALL MAJESTYE. And are wele content to dis-   1315
    obeye hys pryde?

74 *cuculled:* hooded, cowled.   75 *fynde:* fiend.

NOBILYTE. Yea, and his lowsye lawes and decrees to
    sett asyde.

IMPERYALL MAJESTYE. Than must ye be sworne to
    take me for your heade.

CIVYLE ORDER. We wyll obeye yow as our governour
    in Gods steade.

IMPERYALL MAJESTYE. Now that ye are sworne unto
    me your pryncypall,

I charge ye to regarde the wurde of God over all,   1320

And in that alone to rule, to speake, and to judge,

As ye wyll have me your socour and refuge.

CLERGYE. If ye wyll make sure, ye must exyle Se-
    dicyon,

False Dissymulacyon, with all vayne superstycyon,

And put Private Welth out of the monasteryes,   1325

Than Usurpyd Power maye goo a birdynge for
    flyes.

IMPERYALL MAJESTYE. Take yow it in hande, and do
    your true dilygence :

Iche man for hys part, ye shall wante no assys-
    tence.

CLERGYE. I promyse yow here to exyle Usurpyd
    Power,

And yowr supremyte to defende yche daye and   1330
    howre.

NOBILYTE. I promyse also out of the monasteryes

To put Private Welth, and detect hys mysteryes.

CIVYLE ORDER. False Dissymulacyon I wyll hange up
    in Smythfylde,

With suche supersticion as your people hath be-
    gylde.

IMPERYALL MAJESTYE. Than I trust we are at a very   1335
    good conclusyon,

Vertu to have place, and vyce to have confusyon.

Take Veryte wyth ye for every acte ye doo,

So shall ye be sure not out of the waye to goo.[30]

        SEDICYON *intrat.*

[SEDICYON *sings.*]

Pepe,   I   see   ye,   I   am glad I have spyed ye.

NOBILYTE. There is Sedicyon. Stand yow asyde a   1340
      whyle,
  Ye shall see how we shall catche hym by a wyle.
    [IMPERYALL MAJESTYE *stands aside.*]

SEDICYON. No noyse amonge ye? Where is the mery
      chere
  That was wont to be with quaffynge[70] of double
      bere?
  The worlde is not yet as some men woulde it have.
  I have bene abroade, and I thynke I have playde   1345
      the knave.

CIVYLE ORDER. Thu canyst do none other, except thu
      change thy wunte.

SEDICYON. What myschiefe ayle ye that ye are to me
      so blunte?
  I have sene the daye ye have favoured me[76] Per-
      fectyon.

CLERGYE. Thyselfe is not he, thu art of an other com-
      plectyon.
  Sir, thys is the thiefe that first subdued Kyng   1350
      Johan,
  Vexynge other prynces that sens have ruled thys
      regyon,
  And now he doth prate he hath played the knave,
  That the worlde is not yet as some men woulde it
      have.
  It woulde be knowne, sir, what he hath done of
      late.

IMPERYALL MAJESTYE. [*Stepping forward.*] What is   1355
      thy name, frynde, to us here intymate.

SEDICYON. A sayntwary! a sayntwary! for Gods dere
      passion, a sayntwarye!
  Is there none wyll holde me, and I have made so
      manye?

IMPERYALL MAJESTYE. Tell me what thy name is.
      Thu playest the knave, I trowe.

SEDICYON. I am wyndelesse, good man, I have muche
      peyne to blowe.

IMPERYALL MAJESTYE. I saye tell thy name, or the   1360
      racke shall the[e] constrayne.

  76 *favoured me* : called me.

SEDICYON. Holy Perfectyon my godmother called me
　　　　　playne.

NOBILYTE. It is Sedicyon, God gyve hym a very mys-
　　　　　chiefe.

CIVYLE ORDER. Undre heaven is not a more detestable
　　　　　thiefe

SEDICYON. By the Messe ye lye, I see wele ye do not
　　　　　knowe me.

IMPERYALL MAJESTYE. Ah, Brother, art thu come? I   1365
　　　　　am ryght glad we have the[e].

SEDICYON. By bodye, bloude, bones, and sowle, I am
　　　　　not he.

CLERGYE. If swearynge myghte helpe he woulde do
　　　　　we[le] ynough.

IMPERYALL MAJESTYE. He scape not our handes so
　　　　　lyghtly, I waraunde yow.

CLERGYE. Thys is that thiefe, sir, that all Christen-
　　　　　dome hath troubled,

　　And the pope of Rome agaynst all kynges mayn-   1370
　　　　　teyned.

NOBILYTE. Now that ye have hym, no more, but
　　　　　hange hym uppe.

CIVYLE ORDER. If ye so be content, it shall be done
　　　　　ere I suppe.

IMPERYALL MAJESTYE. Loo, the Clergye accuseth
　　　　　the[e], Nobilyte condempneth the[e],

　　And the lawe wyll hange the[e]. What sayst now
　　　　　to me?

SEDICYON. I woulde I were now at Rome at the sygne   1375
　　　　　of the cuppe,

　　For heavynesse is drye. Alas, must I nedes clymbe
　　　　　uppe?
　　　　　　　[SEDICYON *kneels.*]

　　Perdon my lyfe, and I shall tell ye all,

　　Both that is past and that wyll herafter fall.

IMPERYALL MAJESTYE. Aryse. I perdon the[e], so that
　　　　　thu tell the trewthe.

SEDICYON. I wyll tell to yow suche treason as en-   1380
　　　　　sewthe.

　　Yet a ghostly father ought not to bewraye confes-
　　　　　syon.

IMPERYALL MAJESTYE. No confessyon is but ought to
　　　　　discover treason.

SEDICYON. I thynke it maye kepe all thynge save
        heresye.

IMPERYALL MAJESTYE. It maye holde no treason, I
        tell the[e] verelye,

And therfore tell the whole matter by and bye.   1385

Thu saydest now of late that thu haddest played
        the knave,

And that the worlde was not as some men woulde
        it have.

SEDICYON. I coulde playe Pasquyll,[31] but I feare to
        have rebuke.

IMPERYALL MAJESTYE. For utterynge the truthe
        feare neyther byshopp nor duke.

SEDICYON. Ye gave injunctyons that Gods wurde   1390
        myghte be taught,

But who observe them? Full manye a tyme have I
        laught

To see the conveyaunce that prelates and priestes
        can fynde.

IMPERYALL MAJESTYE. And whie do they beare Gods
        wurde no better mynde?

SEDICYON. For if that were knowne, than woulde the
        people regarde

No heade but their prynce; with the churche than   1395
        were it harde.

Than shoulde I lacke helpe to maynteyne their es-
        tate,

As I attempted in the Northe but now of late,[32]

And sens that same tyme in other places besyde,

Tyll my setters on were of their purpose wyde.

A vengeaunce take it, it was never well with me   1400

Sens the cummynge hyther of that same Veryte.

Yet do the byshoppes for my sake vexe hym
        amonge.

IMPERYALL MAJESTYE. Do they so indede? Well,
        they shall not do so longe.

SEDICYON. In your parlement, commaunde yow what
        ye wyll,

The popes ceremonyes shall drowne the Gospell   1405
        styll.

Some of the byshoppes at your injunctyons slepe,

Some laugh and go bye, and some can playe boo
        pepe.

Some of them do nought but searche for here-
        tykes,
Whyls their priestes abroade do playe the scys-
        matykes.
   Tell me in London how manye their othes dis-   1410
           charge
Of the curates there? Yet is it muche wurse at
        large.
If your true subjectes impugne their trecheryes,
They can fatche them in anon for Sacramentaryes,
Or Anabaptystes. Thus fynde they a subtyle shyfte
To helpe proppe up their kyngedome, suche is   1415
        their wyly dryfte.
   Get they false wytnesses, they force not[77] of
         whens they be,
Be they of Newgate, or be they of the Marshall-
        see.[(33)]
Paraventure a thousande are in one byshoppes,
        boke,
And agaynst a daye are readye to the hooke.
IMPERYALL MAJESTYE. Are those matters true that   1420
        thu hast spoken here?
SEDICYON. What can in the worlde more evydent wyt-
        nesse bere?
   First of all consydre, the prelates do not preache
But persecute those that the holye Scriptures
        teache.
And marke me thys wele, they never ponnysh for
        popery,
But the Gospell readers they handle very coursely,   1425
For on them they laye by hondred poundes of
        yron,
And wyll suffer none with them ones for to com-
        mon.
   Sytt they never so longe, nothynge by them
         cometh fourthe
To the truthes furtherance that any thynge ys
        wourthe.
In some byshoppes howse ye shall not fynde a   1430
        testament,
But yche man readye to devoure the innocent.

77 *force not :* care not.

We lyngar a tyme and loke but for a daye

To sett upp the pope, if the Gospell woulde de-
            caye.

CLERGYE. Of that he hath tolde hys selfe is the very
            grounde.

IMPERYALL MAJESTYE. Art thu of counsell in this   1435
            that thu hast spoken?

SEDICYON. Yea, and in more than that, if all secretes
            myght be broken.

For the pope I make so muche as ever I maye do.

IMPERYALL MAJESTYE. I praye the[e] hartely, tell me
            why thu doest so?

SEDICYON. For I perceyve wele the pope is a jolye
            fellawe,

    A trymme fellawe, a ryche fellawe, yea and myry   1440
            fellawe.

IMPERYALL MAJESTYE. A jolye fellawe how dost thu
            prove the pope?

SEDICYON. For he hath crosse keyes with a tryple
            crowne and a cope,

    Trymme as a trencher, havynge his shoes of golde,

    Ryche in hys ryalte and angelyck to beholde.

IMPERYALL MAJESTYE. How dost thu prove hym to   1445
            be a fellawe myrye?

SEDICYON. He hath pipys and belles with kyrye,
            kyrye, kyrye. (34)

    Of hym ye maye bye both salt, creame, oyle and
            waxe,

    And after hygh Masse ye may learne to beare the
            paxe.[78]

IMPERYALL MAJESTYE. Yea, and nothynge heare of
            the Pystle and the Gospell?

SEDICYON. No, Sir, by the Masse, he wyll gyve no   1450
            suche counsell.

IMPERYALL MAJESTYE. Whan thu art abroade where
            doest thy lodgynge take?

SEDICYON. Amonge suche people as God ded never
            make :

    Not only cuckoldes, but suche as folow the popes
            lawes

78 *paxe :* tablet with a repre-
        sentation of the crucifix-
        ion.

In disgysed coates, with balde crownes lyke jacke
  dawes.
IMPERYALL MAJESTYE. Than every where thu art 1455
  the popes altogyther.
SEDICYON. Ye had proved it ere thys, if I had not
  chaunced hyther.
I sought to have served yow lyke as I ded Kyng
  Johan,
But that Veryte stopte me, the devyll hym poyson.
NOBILYTE. He is wurthie to dye and there were men
  nomore.
CIVYLE ORDER. Hange up the vyle knave, and kepe 1460
  hym no longar in store.
IMPERYALL MAJESTYE. Drawe hym to Tyburne, lete
  hym be hanged and quartered.
SEDICYON. Whye, of late dayes ye sayde I shoulde
  not be so martyred.
Where is the pardon that ye ded promyse me?
IMPERYALL MAJESTYE. For doynge more harme thu
  shalt sone pardoned be.
Have hym fourth, Civyle Order, and hang hym 1465
  tyll he be dead,
And on London brydge loke ye bestowe hys head.
CIVYLE ORDER. I shall see it done and returne to yow
  agayne.
SEDICYON. I beshrewe your hart for takynge so muche
  payne.
Some man tell the pope, I besyche ye with all my
  harte,
How I am ordered for takynge the Churches 1470
  parte,
That I maye be put in the holye letanye
With Thomas Beckett, for I thynke I am as
  wurthye.
Praye to me with candels, for I am a saynt al-
  readye.
O blessed saynt Partryck, I see the[e] I verylye.
IMPERYALL MAJESTYE. I see by thys wretche there 1475
  hath bene muche faulte in ye :
Shewe yourselves herafter more sober and wyse
  to be.
Kyng Johan ye subdued for that he ponnyshed
  treason

Rape, theft, and murther in the holye spirytualte :
But Thomas Beckett ye exalted without reason,
Because that he dyed for the Churches wanton   1480
          lyberte,
That the priestes myght do all kyndes of inyquyte,
And be unponnyshed : Marke now the judgement
Of your ydle braynes, and for Gods love repent.
NOBILYTE. As God shall judge me I repent me of my
          rudenesse.
CLERGYE. I am ashamed of my most vayne folyshe-   1485
          nesse.
NOBILYTE. I consydre now that God hath for Sedi-
          cyon
Sent ponnyshmentes great : examples we have in
          Brute,
In Catilyne, in Cassius, and fayer Absolon, [35]
Whome of their purpose God alwayes destytute,
And terryble plages on them ded execute   1490
For their rebellyon. And therfore I wyll beware,
Least his great vengeaunce trappe me in suche
          lyke snare.
CLERGYE. I pondre also that sens the tyme of Adam
The Lorde evermore the governours preserved :
Examples we fynde in Noe and in Abraham,   1495
In Moyses and David, from whome God never
          swerved.
I wyll therfor obeye least he be with me dis-
          pleased.
Homerus doth saye that God putteth fourth hys
          shyelde
The prynce to defende whan he is in the
          fyelde. [36]
CIVYLE ORDER. Thys also I marke : whan the priestes   1500
          had governaunce
Over the Hebrues, the sectes ded first aryse
As Pharisees, Sadducees, and Essees, whych
          wrought muche grevaunce
Amonge the people by their most devylysh prac-
          tyse,
Tyll destructyons the prynces ded devyse,
To the quyetnesse of their faythfull commens all,   1505
As your Grace hath done with the sectes papis-
          tycall.

IMPERYALL MAJESTYE. That poynt hath in tyme
        fallen to your memoryes.

The Anabaptystes, a secte newe rysen of late,

The Scriptures poyseneth with their subtle alle-
        goryes,

The heades to subdue after a sedicyouse rate.   1510

The cytie of Mynster was lost through their de-
        bate.[37]

They have here begonne their pestilent sedes to
        sowe,

But we trust in God to increace they shall not
        growe.

CLERGYE. God forbyd the[y] shoulde, for they myght
        do muche harme.

CIVYLE ORDER. We shall cut them short if they do   1515
        hyther swarme.

IMPERYALL MAJESTYE. The adminystracyon of a
        princes governaunce

Is the gifte of God and hys hygh ordynaunce,

Whome with all your power yow thre ought to ·
        support

In the lawes of God to all hys peoples confort.

First yow, the Clergye, in preachynge of Gods   1520
        worde,

Than yow, Nobilyte, defendynge with the sworde,

Yow, Civyle Order, in executynge justyce.

Thus, I trust, we shall seclude all maner of vyce,

And after we have establyshed our kyngedome

In peace of the Lorde and in hys godly fredome,   1525

We wyll confirme it with wholesom lawes and de-
        crees,

To the full suppressynge of Antichristes vanytees.
    Hic omnes Rex osculatur.[79]

Farwele to ye all, first to yow, Nobilyte,

Than to yow, Clergye, than to yow Civylyte.

And above all thynges, remembre our injunctyon.   1530

OMNES UNA. By the helpe of God, yche one shall do
        hys functyon.

[*Here go out the* KYNG. NOBILYTE, CLERGYE, *and*
    CIVYLE ORDER *turn to the audience.*]

79 *Hic . . . osculatur:* Here
    the king kisses them all.

NOBILYTE. By thys example ye maye see with your
        eyes
    How Antichristes whelpes have noble princes
        used.
    Agayne ye maye see how they with prodigyouse
        lyes
    And craftes uncomely their myschiefes have ex-   1535
        cused.
    Both nature, manhode, and grace they have
        abused,
    Defylynge the lawe, and blyndynge Nobilyte,
    No Christen regyon from their abusyons free.
CLERGYE. Marke wele the dampnable bestowynge of
        their Masses,
    With their foundacyons for poysenynge of their   1540
        kynge.
    Their confessyon driftes, all other traytery
        passes.[80]
    A saynt the[y] can make of the most knave thys
        daye lyvynge,
    Helpynge their market. And to promote the
        thynge
    He shall do myracles. But he that blemysh their
        glorye
    Shall be sent to helle, without anye remedye.   ·1545
CIVYLE ORDER. Here was to be seane what ryseth of
        Sedicyon
    And howe he doth take hys mayntenaunce and
        grounde
    Of ydle persones, brought upp in supersticyon,
    Whose daylye practyse is alwayes to confounde
    Such as myndeth vertu and to them wyll not be   1550
        bounde.
    Expedyent it is to knowe their pestylent wayes,
    Consyderynge they were so busye now of late
        dayes.
NOBILYTE. Englande hath a Quene, thanks to the
        Lorde above,[38]
    Whych maye be a lyghte to other princes all
    For the godlye wayes whome she doth dayle move   1555

80 *traytery passes*: treacher-
    ous devices.

To hir liege people, through Gods wurde specyall.
She is that Angell, as saynt Johan doth hym call,
That with the Lordes seale doth marke out hys
     true servauntes,
Pryntynge in their hartes hys holy wourdes and
     covenauntes.
CLERGYE. In Danyels sprete she hath subdued the   1560
     Papistes,
With all the ofsprynge of Antichristes generacyon.
And now of late dayes, the secte of Anabaptistes
She seketh to suppresse, for their pestiferous
     facyon.
She vanquysheth also the great abhomynacyon
Of supersticyons, witchecraftes, and hydolatrye,   1565
Restorynge Gods honoure to hys first force and
     bewtye.
CIVYLE ORDER. Praye unto the Lorde that hir Grace
     maye contynewe
The dayes of Nestor,[39] to our sowles conso-
     lacyon,
And that hir ofsprynge maye lyve also to subdewe
The great Antichriste, with hys whole generacyon   1570
In Helias sprete,[40] to the confort of thys nacyon,
Also to preserve hir most honourable counsell
To the prayse of God and glorye of the Gospell.

       Thus endeth the ij playes[41]
         of Kynge Johan.

ROYSTER DOYSTER

by

NICHOLAS UDALL

The Prologue.

What Creature is in health, eyther yong or olde,
But som mirth with modestie wil be glad to vse
As we in thys Enterlude shall now vnfolde,
Wherin all scurilitie we vtterly refuse,
Auoiding such mirth wherin is abuse :
Knowing nothing more comedable for a mãs re-
Than Mirth which is vsed in an honest fashion :   (creation
For Myrth prolongeth lyfe, and causeth health.
Mirth recreates our spirites and voydeth pensiuenesse,
Mirth increaseth amitie, not hindring our wealth,
Mirth is to be vsed both of more and lesse,
Being mixed with vertue in decent comlynesse.
As we trust no good nature can gainsay the same :
Which mirth we intende to vse, auoidyng all blame.
The wyse Poets long time heretofore,
Under merrie Comedies secretes did declare,
Wherein was contained very vertuous lore,
With mysteries and forewarnings very rare.
Suche to write neither Plautus nor Terence dyd spare,
Whiche among the learned at this day beares the bell :
These with such other therein dyd excell.
Our Comedie or Enterlude which we intende to play.
Is named Royster Doyster in deede.
Which against the vayne glorious doth inuey,
Whose humour the roysting sort continually doth feede.
Thus by your pacience we intende to procæde
In this our Enterlude by Gods leaue and grace,
And here I take my leaue for a certaine space.

FINIS.

A.ij.   Actus

[DRAMATIS PERSONAE.

RAFE ROYSTER DOYSTER, *a Miles Gloriosus.*[1]
MATHEW MERYGREEKE.[2]
GAWYN GOODLUCKE, *London Merchant, affianced to Custance.*
TRISTRAM TRUSTY, *his friend.*
DOBINET DOUGHTIE, *servant to Royster.*
TOM TRUEPENIE, *servant to Custance.*
SYM SURESBY, *servant to Goodlucke.*
HARPAX[3] *and other Musicians in Royster's service.*
SCRIVENER.
Two ENSIGNS *or standard-bearers.*
DAME CHRISTIAN CUSTANCE,[4] *a wealthy widow.*
MAGE MUMBLE-CRUST, *her old Nurse.*
TIBET TALK-APACE ⎫
ANNOT ALYFACE[5] ⎭ *Maids of Custance.*

THE SCENE
LONDON.]

[Enter] the Prologue.

What Creature is in health, eyther yong or olde,
But som mirth with modestie wil be glad to use
As we in thys Enterlude shall now unfolde,
Wherin all scurilitie we utterly refuse,
Avoiding such mirth wherin is abuse: 5
Knowing nothing more comendable for a mans
        recreation
Than Mirth which is used in an honest fashion:

For Myrth prolongeth lyfe, and causeth health.
Mirth recreates our spirites and voydeth pensive-
        nesse,
Mirth increaseth amitie, not hindring our wealth,   10
Mirth is to be used both of more and lesse,
Being mixed with vertue in decent comlynesse.
As we trust no good nature can gainsay the same:
Which mirth we intende to use, avoidyng all
        blame.

The wyse Poets long time heretofore,   15
Under merrie Comedies secretes did declare,
Wherein was contained very vertuous lore,
With mysteries and forewarnings very rare.

Suche to write neither *Plautus* nor *Terence* dyd
    spare,[1]
Whiche among the learned at this day beares the   20
    bell.[2]
These with such other therein dyd excell.

Our Comedie or Enterlude which we intende to
    play
Is named Royster Doyster in deede.
Which against the vayne glorious doth invey,
Whose humour the roysting sort continually doth   25
    feede.
Thus by your pacience we intende to proceede
In this our Enterlude by Gods leave and grace,
And here I take my leave for a certaine space.
                          [*Exeat.*]

FINIS.

ACTUS I. SCAENA I.

MATHEW MERYGREEKE. *He entreth singing.*
[MATHEW MERYGREEKE.] As long lyveth the mery
    man (they say)
As doth the sory man, and longer by a day.
Yet the Grassehopper for all his Sommer pipyng,
Sterveth in Winter wyth hungrie gripyng,
Therefore an other sayd sawe[1] doth men advise,   5
That they be together both mery and wise.
Thys Lesson must I practise, or else ere long,
Wyth mee Mathew Merygreeke it will be wrong.
In deede men so call me, for by Him that us
    bought,[2]
What ever chaunce betide, I can take no thought,   10
Yet wisedome woulde that I did my selfe bethinke
Where to be provided this day of meate and
    drinke :
For knowe[1] ye, that for all this merie note of
    mine,

ACTUS I. SCAENA I.   2 *bought :* redeemed.
  1 *sayd sawe :* frequently ut-
    tered proverb.

He might appose[3] me now that should aske where
       I dine.
My lyving lieth heere and there, of Gods grace,   15
Sometime wyth this good man, sometyme in that
       place,
Sometime Lewis Loytrer biddeth me come neere,
Somewhyles Watkin Waster maketh us good
       cheere,
Sometime Davy Diceplayer when he hath well
       cast
Keepeth revell route as long as it will last.   20
Sometime Tom Titivile[(1)] maketh us a feast,
Sometime with sir Hugh Pye I am a bidden
       gueast,
Sometime at Nichol Neverthrives I get a soppe,
Sometime I am feasted with Bryan Blinkinsoppe,
Sometime I hang on Hankyn Hoddydodies sleeve,   25
But thys day on Rafe Royster Doysters by hys
       leeve.
For truely of all men he is my chiefe banker
Both for meate and money, and my chiefe shoot-
       anker.[4]
For, sooth Royster Doyster in that he doth say,
And require what ye will ye shall have no nay.   30
But now of Royster Doyster somewhat to expresse,
That ye may esteeme him after hys worthinesse,
In these twentie townes and seke them through-
       out,
Is not the like stocke, whereon to graffe[5] a loute.
All the day long is he facing and craking[6]   35
Of his great actes in fighting and fraymaking:
But when Royster Doyster is put to his proofe,
To keepe the Queenes[(2)] peace is more for his
       behoofe.
If any woman smyle or cast on hym an eye,
Up is he to the harde eares in love by and by,[7]   40

3 *appose* : nonplus, discon-   6 *facing and craking* : swag-
   cert.   gering and bragging.
4 *shootanker* : shot-anchor,   7 *to . . . by* : utterly in love
   i.e. last resort.   at once.
5 *graffe* : graft.

And in all the hotte haste must she be hys wife,
Else farewell hys good days, and farewell his life,
Maister Rafe Royster Doyster is but dead and gon
Excepte she on hym take some compassion,
Then chiefe of counsell, must be Mathew Mery-   45
  greeke,
What if I for mariage to suche an one seeke?
Then must I sooth it, what ever it is :
For what he sayth or doth can not be amisse,
Holde up his yea and nay, be his nowne white
  sonne,[8]
Prayse and rouse him well, and ye have his heart   50
  wonne,
For so well liketh he his owne fonde fashions[9]
That he taketh pride of false commendations.
But such sporte have I with him as I would not
  leese,[10]
Though I should be bounde to lyve with bread
  and cheese.
For exalt hym, and have hym as ye lust[11] in   55
  deede :
Yea to hold his finger in a hole for a neede.
I can with a worde make him fayne or loth,
I can with as much make him pleased or wroth,
I can when I will make him mery and glad,
I can when me lust make him sory and sad,   60
I can set him in hope and eke in dispaire,
I can make him speake rough, and make him
  speake faire.
But I marvell I see hym not all thys same day,
I wyll seeke him out : But loe, he commeth thys
  way,
I have yond espied hym sadly comming,   65
And in love for twentie pounde, by hys glommyng.

8 *nowne white sonne :* own   9 *fonde fashions :* foolish ap-
 darling boy, i.e. close   pearance or behavior.
 friend.   10 *leese :* lose.
          11 *lust :* list, wish.

Actus i.   Scaena ii.

[Enter] RAFE ROYSTER DOYSTER *[to]* MATHEW
                        MERYGREEKE.

RAFE ROYSTER. Come death when thou wilt, I am
                        weary of my life.
MATHEW MERYGREEKE. *[Aside.]* I tolde you I, we
                        should wowe another wife.
RAFE ROYSTER. Why did God make me suche a
                        goodly person?
MATHEW MERYGREEKE. *[Aside.]* He is in by the
                        weke,[1] we shall have sport anon.
RAFE ROYSTER. And where is my trustie friende   5
                        Mathew Merygreeke?
MATHEW MERYGREEKE. *[Aside.]* I wyll make as I
                        sawe him not, he doth me seeke.
RAFE ROYSTER. I have hym espyed me thinketh,
                        yond is hee,
    Hough Mathew Merygreeke my friend, a worde
                        with thee.
MATHEW MERYGREEKE. *[Aside.]* I wyll not heare him,
                        but make as I had haste,
    Farewell all my good friendes, the tyme away   10
                        dothe waste,
    And the tide they say, tarieth for no man.
RAFE ROYSTER. Thou must with thy good counsell
                        helpe me if thou can.
MATHEW MERYGREEKE. God keepe thee worshypfull
                        Maister Royster Doyster,
    And fare well the lustie Maister Royster Doyster.
RAFE ROYSTER. I muste needes speake with thee a   15
                        worde or twaine.
MATHEW MERYGREEKE. Within a month or two I will
                        be here againe,
    Negligence in greate affaires ye knowe may marre
                        all.
RAFE ROYSTER. Attende upon me now, and well re-
                        warde thee I shall.

Actus i.   Scaena ii.
    1 *in by the weke :* far gone.

MATHEW MERYGREEKE. I have take my leave, and the
        tide is well spent.

RAFE ROYSTER. I die except thou helpe, I pray thee   20
        be content,

Doe thy parte wel nowe, and aske what thou wilt,

For without thy aide my matter is all spilt.

MATHEW MERYGREEKE. Then to serve your turne I
        will some paines take,

And let all myne owne affaires alone for your sake.

RAFE ROYSTER. My whole hope and trust resteth   25
        onely in thee.

MATHEW MERYGREEKE. Then can ye not doe amisse
        what ever it bee.

RAFE ROYSTER. Gramercies Merygreeke, most bounde
        to thee I am.

MATHEW MERYGREEKE. But up with that heart, and
        speake out like a ramme,

Ye speake like a Capon that had the cough now :

Bee of good cheere, anon ye shall doe well ynow.   30

RAFE ROYSTER. Upon thy comforte, I will all things
        well handle.

MATHEW MERYGREEKE. So loe, that is a breast to
        blowe out a candle.

But what is this great matter I woulde faine
        knowe,

We shall fynde remedie therefore I trowe.

Doe ye lacke money? ye knowe myne olde offers,   35

Ye have always a key to my purse and coffers.

RAFE ROYSTER. I thanke thee : had ever man suche a
        frende?

MATHEW MERYGREEKE. Ye gyve unto me : I must
        needes to you lende.

RAFE ROYSTER. Nay I have money plentie all things
        to discharge.

MATHEW MERYGREEKE. [*Aside*.] That knewe I ryght   40
        well when I made offer so large.

[RAFE ROYSTER.] But it is no suche matter.[1]

MATHEW MERYGREEKE.   What is it than?

Are ye in daunger of debte to any man?

If ye be, take no thought nor be not afraide,

Let them hardly[2] take thought how they shall be
        paide.

2 *hardly* : by all means.

RAFE ROYSTER. Tut I owe nought.

MATHEW MERYGREEKE. What then? fear ye imprison-   45
        ment?

RAFE ROYSTER. No.

MATHEW MERYGREEKE. No I wist[3] ye offende not so,
        to be shent.[4]

    But if ye[2] had, the Toure[5] coulde not you so
        holde,

    But to breake out at all times ye would be bolde.

    What is it? hath any man threatned you to beate?

RAFE ROYSTER. What is he that durst have put me in   50
        that heate?

    He that beateth me, by His armes, shall well
        fynde,

    That I will not be farre from him nor runne be-
        hinde.

MATHEW MERYGREEKE. That thing knowe all men
        ever since ye overthrewe,

    The fellow of the Lion which *Hercules* slewe.[(1)]

    But what is it than?

RAFE ROYSTER.   Of love I make my mone.   55

MATHEW MERYGREEKE. Ah this foolishe a[(2)] love,
        wilt neare[6] let us alone?

    But bicause ye were refused the last day,

    Ye said ye woulde nere more be intangled that
        way :

    "I would medle no more, since I fynde all so un-
        kinde."

RAFE ROYSTER. Yea, but I can not so put love out of   60
        my minde.

MATHEW MERYGREEKE. But is your love tell me first,
        in any wise,

    In the way of Mariage, or of Merchandise?

    If it may otherwise than lawfull be founde,

    Ye get none of my helpe for an hundred pounde.

RAFE ROYSTER. No by my trouth I would have hir to   65
        my Wife.

MATHEW MERYGREEKE. Then are ye a good man, and
        God save your life,

---

3 *wist* : know.

4 *shent* : blamed.

5 *Toure* : the Tower of Lon-
        don.

6 *neare* : never.

And what or who is she, with whome ye are in
         love?

RAFE ROYSTER. A woman whome I knowe not by
         what meanes to move.

MATHEW MERYGREEKE. Who is it?

RAFE ROYSTER.   A woman yond.

MATHEW MERYGREEKE.   What is hir name?

RAFE ROYSTER. Hir yonder.

MATHEW MERYGREEKE.   Whom?[3]

RAFE ROYSTER.   Mistresse ah—

MATHEW MERYGREEKE.   Fy fy for shame!   70
Love ye, and know not whome? but hir yonde, a
         Woman,

We shall then get you a Wyfe, I can not tell whan.

RAFE ROYSTER. The faire Woman, that supped wyth
         us yesternyght—

And I hearde hir name twice or thrice, and had it
         ryght.

MATHEW MERYGREEKE. Yea, ye may see ye nere take   75
         me to good cheere with you,

If ye had, I coulde have tolde you hir name now.

RAFE ROYSTER. I was to blame in deede, but the
         nexte tyme perchaunce :

And she dwelleth in this house.

MATHEW MERYGREEKE.   What Christian Custance?

RAFE ROYSTER. Except I have hir to my Wife, I shall
         runne madde.

MATHEW MERYGREEKE. Nay unwise perhaps, but I   80
         warrant you for madde.

RAFE ROYSTER. I am utterly dead unlesse I have my
         desire.

MATHEW MERYGREEKE. Where be the bellowes that
         blewe this sodeine fire?

RAFE ROYSTER. I heare she is worthe a thousande
         pounde and more.

MATHEW MERYGREEKE. Yea, but learne this one les-
         son of me afore,

An hundred pounde of Marriage money doubt-   85
         lesse,

Is ever thirtie pounde sterlyng, or somewhat lesse,

So that hir Thousande pounde yf she be thriftie,

Is muche neere about two hundred and fiftie,

Howebeit wowers and Widowes are never poore.

RAFE ROYSTER. Is she a Widowe? I love hir better   90
            therefore.
MATHEW MERYGREEKE. But I heare she hath made
            promise to another.
RAFE ROYSTER. He shall goe without hir, and[7] he
            were my brother.
MATHEW MERYGREEKE. I have hearde say, I am right
            well advised,
    That she hath to Gawyn Goodlucke promised.
RAFE ROYSTER. What is that Gawyn Goodlucke?   95
MATHEW MERYGREEKE.   A Merchant man.
RAFE ROYSTER. Shall he speede afore me? nay sir by
            sweete Sainct Anne.
    Ah sir, Backare quod Mortimer to his sowe,[(3)]
    I wyll have hir myne owne selfe I make God a vow.
    For I tell thee, she is worthe a thousande pounde.
MATHEW MERYGREEKE. Yet a fitter wife for your   100
            maship might be founde :
    Suche a goodly man as you, might get one wyth
            lande,
    Besides poundes of golde a thousande and a thou-
            sande,
    And a thousande, and a thousande, and a thou-
            sande,
    And so to the summe of twentie hundred thou-
            sande,
    Your most goodly personage is worthie of no   105
            lesse.
RAFE ROYSTER. I am sorie God made me so comely
            doubtlesse,
    For that maketh me eche where so highly fa-
            voured,
    And all women on me so enamoured.
MATHEW MERYGREEKE. Enamoured quod you? have
            ye spied out that?
    Ah sir, mary nowe I see you know what is what.   110
    Enamoured ka?[8] mary sir say that againe,
    But I thought not ye had marked it so plaine.
RAFE ROYSTER. Yes, eche where they gaze all upon
            me and stare.

7 *and* : if.   8 *ka* : quotha, said he.

MATHEW MERYGREEKE. Yea Malkyn, I warrant you as
              muche as they dare.

And ye will not beleve what they say in the   115
              streete,

When your mashyp passeth by all such as I meete,

That sometimes I can scarce finde what aunswere
              to make.

Who is this (sayth one) sir *Launcelot du lake?*

Who is this, greate *Guy*[4] of Warwike, sayth an
              other?

No (say I) it is the thirtenth *Hercules* brother.   120

Who is this? noble *Hector* of *Troy,* sayth the
              thirde?

No, but of the same nest (say I) it is a birde.

Who is this? greate *Goliah, Sampson,* or *Col-
              brande?*

No (say I) but it is a brute of the Alie lande.[4]

Who is this? greate *Alexander?* or *Charle le*   125
              Maigne?

No, it is the tenth Worthie, say I to them agayne :

I knowe not if I sayd well.

RAFE ROYSTER.   Yes for so I am.

MATHEW MERYGREEKE. Yea, for there were but nine
              worthies before ye came.

To some others, the thirde *Cato* I doe you call.[5]

And so as well as I can I aunswere them all.   130

Sir I pray you, what lorde or great gentleman is
              this?

Maister Rafe Royster Doyster dame say I, ywis.

O Lorde (sayth she than) what a goodly man it is,

Woulde Christ I had such a husbande as he is.

O Lorde (say some) that the sight of his face we   135
              lacke :

It is inough for you (say I) to see his backe.

His face is for ladies of high and noble parages.[9]

With whome he hardly scapeth great mariages.

With muche more than this, and much otherwise.

RAFE ROYSTER. I can[10] thee thanke that thou canst   140
              suche answeres devise :

But I perceyve thou doste me throughly knowe.

MATHEW MERYGREEKE. I marke your maners for
              myne owne learnyng I trowe,

9 *parages :* ancestry.   10 *can :* give.

But suche is your beautie, and suche are your
    actes,
Suche is your personage, and suche are your
    factes,[11]
That all women faire and fowle, more and less,   145
They[5] eye you, they lubbe[12] you, they talke of
    you doubtlesse,
Your p[l]easant looke maketh them all merie,
Ye passe not by, but they laugh till they be werie,
Yea and money coulde I have the truthe to tell,
Of many, to bryng you that way where they   150
    dwell.

RAFE ROYSTER. Merygreeke for this thy reporting well
    of mee :

MATHEW MERYGREEKE. What shoulde I else sir, it is
    my duetie pardee :

RAFE ROYSTER. I promise thou shalt not lacke, while
    I have a grote.

MATHEW MERYGREEKE. Faith sir, and I nere had
    more nede of a newe cote.

RAFE ROYSTER. Thou shalte have one to morowe, and   155
    golde for to spende.

MATHEW MERYGREEKE. Then I trust to bring the day
    to a good ende.
For as for mine owne parte having money inowe,
I could lyve onely with the remembrance of you.
But nowe to your Widowe whome you love so
    hotte.

RAFE ROYSTER. By Cocke[13] thou sayest truthe, I had   160
    almost forgotte.

MATHEW MERYGREEKE. What if Christian Custance
    will not have you what?

RAFE ROYSTER. Have me? yes I warrant you, never
    doubt of that,
I knowe she loveth me, but she dare not speake.

MATHEW MERYGREEKE. In deede meete it were some
    body should it breake.[14]

RAFE ROYSTER. She looked on me twentie tymes yes-   165
    ternight,

11 *factes* : deeds.   13 *Cocke* : God.
12 *lubbe* : love.   14 *breake* : broach.

And laughed so.

MATHEW MERYGREEKE. That she coulde not sitte
        upright.

RAFE ROYSTER. No faith coulde she not.

MATHEW MERYGREEKE. No even such a thing I cast.[15]

RAFE ROYSTER. But for wowyng thou knowest women
        are shamefast.

But and she knewe my minde, I knowe she would
        be glad,

And thinke it the best chaunce that ever she had.   170

MATHEW MERYGREEKE. Too hir then like a man, and
        be bolde forth to starte,

Wowers never speede well, that have a false harte.

RAFE ROYSTER. What may I best doe?

MATHEW MERYGREEKE. Sir remaine ye a while
        [here].[6]

Ere long one or other of hir house will appere.

Ye knowe my minde.

RAFE ROYSTER.   Yea now hardly lette me alone.   175

MATHEW MERYGREEKE. In the meane time sir, if you
        please, I wyll home,

And call your Musitians, for in this your case

It would sette you forth, and all your wowyng
        grace,

Ye may not lacke your instrumentes to play and
        sing.

RAFE ROYSTER. Thou knowest I can doe that.

MATHEW MERYGREEKE.   As well as any thing.   180

Shall I go call your folkes, that ye may shewe a
        cast?[16]

RAFE ROYSTER. Yea runne I beseeche thee in all pos-
        sible haste.

MATHEW MERYGREEKE. I goe.   *Exeat.*

RAFE ROYSTER. Yea for I love singyng out of measure,

It comforteth my spirites and doth me great
        pleasure.

But who commeth forth yond from my swete   185
        hearte Custance?

My matter frameth well, thys is a luckie chaunce.

15 *cast :* forecast.   16 *cast :* specimen.

ACTUS I.   SCAENA III.

[*Enter*] MAGE MUMBLE-CRUST, *spinning on the
distaffe,* TIBET TALK-APACE, *sowyng.*
            RAFE ROYSTER [*remains.*]

MAGE MUMBLE-CRUST. If thys distaffe were spoonne,
    Margerie Mumble-crust—

TIBET TALK-APACE. [*Interrupting.*] Where good stale
    ale is will drinke no water I trust.

MAGE MUMBLE-CRUST. Dame Custance hath promised
    us good ale and white bread.

TIBET TALK-APACE. If she kepe not promise, I will
    beshrewe hir head :

But it will be starke nyght before I shall have   5
    done.

RAFE ROYSTER. [*Aside.*] I will stande here a while, and
    talke with them anon,

I heare them speake of Custance, which doth my
    heart good,

To heare hir name spoken doth even comfort my
    blood.

MAGE MUMBLE-CRUST. Sit downe to your worke Tibet
    like a good girle.

TIBET TALK-APACE. Nourse, medle you with your   10
    spyndle and your whirle,

No haste but good, Mage Mumble-crust, for whip
    and whurre

The olde proverbe doth say, never made good
    furre.(1)

MAGE MUMBLE-CRUST. Well, ye wyll sitte downe to
    your worke anon, I trust.

TIBET TALK-APACE. Soft fire maketh sweete malte,
    good Mage Mumble-crust.

MAGE MUMBLE-CRUST. And sweete malte maketh joly   15
    good ale for the nones.[1]

TIBET TALK-APACE. Whiche will slide downe the lane
    without any bones.   *Cantet.*[2]

ACTUS I.   SCAENA III.   2 *Cantet :* Let her sing.
  1 *nones :* nonce, present
    time.

Olde browne bread crustes must have much good
>   mumblyng,
But good ale downe your throte hath good easie
>   tumbling.

RAFE ROYSTER. [*Aside.*] The jolyest wench that ere I
>   hearde, little mouse,—
May I not rejoice that she shall dwell in my   20
>   house?

TIBET TALK-APACE. So sirrha, nowe this geare begin-
>   neth for to frame.

MAGE MUMBLE-CRUST. Thanks to God, though your
>   work stand stil, your tong is not lame.

TIBET TALK-APACE. And though your teeth be gone,
>   both so sharpe and so fine
Yet your tongue can renne on patins[3] as well as
>   mine.

MAGE MUMBLE-CRUST. Ye were not for nought named   25
>   Tyb Talk-apace.

TIBET TALK-APACE. Doth my talke grieve you? Alack,
>   God save your grace.

MAGE MUMBLE-CRUST. I holde[4] a grote ye will drinke
>   anon for this geare.

TIBET TALK-APACE. And I wyll pray you the stripes
>   for me to beare.

MAGE MUMBLE-CRUST. I holde a penny, ye will drink
>   without a cup.

TIBET TALK-APACE. Wherein so ere ye drinke, I wote   30
>   ye drinke all up.

[*Enter* ANNOT ALYFACE, *knitting.*]

ANNOT ALYFACE. By Cock and well sowed, my good
>   Tibet Talk-apace.

TIBET TALK-APACE. And een as well knitte my nowne
>   Annot Alyface.

RAFE ROYSTER. [*Aside.*] See what a sort she kepeth
>   that must be my wife!
Shall not I when I have hir, leade a merrie life?

TIBET TALK-APACE. Welcome my good wenche, and   35
>   sitte here by me just.

ANNOT ALYFACE. And howe doth our old beldame
>   here, Mage Mumble-crust?

---

3 *renne on patins:* clatter,   4 *holde:* wager.
>   as when running in
>   wooden shoes.

TIBET TALK-APACE. Chyde, and finde faultes, and
        threaten to complaine.

ANNOT ALYFACE. To make us poore girles shent to hir
        is small gaine.

MAGE MUMBLE-CRUST. I dyd neyther chyde, nor
        complaine, nor threaten.

RAFE ROYSTER. [*Aside.*] It woulde grieve my heart   40
        to see one of them beaten.

MAGE MUMBLE-CRUST. I dyd nothyng but byd hir
        worke and holde hir peace.

TIBET TALK-APACE. So would I, if you coulde your
        clattering ceasse :
But the devill can not make olde trotte holde hir
        tong.

ANNOT ALYFACE. Let all these matters passe, and we
        three sing a song,
So shall we pleasantly bothe the tyme beguile   45
        now,
And eke[5] dispatche all our workes ere we can tell
        how.

TIBET TALK-APACE. I shrew them that say nay, and
        that shall not be I.

MAGE MUMBLE-CRUST. And I am well content.

TIBET TALK-APACE.   Sing on then by and by.

RAFE ROYSTER. [*Aside.*] And I will not away, but
        listen to their song,
Yet Merygreeke and my folkes tary very long.   50
     TIB, AN, *and* MARGERIE, *doe singe here.*

        Pipe mery Annot. etc.[(2)]
Trilla, Trilla. Trillarie.
Worke Tibet, worke Annot, worke Margerie.
Sewe Tibet, knitte Annot, spinne Margerie.
Let us see who shall winne the victorie.   55

TIBET TALK-APACE. This sleve is not willyng to be
        sewed I trowe,
A small thing might make me all in the grounde
        to throwe.
        Then they sing agayne.

     Pipe merrie Annot. etc.
Trilla. Trilla. Trillarie.
What Tibet, what Annot, what Margerie.   60

5 *eke :* also.

Ye sleepe, but we doe not, that shall we trie.
Your fingers be nombde, our worke will not lie.

TIBET TALK-APACE. If ye doe so againe, well I would
advise you nay.
In good sooth one stoppe[6] more, and I make holy
day.[7]
They sing the thirde tyme.

Pipe Mery Annot. etc.   65
Trilla. Trilla. Trillarie.
Nowe Tibbet, now Annot, nowe Margerie.
Nowe whippet[8] apace for the maystrie,[9]
But it will not be, our mouth is so drie.

TIBET TALK-APACE. Ah, eche finger is a thombe to   70
day me thinke,
I care not to let all alone, choose it swimme or
sinke.
They sing the fourth tyme.

Pipe Mery Annot. etc.
Trilla. Trilla. Trillarie.
When Tibet, when Annot, when Margerie.
I will not, I can not, no more can I.   75
Then give we all over, and there let it lye.

Lette hir caste downe hir worke.
TIBET TALK-APACE. There it lieth, the worste is but a
curried cote![10]
Tut I am used therto, I care not a grote.
ANNOT ALYFACE. Have we done singyng since? then
will I in againe,
Here I founde you, and here I leave both twaine.   80
Exeat.
MAGE MUMBLE-CRUST. And I will not be long after :
Tib Talk-apace.
TIBET TALK-APACE. What is the matter?
MAGE MUMBLE-CRUST. Yond stode a man al this space
And hath hearde all that ever we spake togyther.

6 *stoppe :* stitch.   9 *maystrie :* victory.
7 *holy day :* holiday.   10 *a curried cote :* a beating.
8 *whippet :* stitch rap-
    idly (?)

TIBET TALK-APACE. Mary the more loute he for his
        comming hither.
And the lesse good he can to listen maidens talke.   85
I care not and I go byd him hence for to walke :
It were well done to knowe what he maketh here
        away.[11]

RAFE ROYSTER. [*Aside.*] Nowe myght I speake to
        them, if I wist what to say.

MAGE MUMBLE-CRUST. Nay we will go both off, and
        see what he is.

RAFE ROYSTER. One that hath hearde all your talke   90
        and singyng ywis.

TIBET TALK-APACE. The more to blame you, a good
        thriftie husbande[12]
Woulde elsewhere have had some better matters
        in hande.

RAFE ROYSTER. I dyd it for no harme, but for good
        love I beare,
To your dame mistresse Custance, I did your talke
        heare.
And Mistresse nource I will kisse you for ac-   95
        quaintance.

MAGE MUMBLE-CRUST. I come anon sir.

TIBET TALK-APACE. Faith I would our dame Custance
Sawe this geare.

MAGE MUMBLE-CRUST. I must first wipe al cleane,
        yea I must.

TIBET TALK-APACE. Ill chieve[13] it dotyng foole, but
        it must be cust.[14]
        [RAFE *kisses* MAGE.]

MAGE MUMBLE-CRUST. God yelde[15] you sir, chad[16]
        not so much ichotte[17] not whan,
Nere since chwas bore chwine,[18] of such a gay   100
        gentleman.

RAFE ROYSTER. I will kisse you too mayden, for the
        good will I beare you.

---

11 *maketh here away :* is do-
    ing hereabouts.
12 *husbande :* good manager.
13 *chieve :* bring it about
    (that Custance see
    Rafe).

14 *cust :* kissed.
15 *yelde :* reward.
16 *chad :* ich had, I had.
17 *ichotte :* ich wot, I know.
18 *chwas bore chwine :* I was
    born, I ween.

TIBET TALK-APACE. No forsoth, by your leave ye shall
        not kisse me.

RAFE ROYSTER. Yes be not afearde, I doe not dis-
        dayne you a whit.

TIBET TALK-APACE. Why shoulde I feare you? I have
        not so little wit,
Ye are but a man I knowe very well.

RAFE ROYSTER.   Why then?   105

TIBET TALK-APACE. Forsooth for I wyll not, I use not
        to kisse men.

RAFE ROYSTER. I would faine kisse you too maiden,
        if I myght.

TIBET TALK-APACE. What shold that neede?

RAFE ROYSTER.   But to honor you by this light.
I use to kisse all them that I love, to God I vowe.

TIBET TALK-APACE. Yea sir? I pray you when dyd ye   110
        last kisse your cowe?

RAFE ROYSTER. Ye might be proude to kisse me, if ye
        were wise.

TIBET TALK-APACE. What promotion were therin?

RAFE ROYSTER.   Nourse is not so nice.[19]

TIBET TALK-APACE. Well I have not bene taught to
        kissing and licking.

RAFE ROYSTER. Yet I thanke you mistresse Nourse, ye
        made no sticking.

MAGE MUMBLE-CRUST. I will not sticke for a kosse   115
        with such a man as you.

TIBET TALK-APACE. They that lust : I will againe to
        my sewyng now.
          [Re-enter ANNOT ALYFACE.]

ANNOT ALYFACE. Tidings hough, tidings, dame Cus-
        tance greeteth you well.

RAFE ROYSTER. Whome me?

ANNOT ALYFACE. You sir? no sir? I do no suche tale
        tell.

RAFE ROYSTER. But and she knewe me here.

ANNOT ALYFACE.   Tibet Talk-apace,
Your mistresse Custance and mine, must speake   120
        with your grace.

TIBET TALK-APACE. With me?

ANNOT ALYFACE. Ye muste come in to hir out of all
        doutes.

19 *nice* : coy.

TIBET TALK-APACE. And my work not half done? A
      mischief on all loutes.

                        Ex[eant] am[bae.][20]

RAFE ROYSTER. Ah good sweet nourse!

MAGE MUMBLE-CRUST.   A good sweete gentleman!

RAFE ROYSTER. What?

MAGE MUMBLE-CRUST. Nay I can not tel sir, but
      what thing would you?

RAFE ROYSTER. Howe dothe sweete Custance, my   125
      heart of gold, tell me, how?

MAGE MUMBLE-CRUST. She dothe very well sir, and
      commaunde me to you.[21]

RAFE ROYSTER. To me?

MAGE MUMBLE-CRUST. Yea to you sir.

RAFE ROYSTER.   To me? nurse tel me plain
   To me?

MAGE MUMBLE-CRUST. Ye.

RAFE ROYSTER. That word maketh me alive again.

MAGE MUMBLE-CRUST. She commaunde me to one
      last day who ere it was.

RAFE ROYSTER. That was een to me and none other by   130
      the Masse.

MAGE MUMBLE-CRUST. I can not tell you surely, but
      one it was.

RAFE ROYSTER. It was I and none other: this
      commeth to good passe.
   I promise thee nourse I favour hir.

MAGE MUMBLE-CRUST.   Een so sir.

RAFE ROYSTER. Bid hir sue to me for mariage.

MAGE MUMBLE-CRUST.   Een so sir.

RAFE ROYSTER. And surely for thy sake she shall
      speede.

MAGE MUMBLE-CRUST.   Een so sir.   135

RAFE ROYSTER. I shall be contented to take hir.

MAGE MUMBLE-CRUST.   Een so sir.

RAFE ROYSTER. But at thy request and for thy sake.

MAGE MUMBLE-CRUST.   Een so sir.

RAFE ROYSTER. And come hearke in thine eare what
      to say.

20 *Exeant ambae:* Let them   21 *commaunde me to you:*
   both go out.   sends her regards.

MAGE MUMBLE-CRUST.   Een so sir.
Here lette him tell hir a great
long tale in hir eare.

ACTUS I.   SCAENA IIII.

[*Enter*] MATHEW MERYGREEKE, DOBINET
DOUGHTIE, [*and*] HARPAX [*with an-*
other musician.] RAFE ROYSTER
[*and*] MAGE MUMBLE-CRUST
[*continue to whisper.*]

MATHEW MERYGREEKE. Come on sirs apace, and
quite[1] your selves like men,
Your pains shal be rewarded.

DOBINET DOUGHTIE.   But I wot not when.

MATHEW MERYGREEKE. Do your maister worship as
ye have done in time[1] past.

DOBINET DOUGHTIE. Speake to them : of mine office
he shall have a cast.

MATHEW MERYGREEKE. *Harpax*, looke that thou doe   5
well too, and thy fellow.

HARPAX. I warrant, if he will myne example folowe.

MATHEW MERYGREEKE. Curtsie whooresons, douke[2]
you and crouche at every worde.

DOBINET DOUGHTIE. Yes whether our maister speake
earnest or borde.[3]

MATHEW MERYGREEKE. For this lieth upon[4] his pre-
ferment in deede.

DOBINET DOUGHTIE. Oft is hee a wower, but never   10
doth he speede.

MATHEW MERYGREEKE. But with whome is he nowe
so sadly roundyng yond?

DOBINET DOUGHTIE. With *Nobs nicebecetur miserere*[5]
fonde.

MATHEW MERYGREEKE. [*To* RAFE.] God be at your
wedding, be ye spedde alredie?

ACTUS I.   SCAENA IIII.
  1 *quite* : acquit, do justice to.
  2 *douke* : duck, bow.
  3 *borde* : jest.
  4 *lieth upon* : is necessary to.

  5 *Nobs . . . miserere* : non-
    sense Latin, suggesting
    something like "Dainty
    girl, have mercy on us."

I did not suppose that your love was so greedie,
I perceive nowe ye have chose of devotion, 15
And joy have ye ladie of your promotion.

RAFE ROYSTER. Tushe foole, thou art deceived, this
is not she.

MATHEW MERYGREEKE. Well mocke[6] muche of hir,
and keepe hir well I vise[7] ye.

I will take no charge of such a faire piece
keeping.

MAGE MUMBLE-CRUST. What ayleth thys fellowe? he 20
driveth me to weeping.

MATHEW MERYGREEKE. What weepe on the weddyng
day? be merrie woman,

Though I say it, ye have chose a good gentleman.

RAFE ROYSTER. Kocks nownes[8] what meanest thou
man? tut a whistle![9]

[MATHEW MERYGREEKE.][2] Ah sir, be good to hir,
she is but a gristle,[10]

Ah sweete lambe and coney.[11]

RAFE ROYSTER.   Tut thou art deceived. 25

MATHEW MERYGREEKE. Weepe no more lady, ye shall
be well received.

Up wyth some mery noyse sirs, to bring home the
bride.

RAFE ROYSTER. Gogs armes knave, art thou madde? I
tel thee thou art wide.

MATHEW MERYGREEKE. Then ye entende by nyght to
have hir home brought?

RAFE ROYSTER. I tel thee no.

MATHEW MERYGREEKE.   How then?

RAFE ROYSTER.   Tis neither ment ne thought. 30

MATHEW MERYGREEKE. What shall we then doe with
hir?

RAFE ROYSTER.   Ah foolish harebraine,
This is not she.

MATHEW MERYGREEKE. No is? why then unsayde
againe,

6 *mocke* : make.
7 *vise* : advise.
8 *Kocks nownes* : God's
wounds.
9 *a whistle* : whisht, shush.

10 *gristle* : grizzled, aged
lady.
11 *coney* : rabbit (term of affection).

And what yong girle is this with your mashyp so
    bolde?

RAFE ROYSTER. A girle?

MATHEW MERYGREEKE. Yea. I dare say, scarce yet
    three score yere old.

RAFE ROYSTER. This same is the faire widowes nourse   35
    of whome ye wotte.

MATHEW MERYGREEKE. Is she but a nourse of a house?
    hence home olde trotte,

    Hence at once.

RAFE ROYSTER. No, no.

MATHEW MERYGREEKE. What an please your maship
    A nourse talke so homely[12] with one of your wor-
    ship?

RAFE ROYSTER. I will have it so : it is my pleasure
    and will.

MATHEW MERYGREEKE. Then I am content. Nourse,   40
    come againe, tarry still.

RAFE ROYSTER. What, she will helpe forward this my
    sute for hir part.

MATHEW MERYGREEKE. Then ist mine owne pygs
    nie,[13] and blessing on my hart.

RAFE ROYSTER. This is our best friend, man!

MATHEW MERYGREEKE. Then teach hir what to say!

MAGE MUMBLE-CRUST. I am taught alreadie.

MATHEW MERYGREEKE.   Then go, make no delay.

RAFE ROYSTER. Yet hark one word in thine eare.

      [DOBINET *and the musicians crowd*
          around RAFE.]

MATHEW MERYGREEKE.   Back sirs from his taile.   45

RAFE ROYSTER. Backe vilaynes, will ye be privie of my
    counsaile?

MATHEW MERYGREEKE. Backe sirs, so : I told you
    afore ye woulde be shent.

RAFE ROYSTER. She shall have the first day a whole
    pecke of argent.

MAGE MUMBLE-CRUST. A pecke? *Nomine patris*
    [*Crossing herself.*], have ye so much
    spare?

12 *homely :* intimately.   13 *pygs nie :* pig's eye (term
                            of affection).

RAFE ROYSTER. Yea and a carte lode therto,[14] or else   50
        were it bare,
  Besides other movables, housholde stuffe and
      lande.

MAGE MUMBLE-CRUST. Have ye lands too.

RAFE ROYSTER.   An hundred marks.

MATHEW MERYGREEKE.   Yea a thousand.

MAGE MUMBLE-CRUST. And have ye cattell too? and
        sheepe too?

RAFE ROYSTER. Yea a fewe.

MATHEW MERYGREEKE. He is ashamed the numbre of
        them to shewe.
  Een rounde about him, as many thousande sheepe   55
      goes,
  As he and thou and I too, have fingers and toes.

MAGE MUMBLE-CRUST. And how many yeares olde
      be you?

RAFE ROYSTER.   Fortie at lest.

MATHEW MERYGREEKE. Yea and thrice fortie to them.

RAFE ROYSTER.   Nay now thou dost jest.
  I am not so olde, thou misreckonest my yeares.

MATHEW MERYGREEKE. I know that: but my minde   60
        was on bullockes and steeres.

MAGE MUMBLE-CRUST. And what shall I shewe hir
        your masterships name is?

RAFE ROYSTER. Nay she shall make sute ere she know
        that ywis.[15]

MAGE MUMBLE-CRUST. Yet let me somewhat knowe.

MATHEW MERYGREEKE.   This is hee, understand,
  That killed the blewe Spider in Blanchepouder
      lande.(1)

MAGE MUMBLE-CRUST. Yea *Jesus!* William! zee law!   65
        dyd he zo? law!

MATHEW MERYGREEKE. Yea and the last Elephant
        that ever he sawe,
  As the beast passed by, he start out of a buske,[16]
  And een with pure strength of armes pluckt out his
      great tuske.

MAGE MUMBLE-CRUST. *Jesus, nomine patris* [*Crossing herself.*], what a thing was that!

14 *therto* : in addition.   16 *buske* : bush.
15 *ywis* : for sure.

RAFE ROYSTER. Yea but Merygreeke one thing thou   70
      hast forgot.

MATHEW MERYGREEKE.   What?

RAFE ROYSTER. Of thother Elephant.

MATHEW MERYGREEKE.   Oh hym that fledde away.

RAFE ROYSTER. Yea.

MATHEW MERYGREEKE. Yea he knew that his match
      was in place that day

Tut, he bet the king of Crickets on Christmasse
      day,

That he crept in a hole, and not a worde to say.

MAGE MUMBLE-CRUST. A sore[17] man by zembletee.

MATHEW MERYGREEKE.   Why, he wrong[18] a club   75

Once in a fray out of the hande of Belzebub.

RAFE ROYSTER. And how, when, Mumfision?

MATHEW MERYGREEKE.   Oh your coustrelyng[19]

Bore the lanterne a fielde so before the gozelyng.[20]

Nay that is to long a matter now to be tolde :

Never aske his name Nurse, I warrant thee, be   80
      bolde,

He conquered in one day from *Rome*, to *Naples*,

And woonne Townes, nourse, as fast as thou canst
      make Apples.

MAGE MUMBLE-CRUST. O Lorde, my heart quaketh
      for feare : he is to sore.

RAFE ROYSTER. Thou makest hir to much afearde,
      Merygreeke no more.

This tale woulde feare my sweete heart Custance   85
      right evill.

MATHEW MERYGREEKE. Nay let hir take him Nurse,
      and feare not the devill.

But thus is our song dasht. [*To the musicians.*]
      Sirs ye may home againe.

RAFE ROYSTER. No shall they not. I charge you all
      here to remaine :

The villaine slaves! a whole day ere they can be
      founde.

MATHEW MERYGREEKE. Couche on your marybones[21]   90
      whooresons, down to the ground!

17 *sore* : formidable.   20 *gozelyng* : gosling.
18 *wrong* : wrung.   21 *marybones* : marrow bones,
19 *coustrelyng* : lad, groom.   knees.

[DOBINET *and the musicians kneel.*]
Was it meete he should tarie so long in one place
Without harmonie of Musike, or some solace?
Who so hath suche bees as your maister in hys
    head,
Had neede to have his spirites with Musike to be
    fed.
By your maisterships licence.
    [*Picking something from his coat.*]
RAFE ROYSTER.   What is that? a moate?   95
MATHEW MERYGREEKE. No it was a fooles feather
    had light on your coate.[2]
RAFE ROYSTER. I was nigh no feathers since I came
    from my bed.
MATHEW MERYGREEKE. No sir, it was a haire that was
    fall from your hed.
RAFE ROYSTER. My men com when it plese them.
MATHEW MERYGREEKE.   By your leve.
    [*Brushing something from his gown.*]
RAFE ROYSTER.   What is that?
MATHEW MERYGREEKE. Your gown was foule spotted   100
    with the foot of a gnat.
RAFE ROYSTER. Their maister to offende they are
    nothing afearde.
What now?
    [MERYGREEKE *picks something from*
        RAFE's *doublet.*]
MATHEW MERYGREEKE. A lousy haire from your mas-
    terships beard.
OMNES FAMULI.[22, 2] [*Rising.*] And sir for Nurses
    sake pardon this one offence.
We shall not after this shew the like negligence.
RAFE ROYSTER. I pardon you this once, and come   105
    sing nere the wurse.
MATHEW MERYGREEKE. How like you the goodnesse
    of this gentleman, nurse?
MAGE MUMBLE-CRUST. God save his maistership that
    so can his men forgeve,
And I wyll heare them sing ere I go, by his leave.
RAFE ROYSTER. Mary and thou shalt wenche, come we
    two will daunce.

22 OMNES FAMULI: all
    (his) men.

MAGE MUMBLE-CRUST. Nay I will by myne owne   110
        selfe foote the song perchaunce.

RAFE ROYSTER. Go to it sirs lustily.

MAGE MUMBLE-CRUST.   Pipe up a mery note,
  Let me heare it playde, I will foote it for a grote.
       Cantent.(3) [MAGE *dances.*]

RAFE ROYSTER. [*Producing a letter.*] Now nurse take
        thys same letter here to thy mistresse.
  And as my trust is in thee plie my businesse.

MAGE MUMBLE-CRUST. It shal be done!

MATHEW MERYGREEKE.   Who made it?

RAFE ROYSTER.   I wrote it ech whit.   115

MATHEW MERYGREEKE. Then nedes it no mending.

RAFE ROYSTER.   No, no.

MATHEW MERYGREEKE.   No I know your wit.
  I warrant it wel.

MAGE MUMBLE-CRUST. It shal be delivered.
  But if ye speede, shall I be considered?

MATHEW MERYGREEKE. Whough, dost thou doubt of
        that?

MAGE MUMBLE-CRUST.   What shal I have?

MATHEW MERYGREEKE. An hundred times more than   120
        thou canst devise to crave.

MAGE MUMBLE-CRUST. Shall I have some newe geare?
        for my olde is all spent.

MATHEW MERYGREEKE. The worst kitchen wench
        shall goe in ladies rayment.

MAGE MUMBLE-CRUST. Yea?

MATHEW MERYGREEKE. And the worst drudge in the
        house shal go better
  Than your mistresse doth now.

MAGE MUMBLE-CRUST. Then I trudge with your letter.
             [*Exeat.*]

RAFE ROYSTER. Now may I repose me : Custance is   125
        mine owne.
  Let us sing and play homeward that it may be
        knowne.

MATHEW MERYGREEKE. But are you sure, that your
        letter is well enough?

RAFE ROYSTER. I wrote it my selfe.

MATHEW MERYGREEKE. Then sing we to dinner.
     Here they sing, and go out singing.

ACTUS I. SCAENA V.

[*Enter*] CHRISTIAN CUSTANCE [*and*] MAGE
MUMBLE-CRUST.

CHRISTIAN CUSTANCE. Who tooke[1] thee thys letter
Margerie Mumble-crust?

MAGE MUMBLE-CRUST. A lustie gay bachelor tooke it
me of trust,

And if ye seeke to him he will lowe[2] your doing.

CHRISTIAN CUSTANCE. Yea, but where learned he that
manner of wowing?

MAGE MUMBLE-CRUST. If to sue to hym, you will any   5
paines take,

He will have you to his wife (he sayth) for my
sake.

CHRISTIAN CUSTANCE. Some wise gentlemen belike. I
am bespoken :

And I thought verily thys had bene some token

From my dere spouse[3] Gawyn Goodlucke, whom
when him please

God luckily sende home to both our heartes ease.   10

MAGE MUMBLE-CRUST. A joyly[4] man it is I wote well
by report,

And would have you to him for marriage resort :

Best open the writing, and see what it doth speake.

CHRISTIAN CUSTANCE. At thys time nourse I will neither reade ne breake.

MAGE MUMBLE-CRUST. He promised to give you a   15
whole pecke of golde.

CHRISTIAN CUSTANCE. Perchaunce lacke of a pynte
when it shall be all tolde.

MAGE MUMBLE-CRUST. I would take a gay riche husbande, and I were you.

CHRISTIAN CUSTANCE. In good sooth Mage, een so
would I, if I were thou.

But no more of this fond talke now, let us go in,

And see thou no more move me folly to begin.   20

ACTUS I. SCAENA V.   3 *spouse :* affianced.
   1 *tooke :* gave.   4 *joyly :* jolly.
   2 *lowe :* allow.

Nor bring mee no mo letters for no mans pleasure,
But thou know from whom.

MAGE MUMBLE-CRUST.   I warrant ye shall be sure.

[*Exeant.*]

ACTUS II.   SCAENA I.

[*Enter*] DOBINET DOUGHTIE.

DOBINET DOUGHTIE. Where is the house I goe to, be-
   fore or behinde?
I know not where nor when nor how I shal it finde.
If I had ten mens bodies and legs and strength,
This trotting that I have must needes lame me at
   length.
And nowe that my maister is new set on wowyng, 5
I trust there shall none of us finde lacke of doyng :
Two paire of shoes a day will nowe be too litle
To serve me, I must trotte to and fro so mickle.[1]
Go beare me thys token, carrie me this letter,
Nowe this is the best way, nowe that way is 10
   better.
Up before day sirs, I charge you, an houre or
   twaine,
Trudge, do me thys message, and bring worde
   quicke againe,
If one misse but a minute, then His armes and
   woundes,
I woulde not have slacked for ten thousand
   poundes.
Nay see I beseeche you, if my most trustie page, 15
Goe not nowe aboute to hinder my mariage,
So fervent hotte wowyng, and so farre from
   wiving,
I trowe never was any creature livyng,
With every woman is he in some loves pang,
Then up to our lute at midnight, twangledome 20
   twang,
Then twang with our sonets, and twang with our
   dumps,[2]

ACTUS II.   SCAENA I.   2 *dumps :* plaintive melodies.
 1 *mickle :* much.

And heyhough from our heart, as heavie as lead
        lumpes :
Then to our recorder[3] with toodleloodle poope
As the howlet[4] out of an yvie bushe should
        hoope.[5]
Anon to our gitterne,[6] thrumpledum, thrumpledum   25
        thrum,
Thrumpledum,   thrumpledum,   thrumpledum,
        thrumpledum thrum.
Of Songs and Balades also is he a maker,
And that can he as finely doe as Jacke Raker,[(1)]
Yea and *extempore* will he dities compose,
Foolishe *Marsias* nere made the like I suppose,   30
Yet must we sing them, as good stuffe I undertake,
As for such a pen man is well fittyng to make.
Ah for these long nights, heyhow, when will it be
        day?
I feare ere I come she will be wowed away.
Then when aunswere is made that it may not bee,   35
O death why commest thou not? by and by (sayth
        he).
But then, from his heart to put away sorowe,
He is as farre in with some newe love next morowe.
But in the meane season we trudge and we trot,
From dayspring to midnyght, I sit not, nor rest not.   40
And now am I sent to dame Christian Custance :
But I feare it will ende with a mocke for pastance.[7]
I bring hir a ring, with a token in a cloute,[8]
And by all gesse, this same is hir house out of
        doute.
I knowe it nowe perfect, I am in my right way.   45
And loe yond the olde nourse that was wyth us last
        day.

3 *recorder :* wooden instru-   6 *gitterne :* guitarlike instru-
    ment with stops, played   ment.
    like a clarinet.   7 *pastance :* pastime.
4 *howlet :* owl.   8 *cloute :* cloth.
5 *hoope :* hop.

Actus ii. Scaena ii.

[*Enter*] MAGE MUMBLE-CRUST [*to*]
DOBINET DOUGHTIE.

MAGE MUMBLE-CRUST. I was nere so shoke up afore
     since I was borne,
  That our mistresse coulde not have chid I wold
     have sworne :
  And I pray God I die if I ment any harme,
  But for my life time this shall be to me a charme.

DOBINET DOUGHTIE. God you save and see nurse, and   5
     howe is it with you?

MAGE MUMBLE-CRUST. Mary a great deale the worse
     it is for suche as thou.

DOBINET DOUGHTIE. For me? Why so?

MAGE MUMBLE-CRUST. Why wer not thou one of
     them, say,
  That song and playde here with the gentleman last
     day?

DOBINET DOUGHTIE. Yes, and he would know if you
     have for him spoken.
  And prayes you to deliver this ring and token.   10

MAGE MUMBLE-CRUST. Nowe by the token that God
     tokened, brother,
  I will deliver no token one nor other.
  I have once ben so shent for your maisters pleasure,
  As I will not be agayne for all hys treasure.

DOBINET DOUGHTIE. He will thank you woman.

MAGE MUMBLE-CRUST.   I will none of his thanke.   15
                  Ex[*eat.*]

DOBINET DOUGHTIE. I weene I am a prophete, this
     geare will prove blanke :[1]
  But what should I home againe without answere
     go?
  It were better go to *Rome* on my head than so.
  I will tary here this moneth, but some of the house
  Shall take it of me, and then I care not a louse.   20
  But yonder commeth forth a wenche or a ladde,
  If he have not one Lumbardes touche,[1] my
     lucke is bad.

ACTUS ii. SCAENA ii.
  1 *geare . . . blanke :* project
    will come to nothing.

Actus ii.   Scaena iii.

[*Enter*] TRUEPENIE. DOBINET [*remains.*]

TRUEPENIE. I am cleane lost for lacke of mery com-
                panie,
   We gree not halfe well within, our wenches and I,
   They will commaunde like mistresses, they will
                forbyd,
   If they be not served, Truepenie must be chyd.
   Let them be as mery nowe as ye can desire,   5
   With turnyng of a hande, our mirth lieth in the
                mire,
   I can not skill of such chaungeable mettle,
   There is nothing with them but in docke out
                nettle.[1]

DOBINET DOUGHTIE. Whether is it better that I speake
                to him furst,
   Or he first to me, it is good to cast the wurst.   10
   If I beginne first, he will smell all my purpose,
   Otherwise I shall not neede any thing to disclose.

TRUEPENIE. What boy have we yonder? I will see
                what he is.

DOBINET DOUGHTIE. He commeth to me. It is here-
                about ywis.

TRUEPENIE. Wouldest thou ought friende, that thou   15
                lookest so about?

DOBINET DOUGHTIE. Yea, but whether ye can helpe me
                or no, I dout.
   I seeke to one mistresse Custance house here
                dwellyng.

TRUEPENIE. It is my mistresse ye seeke too by your
                telling.

DOBINET DOUGHTIE. Is there any of that name heere
                but shee?

TRUEPENIE. Not one in all the whole towne that I   20
                knowe pardee.

DOBINET DOUGHTIE. A Widowe she is I trow.

TRUEPENIE.   And what and she be?

DOBINET DOUGHTIE. But ensured to an husbande.

TRUEPENIE.   Yea, so thinke we.

DOBINET DOUGHTIE. And I dwell with hir husbande
        that trusteth to be.

TRUEPENIE. In faith then must thou needes be wel-
        come to me,

Let us for acquaintance shake handes togither,   25
And what ere thou be, heartily welcome hither.

[*Enter* TIBET TALK-APACE *and* ANNOT ALYFACE.]

TIBET TALK-APACE. Well Truepenie never but
        flinging.[1]

ANNOT ALYFACE.   And frisking?

TRUEPENIE. Well Tibet and Annot, still swingyng and
        whiskyng?

TIBET TALK-APACE. But ye roile abroade.[2]

ANNOT ALYFACE.   In the streete evere where.

TRUEPENIE. Where are ye twaine, in chambers when 30
        ye mete me there?(2)

But come hither fooles, I have one nowe by the
        hande,

Servant to hym that must be our mistresse hus-
        bande,

Byd him welcome.

ANNOT ALYFACE.   To me truly is he welcome.

TIBET TALK-APACE. Forsooth and as I may say,
        heartily welcome.

DOBINET DOUGHTIE. I thank you mistresse maides.

ANNOT ALYFACE.   I hope we shal better know. 35

TIBET TALK-APACE. And when wil our new master
        come?

DOBINET DOUGHTIE. Shortly I trow.

TIBET TALK-APACE. I would it were to morow: for
        till he resorte

Our mistresse being a Widow hath small comforte,
And I hearde our nourse speak of an husbande to
        day

Ready for our mistresse, a riche man and a gay,   40
And we shall go in our Frenche hoodes every day,
In our silke cassocks (I warrant you) freshe and
        gay,

In our tricke ferdegews[3] and billiments[4] of golde,

ACTUS II. SCAENA III.   3 *ferdegews* : farthingales
  1 *flinging* : running about.   (hoopskirts).
  2 *roile abroade* : gad about.   4 *billiments* : headdresses.

Brave[5] in our sutes of chaunge seven double folde,

Then shall ye see Tibet sirs, treade the mosse so   45
    trimme,

Nay, why sayd I treade? ye shall see hir glide and
    swimme,

Not lumperdee clumperdee like our spaniell Rig.

TRUEPENIE. Mary then prickmedaintie[6] come toste
    me a fig.

Who shall then know our Tib Talk-apace trow ye?

ANNOT ALYFACE. And why not Annot Alyface as fyne   50
    as she?

TRUEPENIE. And what had Tom Truepenie, a father
    or none?

ANNOT ALYFACE. Then our pretty newe come man will
    looke to be one.

TRUEPENIE. We foure I trust shall be a joily mery
    knot.

Shall we sing a fitte to welcome our friende,
    Annot?

ANNOT ALYFACE. Perchaunce he can not sing.

DOBINET DOUGHTIE.   I am at all assayes.[7]   55

TIBET TALK-APACE. By Cocke and the better wel-
    come to us alwayes.

Here they sing.

A thing very fitte
For them that have witte,
And are felowes knitte
Servants in one house to bee,   60
Is fast fast for to sitte,
And not oft to flitte,
Nor varie a whitte,
But lovingly to agree.

No man complainyng,   65
Nor other disdayning,
For losse or for gainyng,
But felowes or friends to bee.
No grudge remainyng,
No worke refrainyng,   70

5 *brave* : elegant.
6 *prickmedaintie* : finical and
    dainty person.

7 *at all assayes* : ready for
    anything.

Nor helpe restrainyng,
But lovingly to agree.

No man for despite,
By worde or by write
His felowe to twite,[8]   75
But further in honestie,
No good turnes entwite,[9]
Nor olde sores recite,
But let all goe quite,
And lovingly to agree.   80

After drudgerie,
When they be werie,
Then to be merie,
To laugh and sing they be free
With chip and cherie   85
Heigh derie derie,
Trill on the berie,[10]
And lovingly to agree.
                Finis.

TIBET TALK-APACE. Wyll you now in with us unto
            our mistresse go?
DOBINET DOUGHTIE. I have first for my maister an er-   90
            rand or two.
  But I have here from him a token and a ring,
  They shall have moste thanke of hir that first doth
            it bring.
TIBET TALK-APACE. Mary that will I.
TRUEPENIE.   See and Tibet snatch not now.
TIBET TALK-APACE. And why may not I sir, get
            thanks as well as you?   *Exeat.*
ANNOT ALYFACE. Yet get ye not all, we will go with   95
            you both.
  And have part of your thanks be ye never so loth.
                        Exeant omnes.
DOBINET DOUGHTIE. So my handes are ridde of it: I
            care for no more.
  I may now return home: so durst I not afore.
                                        Exeat.

8 *twite :* disparage.   10 *Trill . . . berie :* Dance on
9 *entwite :* make a subject   the hillock.
    for disparagement.

ACTUS II.   SCAENA IIII.

[*Enter*] CHRISTIAN CUSTANCE, TIBET [TALK-
APACE,] ANNOT ALYFACE, [*and*] TRUEPENIE.

CHRISTIAN CUSTANCE. Nay come forth all three : and
come hither pretie mayde :

Will not so many forewarnings make you afrayde?

TIBET TALK-APACE. Yes forsoth.

CHRISTIAN CUSTANCE.   But stil be a runner up and
downe,

Still be a bringer of tidings and tokens to towne.

TIBET TALK-APACE. No forsoth mistresse.

CHRISTIAN CUSTANCE.   Is all your delite and joy   5
In whiskyng and ramping[1] abroade like a Tom
boy.

TIBET TALK-APACE. Forsoth these were there too,
Annot and Truepenie.

TRUEPENIE. Yea but ye alone tooke it, ye can not
denie.

ANNOT ALYFACE. Yea that ye did.

TIBET TALK-APACE. But if I had not, ye twaine would.

CHRISTIAN CUSTANCE. You great calfe, ye should have   10
more witte, so ye should :

But why shoulde any of you take such things in
hande?

TIBET TALK-APACE. Because it came from him that
must be your husbande.

CHRISTIAN CUSTANCE. How do ye know that?

TIBET TALK-APACE.   Forsoth the boy did say so.

CHRISTIAN CUSTANCE. What was his name?

ANNOT ALYFACE.   We asked not.

CHRISTIAN CUSTANCE.   No?[1]

ANNOT ALYFACE. He is not farre gone of likelyhod.

TRUEPENIE.   I will see.   15

CHRISTIAN CUSTANCE. If thou canst finde him in the
streete bring him to me.

TRUEPENIE. Yes.   *Exeat.*

ACTUS II.   SCAENA IIII.
  1 *ramping :* gadding immod-
      estly.

CHRISTIAN CUSTANCE. Well ye naughty girles, if ever I
    perceive
That henceforth you do letters or tokens receive,
To bring unto me from any person or place,
Except ye first shewe me the partie face to face, 20
Eyther thou or thou, full truly abye[2] thou shalt.

TIBET TALK-APACE. Pardon this, and the next tyme
    pouder[3] me in salt.

CHRISTIAN CUSTANCE. I shall make all girles by you
    twaine to beware.

TIBET TALK-APACE. If I ever offende againe do not me
    spare.
But if ever I see that false boy any more 25
By your mistreshyps licence I tell you afore
I will rather have my cote twentie times swinged,
Than on the naughtie wag not to be avenged.

CHRISTIAN CUSTANCE. Good wenches would not so
    rampe abrode ydelly,
But keepe within doores, and plie their work 30
    earnestly,
If one would speake with me that is a man likely,
Ye shall have right good thanke to bring me worde
    quickly.
But otherwyse with messages to come in post
From henceforth I promise you, shall be to your
    cost.
Get you in to your work.

TIBET and ANNOT.   Yes forsoth.

CHRISTIAN CUSTANCE.   Hence both twaine. 35
And let me see you play me such a part againe.
[*Exeant* TIBET *and* ANNOT. *Re-enter* TRUEPENIE.]

TRUEPENIE. Maistresse, I have runne past the farre
    ende of the streete,
Yet can I not yonder craftie boy see nor meete.

CHRISTIAN CUSTANCE. No?

TRUEPENIE. Yet I looked as farre beyonde the people.
As one may see out of the toppe of Paules steeple. 40

CHRISTIAN CUSTANCE. Hence in at doores, and let me
    no more be vext.

TRUEPENIE. Forgeve me this one fault, and lay on
    for the next.   [*Exeat.*]

2 *abye* : suffer for it.   3 *pouder* : preserve.

CHRISTIAN CUSTANCE. Now will I in too, for I thinke
        so God me mende,
This will prove some foolishe matter in the ende.
                           Exeat.

ACTUS [I]II.   SCAENA I.

[*Enter*] MATHEW MERYGREEKE.

MATHEW MERYGREEKE. Nowe say thys againe : he
        hath somewhat to dooing
Which followeth the trace of one that is wowing,
Specially that hath no more wit in his hedde,
Than my cousin Royster Doyster withall is ledde.
I am sent in all haste to espie and to marke   5
How our letters and tokens are likely to warke.
Maister Royster Doyster must have aunswere in
        haste
For he loveth not to spende much labour in
        waste.
Nowe as for Christian Custance by this light,
Though she had not hir trouth to Gawyn Good-   10
        lucke plight,
Yet rather than with such a loutishe dolte to marie,
I dare say woulde lyve a poore lyfe solitarie,
But fayne woulde I speake with Custance if I wist
        how
To laugh at the matter, yond commeth one forth
        now.

ACTUS III.   SCAENA II.

[*Enter*] TIBET [TALK-APACE].
MERYGREEKE [*remains.*]

TIBET TALK-APACE. Ah that I might but once in my
        life have a sight
Of him that made us all so yll shent by this light,
He should never escape if I had him by the eare,
But even from his head, I would it bite or teare.
Yea and if one of them were not inowe,   5
I would bite them both off, I make God avow.

MATHEW MERYGREEKE. What is he, whome this little
        mouse doth so threaten?

TIBET TALK-APACE. I woulde teache him I trow, to
        make girles shent or beaten.

MATHEW MERYGREEKE. I will call hir : Maide, with
        whome are ye so hastie?

TIBET TALK-APACE. Not with you sir, but with a little   10
        wag-pastie,[1]

A deceiver of folkes, by subtill craft and guile.

MATHEW MERYGREEKE. [*Aside.*] I knowe where she
        is :[2] Dobinet hath wrought some wile.

TIBET TALK-APACE. He brought a ring and token
        which he sayd was sent

From our dames husbande, but I wot well I was
        shent :

For it liked hir as well to tell you no lies,   15
As water in hir shyppe, or salt cast in hir eies :
And yet whence it came neyther we nor she can
        tell.

MATHEW MERYGREEKE. [*Aside.*] We shall have sport
        anone : I like this very well.

And dwell ye here with mistresse Custance faire
        maide?

TIBET TALK-APACE. Yea mary doe I sir : what would   20
        ye have sayd?

MATHEW MERYGREEKE. A little message unto hir by
        worde of mouth.

TIBET TALK-APACE. No messages by your leave, nor
        tokens forsoth.

MATHEW MERYGREEKE. Then help me to speke with
        hir.

TIBET TALK-APACE. With a good wil that.

Here she commeth forth. Now speake ye know
        best what.

                [*Enter* CHRISTIAN CUSTANCE.]

CHRISTIAN CUSTANCE. None other life with you maide,   25
        but abrode to skip?

TIBET TALK-APACE. Forsoth here is one would speake
        with your mistresship.

ACTUS III.   SCAENA II.   2 *where she is :* what she
    1 *wag-pastie :* mischievous   means.
        rogue.

CHRISTIAN CUSTANCE. Ah, have ye ben learning of mo
        messages now?

TIBET TALK-APACE. I would not heare his minde, but
        bad him shewe it to you.

CHRISTIAN CUSTANCE. In at dores.

TIBET TALK-APACE.   I am gon.   *Ex[eat.]*

MATHEW MERYGREEKE. Dame Custance God ye save.

CHRISTIAN CUSTANCE. Welcome friend Merygreeke: 30
        and what thing wold ye have?

MATHEW MERYGREEKE. I am come to you a little mat-
        ter to breake.

CHRISTIAN CUSTANCE. But see it be honest, else bet-
        ter not to speake.

MATHEW MERYGREEKE. Howe feele ye your selfe
        affected here of late?

CHRISTIAN CUSTANCE. I feele no maner chaunge but
        after the olde rate.

But whereby do ye meane?

MATHEW MERYGREEKE.   Concerning mariage.   35

Doth not love lade you?

CHRISTIAN CUSTANCE.   I feele no such cariage.[3]

MATHEW MERYGREEKE. Doe ye feele no pangues of
        dotage? aunswere me right.

CHRISTIAN CUSTANCE. I dote so, that I make but one
        sleepe all the night.

But what neede all these wordes?

MATHEW MERYGREEKE.   Oh Jesus, will ye see

What dissemblyng creatures these same women be!   40

The gentleman ye wote of, whome ye doe so love,

That ye woulde fayne marrie him, yf ye durst it
        move,

Emong other riche widowes, which are of him
        glad,

Lest ye for lesing of him perchaunce might runne
        mad,

Is nowe contented that upon your sute making,   45

Ye be as one in election of taking.

CHRISTIAN CUSTANCE. What a tale is this? that I wote
        of? whome I love?

MATHEW MERYGREEKE. Yea and he is as loving a
        worme againe as a dove.

Een of very pitie he is willyng you to take,

3 *cariage :* burden.

Bicause ye shall not destroy your selfe for his sake.   50
CHRISTIAN CUSTANCE. Mary God yelde his mashyp
                        what ever he be,
  It is gentmanly spoken.
MATHEW MERYGREEKE.   Is it not trowe ye?
  If ye have the grace now to offer your self, ye
                        speede.
CHRISTIAN CUSTANCE. As muche as though I did, this
                        time it shall not neede,
  But what gentman is it, I pray you tell me plaine,   55
  That woweth so finely?
MATHEW MERYGREEKE.   Lo where ye be againe,
  As though ye knew him not.
CHRISTIAN CUSTANCE.   Tush ye speake in jest.
MATHEW MERYGREEKE. Nay sure, the partie is in good
                        knacking[4] earnest,
  And have you he will (he sayth) and have you he
                        must.
CHRISTIAN CUSTANCE. I am promised duryng my life,   60
                        that is just.
MATHEW MERYGREEKE. Mary so thinketh he, unto him
                        alone.
CHRISTIAN CUSTANCE. No creature hath my faith and
                        trouth but one,
  That is Gawyn Goodlucke : and if it be not hee,
  He hath no title this way what ever he be,
  Nor I know none to whome I have such worde   65
                        spoken.
MATHEW MERYGREEKE. Ye knowe him not, you, by
                        his letter and token!
CHRISTIAN CUSTANCE. In dede true it is, that a let-
                        ter I have,
  But I never reade it yet as God me save.
MATHEW MERYGREEKE. Ye a woman? and your letter
                        so long unredde.
CHRISTIAN CUSTANCE. Ye may therby know what hast   70
                        I have to wedde.
  But now who it is, for my hande I knowe by gesse.
MATHEW MERYGREEKE. Ah well I say.
CHRISTIAN CUSTANCE. It is Royster Doyster doubtlesse.

  4 *knacking* : downright.

MATHEW MERYGREEKE. Will ye never leave this dis-
      simulation?
  Ye know hym not.
CHRISTIAN CUSTANCE. But by imagination,
  For no man there is but a very dolt and loute   75
  That to wowe a Widowe woulde so go about.
  He shall never have me hys wife while he doe live.
MATHEW MERYGREEKE. Then will he have you if he
      may, so mote I thrive,
  And he biddeth you sende him worde by me,
  That ye humbly beseech him, ye may his wife be,   80
  And that there shall be no let[5] in you nor mis-
      trust,
  But to be wedded on Sunday next if he lust,
  And biddeth you to looke for him.
CHRISTIAN CUSTANCE.   Doth he byd so?
MATHEW MERYGREEKE. When he commeth, aske hym
      whether he did or no?
CHRISTIAN CUSTANCE. Goe say, that I bid him keepe 85
      him warme at home
  For if he come abroade, he shall cough me a
      mome.[6]
  My mynde was vexed, I shrew his head, sottish
      dolt.
MATHEW MERYGREEKE. He hath in his head
CHRISTIAN CUSTANCE. As much braine as a burbolt.[7]
MATHEW MERYGREEKE. Well dame Custance, if he
      heare you thus play choploge.[8]
CHRISTIAN CUSTANCE. What will he?
MATHEW MERYGREEKE. Play the devill in the horo- 90
      loge.[9]
CHRISTIAN CUSTANCE. I defye him loute.
MATHEW MERYGREEKE. Shall I tell hym what ye say?
CHRISTIAN CUSTANCE. Yea and adde what so ever thou
      canst, I thee pray,
  And I will avouche it what so ever it bee.
MATHEW MERYGREEKE. Then let me alone, we will
      laugh well ye shall see,

5 *let* : hindrance, objection.
6 *cough me a mome* : show
  what a fool he is.
7 *burbolt* : bird bolt, arrow
  without feathers; hence

a scatterbrained fellow.
8 *choploge* : choplogic, verbal ingenuity.
9 *horologe* : clock.

It will not be long ere he will hither resorte.   95
CHRISTIAN CUSTANCE. Let hym come when hym lust,
                I wishe no better sport.
Fare ye well, I will in, and read my great letter.
I shall to my wower make answere the better.
                                          Exeat.

ACTUS III.   SCAENA III.

MATHEW MERYGREEKE [*remains. Enter*]
                ROYSTER DOYSTER.

MATHEW MERYGREEKE. Nowe that the whole an-
                swere in my devise doth rest,
I shall paint out our wower in colours of the best.
And all that I say shall be on Custances mouth,
She is author of all that I shall speake forsoth.
But yond commeth Royster Doyster nowe in a   5
                traunce.
RAFE ROYSTER. *Juno* sende me this day good lucke
                and good chaunce.
I can not but come see how Merygreeke doth
                speede.
MATHEW MERYGREEKE. [*Aside.*] I will not see him,
                but give him a jutte[1] in deede.
I crie your mastershyp mercie!
                [*Running hard into him.*]
RAFE ROYSTER.   And whither now?
MATHEW MERYGREEKE. As fast as I could runne sir   10
                in poste against you.
But why speake ye so faintly, or why are ye so sad?
RAFE ROYSTER. Thou knowest the proverbe, bycause
                I can not be had.[(1)]
Hast thou spoken with this woman?
MATHEW MERYGREEKE.   Yea that I have.
RAFE ROYSTER. And what will this geare be?
MATHEW MERYGREEKE.   No so God me save.
RAFE ROYSTER. Hast thou a flat answer?
MATHEW MERYGREEKE.   Nay a sharp answer.
RAFE ROYSTER.   What?   15

ACTUS III.   SCAENA III.
   1 *a jutte :* a running against.

MATHEW MERYGREEKE. Ye shall not (she sayth) by
        hir will marry hir cat.
Ye are such a calfe, such an asse, such a blocke,
Such a lilburne,[2] such a hoball,[3] such a lobcocke,[4]
And bicause ye shoulde come to hir at no season,
She despised your maship out of all reason.   20
Bawawe[5] what ye say (ko I)[6] of such a jentman,
Nay I feare him not (ko she) doe the best he can.
He vaunteth him selfe for a man of prowesse
        greate,
Where as a good gander I dare say may him beate.
And where he is louted[7] and laughed to skorne,   25
For the veriest dolte that ever was borne,
And veriest lubber, sloven and beast,
Living in this worlde from the west to the east:
Yet of himselfe hath he suche opinion,
That in all the worlde is not the like minion.   30
He thinketh eche woman to be brought in dotage
With the onely sight of his goodly personage:
Yet none that will have hym: we do hym loute
        and flocke,[8]
And make him among us, our common sporting
        stocke,
And so would I now (ko she) save onely bicause,   35
Better nay (ko I) I lust not medle with dawes.
Ye are happy (ko I) that ye are a woman,
This would cost you your life in case ye were a
        man.
RAFE ROYSTER. Yea an hundred thousand pound
        should not save hir life.
MATHEW MERYGREEKE. No but that ye wowe hir to   40
        have hir to your wife,
But I coulde not stoppe hir mouth.
RAFE ROYSTER.   Heigh how alas,
MATHEW MERYGREEKE. Be of good cheere man, and
        let the worlde passe.

---

2 *lilburne :* lout.
3 *hoball :* clown.
4 *lobcocke :* lubber.
5 *Bawawe :* an exclamation
   of contempt.

6 *ko I :* quoth I, said I.
7 *louted :* mocked.
8 *flocke :* regard as worthless. (Latin *flocci fa-*
   cere)

RAFE ROYSTER. What shall I doe or say nowe that it
        will not bee?

MATHEW MERYGREEKE. Ye shall have choice of a thou-
        sande as good as shee,

And ye must pardon hir, it is for lacke of witte.   45

RAFE ROYSTER. Yea, for were not I an husbande for
        hir fitte?

Well what should I now doe?

MATHEW MERYGREEKE.   In faith I can not tell.

RAFE ROYSTER. I will go home and die.

MATHEW MERYGREEKE.   Then shall I bidde toll the
        bell?

RAFE ROYSTER. No.

MATHEW MERYGREEKE. God have mercie on your
        soule, ah good gentleman,

That er ye shuld th[u]s dye for an unkinde   50
        woman,

Will ye drinke once ere ye goe.[2]

RAFE ROYSTER.   No, no, I will none.

MATHEW MERYGREEKE. How feele your soule to God?

RAFE ROYSTER.   I am nigh gone.

MATHEW MERYGREEKE. And shall we hence streight?

RAFE ROYSTER.   Yea.

MATHEW MERYGREEKE.   *Placebo dilexi.*[9]

Maister Royster Doyster will streight go home and
        die.   *ut infra.*[3]

RAFE ROYSTER. Heigh how, alas, the pangs of death   55
        my hearte do breake.

MATHEW MERYGREEKE. Holde your peace for shame
        sir, a dead man may not speake.

Nequando :[10] What mourners and what torches
        shall we have?

RAFE ROYSTER. None.

MATHEW MERYGREEKE. *Dirige.*[11] He will go darklyng
        to his grave,

Neque lux, neque crux, neque mourners, *neque*
        clinke,[12]

---

9 *Placebo dilexi:* I shall
    please to single out.

10 *Nequando :* Lest (he tear
    my soul like a lion).
    Psalms 7:2.

11 *Dirige :* Direct (O Lord
    my path into your sight).

12 *Neque . . . clinke :* i.e. no
    acolytes with candles,
    no crucifix-bearer, no
    mourners, and no ring-
    ing of the passing bells
    before and after the ser-
    vice.

He will steale to heaven, unknowing to God I   60
    thinke.

A porta inferi,[13] who shall your goodes possesse?

RAFE ROYSTER. Thou shalt be my sectour,[14] and have
    all more and lesse.

MATHEW MERYGREEKE. *Requiem æternam.*[15] Now
    God reward your mastershyp.

And I will crie halfepenie doale for your worshyp.

Come forth sirs, heare the dolefull newes I shall   65
    you tell.

       Evocat servos militis.[16]

Our good maister here will no longer with us
    dwell,

But in spite of Custance, which hath hym weried,

Let us see his mashyp solemnely buried.

And while some piece of his soule is yet hym
    within,

Some part of his funeralls let us here begin.   70

Audivi vocem,[17] All men take heede by this one
    gentleman,

Howe you sette your love upon an unkinde woman.

For these women be all such madde pievishe elves,

They will not be wonne except it please them
    selves.

But in fayth Custance if ever ye come in hell,   75

Maister Royster Doyster shall serve you as well.

And will ye needes go from us thus in very deede?

RAFE ROYSTER. Yea in good sadnesse![18]

MATHEW MERYGREEKE.   Now Jesus
    Christ be your speede.

Good night Roger olde knave, farewell Roger olde
    knave,

Good night Roger olde knave, knave knap.   80

       -ut infra.(4)

Pray for the late maister Royster Doysters soule,

And come forth parish Clarke, let the passing bell
    toll.

13 *A porta inferi*: From the   16 *Evocat . . . militis*: He
    gate of hell.   calls forth the servants
14 *sectour*: executor.   of the soldier.
15 *Requiem æternam*: Rest   17 *Audivi vocem*: I have
    eternal (give to him,   heard a voice (from
    Lord).   heaven saying to me).
                           18 *sadnesse*: seriousness.

Ad servos militis.[19] Pray for your mayster sirs, and
          for hym ring a peale.
He was your right good maister while he was in
          heale.[20]
Qui Lazarum.

RAFE ROYSTER. Heigh how.

MATHEW MERYGREEKE.   Dead men go not so fast.   85
In Paradisum.

RAFE ROYSTER. Heihow.

MATHEW MERYGREEKE. Soft, heare what I have cast.

RAFE ROYSTER. I will heare nothing, I am past.

MATHEW MERYGREEKE.   Whough, wellaway.
Ye may tarie one houre, and heare what I shall
          say,
Ye were best sir for a while to revive againe,
And quite them er ye go.

RAFE ROYSTER.   Trowest thou so?

MATHEW MERYGREEKE.   Ye plain.   90

RAFE ROYSTER. How may I revive being nowe so farre
          past?

MATHEW MERYGREEKE. I will rubbe your temples,
          and fette you againe at last.

RAFE ROYSTER. It will not be possible.

MATHEW MERYGREEKE. [*Rubbing* RAFE's *temples.*]
          Yes for twentie pounde.

RAFE ROYSTER. Armes![21] what dost thou?

MATHEW MERYGREEKE.   Fet you again out of your
          sound.[22]
By this crosse ye were nigh gone in deede, I might   95
          feele
Your soule departing within an inche of your
          heele.
Now folow my counsell.

RAFE ROYSTER.   What is it?

MATHEW MERYGREEKE.   If I wer you,
Custance should eft seeke to me, ere I woulde
          bowe.

RAFE ROYSTER. Well, as thou wilt have me, even so
          will I doe.

---

19 *Ad . . . militis :* To the sol-   21 *Armes :* By God's arms!
          dier's servants.   22 *sound :* swoon.
20 *heale :* health.

MATHEW MERYGREEKE. Then shall ye revive againe   100
    for an houre or two.

RAFE ROYSTER. As thou wilt, I am content for a little
    space.

MATHEW MERYGREEKE. Good happe is not hastie; yet
    in space com[e]th grace,

    To speake with Custance your selfe shoulde be
      very well,

    What good therof may come, nor I, nor you can
      tell.

    But now the matter standeth upon your mariage,   105
    Ye must now take unto you a lustie courage.
    Ye may not speake with a faint heart to Custance,
    But with a lusty breast and countenance,
    That she may knowe she hath to answere to a man.

RAFE ROYSTER. Yes I can do that as well as any can.   110

MATHEW MERYGREEKE. Then bicause ye must Cus-
    tance face to face wowe,

    Let us see how to behave your selfe ye can doe.
    Ye must have a portely bragge after your estate.[23]

RAFE ROYSTER. Tushe, I can handle that after the best
    rate.

            [RAFE *struts.*]

MATHEW MERYGREEKE. Well done, so loe, up man   115
    with your head and chin,

    Up with that snoute man : so loe, nowe ye begin,
    So, that is somewhat like, but, prankie cote,[24]
      nay, whan!

    That is a lustie brute, handes under your side
      man :

    So loe, now is it even as it shoulde[1] bee,
    That is somewhat like, for a man of your degree.   120
    Then must ye stately goe, jetting[25] up and downe,
    Tut, can ye no better shake the taile of your
      gowne?

    There loe, such a lustie bragge[26] it is ye must
      make.

---

23 *portely . . . estate :* a dig-
    nified pompous carriage
    or demeanor to match
    your status in life.

24 *prankie cote :* arrange your
    coat properly.

25 *jetting :* strutting.

26 *lustie bragge :* vigorous
    way of carrying your-
    self.

RAFE ROYSTER. To come behind, and make curtsie,
   thou must som pains take.

MATHEW MERYGREEKE. Else were I much to blame, I 125
   thanke your mastershyp.

The lorde one day all to begrime you with worshyp!

 [MERYGREEKE *pushes the servants.*]

Backe sir sauce,[27] let gentlefolkes have elbowe
   roome,

Voyde sirs, see ye not maister Royster Doyster
   come?

Make place my maisters. [*He shoves* RAFE.]

RAFE ROYSTER.   Thou justlest nowe to nigh.

MATHEW MERYGREEKE. Back al rude loutes.

        [*Bumps* RAFE *again.*]

RAFE ROYSTER.   Tush.

MATHEW MERYGREEKE. I crie your maship mercy. 130

Hoighdagh, if faire fine mistresse Custance sawe
   you now,

Rafe Royster Doyster were hir owne I warrant
   you.

RAFE ROYSTER. Neare an M by your girdle?[(5)]

MATHEW MERYGREEKE. Your good mastershyps

Maistershyp, were hir owne Mistreshyps mistreshyps,

Ye were take up for haukes,[(6)] ye were gone, ye 135
   were gone,

But now one other thing more yet I thinke upon.

RAFE ROYSTER. Shewe what it is.

MATHEW MERYGREEKE. A wower be he never so
   poore

Must play and sing before his bestbeloves doore,

How much more than you?

RAFE ROYSTER. Thou speakest wel out of dout.

MATHEW MERYGREEKE. And perchaunce that woulde 140
   make hir the sooner come out.

RAFE ROYSTER. Goe call my Musitians, bydde them
   high[28] apace.

MATHEW MERYGREEKE. I wyll be here with them ere
   ye can say trey ace.[29]   *Exeat.*

---

27 *sauce* : saucy fellow.   29 *ere . . . ace* : i.e. in a trice.
28 *high* : hie, approach.

RAFE ROYSTER. This was well sayde of Merygreeke,
    I lowe hys wit,
 Before my sweete hearts dore we will have a fit,[30]
 That if my love come forth, that I may with hir 145
    talke,
 I doubt not but this geare shall on my side walke.
 But lo, how well Merygreeke is returned sence.
MATHEW MERYGREEKE. [*Returning with the musi-*
    cians.] There hath grown no grasse on
    my heele since I went hence,
 Lo here have I brought that shall make you
    pastance.
RAFE ROYSTER. Come sirs let us sing to winne my 150
    deare love Custance.
       Cantent.[7]
MATHEW MERYGREEKE. Lo where she commeth, some
    countenaunce to hir make.
 And ye shall heare me be plaine with hir for your
    sake.

     ACTUS III. SCAENA IIII.

 [*Enter* CHRISTIAN] CUSTANCE. MERYGREEKE
  [*and*] ROYSTER DOYSTER [*remain.*]
CHRISTIAN CUSTANCE. What gaudyng and foolyng is
    this afore my doore?
MATHEW MERYGREEKE. May not folks be honest, pray
    you, though they be pore?
CHRISTIAN CUSTANCE. As that thing may be true, so
    rich folks may be fooles.
RAFE ROYSTER. Hir talke is as fine as she had learned
    in schooles.
MATHEW MERYGREEKE. [*Aside to* RAFE.] Looke partly 5
    towarde hir, and drawe a little nere.
CHRISTIAN CUSTANCE. Get ye home idle folkes.
MATHEW MERYGREEKE. Why may not we be here?
 Nay and ye will haze,[1] haze : otherwise I tell you
    plaine,

---

30 *have a fit :* play some
  music.

ACTUS III. SCAENA IIII.
 1 *haze :* have us.

And ye will not haze, then give us our geare
    againe.

CHRISTIAN CUSTANCE. In deede I have of yours much
    gay things God save all.

RAFE ROYSTER. Speake gently unto hir, and let hir   10
    take all.

MATHEW MERYGREEKE. Ye are to tender hearted:
    shall she make us dawes?

Nay dame, I will be plaine with you in my friends
    cause.

RAFE ROYSTER. Let all this passe sweete heart and ac-
    cept my service.[1]

CHRISTIAN CUSTANCE. I will not be served with a
    foole in no wise,

When I choose an husbande I hope to take a man.   15

MATHEW MERYGREEKE. And where will ye finde one
    which can doe that he can?

Now thys man towarde you being so kinde,

You not to make him an answere somewhat to his
    minde.

CHRISTIAN CUSTANCE. I sent him a full answere by
    you dyd I not?

MATHEW MERYGREEKE. And I reported it.

CHRISTIAN CUSTANCE. Nay I must speake it againe.   20

RAFE ROYSTER. No no, he tolde it all.

MATHEW MERYGREEKE.   Was I not metely plaine?

RAFE ROYSTER. Yes.

MATHEW MERYGREEKE. But I would not tell all, for
    faith if I had

With you dame Custance ere this houre it had been
    bad,

And not without cause: for this goodly personage,

Ment no lesse than to joyne with you in mariage.   25

CHRISTIAN CUSTANCE. Let him wast no more labour
    nor sute about me.

MATHEW MERYGREEKE. Ye know not where your pre-
    ferment lieth I see,

He sending you such a token, ring and letter.

CHRISTIAN CUSTANCE. Mary here it is, ye never sawe
    a better.

MATHEW MERYGREEKE. Let us see your letter.

CHRISTIAN CUSTANCE.   Holde, reade it if ye can.   30

And see what letter it is to winne a woman.
MATHEW MERYGREEKE. [*Reads.*] To mine owne deare
    coney, birde, swete heart, and pigsny[2]
Good Mistresse Custance present these by and by.
Of this superscription do ye blame the stile?
CHRISTIAN CUSTANCE. With the rest as good stuffe as   35
    ye redde a great while.
MATHEW MERYGREEKE. [*Reads.*] Sweete mistresse[2]
    where as I love you nothing at all,
Regarding your substance and richesse[3] chiefe
    of all,
For your personage, beautie, demeanour and
    wit,[4]
I commende me unto you never a whit.
Sorie to heare report of your good welfare.   40
For (as I heare say) suche your conditions are,
That ye be worthie favour of no living man,
To be abhorred of every honest man.
To be taken[5] for a woman enclined to vice.
Nothing at all to Vertue gyving hir due price.
Wherfore concerning mariage, ye are thought   45
Suche a fine Paragon, as nere honest man bought.
And nowe by these presentes I do you advertise
That I am minded to marrie you in no wise.
For your goodes and substance,[6] I coulde bee   50
    content
To take you as ye are. If ye mynde to bee my
    wyfe,
Ye shall be assured for the tyme of my lyfe,
I will keepe ye ryght well,[7] from good rayment
    and fare,
Ye shall not be kepte but in sorowe and care.
Ye shall in no wyse lyve at your owne libertie,[8]   55
Doe and say what ye lust,[9] ye shall never
    please me,
But when ye are mery, I will be all sadde,[10]
When ye are sory,[11] I will be very gladde.
When ye seeke your heartes ease, I will be un-
    kinde,

2 *pigsny :* pig's eye (term of
  endearment).

At no tyme,[12] in me shall ye muche gentlenesse   60
    finde.

But all things contrary to your will and minde,

Shall be done : otherwise I wyll not be behinde

To speake. And as for all them[13] that woulde
    do you wrong

I will so helpe and mainteyne, ye shall not lyve
    long.

Nor any foolishe dolte,[14] shall cumbre you but I.   65

I, who ere say nay,[15] wyll sticke by you[16] tyll
    I die,[17]

Thus good mistresse Custance,[18] the lorde you
    save and kepe,

From me Royster Doyster,[19] whether I wake or
    slepe.

Who favoureth you no lesse, (ye may be
    bolde)[20]

Than this letter purporteth,[21] which ye have   70
    unfolde.

CHRISTIAN CUSTANCE. Howe by this letter of love? is
    it not fine?

RAFE ROYSTER. By the armes of Caleys[3] it is none of
    myne.

MATHEW MERYGREEKE. Fie you are fowle to blame,
    this is your owne hand.

CHRISTIAN CUSTANCE. Might not a woman be proude
    of such an husbande?

MATHEW MERYGREEKE. Ah that ye would in a letter   75
    shew such despite.

RAFE ROYSTER. Oh I would I had hym here, the
    which did it endite.

MATHEW MERYGREEKE. Why ye made it your selfe ye
    tolde me by this light.

RAFE ROYSTER. Yea I ment I wrote it myne owne
    selfe yesternight.

CHRISTIAN CUSTANCE. Ywis sir, I would not have sent
    you such a mocke.

RAFE ROYSTER. Ye may so take it, but I ment it not so   80
    by Cocke.

MATHEW MERYGREEKE. Who can blame this woman
    to fume and frette and rage?

  3 *Caleys :* Calais.

Tut, tut, your selfe nowe have marde your owne
  marriage.
Well, yet mistresse Custance, if ye can this re-
  mitte,
This gentleman other wise may your love requitte.
CHRISTIAN CUSTANCE. No God be with you both, and 85
  seeke no more to me.   *Exeat.*
RAFE ROYSTER. Wough, she is gone for ever, I shall
  hir no more see.
MATHEW MERYGREEKE. What weepe? fye for shame,
  and blubber? for manhods sake,
Never lette your foe so muche pleasure of you
  take.
Rather play the mans parte, and doe love refraine.
If she despise you een despise ye hir againe. 90
RAFE ROYSTER. By Gosse[4] and for thy sake I defye
  hir in deede.
MATHEW MERYGREEKE. Yea and perchaunce that way
  ye shall much sooner speede,
For one madde propretie these women have in
  fey,[5]
When ye will, they will not : Will not ye, then will
  they.
Ah foolishe woman, ah moste unluckie Custance, 95
Ah unfortunate woman, ah pievishe Custance,
Art thou to thine harmes so obstinately bent,
That thou canst not see where lieth thine high pre-
  ferment?
Canst thou not lub dis man, which coulde lub dee
  so well?
Art thou so much thine own foe?
RAFE ROYSTER.   Thou dost the truth tell. 100
MATHEW MERYGREEKE. Wel I lament.
RAFE ROYSTER.   So do I.
MATHEW MERYGREEKE.   Wherfor?
RAFE ROYSTER.   For this thing,
  Bicause she is gone.
MATHEW MERYGREEKE. I mourne for an other thing.
RAFE ROYSTER. What is it Merygreeke, wherfore thou
  dost griefe take?

---

4 *Gosse :* God.   5 *in fey :* in faith, verily.

MATHEW MERYGREEKE. That I am not a woman my-
                selfe for your sake,
  I would have you my selfe, and a strawe for yond   105
                Gill,
  And mocke[6] much of you though it were against
                my will.
  I would not I warrant you, fall in such a rage,
  As so to refuse suche a goodly personage.
RAFE ROYSTER. In faith I heartily thanke thee Mery-
                greeke.
MATHEW MERYGREEKE. And I were a woman.
RAFE ROYSTER.   Thou wouldest to me seeke.   110
MATHEW MERYGREEKE. For though I say it, a goodly
                person ye bee.
RAFE ROYSTER. No, no.
MATHEW MERYGREEKE. Yes a goodly man as ere I
                dyd see.
RAFE ROYSTER. No, I am a poore homely man as
                God made mee.
MATHEW MERYGREEKE. By the faith that I owe to
                God sir, but ye bee.
  Woulde I might for your sake, spend a thousande   115
                pound land.
RAFE ROYSTER. I dare say thou wouldest have me to
                thy husbande.
MATHEW MERYGREEKE. Yea: And I were the fairest
                lady in the shiere,[7]
  And knewe you as I know you, and see you nowe
                here.
  Well I say no more.
RAFE ROYSTER.   Grammercies with all my hart.
MATHEW MERYGREEKE. But since that can not be, will   120
                ye play a wise parte?
RAFE ROYSTER. How should I?
MATHEW MERYGREEKE. Refraine from Custance a
                while now.
  And I warrant hir soone right glad to seeke to you,
  Ye shall see hir anon come on hir knees creeping.
  And pray you to be good to hir salte teares weep-
                ing.
RAFE ROYSTER. But what and she come not?

  6 *mocke :* make.   7 *shiere :* shire.

MATHEW MERYGREEKE.   In faith then farewel she.   125
  Or else if ye be wroth, ye may avenged be.
RAFE ROYSTER. By Cocks precious potsticke, and een
        so I shall.
  I wyll utterly destroy hir, and house and all,
  But I woulde be avenged in the meane space,
  On that vile scribler, that did my wowyng dis-   130
        grace.
MATHEW MERYGREEKE. Scribler (ko you) in deede
        he is worthy no lesse.
  I will call hym to you, and ye bidde me doubtlesse.
RAFE ROYSTER. Yes, for although he had as many
        lives,
  As a thousande widowes, and a thousande wives,
  As a thousande lyons, and a thousand rattes,   135
  A thousande wolves, and a thousande cattes,
  A thousande bulles, and a thousande calves,
  And a thousande legions divided in halves,
  He shall never scape death on my swordes point,
  Though I shoulde be torne therfore joynt by joynt.   140
MATHEW MERYGREEKE. Nay, if ye will kyll him, I will
        not fette[8] him,
  I will not in so muche extremitie sette him,
  He may yet amende sir, and be an honest man,
  Therfore pardon him good soule, as muche as ye
        can.
RAFE ROYSTER. Well, for thy sake, this once with his   145
        lyfe he shall passe,
  But I wyll hewe hym all to pieces by the Masse.
MATHEW MERYGREEKE. Nay fayth ye shall promise
        that he shall no harme have,
  Else I will not fet[22] him.
RAFE ROYSTER.   I shall so God me save.
  But I may chide him a good.
MATHEW MERYGREEKE.   Yea that do hardely.
RAFE ROYSTER. Go then.
MATHEW MERYGREEKE. I returne, and bring him to   150
        you by and by.   *Ex[eat]*.

  8 *fette :* fetch.

Actus iii. Scaena v.

ROYSTER DOYSTER [*remains.*]

RAFE ROYSTER. What is a gentleman but his worde
      and his promise?
I must nowe save this vilaines lyfe in any wise,
And yet at hym already my handes doe tickle,
I shall uneth[1] holde them, they wyll be so fickle.
But lo and Merygreeke have not brought him   5
      sens?[2]

[*Enter* MATHEW MERYGREEKE *with the*
SCRIVENER.]

MATHEW MERYGREEKE. Nay I woulde I had of my
      purse payde fortie pens.
SCRIVENER. So woulde I too : but it needed not that
      stounde.[3]
MATHEW MERYGREEKE. But the jentman had rather
      spent five thousande pounde,
For it disgraced him at least five tymes so muche.
SCRIVENER. He disgraced hym selfe, his loutishnesse   10
      is suche.
RAFE ROYSTER. Howe long they stande prating! Why
      comst thou not away?
MATHEW MERYGREEKE. Come nowe to hymselfe, and
      hearke what he will say.
SCRIVENER. I am not afrayde in his presence to ap-
      peere.
RAFE ROYSTER. Arte thou come felow?
SCRIVENER.   How thinke you? am I not here?
RAFE ROYSTER. What hindrance hast thou done me,   15
      and what villanie!
SCRIVENER. It hath come of thy selfe, if thou hast had
      any.
RAFE ROYSTER. All the stocke thou comest of later or
      rather,[4]
From thy fyrst fathers grandfathers fathers father,

ACTUS iii. SCAENA v.   3 *stounde* : eventuality.
  1 *uneth* : with difficulty.   4 *rather* : earlier.
  2 *sens* : since, already.

Nor all that shall come of thee to the worldes
       ende,
Though to three score generations they descende,   20
Can be able to make me a just recompense,
For this trespasse of thine and this one offense.
SCRIVENER. Wherin?
RAFE ROYSTER.   Did not you make me a letter,
       brother?
SCRIVENER. Pay the like hire, I will make you suche
       an other.
RAFE ROYSTER. Nay see and these whooreson Phari-   25
       seys and Scribes
Doe not get their livyng by polling and bribes.[5]
If it were not for shame—
SCRIVENER.[1]   Nay holde thy hands still.
MATHEW MERYGREEKE. Why, did ye not promise that
       ye would not him spill?
SCRIVENER. Let him not spare me. [*Strikes* RAFE.]
RAFE ROYSTER.   Why wilt thou strike me again?
SCRIVENER. Ye shall have as good as ye bring of me,   30
       that is plaine.
MATHEW MERYGREEKE. I can not blame him sir,
       though your blowes wold him greve.
For he knoweth present death to ensue of all ye
       geve.
RAFE ROYSTER. Well, this man for once hath pur-
       chased thy pardon.
SCRIVENER. And what say ye to me? or else I will be
       gon.
RAFE ROYSTER. I say the letter thou madest me was   35
       not good.
SCRIVENER. Then did ye wrong copy it of likelyhood.
RAFE ROYSTER. Yes, out of thy copy worde for worde
       I it wrote.
[RAFE *produces his copy and the* SCRIVENER's
       original draft.]
SCRIVENER. Then was it as ye prayed to have it, I
       wote,[6]
But in reading and pointyng there was made some
       faulte.

5 *polling and bribes:* extor-   6 *wote:* know.
   tion and robbery.

RAFE ROYSTER. I wote not, but it made all my matter   40
        to haulte.

SCRIVENER. How say you, is this mine originall or no?

RAFE ROYSTER. The selfe same that I wrote out of, so
        mote I go.[7]

SCRIVENER. Loke you on your owne fist,[8] and I will
        looke on this,

And let this man be judge whether I reade amisse.

To myne owne dere coney birde, sweete heart,   45
        and pigsny,

Good mistresse Custance, present these by and by.

How now? doth not this superscription agree?

RAFE ROYSTER. Reade that is within, and there ye
        shall the fault see.

SCRIVENER. Sweete mistresse, where as I love you,
        nothing at all

Regarding your richesse and substance:[2] chiefe   50
        of all

For your personage, beautie, demeanour and
        witte

I commende me unto you:[3] Never a whitte

Sory to heare reporte of your good welfare.

For (as I heare say) suche your conditions are,

That ye be worthie favour: of no living man   55

To be abhorred: of every honest man

To be taken[4] for a woman enclined to vice

Nothing at all: to vertue giving hir due price.

Wherefore concerning mariage, ye are thought

Suche a fine Paragon, as nere[5] honest man   60
        bought.

And nowe by these presents[6] I doe you adver-
        tise,

That I am minded to marrie you: In no wyse

For your goodes and[7] substance: I can[8] be
        content

To take you as you are:[9] yf ye will be my wife,

Ye shall be assured for the time of my life,   65

I wyll keepe you right well:[10] from good rai-
        ment and fare,[11]

Ye shall not be kept: but in sorowe and care

---

7 *so mote I go:* so help me.   8 *fist:* the copy in your
                                 handwriting.

Ye shall in no wyse lyve : at your owne libertie,
Doe[12] and say what ye lust : ye shall never
       please me
But when ye are merrie : I will bee all sadde   70
When ye are sorie : I wyll be very gladde
When ye seeke your heartes ease : I will be un-
       kinde
At no time : in me shall ye muche gentlenesse
       finde.
But all things contrary to your will and minde[13]
Shall be done otherwise : I wyll not be behynde   75
To speake : And as for all they[14] that woulde
       do you wrong,
(I wyll so helpe and maintayne ye) shall not lyve
       long.
Nor any foolishe dolte shall cumber you, but I,
I, who ere say nay,[15] wyll sticke by you tyll I die.
Thus good mistresse Custance, the lorde you save   80
       and kepe.[16]
From me Royster Doyster,[17] whether I wake or
       slepe,
Who favoureth you no lesse, (ye may be
       bolde)[18]
Than this letter purporteth,[19] which ye have un-
       folde.
Now sir, what default can ye finde in this letter?
RAFE ROYSTER. Of truth in my mynde there can not   85
       be a better.
SCRIVENER. Then was the fault in readyng, and not in
       writyng,
No nor I dare say in the fourme of endityng,
But who read this letter, that it sounded so
       nought?
MATHEW MERYGREEKE. I redde it in deede.
SCRIVENER.   Ye red it not as ye ought.
RAFE ROYSTER. Why thou wretched villaine, was all   90
       this same fault in thee? [*Offers to strike*
       MERYGREEKE.]
MATHEW MERYGREEKE. I knocke your costarde if ye
       offer to strike me. [*Knocks* RAFE *on the*
       head.]
RAFE ROYSTER. Strikest thou in deede? and I offer but
       in jest?

MATHEW MERYGREEKE. Yea and rappe you againe ex-
          cept ye can sit in rest.

And I will no longer tarie here, me beleve.

RAFE ROYSTER. What wilt thou be angry, and I do   95
          thee forgeve?

Fare thou well scribler, I crie thee mercie[9] in
          deede.

SCRIVENER. Fare ye well bibbler,[10] and worthily
          may ye speede.

RAFE ROYSTER. If it were an other but thou, it were a
          knave.   [*Exit* SCRIVENER.]

MATHEW MERYGREEKE. Ye are an other your selfe sir,
          the Lorde us both save,

Albeit in this matter I must your pardon crave,   100

Alas woulde ye wyshe in me the witte that ye
          have?

But as for my fault I can quickely amende,

I will shewe Custance it was I that did offende.

RAFE ROYSTER. By so doing hir anger may be re-
          formed.

MATHEW MERYGREEKE. But if by no entreatie she will   105
          be turned,

Then sette lyght by hir and bee as testie as shee,

And doe your force upon hir with extremitie.

RAFE ROYSTER. Come on therefore lette us go home
          in sadnesse.

MATHEW MERYGREEKE. That if force shall neede all
          may be in a readinesse,

And as for thys letter hardely[11] let all go,   110

We wyll know where[12] she refuse you for that or
          no.   *Exeant am[bo]*.

9 *I . . . mercie :* I beg your   11 *hardely :* by all means.
  pardon.   12 *where :* whether.
10 *bibbler :* drinker, tippler.

Actus iiii. Scaena i.

[Enter] sym suresby.

sym suresby. Is there any man but I Sym Suresby
    alone,
  That would have taken such an enterprise him
    upon,
  In suche an outragious tempest as this was.
  Suche a daungerous gulfe of the sea to passe.
  I thinke verily *Neptunes* mightie godshyp,
  Was angry with some that was in our shyp,   5
  And but for the honestie which in me he founde,
  I thinke for the others sake we had bene drownde.
  But fye on that servant which for his maisters
    wealth
  Will sticke for to hazarde both his lyfe and his   10
    health.
  My maister Gawyn Goodlucke after me a day
  Bicause of the weather, thought best hys shyppe
    to stay,
  And now that I have the rough sourges so well
    past,
  God graunt I may finde all things safe here at last.
  Then will I thinke all my travaile well spent.   15
  Nowe the first poynt wherfore my maister hath me
    sent
  Is to salute dame Christian Custance his wife
  Espoused : whome he tendreth no lesse than his
    life,
  I must see how it is with hir well or wrong,
  And whether for him she doth not now thinke   20
    long :
  Then to other friendes I have a message or tway,
  And then so to returne and mete him on the way.
  Now wyll I goe knocke that I may dispatche with
    speede,
  But loe forth commeth hir selfe happily in deede.

Actus iiii.   Scaena ii.

[*Enter*] CHRISTIAN CUSTANCE [*to*] SYM SURESBY.

CHRISTIAN CUSTANCE. I come to see if any more
    stirryng be here,

But what straunger is this, which doth to me ap-
    pere?

SYM SURESBY. I will speake to hir : Dame the Lorde
    you save and see.

CHRISTIAN CUSTANCE. What friende Sym Suresby?
    Forsoth right welcome ye be,

  Howe doth mine owne Gawyn Goodlucke, I pray   5
    the tell?

SYM SURESBY. When he knoweth of your health he
    will be perfect well.

CHRISTIAN CUSTANCE. If he have perfect helth, I am
    as I would be.

SYM SURESBY. Such newes will please him well, this
    is as it should be.

CHRISTIAN CUSTANCE. I thinke now long for him.

SYM SURESBY.   And he as long for you.

CHRISTIAN CUSTANCE. When wil he be at home?

SYM SURESBY.   His heart is here een now,   10
  His body commeth after.

CHRISTIAN CUSTANCE.   I woulde see that faine.

SYM SURESBY. As fast as wynde and sayle can cary it
    a maine.

  But what two men are yonde comming hither-
    warde?

CHRISTIAN CUSTANCE. Now I shrew their best Christ-
    masse chekes[1] both togetherward.

Actus iiii.   Scaena iii.

CHRISTIAN CUSTANCE [*and*] SYM SURESBY
[*remain. Enter*] RAFE ROYSTER [*and*]
MATHEW MERYGREEKE.

CHRISTIAN CUSTANCE. [*Aside.*] What meane these
    lewde felowes thus to trouble me stil?

ACTUS IIII.   SCAENA II.
   1 *I . . . chekes :* a ladylike
   imprecation.

Sym Suresby here perchance shal therof deme
        som yll.
And shall suspect[1] in me some point of naughti-
        nesse,
And[1] they come hitherward.

SYM SURESBY.   What is their businesse?

CHRISTIAN CUSTANCE. I have nought to them, nor   5
        they to me, in sadnesse.

SYM SURESBY. Let us hearken them, [*Aside.*] some-
        what there is I feare it.

RAFE ROYSTER. I will speake out aloude best, that she
        may heare it.

MATHEW MERYGREEKE. Nay alas, ye may so feare hir
        out of hir wit.

RAFE ROYSTER. By the crosse of my sworde, I will
        hurt hir no whit.

MATHEW MERYGREEKE. Will ye doe no harme in   10
        deede, shall I trust your worde?

RAFE ROYSTER. By Royster Doysters fayth I will
        speake but in borde.[2]

SYM SURESBY. Let us hearken them, [*Aside.*] som-
        what there is I feare it.

RAFE ROYSTER. I will speake out aloude, I care not
        who heare it :

  Sirs, see that my harnesse, my tergat,[3] and my
        shield,

  Be made as bright now, as when I was last in   15
        fielde,

  As white as I shoulde to warre againe to morrowe :

  For sicke shall I be, but I worke some folke sorow.

  Therfore see that all shine as bright as sainct
        George,

  Or as doth a key newly come from the Smiths
        forge.

  I woulde have my sworde and harnesse to shine so   20
        bright,

  That I might therwith dimme mine enimies sight,

  I would have it cast beames as fast I tell you
        playne,

ACTUS IIII.   SCAENA III.   3 *my harnesse, my tergat :*
  1 *And :* if.   my armor, my light
  2 *borde :* jest.   shield or buckler.

As doth the glittryng grasse after a showre of
  raine.
And see that in case I shoulde neede to come to
  arming,
All things may be ready at a minutes warning,   25
For such chaunce may chaunce in an houre, do ye
  heare?

MATHEW MERYGREEKE. As perchance shall not
  chaunce againe in seven yeare.

RAFE ROYSTER. Now draw we neare to hir, and here
  what shall be sayde.

MATHEW MERYGREEKE. But I woulde not have you
  make hir too muche afrayde.

RAFE ROYSTER. Well founde sweete wife (I trust) for   30
  al this your soure looke.

CHRISTIAN CUSTANCE. Wife, why cal ye me wife?

SYM SURESBY. [*Aside.*] Wife? this gear goth acrook.

MATHEW MERYGREEKE. Nay mistresse Custance, I
  warrant you, our letter
Is not as we redde een nowe, but much better,
And where ye halfe stomaked this gentleman
  afore,
For this same letter, ye wyll love hym now there-   35
  fore,
Nor it is not this letter, though ye were a queene,
That shoulde breake marriage betweene you
  twaine I weene.

CHRISTIAN CUSTANCE. I did not refuse hym for the
  letters sake.

RAFE ROYSTER. Then ye are content me for your husbande to take?

CHRISTIAN CUSTANCE. You for my husbande to take?   40
  nothing lesse truely.

RAFE ROYSTER. Yea say so, sweete spouse, afore
  straungers hardly.

MATHEW MERYGREEKE. And though I have here his
  letter of love with me,
Yet his ryng and tokens he sent, keepe safe with
  ye.

CHRISTIAN CUSTANCE. A mischiefe take his tokens,
  and him and thee too.
But what prate I with fooles? have I nought else   45
  to doo?

Come in with me Sym Suresby to take some re-
      past.

SYM SURESBY. I must ere I drinke by your leave, goe
      in all hast,

To a place or two, with earnest letters of his.

CHRISTIAN CUSTANCE. Then come drink here with me.

SYM SURESBY.   I thank you.

CHRISTIAN CUSTANCE.   Do not misse.

You shall have a token to your maister with you.   50

SYM SURESBY. No tokens this time gramercies, God
      be with you.   *Exeat*.

CHRISTIAN CUSTANCE. Surely this fellowe misdeemeth
      some yll in me,

Which thing but God helpe, will go neere to spill
      me.

RAFE ROYSTER. Yea farewell fellow, and tell thy
      maister Goodlucke

That he commeth to late of thys blossome to   55
      plucke.

Let him keepe him there still, or at least wise
      make no hast,

As for his labour hither he shall spende in wast.

His betters be in place nowe.

MATHEW MERYGREEKE. [*Aside.*] As long as it will hold.

CHRISTIAN CUSTANCE. I will be even with thee thou
      beast, thou mayst be bolde.

RAFE ROYSTER. Will ye have us then?

CHRISTIAN CUSTANCE.   I will never have thee.   60

RAFE ROYSTER. Then will I have you!

CHRISTIAN CUSTANCE. No, the devill shal have thee.

I have gotten this houre more shame and harme
      by thee,

Than all thy life days thou canst do me honestie.

MATHEW MERYGREEKE. [*To* RAFE.] Why nowe may
      ye see what it comth too in the ende,

To make a deadly foe of your most loving frende :   65

[*To* CUSTANCE.] And ywis this letter if ye woulde
      heare it now—

CHRISTIAN CUSTANCE. I will heare none of it.

MATHEW MERYGREEKE.   In faith would ravishe you.

CHRISTIAN CUSTANCE. He hath stained my name for
      ever, this is cleare.

RAFE ROYSTER. I can make all as well in an houre—

MATHEW MERYGREEKE. [*Aside.*]   As ten yeare—
How say ye, wil ye have him?
CHRISTIAN CUSTANCE.   No.
MATHEW MERYGREEKE.   Wil ye take him?   70
CHRISTIAN CUSTANCE. I defie him.
MATHEW MERYGREEKE.   At my word?
CHRISTIAN CUSTANCE.   A shame take him.
Waste no more wynde, for it will never bee.
MATHEW MERYGREEKE. This one faulte with twaine
              shall be mended, ye shall see.
    Gentle mistresse Custance now, good mistresse
              Custance,
    Honey mistresse Custance now, sweete mistresse   75
              Custance,
    Golden mistresse Custance now, white[4] mistresse
              Custance,
    Silken mistresse Custance now, faire mistresse
              Custance.
CHRISTIAN CUSTANCE. Faith rather than to mary with
              suche a doltishe loute,
    I woulde matche my selfe with a begger out of
              doute.
MATHEW MERYGREEKE. Then I can say no more, to   80
              speede we are not like,
    Except ye rappe out a ragge of your Rhetorike.
CHRISTIAN CUSTANCE. Speake not of winnyng me :
              for it shall never be so.
RAFE ROYSTER. Yes dame, I will have you whether ye
              will or no,
    I commaunde you to love me, wherfore shoulde
              ye not?
    Is not my love to you chafing and burning hot?   85
MATHEW MERYGREEKE. Too hir, that is well sayd.
RAFE ROYSTER.   Shall I so breake my braine
To dote upon you, and ye not love us againe?
MATHEW MERYGREEKE. Wel sayd yet.
CHRISTIAN CUSTANCE.   Go to, you goose.
RAFE ROYSTER.   I say Kit Custance,
    In case ye will not haze,[5] well, better yes per-
              chaunce.

    4 *white* : dear.   5 *haze* : have us.

CHRISTIAN CUSTANCE. Avaunt lozell,[6] picke thee
> hence.

MATHEW MERYGREEKE. Wel sir, ye perceive,   90
> For all your kinde offer, she will not you receive.

RAFE ROYSTER. Then a strawe for hir, and a strawe
> for hir againe,
> She shall not be my wife, woulde she never so
> faine,
> No and though she would be at ten thousand
> pounde cost.

MATHEW MERYGREEKE. Lo dame, ye may see what   95
> an husbande ye have lost.

CHRISTIAN CUSTANCE. Yea, no force,[7] a jewell muche
> better lost than founde.

MATHEW MERYGREEKE. Ah, ye will not beleve how
> this doth my heart wounde.
> How shoulde a mariage betwene you be towarde,
> If both parties drawe backe, and become so fro-
> warde?

RAFE ROYSTER. Nay dame, I will fire thee out of thy   100
> house,
> And destroy thee and all thine, and that by and
> by.

MATHEW MERYGREEKE. Nay for the passion of God
> sir, do not so.

RAFE ROYSTER. Yes, except she will say yea to that
> she sayde no.

CHRISTIAN CUSTANCE. And what, be there no officers
> trow we, in towne
> To checke idle loytrers,[1] braggyng up and   105
> downe?
> Where be they, by whome vacabunds shoulde be
> represt?
> That poore sillie[8] Widowes might live in peace
> and rest.
> Shall I never ridde thee out of my companie?
> I will call for helpe, what hough, come forth True-
> penie.
> > [*Enter* TRUEPENIE.]

6 *lozell :* lout.   8 *sillie :* innocent.
7 *no force :* no matter.

TRUEPENIE. Anon. What is your will mistresse? dyd   110
            ye call me?
CHRISTIAN CUSTANCE. Yea, go runne apace, and as
            fast as may be,
   Pray Tristram Trusty, my moste assured frende,
   To be here by and by, that he may me defende.
TRUEPENIE. That message so quickly shall be done
            by Gods grace,
   That at my returne ye shall say, I went apace.   115
                                            Exeat.
CHRISTIAN CUSTANCE. Then shall we see I trowe,
            whether ye shall do me harme.
RAFE ROYSTER. Yes in faith Kitte, I shall thee and
            thine so charme,
   That all women incarnate by thee may beware.
CHRISTIAN CUSTANCE. Nay, as for charming me, come
            hither if thou dare,
   I shall cloute thee tyll thou stinke, both thee and 120
            thy traine,
   And coyle[9] thee mine owne handes, and sende
            thee home againe.
RAFE ROYSTER. Yea sayst thou me that dame? dost
            thou me threaten?
   Goe we, I will see whether I shall be beaten.
MATHEW MERYGREEKE. Nay for the paishe[10] of God,
            let me now treate peace,
   For bloodshed will there be in case this strife in-   125
            creace.
   Ah good dame Custance, take better way with
            you.
CHRISTIAN CUSTANCE. Let him do his worst.
                   [CUSTANCE *beats* RAFE.]
MATHEW MERYGREEKE. [*To* RAFE.] Yeld in time.
RAFE ROYSTER.   Come hence thou.
                   Exeant ROYSTER *et* MERYGREEKE.

   9 *coyle :* beat.   10 *paishe :* Passion.

ACTUS IIII.   SCAENA IIII.

CHRISTIAN CUSTANCE [*remains.*]

CHRISTIAN CUSTANCE. So sirra, if I should not with
  hym take this way,
  I should not be ridde of him I thinke till doomes
  day,
  I will call forth my folkes, that without any mockes
  If he come agayne we may give him rappes and
  knockes.
  Mage Mumble-crust, come forth, and Tibet Talk-   5
  apace.
  Yea and come forth too, mistresse Annot Alyface.
  [*Enter* ANNOT ALYFACE, TIBET TALK-APACE,
      and MAGE MUMBLE-CRUST.]

ANNOT ALYFACE. I come.

TIBET TALK-APACE.   And I am here.

MAGE MUMBLE-CRUST.   And I am here too at length.

CHRISTIAN CUSTANCE. Like warriers if nede bee, ye
  must shew your strength.
  The man that this day hath thus begiled you,
  Is Rafe Royster Doyster, whome ye know well   10
  inowe,
  The moste loute and dastarde that ever on
  grounde trode.

TIBET TALK-APACE. I see all folke mocke hym when
  he goth abrode.

CHRISTIAN CUSTANCE. What pretie maide? will ye
  talke when I speake?

TIBET TALK-APACE. No forsooth good mistresse.

CHRISTIAN CUSTANCE.   Will ye my tale breake?
  He threatneth to come hither with all his force to   15
  fight,
  I charge you if he come, on him with all your
  might!

MAGE MUMBLE-CRUST. I with my distaffe will reache
  hym one rappe.

TIBET TALK-APACE. And I with my newe broome will
  sweepe hym one swappe,
  And then with our greate clubbe I will reache hym
  one rappe.

ANNOT ALYFACE. And I with our skimmer will fling   20
  him one flappe.
TIBET TALK-APACE. Then Truepenies fireforke will
  him shrewdly fray,
 And you with the spitte may drive him quite
  away.
CHRISTIAN CUSTANCE. Go make all ready, that it
  may be een so.
TIBET TALK-APACE. For my parte I shrewe them that
  last about it go. *Exeant* [*the maids*].

ACTUS IIII. SCAENA V.

CHRISTIAN CUSTANCE [*remains.*]

CHRISTIAN CUSTANCE. Truepenie dyd promise me to
  runne a great pace,
 My friend Tristram Trusty to fet into this place.
 Indeede he dwelleth hence a good stert[1] I con-
  fesse :
 But yet a quicke messanger might twice since, as
  I gesse,
 Have gone and come againe. Ah yond I spie him   5
  now.
 [*Enter* TRUEPENIE *with* TRISTRAM TRUSTY.]
TRUEPENIE. Ye are a slow goer sir, I make God avow.
 My mistresse Custance will in me put all the
  blame.
 Your leggs be longer than myne : come apace for
  shame.
CHRISTIAN CUSTANCE. I can[2] thee thanke Truepenie,
  thou hast done right wele.
TRUEPENIE. Maistresse since I went no grasse hath   10
  growne on my hele,
 But maister Tristram Trusty here maketh no
  speede.
CHRISTIAN CUSTANCE. That he came at all I thanke
  him in very deede,
 For now have I neede of the helpe of some wise
  man.

ACTUS IIII. SCAENA V.   *2 can :* give.
 1 *stert :* leap, distance.

TRISTRAM TRUSTY. Then may I be gone againe, for
    none such I [a]m.

TRUEPENIE. Ye may bee by your going : for no Alder-   15
    man

Can goe I dare say, a sadder pace than ye can.

CHRISTIAN CUSTANCE. Truepenie get thee in, thou
    shalt among them knowe,

How to use thy selfe, like a propre man I trowe.

TRUEPENIE. I go.   *Ex*[*eat*].

CHRISTIAN CUSTANCE. Now Tristram Trusty I thank
    you right much.

For at my first sending to come ye never grutch.   20

TRISTRAM TRUSTY. Dame Custance God ye save, and
    while my life shall last,

For my friende Goodluckes sake ye shall not sende
    in wast.

CHRISTIAN CUSTANCE. He shal give you thanks.

TRISTRAM TRUSTY.   I wil do much for his sake.

CHRISTIAN CUSTANCE. But alack, I feare, great dis-
    pleasure shall be take.

TRISTRAM TRUSTY. Wherfore?

CHRISTIAN CUSTANCE.   For a foolish matter.

TRISTRAM TRUSTY.   What is your cause?   25

CHRISTIAN CUSTANCE. I am yll accombred with a cou-
    ple of dawes.

TRISTRAM TRUSTY. Nay weepe not woman : but tell
    me what your cause is

As concerning my friende, is any thing amisse?

CHRISTIAN CUSTANCE. No not on my part : but here
    was Sym Suresby—

TRISTRAM TRUSTY. He was with me and told me so.

CHRISTIAN CUSTANCE.   And he stoode by   30
While Rafe Royster Doyster with helpe of Mery-
    greeke,

For promise of mariage dyd unto me seeke.

TRISTRAM TRUSTY. And had ye made any promise
    before them twaine?

CHRISTIAN CUSTANCE. No I had rather be torne in
    pieces and slaine,

No man hath my faith and trouth, but Gawyn   35
    Goodlucke,

And that before Suresby dyd I say, and there
    stucke,

But of certaine letters there were suche words
    spoken.

TRISTRAM TRUSTY. He tolde me that too.

CHRISTIAN CUSTANCE.   And of a ring and token.

That Suresby I spied, dyd more than halfe sus-
    pect,

That I my faith to Gawyn Goodlucke dyd reject.   40

TRISTRAM TRUSTY. But there was no such matter
    dame Custance in deede?

CHRISTIAN CUSTANCE. If ever my head thought it,
    God sende me yll speede.

Wherfore I beseech you, with me to be a wit-
    nesse,

That in all my lyfe I never intended thing lesse,

And what a brainsicke foole Rafe Royster Doyster   45
    is,

Your selfe know well enough.

TRISTRAM TRUSTY.   Ye say full true ywis.

CHRISTIAN CUSTANCE. Bicause to bee his wife I ne
    graunt nor apply,

Hither will he com he sweareth by and by,

To kill both me and myne, and beate downe my
    house flat.

Therfore I pray your aide.

TRISTRAM TRUSTY.   I warrant you that.   50

CHRISTIAN CUSTANCE. Have I so many yeres lived a
    sobre life,

And shewed my selfe honest, mayde, widowe, and
    wyfe

And nowe to be abused in such a vile sorte,

Ye see howe poore Widowes lyve all voyde of
    comfort.

TRISTRAM TRUSTY. I warrant hym do you no harme   55
    nor wrong at all.

CHRISTIAN CUSTANCE. No, but Mathew Merygreeke
    doth me most appall,[3]

That he woulde joyne hym selfe with suche a
    wretched loute.

TRISTRAM TRUSTY. He doth it for a jest, I knowe hym
    out of doubte,

And here cometh Merygreeke.

CHRISTIAN CUSTANCE.   Then shal we here his mind.

3 *appall:* dismay.

ACTUS IIII.   SCAENA VI.

[*Enter* MATHEW] MERYGREEKE [*to*] CHRISTIAN
          CUSTANCE [*and*] TRISTRAM TRUSTY.

MATHEW MERYGREEKE. Custance and Trusty both, I
          doe you here well finde.

CHRISTIAN CUSTANCE. Ah Mathew Merygreeke, ye
          have used me well.

MATHEW MERYGREEKE. Nowe for altogether[1] ye must
          your answere tell.

Will ye have this man, woman? or else will ye not?

Else will he come never bore so brymme[2] nor tost   5
          so hot.

TRISTRAM *and* CUSTANCE. But why joyn ye with him?

TRISTRAM TRUSTY.   For mirth?

CHRISTIAN CUSTANCE.   Or else in sadnesse?

MATHEW MERYGREEKE. The more fond of you both!
          Hardly the mater gesse.

TRISTRAM TRUSTY. Lo, how say ye dame?

MATHEW MERYGREEKE.   Why, do ye
                    thinke dame Custance

That in this wowyng I have ment ought but
          pastance?

CHRISTIAN CUSTANCE.[1] Much things ye spake, I   10
          wote, to maintaine his dotage.

MATHEW MERYGREEKE. But well might ye judge I
          spake it all in mockage!

For why? Is Royster Doyster a fitte husband for
          you?

TRISTRAM TRUSTY. I dare say ye never thought it.

MATHEW MERYGREEKE.   No to God I vow.

And dyd not I knowe afore of the insurance[3]

Betweene Gawyn Goodlucke, and Christian Cus-   15
          tance?

And dyd not I for the nonce, by my conveyance,[4]

Reade his letter in a wrong sense for daliance?

ACTUS IIII.   SCAENA VI.   2 *bore so brymme :* boar so
     1 *for altogether :* once and   furious.
          for all.   3 *insurance :* engagement.
                            4 *conveyance :* trickery.

That if you coulde have take it up at the first
      bounde,

We should therat such a sporte and pastime have
      founde,

That all the whole towne should have ben the   20
      merier.

CHRISTIAN CUSTANCE. Ill ake your heades both, I was
      never werier,

Nor never more vexte since the first day I was
      borne.

TRISTRAM TRUSTY. But very well I wist he here did
      all in scorne.

CHRISTIAN CUSTANCE. But I feared thereof to take
      dishonestie.

MATHEW MERYGREEKE. This should both have made   25
      sport, and shewed your honestie,

And Goodlucke I dare sweare, your witte therin
      would low.[5]

TRISTRAM TRUSTY. Yea, being no worse than we know
      it to be now.

MATHEW MERYGREEKE. And nothing yet to late, for
      when I come to him,

Hither will he repaire with a sheepes looke full
      grim,

By plaine force and violence to drive you to yelde.   30

CHRISTIAN CUSTANCE. If ye two bidde me, we will
      with him pitche a fielde,

I and my maides together.

MATHEW MERYGREEKE.   Let us see, be bolde.

CHRISTIAN CUSTANCE. Ye shall see womens warre.

TRISTRAM TRUSTY.   That fight wil I behold.

MATHEW MERYGREEKE. If occasion serve, takyng his
      parte full brim,

I will strike at you, but the rappe shall light on   35
      him.

When we first appeare.

CHRISTIAN CUSTANCE.   Then will I runne away
As though I were afeard.

TRISTRAM TRUSTY.   Do you that part wel play
And I will sue for peace.

MATHEW MERYGREEKE.   And I wil set him on.

5 *low :* allow.

Then will he looke as fierce as a Cotssold lyon.[6]
TRISTRAM TRUSTY. But when gost thou for him?
MATHEW MERYGREEKE.   That do I very nowe.   40
CHRISTIAN CUSTANCE. Ye shal find us here.
MATHEW MERYGREEKE. Wel God have mercy on you.
                                    Ex[eat].
TRISTRAM TRUSTY. There is no cause of feare, the
          least boy in the streete :
CHRISTIAN CUSTANCE. Nay, the least girle I have,
          will make him take his feete.
          [*Drum sounds within.*]
But hearke, me thinke they make preparation.
TRISTRAM TRUSTY. No force, it will be a good recrea-   45
          tion.
CHRISTIAN CUSTANCE. I will stande within, and steppe
          forth speedily,
And so make as though I ranne away dreadfully.
                                    [*Exeant.*]

                ACTUS IIII.   SCAENA VII.

[*Enter*] RAFE ROYSTER, [MATHEW] MERYGREEKE
[*with the drum*], DOBINET DOUGHTIE, HARPAX,
          [*and an* ENSIGN.]
RAFE ROYSTER. Nowe sirs, keepe your ray,[1] and see
          your heartes be stoute,
But where be these caitifes, me·think they dare
          not route,[2]
How sayst thou Merygreeke? What doth Kit Cus-
          tance say?
MATHEW MERYGREEKE. I am loth to tell you.
RAFE ROYSTER.   Tushe speake man, yea or nay?
MATHEW MERYGREEKE. Forsooth sir, I have spoken   5
          for you all that I can.
But if ye winne hir, ye must een play the man,
Een to fight it out, ye must a mans heart take.
RAFE ROYSTER. Yes, they shall know, and thou knowe-
          est I have a stomacke.

6 *Cotssold lyon :* i.e. a   ACTUS IIII.   SCAENA VII.
     sheep.   1 *ray :* array, line.
                                    2 *route :* muster.

[MATHEW MERYGREEKE.] A stomacke (quod you)
           yea, as good as ere man had.

RAFE ROYSTER. I trowe they shall finde and feele that   10
           I am a lad.

MATHEW MERYGREEKE. By this crosse[1] I have
           seene you eate your meate as well,
As any that ere I have seene of or heard tell,
A stomacke quod you? he that will that denie
I know was never at dynner in your companie.

RAFE ROYSTER. Nay, the stomacke of a man it is that   15
           I meane.

MATHEW MERYGREEKE. Nay the stomacke of an horse
           or a dogge I weene.

RAFE ROYSTER. Nay a mans stomacke with a weapon
           meane I.

MATHEW MERYGREEKE. Ten men can scarce match
           you with a spoone in a pie.

RAFE ROYSTER. Nay the stomake of a man to trie in
           strife.

MATHEW MERYGREEKE. I never sawe your stomake   20
           cloyed yet in my lyfe.

RAFE ROYSTER. Tushe I meane in strife or fighting to
           trie.

MATHEW MERYGREEKE. We shall see how ye will
           strike nowe being angry.

RAFE ROYSTER. Have at thy pate then, and save thy
           head if thou may! [Strikes MERY-
           GREEKE.]

MATHEW MERYGREEKE. Nay then have at your pate
           agayne by this day. [Strikes RAFE.]

RAFE ROYSTER. Nay thou mayst not strike at me   25
           againe in no wise.

MATHEW MERYGREEKE. I can not in fight make to you
           suche warrantise :
But as for your foes here let them the bargaine
           bie.[3]

RAFE ROYSTER. Nay as for they, shall every mothers
           childe die.
And in this my fume a little thing might make me,
To beate downe house and all, and else the devill   30
           take me.

3 *bie* : aby, suffer.

MATHEW MERYGREEKE. If I were as ye be, by Gogs
        deare mother,
  I woulde not leave one stone upon an other.
  Though she woulde redeeme it with twentie thou-
        sand poundes.
RAFE ROYSTER. It shall be even so, by His lily[4]
        woundes.
MATHEW MERYGREEKE. Bee not at one with hir upon   35
        any amendes.
RAFE ROYSTER. No though she make to me never so
        many frendes.
  Nor if all the worlde for hir woulde undertake,[5]
  No not God hymselfe neither, shal not hir peace
        make,
  [*To his men.*] On therfore, marche forwarde,—
    soft, stay a whyle yet.
MATHEW MERYGREEKE. On.
RAFE ROYSTER.   Tary.
MATHEW MERYGREEKE.   Forth.
RAFE ROYSTER.   Back.
MATHEW MERYGREEKE.   On.
RAFE ROYSTER.   Soft. Now forward set.   40
       [*Enter* CHRISTIAN CUSTANCE.]
CHRISTIAN CUSTANCE. What businesse have we here?
      out! alas, alas!   [*Exeat.*]
RAFE ROYSTER. Ha, ha, ha, ha, ha.
  Dydst thou see that Merygreeke? how afrayde
        she was?
  Dydst thou see how she fledde apace out of my
        sight?
  Ah good sweete Custance I pitie hir by this light.   45
MATHEW MERYGREEKE. That tender heart of yours
        wyll marre altogether,
  Thus will ye be turned with waggyng of a fether.
RAFE ROYSTER. On sirs, keepe your ray.
MATHEW MERYGREEKE. On forth, while this geare is
        hot.
RAFE ROYSTER. Soft, the Armes of Caleys,[6] I have one
        thing forgot.
MATHEW MERYGREEKE. What lacke we now?

---

4 *lily* : lovely.   6 *Caleys* : Calais.
5 *undertake* : intercede.

RAFE ROYSTER.   Retire, or else we be all slain.   50
MATHEW MERYGREEKE. Backe for the pashe[7] of God,
            backe sirs, backe againe.
    What is the great mater?
RAFE ROYSTER.   This hastie forth goyng
    Had almost brought us all to utter undoing,
    It made me forget a thing most necessarie.
MATHEW MERYGREEKE. Well remembered of a cap-   55
            taine by sainct Marie.
RAFE ROYSTER. It is a thing must be had.
MATHEW MERYGREEKE.   Let us have it then.
RAFE ROYSTER. But I wote not where nor how.
MATHEW MERYGREEKE.   Then wote not I when.
    But what is it?
RAFE ROYSTER.   Of a chiefe thing I am to seeke.
MATHEW MERYGREEKE. Tut so will ye be, when ye
            have studied a weke.
    But tell me what it is?
RAFE ROYSTER.   I lacke yet an hedpiece.   60
MATHEW MERYGREEKE. The kitchen collocavit,[8] the
            best hennes to Grece,[9]
    Runne, fet it Dobinet, and come at once withall,
    And bryng with thee my potgunne,[10] hangyng by
            the wall,   [Exit DOBINET.]
    I have seene your head with it full many a tyme,
    Covered as safe as it had bene with a skrine :[11]   65
    And I warrant it save your head from any stroke,
    Except perchaunce to be amased[12] with the
            smoke :
    I warrant your head therwith, except for the mist,
    As safe as if it were fast locked up in a chist :[13]
    And loe here our Dobinet commeth with it nowe.   70
            [Re-enter DOBINET DOUGHTIE.]
DOBINET DOUGHTIE. It will cover me to the shoulders
            well inow.

7 pashe : Passion.
8 collocavit : pail or pot
    (collock). The Latin
    ending is in jest.
9 hennes to Grece : hence to
    Greece, perhaps with
    pun on "hens to grease."

10 potgunne : literally, a
    small cannon, contemp-
    tuous term for a large
    pistol. But this is proba-
    bly a popgun.
11 skrine : strongbox.
12 amased : stupefied.
13 chist : chest.

MATHEW MERYGREEKE. Let me see it on.

RAFE ROYSTER.   In fayth it doth metely well.

MATHEW MERYGREEKE. There can be no fitter thing.
        Now ye must us tell
What to do.

RAFE ROYSTER. Now forth in ray sirs, and stoppe no
        more.

MATHEW MERYGREEKE. Now sainct George to
        borow,[14] Drum dubbe a dubbe afore.   75
        [*Enter* TRISTRAM TRUSTY.]

TRISTRAM TRUSTY. What meane you to do sir, com-
        mitte manslaughter?

RAFE ROYSTER. To kyll fortie such, is a matter of
        laughter.

TRISTRAM TRUSTY. And who is it sir, whome ye in-
        tende thus to spill?

RAFE ROYSTER. Foolishe Custance here forceth me
        against my will.

TRISTRAM TRUSTY. And is there no meane your ex-   80
        treme wrath to slake?
She shall some amendes unto your good mashyp
        make.

RAFE ROYSTER. I will none amendes.

TRISTRAM TRUSTY.   Is hir offence so sore?

MATHEW MERYGREEKE. And he were a loute she
        coulde have done no more.
She hath calde him foole, and dressed[15] him like
        a foole.
Mocked him lyke a foole, used him like a foole.   85

TRISTRAM TRUSTY. Well yet the Sheriffe, the Justice,
        or Constable,
Hir misdemeanour to punishe might be able.

RAFE ROYSTER. No sir, I mine owne selfe will in this
        present cause,
Be Sheriffe, and Justice, and whole Judge of the
        lawes,
This matter to amende, all officers be I shall,   90
Constable, Bailiffe, Sergeant.

MATHEW MERYGREEKE.   And hangman and all.

TRISTRAM TRUSTY. Yet a noble courage, and the

14 *to borow :* aid or protect   15 *dressed :* dressed him
    us.   down.

hearte of a man

Should more honour winne by bearyng with a
woman.

Therfore take the lawe, and lette hir aunswere
therto.

RAFE ROYSTER. Merygreeke, the best way were even   95
so to do.

What honour should it be with a woman to fight?

MATHEW MERYGREEKE. And what then, will ye thus
forgo and lese your right?

RAFE ROYSTER. Nay, I will take the lawe on hir withouten grace.

TRISTRAM TRUSTY. Or yf your mashyp coulde pardon
this one trespace.

I pray you forgive hir.

RAFE ROYSTER.   Hoh?

MATHEW MERYGREEKE.   Tushe tushe sir do not.   100

TRISTRAM TRUSTY. Be good maister to hir.[1]

RAFE ROYSTER.   Hoh?

MATHEW MERYGREEKE.   Tush I say do not.

And what shall your people here returne streight
home?

RAFE ROYSTER. Yea, levie the campe sirs, and hence
againe eche one.[2]

But be still in readinesse if I happe to call,

I can not tell what sodaine chaunce may befall.[3]   105

MATHEW MERYGREEKE. Do not off your harnesse[16] sirs
I you advise,

At the least for this fortnight in no maner wise,

Perchaunce in an houre when all ye thinke least,

Our maisters appetite to fight will be best.

But soft, ere ye go, have once at Custance house.   110

RAFE ROYSTER. Soft, what wilt thou do?

MATHEW MERYGREEKE. Once discharge my harquebouse[17]

And for my heartes ease, have once more with my
potgoon.

RAFE ROYSTER. Holde thy handes! else is all our purpose cleane fordoone.

MATHEW MERYGREEKE. And it cost me my life.

---

16 *harnesse* : armor.   17 *harquebouse* : heavy gun,
                                   usually with a tripod.

RAFE ROYSTER.   I say thou shalt not.
MATHEW MERYGREEKE. By the Matte[18] but I will.   115
              [*Shoots his harquebus.*]
                Have once more with haile shot.
              [*Shoots his potgun.*]
I will have some penyworth, I will not leese all.

              ACTUS IIII.   SCAENA VIII.

    MATHEW MERYGREEKE, RAFE ROYSTER, DOBINET
        DOUGHTIE, [*and*] HARPAX [*remain. Enter*]
              CHRISTIAN CUSTANCE.[1]

CHRISTIAN CUSTANCE. What caitifes are those that so
              shake my house wall?
MATHEW MERYGREEKE. Ah sirrha! now Custance if
              ye had so muche wit
  I woulde see you aske pardon, and your selves
              submit.
CHRISTIAN CUSTANCE. Have I still this adoe with a
              couple of fooles?
MATHEW MERYGREEKE. Here ye what she saith?
CHRISTIAN CUSTANCE. Maidens come forth with your   5
              tooles.
      [*Enter* TIBET TALK-APACE, ANNOT ALYFACE,
      MAGE MUMBLE-CRUST, *and* TRUEPENIE *with
              drum and an* ENSIGN.]
RAFE ROYSTER. In aray.
MATHEW MERYGREEKE. Dubba dub sirrha.
RAFE ROYSTER.   In aray.
  They come sodainly on us.
MATHEW MERYGREEKE.   Dubbadub.
RAFE ROYSTER.   In aray.
  That ever I was borne, we are taken tardie.
MATHEW MERYGREEKE. Now sirs, quite our selves like
              tall men[1] and hardie.
CHRISTIAN CUSTANCE. On afore Truepenie, holde   10
              thyne owne Annot,
  On towarde them Tibet, for scape us they can not.

18 *Matte :* Mass.   quit ourselves like brave
ACTUS IIII.   SCAENA VIII.   men.
  1 *quite . . . men :* let's ac-

Come forth Mage Mumble-crust, so stande fast to-
          gither.

MATHEW MERYGREEKE. God sende us a faire day.

RAFE ROYSTER.   See they marche on hither.

TIBET TALK-APACE. But mistresse.

CHRISTIAN CUSTANCE.   What sayst thou?

TIBET TALK-APACE.   Shall I go fet our goose?

CHRISTIAN CUSTANCE. What to do?

TIBET TALK-APACE. To yonder Captain I will turne   15
          hir loose.

And she gape and hisse at him, as she doth at me,

I durst jeoparde my hande she wyll make him flee.

CHRISTIAN CUSTANCE. On forward.

RAFE ROYSTER. They com.

MATHEW MERYGREEKE. Stand.

RAFE ROYSTER.   Hold.

MATHEW MERYGREEKE.   Kepe.

RAFE ROYSTER.   There.

MATHEW MERYGREEKE.   Strike.

RAFE ROYSTER.   Take heede.

CHRISTIAN CUSTANCE. Wel sayd Truepenie

TRUEPENIE.   Ah whooresons.

CHRISTIAN CUSTANCE.   Wel don in deede.

MATHEW MERYGREEKE. Hold thine owne *Harpax*,   20
          downe with them Dobinet.

CHRISTIAN CUSTANCE. Now Mage, there Annot : now
          sticke them Tibet.

TIBET TALK-APACE. [*Attacking* DOBINET.] All my
          chiefe quarell is to this same little
          knave,

That begyled me last day, nothyng shall him save.

DOBINET DOUGHTIE. Downe with this litle queane,
          that hath at me such spite,

Save you from hir maister, it is a very sprite.   25

CHRISTIAN CUSTANCE. I my selfe will mounsire
          graunde[2] captaine undertake!

RAFE ROYSTER. They win grounde.

MATHEW MERYGREEKE. Save your selfe sir, for Gods
          sake.

          [*Hits* RAFE.]

2 *mounsire graunde* : "Mon-
     sieur le Grand."

RAFE ROYSTER. Out, alas, I am slaine, helpe.

MATHEW MERYGREEKE.   Save your selfe.

RAFE ROYSTER.   Alas.

MATHEW MERYGREEKE. Nay then, have at you mis-
        tresse.
        [*Hits* RAFE *again.*]

RAFE ROYSTER.   Thou hittest me, alas.

MATHEW MERYGREEKE. I wil strike at Custance here.
        [*Hits* RAFE *again.*]

RAFE ROYSTER.   Thou hittest me.

MATHEW MERYGREEKE. [*Aside.*]   So I wil.   30
  Nay mistresse Custance.
        [*Hits* RAFE *again.*]

RAFE ROYSTER.   Alas, thou hittest me still.
  Hold.

MATHEW MERYGREEKE. Save your self sir.

RAFE ROYSTER.   Help, out alas I am slain.

MATHEW MERYGREEKE. Truce, hold your hands, truce
        for a pissing while or twaine :
        [*The fight ceases.*]
  Nay how say you Custance, for saving of your life,
  Will ye yelde and graunt to be this gentmans wife?   35

CHRISTIAN CUSTANCE. Ye tolde me he loved me, call
        ye this love?

MATHEW MERYGREEKE. He loved a while even like a
        turtle dove.

CHRISTIAN CUSTANCE. Gay love God save it, so soone
        hotte, so soone colde,

MATHEW MERYGREEKE. I am sory for you : he could
        love you yet so he coulde.

RAFE ROYSTER. Nay by Cocks precious[3] she shall be   40
        none of mine.

MATHEW MERYGREEKE. Why so?

RAFE ROYSTER. Come away, by the Matte she is
        mankine.[4]
  I durst adventure the losse of my right hande,
  If shee dyd not slee hir other husbande :
  And see if she prepare not againe to fight.

MATHEW MERYGREEKE. What then? sainct George to   45
        borow, our Ladies knight.

3 *Cocks precious :* God's pre-   4 *mankine :* furious.
  cious (wounds).

RAFE ROYSTER. Slee else whom she will, by Gog she
        shall not slee mee.

MATHEW MERYGREEKE. How then?

RAFE ROYSTER.   Rather than to be slaine,
        I will flee.

CHRISTIAN CUSTANCE. Too it againe, my knightesses,
        downe with them all.

RAFE ROYSTER. Away, away, away, she will else kyll
        us all.

MATHEW MERYGREEKE. Nay sticke to it, like an hardie   50
        man and a tall.
             [*Strikes* RAFE.]

RAFE ROYSTER. Oh bones,[5] thou hittest me. Away,
        or else die we shall.

MATHEW MERYGREEKE. Away for the pashe of our
        sweete Lord Jesus Christ.

CHRISTIAN CUSTANCE. Away loute and lubber, or I
        shall be thy priest.[6]
             [*Exeant* RAFE *and his men.*][2]

So this fielde is ours, we have driven them all
        away.

TIBET TALK-APACE. Thankes to God mistresse, ye   55
        have had a faire day.

CHRISTIAN CUSTANCE. Well nowe goe ye in, and make
        your selfe some good cheere.

OMNES PARITER.[7] We goe.

    [*Exeant* TIBET, ANNOT, MAGE, TRUEPENIE, *and
               the* ENSIGN.]

TRISTRAM TRUSTY.   Ah sir, what a field we have
        had heere.

CHRISTIAN CUSTANCE. Friend Tristram, I pray you be
        a witnesse with me.

TRISTRAM TRUSTY. Dame Custance, I shall depose for
        your honestie,[8]

And nowe fare ye well, except some thing else   60
        ye wolde.

CHRISTIAN CUSTANCE. Not now, but when I nede to
        sende I will be bolde.

---

5 *bones:* God's bones.
6 *be thy priest:* preside at
   your death.

7 OMNES PARITER: All at the
   same time.
8 *depose . . . honestie:* tes-
   tify to your virtue.

I thanke you for these paines. [*Exeat* TRUSTY.][3]
                And now I wyll get me in,
Now Royster Doyster will no more wowyng be-
                gin.   *Ex*[*eat*].

                ACTUS V.   SCAENA I.

[*Enter*] GAWYN GOODLUCKE [*and*] SYM SURESBY.
[GAWYN GOODLUCKE.] Sym Suresby my trustie man,
                nowe advise thee well,
And see that no false surmises thou me tell,
Was there such adoe about Custance of a truth?
SYM SURESBY. To reporte that I hearde and sawe, to
                me is ruth,
But both my duetie and name and propretie,[1]   5
Warneth me to you to shewe fidelitie.
It may be well enough, and I wyshe it so to be,
She may hir selfe discharge and trie[2] hir honestie,
Yet their clayme to hir me thought was very large,
For with letters, rings, and tokens, they dyd hir   10
                charge.
Which when I hearde and sawe I would none to
                you bring.
GAWYN GOODLUCKE. No, by sainct Marie, I allowe[3]
                thee in that thing.
Ah sirra, nowe I see truthe in the proverbe olde,
All things that shineth is not by and by[4] pure golde,
If any doe lyve a woman of honestie,   15
I would have sworne Christian Custance had bene
                shee.
SYM SURESBY. Sir, though I to you be a servant true
                and just,
Yet doe not ye therfore your faithfull spouse mys-
                trust.
But examine the matter, and if ye shall it finde,
To be all well, be not ye for my wordes unkinde.   20
GAWYN GOODLUCKE. I shall do that is right, and as I
                see cause why.
But here commeth Custance forth, we shal know
                by and by.

ACTUS V.   SCAENA I.   3 *allowe* : approve.
    1 *propretie* : nature.   4 *by and by* : straightway.
    2 *trie* : prove.

ACTUS V. SCAENA II.

[*Enter*] CHRISTIAN CUSTANCE [*to*] GAWYN
GOODLUCKE [*and*] SYM SURESBY.

CHRISTIAN CUSTANCE. I come forth to see and
      hearken for newes good,
For about this houre is the tyme of likelyhood,
That Gawyn Goodlucke by the sayings of Suresby,
Would be at home, and lo yond I see hym I.
What Gawyn Goodlucke, the onely hope of my   5
      life,
Welcome home, and kysse me your true espoused
      wife.
GAWYN GOODLUCKE. Nay soft dame Custance, I must
      first by your licence,
See whether all things be cleere in your conscience,
I heare of your doings to me very straunge.
CHRISTIAN CUSTANCE. What feare ye? that my faith   10
      towardes you should chaunge?
GAWYN GOODLUCKE. I must needes mistrust ye be
      elsewhere entangled.
For I heare that certaine men with you have
      wrangled
About the promise of mariage by you to them
      made.
CHRISTIAN CUSTANCE. Coulde any mans reporte your
      minde therein persuade?
GAWYN GOODLUCKE. Well, ye must therin declare your   15
      selfe to stande cleere,
Else I and you dame Custance may not joyne this
      yere.
CHRISTIAN CUSTANCE. Then woulde I were dead, and
      faire layd in my grave,
Ah Suresby, is this the honestie that ye have?
To hurt me with your report, not knowyng the
      thing.
SYM SURESBY. If ye be honest my wordes can hurte   20
      you nothing.
But what I hearde and sawe, I might not but re-
      port.

CHRISTIAN CUSTANCE. Ah Lorde, helpe poore widowes,
        destitute of comfort.
Truly most deare spouse, nought was done but for
    pastance.
GAWYN GOODLUCKE. But such kynde of sporting is
        homely[1] daliance.
CHRISTIAN CUSTANCE. If ye knewe the truthe, ye   25
        would take all in good parte.
GAWYN GOODLUCKE. By your leave I am not halfe
        well skilled in that arte.
CHRISTIAN CUSTANCE. It was none but Royster
        Doyster that foolishe mome.[2]
GAWYN GOODLUCKE. Yea Custance, better (they say) a
        badde scuse than none.
CHRISTIAN CUSTANCE. Why Tristram Trusty, sir, your
        true and faithfull frende,
Was privie bothe to the beginning and the ende.   30
Let him be the Judge, and for me testifie.
GAWYN GOODLUCKE. I will the more credite that he
        shall verifie,
And bicause I will the truthe know een as it is,
I will to him my selfe, and know all without misse.
Come on Sym Suresby, that before my friend thou   35
    may
Avouch the same wordes, which thou dydst to me
    say.   *Exeant.*

Actus v. Scaena iii.

CHRISTIAN CUSTANCE [*remains.*]
CHRISTIAN CUSTANCE. O Lorde, howe necessarie it is
        nowe of dayes,
That eche bodie live uprightly all maner wayes,
For lette never so little a gappe be open,
And be sure of this, the worst shall be spoken.
Howe innocent stande I in this for deede or   5
        thought,
And yet see what mistrust towardes me it hath
    wrought.

ACTUS v. SCAENA ii.   2 *mome :* dolt.
  1 *homely :* rude, uncomely.

But thou Lorde knowest all folkes thoughts and
       eke[1] intents
And thou arte the deliverer of all innocentes.
Thou didst helpe the advoutresse[2] that she might
       be amended,
Much more then helpe Lorde, that never yll in-   10
       tended.
Thou didst helpe *Susanna,* wrongfully accused,
And no lesse dost thou see Lorde, how I am now
       abused,
Thou didst helpe *Hester,* when she should have
       died,
Helpe also good Lorde, that my truth may be tried.
Yet if Gawyn Goodlucke with Tristram Trusty   15
       speake,
I trust of yll report the force shall be but weake,
And loe yond they come sadly talking togither,
I wyll abyde, and not shrinke for their comming
       hither.

Actus v.   Scaena iiii.

[*Enter*] GAWYN GOODLUCKE, TRISTRAM TRUSTY
  [*and*] SYM SURESBY. CHRISTIAN CUSTANCE
       [*remains.*]

GAWYN GOODLUCKE. And was it none other than ye
       to me reporte?
TRISTRAM TRUSTY. No, and here were ye wished to
       have[1] seene the sporte.
GAWYN GOODLUCKE. Woulde I had, rather than halfe
       of that in my purse.
SYM SURESBY. And I doe muche rejoyce the matter
       was no wurse,
And like as to open it, I was to you faithfull,   5
So of dame Custance honest truth I am joyfull.
For God forfende that I shoulde hurt hir by false
       reporte.
GAWYN GOODLUCKE. Well, I will no longer holde
       hir in discomforte.

Actus v.   Scaena iii.   2 *advoutresse :* adultress.
1 *eke :* also.

CHRISTIAN CUSTANCE. Nowe come they hitherwarde, I
      trust all shall be well.
GAWYN GOODLUCKE. Sweete Custance neither heart   10
      can thinke nor tongue tell,
Howe much I joy in your constant fidelitie,
Come nowe kisse me the pearle of perfect honestie.
CHRISTIAN CUSTANCE. God lette me no longer to con-
      tinue in lyfe,
Than I shall towardes you continue a true wyfe.
GAWYN GOODLUCKE. Well now to make you for this   15
      some parte of amendes,
I shall desire first you, and then suche of our
      frendes,
As shall to you seeme best, to suppe at home with
      me,
Where at your fought fielde we shall laugh and
      mery be.
SYM SURESBY. And mistresse I beseech you, take with
      me no greefe,
I did a true mans part, not wishyng your repreefe.   20
CHRISTIAN CUSTANCE. Though hastie reportes through
      surmises growyng,
May of poore innocentes be utter overthrowyng,
Yet bicause to thy maister thou hast a true hart,
And I know mine owne truth, I forgive thee for
      my part.
GAWYN GOODLUCKE. Go we all to my house, and of   25
      this geare no more.
Goe prepare all things Sym Suresby, hence, runne
      afore.
SYM SURESBY. I goe.   *Ex[eat].*
GAWYN GOODLUCKE. But who commeth yond, Mathew
      Merygreeke?
CHRISTIAN CUSTANCE. Royster Doysters champion, I
      shrewe his best cheeke.
TRISTRAM TRUSTY. Royster Doyster selfe your wower
      is with hym too.
Surely some thing there is with us they have to doe.   30

Actus v.   Scaena v.

[*Enter*] MATHEW MERYGREEKE [*and*] RAFE
ROYSTER. GAWYN GOODLUCKE, TRISTAM
TRUSTY [*and*] CHRISTIAN CUSTANCE
[*remain.*]

MATHEW MERYGREEKE. Yond I see Gawyn Goodlucke, to whome lyeth my message,
I wyll first salute him after his long voyage,
And then make all thing well concerning your behalfe.

RAFE ROYSTER. Yea for the pashe of God.

MATHEW MERYGREEKE. Hence out of sight, ye calfe,
Till I have spoke with them, and then I will you 5
   fet.

RAFE ROYSTER. In Gods name.   [*Exeat.*]

MATHEW MERYGREEKE. What Master Gawyn Goodlucke wel met,
And from your long voyage I bid you right welcome home.

GAWYN GOODLUCKE. I thanke you.

MATHEW MERYGREEKE. I come to you from an honest
   mome.

GAWYN GOODLUCKE. Who is that?

MATHEW MERYGREEKE. Royster Doyster that doughtie
   kite.

CHRISTIAN CUSTANCE. Fye, I can scarce abide ye 10
   shoulde his name recite.

MATHEW MERYGREEKE. Ye must take him to favour,
   and pardon all past,
He heareth of your returne, and is full yll agast.

GAWYN GOODLUCKE. I am ryght well content he have
   with us some chere.

CHRISTIAN CUSTANCE. Fye upon hym beast, then wyll
   not I be there.

GAWYN GOODLUCKE. Why Custance doe ye hate hym 15
   more than ye love me?

CHRISTIAN CUSTANCE. But for your mynde sir, where
   he were would I not be.

TRISTRAM TRUSTY. He woulde make us al laugh.

MATHEW MERYGREEKE.   Ye nere had better sport.

GAWYN GOODLUCKE. I pray you sweete Custance, let
    him to us resort.

CHRISTIAN CUSTANCE. To your will I assent.

MATHEW MERYGREEKE.   Why, suche a foole it is,

As no man for good pastime would forgoe or misse.   20

GAWYN GOODLUCKE. Fet him to go wyth us.

MATHEW MERYGREEKE.   He will be a glad man.
                                       Ex[*eat*].

TRISTRAM TRUSTY. We must to make us mirth, main-
    taine[1] hym all we can.

And loe yond he commeth and Merygreeke with
    him.

CHRISTIAN CUSTANCE. At his first entrance ye shall see
    I wyll him trim.

But first let us hearken the gentlemans wise talke.   25

TRISTRAM TRUSTY. I pray you marke if ever ye sawe
    crane so stalke.

Actus v.   Scaena vi.

[*Enter*] RAFE ROYSTER [*and*] MATHEW MERY-
GREEKE. CHRISTIAN CUSTANCE, GAWYN GOOD-
    LUCKE, [*and*] TRISTRAM TRUSTY
        [*remain.*]

RAFE ROYSTER. May I then be bolde?

MATHEW MERYGREEKE. I warrant you on my worde,
    They say they shall be sicke, but ye be at theyr
        borde.

RAFE ROYSTER. Thei wer not angry then?

MATHEW MERYGREEKE. Yes at first, and made strange,

But when I sayd your anger to favour shoulde
    change,

And therewith had commended you accordingly,   5

They were all in love with your mashyp by and by.

And cried you mercy that they had done you
    wrong.

RAFE ROYSTER. For why,[1] no man, woman, nor childe
    can hate me long.

Actus v.   Scaena vi.
  1 *For why :* Because.

MATHEW MERYGREEKE. We feare (quod they) he will
          be avenged one day,
Then for a peny give all our lives we may.   10
RAFE ROYSTER. Sayd they so in deede?
MATHEW MERYGREEKE. Did they? yea, even with one
          voice.
     He will forgive all (quod I). Oh how they did re-
          joyce.
RAFE ROYSTER. Ha, ha, ha.
MATHEW MERYGREEKE. Goe fette hym (say they)
          while he is in good moode,
     For have his anger who lust, we will not by the   15
          Roode.
RAFE ROYSTER. I pray God that it be all true, that
          thou hast me tolde,
     And that she fight no more.
MATHEW MERYGREEKE.   I warrant you, be bolde
     Too them, and salute them.
RAFE ROYSTER.   Sirs, I greete you all well.
OMNES. Your maistership is welcom.
CHRISTIAN CUSTANCE.   Savyng my quarell.
     For sure I will put you up into the Eschequer.[1]   20
MATHEW MERYGREEKE. Why so? better nay : Wher-
          fore?
CHRISTIAN CUSTANCE.   For an usurer.
RAFE ROYSTER. I am no usurer good mistresse by His
          armes.
MATHEW MERYGREEKE. When tooke he gaine of
          money to any mans harmes?
CHRISTIAN CUSTANCE. Yes, a fowle usurer he is, ye
          shall see els—
RAFE ROYSTER. [*Aside to* MERYGREEKE.] Didst not   25
          thou promise she would picke no mo
          quarels?
CHRISTIAN CUSTANCE. He will lende no blowes, but
          he have in recompence
     Fiftene for one, whiche is to muche of con-
          science.[2]
RAFE ROYSTER. Ah dame, by the auncient lawe of
          armes, a man
     Hath no honour to foile his handes on a woman.
CHRISTIAN CUSTANCE. And where other usurers take   30
          their gaines yerely,

This man is angry but he have his by and by.

GAWYN GOODLUCKE. Sir, doe not for hir sake beare me
    your displeasure.

MATHEW MERYGREEKE. Well, he shall with you talke
    therof more at leasure.

Upon your good usage, he will now shake your
    hande.

RAFE ROYSTER. And much heartily welcome from a   35
    straunge lande.

MATHEW MERYGREEKE. Be not afearde Gawyn to let
    him shake your fyst.

    [They shake hands.]

GAWYN GOODLUCKE. Oh the moste honest gentleman
    that ere I wist.[2]

I beseeche your mashyp to take payne to suppe
    with us.

MATHEW MERYGREEKE. He shall not say you nay and
    I too, by Jesus.

Bicause ye shall be friends, and let all quarels   40
    passe.

RAFE ROYSTER. I wyll be as good friends with them as
    ere I was.

MATHEW MERYGREEKE. Then let me fet your quier
    that we may have a song.

RAFE ROYSTER. Goe.   *[Exeat* MERYGREEKE.]

GAWYN GOODLUCKE. I have hearde no melodie all this
    yeare long.

    [Re-enter MERYGREEKE *with* DOBINET,
    HARPAX, *and other musicians.*]

MATHEW MERYGREEKE. Come on sirs quickly.

RAFE ROYSTER.   Sing on sirs, for my frends sake.

DOBINET DOUGHTIE. Cal ye these your frends?

RAFE ROYSTER.   Sing on, and no mo words make.   45
    Here they sing.[(3)]

GAWYN GOODLUCKE. The Lord preserve our most no-
    ble Queene of renowne,[(4)]

And hir virtues rewarde with the heavenly crowne.

CHRISTIAN CUSTANCE. The Lorde strengthen hir most
    excellent Majestie,

Long to reigne over us in all prosperitie.

TRISTRAM TRUSTY. That hir godly proceedings the   50
    faith to defende,

  2 *wist :* knew.

He may stablishe and maintaine through to the
      ende.
MATHEW MERYGREEKE. God graunt hir as she doth,
      the Gospell to protect,
Learning and vertue to advaunce, and vice to cor-
      rect.
RAFE ROYSTER. God graunt hir lovyng subjects both
      the minde and grace,
Hir most godly procedyngs worthily to imbrace.   55
HARPAX. Hir highnesse most worthy counsellers God
      prosper,
With honour and love of all men to minister.
OMNES. God graunt the nobilitie hir to serve and love,
With all the whole commontie[3] as doth them be-
      hove.

AMEN.

CERTAINE SONGS TO BE SONG BY THOSE WHICH
SHALL USE THIS COMEDIE OR ENTERLUDE

The Seconde Song.[1]

Who so to marry a minion Wyfe,
Hath hadde good chaunce and happe,
Must love hir and cherishe hir all his life,
And dandle hir in his lappe.

If she will fare well, yf she wyll go gay,   5
A good husbande ever styll,
What ever she lust to doe, or to say,
Must lette hir have hir owne will.

About what affaires so ever he goe,
He must shewe hir all his mynde,   10
None of hys counsell she may be kept fr[o]e,[1]
Else is he a man unkynde.

The Fourth Song.[2]

    I mun be maried a Sunday
    I mun be maried a Sunday,
    Who soever shall come that way,
    I mun be maried a Sunday.

3 *commontie* : commons.

Royster Doyster is my name,   5
Royster Doyster is my name,
A lustie brute I am the same,
I mun be maried a Sunday.

Christian Custance have I founde,
Christian Custance have I founde,   10
A Wydowe worthe a thousande pounde,
I mun be maried a Sunday.

Custance is as sweete as honey,
Custance is as sweete as honey,
I hir lambe and she my coney,   15
I mun be maried a Sunday.

When we shall make our weddyng feast,
When we shall make oure weddyng feast,
There shall bee cheere for man and beast,
I mun be maried a Sunday.   20
           I mun be maried a Sunday, etc.

THE PSALMODIE.[1]

Placebo dilexi,
Maister Royster Doyster wil streight go home and
           die,
Our Lorde Jesus Christ his soule have mercie upon.
Thus you see to day a man, to morow John.

Yet saving for a womans extreeme crueltie,   5
He might have lyved yet a moneth or two or three,
But in spite of Custance which hath him weried,
His mashyp shall be worshipfully buried.
And while some piece of his soule is yet hym within,
Some parte of his funeralls let us here beginne.   10
  Dirige. He will go darklyng to his grave.
Neque lux, neque crux, nisi solum clinke,
Never gentman so went toward heaven I thinke.

Yet sirs as ye wyll the blisse of heaven win,
When he commeth to the grave lay hym softly in,   15
And all men take heede by this one Gentleman,
How you sette your love upon an unkinde woman :
For these women be all suche madde pievish elves,
They wyll not be woonne except it please them
           selves.

But in faith Custance if ever ye come in hell,   20
Maister Royster Doyster shall serve you as well.
  Good night Roger olde knave, Farewel Roger olde
                      knave.
  Good night Roger olde knave, knave, knap.
  Nequando.   Audivi vocem.   Requiem æternam.

THE PEALE OF BELLES RONG BY THE PARISH
        CLERK, AND ROYSTER DOYSTERS
              FOURE MEN.[1]

            The First Bell A Triple.
          When dyed he? When dyed he?

                The Seconde.
          We have hym, We have hym.

                 The Thirde.
          Royster Doyster, Royster Doyster.

               The Fourth Bell.
          He commeth, He commeth.

               The Greate Bell
          Our owne, Our owne.

                   FINIS.

GAMMER GURTONS NEDLE

by

MR. S., MASTER OF ART

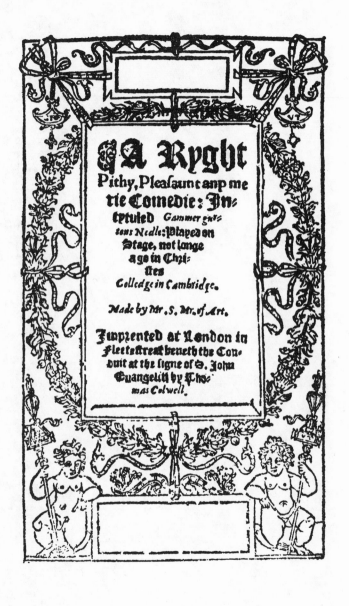

¶A Ryght
Pithy, Pleasaunt and me
rie Comedie: In=
tytuled   *Gammer gur=
tons Nedle*: Played on
Stage, not longe
ago in Chri=
stes
Colledge in Cambridge.

Made by Mr. S. Mr. of Art.

Imprented at London in
Fleetestreat beneth the Con=
duit at the signe of S. Iohn
Euangelist by Tho=
mas Colwell.

The Names of The Speakers in This Comedie.

DICCON, *the Bedlem.*
HODGE, *Gammer Gurtons servante.*
TYB, *Gammer Gurtons mayde.*
GAMMER GURTON.
COCKE,[1] *Gammer Gurtons boye.*
DAME CHAT.
DOCTOR RAT, *the Curate.*
MAYSTER BAYLYE.
DOLL, *Dame Chats mayde.*
SCAPETHRYFT, *mayst Baylyes servante.*
        Mutes.

[THE SCENE
AN ENGLISH VILLAGE.]

GOD SAVE THE QUEENE.

The Prologue

As Gammer Gurton, with manye a wyde styche
Sat pesynge[1] and patching of Hodge her mans
        briche
By chance or misfortune as shee her geare tost[2]
In Hodge lether bryches her needle shee lost.
When Diccon the bedlem[(1)] had hard by report   5
That good Gammer Gurton was robde in thys
        sorte,
He quyetly perswaded with her in that stound[3]
Dame Chat her deare gossyp[4] this needle had
        found,
Yet knew shee no more of this matter (alas)
Then knoeth Tom our clarke what the Priest saith   10
        at Masse.

PROLOGUE
  1 *pesynge :* mending.
  2 *her geare tost :* plied her
    material.

  3 *stound :* predicament.
  4 *gossyp :* buddy.

Here of there ensued so fearfull a fraye,
Mas Doctor was sent for these gossyps to staye,
Because he was Curate, and estemed full wyse
Who found that he sought not, by Diccons device,
When all thinges were tombled and cleane out of   15
    fassion
Whether it were by fortune, or some other constel-
    lacion⁵
Sodenlye the neele Hodge found by the prickynge
And drew it out of his bottocke where he felt it
    stickynge.
Theyr hartes then at rest with perfect securytie,
With a pot of good nale⁶ they stroake up theyr   20
    plauditie.⁷

THE FYRST ACTE.   THE FYRST SCEANE.

[*Enter*] DICCON.

DICCON. Many a myle have I walked, divers and sun-
    dry waies
And many a good mans house have I bin at in my
    daies
Many a gossips cup in my tyme have I tasted
And many a broche and spyt, have I both turned
    and basted.
Many a peece of bacon have I had out of thir   5
    balkes¹
In ronnyng over the countrey, with long and were²
    walkes,
Yet came my foote never, within those doore
    cheekes,
To seeke flesh or fysh, Garlyke, Onyons or Leekes,
That ever I saw a sorte,³ in such a plyght
As here within this house appereth to my syght.   10
There is howlynge and scowlyng, all cast in a
    dumpe,

5 *constellacion*: influence.   FYRST ACTE.   FYRST SCEANE.
6 *nale*: ale.   1 *balkes*: beams (where the
7 *plauditie*: appeal for ap-   bacon was hung).
   plause at the end of the   2 *were*: wary (?)
   play.   3 *sorte*: company, group.

With whewling and pewling, as though they had
    lost a trump.[4]
Syghing and sobbing, they weepe and they wayle,
I marvell in my mynd, what the devill they ayle.
The olde Trot syts groning, with alas and alas,   15
And Tyb wringes her hands, and takes on in worse
    case.
With poore Cocke theyr boye, they be dryven in
    such fyts
I feare mee the folkes be not well in theyr wyts.
Aske them what they ayle, or who brought them
    in this staye?
They aunswer not at all, but alacke and welaway.   20
Whan I saw it booted not, out at doores I hyed
    mee
And caught a slyp of Bacon, when I saw that none
    spyed mee,
Which I intend not far hence, unles my purpose
    fayle
Shall serve for a shoinghorne[5] to draw on two pots
    of ale.

THE FYRST ACTE. THE SECOND SCEANE.

[*Enter*] HODGE [*to*] DICCON.

HODGE. See so cham(1) arayed with dablynge in the
    durt
She that set me to ditchinge, ich wold she had the
    squrt.[1]
Was never poore soule that such a life had?
Gogs bones thys vylthy glaye hase drest[2] mee to
    bad.
Gods soule, see how this stuffe teares.   5
Iche were better to bee a Bearward and set to
    keepe Beares.

---

4 *trump :* i.e. in a game of
    cards.
5 *shoinghorne :* shoehorn, i.e.
    either a means of acquir-
    ing or (OED) an appe-
    tizer.

FYRST ACTE. SECOND SCEANE.
    1 *squrt :* diarrhea.
    2 *glaye hase drest :* clay has
    soiled.

By the Masse here is a gasshe, a shamefull hole
    indeade
And one stytch teare furder, a man may thruste in
    his heade.

DICCON. By my fathers soule Hodge, if I shulde now
    be sworne

I can not chuse but say thy breech is foule be-   10
    torne,
But the next remedye in such a case and hap
Is to plaunche on[3] a piece, as brode as thy cap.

HODGE. Gogs soule man, tis not yet two dayes fully
    ended
Synce my dame Gurton (chem sure) these
    breches amended,
But cham made such[1] a drudge to trudge at   15
    every neede
Chwold rend it though it were stitched with[2]
    sturdy pacthreede.

DICCON. Hodge, let thy breeches go, and speake and
    tell mee soone
What devill ayleth Gammer Gurton, and Tyb her
    mayd to frowne?

HODGE. Tush man thart deceyved, tys theyr dayly
    looke,
They coure[4] so over the coles, theyr eyes be bleard   20
    with smooke.

DICCON. Nay by the Masse, I perfectly perceived as I
    came hether
That eyther Tyb and her dame hath ben by the
    eares together
Or els as great a matter as thou shalt shortly see.

HODGE. Now iche beseeche our Lord they never bet-
    ter agree.

DICCON. By Gogs soule there they syt as still as stones   25
    in the streite
As though they had ben taken[5] with fairies or els
    with some il sprite.

HODGE. Gogs hart, I durst have layd my cap to a
    crowne

3 *plaunche on:* clap on.   5 *taken:* bewitched.
4 *coure:* cower, bend.

Chwould lerne of some prancome[6] as sone as ich
    came to town.

DICCON. Why Hodge art thou inspyred? or dedst thou
    therof here?

HODGE. Nay, but ich saw such a wonder as ich saw   30
    nat this vii. yere.

Tome Tannkards Cow (be Gogs bones) she set me
    up her saile

And flynging about his halfe aker fysking with her
    taile,

As though there had ben in her ars a swarme of
    Bees,

And chad not cryed tphrowh[7] hoore, shead lept
    out of his Lees.[8]

DICCON. Why Hodge lies the connyng[9] in Tom Tank-   35
    ards cowes taile?

HODGE. Well ich chave hard some say such tokens do
    not fayle,

But canst thou not tell[3] in faith Diccon, why she
    frownes or wher at?

Hath no man stolne her Ducks or Henes, or gelded
    Gyb her Cat?

DICCON. What devyll can I tell man, I cold not have
    one word.

They gave no more hede to my talk then thou   40
    woldst to a lorde.

HODGE. Iche can not styll but muse, what mervaylous
    thinge it is.

Chyll in and know my selfe what matters are amys.

DICCON. Then farewell Hodge a while, synce thou
    doest inward hast,

For I will into the good wyfe Chats, to feele how
    the ale dooth taste.   [*Exit* DICCON.]

6 *prancome :* prank.   8 *Lees :* pastures.
7 *tphrowh :* onomatopoeic   9 *connyng :* spell (?)
    term coined by Hodge.

THE FYRST ACTE. THE THYRD SCEANE.

HODGE. [*Enter to him*] TYB.

HODGE. Cham agast by the Masse, ich wot not what
          to do

Chad nede blesse me well before ich go them to.

Perchaunce some felon sprit may haunt our house
          indeed,

And then chwere but a[1] noddy[1] to venter where
          cha no neede.

TYB. Cham worse then mad by the Masse to be at   5
          this staye.[2]

Cham chyd, cham blamd, and beaton all thoures
          on the daye,

Lamed and hunger storved, prycked up all in
          Jagges[3]

Havyng no patch to hyde my backe, save a few
          rotten ragges.

HODGE. I say Tyb, if thou be Tyb, as I trow sure thou
          bee,

What devyll make a doe is this, betweene our   10
          dame and thee?

TYB. Gogsbreade Hodge thou had a good turne thou
          warte not here this whyle.[2]

It had ben better for some of us to have ben hence
          a myle.

My Gammer is so out of course, and frantyke all
          at ones

That Cocke our boy, and I poore wench, have felt
          it on our bones.

HODGE. What is the matter, say on Tyb wherat she   15
          taketh so on?

TYB. She is undone she sayth (alas,) her joye and
          life is gone.

If shee here not of some comfort, she is sayth but
          dead,

Shall never come within her lyps, one inch of
          meate ne bread.

FYRST ACTE. THYRD SCEANE.   2 *staye :* plight.
     1 *noddy :* simpleton.   3 *Jagges :* Tatters.

HODGE. Byr Ladie cham not very glad, to see her in
    this dumpe.
  Cholde a noble[4] her stole hath fallen, and shee   20
    hath broke her rumpe.
TYB. Nay and that were the worst, we wold not
    greatly care
  For bursting of her huckle bone,[5] or breakyng of
    her Chaire,
  But greater, greater, is her grief, as Hodge we
    shall all feele.
HODGE. Gogs woundes Tyb, my Gammer has never
    lost her Neele?
TYB. Her Neele.   25
HODGE. Her Neele?
TYB. Her neele by him that made me, it is true
    Hodge I tell thee.
HODGE. Gogs sacrament, I would she had lost, tharte[6]
    out of her bellie.
  The Devill or els his dame, they ought[7] her sure a
    shame.
  How a murryon[8] came this chaunce, (say Tyb)   30
    unto our dame?
TYB. My Gammer sat her downe on her pes,[9] and
    bad me reach thy breeches
  And by and by, a vengeance in it or[10] she had take
    two stitches
  To clap a clout upon thine ars, by chaunce a syde
    she leares
  And Gyb our cat in the milke pan, she spied over
    head and eares.
  Ah hore, out thefe, she cryed aloud, and swapt   35
    the breches downe.
  Up went her staffe, and out leapt Gyb, at doors
    into the towne,[11]
  And synce that time was never wyght, cold set
    their eies upon it.

---

4 *Cholde a noble :* I wager a
    noble (6s. 8d.).
5 *huckle bone :* hipbone.
6 *tharte :* the heart.
7 *ought :* owed.
8 *murryon :* plague.

9 *pes :* hassock.
10 *or :* ere, before.
11 *towne :* "the enclosed land
    surrounding or belong-
    ing to a single dwelling."
    OED.

Gogs malison chave Cocke and I, byd twenty times
    light on it.

HODGE. And is not then my breches sewid up, to
    morow that I shuld were?

TYB. No in faith Hodge thy breeches lie, for al this   40
    never the nere.

HODGE. Now a vengeance light on al the sort, that
    better shold have kept it,

The cat, the house, and Tyb our maid, that better
    shold have swept it.

Se where she commeth crawling. Come on in
    twenty devils way!

Ye have made a fayre daies worke, have you not?
    pray you say.

THE FYRST ACTE.   THE IIII. SCEANE.

[Enter] GAMMER [to] HODGE [and] TYB.

GAMMER. Alas Hodge, alas I may well cursse and
    ban

This daie that ever I saw it, with Gyb and the
    mylke pan,

For these and ill lucke togather, as knoweth Cocke
    my boye

Have stacke[1] away my deare neele, and robd me
    of my joye,

My fayre longe strayght neele that was myne   5
    onely treasure

The fyrst day of my sorow is, and last end of my
    pleasure.

HODGE. Might ha kept it when ye had it, but fooles
    will be fooles styll.

Lose that is vast in your handes, ye neede not but
    ye will.

GAMMER. Go hie thee Tyb, and run thou hoore, to
    thend here of the towne.

Didst cary out dust in thy lap, seeke wher thou   10
    porest it downe,[1]

And as thou sawest me roking,[2] in the asshes
    where I morned[3]

FYRST ACTE. IIII. SCEANE.   3 *morned*: spent the morn-
  1 *stacke*: stuck.   ing.
  2 *roking*: raking.

So see in all the heape of dust, thou leave no straw
unturned.

TYB. That chal Gammer swythe and tyte,[4] and sone
be here agayne.

GAMMER. Tyb stoope and loke downe to the ground,
to it, and take some paine. [*Exit* TYB.]

HODGE. Here is a prety matter, to see this gere how it
goes.

By Gogs soule I thenk you wold loes your ars, and
it were loose.

Your neele lost, it is pitie you shold lack care and
endlesse sorow.

Gogs deth how shall my breches be sewid, shall I
go thus to morow?

GAMMER. Ah Hodge, Hodge, if that ich cold find my
neele by the reed[5]

Chould sow thy breches ich promise ye, with full
good double threed

And set a patch on either knee, shuld last this
monethes twaine.

Now God and good Saint Sithe I praye, to send it
home againe.

HODGE. Whereto served your hands and eies, but this
your neele to kepe?

What devill had you els to do? ye kept ich wot no
sheepe.

Cham faine abrode to dyg and delve, in water,
myre and claye

Sossing and possing in the durte, styll from day to
daye.

A hundred thinges that be abrode, cham set to see
them weele,

And foure of you syt idle at home, and can not
keepe a neele.

GAMMER. My neele alas ich lost it Hodge, what time
ich me up hasted

To save the milke set up for the, which Gib our
cat hath wasted.

HODGE. The Devill he burst both Gib, and Tyb, with
all the rest.

15

20

25

30

---

4 *swythe and tyte:* rapidly   5 *reed:* rood, cross.
and soon.

Cham always sure of the worst end, who ever have
the best.

Where ha you ben fidging[6] abrode, since you your
neele lost?

GAMMER. Within the house, and at the dore, sitting
by this same post

Wher I was loking a long howre, before these folks   35
came here,

But welaway, all was in vayne, my neele is never
the nere.

HODGE. Set me a candle, let me seeke and grope
where ever it bee.

Gogs hart ye be so folish (ich thinke) you knowe
it not when you it see.

GAMMER. Come hether Cocke, what Cocke I say.
[*Enter* COCKE.]

COCKE.   Howe Gammer.

GAMMER.   Goe hye thee soone,

And grope behynd the old brasse pan, whych   40
thing when thou hast done[2]

Ther shalt thou fynd an old shooe, wher in if thou
looke well

Thou shalt fynd lyeng an inche of a whyte tallow
candell,

Lyght it, and brynge it tite awaye,

COCKE.   That shal be done anone.
[*Exit* COCKE.]

GAMMER. Nay tary Hodge til thou hast light, and
then weele seke ech one.

HODGE. Cum away ye horson boy, are ye a slepe; ye   45
must have a crier.

COCKE. [*Within.*] Ich cannot get the candel light,
here is almost no fier.

HODGE. Chil hold the a peny chil make ye come if
that ich may catch thine eares.

Art deffe thou horson boy? Cocke I say, why canst
not heares?

GAMMER. Beate hym not Hodge but help the boy
and come you two together.
[*Exit* HODGE.]

6 *fidging :* wandering rest-
lessly.

The i. Acte.   The v. Sceane.

GAMMER [*remains. Enter*] TYB.

GAMMER. How now Tyb, quycke lets here, what
        newes thou hast brought hether.

TYB. Chave tost and tumbled yender heap our and
        over againe

  And winowed it through my fingers, as men wold
        winow grain.

  Not[1] so much as a hens turd but in pieces I
        tare it

  Or what so ever clod or clay I found, I did not   5
        spare it

  Lokyng within and eke without, to fynd your neele
        (alas)

  But all in vaine and without help, your neele is
        where it was.

GAMMER. Alas my neele we shall never meete, adue,
        adue for aye.

TYB. Not so Gammer, we myght it fynd if we knew
        where it laye.

          [*Enter* COCKE.]

COCKE. Gogs crosse Gammer if ye will laugh looke in   10
        but at the doore

  And see how Hodge lieth tomblynge and tossing
        amids the floure[1]

  Rakyng there some fyre to find amonge the asshes
        dead

  Where there is not one sparke, so byg as a pyns
        head,

  At last in a darke corner two sparkes he thought he
        sees

  Which were[2] indede nought els but Gyb our   15
        cats two eyes.

  Puffe quod Hodge thinking therby to have fyre
        without doubt.

  With that Gyb shut her two eyes, and so the fyre
        was out

  And by and by them opened, even as they were
        before,

i. Acte. v. Sceane.
  1 *floure :* ashes (?)

With that the sparkes appered even as they had
  done of yore,
And even as Hodge blew the fire as he did thincke 20
Gyb as she felt the blast strayght way began to
  wyncke,
Tyll Hodge fell of swering, as came best to his
  turne,
The fier was sure bewicht and therfore wold not
  burne :
At last Gyb up the stayers, among the old postes
  and pinnes,
And Hodge he hied him after till broke were both 25
  his shinnes :
Cursynge and swering othes, were never of his
  makyng,
That Gyb wold fyre the house, if that shee were
  not taken.

GAMMER. See here is all the thought that the foolysh
  Urchyn taketh,
And Tyb me thinke at his elbowe almost as mery
  maketh.
This is all the wyt ye have when others make their 30
  mone,
Come downe Hodge, where art thou and let the
  Cat alone.

HODGE. [*Within.*] Gogs harte, help and come up, Gyb
  in her tayle hath fyre,
And is like to burne all if shee get a lytle hier :
Cum downe (quoth you,) nay then you might
  count me a patch,[2]
The house commeth downe on your heads if it take 35
  ons the thatch.

GAMMER. It is the cats eyes foole that shineth in the
  darke.

HODGE. [*Within.*] Hath the Cat do you thinke in
  every eye a sparke?

GAMMER. No, but they shyne as lyke fyre as ever
  man see.

HODGE. [*Within.*] By the Masse and she burne all,
  yoush beare the blame for mee.

 2 *patch :* fool.

GAMMER. Cum downe and help to seeke here our   40
    neele that it were found.
    Downe Tyb on the knees I say, downe Cocke to
      the ground.
    To God I make a vowe, and so to good Saint Anne
    A candell shall they have a peece, get it where I
      can,
    If I may my neele find in one place or in other.
          [Enter HODGE.*]*
HODGE. Now a vengeaunce on Gyb light, on Gyb and   45
    Gybs mother
    And all the generacyon of Cats both far and nere.
    Looke on the ground horson, thinks thou the neele
      is here?
COCKE. By my trouth Gammer me thought your
    neele here I saw
    But when my fyngers toucht it, I felt it was a straw.
TYB. See Hodge whats tys,[3] may it not be within it?   50
HODGE. Breake it foole with thy hand and see and
    thou canst fynde it.
TYB. Nay breake it you Hodge accordyng to your
    word.
HODGE. Gogs sydes, fye it styncks; it is a Cats tourd,
    It were well done to make thee eate it by the
      Masse.
GAMMER. This matter amendeth not, my neele is still   55
    where it wasse.
    Our candle is at an ende, let us all in quight
    And come another tyme, when we have more
      lyght.   *[Exeunt.]*

THE II. ACTE.   *Fyrste a Songe.*[1]

Backe and syde go bare, go bare,
    booth foote and hande go colde:
But Bellye God sende thee good ale ynoughe,
    whether it be newe or olde.

I Can not eate, but lytle meate,   5
    my stomacke is not good:

But sure I thinke, that I can drynke
  with him that weares a hood.[1]
Thoughe I go bare, take ye no care,
  I am nothinge a colde :   10
I stuffe my skyn, so full within,
  of joly good Ale and olde.
Backe and syde go bare, go bare,
  booth foote and hand go colde :
But belly God send the good ale inoughe   15
  whether it be new or olde.

I love no rost, but a nut browne toste
  and a Crab[2] layde in the fyre,
A lytle bread, shall do me stead
  much breade I not desyre :   20
No froste nor snow, no winde I trowe
  can hurte mee if I wolde,
I am so wrapt, and throwly lapt
  of joly good ale and olde.
     Backe and syde go bare. &c.   25

And Tyb my wyfe, that as her lyfe
  loveth well good ale to seeke,
Full ofte drynkes shee, tyll ye may see
  the teares run downe her cheekes :
Then dooth she trowle, to mee the bowle   30
  even as a mault worme[3] shuld,
And sayth sweete hart, I tooke my part
  of this joly good ale and olde.
     Backe and syde go bare. &c.

Now let them drynke, tyll they nod and winke,   35
  even as good felowes shoulde doe
They shall not mysse, to have the blisse,
  good ale doth bringe men to :
And all poore soules that have scowred[4] boules
  or have them lustely trolde,[5]   40
God save the lyves, of them and theyr wyves
  whether they be yonge or olde.
     Backe and syde go bare. &c.

Songe.

1 *him . . . hood :* a friar.

2 *Crab :* crab apple roasted
  at the fire.

3 *mault worme :* toper.

4 *scowred :* emptied by
  drinking.

5 *trolde :* passed around.

The Fyrst Sceane.

DICCON. [*Within.*] Well done be Gogs malt, well
        songe and well sayde,
  Come on mother Chat as thou art true mayde,
  One fresh pot of ale lets see to make an ende
  Agaynst this colde wether, my naked armes to
        defende.
        [*Enter with a pot of ale.*]
  This gere it warms the soule, now wind blow on   5
        the worst,
  And let us drink and swill, till that our bellies
        burste.
  Now were he a wyse man, by cunnynge colde
        defyne
  Which way my Journey lyeth or where Diccon will
        dyne,
  But one good turne I have, be it by nyght or daye
  South, East, North or west, I am never out of my   10
        waye.
        [*Enter* HODGE.]
HODGE. Chym goodly rewarded, cham I not, do you
        thyncke?
  Chad a goodly dynner for all my sweate and
        swyncke,
  Neyther butter, cheese, mylke, onyons, fleshe nor
        fyshe
  Save thys poor pece of barly bread, tis a pleasant
        costly dishe.
DICCON. Haile fellow Hodge and well[1] to fare,   15
        with thy meat, if thou have any?
  But by thy words as I them smelled, thy daintrels[1]
        be not manye.
HODGE. Daintrels Diccon (Gogs soule man) save this
        pece of dry horsbred,
  Cha byt no byt this lyve longe daie, no crome
        come in my hed.
  My gutts they yawle crawle and all my belly rum-
        bleth.

II. ACTE.   FYRST SCEANE.
  1 *daintrels :* delicacies.

The puddynges[2] can not lye still, ech one over   20
    other tumbleth.

By Gogs harte cham so vexte, and in my belly
    pende

Chould one peece were at the spittlehouse[3] an-
    other at the castels ende.

DICCON. Why Hodge, was there none at home thy
    dinner for to set?

HODGE. Godgs bread Diccon ich came to late, was
    nothing ther to get.

Gyb (a fowle feind might on her light) lickt the   25
    milke pan so clene

See Diccon, twas not so well washt this .vii. yere as
    ich wene.

A pestilence lyght on all ill lucke, chad thought
    yet for all thys

Of a morsell of bacon behynde the dore at worst
    shuld not misse,

But when ich sought a slyp to cut, as ich was wont
    to do

Gogs soule Diccon, Gyb our Cat had eate the ba-   30
    con to.

    Which bacon DICCON *stole, as is declared*
          before.[1]

DICCON. Ill luck quod he, mary swere it Hodge, this
    day the trueth to tel

Thou rose not on thy right syde, or els blest thee
    not wel,

Thy mylk slopt up, thy bacon filtched, that was
    to bad luck Hodge.

HODGE. Nay, nay, ther was a fowler fault, my Gam-
    mer ga me the dodge.[2]

Seest not how cham rent and torn, my heels, my   35
    knees and my breech?

Chad thought as ich sat by the fire, help here and
    there a stitch,

But there ich was powpte[4] indeede.

DICCON.   Why Hodge?

HODGE.   Bootes not man to tell,

2 *puddynges:* guts.   4 *powpte:* deceived.
3 *spittlehouse:* hospital or
   poorhouse.

Cham so drest amonst a sorte of fooles, chad better
be in hell,

My Gammer (cham ashamed to say) by God
served me not weele.

DICCON. How so Hodge?

HODGE. Hase she not gone trowest now and lost her   40
neele?

DICCON. Her Eele Hodge, who fysht of late? that
was a dainty dysh.

HODGE. Tush tush, her neele, her neele, her neele
man. Tys neyther flesh nor fysh.

A lytle thing with an hole in the end, as bright as
any syller,[5]

Small, longe, sharpe at the poynt, and straight as
any pyller.[6]

DICCON. I know not what a devil thou menest, thou   45
bringst me more in doubt.

HODGE. Knowest not with what Tom Tailers man, sits
broching throughe a clout?

A neele, neele, a neele, my Gammers neele is gone.

DICCON. Her neele Hodge, now I smel thee, that was
a chaunce alone,

By the Masse thou hadst a shamefull losse, and it
wer but for thy breches.

HODGE. Gogs soule man should give a crown chad it   50
but iii. stitches.

DICCON. How sayest thou Hodge, what shuld he have,
again thy neele got?

HODGE. Bem vathers[7] soule, and chad it chould give
him a new grot.

DICCON. Canst thou keepe counsaile in this case?

HODGE. Els chwold my tonge[3] were out.

DICCON. Do thou[4] but then by my advise, and I
will fetch it without doubt.

HODGE. Chyll runne, chyll ryde, chyll dygge, chyl   55
delve, chill toyle, chill trudge shalt
see :

Chill hold chil drawe, chil pull, chill pynche chill
kneele on my bare knee.

---

5 *syller* : silver.   7 *Bem vathers* : By my fa-
6 *pyller* : pillar.   ther's.

Chill scrape, chill scratche, chill syfte, chyll seeke,
      chill bowe, chill bende, chill sweate,
Chil stoop, chil stur, chil cap, chil knele, chil crepe
      on hands and feete,
Chil be thy bondman Diccon, ich sweare by sunne
      and moone
And channot sum what to stop this gap, cham ut-   60
      terly undone
    Pointing behind to his torne breeches.[5]
DICCON. Why, is ther any special cause, thou takest
      hereat such sorow?
HODGE. Kirstian Clack, Tom Simsons maid, bi the
      Masse coms hether to morow.
Chamnot able to say, betweene us what may hap,
She smyled on me the last Sonday when ich put of
      my cap.
DICCON. Well Hodge this is a matter of weight, and   65
      must be kept close,
It might els turne to both our costes as the world
      now gose,
Shalt sware to be no blab Hodge?
HODGE.   Chyll Diccon.
DICCON.   Then go to,
Lay thine hand here, say after me as thou shalt
      here me do.
Haste no booke?
HODGE.   Cha no booke I.
DICCON.   Then needes must force us both,
Upon my breech to lay thine hand, and there to   70
      take thine othe.
HODGE. I Hodge breechelesse,
Sweare to Diccon rechelesse[8]
By the crosse that I shall kysse,
To kepe his counsaile close
And alwayes me to dispose   75
To worke that his pleasure is.
     Here he kysseth[6] DICCONS *breeche.*
DICCON. Now Hodge see thou take heede
And do as I thee byd
For so I judge it meete,

8 *rechelesse :* careless.

This nedle againe to win.   80
There is no shift therin
But conjure up a spreete.
HODGE. What the great devill Diccon I saye?
DICCON. Yea in good faith, that is the waye,
  Fet[9] with some prety charme.   85
HODGE. Softe Diccon be not to hasty yet,
  By the Masse for ich begyn to sweat
  Cham afrayde of some[7] harme.
DICCON. Come hether then and sturre the nat
  One inche out of this Cyrcle plat   90
  But stande as I thee teache.
HODGE. And shall ich be here safe from theyr clawes?
DICCON. The mayster devill with his longe pawes
  Here to thee can not reache :
  Now will I settle me to this geare.   95
HODGE. I saye Diccon, heare me, heare :
  Go softely to thys matter.
DICCON. What devyll man, art afraide of nought.
HODGE. Canst not tarrye a lytle thought
  Tyll ich make a curtesie of water.   100
DICCON. Stand still to it, why shuldest thou feare
      hym?
HODGE. Gogs sydes Diccon, me thinke ich heare him
  And tarrye chal mare all.
DICCON. The matter is no worse then I tolde it.
HODGE. By the Masse cham able no longer to holde it.   105
  To bad iche must beraye the hall.[(2)]
DICCON. Stand to it Hodge, sture not you horson,
  What Devyll, be thine ars strynges brusten?[10]
  Thy selfe a while but staye,
  The devill I smell hym wyll be here anone.   110
HODGE. Hold him fast Diccon, cham gone, cham gone,
  Chyll not be at that fraye.   [*Exit* HODGE.]

9 *Fet :* Fetched.   10 *brusten :* burst, broken.

The ii. Acte.   The ii. Sceane.

DICCON [*remains.*]

DICCON. Fy shytten knave, and out upon thee.
    Above all other loutes fye on thee,
    Is not here a clenly prancke?
    But thy matter was no better
    Nor thy presence here no sweter,   5
    To flye I can the thanke :[1]
    Here is a matter worthy glosynge[2]
    Of Gammer Gurtons nedle losynge
    And a foule peece of warke,
    A man I thyncke myght make a playe   10
    And nede no worde to this they saye
    Being but halfe a Clarke.
    Softe, let me alone, I will take the charge
    This matter further to enlarge
    Within a tyme shorte,   15
    If ye will marke my toyes,[3] and note
    I will geve ye leave to cut my throte
    If I make not good sporte.
    Dame Chat I say, where be ye, within?
                [*Enter* DAME CHAT.]

DAME CHAT. Who have we there maketh such a din?   20
DICCON. Here is a good fellow, maketh no great
                daunger.[4]
DAME CHAT. What Diccon? come nere, ye be no
                straunger,
    We be fast set at trumpe man, hard by the fyre,
    Thou shalt set on the king, if thou come a litle
                nyer.
DICCON. Nay, nay, there is no tarying : I must be gone   25
                againe.
    But first for you in councel I have a word or
                twaine.

ii. Acte.   ii. Sceane.
  1 *can the thanke :* give thee
      thanks.
  2 *glosynge :* interpreting.

  3 *marke my toyes :* watch
      my tricks.
  4 *maketh . . . daunger :* who
      makes himself at home.

DAME CHAT. Come hether Doll. [*Enter* DOLL.] Doll,
        sit downe and play this game,
And as thou sawest me do, see thou do even the
        same.
There is 5. trumps beside the Queene, the hind-
        most thou shalt finde her.[1]
Take hede of Sim Glovers wife, she hath an eie be-   30
        hind her.   [*Exit* DOLL.]
Now Diccon say your will.
DICCON.   Nay softe a litle yet,
I wold not tel it my sister, the matter is so great,
There I wil have you sweare by our dere Lady of
        Bullaine,
S. Dunstone, and S. Donnyke, with the three
        Kinges of Kullaine,
That ye shal keepe it secret.
DAME CHAT.   Gogs bread that will I doo,   35
As secret as mine owne thought, by God and the
        devil two.[5]
DICCON. Here is Gammer Gurton your neighbour, a
        sad and hevy wight,
Her goodly faire red Cock, at home, was stole this
        last night.
DAME CHAT. Gogs soule her Cock with the yelow legs,
        that nightly crowed so just?[6]
DICCON. That cocke is stollen.
DAME CHAT. What was he fet out of the hens ruste?[7]   40
DICCON. I can not tel where the devil he was kept, un-
        der key or locke,
But Tyb hath tykled in Gammers eare, that you
        shoulde steale the cocke.
DAME CHAT. Have I, stronge hoore? by bread and
        salte.
DICCON.   What softe, I say be styl.
Say not one word for all this geare.
DAME CHAT.   By the Masse that I wyl,
I wil have the yong hore by the head, and the old   45
        trot by the throte.

---

5 *two* : too.

6 *so just* : so precisely on the
    hour.

7 *ruste* : roost.

DICCON. Not one word Dame Chat I say, not one word
        for my cote.

DAME CHAT. Shall such a begars brawle[8] as that
        thinkest thou make me a theefe?

  The pocks light on her hores sydes, a pestlence
        and a mischeefe!

  Come out thou hungry nedy bytche, o that my nails
        be short.

DICCON. Gogs bred woman hold your peace, this gere   50
        wil els passe sport.

  I wold not for an hundred pound, this matter shuld
        be knowen,

  That I am auctour of this tale, or have abrode it
        blowen.

  Did ye not sweare ye wold be ruled, before the
        tale I tolde?

  I said ye must all secret keepe, and ye said sure ye
        wolde.

DAME CHAT. Wolde you suffer your selfe Diccon, such   55
        a sort, to revile you

  With slaunderous words to blot your name, and so
        to defile you?

DICCON. No goodwife Chat I wold be loth such drabs
        shulde blot my name

  But yet ye must so order all, that Diccon beare no
        blame.

DAME CHAT. Go to then, what is your rede?[9] say
        on your minde, ye shall mee rule
        herein.

DICCON. Godamercye to Dame Chat, in faith thou   60
        must the gere begin.

  It is twenty pound to a goose turd, my Gammer
        will not tary

  But hetherward she comes as fast as her legs can
        her cary.

  To brawle with you about her cocke, for well I hard
        Tyb say

  The Cocke was rosted in your house, to brea[k]fast
        yesterday,

  And when ye had the carcas eaten, the fethers ye   65
        out flunge

8 *brawle :* brat.   9 *rede :* advice.

And Doll your maid the legs she hid a foote depe
      in the dunge.

DAME CHAT. Oh gracyous God my harte it[1]
      burstes.

DICCON.   Well rule your selfe a space
  And Gammer Gurton when she commeth anon
      into thys place

Then to the Queane lets see tell her your mynd
      and spare not.

So shall Diccon blamelesse bee, and then go to I   70
      care not.

DAME CHAT. Then hoore beware her throte, I can
      abide no longer.

In faith old witch it shal be seene, which of us two
      be stronger,

And Diccon but at your request, I wold not stay
      one howre.

DICCON. Well keepe it in till she be here, and then
      out let it powre,

In the meane while get you in, and make no wordes   75
      of this.

More of this matter within this howre to here you
      shall not misse.

Because I know you are my freind, hide it I cold
      not doubtles.

Ye know your harm, see ye be wise about your
      owne busines.

So fare ye well.[2]

DAME CHAT. Nay soft Diccon and drynke, what Doll
      I say,

Bringe here a cup of the best ale, lets see, come   80
      quicly awaye.

      [DOLL *enters with ale. Exeunt* DOLL *and*
              DAME CHAT.]

The ii. Actt. The iii. Sceane.

DICCON [*remains.*]

DICCON. [*To the audience.*] Ye see masters the one
    end tapt[1] of this my short devise.

Now must we broche thoter to,[2] before the smoke
    arise,

And by the time they have a while run, I trust ye
    need not crave it,

But loke what lieth in both their harts ye ar like
    sure to have it.

[*Enter* HODGE.]

HODGE. Yea Gogs soule, art alive yet? what Diccon   5
    dare ich come?

DICCON. A man is wel hied[3] to trust to thee, I will
    say nothing but mum,

But and ye come any nearer I pray you see all be
    sweete.

HODGE. Tush man, is Gammers neele found? that
    chould gladly weete.

DICCON. She may thanke thee it is not found, for if
    thou had kept thy standing

The devil he wold have fet it out, even Hodge at   10
    thy commaunding.

HODGE. Gogs hart, and cold he tel nothing wher the
    neele might be found?

DICCON. Ye folysh dolt, ye were to seek, ear we had
    got our ground,

Therfore his tale so doubtfull was, that I cold not
    perceive it.

HODGE. Then ich se wel somthing was said, chope one
    day yet to have it,

But Diccon, Diccon, did not the devill cry ho, ho,   15
    ho?

DICCON. If thou hadst taryed where thou stoodst,
    thou woldest have said so.

HODGE. Durst swere of a boke, chard[4] him rore,
    streight after ich was gon.

II. ACTT. III. SCEANE.   3 *hied :* sped.
  1 *tapt :* taped, finished.   4 *chard :* I heard.
  2 *thoter to :* the other too.

But tel me Diccon what said the knave : let me
 here it anon.

DICCON. The horson talked to mee. I know not well
 of what.

One whyle his tonge it ran and paltered of a Cat, 20
Another whyle he stamered styll uppon a Rat,
Last of all there was nothing but every word Chat,
 Chat,
But this I well perceyved before I wolde him rid,
Between Chat, and the Rat, and the Cat, the nedle
 is hyd,
Now whether Gyb our cat have eate it in her 25
 mawe,
Or Doctor Rat our curat have found it in the straw,
Or this Dame Chat your neighbour have stollen it,
 God hee knoweth,
But by the morow at this time, we shal learn how
 the matter goeth.

HODGE. Canst not learn to night man, seest not what
 is here?

 Pointyng behind to his torne breeches.

DICCON. Tys not possyble to make it sooner appere. 30
HODGE. Alas Diccon then chave no shyft, but least ich
 tary to longe

Hye me to Sym Glovers shop, theare to seeke for a
 Thonge,
Ther with this breech to tatche[5] and tye as ich
 may.

DICCON. To morow Hodge if we chaunce to meete,
 shalt see what I will say.

        [Exit HODGE.]

THE II. ACTE. THE IIII. SCEANE.

DICCON [*remains.*]

DICCON. [*To the audience.*] Now this gere must
 forward goe, for here my Gammer
 commeth.

Be still a while and say nothing, make here a litle
 romth.[1]

  [*Enter* GAMMER GURTON.]

5 *tatche :* fasten.

GAMMER. Good lord, shall never be my lucke my
      neele agayne to spye?

Alas the whyle tys past my helpe, where tis still
      it must lye.

DICCON. Now Jesus Gammer Gurton, what driveth   5
      you to this sadnes?

I feare me by my conscience, you will sure fall to
      madnes.

GAMMER. Who is that, what Diccon, cham lost man :
      fye fye.

DICCON. Mary fy on them that be worthy, but what
      shuld be your troble?

GAMMER. Alas the more ich thinke on it, my sorow it
      waxeth doble,

My goodly tossing sporyars[1] neele, chave lost ich   10
      wot not where.

DICCON. Your neele, whan?

GAMMER. My neele (alas) ich myght full ill it spare,

As God him selfe he knoweth nere one besyde
      chave.

DICCON. If this be all good Gammer, I warrant you
      all is save.

GAMMER. Why know you any tydings which way my
      neele is gone?

DICCON. Yea that I do doubtlesse, as ye shall here   15
      anone,

A[2] see a thing this matter toucheth within these
      .xx. howres,

Even at this gate, before my face, by a neyghbour
      of yours,

She stooped me downe, and up she toke a nedle
      or a pyn :

I durst be sworne it was even yours, by all my
      mothers kyn.

GAMMER. It was my neele Diccon ich wot, for here   20
      even by this poste

Ich sat, what time as ich up starte, and so my neele
      it loste :

II. ACTE.   IIII. SCEANE.   2 *A :* I.

    1 *sporyars :* spurrier's, for
      sewing the straps of
      spurs.

Who was it leive[3] son? speke ich pray the, and
    quickly tell me that?

DICCON. A suttle queane as any in thys Towne, your
    neyghboure here dame Chat.

GAMMER. Dame chat Diccon? let me be gone, chil
    thyther in post haste.

DICCON. Take my councell yet or ye go, for feare ye   25
    walke in wast,

It is a murrion crafty drab, and froward to be
    pleased,

And ye take not the better way, our nedle yet ye
    lose it :

For when she tooke it up, even here before your
    doores

What soft Dame Chat (quoth I) that same is none
    of yours.

Avant[4] (quoth she) syr knave, what pratest thou of   30
    that I fynd :

I wold thou hadst kist me I wot whear : (she ment
    I know behind)

And home she went as brag,[5] as it had ben a
    bodelouce,[6]

And I after as bold, as it had ben, the goodman[7]
    of the house :

But there and ye had hard her, how she began to
    scolde,

The tonge it went on patins,[8] by hym that Judas   35
    solde,

Ech other worde I was a knave, and you a hore of
    hores,

Because I spake in your behalfe, and sayde the
    neele was yours.

GAMMER. Gogs bread, and thinks the callet[9] thus to
    kepe my neele me fro?

DICCON. Let her alone, and she minds non other but
    even to dresse you so.

GAMMER. By the Masse chil rather spend the cote   40
    that is on my backe.

---

3 *leive :* dear.

4 *Avant :* Clear out.

5 *brag :* lively.

6 *bodelouce :* body louse.

7 *goodman :* householder.

8 *patins :* wooden shoes, i.e.
    clattering.

9 *callet :* trull.

Thinks the false quean by such a slyght,[1] that
    chill my neele lacke?

DICCON. Slepe not your[2] gere I counsell you, but
    of this take good hede :

Let not be knowen I told you of it, how well so-
    ever ye spede.

GAMMER. Chil in Diccon a cleene aperne[10] to take,
    and set before me,

And ich may my neele once see, chil sure remem-   45
    ber the.   [*Exit* GAMMER.]

THE II. ACTE. THE V. SCEANE.

DICCON [*solus.*]

DICCON. Here will the sporte begin, if these two once
    may meete.

Their chere durst lay money will prove scarsly
    sweete.

My Gammer sure entends, to be uppon her bones,

With[1] staves, or with clubs, or els with coble
    stones.

Dame Chat on the other syde, if she be far behynde   5

I am right far deceived, she is geven to it of kynde.

He that may tarry by it a whyle, and that but
    shorte

I warrant hym trust to it, he shall see all the
    sporte.

Into the towne will I, my frendes to vysit there

And hether straight againe to see thend of this   10
    gere.

In the meane time felowes, pype upp your fiddles,
    I saie take them

And let your freyndes here such mirth as ye can
    make them.   [*Exit.*]
        [*Music.*]

10 *aperne :* apron.

THE III. ACTE.   THE I. SCEANE.

[*Enter*] HODGE [*with a thonge and awl.*]

HODGE. Sym Glover yet gramercy, cham meetlye well
      sped now,

  Thart even as good a felow as ever kyste a cowe,

  Here is a thynge[1] in dede, by the Masse though
      ich speake it,

  Tom Tankards great bald curtal,[1] I thinke could
      not breake it.

  And when he spyed my neede, to be so straight   5
      and hard,

  Hays lent me here his naull,[2] to set the gyb for-
      ward.[3]

  As for my Gammers neele, the flyenge feynd go
      weete,[4]

  Chill not now go to the doore againe with it to
      meete :

  Chould make shyfte good inough and chad a can-
      dels ende,

  The cheefe hole in my breeche, with these two chil   10
      amende.

THE III. ACTE.   THE II. SCEANE.

[*Enter*] GAMMER [*to*] HODGE.

GAMMER. How Hodge, mayst nowe be glade, cha
      newes to tell thee.

  Ich knowe who hais my neele, ich trust soone
      shalt it see.

HODGE. The devyll thou does, hast hard Gammer in
      deede, or doest but jest?

GAMMER. Tys as true as steele Hodge.

HODGE.   Why, knowest well where dydst leese it?

III. ACTE.   I. SCEANE.   2 *naull* : awl.
  1 *bald curtal* : horse with   3 *set . . . forward* : expedite
     white on its head and a   progress (as in sailing)..
     docked tail.   4 *weete* : with it.

GAMMER. Ich know who found it, and took it up shalt   5
    see or it be longe.

HODGE. [*Aside.*] Gods mother dere, if that be true,
    farwel both naule an thong.

  But who hais it Gammer say on: chould faine
    here it disclosed.

GAMMER. That false fixen,[1] that same Dame Chat,
    that counts her selfe so honest.

HODGE. Who tolde you so?

GAMMER. That same did Diccon the bedlam, which
    saw it done.

HODGE. Diccon: it is a vengeable knave Gammer,   10
    tis a bonable[2] horson,

  Can do mo things then that els cham deceyved
    evill:

  By the Masse ich saw him of late cal up a great
    blacke devill,

  O the knave cryed ho, ho, he roared and he
    thundred,

  And yead bene here,[3] cham sure yould murrenly[4]
    ha wondred.

GAMMER. Was not thou afraide Hodge to see him in   15
    this place?

HODGE. No, and chad come to me, chould have laid
    him on the face,

  Chould have promised him.

GAMMER. But Hodge, had he no hornes to pushe?

HODGE. As long as your two armes, saw ye never
    Fryer Rushe

  Painted on a cloth,(1) with a side[5] long cowes
    tayle:

  And crooked cloven feete, and many a hoked   20
    nayle?

  For al the world (if I shuld judg) chould recken
    him his brother.

  Loke even what face Frier Rush had, the devil had
    such another

III. ACTE.   II. SCEANE.
  1 *fixen*: vixen.
  2 *bonable*: abominable.
  3 *And . . . here*: If you had
    been here.

  4 *murrenly*: plaguily, terri-
    bly.
  5 *side*: long, ample.

GAMMER. Now[1] Jesus mercy Hodge, did Diccon
          in him bring?

HODGE. Nay Gammer (heare me speke) chil tel you
          a greater thing.

   The devil (when Diccon had him, ich hard him   25
          wondrous weel)

   Sayd plainly (here before us), that Dame Chat had
          your neele.

GAMMER. Then let us go, and aske her wherfore she
          minds to kepe it,

   Seing we know so much, tware a madnes now to
          slepe it.

HODGE. Go to her Gammer, see ye not where she
          stands in her doores?

           [*Enter* DAME CHAT.]

   Byd her geve you the neele, tys none of hers but   30
          yours.

The III. Acte.   The III. Sceane.

        GAMMER. [DAME] CHAT. HODGE.

GAMMER. Dame Chat cholde praye the fair, let me
          have that is mine.

   Chil not this twenty yeres take one fart that is
          thyne.

   Therfore give me mine owne and let me live be-
          syde the.

DAME CHAT. Why art thou crept from home hether, to
          mine own doores to chide me?

   Hence doting drab, avaunt, or I shall set the fur-   5
          ther.

   Intends thou and that knave, mee in my house to
          murther?

GAMMER. Tush gape not so on[1] me woman, shalt
          not yet eate mee,

   Nor all the frends thou hast, in this shall not in-
          treate mee :

   Mine owne goods I will have, and aske the no[2]
          beleve,[1]

III. Acte.   III. Sceane.
  1 *beleve :* leave, permission.

What woman : pore folks must have right, though   10
    the thing you agreve.

DAME CHAT. Give thee thy right, and hang thee up,
    with al thy baggers broode.

What, wilt thou make me a theefe, and say I stole
    thy good?

GAMMER. Chil say nothing (ich warrant thee), but
    that ich can prove it well.

Thou fet my good even from my doore, cham able
    this to tel.

DAME CHAT. Dyd I (olde witche) steale oft[2] was   15
    thine : how should that thing be
    knowen?

GAMMER. Ich can not tel, but up thou tokest it as
    though it had ben thine owne.

DAME CHAT. Mary fy on thee, thou old gyb,[3] with
    al my very hart.

GAMMER. Nay fy on thee thou rampe, thou ryg,[4] with
    al that take thy parte.

DAME CHAT. A vengeaunce on those lips that laieth
    such things to my charge.

GAMMER. A vengeance on those callats hips, whose   20
    conscience[5] is so large.

DAME CHAT. Come out Hodge.

GAMMER. Come out Hodge, and let me have[3]
    right.

DAME CHAT. Thou arrant Witche.

GAMMER. Thou bawdie bitche, chil make thee cursse
    this night.

DAME CHAT. A bag and a wallet.[1]

GAMMER.   A carte for a callet.[2]

DAME CHAT.   Why wenest thou thus to prevaile?
I hold thee a grote,
        I shall patche thy coate.

GAMMER.   Thou warte as good kysse my tayle :

Thou slut, thou kut,[6] thou rakes, thou iakes : will   25
    not shame make thee hide the?[4]

---

2 *oft* : aught, anything.
3 *gyb* : cat.
4 *rampe* . . . *ryg* : vulgar
    woman . . . wanton.

5 *conscience* : breadth (?)
6 *kut* : gelded or dock-tailed
    horse.

DAME CHAT. Thou skald,[7] thou bald, thou rotten,
            thou glotton, I will no longer chyd the
But I will teache the to kepe home.
GAMMER.   Wylt thou drunken beaste?
              [They fight.]
HODGE. Sticke to her Gammer, take her by the head,
            chil warrant you thys feast.
Smyte I saye Gammer,
       Byte I say Gammer,
             I trow ye wyll be keene :
Where be your nayls? claw her by the jawes, pull   30
       me out bothe her eyen,
Gogs bones Gammer, holde up your head.
DAME CHAT.   I trow drab I shall dresse thee.
   [To HODGE.] Tary thou knave, I hold the a grote, I
      shall make these hands blesse thee.
                   [Exit HODGE.]
Take thou this old hore for amends, and lerne thy
          tonge well to tame
And say thou met at this bickering, not thy fellow
          but thy dame.[8]
        [Knocks down GAMMER *and exit.]*
        [Re-enter HODGE *with a staff.]*
HODGE. Where is the strong stued[9] hore, chil geare[10]   35
       a hores marke,
   [To the audience.] Stand out ones way, that ich
       kyll none in the darke :
Up Gammer and ye be alyve, chil feyght[5] now
       for us bothe,
           [Re-enter DAME CHAT.]
Come no nere me thou scalde callet, to kyll the ich
       wer loth.
DAME CHAT. Art here agayne thou hoddy peke,[11]
       what Doll bryng me out my spitte.
HODGE. Chill broche thee wyth this, bim father soule,   40
       chyll conjure that foule sprete :
           *[*COCKE *appears.]*

7 *skald :* scabby.   10 *geare :* give her.
8 *dame :* mistress, superior.   11 *hoddy peke :* simpleton.
9 *stued :* from the stews,
   whorehouses.

Let dore stand Cocke, why coms in deede? kepe
    dore thou horson boy.

DAME CHAT. Stand to it thou dastard for thine eares,
    ise teche thee a sluttish toye.

HODGE. Gogs woundes hore, chil make the avaunte,
    take heede Cocke, pull in the latche.

                [*Exit* COCKE.]

DAME CHAT. I faith sir loose breche had ye taried, ye
    shold have found your match.

GAMMER. Now ware thy throte losell,[12] thouse pay[6]
    for al.

HODGE.   Well said Gammer by my soule,   45
    Hoyse her, souse her, bounce her, trounce her, pull
    out her throte boule.[13]

DAME CHAT. Comst behynd me thou withered witch,
    and I get once on foote

Thouse pay for all, thou old tarlether,[14] ile teach
    the what longs to it.

Take thee this to make up thy mouth, til time thou
    come by more.

        [*Knocks down* GAMMER *and exit.*]

HODGE. Up Gammer stand on your feete, where is the   50
    olde hore?

Faith woulde chad her by the face choulde cracke
    her callet crowne.

GAMMER. A Hodge, Hodge, where was thy help, when
    fixen had me downe?

HODGE. By the Masse Gammer, but for my staffe Chat
    had gone nye to spyl you.

Ich think the harlot had not cared, and chad not
    com to kill you.

But shall we loose our neele thus?

GAMMER.   No Hodge chwarde[15] lothe doo soo,   55
    Thinkest thou chill take that at her hand? no
    Hodge ich tell the no.

HODGE. Chold yet this fray wer wel take up, and our
    own neele at home.

Twill be my chaunce els some to kil, wher ever it
    be or whome.

12 *losell*: wretch.   14 *tarlether*: piece of old
13 *throte boule*: Adam's   dried salted sheepskin.
    apple.   15 *chwarde*: I were.

GAMMER. We have a parson, (Hodge thou knoes) a
    man estemed wise,

    Mast Doctor Rat, chil for hym send, and let me   60
    here his advise.

    He will her shrive for all this gere, and geve her
    penaunce strait.

    Wese have our neele, els Dame Chat comes nere
    within heaven gate.

HODGE. Ye mary Gammer, that ich think best: wyll
    you now for him send?

    The sooner Doctor Rat be here, the soner wese ha
    an ende,

    And here Gammer Dyccons devill, (as iche re-   65
    member well)

    Of Cat, and Chat, and Doctor Rat: a felloneus
    tale dyd tell.

    Chold you forty pound, that is the way your neele
    to get againe.

GAMMER. Chil ha him strait, call out the boy, wese
    make him take the payn.

HODGE. What Cocke I saye, come out, what devill
    canst not here?

[Enter COCKE.]

COCKE.[7] How now Hodge? how does Gammer,   70
    is yet the wether cleare?

    What wold chave me to doo?

GAMMER.   Come hether Cocke anon:

    Hence swythe to Doctor Rat, hye the that thou
    were gone,

    And pray hym come speke with me, cham not well
    at ease.

    Shalt have him at his chamber, or[8] els at
    mother Bees,

    Els seeke him at Hob Fylchers shop, for as charde   75
    it reported

    There is the best ale in al the towne, and now is
    most resorted.

COCKE. And shal ich brynge hym with me Gammer?

GAMMER.   Yea, by and by[16] good Cocke.

COCKE. Shalt see that shal be here anone, els let me
    have one the docke.[17]   [Exit.]

16 by and by: at once.   17 docke: rump.

HODGE. Now Gammer shal we two go in, and tary for
　　　　hys commynge?

What devill woman, plucke up your hart, and leve   80
　　　　of al this glomming.

Though she were stronger at the first, as ich thinke
　　　　ye did find her,

Yet there ye drest the dronken sow, what time ye
　　　　cam behind her.

GAMMER. Nay, nay, cham sure she lost not all, for set
　　　　thend to the beginning

And ich doubt not, but she will make small bost of
　　　　her winning.

　　　　THE III. ACTE.　　THE IIII. SCEANE.

[Enter] TYB [with Gyb the cat.] HODGE [and]
　　　　GAMMER [remain.]

TYB. Se Gammer, Gammer, Gyb our cat, cham
　　　　afraid what she ayleth.

She standes me gasping behind the doore, as
　　　　though her winde her faileth :

Now let ich doubt what Gyb shuld mean, that[1]
　　　　now she doth so dote.

HODGE. Hold hether,[1] ichould twenty pound, your
　　　　neele is in her throte.

Grope her ich say, me thinkes ich feele it, does   5
　　　　not pricke your hand?

GAMMER. Ich can feele nothing.

HODGE.　　　　No, ich know thars not within this land

A muryner Cat then Gyb is, betwixt the Tems and
　　　　Tyne,

Shase as much wyt in her head almost as chave in
　　　　mine.

TYB. Faith shase eaten some thing, that wil not
　　　　easely downe

Whether she gat it at home, or abrode in the towne   10
Iche can not tell.

GAMMER.　　　　Alas ich feare it be some croked pyn,
And then farewell Gyb, she is undone, and lost al
　　　　save the skyn.

III. ACTE.　　IIII SCEANE.
　　1 Hold hether : Hand
　　　　(her) hither.

HODGE. Tys your[2] neele woman, I say : Gogs soule
　　　　geve me a knyfe
　　And chil have it out of her mawe, or els chal lose
　　　　my lyfe.
GAMMER. What nay Hodge, fy kil not our cat, tis al   15
　　　　the cats we ha now.
HODGE. By the Masse Dame Chat hays me so moved,
　　　　iche care not what I kyll, ma[2] God
　　　　avowe :
　　Go to then Tyb to this geare, holde up her tayle
　　　　and take her,
　　Chil see what devil is in her guts chil take the[3]
　　　　paines to rake her.
GAMMER. Rake a Cat Hodge, what woldst thou
　　　　do?[1]
HODGE.　　　　　What thinckst that cham not able?
　　Did not Tom Tankard rake his Curtal toore[3] day   20
　　　　standing in the stable?
GAMMER. Soft, be content, lets here what newes
　　　　Cocke bringeth from maist Rat.
　　　　　　　　[*Enter* COCKE.]
COCKE. Gammer chave ben ther as you bad, you
　　　　wot wel about what.
　　Twill not be long before he come, ich durst
　　　　sweare of a booke.
　　He byds you see ye be at home, and there for him
　　　　to looke.
GAMMER. Where didst thou find him boy, was he not   25
　　　　wher I told thee?
COCKE. Yes, yes even at Hob Filchers house, by him
　　　　that bought and solde me.
　　A cup of ale had in his hand, and a crab lay in the
　　　　fyer,
　　Chad much a do to go and come, al was so ful of
　　　　myer :
　　And Gammer one thing I can tel, Hob Filchers
　　　　naule was loste
　　And Doctor Rat found it againe, hard beside the   30
　　　　doore poste,
　　I chould a penny can say something, your neele
　　　　againe to fet.

2 *ma :* I make.　　　　　　　3 *toore :* the other.

GAMMER. Cham glad to heare so much Cocke, then
           trust he wil not let,[4]
    To helpe us herein best he can, therfore tyl time
           he come
    Let us go in, if there be ought to get thou shalt
           have some.[4]   [*Exeunt.*]

          THE IIII. ACTE.   THE I. SCEANE.[1]

              [*Enter*] DOCTOR RAT.
DOCTOR RAT. [*To the audience.*] A Man were better
           twenty times be a bandog and barke,
    Then here among such a sort, be parish priest or
           clarke
    Where he shal never be at rest, one pissing while
           a day
    But he must trudge about the towne, this way, and
           that way,
    Here to a drab, there to a theefe, his shoes to teare   5
           and rent
    And that which is worst of al, at every knaves com-
           maundement.
    I had not sit the space, to drinke two pots of ale
    But Gammer Gurtons sory boy, was straite way at
           my taile,
    And she was sicke, and I must come, to do I wot
           not what,
    If once her fingers end but ake, trudge, call for   10
           Doctor Rat,
    And when I come not at their call, I only therby
           loose,
    For I am sure to lacke therfore, a tythe pyg or a
           goose :
    I warrant you when truth is knowen, and told they
           have their tale
    The matter where about I come, is not worth a
           half peny worth of ale,
    Yet must I talke so sage and smothe, as though I   15
           were a glosier[1]

4 *let :* hesitate.   IIII. ACTE.   I SCEANE.
                                  1 *glosier :* flatterer.

Els or the yere come at an end, I shal be sure the
    loser.
What worke ye Gammer Gurton? hoow,[2] here is
    your frend M. Rat.
    [*Enter* GAMMER GURTON.]

GAMMER. A good M. Doctor cha trobled, cha
    trobled you, chwot wel that.

DOCTOR RAT. How do ye woman : be ye lustie, or be
    ye not wel at ease?

GAMMER. By Gys[3] master cham not sick,[2] but   20
    yet chave a disease.
Chad a foule turne now of late, chill tell it you by
    gigs.

DOCTOR RAT. Hath[3] your browne cow cast hir
    calfe, or your sandy sowe her pigs?

GAMMER. No, but chad ben as good they had, as this
    ich wot weel.

DOCTOR RAT. What is the matter?

GAMMER.   Alas, alas, cha lost my good neele,
My neele I say, and wot ye what? a drab came by   25
    and spied it
And when I asked hir for the same, the filth flatly
    denied it.

DOCTOR RAT. What was she that?

GAMMER. A dame ich warrant you : she began to
    scold and brawle—
Alas, alas, come hether Hodge : this wretche[4]
    can tell you all.

THE IIII. ACTE.   THE II. SCEANE.

[*Enter*] HODGE [*to*] DOCTOR RAT [*and*] GAMMER.

HODGE. God morow gaffer Vicar.

DOCTOR RAT.   Come on fellow let us heare.
Thy dame hath sayd to me, thou knowest of all this
    geare,
Lets see what thou canst saie.

HODGE.   Bym fay sir that ye shall,
What matter so ever here was done, ich can tell
    your maship all.[1]

2 *hoow :* how now.   3 *Gys :* Jesus.

My Gammer Gurton heare see now,   5
   sat her downe at this doore, see now:
And as she began to stirre her, see now,
   her neele fell in the floore, see now,
And while her staffe she tooke, see now,
   at Gyb her Cat to flynge, see now,   10
Her neele was lost in the floore, see now
   is not this a wondrous thing, see now?
Then came the queane Dame Chat, see now
   to aske for hir blacke cup, see now:
And even here at this gate, see now: 15
   she tooke that neele up, see now.
My Gammer then she yeede,[1] see now
   hir neele againe to bring, see now
And was caught by the head see now
   is not this a wondrous thing, see now?   20
She tare my Gammers cote see now
   and scratched hir by the face, see now
Chad thought shad stopt hir throte, see now
   is not this a wondrous case, see now?
When ich saw this, ich was wrothe[2] see now   25
   and start betwene them twaine, see now
Els ich durst take a booke othe, see now
   my Gammer had bene slaine, see now.
GAMMER. This is even the whole matter, as Hodge
              has plainly tolde,
And chould faine be quiet for my part, that chould.   30
But helpe us good master, beseech ye that ye doo
Els shal we both be beaten and lose our neele too.
DOCTOR RAT. What wold ye have me to doo? tel me
              that I were gone.
I will do the best that I can, to set you both at one,
But be ye sure Dame Chat hath this your neele   35
              founde?
GAMMER. Here comes the man that see hir take it up
              of the ground,
Aske him your selfe master Rat if ye beleve not
              me :
And helpe me to my neele, for Gods sake and Saint
              Charitie.
            [*Enter* DICCON.]

IIII. ACTE.   II. SCEANE.   1 *yeede :* went.

DOCTOR RAT. Come nere Diccon and let us heare,
>   what thou can expresse.

Wilt thou be sworne thou seest Dame Chat, this   40
>   womans neele have?

DICCON. Nay by S. Benit wil I not, then might ye
>   thinke me rave.

GAMMER. Why, didst not thou tel me so even here,
>   canst thou for shame deny it?

DICCON. I mary Gammer : but I said I wold not abide
>   by it.

DOCTOR RAT. Will you say a thing, and not sticke to
>   it to trie it?

DICCON. Stick to it quoth you Master Rat, mary sir I   45
>   defy it,

Nay there is many an honest man, when he suche
>   blastes hath blowne

In his freindes eares, he woulde be loth the same by
>   him were knowne.[2]

If such a toy be used oft among the honestie[3]

It may beseme a simple man, of[3] your and my
>   degree.

DOCTOR RAT. Then we be never the nearer, for all that   50
>   you can tell.

DICCON. Yes mary sir, if ye will do by mine advise
>   and counsaile.

If mother Chat se al us here, she knoweth how the
>   matter goes.

Therefore I red[4] you three go hence, and within
>   keepe close,

And I will into Dame Chats house, and so the mat-
>   ter use,

That or you cold go twise to church, I warant you   55
>   here news,

She shal looke wel about hir, but I durst lay a
>   pledge,

Ye shal of Gammers neele, have shortly better
>   knowledge.

GAMMER. Now gentle Diccon do so, and good sir let
>   us trudge.

2 *by . . . knowne:* were   3 *the honestie:* "the qual-
>   known to have come   ity."
>   from him.   4 *red:* advise.

DOCTOR RAT. By the Masse I may not tarry so long to
    be your judge.

DICCON. Tys but a litle while man, what take so much   60
    paine,

If I here no newes of it I will come sooner againe.

HODGE. Tary so much, good master Doctor of your
    gentlenes.

DOCTOR RAT. Then let us hie us inward, and Diccon
    speede thy busines.

      [*Exeunt* DOCTOR RAT, GAMMER, *and* HODGE.]

DICCON. [*To the audience.*] Now sirs do you no more,
    but kepe my counsaile iuste,

And Doctor Rat shall thus catch, some good I trust,   65

But mother Chat my gossop, talke first withall I
    must :

For she must be chiefe captaine to lay the Rat in
    the dust.

        [*Enter* DAME CHAT.]

God deven Dame Chat in faith, and wel met in this
    place.

DAME CHAT. God deven my friend Diccon, whether
    walke ye this pace?

DICCON. By my truth even to you, to learne how the   70
    world goeth,

Hard ye no more of the other matter, say me now
    by your troth?

DAME CHAT. O yes Diccon, here the olde hoore, and
    Hodge that great knave,

But in faith I would thou hadst sene, o Lord I
    drest them brave.

She bare me two or three souses behind in the nape
    of the necke

Till I made hir olde wesen, to answere againe   75
    kecke :[5]

And Hodge that dirty dastard, that at hir elbow
    standes,

If one paire of legs had not bene worth two paire
    of hands

He had had his bearde shaven, if my nayles wold
    have served

5 *kecke :* the sound Gam-   pipe) made when Chat
  mer's weasand (wind-   struck it.

And not without a cause, for the knave it well de-
    served.

DICCON. By the Masse I can the thank wench, thou   80
    didst so wel acquite the.

DAME CHAT. And thadst seene him Diccon, it wold
    have made thee beshite the

For laughter. The horsen dolt at last caught up a
    club,

As though he would have slaine the master devil
    Belsabub,

But I set him soone inwarde.

DICCON.   O Lorde there is the thing

That Hodge is so offended, that makes him starte   85
    and flyng.

DAME CHAT. Why? makes the knave any moyling,[6]
    as ye have sene or hard?

DICCON. Even now I sawe him last, like a mad man
    he farde,

And sware by heaven and hell, he would a wreake
    his sorowe

And leve you never a hen on live, by .viii. of the
    clock to morow,

Therefore marke what I say, and my wordes see   90
    that ye trust,

Your hens be as good as dead, if ye leave them on
    the ruste.

DAME CHAT. The knave dare as wel go hang himself,
    as go upon my ground.

DICCON. Wel yet take hede I say, I must tel you my
    tale round,

Have you not about your house, behind your fur-
    nace or leade :[7]

A hole where a crafty knave, may crepe in for   95
    neade?

DAME CHAT. Yes by the Masse, a hole broke down,
    even within these ii. dayes.

DICCON. Hodge, he intendes this same night, to slip
    in there awayes.

DAME CHAT. O Christ that I were sure of it, in faith
    he shuld have his mede.

6 *moyling* : worrying, fidget-   7 *leade* : pot or cauldron.
  ing.

DICCON. Watch wel, for the knave wil be there as sure
          as is your crede.
  I wold spend my selfe a shilling: to have him   100
          swinged well.
DAME CHAT. I am as glad as a woman can be, of this
          thing to here tell.
  By Gogs bones when he commeth, now that I
          know the matter
  He shal sure at the first skip, to leape in scalding
          water:
  With a worse turne besides, when he will, let him
          come.
DICCON. I tell you as my sister, you know what   105
          meaneth mum.   [*Exit* DAME CHAT.]
  Now lacke I but my doctor, to play his part againe.
  And lo where he commeth towards, peradventure
          to his paine.
          [*Enter* DOCTOR RAT.]
DOCTOR RAT. What good newes Diccon? fellow, is
          mother Chat at home?
DICCON. She is syr, and she is not, but it please her
          to whome:
  Yet did I take her tardy, as subtle as she was.   110
DOCTOR RAT. The thing that thou wentst for, hast
          thou brought it to passe?
DICCON. I have done that I have done, be it worse,
          be it better.
  And Dame Chat at her wyts ende, I have almost
          set her.
DOCTOR RAT. Why, hast thou spied the neele? quickly
          I pray thee tell.
DICCON. I have spyed it in faith sir, I handled my   115
          selfe so well,
  And yet the crafty queane, had almost take my
          trumpe.
  But or all came to an ende, I set her in a dumpe:
DOCTOR RAT. How so I pray thee Diccon?
DICCON.   Mary syr will ye heare?
  She was clapt downe on the backside, by Cocks
          mother dere,
  And there she sat sewing a halter, or a bande,   120
  With no other thing save Gammers nedle in her
          hande,

As soone as any knocke, if the filth be in doubte,
She needes but once puffe, and her candle is out :
Now I sir knowing of every doore the pin,
Came nycely, and said no worde, till time I was   125
    within,
And there I sawe the neele, even with these two
    eyes,
Who ever say the contrary, I will sweare he lyes.
DOCTOR RAT. O Diccon that I was not there, then in
    thy steade.
DICCON. Well, if ye will be ordred, and do by my
    reade,
I will bring you to a place, as the house standes,   130
Where ye shall take the drab, with the neele in her
    handes.
DOCTOR RAT. For Gods sake do so Diccon, and I will
    gage my gowne
To geve thee a full pot, of the best ale in the
    towne.
DICCON. Follow me but a litle, and marke what I will
    say,
Lay downe your gown beside you, go to, come on   135
    your way :
    [DOCTOR RAT *removes his clerical gown.*]
Se ye not what is here? a hole wherin ye may
    creepe
Into the house, and sodenly unwares among them
    leape,
There shal ye finde the Bitchfox, and the neele to-
    gether.
Do as I bid you man, come on your wayes hether.
DOCTOR RAT. Art thou sure Diccon, the swil tub   140
    standes not here aboute?
DICCON. I was within my selfe man even now, ther is
    no doubt,
Go softly, make no noyse, give me your foote sir
    John,
Here will I waite upon you, tyl you come out
    anone.
    [DOCTOR RAT *climbs through the hole.*]
DOCTOR RAT. [*Within.*] Helpe Diccon, out alas, I shal
    be slaine among them.

DICCON. If they give you not the nedle, tel them that   145
    ye will hang them.
  Ware that! hoow my wenches, have ye caught the
    Foxe,
  That used to make revel, among your hennes and
    Cocks?
  Save his life yet for his order, though he susteine
    some paine.
  Gogs bread, I am afraide, they wil beate out his
    braine.   [*Exit.*]
    [*Re-enter* DOCTOR RAT *through the hole.*]
DOCTOR RAT. Wo worth the houre that I came heare.   150
  And wo worth him that wrought this geare,
  A sort of drabs and queanes have me blest,
  Was ever creature halfe so evill drest?
  Who ever it wrought, and first did invent it,
  He shall I warrant him, erre long repent it,   155
  I will spend all I have without my skinne
  But he shall be brought to the plight I am in,
  Master Bayly I trow, and he be worth his eares,
  Will snaffle these murderers and all that them
    beares,
  I will surely neither byte nor suppe   160
  Till I fetch him hether, this matter to take up.
                      [*Exit.*]

THE V. ACTE. THE I. SCEANE.

[*Enter*] MAYSTER BAYLYE, DOCTOR RAT,
    [*and* SCAPETHRYFT.]
MAYSTER BAYLYE. I can perceive none other, I speke
    it from my hart,
  But either ye ar in al the fault or els in the greatest
    part.
DOCTOR RAT. If it be counted his fault, besides all his
    greeves
  When a poore man is spoyled : and beaten among
    theeves?
  Then I confesse my fault herein, at this season,   5
  But I hope you wil not judge so much against
    reason.

MAYSTER BAYLYE. And me thinkes by your owne tale,
of all that ye name,
  If any plaid the theefe you were the very same.
  The women they did nothing, as your words make
probation,
  But stoutly withstood your forcible invasion.   10
  If that a theefe at your window, to enter should
begin,
  Wold you hold forth your hand, and helpe to pull
him in :
  Or you wold kepe him out? I pray you answere me.
DOCTOR RAT. Mary kepe him out, and a good cause
why :
  But I am no theefe sir but an honest learned   15
Clarke.
MAYSTER BAYLYE. Yea, but who knoweth that, when
he meets you in the darke?
  I am sure your learning shines not out at your
nose,
  Was it any marvaile, though the poore woman
arose
  And start up, being afraide of that was in hir
purse?
  Me thinke you may be glad that your lucke was   20
no worse.
DOCTOR RAT. Is not this evill ynough, I pray you as
you thinke? *Showing his broken head.*
MAYSTER BAYLYE. Yea but a man in the darke, if
chaunces do wincke,
  As soone he smites his father, as any other man,
  Because for lacke of light, discerne him he ne can,
  Might it not have ben your lucke, with a spit to   25
have ben slaine?
DOCTOR RAT. I thinke I am litle better, my scalpe is
cloven to the braine,
  If there be all the remedy, I know who beares the
knockes.[1]
MAYSTER BAYLYE. By my troth and well worthy, be-
sides to kisse the stockes
  To come in on the backe side, when ye might go
about,
  I know non such, unles they long to have their   30
braines knockt out.

DOCTOR RAT. Well, wil you be so good sir, as talke
    with Dame Chat?

And know what she intended : I aske no more but
    that.

MAYSTER BAYLYE. [*To* SCAPETHRYFT.] Let her be
    called fellow because of master Doctor.
                    [*Exit* SCAPETHRYFT.]

I warrant in this case, she wil be hir owne Proctor,

She wil tel hir owne tale in metter or in prose,   35

And byd you seeke your remedy, and so go wype
    your nose.

THE V. ACTE.   THE II. SCEANE.

[*Enter* SCAPETHRYFT *with* DAME] CHAT [*to*]
    MAYSTER BAYLYE [*and*] DOCTOR RAT.

MAYSTER BAYLYE. Dame Chat, master doctor upon
    you here complained

That you and your maides shuld him much mis-
    order.

And taketh many an oth, that no word he fained,

Laying to your charge, how you thought him to
    murder :

And on his part againe, that same man saith   5
    furder

He never offended you in word nor intent,

To heare you answer hereto, we have now for you
    sent.

DAME CHAT. That I wold have murdered him, fye on
    him wretch,

And evil mought he thee[1] for it, our Lord I be-
    sech,[1]

I will swere on al the bookes that opens and   10
    shuttes

He faineth this tale out of his owne guttes,

For this seven weeks with me, I am sure he sat not
    downe,

Nay ye have other minions, in the other end of the
    towne,

V. ACTE. II. SCEANE.
   1 *thee :* prosper.

Where ye were liker to catch such a blow,
Then any where els, as farre as I know. 15

MAYSTER BAYLYE. Belike then master Doctor, yon
stripe there ye got not?

DOCTOR RAT. Thinke you I am so mad, that where I
was bet,[2] I wot not?
Will ye beleve this queane, before she hath tryd it?
It is not the first dede she hath done and afterward denide it.

DAME CHAT. What man, will you say I broke your 20
head?

DOCTOR RAT. How canst thou prove the contrary?

DAME CHAT. Nay, how provest thou that I did the
deade?

DOCTOR RAT. To plainly, by S. Mary.
This profe I trow may serve, though I no word
spoke.
Showing his broken head.

DAME CHAT. Bicause thy head is broken, was it I that 25
it broke?
I saw thee Rat I tel thee, not once within this fortnight.

DOCTOR RAT. No mary, thou sawest me not, for why
thou hadst no light,
But I felt thee for al the darke, beshrew thy smothe
cheekes,
And thou groped me, this wil declare, any day this
six weekes.
Showing his heade.

MAYSTER BAYLYE. Answere me to this M. Rat, when 30
caught you this harme of yours?

DOCTOR RAT. A while ago sir, God he knoweth,
within les then these ii. houres.

MAYSTER BAYLYE. Dame Chat was there none with
you : (confesse I'faith) about that
season.
What woman, let it be what it wil, tis neither
felony nor treason.

DAME CHAT. Yes by my faith master Baylye, there was
a knave not farre

2 *bet :* beaten.

Who caught one good Philup on the brow, with a   35
    dore barre

And well was he worthy, as it semed to mee,

But what is that to this man, since this was not
    hee?

MAYSTER BAYLYE. Who was it then? lets here.

DOCTOR RAT.   Alas sir, aske you that?

Is it not made plain inough (by the owne mouth
    of Dame Chat)

The time agreeth, my head is broken, her tong can   40
    not lye,

Onely upon a bare nay she saith it was not I.

DAME CHAT. No mary was it not indeede ye shal here
    by this one thing,

This after noone a frend of mine, for good wil gave
    me[2] warning

And bad me wel loke to my ruste, and al my
    Capons pennes,

For if I toke not better heede, a knave wold have   45
    my hennes,

Then I to save my goods, toke so much pains as
    him to watch

And as good fortune served me, it was my
    chaunce him for to catch.

What strokes he bare away, or other what was his
    gaines

I wot not, but sure I am, he had something for
    his paines.

MAYSTER BAYLYE. Yet telles thou not who it was.

DAME CHAT.   Who? it was a false theefe,   50

That came like a false Foxe, my pullaine[3] to kil
    and mischeefe.

MAYSTER BAYLYE. But knowest thou not his name?

DAME CHAT.   I know it but what than?

It was that crafty cullyon Hodge, my Gammer
    Gurtons man.

MAYSTER BAYLYE. [To SCAPETHRYFT.] Cal me the
         knave hether, he shal sure kysse the
         stockes.   [Exit SCAPETHRYFT.]

I shall teach him a lesson, for filching hens or   55
    cocks.

3 *pullaine:* poultry.

DOCTOR RAT. I marvaile Master Baylye, so bleared be
        your eyes.

  An egge is not so ful of meate, as she is ful of lyes :
  When she hath playd this pranke, to excuse al this
        geare,
  She layeth the fault in such a one, as I know was
        not there.

DAME CHAT. Was he not thear? loke on his pate, that   60
        shal be his witnes.

DOCTOR RAT. I wold my head were half so hole, I wold
        seeke no redresse.

        [*Enter* GAMMER GURTON.]

MAYSTER BAYLYE. God bless you Gammer Gurton.

GAMMER.   God dylde[4] you master mine.

MAYSTER BAYLYE. Thou hast a knave within thy
        house, Hodge, a servant of thine.

  They tel me that busy knave, is such a filching one,
  That Hen, Pig, goose or capon, thy neighbour can   65
        have none.

GAMMER. By God cham much ameved, to heare any
        such reporte :

  Hodge was not wont ich trow, to bave[5] him in that
        sort.

DAME CHAT. A theevisher knave is not on live, more
        filching, nor more false.

  Many a truer man then he, hase hanged up by the
        halse.[6]

  And thou his dame of al his theft, thou art the sole   70
        receaver.

  For Hodge to catch, and thou to kepe, I never
        knew none better.

GAMMER. Sir reverence[7] of your masterdome, and
        you were out adoore,

  Chold be so bolde for al hir brags, to cal hir arrant
        whoore,

  And ich knew Hodge so bad as tow,[8] ich wish me
        endlesse sorow

  And chould not take the pains, to hang him up be-   75
        fore to morow?

4 *dylde :* reward.   7 *Sir reverence :* Saving the
5 *bave :* behave.   reverence.
6 *halse :* neck.   8 *tow :* thou.

DAME CHAT. What have I stolne from the or thine?
    thou ilfavored olde trot.

GAMMER. A great deale more (by Gods blest,) then
    chever by the got,

That thou knowest wel I neade not say it.

MAYSTER BAYLYE.   Stoppe there I say,

And tel me here I pray you, this matter by the
    way :

How chaunce Hodge is not here? him wold I faine   80
    have had.

GAMMER. Alas sir, heel be here anon, ha be handled
    to bad.

DAME CHAT. Master Baylye, sir ye be not such a foole
    wel I know,

But ye perceive by this lingring, there is a pad[9] in
    the straw.

Thinking that HODGE *his head was broke, and*
    that GAMMER *wold not let him come*
    before them.

GAMMER. Chil shew you his face, ich warrant the, lo
    now where he is.

[*Enter* SCAPETHRYFT *with* HODGE.]

MAYSTER BAYLYE. Come on fellow, it is tolde me thou   85
    art a shrew iwysse,

Thy neighbours hens thou takest, and playes the
    two legged foxe,

Their chikens and their capons to, and now and
    then their Cocks.

HODGE. Ich defy them al that dare it say, cham as true
    as the best.

MAYSTER BAYLYE. Wart not thou take within this
    houre, in Dame Chats hens nest?

HODGE. Take there? no master chold not dot,[10] for a   90
    house ful of gold.

DAME CHAT. Thou or the devil in thy cote, sweare this
    I dare be bold.

DOCTOR RAT. Sweare me no swearing quean, the devill
    he geve the sorow,

Al is not worth a gnat, thou canst sweare till to
    morow,

9 *pad :* toad. The expression   10 *dot :* do it.
  is proverbial.

Where is the harme he hath? shew it by Gods
    bread,
Ye beat him with a witnes, but the stripes light on   95
    my head.

HODGE. Bet me? Gogs blessed body, chold first ich
    trow have burst the.
Ich thinke and chad my hands loose callet chould
    have crust the.

DAME CHAT. Thou shitten knave I trow thou knowest
    the ful weight of my fist.
I am fowly deceived, onles thy head and my doore
    bar kyste.

HODGE. Hold thy chat whore, thou criest so loude, can   100
    no man else be hard.

DAME CHAT. Well knave, and I had the alone, I wold
    surely rap thy costard.[11]

MAYSTER BAYLYE. Sir answer me to this, is thy head
    whole or broken?

DAME CHAT. Yea master Baylye, blest be every good
    token.

HODGE. Is my head whole? ich warrant you, tis
    neither scurvy nor scald.
What you foule beast, does think tis either pild[12]   105
    or bald?
Nay ich thanke God : chil not for al that thou
    maist spend
That chad one scab on my narse, as brode as thy
    fingers end.

MAYSTER BAYLYE. Come nearer heare.

HODGE.   Yes. That ich dare.

MAYSTER BAYLYE.   By Our Lady here is no harme,
Hodges head is hole ynough, for al Dame Chats
    charme.

DAME CHAT. By Gogs blest how ever the thing he   110
    clockes or smolders,[13]
I know the blowes he bare away, either with head
    or shoulders.
Camest thou not knave within this houre, creping
    into my pens

11 *costard* : pate.   13 *clockes or smolders* :
12 *pild* : shorn.   cloaks or smothers.

And there was caught within my hous, groping
    among my hens?

HODGE. A plage both on thy hens and the, a carte
    whore, a carte,

Chould I were hanged as hie as a tree, and chware   115
    as false as thou art.

Geve my Gammer again her washical,[14] thou stole
    away in thy lap.

GAMMER. Yea Mayster Baylye there is a thing, you
    know not on may hap.

This drab she kepes away my good, the devil he
    might her snare.

Ich pray you that ich might have, a right action on
    her.

DAME CHAT. Have I thy good old filth, or any such   120
    old sowes?

I am as true, I wold thou knew, as skin betwene
    thy browes.

GAMMER. Many a truer hath ben hanged, though you
    escape the daunger.

DAME CHAT. Thou shalt answer by Gods pity, for this
    thy foule slaunder.

MAYSTER BAYLYE. Why, what can ye charge hir
    withal? to say so, ye do not well.

GAMMER. Mary a vengeance to hir hart, that whore   125
    hase stoln my neele.

DAME CHAT. Thy nedle old witch, how so? it were
    almes[15] thy scul to knock.

So didst thou say, the other day, that I had stolne
    thy Cock

And rosted him to my breakfast, which shal not be
    forgotten.

The devil pul out thy lying tong, and teeth that be
    so rotten.

GAMMER. Geve me my neele, as for my cocke, chould   130
    be very loth

That chuld here tel he shuld hang, on thy fals faith
    and troth.

MAYSTER BAYLYE. Your talke is such, I can scarse
    learne who shuld be most in fault.

14 *washical*: whatcha call it.   15 *almes*: charity.

GAMMER. Yet shal ye find no other wight, save she,
    by bred and salt.

MAYSTER BAYLYE. Kepe ye content a while, se that
    your tonges ye holde,

Me thinkes you shuld remembre, this is no place to   135
    scolde.

How knowest thou Gammer Gurton, Dame Chat
    thy nedle had?

GAMMER. To name you sir the party, chould not be
    very glad.

MAYSTER BAYLYE. Yea but we must nedes heare it,
    and therfore say it boldly.

GAMMER. Such one as told the tale, full soberly and
    coldly,

Even he that loked on, wil sweare on a booke: 140

What time this drunken gossip, my faire long neele
    up tooke

Diccon (master) the Bedlam, cham very sure ye
    know him.

MAYSTER BAYLYE. A false knave by Gods pitie, ye
    were but a foole to trow him,

I durst aventure wel the price of my best cap,

That when the end is knowen, all wil turne to a   145
    jape,

Tolde he not you that besides she stole your Cocke
    that tyde?

GAMMER. No master no indede, for then he shuld
    have lyed,

My cocke is I thanke Christ, safe and wel a fine.[16]

DAME CHAT. Yea but that ragged colt, that whore, that
    Tyb of thine

Said plainly thy cocke was stolne, and in my house   150
    was eaten,

That lying cut[17] is lost, that she is not swinged and
    beaten,

And yet for al my good name, it were a small
    amendes.

I picke not this geare (hearst thou) out of my fin-
    gers endes

But he that hard it told me, who thou of late didst
    name

16 *a fine:* in fine, in sum.   17 *cut:* cut-tail horse or geld-
                           ing.

Diccon whom al men knowes, it was the very   155
    same.

MAYSTER BAYLYE. This is the case, you lost your nedle
    about the dores

And she answeres againe, she hase no cocke of
    yours,

Thus in your[3] talke and Action, from that you
    do intend,

She is whole five mile wide, from that she doth de-
    fend :

Will you saie she hath your Cocke?

GAMMER.   No mery[18] sir that chil not.   160

MAYSTER BAYLYE. Will you confesse hir neele?

DAME CHAT.   Will I? no sir will I not.[4]

MAYSTER BAYLYE. Then there lieth all the matter.

GAMMER.   Soft master by the way,

Ye know she could do litle, and she cold not say
    nay.

MAYSTER BAYLYE. Yea but he that made one lie about
    your Cock stealing,

Wil not sticke to make another, what time lies be   165
    in dealing.

I weene, the ende wil prove, this brawle did first
    arise,

Upon no other ground, but only Diccons lyes.

DAME CHAT. Though some be lyes as you belike have
    espyed them,

Yet other some be true, by proof I have wel tryed
    them.

MAYSTER BAYLYE. What other thing beside this, Dame
    Chat?

DAME CHAT.   Mary syr even this,   170

The tale I tolde before, the selfe same tale it was
    his,

He gave me like a frende, warning against my
    losse,

Els had my hens be stolne, eche one, by Gods
    crosse :

He tolde me Hodge wold come, and in he came
    indeede,

18 *mery* : marry, by Mary.

But as the matter chaunsed, with greater hast then   175
  speede,

This truth was said, and true was found, as truly I
  report.

MAYSTER BAYLYE. If Doctor Rat be not deceived, it
  was of another sort.

DOCTOR RAT. By Gods mother thou and he, be a cople
  of suttle foxes,

Betweene you and Hodge, I beare away the boxes,

Did not Diccon apoynt the place, wher thou   180
  shuldst stand to mete him?

DAME CHAT. Yes by the Masse, and if he came, bad
  me not sticke to speet[19] hym.

DOCTOR RAT. Gods sacrament the villain knave hath
  drest us round about,

He is the cause of all this brawle, that dyrty shitten
  loute :

When Gammer Gurton here complained, and made
  a ruful mone

I heard him sweare that you had gotten, hir nedle   185
  that was gone,

And this to try he furder said, he was ful loth how
  be it

He was content with small adoe, to bring me
  where to see it.

And where ye sat, he said ful certain, if I wold
  folow his read

Into your house a privy way, he wold me guide and
  leade,

And where ye had it in your hands, sewing about   190
  a clowte,

And set me in the backe hole, therby to finde you
  out :

And whiles I sought a quietnes, creping upon my
  knees,

I found the weight of your dore bar, for my reward
  and fees,

Such is the lucke that some men gets, while they
  begin to mel[20]

19 *sticke to speet :* hesitate to   20 *mel :* interfere.
 spit.

In setting at one such as were out, minding to make   195
   al wel.

HODGE. Was not wel blest Gammer, to scape that
   stoure?[21, 5] and chad ben there

Then chad ben drest be like, as ill by the Masse,
   as gaffar vicar.

MAYSTER BAYLYE. Mary sir, here is a sport alone, I
   loked for such an end.

If Diccon had not playd the knave, this had ben
   some amend.

My Gammer here he made a foole, and drest hir as   200
   she was,

And goodwife Chat he set to scole, till both partes
   cried alas,

And Doctor Rat was not behind, whiles Chat his
   crown did pare,

I wold the knave had ben starke blind, if Hodge
   had not his share.

HODGE. Cham meetly wel sped alredy amongs, cham
   drest like a coult

And chad not had the better wit, chad bene made   205
   a doult.

MAYSTER BAYLYE. [To SCAPETHRYFT.] Sir knave make
   hast Diccon were here, fetch him
   where ever he bee.

                       [*Exit* SCAPETHRYFT.]

DAME CHAT. Fie on the villaine, fie, fie, that makes
   us thus agree.

GAMMER. Fie on him knave, with al my hart, now fie,
   and fie againe.

DOCTOR RAT. Now fie on him may I best say, whom
   he hath almost slaine.

   [*Re-enter* SCAPETHRYFT *with* DICCON.]

MAYSTER BAYLYE. Lo where he commeth at hand,   210
   belike he was not fare.

Diccon heare be two or three, thy company can
   not spare.

DICCON. God blesse you, and you may be blest so
   many al at once.

DAME CHAT. Come knave, it were a good deed to
   geld the by Cockes bones.

  21 *stoure :* commotion.

Seest not thy handiwarke? Sir Rat can ye forbeare
    him?

DICCON. A vengeance on those hands lite, for my   215
    hands cam not nere hym.

The horsen priest hath lift the pot, in some of
    these ale wyves chayres

That his head wolde not serve him, belyke to come
    downe the stayres.

MAYSTER BAYLYE. Nay soft, thou maist not play the
    knave, and have this language to.

If thou thy tong bridle a while, the better maist
    thou do,

Confesse the truth as I shall aske, and cease a while   220
    to fable.

And for thy fault I promise the, thy handling
    shal be reasonable.

Hast thou not made a lie or two, to set these two
    by the eares?

DICCON. What if I have? five hundred such have I
    seene within these seven yeares :

I am sory for nothing else but that I see not the
    sport

Which was betwene them when they met, as they   225
    them selves report.

MAYSTER BAYLYE. The greatest thing, Master Rat, ye
    se how he is drest.

DICCON. What devil nede he be groping so depe, in
    goodwife Chats hens nest?

MAYSTER BAYLYE. Yea but it was thy drift to bring
    him into the[6] briars.

DICCON. Gods bread, hath not such an old foole, wit
    to save his eares?

He showeth himselfe herein ye see, so very a coxe,[22]   230

The Cat was not so madly alured by the Foxe,

To run into the snares, was set for him doubtlesse,

For he leapt in for myce, and this sir John for
    madnes.

DOCTOR RAT. Well and ye shift no better, ye losel,
    lyther,[23] and lasye,

22 *coxe*: coxcomb, fool.   23 *lyther*: sluggish.

I will go neare for this, to make ye leape at a   235
    Dasye.[24]

In the kings[(1)] name Master Baylye, I charge you
    set him fast.

DICCON. What fast at cardes, or fast on slepe? it is the
    thing I did last.

DOCTOR RAT. Nay fast in fetters false varlet, according
    to thy deedes.

MAYSTER BAYLYE. Master doctor ther is no remedy, I
    must intreat you needes

Some other kinde of punishment.

DOCTOR RAT.   Nay by all Halowes,   240
His punishment if I may judg, shal be naught els
    but the gallous.

MAYSTER BAYLYE. That were to sore, a spiritual man
    to be so extreame.

DOCTOR RAT. Is he worthy any better, sir how do ye
    judge and deame?

MAYSTER BAYLYE. I graunt him worthie[7] punish-
    ment, but in no wise so great.

GAMMER. It is a shame ich tel you plaine, for such   245
    false knaves intreat.

He has almost undone us al, that is as true as
    steele :

And yet for al this great ado cham never the nere
    my neele.

MAYSTER BAYLYE. Canst thou not say any thing to
    that Diccon, with least or most?

DICCON. Yea mary sir, thus much I can say wel, the
    nedle is lost.

MAYSTER BAYLYE. Nay canst not thou tel which way,   250
    that nedle may be found?

DICCON. No by my fay sir, though I might have an
    hundred pound.

HODGE. Thou lier lickdish, didst not say the neele
    wold be gitten?

DICCON. No Hodge, by the same token, you were[8]
    that time beshitten?

For feare of Hobgobling, you wot wel what I
    meane,

24 *leape at a Dasye :* be
    hanged.

As long as it is sence, I feare me yet ye be scarce   255
            cleane.

MAYSTER BAYLYE. Wel Master Rat, you must both
            learne, and teach us to forgeve.

Since Diccon hath confession made, and is so
            cleane shreve,

If ye to me conscent, to amend this heavie
            chaunce,

I wil injoyne him here, some open kind of pen-
            aunce :

Of this condition, where ye know my fee is twenty   260
            pence :

For the bloodshed, I am agreed with you here to
            dispence,

Ye shal go quite,[25] so that ye graunt, the matter
            now to run,

To end with mirth emong us al, even as it was be-
            gun.

DAME CHAT. Say yea master vicar, and he shal sure
            confes to be your detter,

And al we that be heare present, wil love you   265
            much the better.

DOCTOR RAT. My partis the worst, but since you al
            here on agree,

Go even to[26] master Baylye, let it be so for mee.

MAYSTER BAYLYE. How saiest thou Diccon, art con-
            tent this shal on me depend?

DICCON. Go to M. Baylye say on your mind, I know
            ye are my frendl

MAYSTER BAYLYE. Then marke ye wel, to recom-   270
            pence this thy former action

Because thou hast offended al, to make them sat-
            isfaction,

Before their faces, here kneele downe, and as I shal
            the teach.

For thou shalt take on othe, of Hodges leather
            breache

First for master Doctor, upon paine of his cursse,

Where he wil pay for al, thou never draw thy   275
            pursse,

25 *quite :* quit, without hav-   26 *Go even to :* Go ahead
    ing to pay the fee.   then.

And when ye meete at one pot, he shal have the
    first pull,

And thou shalt never offer him the cup, but it be
    full.

To goodwife Chat thou shalt be sworne, even on
    the same wyse,

If she refuse thy money once, never to offer it
    twise.

Thou shalt be bound by the same here, as thou dost   280
    take it

When thou maist drinke of free cost, thou never
    forsake it :

For Gammer Gurtons sake, againe sworne shalt
    thou bee

To helpe hir to hir nedle againe if it do lie in thee

And likewise be bound : by the vertue of that

To be of good abering[27] to Gyb hir great Cat :   285

Last of al for Hodge, the othe to scanne,

Thou shalt never take him, for fine gentleman.

HODGE. Come on fellow Diccon chalbe even with thee
    now.

MAYSTER BAYLYE. Thou wilt not sticke to do this
    Diccon I trow.

DICCON. No by my fathers skin, my hand downe I   290
    lay it!

Loke as I have promised, I wil not denay it,

But Hodge take good heede now, thou do not
    beshite me.

And gave him a good blow on the buttocke.

HODGE. Gogs hart thou false villaine dost thou bite
    me?

MAYSTER BAYLYE. What Hodge doth he hurt the or
    ever he begin?

HODGE. He thrust me into the buttocke, with a bodkin   295
    or a pin,

    [He withdraws the needle.]

I saie Gammer, Gammer!

GAMMER.   How now Hodge, how now?

HODGE. Gods malt Gammer Gurton.

GAMMER.   Thou art mad ich trow.

HODGE. Will you see the devil Gammer?

27 *abering :* conduct.

GAMMER.   The devil, sonne, God blesse us.

HODGE. Chould iche were hanged Gammer.

GAMMER.   Mary so[9] ye might dresse us.

HODGE. Chave it by the Masse Gammer.

GAMMER.   What, not my neele Hodge?   300

HODGE. Your Neele Gammer, your neele.

GAMMER.   No fie, dost but dodge.

HODGE. Cha found your neele Gammer, here in my
               hand be it.

GAMMER. For al the loves on earth Hodge, let me see
               it.

HODGE. Soft Gammer.

GAMMER.   Good Hodge.

HODGE.   Soft ich say, tarie a while.

GAMMER. Nay sweete Hodge say truth, and do not   305
               me begile.

HODGE. Cham sure on it ich warrant you : it goes no
               more a stray.

GAMMER. Hodge when I speake so faire : wilt stil
               say me nay?

HODGE. Go neare the light Gammer, tis[10] wel in
               faith good lucke :

Chwas almost undone; twas so far in my buttocke.

GAMMER. Tis min owne deare neele Hodge, sykerly I   310
               wot.[28]

HODGE. Cham I not a good sonne Gammer, cham I
               not?

GAMMER. Christs blessing light on thee, hast made
               me for ever.

HODGE. Ich knew that ich must finde it, els choud a
               had it never.

DAME CHAT. By my troth Gossyp Gurton, I am even
               as glad

As though I mine owne selfe as good a turne had :   315

MAYSTER BAYLYE. And I by my concience, to see it so
               come forth,

Rejoyce so much at it, as three nedles be worth.

DOCTOR RAT. I am no whit sory to see you so rejoyce.

DICCON. Nor I much the gladder for al this noyce :

Yet say gramercy Diccon, for springing of the   320
               game.

28 *sykerly I wot :* certainly I
   know.

GAMMER. Grammercy Diccon twenty times, o how
              glad cham,
  If that chould do so much, your masterdome to
              come hether,
  Master Rat, goodwife Chat, and Diccon together :
  Cha but one halfpeny, as far as iche know it,
  And chil not rest this night, till ich bestow it.   325
  If ever ye love me, let us go in and drinke.
MAYSTER BAYLYE. I am content if the rest thinke as
              I thinke?
  Master Rat it shal be best for you if we so doo,
  Then shall you warme you and dresse your self too.
DICCON. Soft syrs, take us with you, the company   330
              shal be the more,
  As proude coms behinde they say, as any goes
                     before.   [*Exeunt all but* DICCON.]
  [*To the audience.*] But now my good masters since
              we must be gone
  And leave you behinde us, here all alone :
  Since at our last ending thus mery we bee,
  For Gammer Gurtons nedle sake, let us have a   335
                     plaudytie.   [*Exit.*]

Finis, Gurton. Perused and alowed, &c.
Imprinted at London
in Fleetestreate beneath the Conduite,
at the signe of S. John Evangelist, by
Thomas Colwell.
1575.

FERREX AND PORREX

or

GORBODUC

by

THOMAS SACKVILLE AND THOMAS NORTON

¶ The Tragidie of Ferrex
and Porrex,
ſet forth without addition or alte=
ration but altogether as the ſame was ſhewed
on ſtage before the Queenes Maieſtie,
about nine yeares paſt, *vz.* the
xviij. day of Ianuarie. 1561.
by the gentlemen of the
Inner Temple.

Seen and allowed. &c.

🕭 Imprinted at London by
Iohn Daye, dwelling ouer
Alderſgate.

Gorboduc, king of Brittaine,[1] divided his realme in his lifetime to his sonnes, *Ferrex* and *Porrex.* The sonnes fell to discention.[1] The yonger killed the elder. The mother, that more dearely loved the elder, for revenge killed the   **5** yonger. The people, moved with the crueltie of the fact,[1] rose in rebellion and slew both father and mother. The nobilitie assembled and most terribly destroyed the rebels. And afterwardes for want of issue of the prince whereby the succession of the   **10** crowne became uncertaine, they fell to civill warre,[2] in which both they and many of their issues were slaine, and the land for a long time almost desolate and miserably wasted.

THE P[RINTER] TO THE READER[1]

Where this Tragedie was for furniture of part of the grand Christmasse in the Inner Temple,[1] first written about nine yeares agoe by the right honourable Thomas now Lorde Buckherst, and by T. Norton,[2] and after shewed before her Maj-   **5** estie, and never intended by the authors thereof to be published, yet one W. G.,[3] getting a copie therof at some yongmans hand that lacked a litle money and much discretion, in the last great plage *anno* 1565, about v. yeares past, while the said   **10** Lord was out of England,[4] and T. Norton farre out of London, and neither of them both made privie, put it forth excedingly corrupted,[5] even as if by meanes of a broker for hire, he should have entised into his house a faire maide   **15** and done her villanie, and after all to be-scratched[6] her face, torne her apparell, be-rayed[1] and disfigured her, and then thrust her out of dores dishonested. In such plight after long wan-dring she came at length home to the sight of her   **20** frendes, who scant knew her but by a few tokens and markes remayning. They, the authors I meane,

---

1 *fact :* act, deed.   1 *berayed :* dirtied.

though they were very much displeased that she
so ranne abroad without leave, whereby she caught
her shame, as many wantons do, yet seing the   25
case as it is remedilesse, have for common honestie
and shamefastnesse new apparelled, trimmed, and
attired her in such forme as she was before. In
which better forme since she hath come to me, I
have harbored her for her frendes sake and her   30
owne, and I do not dout her parentes, the authors,
will not now be discontent that she goe abroad
among you good readers, so it be in honest companie. For she is by my encouragement and others
somewhat lesse ashamed of the dishonestie done   35
to her because it was by fraude and force. If she
be welcome among you and gently enterteined,
in favor of the house from whense she is descended,(7) and of her owne nature courteously
disposed to offend no man, her frendes will thanke 40
you for it. If not, but that she shall be still re-
proched with her former missehap, or quarelled
at by envious persons, she poore gentlewoman wil
surely play Lucreces part,(8) and of herself die for
shame, and I shall wishe that she had taried still 45
at home with me, where she was welcome, for she
did never put me to more charge, but this one
poore blacke gowne lined with white that I
have now geven her to goe abroad among you
withall.   50

GORBODUC, *King of Great Brittaine.*
VIDENA, *Queene and wife to king Gorboduc.*
FERREX, *elder sonne to king Gorboduc.*
PORREX, *yonger sonne to king Gorboduc.*
CLOTYN,[1] *Duke of Cornewall.*
FERGUS, *Duke of Albanye.*
MANDUD, *Duke of Loegris.*[2]
GWENARD, *Duke of Cumberland.*
EUBULUS, *Secretarie to the king.*[3]
AROSTUS, *a counsellor to the king.*[4]
DORDAN, *a counsellor assigned by the king to his eldest sonne Ferrex.*
PHILANDER, *a counsellor assigned by the king to his yongest[5] sonne Porrex.*
    (*Both being of the olde kinges counsell before.*)
HERMON, *a parasite remaining with Ferrex.*
TYNDAR, *a parasite remaining with Porrex.*
NUNTIUS, *a messenger of the elder brothers death.*
NUNTIUS, *a messenger of Duke Fergus rising in armes.*
MARCELLA, *a lady of the Queenes privie chamber.*
CHORUS, *foure auncient and sage men of Brittaine.*

[THE SCENE
BRITAIN.]

THE ORDER OF THE DOMME SHEW BEFORE
THE FIRST ACT[1] AND THE
SIGNIFICATION THEROF

First the Musicke of Violenze began to play, during which came in upon the stage sixe wilde men clothed in leaves, of whom the first bare on[1] his necke a fagot[1] of small stickes, which they all both severally and together assayed with all their strengthes to breake, but it could not be broken by them. At the length one of them plucked[2] out one of the stickes and brake it. And the rest, plucking out all the other stickes one

5

1 *fagot :* bundle.

after another, did easely breake them,[3] the   10
same being severed, which being conjoyned they
had before attempted in vaine. After they had this
done, they departed the stage, and the Musicke
ceased. Hereby was signified that a state knit in
unitie doth continue strong against all force but   15
being divided is easely destroyed, as befell upon
Duke Gorboduc, dividing his land to his two
sonnes which he before held in Monarchie, and
upon the discention of the brethren to whom it was
divided.   20

ACTUS PRIMUS. SCENA PRIMA.

[Enter] VIDENA [and] FERREX.

VIDENA. The silent night, that bringes the quiet pawse
From painefull travailes of the wearie day,
Prolonges my carefull[1] thoughtes and makes me
          blame
The slowe *Aurore,* that so for love or shame
Doth long delay to shewe her blushing face,   5
And now the day renewes my griefull[2] plaint.
FERREX. My gracious lady and my[1] mother deare,
Pardon my griefe for your so grieved minde,
To aske what cause tormenteth so your hart.
VIDENA. So great a wrong, and so unjust despite,   10
Without all cause, against all course of kinde![3]
FERREX. Such causelesse wrong and so unjust despite,
May have redresse, or at the least, revenge.
VIDENA. Neither, my sonne. Such is the froward[4] will,
The person such, such my missehappe and thine.   15
FERREX. Mine know I none, but grief for your dis-
          tresse.
VIDENA. Yes, mine for thine, my sonne. A father?
          No.
In kinde a father, not[2] in kindlinesse.[1]
FERREX. My father? Why? I know nothing at all,
Wherein I have misdone unto his grace.   20

ACTUS PRIMUS. SCENA PRIMA.   3 *kinde :* nature.
  1 *carefull :* full of care.   4 *froward :* perverse.
  2 *griefull :* full of grief.

VIDENA. Therefore, the more unkinde to thee and
        mee.
   For, knowing well (my sonne) the tender love
That I have ever borne and beare to thee,
He, greved thereat, is not content alone
To spoile thee of my sight,[2] my chiefest joye,   25
But thee, of thy birthright and heritage
Causelesse, unkindly, and in wrongfull wise,
Against all lawe and right, he will bereave.
Halfe of his kingdome he will geve away.

FERREX. To whom?

VIDENA.   Even to *Porrex*, his yonger sonne,   30
Whose growing pride I do so sore suspect,
That being raised to equall rule with thee,
Meethinkes I see his envious hart to swell,
Filled with disdaine and with ambicious hope.[3]
The end the Goddes do know, whose altars I   35
Full oft have made in vaine of cattell slaine
To send the sacred smoke to heavens throne,
For thee, my sonne, if thinges do[4] so succede,[5]
As now my jelous minde misdemeth sore.[6]

FERREX. Madame, leave care and carefull plaint for   40
        me,
Just hath my father bene to every wight.[7]
His first unjustice he will not extend
To me, I trust, that geve no cause therof.
My brothers pride shall hurt himselfe, not me.

VIDENA. So graunt the Goddes. But yet thy father so   45
Hath firmely fixed his unmoved minde,
That plaintes and prayers can no whit availe,
For those have I assaied, but even this day
He will endevour to procure assent
Of all his counsell to his fonde devise.[8]   50

FERREX. Their ancestors from race to race have borne
True fayth to my forefathers and their seede.
I trust they eke[9] will beare the like to me.

VIDENA. There resteth all. But if they faile thereof,
And if the end bring forth an ill[5] success,   55

5 *succede*: follow.
6 *misdemeth sore*: sorely
   fears.
7 *wight*: creature, person.

8 *fonde devise*: foolish device, plan.
9 *eke*: also.

On them and theirs the mischiefe shall befall,
And so I pray the Goddes requite it them,
And so they will, for so is wont to be.
When lordes, and trusted rulers under kinges,
To please the present fancie of the prince   60
With wrong transpose the course of governance,
Murders, mischiefe, or civill sword at length,
Or mutuall treason, or a just revenge,
When right succeding line returnes againe,
By *Joves* just judgement and deserved wrath,   65
Bringes them to cruell[6] and reprochfull death,
And rootes their names and kindredes from the
          earth.
FERREX. Mother, content you, you shall see the end.
VIDENA. The end? Thy end I feare. *Jove* end me first.
                                        [*Exeunt.*]

ACTUS PRIMUS. SCENA SECUNDA.

[*Enter*] GORBODUC, AROSTUS, PHILANDER,
          EUBULUS, [*and* CHORUS].
GORBODUC. My lords, whose grave advise and faithful
          aide
Have long upheld my honour and my realme
And brought me[1] to this age from[2] tender
          yeres,
Guidyng so great estate with great renowme,
Nowe more importeth mee,¹ than[3] erst,² to use   5
Your fayth and wisedome, whereby yet I reigne,
That when by death my life and rule shall cease,
The kingdome yet may with unbroken course
Have certayne prince, by whose undoubted right
Your wealth and peace may stand in[4] quiet   10
          stay,³
And eke that they whome nature hath preparde,
In time to take my place in princely seate,
While in their fathers tyme their pliant youth
Yeldes to the frame of skilfull governance,

ACTUS PRIMUS.   SCENA   2 *erst :* formerly.
SECUNDA.   3 *stay :* condition.
    1 *more   importeth   me :*   it
        matters more to me.

Maye so be taught and trayned in noble artes,   15
As what their fathers which have reigned before
Have with great fame derived downe to them,
With honour they may leave unto their seede
And not be thought[5] for their unworthy life,
And for their lawlesse swarvynge out of kinde,[4]   20
Worthy to lose what lawe and kind them gave,
But that they may preserve the common peace,
The cause that first began and still mainteines
The lyneall course of kinges inheritance.
For me, for myne, for you, and for the state,   25
Whereof both I and you have charge and care,
Thus do I meane to use your wonted fayth
To me and myne, and to your native lande.
My lordes, be playne without all wrie respect[5]
Or poysonous[6] craft to speake in pleasyng wise,   30
Lest as the blame of yll succedyng thinges
Shall light on you, so light the harmes also.
AROSTUS. Your good acceptance so (most noble king)
Of suche our[7] faithfulnesse as heretofore
We have employed in dueties to your grace,   35
And to this realme whose worthy head you are,
Well proves that neyther you mistrust at all,
Nor we shall neede in[8] boasting wise to shewe,
Our trueth to you, nor yet our wakefull care
For you, for yours, and for our native lande.   40
Wherefore (O kyng) I speake as one for[9] all,
Sithe all as one do beare you egall[6] faith:
Doubt not to use our counsells and our[10] aides,
Whose honours, goods and lyves are whole avowed
To serve, to ayde, and to defende your grace.   45
GORBODUC. My lordes, I thanke you all. This is the
        case :
Ye know, the Gods, who have the soveraigne care
For kings, for kingdomes, and for common weales,
Gave me two sonnes in my more lusty[7] age,
Who nowe in my decayeng[11] yeres are growen   50
Well towardes ryper state of minde and strength,
To take in hande some greater princely charge.

4 *kinde :* nature.   6 *egall :* equal.
5 *wrie respect :* ill-natured   7 *lusty :* vigorous.
     regard.

As yet they lyve and spende[12] hopefull daies,
With me and with their mother here in courte.
Their age nowe asketh other place and trade,   55
And myne also doth aske another chaunge,
Theirs to more travaile, myne to greater ease.
Whan fatall death shall ende my mortall life,
My purpose is to leave unto[13] them twaine
The realme divided into two sondry partes: 60
The one *Ferrex*, myne elder sonne, shall have,
The other shall the yonger[14] *Porrex* rule.
That both my purpose may more firmely[15]
          stande,
And eke that they may better rule their charge,
I meane forthwith to place them in the same,   65
That in my life they may both learne to rule
And I may joy to see their ruling well.
This is in summe, what I woulde have ye[16]
          wey:[8]
First whether ye allowe my whole devise
And thinke it good for me, for them, for you,   70
And for our countrey, mother of us all,
And if ye lyke it, and allowe it well,
Then for their guydinge and their governaunce,
Shew forth such meanes of circumstance[9]
As ye thinke meete to be both knowne and kept.   75
Loe, this is all, now tell me your advise.

AROSTUS. And this is much, and asketh great advise,
But for my part, my soveraigne lord and kyng,
This do I thinke. Your majestie doth know
How under you in justice and in peace   80
Great wealth and honour long we have enjoyed,
So as we can not seeme with gredie mindes
To wisshe for change of Prince or governaunce.
But if we[17] lyke your purpose and devise,
Our lyking must be deemed to proceede   85
Of rightfull reason and of heedefull care,
Not for ourselves, but for the[18] common state,
Sithe our owne state doth neede no better
          change.[10]

8 *wey*: weigh, consider.   10 *better change*: change for
9 *circumstance*: implemen-   the better.
    tation.

I thinke in all as erst your Grace hath saide.
Firste, when you shall unlode your aged mynde   90
Of hevye care and troubles manifolde
And laye the same upon my Lordes your sonnes,
Whose growing yeres may beare the burden long—
And long I pray the Goddes to graunt it so—
And in your life while you shall so beholde   95
Their rule, their vertues, and their noble deedes,
Suche as their kinde behighteth[11] to us all,
Great be the profites that shall growe therof.
Your age in quiet shall the longer last.
Your lasting age shal be their longer stay,   100
For cares of kynges, that rule as you have ruled,
For publique wealth and not for private joye,
Do wast mannes lyfe and hasten crooked age,
With furrowed face and with enfeebled lymmes,
To draw on creepyng death a swifter pace.   105
They two yet yong shall beare the parted[19]
            reigne
With greater ease, than one, nowe olde, alone,
Can welde[12] the whole, for whom muche harder is
With lessened strength the double weight to
            beare.
Your eye, your counsell, and the grave regarde   110
Of Father,[20] yea of such a fathers name,
Nowe at beginning of their sondred reigne,
When is the[21] hazarde of their whole successe,
Shall bridle so their force of youthfull heates,
And so restreine the rage of insolence,   115
Whiche most assailes the yonge and noble minds,
And so shall guide and traine in tempred stay
Their yet greene bending wittes with reverent
            awe,
As[22] now inured[13] with vertues at the first,
Custome (O king) shall bring delightfulnesse.   120
By use of vertue, vice shall growe in hate.
But if you so dispose it, that the daye
Which endes your life, shall first begin their[23]
            reigne,
Great is the perill what will[24] be the ende,

11 *kinde behighteth* : nature   12 *welde* : wield.
      assures, warrants.   13 *inured* : habituated.

When such beginning of such liberties   125
Voide of suche stayes as in your life do lye,
Shall leave them free to[25] randon of their will,
An open praie to traiterous flatterie,
The greatest pestilence of noble youthe.
Whiche perill shal be past, if in your life   130
Their tempred youthe with aged fathers awe,[1]
Be brought in ure[14] of skilfull stayednesse.[15]
And in your life their lives disposed so
Shall length your noble life in joyfulnesse.
Thus thinke I that your grace hath wisely thought,   135
And that your tender care of common weale,
Hath bred this thought, so to divide your lande,
And plant your sonnes to beare the present rule,
While you yet live to see their rulinge well,
That you may longer lyve by joye therein.   140
What furder meanes behovefull are and meete
At greater[26] leisure may your grace devise,
When all have said, and when we be agreed
If this be best to part the realme in twaine,
And place your sonnes in present governement.   145
Whereof as I have plainely said my mynde,
So woulde I here the rest of all my Lordes.
PHILANDER. In part I thinke as hath bene said before,
In parte agayne my minde is otherwise.
As for dividing of this realme in twaine,   150
And lotting out the same in egall partes
To either of my lordes your graces sonnes,
That thinke I best for this your realmes behofe,
For profite and advauncement of your sonnes,
And for your comforte and your honour eke.   155
But so to place them, while your life do[27] last,
To yelde to them your royall governaunce,
To be above them onely in the name
Of father, not in kingly state also,
I thinke not good for you, for them, nor us.   160
This kingdome since the bloudie civill fielde
Where *Morgan* slaine did yeld his conquered parte
Unto his cosins sworde in *Camberland*,[28], [2]
Conteineth all that whilome did suffice
Three noble sonnes of your forefather *Brute*.[3]   165

14 *ure* : use, custom.   15 *stayednesse* : constancy.

So your two sonnes it maye suffice also.[29]
The moe[16] the stronger, if they gree in one.[(4)]
The smaller compasse that the realme doth holde,
The easier is the swey thereof to welde,
The nearer Justice to the wronged poore,   170
The smaller charge,[17] and yet ynoughe for one.
And whan the region is divided so,
That brethren be the lordes of either parte,
Such strength doth nature knit betwene them[30]
        both,
In sondrie bodies by conjoyned love,   175
That not as two, but one of doubled force,
Eche is to other as a sure defence.
The noblenesse and glory of the one
Doth sharpe the courage of the others mynde
With vertuous envie to contende for praise.   180
And suche an egalnesse hath nature made,
Betwene the brethren of one fathers seede,
As an unkindly wrong it seemes to bee,
To throwe the brother[31] subject under feete
Of him whose peere he is by course of kinde,   185
And nature that did make this egalnesse,
Ofte so[32] repineth at so great a wrong,
That ofte she rayseth up a grudginge griefe,
In yonger brethren at the elders state,
Wherby both townes and kingdomes have ben   190
        rased,
And famous stockes of royall bloud destroied.
The brother, that shoulde be the brothers aide
And have a wakefull care for his defence,
Gapes for his death, and blames the lyngering
        yeres
That draw[33] not forth his ende with faster   195
        course,
And oft impacient of so longe delayes,
With hatefull slaughter he preventes[18, 34] the
        fates,
And heapes[35] a just rewarde for brothers
        bloode,
With endlesse vengeaunce on his stocke for aye.[19]

16 *moe :* more.   18 *preventes :* anticipates.
17 *charge :* responsibility.   19 *for aye :* forever.

Suche mischiefes here are wisely mette withall,   200
If egall state maye nourishe egall love,
Where none hath cause to grudge at others good.
But nowe the head to stoupe beneth them bothe,
Ne kinde, ne reason, ne good ordre beares.
And oft it hath ben seene, where natures   205
        course[36]
Hath ben perverted in disordered wise,
When fathers cease to know that they should rule,
The[37] children cease to know they should obey.
And often overkindly[38] tendernesse
Is mother of unkindly stubbornenesse.   210
I speake not this in envie or reproche,
As if I grudged the glorie of your sonnes,
Whose honour I besech the Goddes encrease,[39]
Nor yet as if I thought there did remaine
So filthie cankers in their noble brestes,   215
Whom I esteeme (which is their greatest praise)
Undoubted children of so good a kyng.
Onelie I meane to shewe by[40] certeine rules,
Whiche kinde hath graft within the mind of man,
That nature hath her ordre and her course,   220
Which (being broken) doth corrupt the state
Of myndes and thinges, even in the best of all.(5)
My lordes your sonnes may learne to rule of you.
Your owne example in your noble courte
Is fittest guyder of their youthfull yeares.   225
If you desire to see[41] some present joye
By sight of their well rulynge in your lyfe,
See them obey, so shall you see them rule.
Whoso obeyeth not with humblenesse
Will rule with outrage and with insolence.   230
Longe maye they rule, I do beseche the Goddes,
But longe may they learne, ere they begyn to rule.
If kinde and fates[42] woulde suffre,[20] I would
        wisshe
Them aged princes and immortall kinges.
Wherfore, most noble kynge, I well[43] assent,   235
Betwene your sonnes that you divide your realme,
And as in kinde, so match them in degree.
But while the Goddes prolong your royall life,

20 *suffre :* permit.

Prolong your reigne; for therto lyve you here,
And therfore have the Goddes so long forborne   240
To joyne you to themselves, that still you might
Be prince and father of our common weale.
They, when they see your children ripe to rule,
Will make them roume, and will remove you
           hence,
That yours in right ensuynge of your life   245
Maye rightly honour your immortall[44] name.
EUBULUS. Your wonted true regarde of faithfull
           hartes,
Makes me (O kinge) the bolder to presume,
To speake what I conceive within my brest,
Although the same do not agree at all   250
With that which other here my lordes have said,
Nor which yourselfe have seemed best to lyke.
Pardon I crave, and that my wordes be demed
To flowe from hartie zeale unto your grace,
And to the safetie of your common weale.   255
To parte your realme unto my lordes your sonnes,
I thinke not good for you, ne yet for them,
But worste of all for this our native lande.
Within[45] one land, one single rule is best.
Divided reignes[46] do make divided hartes,   260
But peace preserves the countrey and the prince.
Suche is in man the gredy minde to reigne,
So great is his desire to climbe alofte,
In worldly stage the stateliest partes to beare,
That faith and justice and all kindly love   265
Do yelde unto desire of soveraignitie,
Where egall state doth raise an egall hope
To winne the thing that either wold attaine.
Your grace remembreth how in passed yeres
The mightie *Brute*, first prince of all this lande,   270
Possessed the same and ruled it well in one.
He, thinking that the compasse did suffice
For his three sonnes three kingdoms eke to make,
Cut it in three, as you would now in twaine.
But how much Brittish[47] bloud hath since[48]   275
           bene spilt,
To joyne againe the sondred unitie,
What princes slaine before their timely houre,[49]

What wast[21] of townes and people in the lande,
What treasons heaped on murders and on spoiles
Whose just revenge even yet is scarcely ceased   280
Ruthefull   remembraunce   is   yet   rawe[50]   in
        minde![6]
The Gods forbyd the like to chaunce againe,
And you (O king) geve not the cause therof.
My Lord *Ferrex,* your elder sonne, perhappes
Whome kinde and custome geves a rightfull hope   285
To be your heire and to succede your reigne,
Shall thinke that he doth suffre greater wrong
Than he perchaunce will beare, if power serve.
Porrex, the younger, so upraised[51] in state,
Perhappes in courage[22] will be raysed also.   290
If flatterie, then, which fayles not to assaile
The tendre mindes of yet unskilfull youth,
In one shall kindle and encrease disdaine,
And[52] envie in the others harte enflame,
This fire shall waste their love, their lives, their   295
        land,
And ruthefull[23] ruine shall destroy them both.
I wishe not this (O kyng) so to befall,
But feare the thing that I do most abhorre.
Geve no beginning to so dreadfull ende.
Kepe them in order and obedience,   300
And let them both by now obeying you
Learne such behaviour as beseemes their state,
The elder, myldenesse in his governaunce,
The yonger, a yelding contentednesse.
And kepe them neare unto your presence still,   305
That they, restreyned by the awe of you,
May live in compasse of well tempred staye
And passe the perilles of their youthfull yeares.
Your aged life drawes on to febler[24] tyme,
Wherin you shall lesse able be to beare   310
The travailes that in youth you have susteyned,
Both in your persones and your realmes defence.
If planting now your sonnes in furder partes,
You sende them furder from your present reach,

---

21 *wast:* waste.   23 *ruthefull:* pitiable.
22 *courage:* aspiration, ambi-   24 *febler:* feebler.
    tion.

    Lesse shall you know how they themselves de-   315
            meane.[25, 53]
Traiterous corrupters of their plyant youth
Shall have unspied a muche more free accesse,
And if ambition and inflamed disdaine
Shall arme the one, the other, or them both,
To civill warre, or to usurping pride,   320
Late shall you rue, that you ne recked[26] before.
Good is, I graunt, of all to hope the best,
But not to live still dreadlesse of the worst.
So truste the one, that the other be forsene.
Arme not unskilfulnesse with princely power.   325
But you that long have wisely ruled the reignes
Of royaltie within your noble realme,
So holde them, while the Gods for our avayles
Shall stretch the thred of your prolonged daies.
To soone he clambe[27] into the flaming carre,[54] 330
Whose want of skill did set the earth on fire.[7]
Time and example of your noble grace
Shall teach your sonnes both to obey and rule.
When time hath taught them, time shal make the
            place,[55]
The place that now is full; and so, I pray,   335
Long it remaine, to comforte of us all.
GORBODUC. I take your faithful harts in thankful part.
    But sithe I see no cause to draw my minde
    To feare the nature of my loving sonnes,
    Or to misdeme that envie or disdaine   340
    Can there worke hate where nature planteth love,
    In one selfe[28] purpose do I still abide.
    My love extendeth egally to both,
    My lande suffiseth for them both also.
    Humber shall parte the marches of theyr   345
            realmes.[8]
    The Sotherne part the elder shall possesse.
    The Northerne shall *Porrex*, the yonger, rule.
    In quiet I will passe mine aged dayes,
    Free from the travaile and the painefull cares
    That hasten age upon the worthiest kinges.   350
    But lest the fraude that ye do seeme to feare,

25 *demeane* : behave.   27 *clambe* : climbed.
26 *recked* : took heed.   28 *selfe* : sole.

Of flattering tongues, corrupt their tender youth
And wrythe[29] them to the wayes of youthfull
      lust,[30]
To climyng pride, or to revenging hate,
Or to neglecting of their carefull charge,   355
Lewdely[31] to lyve in wanton recklessnesse,
Or to oppressing of the rightfull cause,
Or not to wreke[32] the wronges done to the poore,
To treade downe truth, or favour false deceite,
I meane to joyne to eyther of my sonnes   360
Some one of those whose long approved faith
And wisdome tryed may well assure my harte,
That mynyng[33] fraude shall finde no way to crepe
Into their fensed[34] eares with grave advise.
This is the ende, and so I pray you all   365
To beare my sonnes the love and loyaltie
That I have founde within your faithfull brestes.
AROSTUS. You, nor your sonnes, our soveraign lord,
        shal want,
   Our faith and service while our lives do last.
            [*Exeunt. The* CHORUS *remains.*]
CHORUS. When settled stay doth holde the royall   370
      throne
In stedfast place, by knowen and doubtles right,
And chiefely when discent on one alone
Makes[56] single and unparted reigne to light,
Eche chaunge of course unjoynts the whole estate,
And yeldes it thrall to ruyne by debate.[35]   375
The strength that knit by faste[57] accorde in one,
Against all forrein power of mightie foes,
Could of itselfe defende itselfe alone,
Disjoyned once, the former force doth lose.
The stickes that sondred brake so soone in twaine,   380
In faggot bounde attempted were in vaine.
Oft tender minde that leades the parciall eye
Of erring parentes in their childrens love,
Destroyes the wrongly[58] loved childe therby.
This doth the proude sonne of *Apollo* prove,   385
Who, rasshely set in chariot of his sire,

29 *wrythe* : twist.
30 *lust* : ambition.
31 *Lewdely* : Rudely.
32 *wreke* : punish.
33 *mynyng* : undermining.
34 *fensed* : fenced, protected.
35 *debate* : strife.

Inflamed the parched earth with heavens fire.
And this great king, that doth devide his land,
And chaunge[59] the course of his discending[36]
    crowne,
And yeldes the reigne into his childrens hande,   390
From blisfull state of joye and great renowne,
A myrrour shall become to Princes all,
To learne to shunne the cause of suche a fall.[9]

THE ORDER AND SIGNIFICATION OF THE DOMME
SHEW BEFORE THE SECOND ACTE

First the Musicke of Cornettes began to playe,
during which came in upon the stage a King ac-
companied with a nombre of his nobilitie and gentlemen. And after he had placed himself in a
chaire of estate prepared for him, there came and   5
kneled before him a grave and aged gentelman
and offred up a cuppe unto him of wyne in a
glasse, which the[1] King refused. After him
commes a brave and lustie yong gentleman and
presentes the King with a cup of[2] golde filled   10
with poyson, which the King accepted, and, drinking the same, immediatly fell downe dead upon
the[3] stage, and so was carried thence away by
his Lordes and gentelmen, and then the Musicke
ceased. Hereby was signified that as glasse by na-   15
ture holdeth no poyson, but is clere and may easely
be seen through, ne boweth by any arte, so a
faythfull counsellour holdeth no treason, but is
playne and open, ne yeldeth to any undiscrete
affection, but geveth[4] holsome counsell, which   20
the yll advised Prince refuseth. The delightfull
golde filled with poyson betokeneth flattery, which
under faire seeming of pleasaunt wordes beareth
deadly poyson, which destroyed the Prince that re-
ceyveth it, as befell in the two brethren Ferrex   25
and Porrex, who refusing the holsome advise of
grave counsellours, credited these yong Paracites
and brought to[5] themselves death and destruction therby.

36 *discending :* hereditary.

ACTUS SECUNDUS.   SCENA PRIMA.

[*Enter*] FERREX, HERMON, [*and*] DORDAN.
FERREX. I mervaile much what reason ledde the
            king
  My father, thus without all my desert,
  To reve[1] me halfe the kingdome, which by course
  Of law and nature should remayne to me.
HERMON. If you with stubborne and untamed pryde   5
  Had stood against him in rebelling[1] wise,
  Or if with grudging minde you had envied
  So slow a slidying of his aged yeres,
  Or sought before your time to haste the course
  Of fatall death upon his royall head,   10
  Or stained your stocke with murder of your kyn,
  Some face of reason might perhaps have seemed
  To yelde some likely cause to spoyle ye thus.
FERREX. The wrekeful[2] Gods powre on my cursed
            head
  Eternall plagues and never dying woes,   15
  The hellish prince adjudge my dampned ghost
  To *Tantales* thirste, or proude *Ixions* wheele,[(1)]
  Or cruell gripe to gnaw my growing[2] harte,
  To during[3] tormentes and unquenched flames,
  If ever I conceyved so foule a thought,   20
  To wisshe his ende of life, or yet of reigne.
DORDAN. Ne yet your father (O most noble Prince)
  Did ever thinke so fowle a thing of you.
  For he, with more than fathers tendre love,
  While yet the fates do lende him life to rule,   25
  (Who long might lyve to see your ruling well)
  To you, my Lorde, and to his other sonne,
  Lo, he resignes his realme and royaltie,
  Which never would so wise a Prince have done,
  If he had once misdemed[4] that in your harte   30
  There ever lodged so unkinde a thought.
  But tendre love (my Lorde) and setled truste

ACTUS SECUNDUS.   SCENA   2 *wrekeful* : revengeful.
PRIMA.   3 *during* : long-lasting.
    1 *reve* : bereave.   4 *misdemed* : suspected.

Of your good nature and your noble minde
Made him to place you thus in royall throne,
And now to geve you half his realme to guide,   35
Yea, and that halfe which in[3] abounding store
Of things that serve to make a welthy realme,
In stately cities, and in frutefull soyle,
In temperate breathing of the milder heaven,
In thinges of nedefull use, which frendly sea   40
Transportes by traffike from the forreine partes,[4]
In flowing wealth, in honour and in force,
Doth passe⁵ the double value of the parte
That *Porrex* hath allotted to his reigne.
Such is your case, such is your fathers love.   45

FERREX. Ah love, my frendes? Love wrongs not whom
          he loves.

DORDAN. Ne yet he wrongeth you, that geveth you
  So large a reigne, ere that the course of time
  Bring you to kingdome by discended right,
  Which time perhaps might end your time before.   50

FERREX. Is this no wrong, say you, to reave from me
  My native right of halfe so great a realme?
  And thus to matche his yonger sonne with me
  In egall power, and in as great degree?
  Yea, and what sonne? The sonne whose swelling   55
          pride
  Woulde never yelde one poinct of reverence,
  Whan I the elder and apparaunt heire
  Stoode in the likelihode to possesse the whole,
  Yea, and that sonne which from his childish age
  Envieth myne honour and doth hate my life.   60
  What will he now do, when his pride, his rage,
  The mindefull malice of his grudging harte,
  Is armed with force, with wealth, and kingly
          state?

HERMON. Was this not wrong, yea, yll advised
          wrong,
  To give so mad a man so sharpe a sworde,   65
  To so great perill of so great missehappe,
  Wide open thus to set so large a waye?

DORDAN. Alas, my Lord, what griefull thing is this,
  That of your brother you can thinke so ill?

5 *passe :* surpass.

I never saw him utter likelie signe,   70
Whereby a man might see or once misdeme
Such hate of you, ne such unyelding pride.
Ill is their counsell, shamefull be their ende,
That raysing such mistrustfull feare in you,
Sowing the seede of such unkindly hate,   75
Travaile by treason[5] to destroy you both.
Wise is your brother, and of noble hope,
Worthie to welde a large and mightie realme.
So much a stronger frende have you therby,
Whose strength is your strength, if you gree in   80
    one.[6]

HERMON. If nature and the Goddes had pinched so
Their flowing bountie, and their noble giftes
Of princelie qualities, from you, my Lorde,
And powrde them all at ones in wastfull wise
Upon your fathers yonger sonne alone,   85
Perhappes there be that in your prejudice
Would say that birth should yeld to worthinesse.
But sithe in eche good gift and princelie arte
Ye are his matche, and in the chiefe of all
In mildenesse and in sobre governaunce   90
Ye farre surmount, and sith there is in you
Sufficing skill and hopefull towardnesse
To weld[7] the whole, and match your elders prayse,
I see no cause why ye should loose[8] the halfe.
Ne would I wisshe you yelde to such a losse,   95
Lest your milde sufferaunce of so great a wronge
Be deemed cowardishe and simple dreade,
Which shall geve courage to the fierie head
Of your yonge brother to invade the whole.
While yet, therfore, stickes in the peoples minde   100
The lothed wrong of your disheritaunce,
And ere your brother have by settled power,
By guilefull cloke of an alluring showe,
Got him some force and favour in the[6] realme,
And while the noble Queene your mother lyves,   105
To worke and practise all for your availe,
Attempt redresse by armes, and wreake yourself
Upon his life, that gayneth by your losse,

6 *gree in one*: agree to-   7 *weld*: wield, rule.
   gether.   8 *loose*: lose.

Who nowe to shame of you, and griefe of us,
In your owne kingdome triumphes over you.   110
Shew now your courage meete for kingly state,
That they which have avowed to spend theyr
　　　goods,
Their landes, their lives and honours in your cause
May be the bolder to mainteyne your parte,
When they do see that cowarde feare in you   115
Shall not betray ne faile their faithfull hartes.
If once the death of *Porrex* ende the strife
And pay the price of his usurped reigne,
Your mother shall perswade the angry kyng,
The Lords your frends eke shall appease his rage.   120
For they be wise, and well they can forsee,
That ere longe time your aged fathers death
Will bryng a time when you shall well requite
Their frendlie favour, or their hatefull spite,
Yea, or their slackenesse to avaunce your cause.   125
Wise men do not so hang on passing state
Of present Princes, chiefely in their age,
But they will further cast their reaching eye,
To viewe and weye the times and reignes to
　　　come.[2]
Ne is it likely, though the kyng be wrothe,   130
That he yet will, or that the realme will beare,
Extreme revenge upon his onely sonne.
Or if he woulde, what one is he that dare
Be minister to such an enterprise?
And here you be now placed in your owne,   135
Amyd your frendes, your vassalles, and your
　　　strength.
We shall defende and kepe your person safe,
Till either counsell turne his tender minde,
Or age, or sorrow end his werie dayes.
But if the feare of Goddes, and secrete grudge   140
Of natures law, repining at the fact,
Withholde your courage from so great attempt,
Know ye, that lust of kingdomes[9] hath no law.
The Goddes do beare and well allow in kinges
The thinges they abhorre in rascall routes.[10]   145

9 *lust of kingdomes :* desire to　　10 *routes :* rabble.
　rule, ambition.

When kinges on slender quarrells runne to warres,
And then in cruell and unkindely wise
Commaund theftes, rapes, murders[7] of inno-
        centes,
The[8] spoile of townes, ruines[9] of mighty
        realmes,
Thinke you such princes do suppose[10] them-   150
        selves
Subject to lawes of kinde, and feare of Gods?
Murders and violent theftes in private men
Are hainous crimes and full of foule reproch,
Yet none offence, but deckt with glorious name
Of noble conquestes, in the handes of kinges.[11]   155
But if you like not yet so hote devise,
Ne list to take such vauntage of the time,
But though with[12] perill of your owne es-
        tate,[13]
You will not be the first that shall invade,
Assemble yet your force for your defence,   160
And for your safetie stand upon your garde.
DORDAN. O heaven, was there ever heard or knowen
So wicked counsell to a noble prince?
Let me (my Lorde) disclose unto your grace
This hainous tale, what mischiefe it containes,   165
Your fathers death, your brothers and your owne,
Your present murder and eternall shame.
Heare me (O king) and suffer not to sinke
So high a treason in your princely brest.
FERREX. The mightie Goddes forbid that ever I   170
Should once conceave such mischiefe in my hart.
Although my brother hath bereft my realme,
And beare perhappes to me an[14] hatefull minde,
Shall I revenge it with his death therefore?
Or shall I so destroy my fathers life   175
That gave me life? The Gods forbid, I say.
Cease you to speake so any more to me.
Ne you my frend with answere once repeate
So foule a tale. In silence let it die.
What lord or subject shall have hope at all,   180
That under me they safely shall enjoye
Their goods, their honours, landes and liberties,
With whom neither one onely brother deare,
Ne father dearer, could enjoye their lives?

But sith I feare my yonger brothers rage,   185
And sith perhappes some other man may geve
Some like advise to move his grudging[11] head
At mine estate, which counsell may perchaunce
Take greater force with him, than this with me,
I will in secrete so prepare myselfe,   190
As if[12] his malice or his lust to reigne
Breake forth in[15] armes or sodeine violence,
I may withstand his rage and keepe mine owne.
            [*Exeunt* FERREX *and* HERMON.]
DORDAN. I feare the fatall time now draweth on
    When civil hate shall end the noble line   195
    Of famous *Brute* and of his royall seede.
    Great *Jove* defend[13] the mischiefes now at hand.
    O that the Secretaries wise advise(3)
    Had erst bene heard when he besought the king
    Not to divide his land, nor send his sonnes   200
    To further partes from presence of his court,
    Ne yet to yelde to them his governaunce.
    Lo, such are they now in the royall throne
    As was rashe[16] *Phaeton* in *Phebus* carre.
    Ne then the fiery stedes did draw the flame   205
    With wilder randon[14] through the kindled skies,
    Than traitorous counsell now will whirle about
    The youthfull heades of these unskilfull kinges.
    But I hereof their father will enforme.
    The reverence of him perhappes shall stay   210
    The growing mischiefes, while they yet are greene.
    If this helpe not, then woe unto themselves,
    The prince, the people, the divided land. [*Exit.*]

Actus Secundus.　Scena Secunda.

[*Enter*] PORREX, TYNDAR, [*and*] PHILANDER.
PORREX. And is it thus? And doth he so prepare,
    Against his brother as his mortall foe?
    And now while yet his aged father lives?
    Neither regardes he him? nor feares he me?

11 *grudging :* begrudging.　　　14 *randon :* violence, impetu-
12 *As if :* So that if.　　　　　　 osity.
13 *defend :* prevent.

Warre would he have? And he shall have it so.   5
TYNDAR. I saw myselfe the great prepared store
Of horse, of armour,[1] and of weapon there,
Ne bring I to my lorde reported tales
Without the ground of seen and searched trouth.
Loe, secrete quarrels runne about his court,   10
To bring the name of you, my lorde, in hate.
Ech man almost can now debate the cause,
And aske a reason of so great a wrong,
Why[2] he so noble and so wise a prince,
Is as unworthy reft his heritage?   15
And why the king, misseledde by craftie meanes,
Divided thus his land from course of right?
The wiser sort holde downe their griefull heades.
Eche man withdrawes from talke and company
Of those that have bene knowne to favour you.   20
To hide the mischiefe of their meaning there,
Rumours are spread of your preparing here.
The rascall numbers of[3] unskilfull sort
Are filled with monstrous tales of you and yours.
In secrete I was counselled by my frendes   25
To hast me thence, and brought you as you know
Letters from those, that both can truely tell,
And would not write unlesse they knew it well.
PHILANDER. My lord, yet ere you move[4] unkindly
                warre,
Send to your brother to demaund the cause.   30
Perhappes some traitorous tales have filled his
                eares
With false reportes against your noble grace,
Which, once disclosed, shall end the growing
                strife,
That els not stayed with wise foresight in time
Shall hazarde both your kingdomes and your lives.   35
Send to your father eke; he shall appease
Your kindled mindes, and rid you of this feare.
PORREX. Ridde me of feare? I feare him not at all,
Ne will to him, ne to my father send.
If danger were for one to tary there,   40
Thinke ye it safetie to returne againe?
In mischiefes, such as *Ferrex* now intendes,
The wonted courteous lawes to messengers
Are not observed, which in just warre they use.

Shall I so hazard any one of mine?   45
Shall I betray my trusty frendes[5] to him,
That have[6] disclosed his treason unto me?
Let him entreate that feares, I feare him not.
Or shall I to the king my father send?
Yea, and send now, while such a mother lives,   50
That loves my brother, and that hateth me?
Shall I geve leasure, by my fonde[1] delayes,
To *Ferrex* to oppresse me all[7] unware?
I will not, but I will invade his realme
And seeke the traitour prince within his court.   55
Mischiefe for mischiefe is a due reward.
His wretched head shall pay the worthy price
Of this his treason and his hate to me.
Shall I abide, and treate,[2, 8] and send, and pray,
And holde my yelden[3] throate to traitours knife?   60
While I with valiant minde and conquering force
Might rid myselfe of foes and winne a realme?
Yet rather, when I have the wretches head,
Then to the king my father will I send.
The bootelesse case[4] may yet appease his wrath   65
If not, I will defend me as I may.
                    [*Exeunt* PORREX *and* TYNDAR.]
PHILANDER. Lo, here the end of these two youthful
                    kings,
The fathers death, the ruine of their realmes.[9]
O most unhappy state of counsellers, [1]
That light on so unhappy lordes and times,   70
That neither can their good advise be heard,
Yet must they beare the blames of ill successe.
But I will to the king their father haste,
Ere this mischiefe come to the[10] likely end,
That if the mindfull wrath of wrekefull Gods,   75
Since mightie *Ilions* fall not yet appeased
With these poore remnantes[11] of the Trojan[12]
                    name,
Have not determined by[13] unmoved fate

ACTUS SECUNDUS. SCENA   3 *yelden :* yielded, surren-
SECUNDA.   dered.
  1 *fonde :* foolish.   4 *bootelesse case :* the situa-
  2 *treate :* entreat.   tion about which he can
                                     do nothing.

Out of this realme to rase[5] the Brittishe line,
By good advise, by awe of fathers name,   80
By force of wiser lordes, this kindled hate
May yet be quentched, ere it consume us all.

                                        [*Exit.*]

CHORUS. When youth not bridled with a guiding stay
Is left to randon of their owne delight,
And welds whole realmes, by force of soveraign   85
      sway,[14]
Great is the daunger of unmaistred might,
Lest skillesse rage throwe downe with headlong
      fall
Their lands, their states, their lives, themselves and
      al.
When growing pride doth fill the swelling brest,
And gredy lust doth rayse the climbing minde,   90
Oh, hardlie maye the perill be represt.
Ne feare of angrie Goddes, ne lawes kinde,[6]
Ne countries[15] care can fiered hartes restrayne,
Whan force hath armed envie and disdaine.
When kinges of foresette[7] will neglect the rede[8]   95
Of best advise, and yelde to pleasing tales,
That do their fansies noysome humour feede,
Ne reason, nor regarde of right availes.
Succeeding heapes of plagues shall teach too late
To learne the mischiefes of misguided[16] state   100
Fowle fall the traitour false that undermines
The love of brethren to destroye them both.
Wo to the prince that pliant eare enclynes,
And yeldes his mind to poysonous tale that floweth
From flattering mouth. And woe to wretched land   105
That wastes itselfe with civil sworde in hand.
Loe, thus it is, poyson in golde to take,[2]
And holsome drinke in homely[9] cuppe forsake.

THE ORDER AND SIGNIFICATION OF THE DOMME
      SHEWE BEFORE THE THIRDE ACT

   Firste the musicke of flutes began to playe, during which came in upon the stage a company of
mourners all clad in blacke, betokening death and

5 *rase* : erase, pluck out.   7 *foresette* : foresight.
6 *lawes kinde* : laws respect-   8 *rede* : counsel.
      ing kindred.   9 *homely* : unpretentious.

sorowe to ensue upon the ill advised misgoverne-
ment and discention of bretherne, as befell upon   5
the murder[1] of Ferrex by his yonger brother.
After the mourners had passed thryse about
the stage, they departed, and than the musicke
ceased.[2]

ACTUS TERTIUS.   SCENA PRIMA.

[*Enter*] GORBODUC, EUBULUS, [*and*] AROSTUS.

GORBODUC. O cruel fates, O mindful wrath of
                 Goddes,
   Whose vengeance neither *Simois* stayned[1]
                 streames
   Flowing with bloud of *Trojan* princes slaine,
   Nor *Phrygian* fieldes made ranck with corpses
                 dead
   Of *Asian* kynges and lordes, can yet appease,   5
   Ne slaughter of unhappie *Pryams* race,
   Nor *Ilions* fall made levell with the soile
   Can yet suffice,[(1)] but still continued rage
   Pursues[2] our lyves,[3] and from the farthest seas
   Doth chase[4] the issues of destroyed *Troye*.   10
   Oh no man happie, till his ende be seene.[(2)]
   If any flowing wealth and seemyng joye
   In present yeres might make a happy wight,
   Happie was *Hecuba*, the wofullest wretch
   That ever lyved to make a myrrour of,[(3)]   15
   And happie *Pryam* with his noble sonnes.
   And happie I, till nowe, alas, I see
   And feele my most unhappye wretchednesse.
   Beholde, my lordes, read ye this letter here.
   Loe, it conteins the ruine of our[5] realme,   20
   If timelie speede provide not hastie helpe.
   Yet (O ye Goddes) if ever wofull kyng
   Might move ye[6] kings of kinges, wreke it on me
   And on my sonnes, not on this giltlesse realme.
   Send down your wasting flames from wrathful   25
                 skies,
   To reve me[1] and my sonnes the hatefull breath.

ACTUS TERTIUS.   SCENA PRIMA.
   1 *reve me :* bereave me (of).

Read, read my lordes. This is the matter why
I called ye nowe to have your good advyse.
          The letter from DORDAN the Counsellour
                    of the elder prince.
                EUBULUS *readeth the letter.*
My soveraigne lord, what I am loth to write,
But lothest am to see, that I am forced   30
By letters nowe to make you understande.
My lord *Ferrex,* your eldest sonne, misledde
By traitorous fraude[7] of yong untempred wittes,
Assembleth force agaynst your yonger sonne,
Ne can my counsell yet withdrawe the heate   35
And furyous panges of hys enflamed head.
Disdaine (sayth he) of his disheritance
Armes him to wreke the great pretended[2] wrong,
With civyll sword upon his brothers life.
If present helpe do not restraine this rage,   40
This flame will wast your sonnes, your land, and
          you.
                    Your majesties faithfull and most
                    humble subject, Dordan.
AROSTUS. O king, appease your griefe and stay your
                    plaint.
Great is the matter, and a wofull case.
But timely knowledge may bring timely helpe.[8]
Sende for them both unto your presence here.
The reverence of your honour, age,[9] and state,   45
Your grave advice, the awe of fathers name,
Shall quicklie knit agayne this broken peace.
And if in either of my lordes your sonnes
Be suche untamed and unyelding pride,   50
As will not bende unto your noble hestes,[3]
If *Ferrex,* the elder sonne, can beare no peere,
Or *Porrex,* not content, aspires to more
Than you him gave above his native right,
Joyne with the juster side. So shall you force   55
Them to agree, and holde the lande in stay.
EUBULUS. What meaneth this? Loe, yonder comes in
                    hast
Philander from my lord your yonger sonne.
                [*Enter* PHILANDER.]

2 *pretended* : offered.   3 *hestes* : behests.

GORBODUC. The Goddes sende joyfull newes.

PHILANDER.   The mightie *Jove*
  Preserve your majestie, O noble king.   60

GORBODUC. *Philander*, welcome. But how doth my
        sonne?

PHILANDER. Your sonne, sir, lyves, and healthie I him
        left.
  But yet (O king) the[10] want of lustfull[4] health
  Could not be halfe so griefefull to your grace,
  As these most wretched tidynges that I bryng.   65

GORBODUC. O heavens, yet more? Not[11] ende of
        woes to me?

PHILANDER. *Tyndar*, O king, came lately from the
        court
  Of *Ferrex*, to my lord your yonger sonne,
  And made reporte of great prepared store
  For[12] warre, and sayth that it is wholly ment   70
  Agaynst *Porrex*, for high disdayne that he
  Lyves now a king and egall in degree
  With him that claimeth to succede the whole,
  As by due title of discending right.
  Porrex is nowe so set on flaming fire,   75
  Partely with kindled rage of cruell wrath,
  Partely with hope to gaine a realme thereby,
  That he in hast prepareth to invade
  His brothers land, and with unkindely warre
  Threatens the murder of your elder sonne.   80
  Ne could I him perswade that first he should
  Send to his brother to demaunde the cause,
  Nor yet to you to staie this[13] hatefull strife.
  Wherfore sithe there no more I can be hearde,
  I come myselfe now to enforme your grace,   85
  And to beseche you, as you love the life
  And safetie of your children and your realme,
  Now to employ your wisdome and your force
  To stay this mischiefe ere it be to late.

GORBODUC. Are they in armes? Would he not sende   90
        to[14] me?
  Is this the honour of a fathers name?
  In vaine we travaile to asswage their mindes,
  As if their hartes, whome neither brothers love,

---

4 *lustfull*: vital, lively.

Nor fathers awe, nor kingdomes cares,[15] can
      move,
Our counsels could withdraw from raging heat.   95
Jove slay them both, and end the cursed line.
For though perhappes feare of such mightie force
As I, my lordes, joyned with your noble aides,
Maye yet raise, shall represse[16] their present
      heate,
The secret grudge and malice will remayne,   100
The fire not quenched, but kept in close restraint,
Fedde still within, breakes forth with double
      flame.
Their death and myne must peaze⁵ the angrie
      Gods.
PHILANDER. Yelde not, O king, so much to weake
      dispeire.
Your sonnes yet lyve, and long, I trust, they shall.   105
If fates had taken you from earthly life,
Before beginning of this civyll strife,
Perhaps your sonnes in their unmaistered youth,
Loose from regarde of any lyving wight,
Would runne on headlong, with unbridled race,   110
To their owne death and ruine of this realme.
But sith the Gods, that have the care for kinges,
Of thinges and times dispose the order so
That in your life this kindled flame breakes forth,
While yet your lyfe, your wisdome, and your   115
      power
May stay the growing mischiefe, and represse
The fierie blaze of their inkindled[17] heate,
It seemes, and so ye ought to deeme therof,
That lovyng *Jove* hath tempred so the time
Of this debate to happen in your dayes,   120
That you yet lyving may the same appeaze,
And adde it to the glory of your latter age,
And they your[18] sonnes may learne to live in
      peace.
Beware (O king) the greatest harme of all,
Lest by your waylefull plaints your hastened death   125
Yelde larger roume unto their growing rage.
Preserve your life, the onely hope of stay.

5 *peaze :* appease.

And if your highnes herein list to use
Wisdome or force, counsell or knightly aide,
Loe, we, our persons, powers and lyves are yours,   130
Use us tyll death, O king, we are your owne.
EUBULUS. Loe, here the perill that was erst foresene,
    When you (O king) did first devide your lande,
    And yelde your present reigne unto your sonnes,
    But now (O noble prince) now is no time   135
    To waile and plaine, and wast your wofull life.
    Now is the time for present good advise.
    Sorow doth darke the judgement of the wytte.
    The hart unbroken and the courage free
    From feble faintnesse of bootelesse despeire,   140
    Doth either ryse to safetie or renowme
    By noble valure of unvanquisht minde,
    Or yet doth perishe in more happy sort.
    Your grace may send to either of your sonnes
    Some one both wise and noble personage,   145
    Which with good counsell and with weightie name
    Of father shall present before their eyes
    Your hest, your life, your safetie, and their owne,
    The present mischiefe of their deadly strife.
    And in the while, assemble you the force   150
    Which your commaundement and the spedy hast
    Of all my lordes here present can prepare.
    The terrour of your mightie power shall stay
    The rage of both, or yet of one at lest.
            [*Enter* NUNTIUS.]
NUNTIUS. O king, the greatest griefe that ever prince   155
           dyd heare,
    That ever wofull messenger did tell,
    That ever wretched lande hath sene before,
    I bryng to you. *Porrex,* your yonger sonne,
    With soden force invaded hath the lande
    That you to *Ferrex* did allotte to rule,   160
    And with his owne most bloudy hand he hath
    His brother slaine, and doth possesse his realme.
GORBODUC. O heavens, send down the flames of your
           revenge,
    Destroy I say with flash of wrekefull fier
    The traitour sonne, and then the wretched sire.   165
    But let us go, that yet perhappes I may

Die with revenge, and peaze the hatefull gods.

[*Exeunt.*]

CHORUS. The lust of kingdome knowes no sacred faith,
No rule of reason, no regarde of right,
No kindely love, no feare of heavens wrath,   170
But with contempt of Goddes, and mans despite,
Through blodie slaughter doth prepare the waies
To fatall scepter and accursed reigne.
The sonne so lothes the fathers lingering daies,
Ne dreades his hand in brothers blode to staine.   175
O wretched prince, ne doest thou yet recorde
The yet fresh murthers done within the lande
Of thy forefathers, when the cruell sworde
Bereft *Morgan* his life with cosyns hand?
Thus fatall plagues pursue the giltie race,   180
Whose murderous hand imbrued with giltlesse
          blood
Askes vengeaunce still[19] before the heavens
          face,
With endlesse mischiefes on the cursed broode.
The wicked childe thus[20] bringes to wofull sire
The mournefull plaintes, to wast his very[21] life.   185
Thus do the cruell flames of civyll fier
Destroy the parted reigne with hatefull strife.
And hence doth spring the well from which doth
          flow
The dead black streames of mourning, plaints and
          woe.

THE ORDER AND SIGNIFICATION OF THE DOMME
SHEW BEFORE THE FOURTH ACT

First the musick of Howboies[1] began to plaie,
during which there came[1] from under the stage,
as though out of hell, three furies—Alecto, Megera,
and Ctesiphone—clad in black garmentes sprinkled
with bloud and flames, their bodies girt with   5
snakes, their heds spred with serpentes instead of
heare, the one bearing in her hand a Snake, the
other a Whip, and the third a burning Firebrand,
ech driving before them a king and a queene,
which, moved by furies, unnaturally had slaine   10

1 *Howboies:* wind instru-
    ments of high pitch.

their owne children. The names of the kings and
queenes were these : Tantalus, Medea, Athamas,
Ino, Cambises, Althea.[1] After that the furies
and these had passed about the stage thrise, they
departed, and than the musicke ceased. Hereby   15
was signified the unnaturall murders to follow, that
is to say [of] Porrex, slaine by his owne mother,
and of king Gorboduc and queene Videna, killed
by their owne subjectes.

Actus Quartus.   Scena Prima.[1]

[Enter] VIDENA, *sola.*

VIDENA. Why should I lyve, and linger forth my time
   In longer life to double my distresse?
   O me, most wofull wight, whom no mishappe
   Long ere this day could have bereved hence.
   Mought not these handes by fortune, or by fate,   5
   Have perst this brest, and life with iron reft?
   Or in this palace here, where I so long
   Have spent my daies, could not that happie houre
   Once, once have hapt in which these hugie frames[2]
   With death by fall might have oppressed me?   10
   Or should not this most hard and cruell soile,
   So oft where I have prest my wretched steps,
   Sometime had ruthe of myne accursed life,
   To rende in twayne and[1] swallow me therin?
   So had my bones possessed now in peace   15
   Their happie grave within the closed grounde,
   And greadie wormes had gnawen this pyned hart
   Without my feeling payne. So should not now
   This lyving brest remayne the ruthefull tombe,
   Wherin my hart yelden[1] to death is graved.   20
   Nor driery[2] thoughts with panges of pining griefe
   My dolefull minde had[2] not afflicted thus.
   O my beloved sonne, O my swete childe,
   My deare *Ferrex,* my joye, my lyves delyght.
   Is my beloved[3] sonne, is my sweete childe,   25
   My deare *Ferrex,* my joye, my lyves delight,

Actus Quartus.   Scena   2 *driery :* dreary, gloomy.
Prima.
  1 *yelden :* yielded.

Murdered with cruell death? O hatefull wretch,
O heynous traitour both to heaven and earth,
Thou, *Porrex,* thou this damned dede hast
    wrought,
Thou, *Porrex,* thou shalt dearely bye.[3], [4] the   30
    same.
Traitour to kinne and kinde, to sire and me,
To thine owne fleshe, and traitour to thyselfe!
The Gods on thee in hell shall wreke their wrath,
And here in earth this hand shall take revenge,
On thee, *Porrex,* thou false and caitife wight.[4]   35
If after bloud so eigre[5] were thy thirst,
And murderous minde had so possessed thee,
If such hard hart of rocke and stonie flint
Lived in thy brest, that nothing els could like
Thy cruell tyrantes thought but death and bloud,   40
Wilde savage beasts, mought not their[5] slaugh-
    ter serve
To fede thy gredie will, and in the middest
Of their entrailes to staine thy deadly handes
With bloud deserved, and drinke thereof thy fill?
Or if nought els but death and bloud of man   45
Mought please thy lust, could none in Brittaine
    land,
Whose hart betorne out of his panting[6] brest
With thine owne hand, or worke what death thou
    wouldest,
Suffice to make a sacrifice to peaze[7]
That deadly minde and murderous thought in thee   50
But he who in the selfe same wombe was
    wrapped,
Where thou in dismall hower receivedst life?
Or if nedes, nedes, thy[8] hand must[9] slaughter
    make,
Moughtest thou not have reached a mortall
    wound,
And with thy sword have pearsed[6] this cursed   55
    wombe,
That the accursed *Porrex* brought to light,
And geven me a just reward therefore?

3 *bye:* aby, regret.   5 *eigre:* sharp.
4 *caitife wight:* treacherous   6 *pearsed:* pierced.
    creature.

So *Ferrex* yet[10] sweete life mought have en-
      joyed.
And to his aged father comfort brought,
With some yong sonne in whom they both might   60
      live.
But whereunto waste I this ruthfull speche,
To thee that hast[11] thy brothers bloud thus
      shed?
Shall I still thinke that from this wombe thou
      sprong?
That I thee bare? Or take thee for my sonne?
No traitour, no. I thee refuse for mine.   65
Murderer, I thee renounce, thou art not mine.
Never, O wretch, this wombe conceived thee,
Nor never bode[7] I painfull throwes for thee.
Changeling[8] to me thou art, and not my childe,
Nor to no wight that sparke of pitie knew.   70
Ruthelesse, unkinde, monster of natures worke,
Thou never suckt the milke of womans brest,
But from thy birth the cruell tigers teates
Have nursed thee.[12] Nor yet of fleshe and bloud
Formde is thy hart, but of hard iron wrought,   75
And wilde and desert woods bredde thee to life.
But canst thou hope to scape my just revenge?
Or that these handes will not be wrooke[9], [13] on
      thee?
Doest thou not know that *Ferrex* mother lives
That loved him more dearly than herselfe?   80
And doth she live, and is not venged on thee?

Actus Quartus. Scena Secunda.

[*Enter*] gorboduc [*and*] arostus.
gorboduc. We marvell much wherto this lingring
      stay
Falles out so long. *Porrex* unto our court
By order of our letters is returned,
And *Eubulus* received from us by hest[1]

7 *bode* : endured.   9 *wrooke* : revenged.
8 *changeling* : child which   Actus Quartus. Scena
    fairies exchanged in his   Secunda.
    infancy for the true   1 *hest* : behest.
    child.

At his arrivall here to geve him charge   5
Before our presence straight to make repaire,[2]
And yet we have[1] no worde whereof he stayes.
AROSTUS. Lo, where he commes and *Eubulus* with
       him.
     [*Enter* PORREX *and* EUBULUS.]
EUBULUS. According to your highnesse hest to me,
  Here have I *Porrex* brought, even in such sort   10
  As from his weried horse he did alight,
For that your grace did will such hast therein.
GORBODUC. We like and praise this spedy will in you,
  To worke the thing that to your charge we gave.
Porrex, if we so farre should swarve from kinde,   15
  And from those[2] boundes which lawe[3] of na-
       ture sets,
As thou hast done by vile and wretched deede,
In cruell murder of thy brothers life,
Our present hand could stay no longer time,
But straight should bathe this blade in bloud of   20
       thee
As just revenge of thy detested crime.
No, we should not offend the lawe of kinde,
If now this sworde of ours did slay thee here.
For thou hast murdered him, whose heinous death
Even natures force doth move us to revenge   25
By bloud againe, and[4] justice forceth us
To measure death for death, thy due desert.
Yet sithens[3] thou art our childe, and sith as yet
In this hard case what worde thou canst alledge
For thy defence by us hath not bene heard,   30
We are content to stave our will for that
Which justice biddes us presently to worke,
And geve thee leave to use thy speche at full
If ought thou have to lay for thine excuse.
PORREX. Neither, O king, I can or will denie   35
  But that this hand from *Ferrex* life hath reft,
Which fact how much my dolefull hart doth waile,
Oh would it mought as full appeare to sight
As inward griefe doth poure it forth to me.
So yet perhappes if ever ruthefull hart   40
Melting in teares within a manly brest,

---

2 *make repaire :* come.   3 *sithens :* since.

Through depe repentance of his bloudy fact,
If ever griefe, if ever wofull man[5]
Might move regreite with sorrowe of his fault,
I thinke the torment of my mournefull case   45
Knowen to your grace, as I do feele the same,
Would force even wrath herselfe to pitie me.
But as the water troubled with the mudde
Shewes not the face which els the eye should see,
Even so your irefull minde with stirred thought   50
Can not so perfectly discerne my cause.
But this unhappe, amongest so many heapes,
I must content me with, most wretched man,
That to myselfe I must reserve[6] my woe
In pining thoughtes of mine accursed fact,   55
Since[7] I may not shewe here my smallest griefe
Such as it is, and as my brest endures,
Which I esteeme the greatest miserie
Of all missehappes that fortune now can send.
Not that I rest in hope with plaint and teares   60
To[8] purchase life, for to the Goddes I clepe⁴
For true recorde of this my faithfull speche,
Never this hart shall have the thoughtfull dread
To die the death that by your graces dome⁵
By just desert shall be pronounced to me.   65
Nor never shall this tongue once spend the[9]
              speche
Pardon to crave, or seeke by sute to live.
I meane not this, as though I were not touchde
With care of dreadfull death, or that I helde
Life in contempt, but that I know the minde   70
Stoupes to no dread, although the fleshe be fraile.
And for my gilt, I yelde the same so great
As in myselfe I finde a feare to sue
For graunt of life.

GORBODUC.   In vaine, O wretch, thou shewest
A wofull hart. *Ferrex* now lies in grave,   75
Slaine by thy hand.

PORREX.   Yet this, O father, heare :
And then I end. Your majestie well knowes
That when my brother *Ferrex* and myselfe

4 *clepe :* call.   5 *dome :* judgment, sen-
                                              tence.

By your owne hest were joyned in governance
Of this your graces realme of Brittaine land,   80
I never sought nor travailled for the same,
Nor by myselfe, nor[10] by no frend I wrought,
But from your highnesse will alone it sprong,
Of your most gracious goodnesse bent to me,
But how my brothers hart even then repined   85
With swollen disdaine against mine egall rule,
Seing that realme, which by discent should grow
Wholly to him, allotted halfe to me.
Even in your highnesse court he now remaines,
And with my brother then in nearest place,   90
Who can recorde what proofe thereof was shewde,
And how my brothers envious hart appearde.
Yet I that judged it my part to seeke
His favour and good will, and loth to make
Your highnesse know the thing which should have   95
          brought
Grief to your grace, and your offence to him,
Hoping my[11] earnest sute should soone have
          wonne
A loving hart within a brothers brest,
Wrought in that sort that for a pledge of love
And faithfull hart, he gave to me his hand.   100
This made me thinke that he had banisht quite
All rancour from his thought and bare to me
Such hartie love as I did owe to him.
But after once we left your graces court,
And from your highnesse presence lived apart,   105
This egall rule still, still, did grudge him so
That now those envious sparkes which erst lay
          raked
In living cinders of dissembling brest,
Kindled so farre within his hart[12] disdaine,
That longer could he not refraine from proofe   110
Of secrete practise to deprive me[13] life
By poysons force, and had bereft me so,
If mine owne servant hired to this fact
And moved by trouth with hate to worke the same,
In[14] time had not bewrayed[6] it unto me.   115
Whan thus I sawe the knot of love unknitte,

6 *bewrayed :* revealed.

All honest league and faithfull promise broke,
The law of kinde and trouth thus rent in twaine,
His hart on mischiefe set, and in his brest
Blacke treason hid, then, then did I despeire   120
That ever time could winne him frend to me.
Then saw I how he smiled with slaying knife
Wrapped under cloke, then saw I depe deceite
Lurke in his face and death prepared for me.
Even nature moved me than to holde my life   125
More deare to me than his, and bad this hand,
Since by his life my death must nedes ensue,
And by his death my life to be preserved,
To shed his bloud, and seeke my safetie so.
And wisedome willed me without protract[7]   130
In spedie wise to put the same in ure.[8]
Thus have I tolde the cause that moved me
To worke my brothers death, and so I yeld
My life, my death, to judgement of your grace.

GORBODUC. Oh cruell wight, should any cause pre-   135
      vaile
To make thee staine thy hands with brothers
      bloud?
But what of thee we will resolve to doe,
Shall yet remaine unknowen. Thou in the meane
Shalt from our royall presence banisht be,
Untill our princely pleasure furder shall   140
To thee be shewed. Depart therefore our sight,
Accursed childe. What cruell destenie,
What froward fate hath sorted us this chaunce,
That even in those where we should comfort find,
Where our delight now in our aged dayes   145
Sould rest and be, even there our onely griefe
And depest sorrowes to abridge our life,
Most pyning cares and deadly thoughts do
      grow?[15]   [*Exit* PORREX.]

AROSTUS. Your grace should now in these grave yeres
      of yours
Have found ere this the price of mortall joyes,   150
How short they be, how fading here in earth,
How full of chaunge, how brittle our estate,
Of nothing sure, save onely of the death,

---

7 *protract :* delay.   8 *ure :* use, practice.

To whom both man and all the world doth owe
Their end at last. Neither should[16] natures   155
    power
In other sort against your hart prevaile,
Than as the naked hand whose stroke assayes
The armed brest where force doth light in vaine.
GORBODUC. Many can yelde right sage and grave ad-
    vise
Of pacient sprite to others wrapped in woe,   160
And can in speche both rule and conquere kinde,
Who if by proofe they might feele natures force,
Would shew themselves men as they are in dede,
Which now wil nedes be gods. But what doth
    meane
The sory chere[9] of her[17] that here doth come?   165
    [Enter MARCELLA.]
MARCELLA. Oh where is ruth? Or where is pitie now?
Whether is gentle hart and mercy fled?
Are they exiled out of our stony brestes,
Never to make returne? Is all the world
Drowned in bloud, and soncke in crueltie?   170
If not in women mercy may be found,
If not (alas) within the mothers brest,
To her owne childe, to her owne fleshe and bloud,
If ruthe be banished thence, if pitie there
May have no place, if there no gentle hart   175
Do live and dwell, where should we seeke it then?
GORBODUC. Madame (alas) what meanes your woful
    tale?
MARCELLA. O sillie[10] woman I, why to this houre
Have kinde and fortune thus deferred[11] my breath,
That I should live to see this dolefull day?   180
Will ever wight beleve that such hard hart
Could rest within the cruell mothers brest,
With her owne hand to slay her onely sonne?
But out (alas) these eyes behelde the same,
They saw the driery[12] sight, and are becomen   185
Most ruthfull recordes of the bloudy fact.

---

9 *sory chere*: sorrowful man-   12 *driery*: horrid, perhaps
   ner.   with something of the
10 *sillie*: innocent, harmless.   old sense of "bloudy."
11 *deferred*: prolonged.

Porrex (alas) is by his mother slaine,
And with her hand, a wofull thing to tell,
While slumbring on his carefull bed he restes
His hart stabde[18] in with knife is reft of life.   190
GORBODUC. O *Eubulus,* oh draw this sword of ours,
And pearce this hart with speed. O hatefull light,
O lothsome life, O sweete and welcome death.
Deare *Eubulus,* worke this we thee besech.
EUBULUS. Pacient, your grace, perhappes he liveth   195
yet,
With wound receaved, but not of certaine death.
GORBODUC. O let us then repayre unto the place,
And see if[19] *Porrex* live,[20] or thus be slaine.
                [*Exeunt* GORBODUC *and* EUBULUS.]
MARCELLA. Alas, he liveth not, it is too true,
That with these eyes of him a perelesse prince,   200
Sonne to a king, and in the flower of youth,
Even with a twinke[13] a senselesse stocke I saw.
AROSTUS. O damned deede.
MARCELLA.   But heare hys[21] ruthefull end.
The noble prince, pearst with the sodeine
wound,[22]
Out of his wretched slumber hastely start,   205
Whose strength now fayling straight he over-
threw,[14]
When in the fall his eyes even new unclosed
Behelde the Queene, and cryed to her for helpe.
We then, alas, the ladies which that time
Did there attend, seing that heynous deede,   210
And hearing him oft call the wretched name
Of mother, and to crye to her for aide,
Whose direfull hand gave him the mortall wound,
Pitying (alas) for nought els could we do
His ruthefull[23] end, ranne to the wofull bedde,   215
Dispoyled straight[15] his brest, and all we might
Wiped in vaine with napkins next at hand,
The sodeine streames of bloud that flushed fast
Out of the gaping wound. O what a looke,
O what a ruthefull, stedfast eye methought   220
He fixt upon my face, which to my death

---

13 *with a twinke :* in a twin-   14 *overthrew :* fell down.
   kling.   15 *straight :* directly.

Will never part fro me, when with a braide[16]
A deepe fet[17] sigh he gave, and therewithall
Clasping his handes, to heaven he cast his sight.
And straight pale death pressing within his face   225
The flying ghost his mortall corpes forsooke.

AROSTUS. Never did age bring forth so vile a fact.[18]

MARCELLA. O hard and cruell happe, that thus as-
          signed
Unto so worthy a wight so wretched end.
But most hard, cruell hart, that could consent   230
To lend the hatefull destenies that hand,
By which, alas, so heynous crime was wrought.
O Queene of adamant, O marble brest,
If not the favour of his comely face,
If not his princely chere and countenance,   235
His valiant, active armes, his manly brest,
If not his faire and seemely personage,
His noble limmes in such proportion[24] cast
As would have wrapt[19] a sillie womans thought,
If this mought not have moved thy bloudy hart   240
And that most cruell hand the wretched weapon
Even to let fall, and kiste him in the face,
With teares for ruthe to reave such one by death,
Should nature yet consent to slay her sonne?
O mother, thou to murder thus thy childe?   245
Even *Jove* with justice must with lightning flames
From heaven send downe some strange revenge on
          thee.
Ah, noble prince, how oft have I behelde
Thee mounted on thy fierce and traumpling stede,
Shining in armour bright before the tilt,   250
And with thy mistresse sleve tied on thy helme,
And charge thy staffe to please thy ladies eye,
That bowed the headpeece of thy frendly foe?
How oft in armes on horse to bend the mace?
How oft in armes on foote to breake the sworde,   255
Which never now these eyes may see againe?

AROSTUS. Madame, alas, in vaine these plaints are
          shed.

---

16 *braide*: sudden movement,   18 *fact*: deed.
     spasm.   19 *wrapt*: made rapt.
17 *fet*: fetched, drawn.

Rather with me depart, and helpe to swage[20]
The thoughtfull griefes that in the aged king
Must needes by nature growe, by death of this   260
His onely sonne, whom he did holde so deare.
MARCELLA. What wight is that which saw that I did
                   see,
And could refraine to waile with plaint and teares?
Not I, alas, that hart is not in me.
But let us goe, for I am greved anew,   265
To call to minde the wretched fathers woe.
                              [*Exeunt.*]
CHORUS. Whan greedy lust in royall seate to reigne
Hath reft all care of Goddes and eke of men,
And cruell hart, wrath, treason, and disdaine
Within[25] ambicious brest are lodged, then   270
Beholde how mischiefe wide herselfe displayes,
And with the brothers hand the brother slayes.
When bloud thus shed doth staine the[26] heav-
                   ens face,
Crying to *Jove* for vengeance of the deede,
The mightie God even moveth from his place,   275
With wrath to wreke. Then sendes[27] he forth
                   with spede
The dreadfull furies, daughters of the night,
With serpentes girt, carying the whip of ire,
With heare[21] of stinging snakes, and shining bright
With flames and bloud, and with a brand of fire.   280
These for revenge of wretched murder done,
Do make[28] the mother kill her onely sonne.
Blood asketh blood, and death must death requite.
Jove by his just and everlasting dome
Justly hath ever so requited it.   285
The[29] times before recorde, and times to come
Shall finde it true, and so doth present proofe
Present before our eyes for our behoofe.
O happy wight that suffres not the snare
Of murderous minde to tangle him in blood.   290
And happy he that can in time beware
By others harmes and turne it to his good.
But wo to him that fearing not to offend
Doth serve his lust, and will not see the end.
                              [*Exeunt* CHORUS.]

20 *swage* : assuage.   21 *heare* : hair.

THE ORDER AND SIGNIFICATION OF THE DOMME
SHEW BEFORE THE FIFTH ACT.

First the drommes and fluites began to sound,
during which there came forth upon the stage a
company of Hargabusiers[1] and of Armed men
all in order of battaile. These, after their peeces
discharged and that the armed men had three   5
times marched about the stage, departed, and then
the drommes and fluits did cease. Hereby was signified tumults, rebellions, armes and civill warres
to follow, as fell in the realme of great Brittayne,
which by the space of fiftie yeares and more con-   10
tinued in civill warre betwene the nobilitie after
the death of king Gorboduc, and of his issues, for
want of certayne limitacion in the[1] succession
of the crowne, till the time of Dunwallo Mol-
mutius,[2] who reduced the land to monarchie.   15

ACTUS QUINTUS. SCENA PRIMA.

[Enter] CLOTYN, MANDUD, GWENARD, FERGUS,
                   [and] EUBULUS.

CLOTYN. Did ever age bring forth such tirants harts?
   The brother hath bereft the brothers life,
   The mother she hath died[1] her cruell handes
   In bloud of her owne sonne, and now at last
   The people, loe, forgetting trouth and love,   5
   Contemning quite both law and loyall hart,
   Even they have slaine their soveraigne lord and
                   queene.
MANDUD. Shall this their traitorous crime unpunished
                   rest?
   Even yet they cease not, caryed on[1] with rage,
   In their rebellious routes, to threaten still   10
   A new bloudshed unto the princes kinne,
   To slay them all, and to uproote the race
   Both of the king and queene, so are they moved
   With Porrex death, wherin they falsely charge

ACTUS QUINTUS. SCENA
PRIMA.
   1 died: dyed.

The giltlesse king without desert at all,   15
And traitorously have murdered him therfore,
And eke the queene.

GWENARD.   Shall subjectes dare with force
To worke revenge upon their princes fact?
Admit the worst that may, as sure in this
The deede was fowle, the queene to slay her sonne,   20
Shall yet the subject seeke to take the sworde,
Arise agaynst his lord, and slay his king?
O wretched state, where those rebellious hartes
Are not rent out even from their living breastes,
And with the body throwen unto the foules   25
As carrion foode, for terrour of the rest.

FERGUS. There can no punishment be thought too
            great
For this so grevous cryme; let spede therfore
Be used therin, for it behoveth so.

EUBULUS. Ye, all my lordes, I see, consent in one,   30
And I as one consent with ye in all.
I holde it more than neede with[2] sharpest law
To punish this[3] tumultuous bloudy rage.
For nothing more may shake the common state,
Than sufferance of uproares without redresse,   35
Wherby how some kingdomes of mightie power
After great conquestes made, and florishing
In fame and wealth, have ben to ruine brought.
I pray to *Jove* that we may rather wayle
Such happe in them than witnesse in ourselves.   40
Eke fully with the duke my minde agrees.[4]
Though kinges forget to governe as they ought,
Yet subjectes must obey as they are bounde.
But now, my lordes, before ye farder wade,
Or spend your speach what sharpe revenge shall   45
            fall
By justice plague on these rebellious wightes,
Methinkes ye rather should first search the way
By which in time the rage of this uproare
Mought be repressed, and these great tumults
            ceased.
Even yet the life of Brittayne land doth hang   50
In traitours balaunce of unegall weight.
Thinke not, my lordes, the death of *Gorboduc,*
Nor yet *Videnas* bloud will cease their rage.

Even our owne lyves, our wives and children
    deare,[5]
Our countrey dearest of all, in daunger standes,   55
Now to be spoiled, now, now made desolate,
And by ourselves a conquest to ensue.
For geve once swey unto the peoples lustes,
To rush forth on, and stay them not in time,
And as the streame that rowleth downe the hyll,   60
So will they headlong ronne with raging thoughtes
From bloud to bloud, from mischiefe unto moe,[2]
To ruine of the realme, themselves and all,
So giddy are the common peoples mindes,
So glad of chaunge, more wavering than the sea.   65
Ye see (my lordes) what strength these rebelles
    have,
What hugie nombre is assembled still,
For though the traiterous fact, for which they rose
Be wrought and done, yet lodge they still in field.
So that how farre their furies yet will stretch   70
Great cause we have to dreade. That we may seeke
By present battaile to represse their power,
Speede must we use to levie force therfore.
For either they forthwith will mischiefe worke,
Or their rebellious roares forthwith will[6] cease.   75
These violent thinges may have no lasting long.
Let us therfore use this for present helpe,
Perswade by gentle speach, and offre grace
With gift of pardon save unto the chiefe,
And that upon condicion that forthwith   80
They yelde the captaines of their enterprise,
To beare such guerdon[3] of their traiterous fact,
As may be both due vengeance to themselves,
And holsome terrour to posteritie.
This shall, I thinke, scatter[7] the greatest part,   85
That now are holden with desire of home,
Weried in field with cold of winters nightes,
And some (no doubt) striken with dread of law.
Whan this is once proclaimed, it shall make
The captaines to mistrust the multitude,   90
Whose safetie biddes them to betray their heads,
And so much more bycause the rascall routes

2 *moe* : more.

3 *guerdon* : reward, i.e. pun-
    ishment.

In thinges of great and perillous attemptes
Are never trustie to the noble race.
And while we treate and stand on termes of grace,   95
We shall both stay their furies rage the while,
And eke⁴ gaine time, whose onely helpe⁵ sufficeth
Withouten warre to vanquish rebelles power.
In the meanewhile, make you in redynes
Such band of horsemen as ye may prepare.   100
Horsemen (you know) are not the commons
            strength,
But are the force and store of noble men,
Wherby the unchosen and unarmed sort
Of skillesse rebelles, whome none other power
But nombre makes to be of dreadfull force,   105
With sodeyne brunt may quickely be opprest.
And if this gentle meane of proffered grace
With stubborne hartes cannot so farre avayle
As to asswage their desperate courages,
Then do I wish such slaughter to be made,   110
As present age and eke posteritie
May be adrad with horrour of revenge
That justly then shall on these rebelles fall.
This is, my lordes,[8] the summe of mine advise.

CLOTYN. Neither this case admittes debate at large,   115
    And though it did, this speach that hath ben sayd
    Hath well abridged the tale I would have tolde.
    Fully with *Eubulus* do I consent
    In all that he hath sayd, and if the same
    To you, my lordes, may seeme for best advise,   120
    I wish that it should streight be put in ure.

MANDUD. My lordes, than let us presently depart,
    And follow this that liketh us⁶ so well.

                    [*Exeunt all but* FERGUS.]

FERGUS. If ever time to gaine a kingdome here
    Were offred man, now it is offred mee.   125
    The realme is reft both of their king and queene,
    The ofspring of the prince is slaine and dead,
    No issue now remaines, the heire unknowen,
    The people are in armes and mutynies,
    The nobles they are busied how to cease   130
    These great rebellious tumultes and uproares,

---

4 *eke* : also.   6 *liketh us* : pleases us.
5 *onely helpe* : help alone.

And *Brittayne* land now desert left alone
Amyd these broyles uncertayne where to rest,
Offers herselfe unto that noble hart
That will or dare pursue to beare her crowne.   135
Shall I that am the duke of *Albanye*,
Discended from that line of noble bloud, [1]
Which hath so long florished in worthy fame,
Of valiaunt hartes, such as in noble brestes
Of right should rest above the [9] baser sort,   140
Refuse to venture [10] life to winne a crowne?
Whom shall I finde enmies that will withstand
My fact herein, if I attempt by armes
To seeke the same [11] now in these times of
          broyle?
These dukes power can hardly well appease   145
The people that already are in armes.
But if perhappes my force be once in field,
Is not my strength in power above the best
Of all these lordes now left in *Brittayne* land?
And though they should match me with power of   150
          men,
Yet doubtfull is the chaunce of battailles joyned.
If victors of the field we may depart,
Ours is the scepter then of great Brittayne.
If slayne amid the playne this body lye, [12]
Mine enemies yet shall not deny me this,   155
But that I dyed geving the noble charge
To hazarde life for conquest of a crowne.
Forthwith therefore will I in post[7] depart
To *Albanye*, and raise in armour there
All power I can. And here my secret friendes   160
By secret practise shall sollicite still
To seeke to wynne to me the peoples hartes. [*Exit.*]

ACTUS QUINTUS.   SCENA SECUNDA.

[*Enter*] EUBULUS, [*solus.*]

EUBULUS.   O *Jove*, how are these peoples harts
          abusde?
What blind fury thus headlong caries them?
That though so many bookes, so many rolles

7 *in post :* in haste.

Of auncient time[1] recorde what grevous plagues
Light on these rebelles aye, and though so oft   5
Their eares have heard their aged fathers tell
What juste reward these traitours still receyve,
Yea, though themselves have sene depe death and
          bloud,
By strangling cord and slaughter of the sword,
To such assigned, yet can they not beware,   10
Yet can[2] not stay their lewde,[3] rebellious
          handes,
But suffring, loe[4] fowle treason to distaine¹
Their wretched myndes, forget their loyall hart,
Reject all truth, and rise against their prince.
A ruthefull case, that those, whom duties bond,[5]   15
Whom grafted law by nature, truth, and faith,
Bound to preserve their countrey and their king,
Borne to defend their commonwealth and prince,
Even they should geve consent thus to subvert
Thee, Brittaine land, and from thy[6] wombe   20
          should spring[7]
(O native soile) those, that will needs destroy
And ruyne thee and eke themselves in fine.
For lo, when once the dukes had offred grace
Of pardon sweete, the multitude, missledde
By traitorous fraude of their ungracious heades,²   25
One sort that saw the dangerous successe³
Of stubborne standing in rebellious warre,
And knew the difference of princes power
From headlesse nombre of tumultuous routes,⁴
Whom common countreies care and private feare   30
Taught to repent the errour[8] of their rage,
Layde handes upon the captaines of their band,
And brought them bound unto the mightie dukes.
And other[9] sort, not trusting yet so well
The truth of pardon, or mistrusting more   35
Their owne offence than that they could[10]
          conceive
Such hope of pardon for so foule misdede,
Or for that they their captaines could not yeld,

Actus Quintus. Scena
Secunda.
  1 *distaine*: stain.
  2 *fraude* . . . *heades*: de-

ception of their unso-
phisticated minds.
3 *successe*: aftermath.
4 *routes*: hordes.

Who, fearing to be yelded, fled before,
Stale[5] home by silence of the secret night.   40
The thirde unhappy and enraged sort
Of desperate hartes, who, stained in princes bloud
From trayterous furour could not be withdrawen
By love, by law, by grace, ne yet by feare,
By proffered life, ne yet by threatned death,   45
With mindes hopelesse of life, dreadlesse of death,
Carelesse of countrey, and awelesse of God,
Stoode bent to fight, as furies did them move,
With violent death to close their traiterous life.
These all by power of horsemen were opprest   50
And with revenging sworde slayne in the field,
Or with the strangling cord hangd on the tree,[11]
Where yet their[12] carryen carcases do preach
The fruites that rebelles reape of their uproares
And of the murder of their sacred prince.   55
But, loe, where do approche the noble dukes,
By whom these tumults have ben thus appeasde.

> [*Enter* CLOTYN, MANDUD, GWENARD,
> *and* AROSTUS.]

CLOTYN. I thinke the world will now at length be-
          ware
    And feare to put on armes agaynst their prince.
MANDUD. If not, those trayterous hartes that dare[13]   60
          rebell,
    Let them beholde the wide and hugie fieldes
    With bloud and bodies[14] spread of[15] rebelles
          slayne,
    The lofty[16] trees clothed with the[17] corpses
          dead
    That strangled with the corde do hang theron.[18]
AROSTUS. A just rewarde, such as all times before   65
    Have ever lotted[6] to those wretched folkes.
GWENARD. But what meanes he that commeth here
          so fast?

> [*Enter* NUNTIUS.]

NUNTIUS. My lordes, as dutie and my trouth doth
          move
    And of my countrey worke a[19] care in mee,
    That if the spending of my breath availed[20]   70

---

5 *Stale*: Stole.   6 *lotted*: allotted.

To do the service that my hart desires,
I would not shunne to imbrace a present death.
So have I now in that wherein I thought
My travayle mought performe some good effect,
Ventred my life to bring these tydinges here.   75
Fergus, the mightie duke of Albanye,
Is now in armes and lodgeth in the fielde
With twentie thousand men. Hether he bendes
His spedy marche, and mindes to invade the
    crowne.
Dayly he gathereth strength and spreads abrode   80
That to this realme no certeine heire remaines,
That Brittayne land is left without a guide,
That he the scepter seekes, for nothing els
But to preserve the people and the land,
Which now remaine as ship without a sterne.[7]   85
Loe, this is that which I have here to say.[21]
CLOTYN. Is this his fayth? And shall he falsely thus
Abuse the vauntage of unhappie times?
O wretched land, if his outragious pride,
His cruell and untempred wilfulnesse,   90
His deepe dissembling shewes of false pretence,
Should once attaine the crowne of Brittaine land.
Let us, my lordes, with timely force resist
The new attempt of this our common foe,
As we would quench the flames of common fire.   95
MANDUD. Though we remaine without a certain
    prince
To weld the realme or guide the wandring rule,
Yet now the common mother of us all,
Our native land, our countrey, that conteines
Our wives, children, kindred, ourselves and all   100
That ever is or may be deare to man,
Cries unto us to helpe ourselves and her.
Let us advaunce our powers to represse
This growing foe of all our liberties.
GWENARD. Yea, let us so, my lordes, with hasty   105
    speede.
And ye (O Goddes) send us the welcome death
To shed our bloud in field, and leave us not
In lothesome life to lenger out our dayes,[22]

7 *sterne :* rudder.

To see the hugie heapes of these unhappes[23]
That now roll downe upon the wretched land   110
Where emptie place of princely governaunce,
No certaine stay now left of doubtlesse heire
Thus leave this guidelesse realme an open pray
To endlesse stormes and waste of civill warre.
AROSTUS. That ye (my lordes) do so agree in one,   115
To save your countrey from the violent reigne
And wrongfully usurped tyrannie
Of him that threatens conquest of you all,
To save your realme, and in this realme yourselves,
From forreine thraldome of so proud a prince,(1)   120
Much do I prayse, and I besech the Goddes,
With happy honour to requite it you.
But (O my lordes) sith now the heavens wrath
Hath reft this land the issue of their prince,
Sith of the body of our late soveraigne lorde   125
Remaines no moe, since the yong kinges be slaine,
And of[24] the title of discended crowne
Uncertainly the diverse mindes do thinke
Even of the learned sort, and more uncertainly
Will parciall8 fancie and affection deeme,   130
But most uncertainly will climbing pride
And hope of reigne withdraw to[25] sundry partes
The doubtfull right and hopefull lust to reigne,
When once this noble service is atchieved
For Brittaine land, the mother of ye all,   135
When once ye have with armed force represt
The proude attemptes of this Albanian prince
That threatens thraldome to your native land,
When ye shall vanquishers returne from field,
And finde the princely state an open pray   140
To gredie lust and to usurping power,
Then, then (my lordes) if ever kindly care
Of auncient honour of your auncesters,
Of present wealth and noblesse of your stockes,
Yea, of the lives and safetie yet to come   145
Of your deare wives, your children, and yourselves
Might move your noble hartes with gentle ruth,
Then, then, have pitie on the torne estate,
Then helpe to salve the welneare9 hopelesse sore

8 *parciall:* biased.   9 *welneare:* well-nigh.

Which ye shall do, if ye yourselves withholde   150
The slaying knife from your owne mothers throate.
Her shall you save, and you, and yours in her,
If ye shall all with one assent forbeare
Once to lay hand or take unto yourselves
The crowne, by colour of pretended right,   155
Or by what other meanes so ever it be,
Till first by common counsell of you all
In Parliament the regall diademe
Be set in certaine place of governaunce,
In which your Parliament and in your choise,   160
Preferre the right (my lordes) without[26] re-
                    spect
Of strength of[27] frendes, or whatsoever cause
That may set forward any others part.
For right will last, and wrong can not endure.
Right meane I his or hers, upon whose name   165
The people rest by meane of native line,
Or by the vertue of some former lawe
Already made their title to advaunce.[2]
Such one (my lordes) let be your chosen king,
Such one so borne within your native land,   170
Such one preferre, and in no wise admitte
The heavie yoke of forreine governance.
Let forreine titles yelde to publike wealth.
And with that hart wherewith ye now prepare
Thus to withstand the proude, invading foe,   175
With that same hart (my lordes) keepe out also
Unnaturall thraldome of strangers reigne,
Ne suffer you against the rules of kinde
Your mother land to serve a forreine prince.
EUBULUS. [*Steps forward.*] Loe, here the end of   180
                    Brutus royall line,
And, loe, the entry to the wofull wracke
And utter ruine of this noble realme.
The royall king and eke his sonnes are slaine.
No ruler restes within the regall seate.
The heire, to whom the scepter longes, unknowen,   185
That to eche force of forreine princes power,
Whom vauntage of our[28] wretched state may
                    move[29]
By sodeine armes to gaine so riche a realme,
And to the proud and gredie minde at home,

Whom blinded lust to reigne leades to aspire,   190
Loe, Brittaine realme is left an open pray,
A present spoyle by conquest to ensue.
Who seeth not now how many rising mindes
Do feede their thoughts with hope to reach a
      realme?
And who will not by force attempt to winne   195
So great a gaine, that hope perswades to have?
A simple colour shall for title serve.
Who winnes the royall crowne will want no right,
Nor such as shall display by long discent
A lineall race to prove him lawfull[30] king.   200
In the meanewhile these civil armes shall rage,
And thus a thousand mischiefes shall unfolde,
And farre and neare spread thee (O Brittaine
      land)
All right and lawe shall cease, and he that had
Nothing to day, to morrowe shall enjoye   205
Great heapes of golde[31] and he that flowed in
      wealth,
Loe, he shall be bereft[32] of life and all,
And happiest he that then possesseth least.
The wives shall suffer rape, the maides defloured,
And children fatherlesse shall weepe and waile,   210
With fire and sworde thy native folke shall perishe,
One kinsman shall bereave anothers[33] life,
The father shall unwitting slay the sonne,
The sonne shall slay the sire and know it not,
Women and maides the cruell souldiers sword   215
Shall perse to death, and sillie children, loe,
That playinge[34] in the streetes and fieldes are
      found,
By violent hand shall close their latter day.
Whom shall the fierce and bloudy souldier
Reserve to life? Whom shall he spare from death?   220
Even thou (O wretched mother) halfe alive,
Thou shalt beholde thy deare and onely childe
Slaine with the sworde while he yet suckes thy
      brest.
Loe, giltlesse bloud shall thus eche where be shed.
Thus shall the wasted soile yelde forth no fruite,   225
But dearth and famine shall possesse the land.
The townes shall be consumed and burnt with fire,

The peopled cities shall waxe desolate,
And thou, O Brittaine,[35] whilome in renowme,
Whilome in wealth and fame, shalt thus be torne,   230
Dismembred thus, and thus be rent in twaine,
Thus wasted and defaced, spoyled and destroyed.
These be the fruites your civil warres will bring.
Hereto it commes when kinges will not consent
To grave advise, but followe wilfull will.   235
This is the end, when in fonde[36] princes hartes
Flattery prevailes and sage rede hath no place.
These are the plages, when murder is the meane
To make new heires unto the royall crowne.
Thus wreke the Gods, when that the mothers   240
        wrath
Nought but the bloud of her owne childe may
        swage.
These mischiefes spring[37] when rebells will
        arise,
To worke revenge and judge their princes fact.
This, this ensues, when noble men do faile
In loyall trouth, and subjectes will be kinges.   245
And this doth growe when, loe, unto the prince,
Whom death or sodeine happe of life bereaves,
No certaine heire remaines, such certaine
        heire,[38]
As not all onely is the rightfull heire
But to the realme is so made knowen[39] to be,   250
And trouth therby vested in subjectes hartes,
To owe fayth there where right is knowen to rest.
Alas, in Parliament what hope can be,
When is of Parliament no hope at all?
Which, though it be assembled by consent,   255
Yet is[40] not likely with consent to end,
While eche one for himselfe, or for his frend,
Against his foe, shall travaile what he may.
While now the state left open to the man
That shall with greatest force invade the same   260
Shall fill ambicious mindes with gaping hope,
When will they once with yelding hartes agree?
Or in the while, how shall the realme be used?
No, no. Then Parliament should have bene holden,
And certeine heires appointed to the crowne   265

To stay[10] the[41] title of established right
And in the people plant[42] obedience,
While yet the prince did live, whose name and
                power
By lawfull sommons and authoritie
Might make a Parliament to be of force   270
And might have set the state[43] in quiet stay.
But now, O happie man, whom[44] spedie death
Deprives of life, ne is enforced to see
These hugie mischiefes and these miseries,
These civil warres, these murders, and these   275
                wronges.
Of justice yet must God[45] in fine restore
This noble crowne unto the lawfull heire,
For right will alwayes live and rise at length,
But wrong can never take deepe roote to last.

                                        [*Exeunt.*]

              The ende of the Tragedie of Kynge
                      Gorboduc.[46]

10 *stay :* sustain.

CAMBISES

by

THOMAS PRESTON

A lamentable tragedy

mixed ful of pleasant mirth, conteyning the life of
CAMBISES king of PERCIA, from the beginning
of his kingdome vnto his death, his one good deed of execution, after that many wicked deeds
and tirannous murders, committed by and
through him, and laſt of all, his odious
death by Gods Juſtice appoin-
ted. Don in ſuch order as
foloweth. By
Thomas Preston.

❦ *The diuiſion of the partes.*

Councel. Huf. Praxaſpes. Murder. Lob, the 3. Lord.	*For one man.*	Prologue. Siſamnes. Diligence. Crueltie. Hob. Preparatiō the 1. Lord.	*For one man.*	
Lord. Ruf, Commons cry, Cōmōs cōplaint Lord ſmirdis. Venus.	*For one man.*	Ambidexter, Triall.	*For one man.*	
Knight, Snuf, ſmall habilitie. Proof. Execution. Attendance. ſecond Lord.	*For one man.*	Meretrix, Shame. Otian. Mother. Lady. Queene.	*For one man.*	
Cambiſes. Epilogus.	*For one man.*	Yung childe Cupid.	*For one man.*	

CAMBISES, *King of Persia.*
SMIRDIS, *his brother.*
SISAMNES, *a judge.*
OTIAN, *his son.*
PRAXASPES, *a councellor.*
YUNG CHILDE, *his son.*
MOTHER *to the Yung Childe.*
LADY, *afterwards* QUEENE *and wife to Cambises.*
WAITING MAID.
AMBIDEXTER, *the Vice.*
VENUS.
CUPID, *her son.*

SHAME.	COMMONS COMPLAINT.
COUNCELL.	TRIALL.
ATTENDANCE.	PROOF.
DILIGENCE.	EXECUTION.
PREPARATION.	CRUELTIE.
SMALL HABILITIE.	MURDER.
COMMONS CRY.	HOB ⎫ *Country bumpkins.*
HUF ⎫	LOB ⎭
RUF ⎬ *Ruffians.*	MARIAN MAY-BE-GOOD, *wife*
SNUF ⎭	*to Hob.*
MERETRIX, *a prostitute.*	*Three* LORDS, KNIGHT.

THE SCENE
PERSIA.]

The PROLOGUE *entreth.*

Agathon,(1) he whose counsail wise to princes
        weal¹ extended,
By good advice unto a prince three things he hath
        commended :
First, is that he hath government and ruleth over
        men,
Secondly, to rule with lawes, eke² Justice (saith
        he) then,

PROLOGUE.   2 *eke :* also.
1 *weal :* welfare, or perhaps
   rule.

Thirdly, that he must wel conceive he may not   5
    alwaies raigne.

Lo, thus the rule unto a prince Agathon squared[3]
    plaine.

Tully[2] the wise, whose sapience in volumes
    great dooth tell,

Who in wisdome in that time did many men excel,

A Prince (saith he) is of himself a plaine and
    speaking law,

The law, a schoolemaister devine—this by his rule   10
    I draw.[4]

The sage and wittie Seneca[3] his woords therto
    did frame :[5]

The honest excercise of kings, men wil insue the
    same,

But contrary wise if that a king abuse his kingly
    seat,

His ignomy and bitter shame in fine shal be more
    great.

   In Percia there reignd a king who Cirus hight[6]   15
    by name,

Who did deserve, as I doo read, the lasting blast[7]
    of Fame,

But he, when Sisters Three[4] had wrought to
    shere his vitall thred,

As heire due, to take the crowne Cambises did
    proceed.

He in his youth was trained up by trace[8] of ver-
    tues lore,

Yet (beeing king) did clene forget his perfect race   20
    before,[9]

Then, cleving more unto his wil, such vice did im-
    mitate

As one of Icarus his kind,[5] forewarning then
    did hate.

Thinking that none could him dismay, ne none his
    fact[10] could see,

---

3 *squared :* set forth, or pos-
    sibly fitted.

4 *draw :* derive.

5 *frame :* address.

6 *hight :* was called.

7 *blast :* trump, tribute.

8 *by trace :* in the path.

9 *perfect race before :* previ-
    ously admirable behav-
    ior.

10 *fact :* deed.

Yet at the last a fall he took, like Icarus to bee.

Els—as the fish which oft had take the pleasant   25
    bait from hook

In safe[11] did spring and pearce the streams when
    fisher fast did looke

To hoist up from the watry waves unto the dryed
    land

Then skaepte,[12] at last by suttle baight come to
    the fishers hand—

Even so this King Cambises heer, when he had
    wrought his wil,

Taking delight the innocent his guiltlesse blood to   30
    spil,

Then mightie Jove would not permit to procecute
    offence,

But what mesure the king did meat,[13] the same
    did Jove commence,

To bring to end with shame his race. Two yeeres
    he did not reign.

His crueltie we wil delate[14] and make the matter
    plain,

Craving that this may suffise now your patience to   35
    win.

I take my way. Beholde, I see the players com-
    ming in.   [*Exit.*]

FINIS.

First enter CAMBISES *the King,* KNIGHT, [LORD,]
    and COUNCELL.[1]

CAMBISES. My Councell[2] grave and sapient, with
    lords of legal train,

Attentive ears towards me[3] bend, and mark
    what shal be sain.

So you likewise, my valiant knight, whose manly
    acts doth fly

By brute[1] of Fame that, sounding tromp, doth
    perse the azure sky.

---

11 *safe :* safety.   14 *delate :* relate.
12 *skaepte :* escaped.   CAMBISES.
13 *meat :* mete, measure out.   1 *brute :* report.

My sapient woords, I say, perpend,[2] and so your   5
    skil delate.

You knowe that Mors[3] vanquished hath Cirus,
    that king of state,

And I by due inheritance possesse that princely
    crowne,

Ruling by swoord of mighty force in place of great
    renown.

You knowe and often have heard tell my fathers
    worthy facts.

A manly Marsis[4] heart he bare, appeering by his   10
    acts.

And what, shall I to ground let fall my fathers
    golden praise?

No, no! I meane for to attempt this same more
    large to raise.

In that that I, his sonne, succeed his kingly seat, as
    due,

Extend your councel unto me in that I aske of you :

I am the king of Persia, a large and fertil soile.   15

The Egyptians against us repugne[5] as varlets[4]
    slave[6] and vile.

Therefore I meane with Marsis hart with warres
    them to frequent,

Them to subdue as captives mine, this is my harts
    intent.

So shall I win honors delight, and praise of me
    shall go.

My Councell, speake, and lordings eke, is it not   20
    best doo so?

COUNCELL. O puisant[5] king, your blisful woords
    deserves abundant praise,

That you in this doo go about your fathers fame to
    raise.

O blisful day, that king so yung such profit should
    conceive,

His fathers praise and his to win from those that
    would deceive!

---

2 *perpend* : heed.   5 *repugne* : are contemptu-
3 *Mors* : Death.   ous.
4 *Marsis* : of Mars, Mars-like.   6 *slave* : slavish.

Sure, my true and soveraine king, I fall before you   25
          prest,
Answere to give, as dutie mine, in that your Grace
          request.
If that your hart adicted be the Egyptians to con-
          vince[7]
Through Marsis aid the conquest wun, then deed
          of happy prince
Shall pearce the skyes unto the throne of the su-
          pernall seat
And merite there a just rewarde of Jupiter the   30
          Great.
But then your Grace must not turn back from this
          pretenced[8] wil.
For to proceed in vertuous life imploy indevour
          stil.
Extinguish vice, and in that cup to drink have no
          delight.
To martiall feats and kingly sporte fix all your
          whole delight.

CAMBISES.[6] My Councell grave, a thousand thanks   35
          with hart I doo you render,
That you my case so prosperouse intierly doo
          tender.
I wil not swarve from those your steps wherto you
          wold me train.
But now, my lord and valiant knight, with woords
          give answer plain :
Are you content with me to go the Marsis games to
          try?

LORD. Yea, peerlesse prince! To aid your Grace my-   40
          self wil live and dye.

KNIGHT. And I for my habilitie[9] for feare will not
          turn back,
But as the ship against the rocks sustain and bide
          the wrack.[10]

CAMBISES. O willing harts, a thousand thanks I render
          unto you!
Strik up your drummes with courage great, we
          wil march foorth even now.

---

7 *convince* : vanquish.   9 *for my habilitie* : as for my
8 *pretenced* : intended.   willingness.
                                   10 *wrack* : wreck.

COUNCELL. Permit (O king) few woords to heer, my   45
    duty serves no lesse,
    Therefore give leave to Councell thine his minde
      for to expresse.
CAMBISES. Speake on, my Councell, what it be[11] you
    shal have favour mine.
COUNCELL. Then wil I speake unto your Grace as
    duty dooth me binde.
    Your Grace dooth meane for to attempt of war the
      manly art :
    Your Grace therein may hap receive with others   50
      for your parte
    The dent[12] of death, in those affaires all persons
      are alike,
    The hart couragious oftentimes his detryment
      dooth seek.
    Its best therfore for to permit a ruler of your land
    To sit and judge with equitie when things of right
      are scand.
CAMBISES. My Grace dooth yeeld to this your talk, to   55
    be thus now it shall.
    My knight, therefore, prepare yourself Sisamnes
      for to call.
    A judge he is of prudent skil, even he shal beare
      the sway
    In absence mine, when from the land I doo de-
      parte my way.
KNIGHT. Your knight before your Grace even heer
    himself hath redy prest
    With willing hart for to fulfil as your Grace made   60
      request.   *Exit.*
COUNCELL. Pleaseth your Grace, I judge of him to be
    a man right fit,
    For he is learned in the law, having the gift of wit.
    In your Graces presinct[13] I doo not view for it a
      meeter man.
    His learning is of good effect, bring proofe thereof
      I can.
    I doo not knowe what is his life, his conscience hid   65
      from me.

11 *what it be :* whatever it is.   13 *presinct :* vicinity, en-
12 *dent :* blow.   virons.

    I dout not but the feare of God before his eyes to
          be.

LORD. Report[7] declares he is a man that to himself
          is nye,[14]

    One that favoureth much the world and too much
          sets therby.[8]

    But this I say of certainty : if he your Grace suc-
          ceed

    In your absence but for awhile, he wil be warnd   70
          indeed

    No injustice for to frequent, no partiall judge to
          proove,

    But rule all things with equitie to win your Graces
          loove.

CAMBISES. Of that he shall a warning have my
          heasts[15] for to obay.

    Great punishment for his offence against him wil I
          lay.

COUNCELL. Beholde, I see him now agresse[16] and   75
          enter into place.

             [*Enter* SISAMNES.]

SISAMNES. O puisant prince and mightie king, the
          gods preserve your Grace!

    Your Graces message came to me your wil pur-
          porting foorth.

    With grateful minde I it received according to
          mine othe,

    Erecting then myself with speed before your
          Graces eyes,

    The tenor of your princely wil from you for to   80
          agnise.[17]

CAMBISES. Sisamnes, this the whole effect the which
          for you I sent :

    Our mind it is to elevate you to great preferment.

    My Grace and gratious Councell eke hath chose
          you for this cause.

    In judgment you doo office beare, which[18] have
          the skil in lawes.

14 *nye :* nigh. (He thinks only   16 *agresse :* enter.
    of himself.)   17 *agnise :* learn.
15 *heasts :* behests.   18 *which :* who.

We think that you accordingly by justice rule wil   85
    deale,

That for offence none shal have cause of wrong
    you to appeale.[19]

SISAMNES. Abundant thanks unto your Grace for this
    benignitie!

To you his Councell, in like case, with lords of
    clemency.

What so your Grace to me permits, if I therin
    offend,

Such execution then commence, and use it to this   90
    end,

That all other by that my deed example so may
    take

To admonish them to flee the same by fear it may
    them make.

CAMBISES. Then, according to your woords, if you
    therein offend,

I assure you even from my brest, correction shall
    extend.

From Persia I meane to go into the Egipt land   95

Them to convince by force of armes and win the
    upper hand.

While I therfore absent shall be I doo you ful
    permit

As governour in this my right in that estate to sit

For to detect and eke correct those that abuse my
    Grace.

This is the totall of my wil. Give answere in this   100
    case.

SISAMNES. Unworthy much (O prince) am I and for
    this gift unfit,

But sith that it hath pleasd your Grace that I in
    it must sit,

I doo avouch unto my death according to my skil

With equitie for to observe your Graces minde and
    wil,

And nought from it to swarve, indeed, but sin-   105
    cerely to stay,

Els let me taste the penaltie, as I before did say.

CAMBISES. Wel then, of this authoritie I give you ful
    possession.

19 *appeale :* accuse.

SISAMNES. And I will it fulfil also, as I have made pro-
    fession.

CAMBISES. My Councell, then let us departe a final
    stay to make.

To Egypt[9] land now foorth with speed my voy- 110
    age I wil take.

Strike up your drummes us to rejoyce to hear the
    warlike sound.

Stay you heere, Sisamnes judge, and looke wel to
    your bound![20]

Exeunt King, LORD *and* COUNCELL [*to the sound
    of drums.*]

SISAMNES. Even now the king hath me extolde and
    set me up aloft.

Now may I were the brodered garde[10], (1) and
    lye in down bed soft.

Now may I purchase house and land and have all 115
    at my wil.

Now may I build a princely place my minde for
    to fulfil.

Now may I abrogate the law as I shall think it
    good.

If anyone me now offend, I may demaund his
    blood.

According to the proverb olde, my mouth I wil
    up-make. (2)

Now it dooth lye all in my hand to leave or els to 120
    take,

To deale with justice to my[11] bound and so to
    live in hope.

But oftentimes the birds be gone while one for
    nest dooth grope. (3)

Doo wel or il, I dare avouch some evil on me wil
    speake.

No, truely, yet I doo not meane the kings precepts
    to breake.

To place I meane for to returne my duty to ful- 125
    fil. (4)   *Exit.*

Enter [AMBIDEXTER] *the Vice, with an olde
  capcase on his hed, an olde pail about
  his hips for harnes,*[21] *a scummer*

20 *bound :* bond, promise.   21 *harnes :* armor.

and a potlid by his side, and
a rake on his shoulder.[12]

AMBIDEXTER. Stand away! stand away![5] for the
passion of God.
Harnessed I am, prepared to the field.
I would have bene content at home to have bod,[22]
But I am sent forth with my speare and sheeld.
I am appointed to fight against a snail.[6]   130
And Wilken Wren the ancient[23] shall beare;
I dout not but against him to prevail.
To be a man my deeds shall declare.
If I overcome him, then a butterflye takes his
parte.
His weapon must be a blew-speckled[13] hen.   135
But you shall see me overthrowe him with a fart.
So without conquest he shal go home againe.
If I overcome him, I must fight with a flye,
And a black pudding the flyes weapon must be
At the first blowe on the ground he shall lie.   140
I wil be sure to thrust him through the mouth to
the knee.
To conquest these fellowes the man I wil play.
Ha, ha, ha, now ye wil make me to smile
To see if I can all men beguile.[7]
Ha! my name, my name would you so faine   145
knowe?
Yea, iwis,[24] shal ye, and that with all speed—
I have forgot it, therefore I cannot showe.
A, a, now I have it. I have it indeed!
My name is Ambidexter. I signifie one
That with bothe hands finely can play,   150
Now with king Cambises and by and by[25] gone.
Thus doo I run this way and that way.
For [a] while I meane with a souldier to be,
Then give I a leape to Sisamnes the judge.
I dare avouch you shall his destruction see.   155
To all kinde of estates I meane for to trudge.
Ambidexter? Nay, he is a fellow, if ye knew all!
Ceasse for a while, heerafter hear more ye shall.
[*Steps aside.*]

22 *bod:* abided, remained.   24 *iwis:* certainly.
23 *ancient:* flag.   25 *by and by:* at once.

Enter [as soldiers] three ruffians, HUF, RUF,
and SNUF, *singing.*

HUF. Gogs flesh and His wounds, these warres re-
      joyce my hart!

By His wounds, I hope to doo wel for my parte.   160

By Gogs hart, the world shall go evil[14] if I doo
      not shift.[26]

At some olde carles bouget[27, [15] I meane for to
      lift.

RUF. By his flesh, nose, eyes, and eares,

I will venter[28] void of all cares!

He is not a souldier that dooth feare any dout   165

If that he would bring his purpose about.

SNUF. Feare that feare list, it shall not be I.

By Gogs wounds, I will make some neck stand
      awry,

If I lose my share, I sweare by Gogs hart,

Then let another take up my parte.   170

HUF. Yet I hope to come the richest souldier away.

RUF. If a man aske ye, ye may hap to say nay.

SNUF. Let all men get what they can, not to leese[29]
      I hope.

Wheresoever I go, in eche corner I wil grope.

AMBIDEXTER. [*Advancing.*] What and ye run into[16]   175
      the corner of some prety maid?

SNUF. To grope there, good fellow, I wil not be
      afraid!

HUF. Gogs wounds, what art thou that with us doost
      mel?[30]

Thou seemest to be a soldier, the trueth to tel.

Thou seemest to be harnessed, I cannot tel how.

I think he came lately from riding some cow.   180

Such a deformed slave did I never see!

Ruf, doost thou knowe him? I pray thee tel mee.

RUF. No, by my troth, fellow Huf, I never see him
      before.

SNUF. As for me, I care not if I never see him more.

Come, let us run his arse against the poste!   185

---

26 *shift* : prosper.   29 *leese* : lose.
27 *bouget* : wallet.   30 *mel* : mix, intrude.
28 *venter* : venture.

AMBIDEXTER. A, ye slaves! I wil be with you at
    the[17] oste![31]

A, ye knaves! I wil teach ye how ye shal me de-
    ride!

    Heer let him swinge them about.[18]

[*To* RUF.] Out of my sight! I can ye not abide!

[*To* HUF.] Now, goodman pouchmouth,[32] I am a
    slave with you?

Now have at ye afresh, again even now!   190

[*To* SNUF.] Mine arss against the poste you wil
    run?

But I wil make ye[19] from that saying to turn!

HUF. I beseech ye hartely to be content.

RUF. I insure you, by mine honesty, no hurt we ment.

Beside that, again, we do not knowe what ye are.   195

Ye knowe that souldiers their stoutnes wil declare.

Therefore, if we have any thing[33] offended,

Pardon our rudenes, and it shal be amended.

AMBIDEXTER. Yea, Gods pitie, begin ye to intreate
    me?

Have at ye once again! By the Masse, I wil beat   200
    ye!

    Fight again.

HUF. Gogs hart, let us kil him, suffer[34] no longer!

    Draw their swords.

SNUF. Thou slave, we wil see if thou be the strongar!

RUF. Strike of[f] his hed at one blowe!

That we be souldiers, Gogs hart, let him knowe!

AMBIDEXTER. O the passion of God, I have doon, by   205
    mine honesty.

I wil take your parte heerafter, verily.

ALL. Then content[20] let us agree.

AMBIDEXTER. Shake hands with me, I shake hands
    with thee.

Ye are ful of curtesye that is the best.

And you take great pain, ye are a mannerly   210
    gest.[35]

---

31 *at the oste:* at the same
    inn, hence intimately.

32 *pouchmouth:* with pro-
    truding lips.

33 *any thing:* in any way.

34 *suffer:* put up with (him).

35 *gest:* fellow.

Why, maisters, doo you not knowe me? The trueth
to me tel.

ALL. No, trust us, not very wel.

AMBIDEXTER. Why, I am Ambidexter, who many
souldiers doo love.

HUF. Gogs hart, to have thy company needs we must
proove.

We must play with bothe hands, with our hostes[36] 215
and host,

Play with bothe hands, and score on the poste.[8]

Now and then with our captain for many a delay

We wil not stick with bothe hands to play.

AMBIDEXTER. The honester man ye, ye[21] may me
trust.

Enter MERETRIX, with a staf on her shoulder.

MERETRIX. What, is there no lads heer that hath a 220
lust

To have a passing trul to help at their need?

HUF. Gogs hart, she is come indeed!

What, Mistres Meretrix, by His wounds, welcome
to me.

MERETRIX. What wil ye give me? I pray you, let me
see.

RUF. By His hart, she lookes for gifts by and by. 225

MERETRIX. What, Maister Ruf? I cry you mercy!

The last time I was with you I got a broken hed

And lay in the street all night for want of a bed!

SNUF. Gogs wounds, kisse me, my trul so white.[37]

In thee, I sweare, is all my delight. 230

If thou shouldest have had a broken hed for my
sake,

I would have made his head to ake!

MERETRIX. What, Maister Ambidexter? Who looked
for you?

AMBIDEXTER. Mistres Meretrix, I thought not to see
you heer now.

There is no remedy, at meeting I must have a 235
kisse.

MERETRIX. What, man? I wil not stick for that, by
Gissel

Kisse

36 *hostes* : hostess.   37 *white* : fair.

AMBIDEXTER. So now, gramercy! I pray thee be gone.

MERETRIX. Nay, soft, my freend. I meane to have
one.

[AMBIDEXTER *resists*.]

Nay, soft! I swere, and if ye were my brother,
Before I let go I wil have another.   240

Kisse, kisse, kisse.

RUF. Gogs hart, the whore would not kisse me yet!

MERETRIX. If I be a whore, thou art a knave. Then it
is quit.[38]

HUF. But hearst thou, Meretrix? With who this night
wilt thou lye?

MERETRIX. With him that giveth me the moste
monye.

HUF. Gogs hart, I have no money in pursse, ne yet in   245
clout.[39]

MERETRIX. Then get thee hence and pack, like a lout!

HUF. Adieu, like a whore!   *Exit* HUF.

MERETRIX. Farwell, like a knave!

RUF. Gogs nailes, Mistres Meretrix, now he is gone,
A match ye shall make straight with me.   250
I wil give thee sixpence to lye one night with thee.

MERETRIX. Gogs hart, slave, doost thinke I am a six-
peny jug?[(9)]

No, wis ye, Jack, I look a little more smug.[40]

SNUF. I will give her xviii pence to serve me first.

MERETRIX. Gramercy, Snuf, thou art not the wurst.   255

RUF. By Gogs hart, she were better be hanged to
forsake me and take thee.

SNUF. Were she so? That shall we see.

RUF. By Gogs hart, my dagger into her I wil thrust.

SNUF. A, ye boy, ye would doo it and ye durst!

AMBIDEXTER. Peace, my maisters, ye shall not fight.   260
He that drawes first, I wil him smite.

RUF. Gogs wounds, Maister Snuf, are ye so lusty?

SNUF. Gogs sides, Maister Ruf, are ye so crusty?

RUF. You may happen to see.

SNUF. Doo what thou darest to me!   265

Heer [SNUF *and* RUF] *draw and fight. Heere she*

38 *quit* : even.   40 *smug* : attractive, trim,
39 *clout* : cloth.   smart.

>   *must lay on and coyle*[41] *them both, the*
>   *Vice must run his way for feare,*
>   SNUF *fling down his swoord and*
>   *buckler and run his way.*

MERETRIX. Gogs sides, knaves, seeing to fight ye be
                 so rough,
  Defend yourselves, for I will give ye bothe inough.
  I wil teach ye how ye shall fall out for me!
  Yes, thou slave, Snuf, no more blowes wilt thou
                 bide?
  To take thy heeles a time hast thou spied?   270
  [*To* RUF.] Thou villain, seeing Snuf has gone away,
  A little better I meane thee to pay!

>   *He falleth down, she falleth upon him and*
>   *beats*[22] *him and taketh away his*
>   *weapon.*[23]

RUF. Alas, good Mistres Meretrix, no more!
  My legs, sides, and armes with beating be sore!
MERETRIX. Thou a souldier, and loose thy weapon?   275
  Goe hence, sir boy. Say a woman hath thee
                 beaten.
RUF. Good Mistres Meretrix, my weapon let me have.
  Take pitie on me, mine honestie to save.
  If it be knowen this repulse[24] I sustain,
  It wil redound to my ignomy and shame.   280
MERETRIX. If thou wilt be my man and wait upon
                 mee,
  This sword and buckler I wil give thee.
RUF. I wil doo all at your commaundement.
  As servant to you I wil be obedient.
MERETRIX. Then let me see how before me you can   285
                 go.
  When I speake to you, ye[25] shall doo so:
  Of[f] with your cap at place and at boord,[42]
  "Forsooth, Mistres Meretrix" at every woord.
  Tut, tut, in the campe such soldiers there be
  One good woman would beat away two or three.   290
  Wel, I am sure customers tary at home.
  Manerly before, and let us be gone!

41 *coyle :* thrash.   42 *at place and at boord :* at
                                       post and at table.

Exeunt [RUF *and* MERETRIX, RUF *acting as her
gentleman-usher.*]
[*Re-*]*enter* AMBIDEXTER.

AMBIDEXTER. [*To the audience.*] O the passion of
   God! be they heer stil or no?
I durst not abide to see her beat them so!
I may say to you I was[26] in such a fright,[27]   295
Body of me, I see the heare of my hed stand up-
   right.
When I saw her so hard upon them lay on,
O the passion of God! thought I, she wil be with
   me anon!
I made no more adoo but avoided the thrust,
And to my legges began for to trust,   300
And fell a-laughing to myself when I was once
   gone.
It is wisdome (quoth I) by the Masse, to save one!
Then into this place I intended to trudge,
Thinking to meet Sisamnes the judge.
Beholde where he commeth! I wil him meet,   305
And like a gentleman I meane him to greet.
   Enter SISAMNES.
SISAMNES. Since that the Kings Graces Majestie in
   office did me set,
What abundance of welth to me might I get!
Now and then some vantage I atchive, much more
   yet may I take,
But that I fear unto the king that some complaint   310
   wil make.
AMBIDEXTER. Jesu, Maister Sisamnes, you are unwise.
SISAMNES. Why so, I pray ye[28] let me agnise.[43]
What, Maister Ambidexter, is it you?
Now welcome to me, I make God avow!
AMBIDEXTER. Jesu, Maister Sisamnes, with me you   315
   are wel acquainted.
By me rulers may be trimly painted.
Ye are unwise if ye take not time while ye may.
If ye wil not now, when ye would ye shall have
   nay.
What is he that of you dare make exclamation
Of your wrong-dealing[29] to make explication?   320

43 *agnise :* know, learn.

Can you not play with bothe hands and turn with
    the winde?

SISAMNES. Beleeve me, your woords draw deepe in
    my minde.

In colloure[44] wise unto this day, to bribes I have
    inclyned.

More the same for to frequent,[45] of trueth, I am
    now minded.

Beholde, even now unto me suters doo proceed.   325
    [*Enter* SMALL HABILITIE.]

SMALL HABILITIE. I beseech you heer, good Maister
    Judge, a poor mans cause to tender.

Condemne me not in wrongful wise that never was
    offender.

You knowe right wel my right it is. I have not for
    to give.

You take away from me my due, that should my
    corps[46] releeve.

The Commons of you doo complain from them   330
    you devocate[47]

With anguish great and grevos words their harts
    doo penetrate.

The right you sel unto the wrong, your private
    gain to win.

You violate the simple man and count it for no sin.

SISAMNES. Hold thy tung, thou pratling knave, and
    give to me reward.

Els, in this wise, I tell thee trueth, thy tale wil not   335
    be heard.

Ambidexter, let us go hence and let the knave
    alone.

AMBIDEXTER. Farwell, Small Habilitie, for help now
    get ye[30] none.

Bribes hath corrupt him good lawes to pollute.
    Exeunt [SISAMNES *and* AMBIDEXTER.]

SMALL HABILITIE. A naughtie man, that wil not obay
    the kings constitute![48]

---

44 *in colloure* : in pretext.
45 *frequent* : indulge in.
46 *corps* : body, bodily needs.

47 *devocate* : turn away, opp.
    of *advocate* (?)
48 *constitute* : law or consti-
    tuted authority.

With hevy hart I wil return, til God redresse my   340
　　　　pain.   *Exit.*

Enter SHAME, *with a trump black.*

SHAME. From among the grisly ghosts[31] I come,
　　　　from tirants testy train.[49]
Unseemly Shame, of sooth I am, procured to make
　　　　plain
The odious facts and shamelesse deeds that Cam-
　　　　bises king dooth use.
All pietie and vertuouse life, he dooth it clene
　　　　refuse.
Lechery and drunkennes, he dooth it much fre-   345
　　　　quent.
The tigers kinde to immitate he hath given ful
　　　　consent.
He nought esteemes his Councel grave ne vertuous
　　　　bringing-up,
But dayly stil receives the drink of damned vices
　　　　cup.
He can bide no instruction, he takes so great de-
　　　　light
In working of iniquitie for to frequent his spight.   350
As Fame dooth sound the royal trump of worthy
　　　　men and trim,
So Shame dooth blowe with strained blast the
　　　　trump of shame on him.
　　　　　　　　　　Exit [*sounding the trump.*]

Enter [CAMBISES] *the King,* LORD, PRAXASPES,
　　　　　　and SISAMNES.

CAMBISES. My Judge, since my departure hence,
　　　　have you used judgement right?
If faithful steward[32] I ye find, the same I wil
　　　　requite.
SISAMNES. No dout your Grace shal not once hear   355
　　　　that I have done amis.
PRAXASPES. I much rejoyce to heare so good newes as
　　　　this.

Enter COMMONS CRY *running in. Speak this verse
　　　　and*[33] *goe out again hastely.*

COMMONS CRY. Alas! alas! how are the Commons op-
　　　　pressed

49 *testy train:* irascible pro-
　　cession.

By that vile judge, Sisamnes by name!
I doo not knowe how it should be redressed.
To amend his life no whit he dooth frame.   360
   We are undoon and thrown out of doore,
His damnable dealing dooth us so torment.
At his hand we can finde no releef nor succoure.
God graunt him grace for to repent.

Run away crying.

CAMBISES. What doleful cryes be these, my lord, that   365
    sound doo in mine eare?
  Intelligence if you can give, unto your king de-
    clare.
  To me it seemeth my Commons all they doo la-
    ment and cry
  Out of Sisamnes, judge moste cheefe, even now
    standing us by.
PRAXASPES. Even so (O king) it seemd to me, as you
    rehersall made.
  I dout[50] the judge culpable be in some respect or   370
    trade.[51]
SISAMNES. Redouted king, have no mistrust. No whit
    your minde dismay.
  There is not one that can me charge or ought
    against me lay.

Enter COMMONS COMPLAINT, with PROOF and
TRIALL.

COMMONS COMPLAINT. Commons complaint I repre-
    sent, with thrall[52] of dolful state.
  My urgent cause erected foorth my greefe for to
    dilate.
  Unto the king I wil prepare my misery to tel,   375
  To have releef of this my greef and fettered feet so
    fel.[53]
  Redouted prince and mightie king, myself I pros-
    trate heer.

[Kneels.]

  Vouchsafe (O king) with me to beare for this that
    I appeer.
  With humble sute I pardon crave of your most
    royall Grace,

50 *dout :* suspect.   52 *thrall :* thralldom, op-
51 *trade :* way, manner.   pression.
                        53 *fel :* dreadful.

To give me leave my minde to breke before you   380
    in this place.

CAMBISES. Commons Complaint, keep nothing back.
    Fear not thy tale to tel.

What ere he be within this land that hath not used
    thee wel.

As princes mouth shall sentence give, he shal re-
    ceive the same.

Unfolde the secrets of thy brest, for I extinguish
    blame.

COMMONS COMPLAINT. God preserve your royall   385
    Grace, and send you blisfull dayes,

That all your deeds might stil accord to give the
    gods[34] the praise.

My complaint is (O mightie king) against that
    judge you by,

Whose careles deeds, gain to receive, hath made
    the commons cry.

He, by taking bribes and gifts, the poore he dooth
    oppresse,

Taking releef from infants yung, widowes, and   390
    fatherlesse.

CAMBISES. [*To* SISAMNES.] Untrustful traitor and cor-
    rupt judge, how likest thou this com-
    plaint?

Forewarning I to thee did give of this to make
    restraint.

And hast thou doon this divelish deed mine ire for
    to augment?

I sentence give, thou Judas judge. Thou shalt thy
    deed repent.

SISAMNES. O pusant[54] prince, it is not so! His com-   395
    plaint I deny.

COMMONS COMPLAINT. If it be not so (moste mightie
    king) in place then let me dye.

Beholde that I have brought with me bothe Proof
    and Triall true

To stand even heer and sentence give what by
    him did insue.

PROOF. I, Proof, doo him in this appeal,[55] he did the
    Commons wrong.

54 *pusant :* puissant, power-   55 *appeal :* accuse.
    ful.

Unjustly he with them hath delt, his greedy[56]   400
    was so strong.

His hart did covet in to get, he cared not which
    way.

The poor did leese[57] their due and right because
    they want to pay[58]

Unto him for bribes. Indeed, this was his wunted
    use.[59]

Wheras your Grace good lawes did make, he did
    the same abuse.

TRIALL. I, Triall, heer to verify what Proof dooth   405
    now unfolde,

[*Pointing to* SISAMNES.] To stand against him in
    his wrong as now I dare be bolde.

CAMBISES. How likest thou this, thou caitive vile?
    Canst thou the same deny?

SISAMNES. O noble king, forgive my fact. I yeeld to
    thy mercy.

CAMBISES. Complaint[35] and Proof, redresse will I
    all this your misery.

Departe with speed from whence you came, and   410
    straight commaund by me

The execution man to come before my Grace with
    haste.

ALL. For to fulfil this your request no time we meane
    to waste.   *Exeunt they three.*

CAMBISES. My lord, before my Grace go call Otian,
    this judges sonne,

And he shal heare and also see what his father
    hath doon.

The father he shall suffer death, the sonne his   415
    roume succeed.[60]

And if that he no better proove, so likewise shall
    he speed.

PRAXASPES. As your Grace hath commaundment
    given, I meane for to fulfil.
        Step aside and fetch him.

CAMBISES. Accursed judge, couldst thou consent to
    do this cursed il?

56 *greedy :* greediness.
57 *leese :* lose.
58 *want to pay :* lack the
    wherewithal to pay.

59 *wunted use :* accustomed
    practice.
60 *roume succeed :* take his
    place.

According unto thy demaund thou shalt, for this
    thy gilt,

Receive thy death before mine eyes. Thy blood it   420
    shal be spilt.

    [PRAXASPES *brings in* OTIAN.]

PRAXASPES. Beholde (O king) Sisamnes sonne be-
    fore you dooth appeere.

CAMBISES. Otian, this is my minde, therfore to me
    come neer:

Thy father heer for judgment wrong procured
    hath his death,

And thou, his sonne, shalt him succeed when he
    hath lost his breth.

And if that thou doost once offend, as thou seest   425
    thy father have,

In like wise thou shalt suffer death. No mercy shal
    thee save.

OTIAN. O mightie king, vouchsafe your Grace my fa-
    ther to remit.

Forgive his fault. His pardon I doo aske of you as
    yet.

Alas, although my father hath your princely hart
    offended,

Amends for misse[61] he wil now make, and faults   430
    shal be amended.

Insted of his requested life, pleaseth your Grace
    take mine!

This offer I as tender childe, so duty dooth me
    binde.

CAMBISES. Doo not intreat my Grace no more, for he
    shall dye the death.

Where is the execution man him to bereave of
    breath?

    Enter EXECUTION.

EXECUTION. At hand, and if it like your Grace, my   435
    duty to dispatch,

In hope that I when deed is doon a good rewarde
    shall catch.

CAMBISES. Dispatch with swoord this judges life, ex-
    tinguish fear and cares.

So doon, draw thou his cursed skin strait over
    bothe his eares.

61 *misse :* mistake, misdeed.

I wil see the office doon, and that before mine
eyes.

EXECUTION. To doo the thing my king commaunds I   440
give the enterprise.[62]

SISAMNES. Otian, my sonne, the king to death by law
hath me condemned,

And you in roume and office mine his Graces wil
hath placed.

Use justice, therfore, in this case, and yeeld unto
no wrong,

Lest thou doo purchase the like death or[63] ever
it be long.[36]

OTIAN. O father deer, these words to hear, that you   445
must dye by force,

Bedewes my cheeks with stilled[64] teares. The king
hath no remorce.

The greevous greefs and strained sighes my hart
doth breke in twain,

And I deplore, moste woful childe, that I should
see you slaine.

O false and fickle frowning Dame, that turneth
as the winde,[10]

Is this the joy in fathers age thou me assignest to   450
finde?

O doleful day, unhappy houre, that loving childe
should see

His father deer before his face thus put to death
should bee.

Yet, father, give me blessing thine, and let me
once imbrace

Thy comely corps in foulded armes and kisse thy
ancient face!

SISAMNES. O childe, thou makes my eyes to run as   455
rivers doo by streme.[65]

My leave I take of thee, my sonne. Beware of this
my beame.[66]

---

62 *give the enterprise :* promise to undertake.

63 *or :* before.

64 *stilled :* distilled.

65 *by streme :* in streams,
flowing.

66 *beame :* misfortune (?)
(Cf. "bote of beam,"
remedy or improve-
ment.)

CAMBISES. Dispatch even now, thou man of death,
no longer seeme to stay.[67]

EXECUTION. Come, M[aster] Sisamnes, come on your
way, my office I must pay.

Forgive therefore my deed.

SISAMNES. I doo forgive it thee, my freend. Dispatch   460
therfore with speed.

Smite him in the neck with a swoord to signify
his death.

PRAXASPES. Beholde (O king) how he dooth bleed,
being of life bereft.

CAMBISES. In this wise he shall not yet be left.

Pul his skin over his eares[37] to make his death
more vile.

A wretch he was, a cruel theef, my Commons to
begile.

Flea him[68] with a false skin.

OTIAN. What childe[38] is he of natures mould   465
could bide the same to see,

His father fleaed in this wise? Oh, how it greeveth
me!

CAMBISES. Otian, thou seest thy father dead, and
thou art in his roume.

If thou beest proud, as he hath been, even therto
shalt thou come.

OTIAN. O king, to me this is a glasse, [11] with greefe
in it I view

Example that unto your Grace I doo not proove   470
untrue.

PRAXASPES. Otian, convay your father hence to tomb
where he shall lye.

OTIAN. And if it please your lordship, it shall be done
by and by.

Good execution man, for need, helpe me with him
away.

EXECUTION. I wil fulfil as you to me did say.

They take him away.

CAMBISES. My lord, now that my Grace hath seen   475
that finisht is this deed,

67 *stay :* hold off, delay.   68 *Flea him :* Flay him, skin
                                                                      him.

To question mine give tentive[69] eare, and answere
     make with speed:

Have not I doon a gratious deed, to redresse my
     Commons wo?

PRAXASPES. Yea, truely, if it please your Grace, you
     have indeed doon so.

But now (O king) in freendly wise I councel you
     in this:

Certain vices for to leave that in you placed is—   480

The vice of drunkennes (Oh king) which doth
     you sore infect

With other great abuses which I wish you to de-
     tect.

CAMBISES. Peace, my lord! What needeth this? Of
     this I wil not hear!

To pallaice now I wil return and there to make
     good cheer.

God Baccus he bestowes his gifts, we have good   485
     store[70] of wine,

And also that the ladyes be both passing brave[71]
     and fine.

But stay, I see a lord now come and eke a valiant
     knight.

What newes, my lord? To see you heer my hart it
     dooth delight.

Enter LORD *and* KNIGHT *to meet the King.*

LORD. No newes (O king) but of duty come to wait
     upon your Grace. ·

CAMBISES. I thank you, my lord and loving knight.   490
     I pray ye[39] with me trace.[72]

My lords and knight, I pray ye tel, I wil not be
     offended,

Am I worthy of any crime once to be reprehended?

PRAXASPES. The Persians much praise[40] your
     Grace, but one thing discommend,

In that to wine subject you be, wherin you doo
     offend.

Sith that the might of wines effect dooth oft sub-   495
     due your brain,

---

69 *tentive*: attentive.
70 *store*: reserve, plenteous
     supply.

71 *passing brave*: surpass-
     ingly elegant.
72 *trace*: walk along.

My councel is to please their harts from it you
    would refrain.

LORD. [*To* PRAXASPES.] No, no, my lord, it is not so!
    For this of prince they tel:

For vertuous proof and princely facts Cirus he
    dooth excel.

By that his Grace by conquest great the Egiptians
    did convince,[73]

Of him reporte abrode dooth passe to be a worthy   500
    prince.

KNIGHT. In person of Cresus I answer make: we
    may not his Grace compare

In whole respect for to be like Cirus, the kings
    father,

Insomuch your Grace hath yet no childe as Cirus
    left behinde,

Even you I meane, Cambises king, in whom I
    favour finde.

CAMBISES. Cresus said wel in saying so. But Praxas-   505
    pes, tel me why

That to my mouth in such a sort thou should
    avouch a lye,

Of drunkennes me thus to charge, but thou with
    speed shalt see

Whether that I a sober king or els a drunkard bee.

I knowe thou haste a blisful babe, wherin thou
    doost delight.

Me to revenge of these thy woords I wil go wreke   510
    this spight:

When I the moste have tasted wine, my bowe it
    shal be bent

At hart of him even then to shoot is now my whole
    intent.

And if that I his hart can hit, the king no drunk-
    ard is.

If hart of his I doo not kil, I yeeld to thee in this.

Therfore, Praxaspes, fetch to me thy yungest   515
    sonne with speed.

There is no way, I tel thee plain, but I wil doo this
    deed.

73 *convince:* vanquish.

PRAXASPES. Redouted prince, spare my sweet childe.
He is mine only joy!

I trust your Grace to infants hart no such thing wil
imploy.

If that his mother hear of this, she is so nigh her
flight

In clay her corps wil soon be shrinde[74] to passe   520
from worlds delight.

CAMBISES. No more adoo. Go fetch me him. It shal
be as I say.

And if that I doo speak the word, how dare ye once
say nay?

PRAXASPES. I wil go fetch him to your Grace, but so
I trust it shall not be!

CAMBISES. For feare of my displeasure great, goe
fetch him unto me. [*Exit* PRAXASPES.]

Is he gone? Now, by the gods, I will doo as I say!   525

My lord, therfore fil me some wine, I hartely you
pray,

For I must drink to make my brain somewhat in-
toxicate.(12)

When that the wine is in my head, O trimly I can
prate!

LORD. Heere is the cup, with filled wine, therof to
take repaste.

CAMBISES. Give it me to drink it off,[41] and see no   530
wine be wast.
Drink.

Once again inlarge[75] this cup, for I must taste it
stil.
Drink.

By the gods, I think of pleasant wine I cannot take
my fill!

Now drink is in, give me my bowe and arrowes
from sir knight.

At hart of childe I meane to shoot, hoping to cleve
it right.

KNIGHT. Beholde (O king) wher he dooth come, his   535
infant yung in hand.

[*Re-enter* PRAXASPES *leading his* YUNG CHILDE.]

74 *shrinde :* enshrined.   75 *inlarge :* fill.

PRAXASPES. O mightie king, your Grace behest with
   sorow I have scand[76]

And brought my childe fro mothers knee before
   you to appeer,

And she therof no whit dooth knowe that he in
   place is heer.

CAMBISES. Set him up my mark to be! I wil shoot at
   his hart.

PRAXASPES. I beseech your Grace not so to doo! Set   540
   this pretence[77] apart!

Farewel, my deer and looving babe! Come kisse
   thy father deer.

A greevous sight to me it is to see thee slain even
   heer.

Is this the gain now from the king for giving councel good,

Before my face with such despight to spil my sons
   hart blood?

O heavy day to me this is, and mother in like case!   545

YUNG CHILDE. O father, father, wipe your face.

I see the teares run from your eye.

My mother is at home sowing of a band.[78]

Alas, deer father, why doo you cry?

CAMBISES. Before me as a mark[42] now let him   550
   stand!

I wil shoot at him my minde to fulfil.[43]

YUNG CHILDE. Alas, alas, father, wil you me kil?

Good master king, doo not shoot at me, my mother
   looves me best of all!

      Shoot.

CAMBISES. I have dispatched him! Down he dooth
   fall!

As right as a line his hart I have hit.   555

Nay, thou shalt see, Praxaspes, straunger newes
   yet.

My knight, with speed his hart cut out and give it
   unto me.

KNIGHT. It shal be doon (O mightie king) with all
   seleritie.

---

76 *scand*: considered.
77 *pretence*: intention.

78 *sowing . . . band*: sewing
  a ruff or a strip to go
  around a hat or dress.

LORD. My lord Praxaspes, this had not been but your
    tung must be walking.

To the king of correction you must needs be   560
    talking.

PRAXASPES. No correction (my lord) but councel for
    the best.

KNIGHT. Heere is the hart, according to your Graces
    behest. [*Gives it to* CAMBISES.]

CAMBISES. Beholde, Praxaspes, thy sonnes owne hart.
    Oh how wel the same was hit!

After this wine to doo this deed I thought it very
    fit.

Esteeme thou maist right wel therby no drunkard   565
    is the king.

That in the midst of all his cups could doo this
    valiant thing.

My lord and knight, on me attend, to pallaice we
    wil go

And leave him heer to take his sonne when we are
    gone him fro.[79]

ALL. With all our harts we give consent to wait
    upon your Grace.

            [*Exeunt all but* PRAXASPES.]

PRAXASPES. A woful man (O Lord) am I to see him   570
    in this case.

My dayes, I deem, desires their end. This deed
    wil help me hence.

To have the blossoms of my feeld destroyd by
    violence!

          Enter MOTHER.

MOTHER. Alas, alas, I doo heare tell the king hath
    kild my sonne.

If it be so, wo worth[80] the deed that ever it was
    doon!

It is even so! My lord I see how by him he dooth   575
    weep.

What ment I, that from hands of him this childe I
    did not keep?

Alas, husband and lord, what did you meane, to
    fetch this child away?

79 *fro :* from.   80 *worth :* become, come to.

PRAXASPES. O lady wife, I little thought for to have
         seen this day.

MOTHER. O blisful babe! O joy of womb! Harts com-
         fort and delight!

For councel given unto the king is this thy just   580
         requite?

O hevy day and dolefull time, these mourning
         tunes to make.

With blubred eyes into mine armes from earth I
         wil thee take

And wrap thee in mine apron white. But oh, my
         hevy hart!

The spightful pangs that it sustains wold make it
         in two to part,

The death of this my sonne to see! O hevy mother   585
         now,

That from thy sweet and sugred joy to sorow so
         shouldst bow.

What greef in womb did I retain before I did thee
         see!

Yet at the last when smart was gone what joy wert
         thou to mee!

How tender was I of thy food, for to prepare thy
         state,

How stilled[81] I thy tender hart at times earely and   590
         late!

With velvet paps I gave thee suck with issue from
         my brest,

And daunced thee upon my knee to bring thee
         unto rest.

Is this the joy of thee I reap (O king) of tigers
         brood?

Oh tigers whelp, hadst thou the hart to see this
         childes hart blood?

Nature inforseth me, alas, in this wise to deplore,   595

To wring my hands, O wele away, that I should
         see this houre!

Thy mother yet wil kisse thy lips, silk soft and
         pleasant white,

With wringing hands lamenting for to see thee in
         this plight.

81 *stilled*: quieted.

My lording deer, let us go home our mourning to
    augment.

PRAXASPES. My lady deer, with hevy hart to it I doo   600
    consent,

Between us bothe the childe to bere unto our
    lordly place. *Exeunt [with the body.]*
        Enter AMBIDEXTER.

AMBIDEXTER. [*To the audience.*] Indeed, as ye say, I
    have been absent a long space.

But is not my cosin Cutpurse[13] with you in the
    menetime?

To it, to it, cosin, and doo your office fine!

How like you Sisamnes for using of me?   605

He plaid with bothe hands, but he sped il fa-
    vouredly.

The king himself was godly up trained.

He professed vertue, but I think it was fained.

He playes with bothe hands, good deeds and il.

But it was no good deed Praxaspes sonne for to kil.   610

As he for the good deed on the judge was com-
    mended,

For all his deeds els he is reprehended.

The moste evill disposed person that ever was

All the state of his life he would not let passe.

Some good deeds he will doo, though they be but   615
    few.

The like things this tirant Cambises dooth
    shew.[14]

No goodnes from him to none is exhibited,

But stil malediction abrode is distributed.

And yet ye shall see in the rest of his race[82]

What infamy he wil woork against his owne grace.   620

Whist, no more woords! Heer comes the kings
    brother.

    Enter Lord SMIRDIS *with* ATTENDANCE *and*
        DILIGENCE.

SMIRDIS. The kings brother by birth am I, issued from
    Cirus loynes.

A greef to me it is to hear of this the kings re-
    pines.[83]

---

82 *race :* career, life.   83 *repines :* discontents or
                                  lapses from virtue.

I like not wel of those his deeds that he dooth stil
    frequent.
I wish to God that other waies his minde he could   625
    content.
Yung I am and next to him, no mo of us there be.
I would be glad a quiet realme in this his reign to
    see.
ATTENDANCE. My lord, your good a[nd] willing[44]
    hart the gods wil recompence
In that your minde[45] so pensive is for those
    his great offence.
My lord, His Grace shall have a time to pair[84]   630
    and to amend.
Happy is he that can escape and not his Grace
    offend.
DILIGENCE. If that wicked vice he could refrain,[85]
    from wasting wine forbere,
A moderate life he would frequent, amending this
    his square.[86]
AMBIDEXTER. My lord, and if your Honor it shall
    please,
I can informe you what is best for your ease: 635
Let him alone, of his deeds doo not talke,
Then by his side ye may quietly walke.
After his death you shal be king.
Then may you reforme eche kinde of thing.
In the meanetime live quietly, doo not with him   640
    deale.
So shall it redownd much to your weale.
SMIRDIS. Thou saist true, my freend, that is the best.
I knowe not whether he loove me or doo me de-
    test.
ATTENDANCE. Leane from[87] his company all that you
    may.
I, faithful Attendance, wil your Honor obay.   645
If against your Honor he take any ire,
His Grace is as like to kindle his fire
To your Honors destruction as otherwise.
DILIGENCE. Therefore, my lord, take good advise,

84 *pair*: repair, improve him-   86 *square*: perverse.
    self.   87 *Leane from*: Avoid.
85 *refrain*: refrain from.

And I, Diligence, your case wil so tender 650
That to his Grace your Honor shal be none
offender.

SMIRDIS. I thank you both, intire freends. With my
Honor stil remain.

AMBIDEXTER. Beholde where the king dooth come
with his train.

Enter King [CAMBISES] *and* I. LORD.[46]

CAMBISES. O lording deer and brother mine, I joy your
state to see,

Surmising much what is the cause you absent[88] 655
thus from mee.

SMIRDIS. Pleaseth your Grace, no absence I, but
redy to fulfil,

At all assayes,[89] my prince and king, in that your
Grace me wil.

What I can doo in true defence to you, my prince
aright,

In readynes I alwaies am to offer foorth my might.

CAMBISES. And I the like to you again doo heer 660
avouch the same.

ALL. For this your good agreement heer, now praised
be Gods name.

AMBIDEXTER. [*Aside to* SMIRDIS.] But hear ye, noble
prince, harke in your[47] eare:

It is best to doo as I did declare.

CAMBISES. My lord and brother Smirdis, now this is
my minde and wil,

That you to court of mine return and there to tary 665
stil,

Til my return within short space your Honor for to
greet.

SMIRDIS. At your behest so wil I doo till time again
wee meet.

My leave I take from you (O king), even now I
doo departe.

Exeunt SMIRDIS, ATTENDANCE, *and* DILIGENCE.

CAMBISES. Farwel, lord and brother mine, farwel with
all my hart!

My lord, my brother Smirdis is of youth and manly 670
might,

88 *absent*: absent yourself.　　89 *At all assayes*: In every
task.

And in his sweet and pleasant face my hart dooth
    take delight.

LORD. Yea, noble prince, if that your Grace before his
    Honor dye,

He wil succeede, a vertuous king, and rule with
    equitie.

CAMBISES. As you have said, my lord, he is cheef heire
    next my Grace,

And if I dye tomorrow next he shall succeed my   675
    place.

AMBIDEXTER. And if it please your Grace (O king) I
    herd him say

For your death unto the gods[48] day and night
    he did pray,

He would live so vertuously and get him such a
    praise

That Fame by trump his due deserts his[49]
    honor should upraise.

He said your Grace deserved had the cursing of   680
    all men,

That ye should never after him get any praise
    agen.

CAMBISES. Did he speake thus of my Grace in such
    dispightful wise?

Or els doost thou presume to fil my princely eares
    with lyes?

LORD. I cannot think it in my hart that he would
    report so.

CAMBISES. How sayst thou? Speake the trueth, was   685
    it so or no?

AMBIDEXTER. I think so, if it please your Grace, but
    I cannot tel.

CAMBISES. Thou plaist with bothe hands, now I per-
    ceive well

But, for to put all doutes aside and to make him
    leese his hope,

He shall dye by dent[90] of swoord or els by
    choking rope.

Shall he succeed when I am gone to have more   690
    praise then I?

90 *dent:* dint, blow.

Were he father, as brother, mine, I swere that he
    shall dye.
To pallaice mine I wil therfore, his death for to
    pursue.

Exit [CAMBISES *with the* LORD.]

AMBIDEXTER. Are ye gone? Straightway I wil followe
    you.
[*Turning to the audience.*] How like ye now, my
    maisters? Dooth not this geer cotten?[91]
The proverbe olde is verified : soon ripe and soon   695
    rotten.
He wil not be quiet til his brother be kild.
His delight is wholly to have his blood spild.
[*To one in the audience.*] Mary, sir, I tolde him
    a notable lye.
If it were to doo again, man,[50] I durst not[51]
    doo it, I.
Mary, when I had doon, to it I durst not stand.   700
Therby ye may perceive I use to play with eche
    hand.
But how now, cosin Cutpursse, with whome play
    you?
Take heed, for his hand is groping even now!
Cosin, take heed, if you doo secretly grope,
If ye be taken, cosin, ye must looke through a   705
    rope.   *Exit.*

Enter Lord SMIRDIS *alone.*

SMIRDIS. I am wandring alone, heer and there to
    walke.
The court is so unquiet, in it I take no joy.
Solitary to myself now I may talke.
If I could rule, I wist what to say.

Enter CRUELTIE *and* MURDER *with*
bloody hands.

CRUELTIE. My coequall partner, Murder, come away.   710
From me long thou maist not stay.
MURDER. Yes, from thee I may stay, but not thou from
    me.
Therfore I have a prerogative aboove thee.
CRUELTIE. But in this case we must togither abide.

91 *geer cotten :* plot thicken,
    plan begin to take effect.

Come, come, Lord Smirdis I have spide. 715
Lay hands on him with all festination,[92]
That on him we may work our indignation.
SMIRDIS. How now, my freends? What have you to
doo with me?
MURDER. King Cambises hath sent us unto thee,
Commaunding us straightly, without mercy or fa- 720
vour,
Upon thee to bestow our behaviour[(15)]
With crueltie to murder you and make you away.
SMIRDIS. Yet pardon me, I hartely you pray!
Consider, the king is a tirant tirannious,
And all his dooings be damnable and parnitious. 725
Favour me, therfore, I did him never offend.
CRUELTIE. No favour at all! Your life is at an end.
Even now I strike his body to wound.
Strike him in divers places.[52]
Beholde, now his blood springs out on the ground!
A little bladder of vineger prikt.[53]
MURDER. Now he is dead, let us present him to the 730
king.
CRUELTIE. Lay to your hand away him to bring.
Exeunt [with the body.]
Enter AMBIDEXTER.
AMBIDEXTER. O the passion of God, yunder is a hevy
court.
Some weeps, some wailes, and some make great
sport.
Lord Smirdis by Crueltie and Murder is slain,
But, Jesus, for want of him how some doo com- 735
plain!
If I should have had a thousand pound I could not
forbeare weeping.
Now Jesus have his blessed soule in keeping!
Ah, good Lord, to think on him, how it dooth me
greeve!
I cannot forbeare weeping, ye may me beleeve.
Weep.
O my hart, how my pulses doo beat, 740
With sorowful lamentations I am in such a heat!
Ah, my hart, how for him it dooth sorow!

92 *festination :* haste.

[*Starting to laugh.*] Nay, I have doon, in faith,
    now, and God give you[54] good
    morow!
Ha ha, weep? Nay, laugh, with both[55] hands to
    play.
The king through[56] his crueltie hath made him 745
    away,
But hath not he wrought a moste wicked deed,
Because[93] king after him he should not proceed,
His owne naturall brother and having no more,
To procure his death by violence sore?
In spight, because his brother should never be 750
    king,
His hart, beeing wicked, consented to this thing.
Now he hath no more brothers nor kinred alive.
If the king use this geer stil, he cannot long thrive.
    Enter HOB *and* LOB.
HOB. Gods hat, naibor, come away. Its time to mar-
    ket to go.
LOB. Gods vast,[94] naybor, zay ye zo?(16) 755
The clock hath striken vive, ich think, by Laken.[95]
Bum vay,[96] vrom sleep cham not very wel waken.
But, naybor Hob, naybor Hob, what have ye to
    zel?
HOB. Bum troth, naybor Lob, to you I chil tel:
Chave two goslings and a chine of porke, 760
There is no vatter between this and Yorke,
Chave a pot of strawberyes and a calves hed,
A zennight since tomorrow[97] it hath been dead.
LOB. Chave a score of egges and of butter a pound.
Yesterday a nest of goodly yung rabits I vound. 765
Chave vorty things mo, of more and of lesse,
My brain is not very good them to expresse.
But, Gods hat, naybor, wotst what?
HOB. No, not wel, naybor, whats that?
LOB. Bum vay, naybor, maister king is a zhrode[98] lad! 770
Zo God help me and holidam, I think the vool be
    mad.

93 *Because:* So that.
94 *vast:* fist.
95 *by Laken:* by Our Lady.
96 *Bum vay:* By my faith.
97 *A . . . tomorrow:* A week
  ago tomorrow.
98 *zhrode:* shrewd, harsh.

Zome zay he deale cruelly his brother he did kill,
And also a goodly vung lads hart-blood he did spil.

HOB. Vorbod[99] of God, naibor, has he plaied zuch a
        volish deed?

AMBIDEXTER. Goodman Hob and goodman Lob, God   775
        be your speed!

As you twoo towards market doo walke
Of the kings crueltie I did hear you talke.
I insure you he is a king most vile and parnitious.
His dooings and life are odious and vicious.

LOB. It were a good deed zome body would breke his   780
        hed.

HOB. Bum vay, naybor Lob, I chould he were dead.

AMBIDEXTER. So would I, Lob and Hob, with all
        my hart!

[*To the audience.*] Now with bothe hands wil
        ye[57] see me play my parte!—

A, ye whorson traitorly knaves,
Hob and Lob, out upon you, slaves!   785

LOB. And[100] thou calst me knave, thou art another!
My name is Lob, and Hob my next naybor.

AMBIDEXTER. Hob and Lob, a, ye cuntry patches![101]
A, ye fooles! ye have made wrong matches!
Ye have spoken treason against the kings Grace.   790
For it I wil accuse ye before his face.
Then for the same ye shal be martered.
At the least ye shal be hangd, drawn, and
        quartered!

HOB. O gentleman, ye shal have two peare pyes, and
        tel not of me!

LOB. By God, a vat gooce chil give thee.   795
I think no hurt, by my vathers soule I zweare!

HOB. Chave lived wel all my lifetime my naybors
        among,
And now chuld be lothe to come to zuch wrong,
To be hanged and quartered the greef would be
        great.

LOB. A foule evil on thee, Hob! Who bid thee on it   800
        treat?
Vor it was thou that first did him name.

---

99 *Vorbod*: For the body.   101 *patches*: clowns.
100 *And*: If.

HOB. Thou lyest like a varlet and thou zaist the zame!
    It was zuch a voolish Lob as thou.
LOB. Speak many woords and by Cods nailes I vow
    Upon thy pate my staffe I wil lay!   805
AMBIDEXTER. [*To the audience.*] By the Masse, I wil
                cause them to make a fray.—
    Yea, Lob, thou sayest true, all came through him.
LOB. Bum vay, thou Hob,[58] a little would make me
                ye trim,
    Give thee a zwap[59] on thy nose til thy hart
                ake!
HOB. If thou darest, doo it! Els, man, cry creke![102]   810
    I trust before thou hurt me
    With my staffe chil make a Lob of thee!
    Heer let them fight with their staves, not come
    neer another by three or foure yardes, the Vice
        set them on as hard as he can, one of their
            wives come out, and all to beat[103] the
                    Vice, he run away.
    Enter MARIAN MAY-BE-GOOD, HOBS *wife, run-*
        ning in with a broome, and parte them.
            [AMBIDEXTER *runs but remains*
                    in sight.]
MARIAN. O the body of me, husband Hob, what
                meane you[60] to fight?
    For the passion of God, no more blowes smite!
    Neighbours and freends so long, and now to fall   815
                out?
    What, in your age to seeme so stout?
    If I had not parted ye, one had kild another.
LOB. I had not cared, I swere by Gods Mother!
MARIAN. Shake hands again at the request of me.
    As ye have been freends, so freends stil be.   820
HOB. Bum troth, cham content and zaist woord,[104]
                neighbour[61] Lob.
LOB. I am content, agreed, neighbor Hob.
    Shake hands and laugh hartely one at another.
MARIAN. So, get you to market, no longer stay.
    And with yonder knave let me make a fray.

102 *cry creke :* give up, "say   104 *and . . . woord :* if you
        uncle."   say the word.
103 *to beat :* beat all over.

HOB. Content, wife Marian, chill doo as thou doost   825
        say.
  But busse me, ich pray thee, at going away.
                        Exeunt HOB, LOB.
MARIAN. Thou whorson knave and prickeard boy,
        why didst thou let them fight?
  If one had kild another heer, couldst thou their
        deaths requite?
  It beares a signe by this thy deed a cowardly
        knave thou art,
  Els wouldst thou draw that weapon thine, like a   830
        man them to parte.
AMBIDEXTER. What, Marian May-be-good, are you
        come pratling?
  Ye may hap get a box on the eare with your
        talking.
  If they had kilde one another, I had not cared a
        pease.[105]
  Heer let her swinge him in her brome, she gets
  him down, and he her down, thus one on the
        top of another make pastime.
MARIAN. A, villain, myself on thee I must ease!
  Give me a box on the eare? That wil I try.   835
  Who shal be maister thou shalt see by and by.
AMBIDEXTER. O, no more, no more, I beseech you
        hartely!
  Even now I yeeld and give you the maistery.[106]
    Run his way out while she is down.
MARIAN. A, thou knave, doost thou throw me down
        and run thy[62] way?
  If he were heer again, oh, how I would him pay!   840
  I wil after him, and if I can him meet
  With these my nailes his face I wil greet. [*Exit.*]
  Enter VENUS *leading out her sone* CUPID, *blinde.*
    He must have a bowe and two shafts, one
      hedded with golde and th'other
        hedded with lead.
VENUS. Come foorth, my sonne. Unto my words atten-
        tive eares resigne.

105 *a pease:* the worth of a   106 *give . . . maistery:* con-
    pea.   cede your superiority.

What I pretend, see you frequent,[107] to force this
        game of mine.

The king a kinswoman hath, adornd with beautie   845
        store,[108]

And I wish that Dianas gifts they twain shal keep
        no more,

But use my silver sugred game their joyes for to
        augment.

When I doo speake, to wound his hart, Cupid my
        sonne, consent,

And shoot at him the shaft of loove that beares the
        hed of golde,

To wound his hart in loovers wise, his greef for   850
        to unfolde.

Though kin she be unto his Grace, that nature me
        expel,

Against the course therof he may in my game
        please me wel.

Wherefore, my sonne, doo not forget, foorthwith
        pursue the deed.

CUPID. Mother, I meane for to obay as you have
        whole decreed,

But you must tel me, mother deer, when I shal   855
        arrow draw,

Els your request to be attaind wil not be worth a
        straw.

I am blinde and cannot see but stil doo shoot by
        gesse,

The poets wel, in places store, of my might doo
        expresse.

VENUS. Cupid, my sonne, when time shall serve that
        thou shalt doo this deed,

Then warning I to thee wil give, but see thou   860
        shoot with speed.

Enter a LORD, *a* LADY, *and a* WAITING MAID.[63]

LORD. Lady deer, to king akin, forwith let us proceed

To trace abrode the beauty feelds[109] as erst we had
        decreed.

107 *What . . . frequent :*   109 *trace . . . feelds :* to stroll
    What I intend, see that   abroad in the beautiful
    you carry out.   fields.
108 *store :* in great supply.

The blowing buds whose savery sents our sence
      wil much delight,

The sweet smel of musk white rose to plese the
      appetite,

The chirping birds whose plesant tunes therein   865
      shal hear record,[17]

That our great joy we shall it finde in feeld to
      walke abrode,

On lute and cittern there to play a heavenly
      harmony,[64]

Our eares shall heare, hart to content, our sports
      to beautify.[65]

LADY. Unto your woords, moste comely lord, myself
      submit doo I,

To trace with you in feeld so green I meane not   870
      to deny.

   *Heere trace up and down playing [the lute and
             cittern.]*

MAID. And I, your waiting maid, at hand with dili-
      gence wil be

For to fulfil with hart and hand when you shall
      commaund me.

   *Enter [CAMBISES the] King, LORD, and
             KNIGHT.*[18]

CAMBISES. Come on, my lord and knight, abrode our
      mirth let us imploy.

Since he is dead, this hart of mine in corps I feel
      it joy.

Should brother mine have reigned king when I   875
      had yeelded breth?

A thousand brothers I rather had to put them all
      to death.

But, oh, beholde, where I doo see a lord and lady
      fair!

For beauty she moste worthy is to sit in princes
      chaire.

VENUS. Shoot forth, my sonne! Now is the time that
      thou must wound his hart.

CUPID. Content you, mother, I wil doo my parte.   880
   Shoot ther, and go out VENUS and CUPID.

CAMBISES. Of trueth, my lord, in eye of mine all
      ladyes she dooth excel.

Can none reporte what dame she is and to my
    Grace it tel?

LORD. Redouted prince, pleaseth your Grace, to you
    shee is akin.

Cosin-jarmin,[110] nigh of birth, by mothers side
    come in.

KNIGHT. And that her waiting maiden is, attending   885
    her upon.

[*Indicating the first* LORD.] He is a lord of princes
    court and wil be there anon.

They sport themselves in pleasant feeld, to former
    used use.[111]

CAMBISES. My lord and knight, of trueth I speake,
    my hart it cannot chuse

But with my lady I must speake and so expresse
    my minde.

[*Calling to them.*] My lord and ladyes walking   890
    there, if you wil favour finde,

Present yourselves unto my Grace and by my side
    come stand.

FIRST LORD. We wil fulfil, moste mightie king, as your
    Grace doth commaund.

CAMBISES. Lady deer, intelligence my Grace hath got
    of late

You issued out of mothers stocke and kin unto my
    state.

According to rule of birth you are cosin-jarmin   895
    mine,

Yet doo I wish that farther of this kinred I could
    finde,

For Cupid he, that eyelesse boy, my hart hath so
    enflamed

With beauty you me to content the like cannot be
    named.

For since I entred in this place and on you fixt
    mine eyes,

Moste burning fits about my hart in ample wise   900
    did rise.

The heat of them such force dooth yeeld, my
    corps they scorch, alas,

---

110 *Cosin-jarmin:* Cousin-ger-   111 *to . . . use:* according to
man, first cousin.   well-established custom.

And burnes the same with wasting heat as Ti-
    tan[19] dooth the grasse.

And sith this heat is kindled so and fresh in hart
    of me,

There is no way but of the same the quencher you
    must be.

My meaning is that beauty yours my hart with   905
    loove[66] dooth wound.

To give me loove minde to content, my hart hath
    you out found

And you are shee must be my wife, els shall I end
    my dayes.

Consent to this and be my queen, to were the
    crown with praise.

LADY. If it please your Grace (O mightie king) you
    shall not this request.

It is a thing that Natures course dooth utterly de-   910
    test,

And high it would the gods[67] displease of all
    that is the worst.

Yet humble thanks I render now unto you, mightie
    king,

That you vouchsafe to great estate so gladly
    would me bring.[20]

Were it not it were offence, I would it not deny,

But such great honor to atchive my hart I would   915
    apply.

Therfore (O king) with humble hart in this I par-
    don crave.

Mine[68] answer is, in this request your minde ye
    may not have.

CAMBISES. May I not? Nay, then I wil, by all the gods
    I vow!

And I wil mary thee as wife, this is mine answere
    now.

Who dare say nay that I pretend,[112] who dare   920
    the same withstand,

Shall lose his hed and have reporte as traitor
    through my land.

112 *that . . . pretend:* to what
    I intend.

There is no nay. I wil you have, and you my
        queen shal be.

LADY. Then, mightie king, I crave your Grace to
        hear the words of me:

Your councel take of lordings wit, the lawes aright
        peruse.

If I with safe may graunt this deed, I wil it not   925
        refuse.

CAMBISES. No, no, what I have said to you, I meane
        to have it so.

For councel theirs I mean not, I, in this respect to
        go.

But to my pallaice let us go the mariage to pre-
        pare,

For to avoid my wil in this I can it not forbeare.

LADY. O God, forgive me if I doo amisse!   930

The king by compultion inforseth me this.

MAID. Unto the gods for your estate I wil not cease to
        pray,

That you may be a happy queen and see moste
        joyful day.

CAMBISES. Come on, my lords, with gladsome harts
        let us rejoyce with glee.

Your musick showe to joy this deed at the request   935
        of me!

BOTHE [LORDS.] For to obey your Graces woords our
        honours doo agree.   *Exeunt.*
        Enter AMBIDEXTER.

AMBIDEXTER. O the passion of me! Mary, as ye say,
        yonder is a royal court.

There is triumphing and sport upon sporte,

Such loyall lords with such lordly exercise,

Frequenting such pastime as they can devise,   940

Running at tilt, justing, with running at the
        ring, [21]

Masking and mumming, [22] with eche kinde of
        thing,

Such dauncing, such singing, with musicall har-
        mony—[69]

Beleeve me, I was loth to absent their company.

But wil you beleve? Jesu, what haste they made   945
        til they were maried!

Not for a million of pounds one day longer they
      would have taried![70]

Oh, there was a banquet royall and super ex-
      celent!

Thousands and thousands at that banquit was
      spent.

I muse of nothing but how they can be maried so
      soon.

I care not if I be maried before tomorow at noon,   950

If mariage be a thing that so may be had.

[*To one of the audience.*] How say you, maid? To
      mary me wil ye be glad?

Out of dout, I beleeve it is some excellent treasure,

Els to the same belongs abundant pleasure.

Yet with mine eares I have heard some say,   955

"That ever I was maried, now cursed be the day!"

Those be they that[71] with curst[113] wives be
      matched,

That husband for haukes meat[23] of them is up
      snatched,

Hed broke with a bedstaf, face all to-be-
      scratched,[114]

"Knave," "slave," and "villain" a coild[115] cote now   960
      and than,

When the wife hath given it she wil say, "Alas,
      good man!"

Such were better unmaried, my maisters, I trowe,

Then all their life after to[72] be matched with a
      shrowe.[116]

Enter PREPARATION.

PREPARATION. With speed I am sent all things to
      prepare,

My message to doo as the king did declare.   965

His Grace dooth meane a banquit to make,

Meaning in this place repaste for to take.

Wel, the cloth shal be laid and all things in redy-
      nes,

To court to return when doon is my busines.

AMBIDEXTER. A proper man and also a[73] fit   970

For the kings estate to prepare a banquit.

---

113 *curst :* shrewish.   115 *coild :* beaten, thrashed.
114 *to-bescratched :* scratched   116 *shrowe :* shrew.
    asunder.

PREPARATION. What, Ambidexter! Thou art not unknowen.

A mischief on all good faces, so that I curse not
mine owne.

Now, in the knaves name, shake hands with me.

AMBIDEXTER. Wel said, goodman pouchmouth, your   975
reverence I see.

I wil teach ye, if your manners no better be.

A, yee slave, the king dooth me a gentleman alow.

Therfore I look that to me ye should bow.

Fight.

PREPARATION. Good Maister Ambidexter, pardon my
behaviour.

For this your deeds, ye[74] are a knave for your   980
labour.

AMBIDEXTER. Why, ye stale counterly[117] villain,[75]
nothing but "knave"?

Fight.

PREPARATION. I am sory your maistership offended I
have.

Shake hands, that betweene us agreement may
bee.

I was over-shot with myself,[118] I doo see.

Let me have your help this furniture to provide.   985

The king from this place wil not long abide.

Set the frute on the bord.[119]

AMBIDEXTER. Content. It is the thing that I would
wish.

I myself wil go fetch one[76] dish.

*Let the Vice fetch[77] a dish of nuts and let
them fall in the bringing of them in.*

PREPARATION. Clenly, Maister Ambidexter, for fair
on the ground they lye.

AMBIDEXTER. I wil have them up again by and by.   990

PREPARATION. To see all in redynes I wil put you in
trust.

There is no nay, to the court needs I must.

Exit PREPARATION.

AMBIDEXTER. Have ye no dout but all shal be wel.

Mary, sir, as you say, this geer dooth excel.

---

117 *counterly*: jailbird.   119 *bord*: table.
118 *was . . . myself*: went
   too far.

All things is in a redynes when they come   995
        hither.[78]

The kings Grace and the queen bothe togither.

[*To the audience.*] I beseech ye, my maisters, tel
        me, is it not best

That I be so bolde as to bid a gest?

He is as honest a man as ever spurd cow,

My cosin Cutpurse I meane. I beseech ye, judge   1000
        you.

Beleeve me, cosin, if to be the kings gest ye could
        be taken,

I trust that offer would not[79] be forsaken.

But, cosin, because to that office ye are not like to
        come,

Frequent your exercises—a horne on your
        thumb,(24)

A quick eye, a sharp knife, at hand a receiver.[120]   1005

But then take heed, cosin, ye be a clenly con-
        vayour.[121]

Content yourself, cosin, for this banquit you are
        unfit,

When such as I at the same am not worthy[80] to
        sit.

   Enter [CAMBISES *the*] *King,* QUEENE, *and his*
        traine [*of two* LORDS.][81]

CAMBISES. My queen and lords to take repast let us
        attempt the same.

Heer is the place, delay no time, but to our pur-   1010
        pose frame.

QUEENE. With willing harts your whole behest we
        minde for to obay.

ALL. And we, the rest of princes train, wil doo as you
        doo say.

        Sit at the banquit.

CAMBISES. Methink mine eares dooth wish the sound
        of musicks harmony.[82]

Heer for to play before my Grace in place I would
        them spy.

AMBIDEXTER. They be at hand, sir, with stick and   1015
        fidle.

---

120 *receiver :* "fence."   121 *clenly convayour :* adroit
                             thief.

They can play a new daunce called Hey didle
didle.

[Enter musicians and] play at the banquet.[83]

CAMBISES. My queene, perpend.[84] What I pro-
nounce I wil not violate,

But one thing which my hart makes glad I minde
to explicate :

You knowe in court uptrained is a lyon very yung,

Of one[85] litter two whelps[122] beside, as yet not   1020
very strong.[86]

I did request one whelp to see and this yung lion
fight,

But lion did the whelp convince by strength of
force and[87] might.

His brother whelpe,[88] perceiving that the lion
was to[o] good,

And he by force was like to see the other whelp
his blood,[123]

With force to lyon he did run, his brother for to   1025
help.

A wunder great it was to see that freendship in a
whelp.

So then the[89] whelpes between them both the
lyon did convince,

Whiche thing to see before mine eyes did glad the
hart of prince.

At this tale tolde, let the Queene weep.

QUEENE. These woords to hear makes stilling[124]
teares issue from christal eyes.(25)

CAMBISES. What doost thou meane, my spouse, to   1030
weep for losse of any prise?

QUEENE. No, no (O king) but as you see, freendship
in brothers whelp.

When one was like to have repulse the other
yeelded help.

And was this favour showd in dogs to shame of
royall king?

---

122 *whelps:* young dogs.
123 *by . . . blood:* perforce
    was likely to see the
    blood of the other
    whelp.

124 *stilling:* distilling, trick-
    ling.

Alack, I wish these eares of mine had not once
    heard this thing!

Even so should you (O mightie king) to brother   1035
    been a stay,

And not, without offence to you, in such wise him
    to slay.

In all assayes it was your parte his cause[90] to
    have defended,

And whosoever had him misused, to have them
    reprehended.

But faithful loove was more in dog then it was in
    your Grace.

CAMBISES. O cursed caitive, vicious, vile![91] I hate   1040
    thee in this place!

This banquit is at an end.[92] Take all these
    things away.

Before my face thou shalt repent the woords that
    thou doost say.

O wretch moste vile, didst thou the cause of
    brother mine so tender

The losse of him should greeve thy hart, he beeing
    none offender?

It did me good his death to have, so wil it to have   1045
    thine.

What freendship he had at my hands, the same
    even thou shalt finde.

I give consent and make a vow that thou shalt dye
    the death.

By Cruels swoord and Murder fel even thou shalt
    lose thy[93] breth.

Ambidexter, see with speed to Crueltie ye go:

Cause him hether to approch, Murder with him   1050
    also.

AMBIDEXTER. I redy am[94] for to fulfil, if that it be
    your Graces wil.

CAMBISES. Then nought oblight[125] my message
    given, absent thyself away.

AMBIDEXTER. Then in this place I wil no longer stay.

    [*Aside to the* QUEENE.] If that I durst I would
    mourne your case,

125 *oblight :* forget.

But, alas, I dare not for feare of his Grace.   1055

Exit AMBIDEXTER.

CAMBISES. Thou cursed Jil, by all the gods I take an
    othe and swere

That flesh of thine these hands of mine in peeces
    small could tere!

But thou shalt dye by dent of swoord, there is no
    freend ne fee

Shall finde remorce at princes hand to save the life
    of thee.

QUEENE. O mightie king and husband mine, vouch-   1060
    safe to heer me speke,

And licence give to spouse of thine her patient
    minde to breke.[126]

For tender loove unto your Grace my woords I did
    so frame.

For pure loove doth hart of king me violate and
    blame.

And to your Grace is this offence that I should pur-
    chase death?

Then cursed time that I was queen, to shorten this   1065
    my breth!

Your Grace doth know by mariage true I am your
    wife and spouse,

And one to save anothers helth (at troth plight)
    made our vowes.

Therfore, O king, let looving queen at thy hand
    finde remorse,

Let pitie be a meane to quench that cruel raging
    force,

And pardon, plight from princes mouth, yeeld   1070
    grace unto your queen

That amitie with faithful zeal may ever be us be-
    tween.

CAMBISES. A, caitive vile, to pitie thee my hart it is
    not bent,

Ne yet to pardon your offence it is not mine intent.

FIRST LORD. Our mightie prince, with humble sute of
    your Grace this I crave:

That this request it may take place your favour for   1075
    to have.

126 *breke*: express.

Let mercy yet abundantly the life of queen pre-
      serve,

Sith she in moste obedient wise your Graces wil
      dooth serve.

As yet your Grace but while with her hath had
      cohabitation,

And sure this is no desert why to yeeld her indig-
      nation.

Therfore (O king) her life prolong to joy her   1080
      dayes in blisse.

SECOND LORD. Your Grace shal win immortall fame in
      graunting unto this.

She is a queene whose goodly hue excelles the
      royall rose,

For beautie bright Dame Nature she a large gift
      did dispose.

For comelynes who may compare? Of all she
      beares the bell.[26]

This should give cause to moove your Grace to   1085
      loove her very wel.

Her silver brest in those your armes to sing the
      songs of loove,

Fine quallities moste excellent to be in her you
      proove,

A preciouse pearle of prise to prince, a jewel pass-
      ing all!

Therfore (O king) to beg remorce on both my
      knees I fall.

To graunt her grace to have her life with hart I   1090
      doo desire.

CAMBISES. You villaines twain, with raging force ye
      set my hart on fire!

If I consent that she shall dye, how dare ye crave
      her life?

You two to aske this at my hand dooth much in-
      large my strife.

Were it not for shame, you two should dye that
      for her life doo sue.

But favour mine from you is gone, my lords, I tel   1095
      you true.

I sent for Crueltie of late. If he would come away

I would commit her to his hands his cruel parte to
      play.

Even now I see where he dooth come. It dooth my
　　hart delight.
　　　　Enter CRUELTIE *and* MURDER.
CRUELTIE. Come, Murder, come, let us go foorth with
　　might.
Once again the kings commaundement we must   1100
　　fulfil.
MURDER. I am contented[95] to doo it with a good
　　wil.
CAMBISES. Murder and Crueltie, for bothe of you I
　　sent
With all festination your offices to frequent.
Lay holde on the queen, take her to your power,
And make her away within this houre!   1105
Spare for no feare, I doo you ful permit.
So I from this place doo meane for to flit.
BOTHE. With couragious harts (O king) we wil obey.
CAMBISES. Then come, my lords, let us departe away.
BOTHE THE LORDS. With hevy harts we wil doo all   1110
　　your Grace dooth say.
　　　　Exeunt King [CAMBISES] *and* LORDS[96]
CRUELTIE. Come, lady and queen, now are you in our
　　handling.[97]
In faith, with you we wil use no dandling.[127]
MURDER. With all expedition I, Murder, wil take
　　place.
Though thou be a queene, ye be under my grace.
QUEENE. With patience I wil you bothe obey.[98]   1115
CRUELTIE. No more woords, but go with us away.[99]
QUEENE. Yet before I dye some psalme to God let me
　　sing.
BOTHE. We be content to permit you that thing.
QUEENE. Farwell, you ladyes of the court,
With all your masking hew.[100]   1120
I doo forsake these brodered gardes[128]
And all the facions new,
The court and all the courtly train
Wherein I had delight.
I banished am from happy sporte,   1125

127 *dandling*: toying, delay-   128 *brodered gardes*: embroi-
　　ing.   dered trim or borders on
　　　　　　　　　　　　　　　　　　　　　　　garments.

And all by spitefull spite.
Yet with a joyful hart to God
A psalme I meane to sing,
Forgiving all men[101] and the king
Of eche kinde of thing.   1130
          Sing and exeunt.
          Enter AMBIDEXTER, *weping.*
AMBIDEXTER. A, a, a, a, I cannot chuse but weep for
          the queene.
Nothing but mourning now at the court there is
          seen.
Oh, oh, my hart, my hart! Oh, my bum wil break!
Very greef so torments me that scarce I can
          speake.
Who could but weep for the losse of such a lady?   1135
That cannot I doo, I sweare by mine honesty.
But Lord, so the ladyes mourn, crying "Alack!"
Nothing is worne now but onely black.
I beleeve all the[102] cloth in Watling Street(27)
          to make gownes would not serve.
If I make a lye, the devil let ye sterve![129]   1140
All ladyes mourne, bothe yung and olde.
There is not one that weareth a points worth of
          gold.
There is a sorte for feare for the king doo pray
That would have him dead, by the Masse, I dare
          say.
What a king was he that hath used such tiranny!   1145
He was akin to Bishop Bonner,(28) I think verely!
For bothe their delights was to shed blood,
But never intended to doo any good.
Cambises put a judge to death, that was a good
          deed,
But to kil the yung childe was worse to proceed,   1150
To murder his brother and then his owne wife,
So help me God and holidom, it is pitie of his life!
Heare ye? I wil lay twentie thousand pound
That the king himself dooth dye by some wound.
He hath shed so much blood that his wil be shed.   1155
If it come so[103] to passe, in faith, then he is
          sped.

129 *sterve :* perish.

Enter [CAMBISES] *the King, without a gown, a swoord thrust up into his side, bleeding.*

CAMBISES. Out, alas! What shal I doo? My life is finished!

Wounded I am by sudain chaunce, my blood is minished.[130]

Gogs hart, what meanes might I make my life to preserve?

Is there nought to be my help, nor is there nought   1160
to serve?

Out upon the court and lords that there remain!

To help my greef in this case wil none of them take pain?

Who but I, in such a wise, his deaths wound could have got?

As I on horseback up did leape, my swoord from scabard shot

And ran me thus into the side, as you right wel   1165
may see.

A mervels chaunce unfortunate[131] that in this wise should bee!

[*The King falls to the ground.*]

I feele myself a-dying now, of life bereft am I,

And Death hath caught me with his dart, for want of blood, I spy.

Thus gasping heer on ground I lye, for nothing I doo care.

A just reward[104] for my misdeeds my death   1170
dooth plain declare.

Heer let him quake and stir.

AMBIDEXTER. How now, noble king? Pluck up your hart!

What, wil you dye and from us departe?

Speake to me and[132] ye be alive.

He cannot speak. But beholde, how with Death he dooth strive.

[*The King dies.*]

Alas, good king, alas, he is gone.   1175

The devil take me if for him I make any mone.

---

130 *minished :* diminished, reduced in quantity.
131 *A . . . unfortunate :* A remarkable piece of bad
luck.
132 *and :* if.

I did prognosticate of his end, by the Masse.
Like as I did say, so is it come to passe.
I wil be gone. If I should be found heer,
That I should kil him it would appeer.   1180
For feare with his death they doo me charge
Farewel, my maisters, I wil goe take barge.
I meane to be packing, now is the tide.
Farewel, my maisters, I wil no longer abide!

> *Exit* AMBIDEXTER.

> *Enter three* LORDS.

FIRST LORD. Beholde, my lords,[105] it is even so as   1185
    he to us did tel:
His Grace is dead upon the ground by dent of
    swoord moste fel.
SECOND LORD. As he in saddle would have lept, his
    sword from sheath did go,
Goring him up into the side, his life was ended so.
THIRD LORD. His blood so fast did issue out that
    nought could him prolong.
Yet, before he yeelded up the ghost, his hart was   1190
    very strong.
FIRST LORD. A just rewarde for his misdeeds the God
    aboove hath wrought,
For certainly the life he led was to be counted
    nought.
SECOND LORD. Yet a princely buriall he shall have ac-
    cording[106] his estate,
And more of him heer at this time we have not to
    dilate.
THIRD LORD. My lords, let us take him up to cary[107]   1195
    him away.
BOTHE. Content we are with one accord to doo as you
    doo say.

> *Exeunt all* [*bearing away the body of* CAMBISES.]

EPILOGUS[1]

Right gentle audience, heere have you perused[1]
The tragicall history of this wicked king.
According to our duety we have not refused
But to our best intent exprest every thing.

EPILOGUS.
   1 *perused :* viewed in detail.

We trust none is offended for this our dooing.   5
    Our author craves likewise if he have squared
        amisse
    By gentle admonicion to knowe where the
        fault is.

  His good wil shall not be neglected to amend
    the same.
Praying all to beare therfore with his[2] simple
    deed
Until the time serve a better he may frame,   10
Thus yeelding you thanks to end we decreed.
That you so gently have[3] suffred us to proceed
    In such patient wise as to hear and see
    We can but thank ye therfore, we can doo no
        more, we.[4]

  As duty bindes us for our noble Queene let us   15
    pray,
And for her honerable councel the trueth that they
    may use[5]
To practise justice and defend her Grace eche day.
To maintain Gods woord they may not refuse
To correct all those that would her Grace and
        Graces lawes abuse,
    Beseeching God over us she may reign long   20
    To be guided by trueth and defended from
        wrong.
    Amen quod Thomas Preston

Imprinted at London by John Allde.[6]

VARIANTS

FULGENS AND LUCRES

The text is based upon the Huntington facsimile of the unique copy of the first edition, printed by John Rastell between 1513 and 1519.

Q   Rastell's quarto.

B   Two leaves preserved in the Bagford fragments, British Museum, from another, uncorrected copy of the same edition.

BR   Edition of Boas and Reed.

Pars Prima

[1] fill] full Q.

[2] *Ll. 30 and 31 appear twice in Q by mistake.*

[3] Publius] publins Q.

[4] BR *wrongly prints this line :* whiche of these ye .ii. men sholde haue pre-eminence.

[5] convenience] couenience Q.

[6] process] p[ro]ces Q.

[7] I] y Q.

[8] and] ad Q.

[9] pleasure] pleasnre Q.

[10] then] than Q.

[11] parish] parisish Q.

[12] A.] *Omitted in Q but added by hand.*

[13] help] selp Q.

[14] on] ou Q.

[15] or] of Q.

[16] th'emperiall] hemperiall Q.

[17] worldly] wordly Q.

[18] male] mase Q.

[19] Q *prints this line with the following stanza.*

[20] reson] resou Q.

[21] intend] nitend Q.

[22] To the promocyon] To : repromocyon Q.

[23] substance] subslace Q.

[24] counsellyng] counsell Q, yng *added by hand.*

[25] Q *puts the speech heading before l. 347.*

[26] A.] *inserted in Q by hand.*

[27] FULGENS] fulgeus Q.

[28] facta] fctā Q.

[29] lu *unnecessarily prefixed to this line in Q.*

[30] ANCILLA] Q *places this over the speech as well as using the regular tag :* an.

[31] GAYUS.] Gaius Q, *inserted by hand.*

[32] that that ye] that y̆e ye Q.

[33] gentilwoman] gentilman Q.

[34] *Q prefixes the tag,* ga., *to l.* 559. *The error is corrected by hand.*

[35] Upon] wpon Q.

[36] FLAMYNEUM, *dicat ei*] fla. & dicat ci Q.

[37] Upon] wpon Q.

[38] But] Bnt Q.

[39] substaunce] substanuce Q.

[40] entente] entete Q.

[41] undertake] wndertake Q.

[42] yes] Bves Q.

[43] GAYUS.] Ga *prefixed to l.* 652 *in* Q, *corrected by hand.*

[44] A.] R. Q.

[45] A.] *Q omits; added by hand.*

[46] and] aud Q.

[47] Ey, God gyve it a very very vengeaunce] Q. BR *emends to* By god gyue it a very vengeaunce! *Compare l.* 1028.

[48] faythfully] faytfully Q.

[49] Q. *prefixes* an. *here as well as to* Se the man!

[50] B.] *Omitted in* Q, *added by hand.*

[51] *speech tag omitted in* Q, Anc *added by hand and in the right margin* ye mayde spek.

[52] B.] Q. BR *gives the speech to* A. *Since there are difficulties of coherence either way, it seems best not to emend.*

[53] I] y Q.

[54] *Written over this line as if to emend it is* a Pece ey. *The tag* A *is also apparently inserted by hand.*

[55] B.] *Q omits, added by hand.*

[56] Let] Q. BR *misprints* Le.

[57] A.] *Q omits, added by hand.*

[58] then] Q. BR *emends to* than.

[59] gentylwoman] gentylman Q. BR *emends to* gentilwoman.

[60] he] BR. I Q.

[61] *Et exeat* GAYUS.] Et exeat Gaius & A Q.

[62] B.] *Prefixed to the following line in* Q. BR *corrects.*

[63] And] An Q.

[64] agayne] agayue Q.

[65] And] Bnd Q.

Pars Secunda

[1] That] This Q.

[2] lo] Q. BR *emends to* so.

[3] nought] uoght Q.

[4] *Q repeats* B *before this line, which begins a page.*

[5] thinke] thiuke Q.

[6] Cokkis] Q. collis B.

[7] or] Q. ar B.

[8] musc] Q. must B.
[9] sad] Q. sayd B.
[10] ernest] Q. hernest B.
[11] Tyl] Tyl I Q.
[12] togeder] to geer Q.
[13] gestis] geftis Q.
[14] contray] contrary Q.
[15] those fygures] that fygures Q.
[16] understoode] vnderstonde Q.
[17] GAYUS] B Q.
[18] have] hane Q.
[19] my] me Q.
[20] thryse] thyrse Q.
[21] starve] starce Q.
[22] scarecenes] scaecenes Q.
[23] PUBLIUS CORNELIUS] pub. cornelus Q.
[24] women] woman Q.
[25] for] far Q.

JOHAN JOHAN THE HUSBANDE

The text is based upon Farmer's facsimile of the copy of Rastell's edition (1533) in the library of Magdalene College. There exists another copy of this edition formerly in the Ashmolean Museum, now in the Bodleian Library, Oxford. I have collated Xerox prints of this with the Magdalene text, which exhibits a few minor corrections.

M   Rastell's folio edition of 1533 (Magdalene).
A   Ashmolean copy of the same edition.
P   Edition of Pollard.

[1] Whan she offendeth] *Missing from* A *because of cropping.* When she offendeth *written in margin.*

[2] *This and the three preceding speech tags are mistakenly raised by one line in* M *and* A.

[3] JOHAN] Tyb M *and* A. *A verse may be missing after l. 201, judging from the lack of a rhyme for* part.

[4] TYB] Jhān M *and* A.

[5] P *needlessly inserts* thou *before* what.

[6] JOHAN JOHAN] M *and* A. P *assigns this speech to Tyb, l. 245 to Johan, ll. 246–57 to Tyb, ll. 258–59 to Tyb. Whittingham's reprint* (1819?) *reapportions the speeches still differently. But the passage* (ll. 242–59) *is characteristic of Johan, though at least one scholar* (S. Sultan, *JEGP,* LII (1953), 491–97) *would assign ll. 252–59 to Tyb.*

Confused, however, by the paragraph signs, Rastell or his printer repeats Jhān *before l. 252, assigns ll. 258–59 to Tyb and ll. 260 through the first part of l. 263 to Johan.*

[7] Now] M *and* A How.

[8] Now] M *and* A How.

[9] me] M *and* A. P, *followed by* J. Q. Adams, *emends to* my, *and again at l. 376.*

[10] stynte] P. stynk M *and* A.

[11] thought] P. though M *and* A.

[12] he] M *and* A. *Adams emends to* she, *following a suggestion of* P, *who assumes the reference to be to* Tyb.

[13] P, *followed by Adams, inserts* it *after* take.

[14] Ye] M. Je A.

[15] chafe] M. chefe A.

[16] TYB] *So placed in* M. A *has it before l. 512.*

[17] ryft] M. ryftt A.

[18] beyond] M. beand A.

[19] beyond] M. beyand A.

[20] wonderous] monderous M *and.* A.

[21] notwithstandyng] not withstankyng M *and* A.

[22] thee] thy M *and* A. P *and Adams emend to* thou.

[23] you] *emendation of Adams.* your M, A, *and* P.

KYNG JOHAN

The basis of the text is Bang's facsimile of the MS. For innumerable readings and for guidance in arranging parts of the difficult MS. in the order intended for the stage, I am indebted to the Malone Society transcription edited by John Henry Pyle Pafford. The MS. now resides in the Huntington Library.

The play was first printed in 1838, in an edition prepared by J. P. Collier for the Camden Society. Collier lacked two leaves not discovered until 1847 and made a number of errors, including omission of a whole line. I list only sample variants from Collier, but adopt a few of his readings. Manly's edition is a reprint of Collier with no independent value.

This edition is the first to present the whole of the play in Bale's final recension and with his substitutions and interpolations arranged as they were meant to be acted. The MS. is a scribal copy done about 1538–40; the early version of the play which it represents may be some years older still. Bale himself, however, revised the MS. in his own hand, perhaps during the reign of Edward VI as well as after Elizabeth's accession. I have endeavored to present the play as Bale left it, listing in the variants everything amounting to an entire word or more which he thought fit to change. His great care is evident. It will be noted that at first he altered words and phrases, then began to make insertions in the margin and on new sheets, and finally abandoned the scribal version to write a new conclusion. Of the original conclusion canceled by Bale, only the 139 lines printed below survive.

I have made the spelling of characters' names consistent by adopting throughout the form favored by Bale (thus "Englande" for the scribe's "Ynglond") whenever that can be determined from his revisions, otherwise by adopting the most frequent spelling. Bale's paragraph signs are represented by indentation. They mark off stanzas of verse and occasionally indicate turns of thought.

A   MS. as written by the scribe.
B   MS. as revised by Bale.
C   Edition of Collier.
M   Malone Society edition.

Actus Primus.

[1] their force] B. the strenght A.

[2] doth] B. to A.

[3] cauteles] B. fantesyes A.

[4] over] B. of A.

[5] lycherye] C. M *reads* bycherye.

[6] as it doth] B. yt do A.

[7] Truly] trwly A.

[8] ther] p^t A. C *prints* that.

[9] *Collier suggests that this line should read:* Seke ryght to procure to the weake and faterless.

[10] thu] B, *inserted.*

[11] *This and the preceding line are written by mistake in* A *after l. 166, crossed out, and repeated here.*

[12] a] B, *inserted.*

[13] over] B. of A.

[14] in] B. yn A.

[15] Scotland] scotlond A.

[16] more] B, *inserted. The line is written in the margin.*

[17] knowe] B, *omitted in* A.

[18] worlde] B, *omitted in* A.

[19] here] B, *inserted.*

[20] both] B. A *has by mistake* I hath.

[21] have] B. hathe A.

[22] is] B, *inserted.*

[23] abhorre] B. abore A.

[24] it] B, *omitted in* A.

[25] and more] B. d A.

[26] *Here begins a marginal addition by Bale running to l. 458.* C *accidentally omits l. 450.*

[27] B. *Before revision the line read:* And to thynke that Christes deth ys unsufficient.

[28] the] B, *inserted.*

[29] calke] A. talke C.

[30] Are] B, *omitted in* A.

[31] gyveth] B. geve A.

[32] eyther] B. owther A.

[33] Ded] sayd A.

[34] trybute] trybytt A. trybutt C.

[35] in] B, *inserted. Bale crossed out the* In *mistakenly placed after* onys.

[36] I] B, *inserted.*

[37] hether] *canceled in* A.

[38] are] B, *inserted.*

[39] letany] leany A.

[40] vengeable] B. *Bale presumably meant this to replace* horeble *which precedes it in* A *but is not deleted.*

[41] nose] B. fase A.

[42] wherfor] B. why A.

[43] beare] B. bare A.

[44] We] B. whe A.

[45] profyghtes] A. C *misreads as* slyghtes. *Compare l. 958.*

[46] yet] B, *inserted.*

[47] fast] B, *inserted.*

[48] saynt] B, *inserted.*

[49] what] B. all A.

[50] becam] M. C *reads* began.

[51] for] B, *inserted.*

[52] thretned] threned A.

[53] feche] M. C *reads* seche.

[54] them] B, *inserted.*

[55] for] B, *inserted.*

[56] croked] B. myghty A.

[57] I am alofte] *Emendation suggested by Collier.* thu art alofte B, a lofte A. *Bale must have nodded, since clearly the speaker Sedicyon is aloft. Kittredge, according to Manly, suggested giving the line to Dissymulacyon.*

[58] desyre] B. dyssyre A.

[59] have] B, *inserted.*

[60] farre] B, *inserted.*

[61] truly] B, *inserted.*

[62] hose] B. hosse A.

[63] lose] B. losse A.

[64] horryble] B. horebyll A.

[65] ceremony] B. cerymōy A.

[66] knave] knove A.

[67] alwayes] B. euer A.

[68] their] B, *inserted.*

[69] *Here starts a passage written by Bale on a blank leaf for insertion at this point and extending to l. 1011.*

[70] do] B, *inserted.*

[71] so] B, *inserted.*

[72] *The original direction reads :* Here the pope go owt & dys-symulacyon & nobylyte cū in & say. *After the insertion of the Interpretour's speech just before it this is no longer appropriate since the Pope is not to remain onstage while the Interpretour speaks. I have divided the direction to fit the new situation, changing* dys-symulacyon *to* SEDICYON, *since it is Sedicyon who speaks with Nobilyte at the start of Act II. &* dyssymulacyon *may mean that Dissymulacyon is to go off with the Pope, not that he is to enter with Nobilyte.*

[73] *All of the Interpretour's speech is written by Bale on a separate leaf for insertion here.*

ACTUS SECUNDUS.

[1] contyneally] contymeally M.

[2] cleane] B, *inserted.*

[3] move] B. show A.

[4] ryghtfull] *the* -full *added by Bale.*

[5] whole] B. hole A.

[6] magnifycence] B. p[re]hemyne[n]ce A.

[7] In] B. A A.

[8] to] B, *inserted.*

[9] same] B, *inserted.*

[10] the] B, a A.

[11] an holy and] B, *inserted.*

[12] loade B. Rode A. *Bale at first supplied* broode *but deleted it.*

[13] my] B, *inserted.*

[14] tyckle] B. tycle A, *not however deleted.*

[15] after a pared] M. a ster apared C.

[16] I] y A.

[17] sturdynesse] B. rumer A.

[18] it] B. pᵗ (*that*) A.

[19] *Ll. 261–64 are a marginal insertion by Bale.*

[20] it] B, *inserted.*

[21] iwys] B, *inserted.*

[22] seke] B. laber A.

[23] so] B, *inserted.*

[24] to] B, *inserted.*

[25] shall] B, *inserted.*

[26] thu] B, yow A.

[27] feed] B. frend A.

[28] her] B, *inserted.*

[29] of] B. o A.

[30] is] B. sheweth A.

[31] as] B, *inserted.*

[32] swete] B, *inserted.*

[33] *Ll. 417–22 are a marginal addition by Bale to replace this line in* A: now wold I fayne know the mynd of my commynalte.

[34] *In* A *this direction occurs with the preceding one. The insertion of Johan's soliloquy requires moving it to this position.*

[35] my] B. good A.

[36] lyvely] B. owne A.

[37] two] B. to A.

[38] to] B, *inserted.*

[39] me] B, *inserted.*

[40] have] B, *inserted.*

[41] covenaunt] convaunt A, connaunt C.

[42] *In the MS. this direction occurs between ll. 492 and 493.*

[43] here, for whye] B. thowght, for A.

[44] so have ye] B. so ye have A.

[45] interdyct] C. M *reads* interdyet.

[46] the] B, *inserted.*

[47] their] B. be A.

[48] we have] B, *inserted.*

[49] landynge] B. commyng A.

[50] *Ll. 523–32 are a marginal insertion by Bale.*

[51] grace, mercye] B. great grace A.

[52] leede] B, *inserted.*

[53] *Ll. 549–607 constitute a major addition written by Bale on a separate leaf for insertion here.*

[54] Innocent] B. inosent A.

[55] than,] B, *inserted.*

[56] here] B. wpe A.

[57] With] B. In A.

[58] great] B, *inserted.*

[59] the] B. ye A.

[60] *Ll. 638–41 are an addition by Bale.*

[61] we shall commen] B. I wyll show yow A.

[62] bonde] B. hand A.

[63] a] B, *inserted.*

[64] *Ll. 656–59 are an addition by Bale.*

[65] is] B. ys A.

[66] *et*] B. e A.

[67] *hac*] B. ac A.

[68] *mihi*] B. w A.

[69] *From this point on I print as the text the revised conclusion of the play in Bale's own hand. Of the corresponding section in* A *only the first four pages are preserved, so that the original ending is lost. The canceled text in Hand* A *from l. 687 until it breaks off runs as follows:*

STEVYN LANGTON. I passe not on yt now that ye are   687
    amendyd.

ENGLANDE. Ser, yender is a clarke which ys condempnyd
    for treason.

The sreyves wold fayne know what to do with hym
    this season.

KYNG JOHAN. For so moch as he hath falsefyed owr   690
    coyne

As he is worthy late hym with a halter joyne.

CARDYNALL. What styll agaynst the chirch? Get me
    bocke, bell and candell,

And as I am a trew prist I shall yow yet bett handell.

Remember ye not how ye used Peter Punfret,

A good symple man and as they say a prophet?   695

KYNG JOHAN. I ded prove hym ser a verye supsticyose
    wreche.

STEVYN LANGTON. He prophesyed of yow and therfor ye
    ded hym up streche.

Ded he any more than call yow a devyll Incarnate?

KYNG JOHAN. Yes, he toke uppon hym my yeares to
    predestynate.

Well, as for this man, he cawse that he is a prist   700

I geve hym to yow, do with hym what ye lyst.

CARDYNALL. Than forth and byd them to set hym at
    lyberte.

ENGLANDE. I shall be full glad to do as ye commaund
    me.

CARDYNALL. Ere I releace yow of the interdiccyon here

In the whych yowr realme contynewed hath this vij.   705
    yere

Ye shall make Julyane yowr syster in law this bonde,

To geve hyr the thyrd parte of Englande and of
    Yerlond.

KYNG JOHAN. Oh, ye undo me upp, consyderyng my
    great paymentes.

ENGLANDE. Ser, dyscomfort not, for God hath sett de-
    baytementes.

The woman ys ded, soch tydynges is hether browght.   710

Go owt ENGLANDE *and dresse for* DISSYMULACYON.

KYNG JOHAN. Oh Lord, for me wreche, what a myracle
    hast thou wrowght.

Lyke as David sayth, thou dost not leve that servont

That wyll trust in the or in thy blessed covenant.

CARDYNALL. Than I here releace yow of the Interdic-
    cyons all,

Straytly chargyng yow uppon danger that may fall   715

No more to meddle with the chyrchis reformacyon

Nor kepe them from Rome for any appelacyon
By God and by all the contentesin this boke.

KYNG JOHAN. Ageynst Holy Churche I wyll nowther
    speke nor loke.

STEVYN LANGTON. Opyn the churche dorys and let the   720
    belles be ronge,

And throwgh owt the realme se that *Te Deum* be
    songe.

CARDYNALL. Go yowr wayes a pace and see that yt be
    done.

KYNG JOHAN. At yowr commaundement yt shall be per-
    formyde sone.   *Here go owt the Kyng.*

CARDYNALL. By the Messe I lawght to se this clene con-
    vayance.

He is now full glad as owr pype gothe to daunce.   725

STEVYN LANGTON. I promyse the suer yet wyll I not leve
    hym soo.

CARDYNALL. Why, felow Sedicyon, with hym what wylte
    thou doo?

STEVYN LANGTON. Mary feche yn Lewes, kyng Philyppes
    son in Fraunce,

To fall uppon hym with his men and ordynaunce.

I wyll not leve hym tell I bryng hym to his ende.   730

CARDYNALL. Well God be with the, do as shall lye in thi
    mend.

Here the CARDYNALL *go owt and dresse for* NOBILYTE.

STEVYN LANGTON. I mervell greatly wher Dissymula-
    cyon ys.

        [*Enter* DISSYMULACYON.]

DISSYMULACYON. I wyll cum anone, yf thow tary whyll
    I pysse.

STEVYN LANGTON. I beshrow yowr hart. Wher have ye
    ben so longe?

DISSYMULACYON. In the gardyn man the herbysse and   735
    wedes amonge,

And ther have I gott the poysson of a toode.

I hope at the last to worke sum myscheffe abroode.

STEVYN LANGTON. I was wonte sumtyme of thi secrett
    cownsell to be.

Am I now a dayes be cum a stranger to the?

DISSYMULACYON. I wyll tell the all undernethe bene-   740
    dicite,

What I mynd to do in cace thou wylt asoyle me.

STEVYN LANGTON. Thow shalt be assoylyd by the Popys
    auctoryte.

DISSYMULACYON. Shall I so in dede? Be the Messe than
    have at the.

Benedicite.

STEVYN LANGTON. *Dominus. In nomine Domine pape*
      amen.

DISSYMULACYON. Syr this is my mende. I wyll geve Kyng   745
      Johan this poyson

And make hym suer that he shall never have good
      foyson,

And this must thow say to colur with the thyng,

That he wold have mad a loffe worth xx shelyng.

STEVYN LANGTON. Nay that is soch a lye as esly maye
      be felt.

DISSYMULACYON. Tushe man, among folys yt shall never   750
      be owt smelt.

STEVYN LANGTON. I am swer than thou wylt geve hym yt
      in a drynke.

DISSYMULACYON. Mary that I wyll and the ton halfe with
      hym swynke

To corage hym to drynke the botome off.

STEVYN LANGTON. Yf thow serve hym so thou shalt knav-
      yshly with hym scoffe.

Thyn owne carkas than ys lyke to suffor lasshes.   755

DISSYMULACYON. Tushe, what thow I dye man, there
      shall rysse more of myn asshes.

I am suer the prystes wyll pray for me so bytterlye

That I shall not cum in hell nor in purgatory.

STEVYN LANGTON. Nay to kepe the frothens thou shalt
      have v. monkes synggyng

In Swynshed abbey so long as the world ys dwryng.   760

DISSYMULACYON. Whan the world ys done what helpe
      shall I have than?

STEVYN LANGTON. Than shyft for thi selfe, so well as
      ever thow can.

DISSYMULACYON. Cockes sowle he comyth here, assoyle
      me that I were gon then.

STEVYN LANGTON. *Ego absolvo te. In nomine Domini*
      pape amen.

    Here go owt DISSYMULACYON *and* STEVYN LANGTON
    together and KYNG JOHAN *cum in* [*with* ENGLANDE.]

KYNG JOHAN. No prince in the world in soche captyvyte   765

As I am this hower, and all for ryghtosnes.

Agenst me I have both the lordes and commynalte,

Bysshoppes and lawers, whych in ther cruell madnes

Hathe browght in hyther the French kynges fyrst son
      Lewes.

The chance unto me ys not so dolorowsse   770

But my lyfe this howr ys moche more tedyowse.

    More of compassyon for shedyng of Christen blood

Than anye thyng els my crowne I gave up lately

To the Pope of Rome, whych hath no tyttle good
Of jurysdyccon, but usurpacyon onlye.   775
And now to the Lord I wold resygne upp gladlye
Bothe my crowne and lyfe, for thyne owne ryght it ys
Yf yt wold please the, to take my sowle to thi blys.

ENGLANDE. Sur dyscomfort not. In the honore of Christ
            Jesu

God wyll never fayle yow entendynge not els but   780
            vertu.

KYNG JOHAN. The anguysh of spyrytt so pangeth me
            every wher
That incessantlye I thyrst tyll I be ther.

DISSYMULACYON *syng this.* Wassayle, wassayle in snowe,
            frost, and hayle,
Wassayle, wassayle that moch dothe avayle,
Wassayle, wassayle that never wyll fayle.   785

KYNG JOHAN. Who is that Englande? I pray the stepe
            forth and se.

ENGLANDE. He dothe seme a farre of, sum relygyose
            mann to be.

            [*Enter* DISSYMULACYON *with a cup.*]

DISSYMULACYON. Now Jesus preserve yowr worthy excel-
            ent Grace,
For dowtles ther is a very angelycke face.
Now for sothe and God I wold thynk my selfe in   790
            hevyn
Yf I myght remayn with yow but yeres alevyn.
I wold covyt here non other felycyte.

KYNG JOHAN. A lovyng person thow shuldest seme for
            to be.

DISSYMULACYON. I am as jentell a worme as ever yow
            dyd se.

KYNG JOHAN. But what is thy name, I besych the hartyly   795
            shew me.

DISSYMULACYON. My name ys callyd Monastycall Devo-
            cyon.
Here have I browt yow a very helsum porsheon,
For I hard yow say that ye were very drye.

KYNG JOHAN. In dede I am thyrstye. I pray the good
            moncke cum nygh.

DISSYMULACYON. The dayes of yowr lyfe never felt yow   800
            such a cuppe,
So good and holsom yf ye wold drynke yt uppe.
Yt passyth maumsey, capryke, tyrre or ypocras.
Be my fayth I trow suche a drynke never was.

KYNG JOHAN. Begynne gentyll monke. I pray the drynk
            halfe to me.

DISSYMULACYON. Yf ye wold drynke all, yt ware the   805
    better for ye.

KYNG JOHAN. Nay, thow shalt drynke halfe, ther is no
    remedy.

DISSYMULACYON. Good lucke to yow than, have at yt
    evyn harttely.

KYNG JOHAN. God seynt the, good monke, with all my
    very hart.

    [DISSYMULACYON] *drynke to the K[y]ng.*

DISSYMULACYON. Loo I have dronk yow halfe, now
    drynke yow owt that part.

    [*Aside.*] Where art thou Sedicyon? I dye man, I dye.   810
        [*Enter* SEDICYON.]

SEDICYON. Cum of apace than, and gett the to the
    farmary.

  I have provyded for the be swet Saynt Powle,

  v. monkes that shall syng perpetualy for thi sowle

  That I warant the thow shalt never cum in hell.

               Here have hym owt of the place.

DISSYMULACYON. To send me to hevyn I pray the go ryng   815
    the holy bell.

KYNG JOHAN. My body sore grogeth, of the collyck I am
    afrayed.

ENGLANDE. Alas sur alas, I fere that ye are betrayed.

KYNG JOHAN. Why, where is the monke that dranke with
    me here lately?

ENGLANDE. He is poysond ser, and lyeth a dyyng suerly.

KYNG JOHAN. What, yt is not so, for he was with me   820
    here now.

ENGLANDE. Dowghtles yt is so. trew, as I have told yow.

KYNG JOHAN. Ther is no malyce, to the malyce of the
    clargy.

  Well, the swete Lord of hevyn on me and them have
    marcy.

  For ryghtosnes sake, they have ever hated me.

  They causyd my londe to be excommynycate.   825

[70] quaffynge] C. quassynge B.

ROYSTER DOYSTER

The text is taken from Xerox prints made from microfilm of the
unique Eton copy.

E   Eton quarto.

M Malone Society reprint.

A Arber's reprint of July 1, 1869.

F   Edition of Ewald Flügel.

W Rafe's letter in its two versions as printed in Wilson's *Arte of Logique* (ed. 1553). Here I do not list the many variations of mere spelling.

ACTUS I. SCAENA I.

[1] knowe] E, M. know A.

ACTUS I. SCAENA II.

[1] *This half line is not assigned to Rafe in* E.
[2] ye] he E, M, A.
[3] Whom] E, M, A. Who F.
[4] Guy] M, F. Cuy E, A.
[5] They] E, M, F. That A.
[6] here] *Omitted in* E. *Added by Cooper.*

ACTUS I. SCAENA IIII.

[1] time] itme E.
[2] E *assigns this line and a half to Rafe.*

ACTUS II. SCAENA IIII.

[1] No] F. No did E, M, A.

ACTUS III. SCAENA III.

[1] shoulde] E, M. should A.

ACTUS III. SCAENA IIII.

[1] service] sernice E. *Corrected by Cooper.*
[2] Sweete mistresse] E. Swete maistresse,] W.
[3] substance and richesse] E. richesse and substaunce W.
[4] demeanoure and wit,] E. demeanoure, & witte,] W.
[5] taken] E. take W.
[6] substance,] E. substaunce] W.
[7] well,] E. wel] W.
[8] E *has the comma,* W *a period.*
[9] W *omits the comma.*
[10] E *has comma,* W *a period.*
[11] W *omits the comma.*
[12] W *omits the comma.*
[13] them] E. them,] W.
[14] W *omits the comma.*
[15] who ere say nay,] E. (who ere saie naie)] W.
[16] you] E. you,] W.
[17] *This line is omitted in Arber's reprint of July 24, 1869.*
[18] W *omits the comma.*
[19] Royster Doyster,] Roister Doister] E. Roisterdoister] W.
[20] (ye may be bolde) E. ye maie be bolde,] W.
[21] W *omits the comma.*
[22] fet] F *misreads* set.

ACTUS III. SCAENA V.

[1] SCRIVENER E. A *gives this half line to Merygreeke.*
[2] substance :] E. substaunce,] W.
[3] you :] E. you.] W.
[4] taken] E. take W.
[5] nere] E. neuer W.
[6] presents] E. presentes,] W.
[7] and] E. an W.
[8] can] E. could W.
[9] are :] E. are.] W.
[10] well :] E. wel.] W.
[11] W *omits comma.*
[12] Doe] E. Dooe,] W.
[13] W *has comma.*
[14] they] E. them] W.
[15] who ere say nay,] E. (who ere saie naie)] W.
[16] W *omits the period.*
[17] Royster Doyster,] Roister Doister,] E. Roisterdoister,] W.
[18] (ye may be bolde) E. ye maie be bolde,] W.
[19] W *omits the comma.*

ACTUS IIII. SCAENA III.

[1] suspect] A *and all editors.* supect E.

ACTUS IIII. SCAENA VI.

[1] E *reverses the names of the speakers for ll.* 10 *and* 11.

ACTUS IIII. SCAENA VII.

[1] F *omits the heading assigning this half line to Trusty.*
[2] F *assigns this line to Trusty,* E *to Royster.*
[3] E *mistakenly prints* T. Trustie *before l.* 104; *the words from* But *to* befall *must however belong to Rafe.*

ACTUS IIII. SCAENA VIII.

[1] *To the names of the characters* E *adds* Two drummes with their Ensignes.
[2] E *has* Exeant om.
[3] E *has instead* Exeat *at the end of l.* 61.

ACTUS V. SCAENA IIII.

[1] here . . . have] E. F *needlessly emends to* here were y^at wished ye to have.

ACTUS V. SCAENA V.

[1] maintaine] maintaiue E.

SECONDE SONG

[1] froe] *Emendation of Cooper.* free E.

GAMMER GURTONS NEDLE

I have used Farmer's facsimile of the British Museum copy of the edition of 1575, listing the variants from microfilm of the Huntington Library copy. Though probably not the first edition (the play was entered to T. Colwell in the Stationers' *Registers* in 1563) this is the only one surviving from the sixteenth century. The reprint of 1661 lacks independent value.

BM British Museum copy, edition of 1575.
H Huntington copy of the same edition.
BS Edition of Brett-Smith (reprint of the Bodleian copy).
B Edition of Henry Bradley.

NAMES OF THE SPEAKERS

[1] COCKE] Docke BM, H.

FYRST ACTE, SECOND SCEANE.

[1] such] suce BM, H.
[2] with] what BM, H.
[3] canst thou not tell] cast $\overset{u}{y}$ not till BM, H.

FYRST ACTE, THYRD SCEANE.

[1] a] at BM, H.
[2] this whyle] *cropped in* BM, *supplied from* H.

FYRST ACTE, IIII SCEANE.

[1] downe] dowde BM, H. *Emendation of Dodsley.*
[2] *In arranging ll. 39–40 according to rhyme I follow Manly and* B. BM *and* H *print as follows:*

Cocke. Howe Gammer.
Gāmer. Goe hye thee soone, and grope behynd the old
      brasse pan,
  Whych thing When thou hast done

THE I. ACTE, V. SCEANE.

[1] Not] BM. No H, BS.
[2] were] where BM, H.
[3] tys] BM, H. B *and* BS *emend to* thys.

THE II. ACTE, FYRST SCEANE.

[1] well] will BM, H.
[2] dodge] dogde BM, H.
[3] tonge] thonge BM, thouge H.

[4] thou] than BM, H.
[5] *breeches*] kreeches BM, H.
[6] *kysseth*] kyssech BM, H.
[7] some] syme BM, H.

THE II. ACTE, II. SCEANE.

[1] it] is BM, H.
[2] well] will BM, H.

THE II. ACTE, IIII. SCEANE.

[1] slyght] slygh BM, H.
[2] your] you BM, H.

THE II. ACTE, V. SCEANE.

[1] With] Wich BM, H.

THE III. ACTE, I. SCEANE.

[1] thynge] BM, H. *Editors generally emend to* thonge.

THE III. ACTE, II. SCEANE.

[1] Now] New BM, H.

THE III. ACTE, III. SCEANE.

[1] on] no BM, H.
[2] no] on BM, H.
[3] me have] haue me BM, H.
[4] the] BS. *Omitted from* BM, H.
[5] feyght] feygh BM, H.
[6] pay] pray BM, H.
[7] COCKE] Gāmer BM, H.
[8] or] of BM, H.

THE III. ACTE, IIII. SCEANE.

[1] that] *Expanded as if from* $\overset{t}{y}$. $\overset{e}{y}$ BM, H.
[2] Tys your] Tyb, your BM, H. *Emendation of Hawkins.*
[3] the] *Expanded as if from* $\overset{e}{y}$. $\overset{u}{y}$ BM, H.
[4] Let . . . some.] *Cropped in* BM. *Supplied from* H.

THE IIII. ACTE, I. SCEANE.

[1] *In* BM *and* H *the heading reads:* The ii. Acte. The iiii. Sceane.
[2] sick] sich BM, H.
[3] Hath] Hach BM, H.
[4] wretche] wrtche BM, H.

THE IIII. ACTE, II. SCEANE.

[1] all] *omitted in* BM, H.
[2] wrothe] worthe BM, H.
[3] of] if BM, H.

THE V. ACTE, I. SCEANE.

[1] knockes] kockes BM, H.

THE V. ACTE, II. SCEANE.

[1] besech] besēch BM, H.
[2] me] we BM, H.
[3] your] you BM, H.
[4] will I not] BM, H. BS *emends to* I will not.
[5] that stoure] y scoure BM, H.
[6] the] *Expanded as if from* $\overset{e}{y}$. $\overset{t}{y}$ BM, H.
[7] worthie] wortie BM, H.
[8] were] where BM, H.
[9] so] se BM, H.
[10] tis] this BM, H.

FERREX AND PORREX or GORBODUC

The text is based upon Farmer's photographic facsimile of the second edition (evidently 1570–71), authorized, according to the printer's note to the reader, by Sackville and Norton themselves. Farmer used the copy in the British Museum. The title page of the surreptitious first edition (1565) calls the play "The TRAGEDIE OF GORBODVC, Where of three Actes were wrytten by Thomas Nortone, and the two laste by Thomas Sackuyle." The third edition (1590)—annexed to another work, *The Serpent of Deuision*— is a reprint of the first. All were issued in the small octavo size rather than the usual quarto.

Variants are supplied here from the copy of the 1565 edition in the Huntington Library and from the film of the 1590 edition (Huntington copy) supplied by University Microfilms. They reveal the close relationship of the first and third editions and tend to confirm the opinion of W. W. Greg that the authorized edition itself was probably set up from a corrected copy of the corrupt first edition.

A   Edition of 1565, printed by William Griffith.
B   Edition of 1570–71, printed by John Daye.
C   Edition of 1590, printed by Edward Allde for John Perrin.

ARGUMENT

[1] discention] B. dyuision and discention A, deuision and dissention C.

TO THE READER

[1] *This letter to the reader appears only in* B.

THE NAMES OF THE SPEAKERS

[1] CLOTYN] A *and* C. CLOYTON B.
[2] Loegris] B. Leagre A *and* C.
[3] king] B. king Gorboduc A *and* C.
[4] to the king] B. of king Gorboduc A *and* C.
[5] yongest] B. yonger A *and* C.

DOMME SHEW BEFORE THE FIRST ACT

[1] on] C. in A *and* B.
[2] plucked] A *and* B. pulled C.
[3] them] B. *omitted from* A *and* C.

ACTUS PRIMUS. SCENA PRIMA.

[1] my] B. *omitted from* A *and* C.
[2] not] B. but not A *and* C.
[3] hope] B. pride A *and* C.
[4] do] B. *omitted from* A *and* C.
[5] ill] B. euill A *and* C.
[6] cruell] B. ciuill A *and* C.

ACTUS PRIMUS. SCENA SECUNDA.

[1] to] B from A *and* C.
[2] from] A *and* B. and C.
[3] than] B. the A *and* C.
[4] in] A *and* B. at C.
[5] thought] B. taught A *and* C.
[6] poysonous] A *and* B. poysons C.
[7] our] B. your A *and* C.
[8] in] B. no A *and* C.
[9] as one for] B. for one as A *and* C.
[10] our . . . our] B. their . . . their A *and* C.
[11] decayeng] B. deceyuynge A, deceiuing C.
[12] spende] B. spende their A, spend their C.
[13] unto] A *and* B. betweene C.
[14] yonger] B. other A *and* C.
[15] firmely] B *and* C. framelie A.
[16] ye] A *and* B. you C.
[17] we] B. ye A *and* C.
[18] the] B *and* C. our A.
[19] parted] B. partie A *and* C.
[20] Father] B. fathers A *and* C.
[21] is the] B. it is A *and* C.

[22] As] B. And A *and* C.
[23] their] A *and* B. the C.
[24] will] A *and* B. shall C.
[25] free to] B. to free A *and* C.
[26] greater] B *and* C. great A.
[27] do] A *and* B. doth C.
[28] Camberland] A *and* B. Cumberland C.
[29] suffice also] B. also suffise A *and* C.
[30] them] B *and* C. the A.
[31] brother] B. other A *and* C.
[32] Ofte so] A *and* B. Oft sore C.
[33] draw] B. brings A *and* C.
[34] preventes] B. presentes A, presents C.
[35] heapes] B. keepes A *and* C.
[36] where natures course] B. that where Nature A *and* C.
[37] The] B. And A *and* C.
[38] overkindly] B. our vnkindly A *and* C.
[39] encrease] B. to encrease A, to increase C.
[40] by] B. my A *and* C.
[41] see] B. seeke A *and* B.
[42] fates] A *and* B. saies C.
[43] well] A *and* B. will C.
[44] immortall] B. mortall A *and* C.
[45] Within] B. For with A *and* C.
[46] reignes] A *and* B. Regions C.
[47] Brittish] B. Brutish A *and* C.
[48] since] B. sithence A *and* C.
[49] houre] B. honour A *and* C.
[50] rawe] B. had A *and* C.
[51] upraised] B. vnpaised A *and* C.
[52] And] A *and* B. In C.
[53] demeane] B. demaund A *and* C.
[54] carre] B. Carte A *and* C.
[55] place] B. pace A *and* C.
[56] Makes] B. Make A *and* C.
[57] faste] B. laste A, last C.
[58] wrongly] B. wrongfull A *and* C.
[59] chaunge] B. chaunged A, chaungde C.

DOMME SHEW BEFORE THE SECOND ACT.

[1] the] A *and* C. the the B.
[2] of] A *and* B. *omitted from* C.
[3] the] A *and* C. the the B.
[4] geveth] A *and* B. giueth any C.
[5] to] A *and* B. vnto C.

ACTUS SECUNDUS. SCENA PRIMA.

[1] rebelling] B. rebellious A *and* C.

[2] growing] A *and* B. groaning C.

[3] which in] B. within A *and* C.

[4] partes] B. portes A *and* C.

[5] treason] B. reason A *and* C.

[6] the] B. this A *and* C.

[7] murders] B. murder A *and* C.

[8] The] B. To A *and* C.

[9] ruines] B. and reignes A *and* C.

[10] suppose] B. suppresse A *and* C.

[11] *Ll. 154–55 precede ll. 152–53 in* A *and* C.

[12] with] B. with great A *and* C.

[13] owne estate] B. state A *and* C.

[14] an] B *and* C. and A.

[15] in] B. with A *and* C.

[16] rashe] A *and* B. that C.

ACTUS SECUNDUS. SCENA SECUNDA.

[1] armour] B. Armours A *and* C.

[2] Why] B. While A *and* C.

[3] of] A *and* B. of the C.

[4] move] B. nowe A, now C.

[5] frendes] B. friende A, frend C.

[6] have] B. hath A *and* C.

[7] all] B. at A *and* C.

[8] and treate] B. entreate A, intreat C.

[9] ruine of their realmes] B. reigne of their two realmes A *and* C.

[10] the] B. that A *and* C.

[11] remnantes] B. remnant A *and* C.

[12] Trojan] B. Troians A *and* C.

[13] determined by] B. determinedlie A, determinedly C.

[14] sway] B. fraie A, fray C.

[15] countries] B. Countrie A, Country C.

[16] misguided] B. misguydinge A, misguiding C.

DOMME SHEWE BEFORE THE THIRDE ACT

[1] murder] A *and* C. murderer B.

[2] ceased] A *and* B. caused C.

ACTUS TERTIUS. SCENA PRIMA.

[1] stayned] B. streined A *and* C.

[2] Pursues] B. Pursue A *and* C.

[3] lyves] A. lynes B, liues C.

[4] chase] B. chast A *and* C.
[5] our] A *and* B. this C.
[6] ye] B. you A *and* C.
[7] traitorous fraude] B. traitours framde A *and* C.
[8] timely help] A *and* B. manly help C.
[9] honour, age] A *and* C. honourage B.
[10] the] B. this A *and* C.
[11] Not] not B, no A *and* C.
[12] For] B. Of A *and* C.
[13] this] B. his A *and* C.
[14] to] B. for A *and* C.
[15] cares] B. care A *and* C.
[16] represse] A *and* B. expresse C.
[17] inkindled] A *and* B. vnkindled C.
[18] your] A *and* C. our B.
[19] still] B. *omitted from* A *and* C.
[20] thus] B. this A *and* C.
[21] very] B. wery A, weary C.

Domme Shew Before The Fourth Act

[1] came] B. came forth A *and* C.

Actus Quartus. Scena Prima.

[1] and] *omitted in error by Cunliffe.*
[2] had] A *and* B. hath C.
[3] beloved] B. wel beloued A *and* C.
[4] bye] B. abye A *and* C.
[5] their] B. the A *and* C.
[6] panting] B. louying A, louing C.
[7] peaze] B. appeaze A, appease C.
[8] thy] B. thie A, this C.
[9] must] A *and* B. might C.
[10] yet] B. if A *and* C.
[11] hast] A *and* B. hath C.
[12] thee] B. *omitted from* A *and* C.
[13] wrooke] A *and* B. wrekte C.

Actus Quartus. Scena Secunda.

[1] have] A *and* B. heare C.
[2] those] B. these A *and* C.
[3] lawe] B. lawes A *and* C.
[4] and] B. But A *and* C.
[5] man] A *and* B. men C.
[6] reserve] B. referre A *and* C.
[7] Since] B. Sithens A, Sithence C.
[8] To] B. Should A *and* C.

[9] the] B. this A *and* C.
[10] nor] A *and* B. or C.
[11] my] B. by A *and* C.
[12] hart] B. hartes A *and* C.
[13] me] A *and* B. my C.
[14] In] A *and* B. If C.
[15] grow] B. graue A *and* C.
[16] should] B. shall A *and* C.
[17] of her] A *and* B. *omitted from* C.
[18] stabde] B. stalde A *and* C.
[19] if] B. if that A *and* C.
[20] live] B. *omitted from* A *and* C.
[21] hys] B. this A *and* C.
[22] wound] B. wounde A, wounds C.
[23] ruthefull] A *and* B. rufull C.
[24] proportion] B *and* C. preparacion A.
[25] Within] B. Within the A *and* C.
[26] the] B. this A *and* C.
[27] sendes] A *and* B. send C.
[28] Do make] A *and* B. Dooth cause C.
[29] The] B. These A *and* C.

DOMME SHEW BEFORE THE FIFTH ACT

[1] in the] A *and* C. in B.

ACTUS QUINTUS. SCENA PRIMA.

[1] on] B. out A *and* C.
[2] with] B. with the A *and* C.
[3] this] B. the A *and* C.
[4] *After this line the following passage appears in* A *and* C :
    that no cause serues, wherby the Subiect may
    Call to accompt the dooinges of his Prince,
    Muche lesse in blood by swoorde to woorke reuenge
    No more then maye the hande cut of the head,
    In Acte nor speech, no : not in secret thought
    The Subiect may rebell against his Lord,
    Or Judge of him that sits in *Ceasars* Seate.
    With grudging mind [to] damne those He mislikes.
A *prints* do *and* C *prints* doo *for* to *in the final line.*
[5] deare] B. *omitted in* A *and* C.
[6] will] A *and* B. must C.
[7] scatter] B. flatter A *and* C.
[8] lordes] A *and* C. lord B.
[9] the] A *and* C. the the B.
[10] venture] B. aduenture A *and* C.
[11] same] B. Fame A *and* C.
[12] lye] B. be A *and* C.

ACTUS QUINTUS. SCENA SECUNDA.

[1] time] A *and* B. time of C.
[2] can] B. can they A *and* C.
[3] lewde] B. *omitted from* A *and* C.
[4] loe] B. to A, too C.
[5] bond] B. bounde A, bound C.
[6] thy] B. the A *and* C.
[7] spring] B. bring A *and* C.
[8] errour] B. terrour A *and* C.
[9] And other] B. An other A, Another C.
[10] could] A *and* B. should C.
[11] tree] B. trees A *and* C.
[12] their] B. the A *and* C.
[13] dare] A *and* B. doo C.
[14] bodies] B. bodie A *and* C.
[15] of] B. with A *and* C.
[16] lofty] B. lustie A *and* C.
[17] the] B. *omitted from* A *and* C.
[18] theron] B. therin A, therein C.
[19] a] B. and A *and* C.
[20] availed] B. auaile A *and* C.
[21] here to say] B. hereto saide A, hereto said C.
[22] dayes] B. lyues A, liues C.
[23] unhappes] A *and* B. mishaps C.
[24] of] B. of the A *and* C.
[25] to] B. from A *and* C.
[26] without] A *and* C. with B.
[27] or] B. of A *and* C.
[28] our] B. your A *and* C.
[29] may move] B. *omitted from* A *and* C.
[30] lawfull] B. selfe a A *and* C.
[31] golde] B. good A *and* C.
[32] bereft] B. reft A *and* C.
[33] anothers] an others B *and* C, an other A.
[34] playinge] A *and* C. play B.
[35] Brittaine] B. Brittaine Land A *and* C.
[36] fonde] B. yonge A, yong C.
[37] spring] B. springs A, springes C.
[38] such certaine heire] B. suche certentie A, such certeintie C.
[39] knowen] B. vnknowen A, vnknowne C.
[40] is] B. is it A *and* C.
[41] the] B. their A *and* C.
[42] in the people plant] B. plant the people in A *and* C.
[43] state] A *and* B. Realme C.
[44] whom] B. whome A, what C.
[45] God] B. Ioue A *and* C.
[46] The . . . Gorboduc] A *and* C. omitted *in* B.

CAMBISES

The text is taken from microfilm of the Huntington Library copy of the first edition (about 1570). Variants are listed from the second quarto (about 1585), again from microfilm of the Huntington copy. They do not include variations of punctuation or mere spelling except in a few instances in which I have adopted the spelling of the second quarto.

A   Quarto of about 1570, printed by John Allde.

B   Quarto of about 1585, printed by Edward Allde.

Ad   Edition of Adams.

M   Edition of Manly.

[1] COUNCELL] Ad. Councellor A, B, M.

[2] Councell] Counsaile A *and* B.

[3] me] B. *omitted from* A.

[4] varlets] B. verlets A.

[5] puisant] B. pusant A.

[6] CAMBISES] *Here* A *and* B *switch to King, which designates Cambises' speeches for the rest of the play.*

[7] Report] B. Reparte A.

[8] too much sets thereby] to much sets therby A, sets to much sets thereby B.

[9] Egypt] B. Egit A.

[10] were the brodered garde] A. weare the brodered guard B.

[11] my] A. me B.

[12] shoulder] B. shhulder A.

[13] speckled] A. specked B.

[14] evil] A. hard B.

[15] bouget] A. budget B.

[16] into] A. in B.

[17] the] A. *omitted from* B.

[18] about] B. ahout A.

[19] ye] A. you B.

[20] content] A. come B.

[21] ye, ye] A. ye B, *which seems not to make sense.*

[22] beats] B. beat A.

[23] weapon] A. weapons B.

[24] repulse] B. repulle A.

[25] ye] A. you B.

[26] was] A. wis B.

[27] fright] *Hawkins, followed by subsequent editors.* flight A *and* B.

[28] ye] A. thee B.

[29] -dealing] A, B, M. Ad *prints* doing. *Hawkins and Hazlitt* dealings.

[30] ye] A. you B.

[31] ghosts] B. gosts A.

[32] steward] B. stuard A.

[33] and] B. *omitted from* A.

[34] gods] God A *and* B.

[35] Complaint] Complaints A *and* B.

[36] Lest . . . long.] *The line is missing from* B.

[37] eares] A. eyes B.

[38] childe] A. thilde B.

[39] ye] A. you B.

[40] much praise] A. much doo praise B.

[41] off] B. of A.

[42] a mark] B. mark A.

[43] I . . . fulfil.] A *and* B *make this line part of the preceding line.*

[44] a[nd] willing] M. awilling A, a willing B.

[45] minde] B. mnde A.

[46] 1. LORD] A. a Lord B.

[47] your] B. you A.

[48] gods] God A *and* B.

[49] his] A. in B.

[50] man] A. *omitted from* B.

[51] not] M *and* Ad. *lacking in* A *and* B.

[52] *In* A *and* B *this direction is opposite l.* 722.

[53] *In* A *and* B *this direction is opposite l.* 726.

[54] you] A. ye B.

[55] both] A. buth B.

[56] through] B. througe A.

[57] ye] A. you B.

[58] Hob] A. Hod B.

[59] zwap] B. zawp A.

[60] you] A. ye B.

[61] neighbour] B. neigbor A.

[62] thy] A. the B.

[63] *This direction is from* B. A *has merely* Lord, Lady, waiting maid.

[64] harmony] B. hermony A.

[65] beautify] B. beautie A.

[66] loove] loone A, loue B.

[67] gods] God A *and* B.

[68] Mine] A *and* B. M *and* Ad *print* My.

[69] harmony] B. hermony A.

[70] taried] A. tared B.

[71] that] A. *omitted from* B.

[72] to] A *and* B. M *and* Ad *omit.*

[73] a] A. *omitted from* B.

[74] deeds, ye] A. deeds, you B. deede, you Ad, deed you M.

[75] villain] B. vaillain A.

[76] one] B. on A.

[77] fetch] B. fet A.

[78] hither] B. hether A.

[79] would not] A. will never B.

[80] not worthy] A. unworthy B.

[81] *The direction is from* B. A *has merely* Enter.

[82] harmony] B. hermony A.

[83] *In* A *and* B *the direction occurs after l. 1014.*

[84] perpend] B. parpend A.

[85] one] B. on A.

[86] strong] B. streng A.

[87] and] & B. a A.

[88] whelpe] B. welp A.

[89] the] B. the the A.

[90] cause] B. canse A.

[91] vile] A. and vile B.

[92] is at an end] B. it is an end A. M *emends to* now is at an end.

[93] lose thy] B. dye the A.

[94] I redy am] A *and* B. M, *followed by* Ad, *divides this line into two after* fulfil *and prints* I am redy.

[95] contented] A. contended B.

[96] LORDS] A. Lord B.

[97] handling] B. haudling A.

[98] obey] A. away B.

[99] away] A. obay B.

[100] *This and the line above are printed as one in* A *and* B, *and so for the rest of the speech.*

[101] men] *emendation of* M, *lacking in* A *and* B.

[102] the] *emendation of Hazlitt, lacking in* A *and* B.

[103] so] A. *omitted from* B.

[104] reward] B. rewad A.

[105] lords] A. Lord B.

[106] according] A, M. according to B, Ad.

[107] to cary] A. and carry B.

EPILOGUS

[1] EPILOGUS] A. Epilogue B.

[2] his] A. this B.

[3] have] A. huue B.

[4] we] B. *omitted from* A.

[5] use] B. u (*the rest missing*) A.

[6] John Allde] A. Edward Allde B.

NOTES

NOTES

FULGENS AND LUCRES

Dramatis Personae.

(1) A and B are not the youths' names but merely designate their speeches. I am not certain why Medwall does not name the lads, especially when he gives Lucres' servant the non-Roman name Jone. A calls B "what cal't" and evades telling his own name to Lucres (II, ll. 345 ff.). Such evasiveness became one of the characteristics of the Vice.

Pars Prima.

(1) Boas and Reed remark that this allusion to Psalms 19 (Vulgate 18) in such a context is a fitting touch of humor for a chaplain-playwright.

(2) Presumably a line has been omitted just before this, rhyming with "tell" and "damesell," and saying what the banqueters mused about besides the dancing girl.

(3) B's disclaimer, as Boas and Reed note, is presumably only a blind. That is, he is a member of the troupe of players who have come to the hall. At the beginning of Part II, A admits that he is himself one of the troupe. On their probable appearance—particolored knee-length coats sometimes with capes and hoods, shaven faces, close-clipped hair, flat shoes—see Chambers, *Mediaeval Stage,* I, 44–45. A. W. Pollard, *Fifteenth Century Prose and Verse* (London, 1903), pp. 307–21, prints documents relating to a suit by John Rastell, printer of *Fulgens,* for recovery from Henry Walton of the following : "a player's garment of green sarcenet lined with red tuke and with roman letters stitched upon it of blue and red sarcenet, and another garment paned with green and blue sarcenet lined with red buckram, and another garment paned likewise and lined as the other, with a cape furred with white cats, and another garment paned with yellow, green, blue, and red sarcenet, and lined with red buckram. Another garment for a priest to play in, of red Say, and a garment of red and green Say, paned and guarded with gold skins, and fustians of Naples black, and sleeved with red, green, yellow, and blue sarcenet. And another garment, spangled, of blue satin of Bruges, and lined with green sarcenet," etc. Cf. *Kyng Johan,* I, l. 65.

(4) Note the shift from *rime couée* to rhyme royal as the tone changes from colloquial to stately. The beginning of this section is adapted from Tiptoft, "'auctor" of l. 75: "When Thempyre of Rome moste floured and was in the age of his force and strengthe." Boas and Reed think that "empire" here means merely "rule" and that, since in Tiptoft Gayus fought against Mithridates, the plot takes place during the closing period of the Republic, not during the Empire.

(5) Boas and Reed compare Tiptoft : "There was in her so grete attemperaunce of lyf . . . that it shewed her to lacke nothyng that coude be wylled."

(6) In fact it is Lucres herself who chooses Gayus. (See the general Introduction.) Possibly Medwall had not yet decided how to effect the resolution in the play. In Tiptoft the matter is brought before the senate for a "sentence dyffynytyf," but their decision is not disclosed.

(7) "An officer charged with the arrangement of ceremonies, *esp.* with the ordering of guests at a banquet." OED.

(8) The season was Christmas, the usual time for plays and other entertainments in the halls of the great, at court, and in schools, universities, and Inns of Court.

(9) The audience must make room so that Fulgens can pass among them to the place of the performance. It is noteworthy that while A and B often acknowledge the presence of the spectators, even when the place represents Rome, the "Romans" seldom do so.

(10) One of many anachronisms. The Tudor chaplain betrays himself. Compare Matthew 6:45 and I Corinthians 12:4–11 with the lines following.

(11) A fears that B will shatter the dramatic illusion if he enters the play world from the banquet hall. The participation of A and B in the lives of ancient Romans constitutes the most striking feature of Medwall's dramaturgy. He formalizes what Sir Thomas More, according to Roper's *Life*, had done extempore in Morton's household before leaving it in 1492. More would "sodenly sometymes slip in among the players and make a parte of his owne there presently among them."

(12) An anachronistic allusion to the Marriage Service. The original "departe," meaning to part or separate, was altered in 1662 to "do part."

(13) The tale which A now tells is of course a lie, providing an early instance of what E. E. Stoll, in connection with *Othello*, calls the calumniator-believed.

(14) A sly joke in the later manner of Heywood, a dig at A's ignorance rather than praise of his honesty.

(15) Manifestly the fashion described by B is not that represented by the man on the woodcut on the title page, with his full-length brocaded gown, feather, and chain. Possibly he is in-

tended as Gayus or Fulgens; most likely the illustration was not prepared specially for the play. Boas and Reed point out its resemblance to Flemish miniatures of the end of the fifteenth century.

(16) This and the next stage direction (after l. 853) are the only ones in English in the original edition.

(17) In having B remark that the Roman lady's maid sings better than anyone hence to York, Medwall thinks extra-dramatically in terms of English geography and of Morton's residence at Lambeth, not of Rome.

(18) Such a facetious slip of the tongue is characteristic of the Vice of later Tudor drama and of the witty parasite in Roman comedy.

(19) Land worth £20 in annual income to be settled upon Jone for her use in the event of B's death.

(20) "Our English plain Proverb, *De Puerperis* [about childbirth], they are in the Straw; shows Feather-Beds to be of no ancient use amongst the Common sort of our Nation." Fuller's *Worthies*, quoted in OED. The point of Jone's anecdote, I think, lies in the double meaning of "in the strawe." Like the couple in B's "marvelous case," this couple went from poor to poorer, from half a bed to straw, for their "greate encrease and gayne" was only in the form of offspring.

(21) The wild fire is erysipelas, also called St. Anthony's fire, a disease involving inflammation of the skin.

(22) What follows is a mock jousting for the favor of the "lady," who was traditionally the judge of such encounters. It resembles the childrens' imitation of the serious tilting of knights pictured in Strutt, *Sports and Pastimes of the People of England*, opposite p. 126. In the picture from a fourteenth-century book of prayers two boys hold a switch or staff between their legs (cf. "put me a staffe thorow here") which represents the horse, and a smaller staff under one arm in place of a lance. But here the hands or arms of A and B are bound in some manner, and Gayus must untie them when he enters a few lines later. The description of the sport as jousting "at farte pryke in cule" (i.e. target in the buttocks) would suggest that A presents his posterior to the charge of B, and the suggestion is re-enforced by his complaint (l. 1262) that he has "a grete garce here byhynde." But the dialogue during the tilt does not seem to indicate that A is merely a target, a human quintain. The one direction *"Et proiectus dicat* A" is no help in visualizing the encounter, and the few directions that I have ventured to insert are tentative.

(23) These symbols probably invite an *ad lib.* expression of olefactory displeasure, as "faugh, faugh."

(24) A traditional uncouth pun. Baskerville compares the *Revesby Sword Play*, Manly's *Specimens*, I, 309:

PICKLE HERRING. Nay, then sweet Ciss, ne'er trust me more,

For I never loved lass like the[e] before.

FOOL. No, nor behind, neither.

(25) The lie which A now tells Gayus is one of Medwall's interesting foreshadowings of Shakespeare. Compare *I Henry IV*, II, iv, ll. 180 ff.

(26) Another of A's facetious slips of the tongue.

(27) The fire actually blazing in the hall against the winter cold, one of many extra-dramatic references in the play.

Pars Secunda.

(1) The present plurals in -s are a feature of the Northern dialect. Here they are useful for the rhyme, but Medwall's language has a Northern flavor generally.

(2) From this long apology and expressed wish that the audience will "alowe" (i.e. approve) the low-comic matter it would seem that Medwall himself was unaware that the material was not really "impertinent" but artistically relevant as parody of the high plot. He espouses a kind of "groundlings" theory.

· (3) Real or feigned uncertainty about his own name characterizes the later Vice in Tudor drama. Compare Ambidexter in *Cambises*, l. 147. Of course "A" has no name that we know of.

(4) A base dance is one in slow time requiring four steps : "syngle, double : repryse and braule" (OED). If, as Boas and Reed believe, the performance was at Christmas 1497, Morton would have had Spanish guests at Lambeth, for the Spanish envoy had made peace between Henry VII and the Scottish king James IV, and a marriage was hoped for between Catherine of Aragon and Prince Arthur.

(5) Presumably one of the musicians actually had a sore lip.

(6) A line of Flemish : "Play up drum, I bid you merrily." Boas and Reed point out that special payments were made to the ambassadors of Spain and Flanders at Christmas, 1497, and that the Magnus Intercursus had re-established trade relations with Flanders. Flemish officials were probably in the audience.

(7) "A species of Portuguese unknown to the ethnologist." Boas and Reed. The dance is really a "mummynge" (II, l. 126) or disguising, a form of entertainment much in vogue under Henry VII and young Henry VIII. See Chambers, *Mediaeval Stage*, I, 398 ff.; J. P. Collier, *English Dramatic Poetry and Annals of the Stage*, I, 50–83; and especially R. J. E. Tiddy, *The Mummer's Play*, Oxford, 1923.

(8) Cornelius' comparison of stories about his ancestors to the medieval romances of Arthur and Alexander is independent of Tiptoft and of course anachronistic.

(9) The remaining forty lines of Cornelius' speech paraphrase the speech he makes to Lucres before the Senate in Tiptoft.

(10) Actually Lucres just before her last exit instructs B to tell

his master. B soon forgets the errand. There is no later mention of informing the fortunate Gayus. The play dissolves and returns us to the banquet hall.

(11) Boas and Reed put the return of B after l. 767, assuming that he has been in the hall and heard her make her choice. B left the stage after l. 403 to get refreshment for the mummers.

(12) Again, the implicit locality of the action is Lambeth, not Rome.

(13) An unusual reference to an off-stage conversation and a suggestion of another time scheme than that of dinner and supper.

(14) Paul's Chain was one of six gates in the Cathedral Close, the wall around the churchyard. It was so named because of the chain hung across the gateway during service to keep out traffic.

JOHAN JOHAN THE HUSBANDE

DRAMATIS PERSONAE.

(1) Maxwell, *French Farce and John Heywood*, pp. 68–69, suggests that in so naming his hero Heywood has in mind French usage. Janot and Jeninot, diminutives of Jean, may mean "sot" or "cuckold." And in at least one farce Jehan is used colloquially for a husband who must take his wife's orders.

THE PLAY.

(1) "St. Anthonie is notoriously known for the patron of hogs, having a pig for his page in all pictures." Fuller, quoted in OED.

(2) Probably an invented oath to make the rhyme. "There are three Croomes in the manor of Ripple, Worcestershire, and the church of Ripple is dedicated to the B. Virgin, but Nash's *History of Worcestershire* says nothing of 'Our Lady of Crome.'" Pollard.

(3) By figurative analogy with potstick, bung-stick, etc. It will be convenient for Johan to beat her for her chiding.

(4) Dried stockfish might be so stiff as to require beating before it could be cooked. The reference to Temmes Strete along with that to St. Paul's (l. 153) establishes the locale as London.

(5) Chafe means both to rub and to warm. Maxwell notes that the farce *Pernet* turns upon the expression "chauffer le cire" in its sense of attending upon some good result "as one might await the warming of the wax with which a charter was to be sealed." Heywood borrows the incident, but his changes in the plot rob it of this original significance.

(6) The husband's frustrated attempt to bless the table is another detail borrowed from *Pernet,* heightened by the change of the Cousin to Syr Johan the Preest.

(7) The "miracles" form a link with *The Pardoner and the Frere* and *The Foure P. P.* and strengthen the case for Heywood's

authorship of *Johan Johan*. (See the Introduction. Compare *Fulgens and Lucres*, I, ll. 947–64.)

(8) "S. Modwena, an Irish virgin, who died A.D. 518. She is said to have been the patroness of Burton-upon-Trent, and Henry VIII's commissioners sent thence to London 'the image of seint Moodwyn with her red kowe and hir staff, whych wymen labouryng of child in those parties were very desirous to have with them to lean upon." Pollard.

(9) The teasing of Johan which begins here suggests that his suffering was prearranged by Tyb and Syr Johan; there is an unusual amount of implication for a Tudor play. Comparison of Tyb's sending of Johan to the Priest with the scene between the two men implies that Syr Johan's invitation to dinner was arranged off stage, perhaps also the leak in the pail and the two convenient candles to supply wax. It is noteworthy in this connection that Margery and Anne are not to taste the pie which they allegedly helped prepare.

KYNG JOHAN

FACSIMILE.

This section of the MS. contains II, ll. 1338–55. It is from the revised ending of the play and is written in the playwright's own hand.

DRAMATIS PERSONAE.

(1) Civyle Order represents the class of lawyers and judges. The three estates of the realm are Nobilyte, Clergye, and Commynalte.

The particular individuals mentioned here are identified in the notes to the play itself.

ACTUS PRIMUS.

(1) The powers, that is, of a king, the "hygh powres" referred to in l. 7 which even Christ obeyed. The necessary supremacy of crown over church is the theme of the play.

(2) Bale himself later cites the following writers of chronicles (II, ll. 1077 ff.) : Polydore Vergil, Sigebertus, Vincentius, Nauclerus, Giraldus, Matthew Paris, Paulus Phrigio, Johan Major, Hector Boethius. There are innumerable others whom he also may have used, notably Radulph of Coggeshall, Ranulph Higden (trans. Trevisa), Robert Fabyan. The chronicle of Edward Hall (1542) merely touches on John's reign, and those of Grafton (1568), Holinshed (1577) and Stow (1580) are later than *Kyng Johan*, as is the Bale-like defense of John in Foxe's *Acts and Monuments of Martyrs* (Latin ed., 1554, English ed. 1563).

(3) Ireland, Wales, the county of Anjou, and the duchy of Normandy, as well as England, were parts of the Angevin domin-

ions which John inherited. He lost Normandy in 1204. The loss is mentioned later in this scene (ll. 595–96), and the election of Stephen Langton as Archbishop of Canterbury (1204 or 1205 according to early chroniclers, actually 1207) occurs at Rome in the next scene. John ruled from 1199 until his death in 1216.

(4) John's most conspicuous victory had been in 1202 at Mirabeau, where he rescued his mother, Eleanor, from the French and took prisoner his rebellious nephew Arthur.

(5) Matthew 15:14.

(6) Colossians 4:6.

(7) Matthew 23:14, Mark 12:40, Luke 20:47.

(8) Isaiah 1:17, translated in Bale's next couplet.

(9) Such a direction for the doubling of parts by a single actor shows that the MS. is intended for players. Since Englande, the only female part, is doubled with Clergye, evidently the company had no boy for women's roles. The reader will note that the play is written to permit doubling of other parts as well, much of it specified in the text. The maximum number of players on stage at any one time is five, the probable size of the troupe.

(10) Psalms 45:9–13.

(11) All of the sects or orders of the Church in this satirical passage are real, but most, e.g. the Jesuits, do not date back to the reign of John. See J. S. Farmer's long note on "Religions" in *The Dramatic Works of John Bale*, London, 1907.

(12) The early Christians believed that Antichrist, a great antagonist of Christ, would appear toward the end of the world and fill it with wickedness until banished at Christ's second coming. See I John 2:18. Bale follows Thomas Kirchmayer in identifying Antichrist with the pope.

(13) John can scarcely be said to have given Anjou to Arthur at all, much less "in chaunge," in exchange. Higden says that Thomas of Thornay ceded the county to Arthur, Fabyan that after Philip of France to John's great irritation made Arthur Duke of Brittany, Arthur entered Anjou and took possession of it. Moreover, as Bale is careful not to say, John had Arthur killed, or killed him with his own hands, not long after the battle of Mirabeau. It is true that John brought Ireland under royal authority by a military expedition, cowed Scotland, and married his illegitimate daughter Joan to Llewelyn ap Ioworth of Wales.

(14) The Latin words are from the Lord's prayer : "Our Father, which art in heaven, hallowed be (thy name)."

(15) "Upon my honor, my friend, I (am) wholly at your pleasure." Sedicyon probably strikes an affected pose as he employs the language of compliment.

(16) Benno II, bishop of Osnabrück in Lower Saxony (d. 1088). An anonymous translation from the German entitled *The*

Newe Idole, and Old Devyll (London, 1534) objected to his canonization as a saint.

(17) These are meant as names of mock saints. There was however a church of St. Saviour's, mentioned in Heywood's *The Foure P. P.* (l. 47) and now the cathedral church of Southwark. St. Spryte, i.e. St. Spirit, may refer to the Holy Ghost or to St. Speratus, d. 200 A.D.

(18) Sedicyon prophesies three centuries of papal domination in England, ended by Henry VIII.

(19) Chronicle material. Fabyan writes that in 1205 "came downe a strayght commaundement from the pope, that except the kynge wolde peasablye suffre the archebisshop of Cauntorbury to occupye his see . . . that the lande shulde be entyrdyted; chargynge theyse iiii. bysshopys folowynge, that is to saye, Wyllyam, then bysshop of London, Eustace, bysshop of Ely, Waltyr, bisshop of Wynchestre, and Gylys, bisshop of Herforde, to denounce the kynge and his lande accursyd, if he the commaundement disobeyed . . . ; but all was in vayne." The interdict ended with John's capitulation in 1214.

(20) The twenty-one-line addition to the MS. which starts here is doubtless intended to allow time for the changes of costume specified in the preceding direction.

(21) The "Albygeanes" are the Albigenses, a heretical sect in southern France, centered in Toulouse. They were extirpated in mid-thirteenth century by the Inquisition, but after the death of Innocent III. Nor was it through St. Dominic's preaching that they were burnt, though he lived in Toulouse.

(22) Pandulph was the papal legate sent to induce John to accept Stephen Langton as Archbishop of Canterbury. Raymundus has not been identified, though Bale may have had in mind the Spanish Dominican St. Raymund of Pennaforte, who was instrumental in bringing the Inquisition to Aragon a few years after the deaths of John and Innocent.

(23) The four chief mendicant orders are the Franciscans or Gray Friars (founded 1209), the Dominicans (founded 1216), the Carmelites or White Friars and Augustinian Hermits or Black Friars (both ca. 1250).

(24) If John was the Moses of the Reformation, then Henry VIII becomes the Joshua who led the English into the land of milk and honey (cf. Joshua 5:6) and also, the Interpretour continues, the David who struck down Goliath the pope. The reference to "our late Kynge Henrye" and the division of the play into two parts both belong to a revision undertaken most likely under Edward VI but possibly under Elizabeth of the one-part play written under Henry VIII.

ACTUS SECUNDUS.

(1) The expression "In the name of (our) Lord the pope" is rendered satirical by its substitution of the pope for God the Father. The benediction is properly *In nomine patrii et filii et spiritus sancti.*

(2) The New Learning is generally taken to be the Tudor term for what we call humanism. Some scholars however think it limited to Lutheranism. This passage may be read from either point of view.

(3) The passage following is Heywoodian. Compare the "relics" speeches of the pardoners in *Pardoner and Frere* and *Foure P. P.*

(4) J. S. Farmer collects three other references to John Shorne, whom Sedicyon here credits with uprooting the figurative tree of Jesse (Isaiah 11:1, 10.). See Heywood's *Foure P. P.*, l. 45. If Shorne was not, as his name suggests, fictional, he may have been a priest of Shorne in Kent.

(5) "Darvell Gathyron, or Gatherin, was 'an huge great image,' to which miraculous powers were imputed, brought out of Wales, and burnt in 1538, with a Priest of the name of Forest. *Vide* Hall's and Stow's Chronicles, and Sir H. Ellis's *Letters on English History*, Ist Series, ii, 82." Collier.

(6) Thomas Becket, Archbishop of Canterbury, murdered in the cathedral in 1170 for opposing Henry II, John's father. Bale wrote a play now lost on the impostures of Thomas Becket.

(7) Ecclesiastes 10:20. The reference in the following couplet is to Romans 13:1, 2.

(8) Dathan and Abiram rebelled against Moses, and the ground swallowed them up. Numbers 16.

(9) A Loller, or Lollard, is a member of the reform movement initiated long after King John by John Wycliffe (d. 1384). The term means "mumbler" (of prayers).

(10) To be held in feudal tenure, as a fief. With the ceremony that follows compare Fabyan (*anno* 1212) : "the kyng knelyng upon his knees, toke the crowne from his hede, & sayd theyse wordis folowynge to the legat, delyverynge hym the crowne, 'Here I resygne up the crowne of the realme of Englande & Irelande, into the popis handys, Innocent the thyrde, & put me hole in his mercy and ordynaunce.' After rehersayll of which wordis, Pandulph toke the crowne of the kynge, and kepte the possessyon thereof v. dayes after, in token of possessyon of the sayd realme of Englande; and when the sayd v. dayes were expyred, the kynge reassumyd the crowne of Pandulph, by vertue of a bande, or instrument, made unto the pope . . . whereof, the effecte is, that the sayd kynge John & his heyres shulde ever after be feodaryes unto the fore namyd pope Innocent . . . and to pay yerely to the Churche of Rome, a M. marke of sylver, that is to saye, for Englande vii. C. marke, & for Irelande CCC. marke . . . for the which summes . . .

the money callid Petyr pens, are at this day gatheryd in sondry placis of Englande."

(11) As with the benediction earlier, this absolution is rendered satirical by the substitution of pope for Deity, cardinals for saints, etc.

(12) The unconscious shift from Stevyn Langton to Sedicyon in the speech headings is characteristic of Bale's ambivalent state of mind in relation to literal and allegorical modes of drama.

(13) Compare Acts 23:2.

(14) Compare Trevisa's translation of Higden's *Polychronicon*: "About þat tyme [of Langton's coming to England] kyng John made honge and drawe an holy man þat heet Peeris of Pountfreiyt, for he hadde i-warnede hym of meny myshappes þat shulde falle hem for his cruelnes and for his fornicacioun. Also for he hadde i-warnede hym þat he schulde regne but fourtene yere, and he regnede almost ey3tene yere; but he knewe nou3t in þat doynge þat he regnede freliche but fourtene yere; . . . for . . . þre yere was tributarie to þe pope."

(15) The fable about master Morris, with the Latin verse, is told in several chronicles more fully than Bale tells it. It appears in Pynson's edition of Fabyan in 1516 but is omitted in the editions of 1542 and 1559.

(16) Neither barrel better herring, a proverbial expression meaning that there is nothing to choose between the two.

(17) Richard's widow was actually Berengaria of Navarre. This scheme of the Church to gain through her death lacks historical basis, and I have not been able to find it in the English chroniclers. The proverb means that a person will be sure to profit if he leaves nothing to chance.

(18) "St. Anthonie is notoriously known as the patron of hogs, having a pig for his page in all pictures." Fuller, quoted in OED.

(19) John died of natural causes, of "the flux" as the chroniclers say, but they also cite a rumor, which Bale of course prefers, that John was poisoned by a monk named Simon at Swineshead abbey, Simon having received absolution in advance.

(20) When John became his vassal, Innocent III became to some degree his ally against his rebellious barons and Louis, the son of Philip of France. The pope sent the legate Gualo to France to try to dissuade Louis from invading England, and when this dissuasion failed and Louis took Rochester and other towns Gualo excommunicated John's enemies.

(21) Otto was Duke of Saxony and Holy Roman Emperor. He was also John's nephew, a grandson of Henry II. He shared in the general defeat of John's forces against Philip at Bouvine in 1214. According to Fabyan he was excommunicated "for his rapyne & extorcion done to the churche of Rome."

(22) Enoch and Helye, or Helias, denounce Antichrist and re-

veal him for what he is in the Chester play *The Coming of Anti-christ*. A Mass of Scala Celi (the ladder to heaven) is one in which the introit begins with these words, drawn from Jacob's vision, Genesis 28:12.

(23) Polydore Vergil in his *Anglica Historia* (1513, printed 1534).

(24) John Leland (d. 1552) was an eminent historian and the king's antiquary. Here Bale calls upon him to awaken to his historian's responsibility to clear the name of John. The Malone Society editors think that "slumbre" refers to Leland's insanity (1546–52) and that the lines were written during the reign of Edward VI.

(25) This list of authorities for John's valor and virtue is misleading to say the least. Matthew Paris' *Chronica Majora*, a revision in its early sections of the *Chronica* of Roger of Wendover, offers in fact the first full portrait of John as a villain-king, and Hector Boethius regards John from the Scottish point of view (*Historia Scotorum*, Book 13, Chapters 9–11) with unrelieved detestation.

(26) Veryte is in error in asserting that John exiled the Jews from England. On the contrary, they were under his special protection—for purely financial reasons. They were banished in 1292 and not permitted to return until the time of Oliver Cromwell.

(27) The authorities cited by Veryte make this speech a good example of Bale's Christian humanism, though the sentiments attributed to Plato, presumably in the *Republic*, and Seneca are suspiciously uncharacteristic. For Eglon see Judges 3.

(28) Probably a reference to stained-glass windows showing the punishment accorded to evil kings at the Last Judgment.

(29) Matthew 16:17. Translated in the next couplet.

(30) Possibly in a pre-Elizabethan version the play ended at this point.

(31) That is, play the satirist. Pasquino was the name given to a statue disinterred (1501) in Rome, on which satirical verses were pasted.

(32) Henry VIII's suppression of the monasteries led to a rebellion in Yorkshire and Lincolnshire in 1536.

(33) That is, even if the witnesses were criminals. Newgate and the Marshalsea were prisons in London.

(34) Kyrie eleison, "Lord, have mercy," is a petition used in various offices of the Catholic Church.

(35) Brutus and Cassius rebelled against Julius Caesar, Catiline conspired against Caesar and the consul Cicero and so threatened the Republic, and Absalom (II Samuel 15) conspired against his father, David.

(36) An allusion presumably to the *Iliad*, Book 18, but vague like many of Bale's classical references and probably indebted to a commonplace book.

(37) The Anabaptists, "re-baptizers," took over Münster in West-

phalia (1532–35) and the town became the scene of great disorder. Those who fled persecution in Germany and the Netherlands after 1535 and came to England were persecuted there.

(38) The passage following shows that Bale revised the play for performance in Elizabethan times, and it may imply a performance before the queen herself, perhaps at Ipswich on her visit there in August 1561. The MS. was found among the archives of the corporation of Ipswich.

(39) That is, the days of wise government. Nestor was the wisest of the Greeks during and after the Trojan war.

(40) In the spirit of Helias, who with Enoch denounced Antichrist. (See note 22.)

(41) By "plays" Bale most likely means "acts." He wrote *finit actus primus* at the close of the first part. In his own *Scriptores* he describes his play *Pro Joanne Anglorum rege* as in two books ("Lib. 2"). But he also says that it begins with words equivalent to *Quum Dominus aeterno beneficio,* "When the Lord through his eternal beneficence . . . ," which is not the beginning of *Kyng Johan.* Conceivably, then, there was another play antecedent to this and now lost.

ROYSTER DOYSTER

DRAMATIS PERSONAE.

(1) Udall probably coined the name Royster from the verb "to roist," meaning to bluster or swagger. Compare Prologue, l. 25. The old copy uses the spellings Ralph, Raufe, and Rafe, and I have adopted the latter as representing the Tudor pronunciation. The Miles Gloriosus, the boastful warrior or captain, is a type from New Comedy best represented in Plautus' *Miles Gloriosus,* one of Udall's sources. The type became common on the Tudor stage.

(2) The name of the intriguer suggests his joint heritage from Heywood's Vice (cf. Mery-reporte) and from the Greek parasite or witty servant in Roman comedy. "Greek" had long typified a wily or cunning person.

(3) The name Harpax is borrowed from the *Pseudolus* of Plautus.

(4) The heroine's name suggests Christian constancy.

(5) Alyface means either Holy-face (cf. Alie lande, I, ii, l. 124) or Ale-face (the face achieved from drinking too much ale), or perhaps a combination of the two.

PROLOGUE.

(1) Plautus and Terence are the writers of the extant Roman comedies. Udall's idea that their comedies contain hidden meanings belongs to a Renaissance tradition of interpretation that goes back to Petrarch and finds English expression in works like Reynold's

Mythomystes and Bacon's *De Veterum Sapientia*. Presumably he did not apply the idea to his own comedy.

(2) The ram with a bell about its neck, i.e. the bellwether, leads the flock of sheep.

ACTUS I. SCAENA I.

(1) This like most of the other names in the passage is a traditional literary name for a country or low-life fellow. Titivillus is a devil in the mysteries and in the morality *Mankind*, but in secular literature the name connotes simply a worthless fellow. Cooper compares Latin *titivillitium*, something vile or worthless.

(2) Since Udall died before Elizabeth became queen and since the play with its anti-Catholic satire is unlikely to be Marian, the reading must have been originally "Kinges," altered by the Elizabethan printer. Merygreeke means that Rafe uses the monarch's prohibition against fighting as a pretext for not really having to fight.

ACTUS I. SCAENA II.

(1) Rafe overthrew a lion just like the one that Hercules killed. Flügel compares *Thersytes* in Hazlitt's Dodsley, I, 403.

(2) An unusual but recognized use of the article. But some editors omit the "a."

(3) The proverb is in Heywood, ed. Habenicht, l. 1060.

(4) Holy Land. Colbrand was a Danish giant whom Guy of Warwick fought upon his return from the Holy Land. Brutus, the descendant of Aeneas from whom in turn according to legend the British themselves are descended, was also called Brute, and the term came to mean simply a hero. The Nine Worthies were Hector, Alexander, Caesar; Joshua, Daniel, Judas Macchabaeus; and Arthur, Charlemaigne, and Godfrey of Bouillon.

(5) Juvenal, *Satires*, II, l. 40, speaks of *Tertius e caelo cecidit Cato*. The other two were Marcus Porcius Cato the statesman and his great-grandson of the same name, a patriot and philosopher.

ACTUS I. SCAENA III.

(1) A proverbial expression, in which "furre" is equivalent to "furwe," an old form of "furrow."

(2) This is the beginning of a refrain once familiar but now apparently unrecorded.

ACTUS I. SCAENA IIII.

(1) The name mimics the exotic places in medieval romances. *Pouldre blanche* is composed of ginger, cinnamon, and nutmeg. Here the reference is to the place where such powder is used, to wit, the kitchen.

(2) There is a picture of a fool's feather in Douce, *Illustrations of Shakespeare, and of Ancient Manners,* II, Plate iv.

(3) What they sing is the Seconde Song printed at the end of the play.

ACTUS II. SCAENA I.

(1) Proverbial name for a poetaster, one who rakes together bad verses.

ACTUS II. SCAENA II.

(1) A banker's touch, perhaps with reference to ability to deliver the ring and token. The Lombards were famous bankers. The phrase "a wenche or a ladde," incidentally, reminds us that the play was written for performance by schoolboys.

ACTUS II. SCAENA III.

(1) Heywood's proverbs, ed. Habenicht, l. 1416. The proverb derives from the practice of curing nettle stings with dock leaves.

(2) "Are you two in-doors when you meet me in the street?" Adams.

ACTUS III. SCAENA III.

(1) Scheurwegh suggests that the proverb was something like "I am so sad, because I can not be had."

(2) Reference to the custom of offering a condemned man a drink before his execution.

(3) "As below," referring to the PSALMODIE printed at the end of the play. But that is another version of the mock requiem for Rafe which follows here. The Latin phrases of the parody of the service for the dead, the *Officium Defunctorum,* are taken unsystematically from the following :

Placebo Domine in regione vivorum. First antiphon of the Vespers of the *Officium.*

Nequando rapiat ut leo animam meam. Beginning of the third antiphone of the Matins.

A porta inferi Erue, Domine, animam eius. Versicle recited before the Oration.

Requiem aeternam dona eis, Domine, et lux perpetua luceat eis. Another versicle of the *Officium.*

Audivi vocem de coelo dicentem mihi beate mortui qui in Domino moriuntur. Versicle of the Lauds.

Qui Lazarum resuscitasti in monumento foetidum. Second responsory of the Matins.

In paradisum deducant te Angeli. Beginning of the antiphon sung when leaving the church with the body on the way to the grave.

(4) Here, or after l. 82, is meant to be inserted the PEALE OF BELLES printed at the very end of the play.

(5) "Never an M by your girdle?" means, proverbially, "Why don't you show proper respect and call me Master?" Merygreeke makes up for his lack of ceremony in his next speech.

(6) This probably refers to the practice of using old horses as quarry for hawks.

(7) They sing the Fourth Song printed after the play.

ACTUS IIII. SCAENA III.

(1) According to Flügel, of all the statutes against vagrants the closest to Custance's humorous and resolute words is one passed under Edward VI in 1547. It mentions persons "living idle and loiteringly."

ACTUS IIII. SCAENA VII.

(1) I do not know what cross Merygreeke swears by. Since he swears by it earlier as well (III, iii, l. 95) he may point to something in the hall. It is not inconceivable that the play was performed in the school chapel. Rafe swears by the cross on his sword (IV, iii, l. 9).

ACTUS V. SCAENA VI.

(1) Flügel cites Pollock and Maitland, *History of English Law*, I, 171 : "The Exchequer is called a curia . . . it receives and audits the accounts of the sheriffs and other collectors; it calls the King's debtors before it."

(2) "The passage refers to 37 Henry VIII., c. 20 (1545), to a law which allows ten per cent interest : 'The sum of ten pound in the hundred, and so after that rate and not above,' and which forbids the lender 'to receive, accept or take in Lucre or Gain for the forbearing of giving Day of Payment of one whole year of and for his or their money. . . .'" Flügel.

(3) Either the song is not supplied or else (which is unlikely) the following prayer is to be sung.

(4) Almost certainly Queen Elizabeth. Udall, it is true, was on good terms with Mary despite his Protestant leanings. Both he and Mary had labored before her accession on the translation of Erasmus' paraphrase of the New Testament. But still it is unlikely that he would call upon her "the Gospell to protect." Probably the prayer was written or adapted by whoever prepared the play for printing after 1558.

SONGS

(1) The Seconde Song is sung at I, iv, l. 112.

(2) The Fourth Song belongs at III, iii, l. 150. The first and

third are included in the text, and the fifth, if it is not the final prayer, is lacking.

PSALMODIE

(1) A variant version of the mock requiem (III, iii, ll. 57 ff.)

PEALE OF BELLES

(1) For insertion after III, iii, l. 82.

GAMMER GURTONS NEDLE

PROLOGUE.

(1) Diccon is an old form of Dick, nickname for Richard. A bedlam technically was a patient discharged from Bethlehem Hospital for the insane and permitted to live as a licensed vagabond or beggar. But Diccon little resembles the type. (See the Introduction.)

FYRST ACTE. SECOND SCEANE.

(1) A dialect form of the Southwest of England, abbreviated from "ich am," I am. Among the other such forms in the play are "chave" (I have), "chad" (I had), "chil" (I will), "chard" (I heard), "chwot" (I wot). The language is conventional rather than philological, however, and the playwright makes blunders, such as "ich chave hard" (I, ii, l. 36.).

THE II. ACTE. Songe.

(1) Perhaps the acts in academic plays were generally separated by music, as here and with fiddle music between Acts II and III. The song was borrowed by the playwright, and Bradley prints a longer and superior version of it after his edition of the play.

THE II. ACTE. FYRST SCEANE.

(1) Such a direction shows that the printed play is for readers, not for the use of actors.

(2) An extra-dramatic reference, to the auditorium rather than to Hodge's village.

THE II. ACTE. THE II. SCEANE.

(1) Trump, as the card-playing reader will have noted for himself, was a game closely related to whist.

THE II. ACTE. THE IIII. SCEANE.

(1) This kind of injunction to the audience to make room for players to enter was frequently necessary in plays performed in halls and innyards; it is interesting that it should be written into

the text. The cry for room goes back at least to *Mankind* (ca. 1475), l. 324 : "Make rom, sers, for we have be longe!" Cf. *Fulgens*, I, ll. 193–94; *Cambises*, l. 126 ("Stand away! stand away!"); and Falstaff's "Stand aside Nobilitie" in *I Henry IV*, II, iv, l. 428.

THE III. ACTE. THE II. SCEANE.

(1) In a popular German tale a devil takes the name and guise of Friar Rush and makes mischief in a monastery. Evidently his likeness was painted on the cloth hangings used as substitutes for tapestry.

THE III. ACTE. THE III. SCEANE.

(1) "The accoutrements of an itinerant trull." Steevens in Hazlitt's Dodsley, III, 215.

(2) Whores were whipped at the back of a cart.

THE III. ACTE. THE IIII. SCEANE.

(1) Rake is a term from farriery : "To clean (a costive horse or its fundament) from ordure by scraping with the hand." OED.

THE V. ACTE. THE II. SCEANE.

(1) Edward VI was probably the king when the play was composed though the first known edition was printed in 1575. (See the Introduction.)

FERREX AND PORREX or GORBODUC

ARGUMENT.

(1) Gorboduc is a legendary king of ancient Britain like Leir, whose reign is described shortly before that of Gorboduc in the ultimate source of such material, the *Historia Regum Britanniae* of Geoffrey of Monmouth. Geoffrey's account is paraphrased in the Introduction. The playwrights borrowed from the reign of Leir the king's division of the realm during his children's lifetime; hence the resemblance of the opening of the tragedy to Shakespeare's *King Lear*.

(2) The chief immediate political purpose of *Gorboduc* was to induce Elizabeth to limit the succession and so avoid the risk of civil war in England if she should die. Compare the long sermon by Eubulus at the close of Act V.

TO THE READER

(1) One of the four Inns of Court in London. For the date and some details of this grand Christmas, see note 20 of the Introduction.

(2) Both the entry in the Stationers' *Registers* and the title page

of the unauthorized first edition state that Thomas Norton wrote the first three acts and Thomas Sackville (later Lord Buckherst) wrote the last two.

(3) The colophon of the first edition says that the play was printed "at the Signe of the Faucon by William Griffith."

(4) Sackville traveled in France and Italy from 1563 to 1566. See F. W. Maitland, "Thomas Sackville's Message from Rome," *EHR*, Oct., 1900, pp. 757–60.

(5) A glance at the variants will show that the edition of 1565 was not very corrupt. W. W. Greg believed that the authorized edition was set up from a corrected copy of the unauthorized.

(6) "To" here is an archaic usage, meaning "asunder," "to pieces."

(7) The house is the Inner Temple.

(8) Lucrece, ravished by Tarquin, stabbed herself in shame.

DOMME SHEW

(1) The idea for staging an allegorical dumb show between the acts was suggested by the *intermedii* so used in Italian tragedy. *Intermedii,* however, were often irrelevant to the action of the play. The dumb shows in *Gorboduc* doubtless owe something to English allegorical pageants (now lost) staged on political and state occasions. (See the Introduction on Heywood and Udall.)

ACTUS PRIMUS. SCENA PRIMA.

(1) Compare the first line spoken by Hamlet: "A little more then kin, and lesse then kind."

(2) H. A. Watt points out that "to spoile *me* of *thy* sight" would make better sense. The reading may be a printer's error.

ACTUS PRIMUS. SCENA SECUNDA.

(1) That is, their youth tempered with awe or respect for their father.

(2) According to Geoffrey of Monmouth, Morgan, son of Leir's eldest daughter, Gonorilla, and the Duke of Albany, was slain by Cunedagius, son of Leir's second daughter, Regan, in civil war "in pago Kambria," that is, in Wales. The form Cumberland in Duke Gwenard's title designates Wales, not the county on the Scottish border in England.

(3) In Geoffrey, Brute, great-grandson of Aeneas, upon his death left Britain to be divided among his three sons Locrinus, Kamber, and Albanactus.

(4) A reminder of the application of the lesson of the preceding dumb show.

(5) An early statement in drama of one of the ruling ideas in *King Lear.*

(6) Watt remarks that an Elizabethan audience would see in this a reference to the Wars of the Roses.

(7) Phaeton, son of Phoebus, in attempting prematurely to drive his father's sun-chariot set fire to the earth.

(8) The river Humber separates Yorkshire and Lincolnshire in eastern Britain. Porrex's share, corresponding roughly to the Anglo-Saxon kingdom of Northumbria, would include much of Scotland.

(9) The first edition of *A Mirrour for Magistrates*, a great collection continuing into English history Boccaccio's and Lydgate's stories of the Falls of Princes, had appeared in 1559. A mirror permits the Elizabethan magistrate to see himself in the fall of an historical figure through political misjudgment.

ACTUS SECUNDUS. SCENA PRIMA.

(1) Tantalus, for serving his son Pelops to the gods, stands in the underworld, tantalized by water and fruit that he cannot reach, and Ixion, for trying to seduce Hera, turns forever on a wheel. Pluto, or Dis, the "hellish prince" presides over the underworld.

(2) Hermon's words from "Wise men" to "come" are placed in quotation marks in the original editions to indicate that they are especially sententious—even though spoken by a traitor. I have omitted the quotation marks here and at a few other places in the tragedy.

(3) The Secretary is Eubulus, who opposed division of the kingdom in I, ii, ll. 247 ff.

ACTUS SECUNDUS. SCENA SECUNDA.

(1) A recurrent theme in Tudor drama. Compare the fate of Praxaspes in *Cambises*.

(2) An echo of Seneca's *Thyestes* (453), *venenum in auro bibitur*. Watt, in his notes to Cunliffe's edition, indicates several more such borrowings.

ACTUS TERTIUS. SCENA PRIMA.

(1) This passage depends on the belief of the Britons that as descendants of Brute they are direct "issues of destroyed Troye." Simois is a river near Troy, Phrygia the country in Asia Minor in which Troy stood.

(2) An idea expressed in the last line of Sophocles *Oedipus* and echoed in the Senecan version.

(3) To become an example (of suffering) for contemporaries.

DOMME SHEW BEFORE THE FOURTH ACT.

(1) Tantalus fed his son Pelops to the gods; Medea killed her children when Jason planned to desert her; Athamus, son of Aeolus, slew his son Learchus; Ino, Athamus' wife, drowned herself and their remaining son; and Althea brought about the death of her

son Meleager after he had killed her brothers. Cambises' murders of his brother and wife are amply dramatized in Preston's play, but he did not to my knowledge slay his offspring.

Actus Quartus. Scena Prima.

(1) Here begins the part of the play attributed to Sackville.

(2) That is, the very structure of the palace. The speech resembles the opening lines of Seneca's *Medea* and anticipates the beauty of Sackville's contributions to the 1563 edition of the *Mirrour*.

Domme Shew Before The Fifth Act.

(1) Harquebusiers are soldiers bearing light cannon fired from a tripod or trestle. In later chronicle plays the noisy stage action here isolated from the Senecan drama proper became part of the play.

(2) Fabyan, in his *Chronicles,* specifies that the strife among rival kings lasted for fifty-one years after the death of Gorboduc. Dunwallo, in Geoffrey and the subsequent chroniclers, is the son of Clotyn, Duke of Cornwall in the play.

Actus Quintus. Scena Prima.

(1) The Duke of Albany was a descendant of Albanactus, son of Brute, and so in the Trojan line. Geoffrey calls him Staterius and makes him the last of the five kings to hold out against Dunwallo.

Actus Quintus. Scena Secunda.

(1) Very likely an allusion to the Elizabethan fear of thralldom to Philip of Spain.

(2) A covert argument for the right of Katherine Grey to the succession. She was, as H. L. Courtney notes, in the native line, whereas Mary Stuart was a foreigner, and a "former lawe" made by Henry VIII supported her claim. Watt points to the significant phrasing "his or *hers*" in l. 165.

CAMBISES

Prologue.

(1) Agathon was a writer of Greek tragedy. Ll. 3–5 following are translated from the *Eclogae* of Stobaeus (ca. 500 A.D.).

(2) Tully is Marcus Tullius Cicero, the orator and consul.

(3) Lucius Annaeus Seneca, the philosopher and author of the extant Roman tragedies. Cunliffe locates the reference in *Thyestes*, ll. 213–17.

(4) The three old women called the Fates. Clotho spins the thread of life, Lachesis determines its length, and Atropos cuts it.

(5) Icarus flew too near the sun with the wings made by his father, Daedalus, and the wax holding them together melted. Daedalus had forewarned him not to do so.

(THE PLAY)

(1) Embroidered trim on the borders of garments, a symbol of luxury.

(2) That is, take on the expression of someone eating something tasty. But see Heywood's *Proverbs*, ed. Habenicht, l. 1121, and comment.

(3) The meaning is that one must not count his chickens before they are hatched.

(4) The last six lines are a primitive attempt to depict inner moral struggle through soliloquy, anticipating the similar soliloquies of Macbeth.

(5) The traditional request for the audience to make room for the actor to get to the stage and perform.

(6) An allusion to the old play of *Thersites* (1537), in which the hero, a Miles Gloriosus, fights a snail.

(7) The line suggests Ambidexter's kinship to the vices who tempted Mankynde in the theological plays of the fifteenth century.

(8) "The door-post in a tavern on which was scored up the reckonings of the guests." Adams.

(9) That is, "Do you think I am such a cheap vessel or drink?" —with pun on "jug," pet name for Joan, used to mean "a woman."

(10) An allusion to Dame Fortune.

(11) A mirror in the technical Elizabethan sense, one which serves to present the magistrate with a fearful object lesson lest he fall like the transgressor reflected in it.

(12) Shakespeare alludes to this scene in *I Henry IV*, II, iv: "Give me a Cup of Sacke to make mine eyes looke redde, that it may be thought I have wept, for I must speake in passion, and I will doe it in King *Cambyses* vaine."

(13) A reference to pickpockets in the audience, and a suggestion that the moral uncertainty on stage exists there too.

(14) The notion that a magistrate no matter how evil must occasionally do good is a ruling idea in Preston's source, Taverner's *Garden of Wysedome*. (See the Introduction.)

(15) This line shows that Murder and Crueltie are still thought of as personified abstractions inflicting their effects upon the human individual as in allegorical drama. They are not yet, that is, equivalent to the 1. and 2. Murderers in Shakespeare.

(16) Lob and Hob speak the conventionalized language of the stage rustic much as in *Gammer Gurtons Nedle*. It approximates the dialect of the Southwest: "z" for "s," "v" for "f," and "ich" for "I," generally contracted with the verb as in "cham," "I am."

(17) A difficult line, probably meaning that here in the fields the birds shall be heard to warble (record) their pleasant tunes.

(18) At this point all eight members of the troupe are on stage together. The actor who played Ambidexter must therefore take another role here, and it is not Trial, as specified in the "Division of the Parts." The only part not included there is that of the Waiting Maid, but if the sixth player takes it he has little time for a change of costume before his entrance as Ambidexter after l. 936.

(19) Titan means the sun, perhaps because Hyperion, one of the twelve Titans, was the sun god.

(20) The line is ungrammatical or elliptical (with "that you" understood after "vouchsafe").

(21) "Running at tilt" means combating at the quintain, a staff in the ground with a shield attached, or some other stationary object, which the man on horseback was to strike dexterously with his lance. Jousting is between two men with lances on horseback. Of running at the ring, Strutt writes : "The excellency of the pastime was to ride at full speed, and thrust the point of the lance through the ring, which was supported in a case or sheath, by the means of two strings, but might be readily drawn out by the force of the stroke, and remain upon the top of the lance." *Sports and Pastimes of the People of England,* p. 112, with an illustration opposite.

(22) See note 7 to part II of *Fulgens and Lucres.*

(23) Hawk's meat is anything snatched at viciously or torn apart.

(24) "A casing of horn was worn over the thumb by the cutpurse, apparently to resist the sharp edge of the knife in cutting purses. *Horn-thumb* became a cant term for a cutpurse." Adams.

(25) Again, Shakespeare parodies Preston in *I Henry IV :*

> FALLSTAFF. For Gods sake Lords, convey my tristfull Queen,
> For teares doe stop the floud-gates of her eyes.
>
> HOSTESSE. O rare, he dooth it as like one of these harlotry
> Players, as ever I see. (II, iv, ll. 434–36)

(26) She is the bellwether, the leader.

(27) Watling Street in London (not in Persia) was noted for its tailors.

(28) Edmund Bonner, Bishop of London, became notorious for his cruelty in burning heretics during Mary's reign. He refused the Oath of Supremacy in 1559 and was deprived of his bishopric and cast into the Marshalsea, where he died in 1569. It is possible then that he was still alive when the play was first performed.

SELECTED BIBLIOGRAPHY

SELECTED BIBLIOGRAPHY

The list includes the works cited earlier in the book. It uses the following standard abbreviations of the titles of periodicals :

ELH   Journal of English Literary History.
ES   English Studies.
HLQ   Huntington Library Quarterly.
JEGP Journal of English and Germanic Philology.
MLN   Modern Language Notes.
MLR   Modern Language Review.
MP   Modern Philology.
N&Q   Notes and Queries.
PMLA Publications of the Modern Language Association of America.
PQ   Philological Quarterly.
RES   Review of English Studies.
SP   Studies in Philology.
TSE   Tulane Studies in English.

I. GENERAL

Arber, Edward, ed. A *Transcript of the Registers of the Company of Stationers of London, 1554–1640 A. D.* London, 1875–94. Reprinted New York, 1950. 5 vols.

Bale, John. *Index Britanniae Scriptorum.* Ed. R. L. Poole and Mary Bateson. Oxford, 1902.

Bernard, J. E. *The Prosody of the Tudor Interlude.* New Haven, 1939. (Yale dissertation)

Bevington, D. M. *From "Mankind" to Marlowe.* Cambridge, Mass., 1962.

Boas, Frederick S. *An Introduction to Tudor Drama.* Oxford, 1933.
Shakspere and his Predecessors. London, 1896.
University Drama in the Tudor Age. Oxford, 1914.

Bradbrook, M. C. *The Rise of the Common Player. A Study of Actor and Society in Shakespeare's England.* London, 1962.

Brooke, C. F. Tucker. *The Tudor Drama.* Boston, 1911.

Campbell, Lily B., ed. *The Mirror for Magistrates.* Cambridge, 1938.

Shakespeare's Histories, Mirrors of Elizabethan Policy. San Marino, 1947.

Caspari, Fritz. *Humanism and the Social Order in Tudor England.* Chicago, 1954.

Chambers, E. K. *The Elizabethan Stage.* Oxford, 1923. 4 vols. *The Mediaeval Stage.* Oxford, 1903. 2 vols.

Clemen, Wolfgang. *English Tragedy before Shakespeare : The Development of Dramatic Speech.* Tr. T. S. Dorsch. London and New York, 1961.

Collier, John P. *The History of English Dramatic Poetry to the Time of Shakespeare and Annals of the Stage to the Restoration.* London, 1879. 3 vols.

Craik, T. W. *The Tudor Interlude : Stage, Costume, and Acting.* Leicester, 1958.

Cunliffe, J. W. *The Influence of Seneca on Elizabethan Tragedy* (1893). Reprinted New York, 1925.

Cushman, L. W. *The Devil and the Vice in the English Dramatic Literature before Shakespeare.* Halle, 1900.

Eckhardt, Eduard. *Die lustige Person imm älteren englische Drama.* Berlin, 1902.

Erasmus, Desiderius. *The Education of a Christian Prince.* Trans. L. K. Born. New York, 1936.

Farnham, Willard. *The Medieval Heritage of Elizabethan Tragedy.* Berkeley, 1936.

Gayley, C. M. *Plays of Our Forefathers.* New York, 1907.

Greg, W. W. *A Bibliography of English Printed Drama to the Restoration.* Vol. I (to 1616). London, 1939.

Harbage, A. *Annals of English Drama, 975–1700.* Philadelphia and London, 1940. Revised by S. Schoenbaum. London, 1964.

Herford, C. H. *Studies in the Literary Relations of England and Germany in the Sixteenth Century.* Cambridge, 1886.

Heywood, John. *A Dialogue of Proverbs.* Ed. R. E. Habenicht. Berkeley and Los Angeles, 1963. (University of California Publications, English Studies 25.)

Inderwick, F. A. *A Calendar of the Inner Temple Records.* London, 1896. Vol. I.

Kernodle, G. R. *From Art to Theatre : Form and Convention in the Renaissance.* Chicago, 1944.

Mares, F. H. "The Origin of the Figure Called 'the Vice' in Tudor Drama." *HLQ,* XXII (1958), 289–302.

Motter, T. H. Vail. *The School Drama in England.* New York, 1929.

Murray, J. A. H. et al. *The Oxford English Dictionary.* Oxford, 1933. 13 vols. (OED)

Nungezer, Edwin. *A Dictionary of Actors and Other Persons Associated with the Public Representation of Plays in England before 1642.* New Haven, 1929.

Pollard, A. W., ed. *Fifteenth Century Prose and Verse*. Westminster, 1903.

Pollard, A. W. and G. R. Redgrave. *A Short-Title Catalogue of Books Printed in England, Scotland, and Ireland and of English Books Printed Abroad, 1475–1640*. London, 1926.

Reed, A. W. *Early Tudor Drama*. London, 1926.

Ribner, I. "Morality Roots of the Tudor History Play." *TSE*, IV (1954), 21–43.

Righter, Anne. *Shakespeare and the Idea of the Play*. London, 1962.

Rossiter, A. P. *English Drama from Early Times to the Elizabethans*. London, 1950.

Smith, Gregory, ed. *Elizabethan Critical Essays*. Oxford, 1904. 2 vols.

Spivack, Bernard. *Shakespeare and the Allegory of Evil*. New York, 1958.

Stratman, Carl J., C. S. V. *Bibliography of Medieval Drama*. Berkeley and Los Angeles, 1954.

Strutt, Joseph. *The Sports and Pastimes of the People of England*. 1801. New Edition, London, 1903.

Thompson, E. N. S. "The English Moral Plays." *Transactions of the Connecticut Academy of Arts and Sciences*. XIV (1910), 291–413.

Tiddy, R. J. E. *The Mummer's Play*. Oxford, 1923.

Ward, A. W. *A History of English Dramatic Literature*. Vol. I. London, 1899.

Welsford, Enid. *The Court Masque*. New York, 1962.

Wickham, Glynne. *Early English Stages*. Vol. I, 1300–1576. London, 1959.

II. COLLECTIONS OF PLAYS

(IN SEPARATE VOLUMES AND IN SERIES)

Adams, Joseph Q. *Chief Pre-Shakespearean Dramas*. Boston, etc., 1924.

Bang, W., et al. *Materialien zur kunde des älteren englischen Dramas*. Louvain, 1902–14. 44 vols. Continued as *Materials for the Study of Old English Drama*. 1927–.

Boas, F. S. *Five Pre-Shakespearean Comedies*. London, 1934. (The World's Classics)

Bond, R. W. *Early Plays from the Italian*. Oxford, 1911.

Brandl, Alois. *Quellen des Weltlichen Dramas in England vor Shakespeare*. Strassburg, 1898.

Cunliffe, J. W. *Early English Classical Tragedies*. Oxford, 1912.

Dodsley, Robert. *A Select Collection of Old English Plays.* 1744. Ed. W. C. Hazlitt, London, 1874. Vols. I–IV.

Farmer, J. S. Early English Drama Society publications. London, 1905–8. Nine volumes of Tudor plays, with note-books and word-lists.
    Tudor Facsimile Texts. London, 1907–14. 143 volumes of photo-lithographic facsimiles.

Furnivall, F. J. and A. W. Pollard. *The Macro Plays.* E. E. T. S. Extra Series 91. London, 1904.

Gayley, C. M. *Representative English Comedies, with Introductory Essays and Notes, An Historical View of Our Earlier Comedy, and Other Monographs, by Various Writers.* New York, 1907. Vol. I, From the Beginnings to Shakespeare.

Greg, W. W. et al. Malone Society Reprints. London and Oxford, 1907.— Facsimile reprints with textual introductions.

Manly, J. M. *Specimens of the Pre-Shaksperean Drama.* Boston and London, 1900. 2 vols.

III. HENRY MEDWALL

EDITIONS

Boas, F. S. and A. W. Reed. *Fulgens & Lucres, a Fifteenth-Century Secular Play.* Oxford, 1926. (Tudor and Stuart Library)

Boas, F. S. *Fulgens and Lucrece.* In : *Five Pre-Shakespearean Comedies.* [See Section II, COLLECTIONS.]

Brandl, A. *A Goodly Interlude of Nature.* In : *Quellen.* [See Section II, COLLECTIONS.]

Farmer, J. S. *A Goodly Interlude of Nature.* In : *Recently Discovered "Lost" Tudor Plays.* London, 1907. (Early English Drama Society)
    Nature, by Henry Medwall. London, 1908. (Tudor Facsimile Texts)

Fulgens and Lucres, by Henry Medwall. New York, 1920. (Henry E. Huntington Facsimile Reprints, I. Introductory note by Seymour de Ricci)

STUDIES

Baskervill, C. R. "Conventional Features of Medwall's *Fulgens and Lucres.*" *MP*, XXIV (1927), 419–42.

Lowers, J. K. "High Comedy Elements in Medwall's *Fulgens and Lucres.*" *ELH*, VIII (1941), 103–6.

Von Hecht, Hans. *Medwalls Fulgens and Lucres. Eine Studie zu den Anfangen des weltlichen Dramas in England.* Leipzig, 1925. (*Palaestra*, Vol. 148)

IV. JOHN HEYWOOD

Tannenbaum, Samuel A. and Dorothy R. *John Heywood, A Concise Bibliography.* New York, 1946.

EDITIONS

Adams, J. Q. *The Foure P. P., Johan Johan,* and *Wether.* In : *Chief Pre-Shakespearean Dramas.* [See Section II, COLLECTIONS.]

Brandl, A. *The Play of Love, Wether,* and *Johan Johan.* In : *Quellen.* [See Section II, COLLECTIONS.]

Cameron, K. W. *John Heywood's "Play of the Wether."* Raleigh, N. C., 1941.

De la Bère, R. *John Heywood, Entertainer.* London, 1937. (Texts of *Wytty and Wyttles, Pardoner and the Frere, Johan Johan*)

Farmer, J. S. *The Dramatic Writings of John Heywood.* London, 1905. (Early English Drama Society)
Tudor Facsimile Texts of all Heywood's plays except *Wytty and Wyttles.* [See Section II, COLLECTIONS.]

Manly, J. M. *The Foure PP.* In : *Specimens,* Vol. I. [See Section II, COLLECTIONS.]

Pollard, A. W. *Wether, Johan Johan.* In : Gayley's *Representative English Comedies,* Vol. I. [See Section II, COLLECTIONS.]

STUDIES

Bolwell, R. W. *The Life and Works of John Heywood.* New York, 1921.

Cameron, K. W. *The Background of John Heywood's "Witty and Witless," a Study in Early Tudor Drama.* Raleigh, N. C., 1941. (Includes specialized bibliography of Heywood scholarship.)

Craik, T. W. "The True Source of John Heywood's *Johan Johan.*" *MLR,* XLV (1950), 289–95.

De la Bère, R. *John Heywood, Entertainer.* London, 1937.

Hillebrand, H. N. "On the Authorship of the Interludes Attributed to John Heywood." *MP,* XIII (1915), 267–80.

Maxwell, Ian C. *French Farce and John Heywood.* Melbourne and London, 1946.

Sultan, S. "The Audience Participation Episode in *Johan Johan.*" *JEGP,* LII (1953), 491–97.

Swoboda, Wilhelm. *John Heywood als Dramatiker.* Vienna, 1888.

Young, Karl. "The Influence of French Farce Upon the Plays of John Heywood." *MP,* II (1904–5), 97–124.

V. JOHN BALE

Davies, W. T. *A Bibliography of John Bale.* Oxford, 1939.

EDITIONS

Bang, W. *Bales Kynge Johan, nach der Handschrift in der Chats-worth Collection in faksimile hrsg.* Louvain, 1909. (*Materialien,* Vol. 25)
Collier, J. P. *Kynge Johan, a Play in Two Parts.* London, 1838. (Camden Society)
Farmer, J. S. *The Dramatic Writings of John Bale, Bishop of Os-sory.* London, 1907. (Early English Drama Society)
   Tudor Facsimile Texts of *God's Promises, The Temptation of Our Lord,* and *Three Laws.* [See Section II, COLLECTIONS.]
Manly, J. M. *Kynge Johan.* In : *Specimens.* Vol. I. [See Section II, COLLECTIONS.]
Pafford, J. H. P. and W. W. Greg. *King Johan, by John Bale.* Ox-ford, 1931. (Malone Society Reprints)
Schwemmer, P. *A Brefe Comedy or Enterlude Concernynge the Temptacyon of Our Lorde and Saver Jesus Christ by Sathan in the Desart.* Nürnberg, 1919.

STUDIES

Barke, Herbert. *Bales "Kynge Johan" und sein Verhältnis zur zeitgenössischen Geschichtsschreibung.* Würzburg, 1937.
Cason, C. E. "Additional Lines for Bale's *Kynge Johan.*" *JEGP,* XXVII (1928), 42–50.
Harris, J. W. *John Bale, a Study in the Minor Literature of the Reformation.* Urbana, 1940.
McClusker, Honor. *John Bale, Dramatist and Antiquary.* Bryn Mawr, 1942.
Miller, E. S. "The Roman Rite in Bale's *King John.*" *PMLA,* LXIV (1949), 802–22.

VI. NICHOLAS UDALL

EDITIONS

Adams, J. Q. *Roister Doister.* In : *Chief Pre-Shakespearean Dramas.* [See Section II, COLLECTIONS.]
Arber, Edward. *Roister Doister.* London, July 1, 1869. (English Reprints, 17)
Boas, F. S. *Ralph Roister Doister.* In : *Five Pre-Shakespearean Comedies.* [See Section II, COLLECTIONS.]

Child, C. G. *Ralph Roister Doister*. Boston, etc., 1912. (Riverside College Classics)

Cooper, W. D. *Ralph Roister Doister . . . and The Tragedie of Gorboduc*. London, 1847. (Shakespeare Society)

Farmer, J. S. *The Dramatic Writings of Nicholas Udall*. London, 1906. (Early English Drama Society)

Flügel, Ewald. *Roister Doister*. In : Gayley's *Representative English Comedies*, Vol. I. [See Section II, COLLECTIONS.]

Greg, W. W. *Roister Doister*. London, 1935. (Malone Society Reprints)

Manly, J. M. *Roister Doister*. In : *Specimens*, Vol. II. [See Section II, COLLECTIONS.]

Scheurweghs, G. *Nicholas Udall's Roister Doister*. Louvain, 1939. (Materials for the Study of Old English Drama, Vol. 16)

STUDIES

Baldwin, T. W. and M. C. Linthicum. "The Date of *Ralph Roister Doister*." *PQ*, VI (1927), 379–95.

Flügel, E. "Nicholas Udall's Dialogues and Interludes." In : W. P. Ker, et al., eds., *An English Miscellany, Presented to Dr. Furnivall*. Oxford, 1901. Pp. 81–85.

Hales, J. W. "The Date of the 'First English Comedy.' " *Englische Studien*, XVIII (1893), 408–21.

Hinton, J. "The Source of *Ralph Roister Doister*." *MP*, XI (1913–14), 273–78.

Maulsby, D. L. "The Relation between Udall's *Roister Doister* and the Comedies of Plautus and Terence." *Englische Studien*, XXXVIII (1907), 251–77.

Miller, E. S. "Roister Doister's 'Funeralls.' " *SP*, XLIII (1946), 42–58.

Reed, A. W. "Nicholas Udall and Thomas Wilson." *RES*, I (1925), 275–78.

VII. MR. S., MASTER OF ART

EDITIONS

Adams, J. Q. *Gammer Gurtons Nedle*. In : *Chief Pre-Shakespearean Dramas*. [See Section II, COLLECTIONS.]

Boas, F. S. *Gammer Gurton's Needle*. In : *Five Pre-Shakespearean Comedies*. [See Section II, COLLECTIONS.]

Bradley, Henry. *Gammer Gurtons Nedle*. In : Gayley's *Representative English Comedies*, Vol. I. [See Section II, COLLECTIONS.]

Brett-Smith, H. F. B. *Gammer Gvrtons Nedle*. Oxford, 1920. (The Percy Reprints)

Farmer, J. S. *Gammer Gurton's Needle*. In : *Anonymous Plays*,

Third Series. London, 1906. (Early English Drama Society)
Gammer Gurton's Needle. London, 1910. (Tudor Facsimile
Texts)

Manly, J. M. *Gammer Gurtons Nedle.* In : *Specimens,* Vol. II. [See
Section II, COLLECTIONS.]

STUDIES

Boas, F. S. "Early Academic Comedy." Chap. IV of *University
Drama in the Tudor Age.* Oxford, 1914.

Roberts, C. W. "The Authorship of *Gammer Gurton's Needle. PQ,*
XIX (1940), 97–113.

VIII. THOMAS NORTON AND THOMAS SACKVILLE

EDITIONS

Adams, J. Q. *The Tragidie of [Gorboduc; or of] Ferrex and Porrex.* In : *Chief Pre-Shakespearean Dramas.* [See Section II, COL-
LECTIONS.]

Cooper, W. D. *Ralph Roister Doister . . . and The Tragedie of
Gorboduc.* London, 1847. (Shakespeare Society)

Cunliffe, J. W. *Gorboduc.* In : *Early English Classical Tragedies.*
[See Section II, COLLECTIONS.]

Farmer, J. S. *The Dramatic Writings of Richard Edwards, Thomas
Norton, and Thomas Sackville.* London, 1906. (Early English
Drama Society)
Ferrex and Porrex (or Gorboduc). London, 1908. (Tudor Fac-
simile Texts)

Sackville-West, R. W. *The Works of Thomas Sackville.* London,
1859.

Watt, H. A. *Gorboduc.* Madison, Wis., 1910.

STUDIES

Courtney, L. H. "The Tragedy of *Ferrex and Porrex." N&Q,* Second Series, X (1860), 261–63. (On political applications and
authorship)

Gillet, J. E. "The Authorship of *Gorboduc." MLN,* XXXI (1916),
377–78.

Small, A. "The Political Import of the Norton Half of *Gorboduc."
PMLA,* XLVI (1931), 641–46.

Wilson, S. R. *"Gorboduc* and the Theory of Tyrannicide." *MLR,*
XXXIV (1939), 355–66.

IX. THOMAS PRESTON

EDITIONS

Adams, J. Q. *Cambises, King of Percia.* In : *Chief Pre-Shakespearean Dramas.* [See Section II, COLLECTIONS.]

Farmer, J. S. *Cambises King of Persia, by Thomas Preston.* London, 1910. (Tudor Facsimile Texts)

Manly, J. M. *Cambises King of Percia.* In : *Specimens,* Vol. II. [See Section II, COLLECTIONS.]

STUDIES

Allen, D. C. "A Source for *Cambises*." *MLN,* XLIX (1934), 384–87.

Armstrong, W. A. "The Background and Sources of Preston's *Cambises*." *ES,* XXXI (1950), 129–35.

"The Authorship and Political Meaning of *Cambises*." *ES,* XXXVI (1955), 289–99.

Feldman, A. "King Cambises' Vein." *N&Q,* CXCVI (1951), 98–100.

Linthicum, M. C. "The Date of *Cambyses*." *PMLA,* XLIX (1934), 959–61.

Tilley, M. P. "Shakespeare and his Ridicule of *Cambyses*." *MLN,* XXIV (1909), 244–47.

THE NORTON LIBRARY
SEVENTEENTH-CENTURY SERIES

J. MAX PATRICK, *General Editor*

JACOBEAN DRAMA: *An Anthology* Volume I N559
Edited with an Introduction, Notes, and Variants by Richard C. Harrier (*Every Man in His Humour* by Ben Jonson; *The Malcontent* by John Marston; *The White Devil* by John Webster; and *Bussy D'Ambois* by George Chapman)

JACOBEAN DRAMA: *An Anthology* Volume II N560
Edited with an Introduction, Notes, and Variants by Richard C. Harrier (*The Changeling* by Thomas Middleton and William Rowley; *The Revenger's Tragedy* by Cyril Tourneur; *The Broken Heart* by John Ford; and *The Lady of Pleasure* by James Shirley)

THE COMPLETE POETRY OF ROBERT HERRICK N435
Edited with an Introduction and Notes by J. Max Patrick

THE COMPLETE POETRY OF BEN JONSON N436
Edited with an Introduction, Notes, and Variants by William B. Hunter, Jr.

SHORT FICTION OF THE SEVENTEENTH CENTURY: *An Anthology* N437
Selected and edited by Charles C. Mish

THE COMPLETE POETRY OF HENRY VAUGHAN N438
Edited with an Introduction, Notes, and Variants by French Fogle

THE WORKS OF THOMAS CAMPION N439
Edited with an Introduction and Notes by Walter R. Davis

THE COMPLETE PLAYS OF WILLIAM WYCHERLEY N440
Edited with an Introduction, Notes, and Variants by Gerald Weales

SEVENTEENTH-CENTURY AMERICAN POETRY N620
Edited with an Introduction, Notes, and Comments by Harrison T. Meserole

THE PROSE OF SIR THOMAS BROWNE N619
Edited with an Introduction, Notes, and Variants by Norman J. Endicott